Composition
& Literary
Form

Composition & Literary Form: an Anthology

Second Edition

Nicholas A. Salerno
Arizona State University

Nancy J. Hawkey
Scottsdale Community College

Winthrop Publishers, Inc.
Cambridge, Massachusetts

Library of Congress Cataloging in Publication Data

Salerno, Nicholas A   Comp.
   Composition and literary form.

   Includes index.
   1. College readers. I. Hawkey, Nancy J.
II. Title.
PE1122.S16 1978   808′.04275   77-17470
ISBN 0-87626-160-8

Cover design by Karyl Klopp

Acknowledgments

Conrad Aiken, "Silent Snow, Secret Snow." Reprinted by permission of Brandt & Brandt. Copyright © 1932, 1960 by Conrad Aiken.

Woody Allen, "A Brief, Yet Helpful Guide to Civil Disobedience." © 1972 by the New York Times Company. Reprinted by permission.

W. H. Auden, "Schoolchildren," "The Unknown Citizen," and "Musée des Beaux Arts." Copyright © 1940 and renewed 1968 by W. H. Auden. Reprinted from *Collected Shorter Poems 1927–1957*, by W. H. Auden, by permission of Random House, Inc.

James Baldwin, "Sonny's Blues." Excerpted from *Going to Meet the Man* by James Baldwin. Copyright © 1948, 1951, 1957, 1958, 1960, 1965 by James Baldwin. Originally appeared in *Partisan Review*. Reprinted by permission of The Dial Press.

Imamu Amiri Baraka (LeRoi Jones), "Jazz and the White Critic." From *Black Music*, 1967. Copyright 1963 by Imamu Amiri Baraka. Reprinted by permission of the Sterling Lord Agency, Inc.

Donald Barthelme, "The Police Band." Reprinted with the permission of Farrar, Straus & Giroux, Inc. from *Unspeakable Practices, Unnatural Acts* by Donald Barthelme. Copyright © 1964, 1968 by Donald Barthelme.

Ray Bradbury, "Dwellers in Silence." Copyright by Ray Bradbury, reprinted by permission of Harold Matson Company, Inc.

Richard Brautigan, "The Cleveland Wrecking Yard." Excerpted from *Trout Fishing in America* by Richard Brautigan. Copyright © 1967 by Richard Brautigan. Reprinted by permission of Delacorte Press/Seymour Lawrence.

Robert Bridges, "London Snow." From *The Poetical Works of Robert Bridges* by permission of Oxford University Press.

Gwendolyn Brooks, "We Real Cool." From *The World of Gwendolyn Brooks* (1971) by Gwendolyn Brooks. Copyright © 1959 by Gwendolyn Brooks. Reprinted by permission of Harper & Row, Publishers.

Anthony Burgess, "The Private Dialect of Husbands and Wives." Reprinted by permission of International Creative Management. Copyright © 1968 by Conde Nast.

Kuangchi C. Chang, "Garden of My Childhood." Reprinted from *The American Scholar*, Volume 26, Number 3, Summer, 1957. Copyright © 1957 by the United Chapters of Phi Beta Kappa. By permission of the publishers.

Walter Van Tilburg Clark, "Hook." From *Hook* by Walter Van Tilburg Clark. Reprinted by permission of International Creative Management. Copyright © 1940, 1968 by Walter Van Tilburg Clark.

Arthur C. Clarke, "The Star of the Magi." Copyright 1972 by Arthur C. Clarke. Reprinted by permission of the author and the author's agents, Scott Meredith Literary Agency, Inc.

Judy Collins, "Since You've Asked." Copyright © 1967 Rocky Mountain National Park Music Co., Inc. All rights reserved. Used by permission.

Victor Hernández Cruz, "The Cha Cha Cha at Salt Lake City Bus Terminal." Reprinted by permission of the author.

Emily Dickinson, "A Bird Came Down the Walk," "I Heard a Fly Buzz When I Died," "A Narrow Fellow in the Grass," "She Rose to His Requirement," and "To Make a Prairie It Takes a Clover and One Bee." Reprinted by permission of the publishers and the Trustees of Amherst College from *The Poems of Emily Dickinson*, edited by Thomas H. Johnson, Cambridge, Mass.: The Belknap Press of Harvard University Press, Copyright © 1951, 1955 by the President and Fellows of Harvard College.

William D. Eastlake, "Whitey's on the Moon Now." Reprinted by permission of the author.

Loren Eiseley, "The Bird and the Machine." Copyright © 1955 by Loren Eiseley. Reprinted from *The Immense Journey* by Loren Eiseley, by permission of Random House, Inc.

T. S. Eliot, "The Journey of the Magi" and "The Love Song of J. Alfred Prufrock." From *Collected Poems 1909–1962* by T. S. Eliot, copyright 1936 by Harcourt Brace Jovanovich, Inc., copyright 1963, 1964 by T. S. Eliot. Reprinted by permission of the publishers.

Eugene Field, "Little Boy Blue." From *Poems of Childhood* by permission of Charles Scribner's Sons.

Robert Frost, "Desert Places" and "Departmental." From *The Poetry of Robert Frost*, edited by Edward Connery Lathem. Copyright 1936 by Robert Frost. Copyright © 1964 by Lesley Frost Ballantine. Copyright © 1969 by Holt, Rinehart and Winston. Reprinted by permission of Holt, Rinehart and Winston, Publishers.

Nikki Giovanni, "Nikki-Rosa." Reprinted by permission of Broadside Press.

Rose K. Goldsen, "Toys and the Imagination of Children." From *Human Behavior*, Vol. V (December, 1976). Reprinted by permission of the author.

José Angel Gutiérrez, "22 Miles. . . ." From *El Grito*, © 1968. Reprinted by permission of the author.

Adrian Henri, "Poem for Roger McGough." © Adrian Henri, published in *Penguin Modern Poets 10: The Mersey Sound*.

Eric Hoffer, "Man, Play, and Creativity." Reprinted by permission from *Think* magazine, published by IBM, copyright 1967 by International Business Machines Corporation.

Robert Hogan, "After Sending Freshmen to Describe a Tree." Reprinted from the *AAUP Bulletin*, Winter, 1957, by permission of the American Association of University Professors.

Gerard Manley Hopkins, "God's Grandeur." From *The Poems of Gerard Manley Hopkins*, published by Oxford University Press.

Arthur Hoppe, "The Greatest Generation." Copyright 1970 by Chronicle Publishing Company.

Langston Hughes, "Dream Boogie." Reprinted by permission of Harold Ober Associates, Incorporated. © 1951 by Langston Hughes.

Ted Hughes, "Hawk Roosting." From *Lupercal* by Ted Hughes. Copyright © 1959 by Ted Hughes. Reprinted by permission of Harper & Row, Publishers.

Bruce Ignacio, "Lost." First published in *South Dakota Review*, Summer 1969. Reprinted by permission of *South Dakota Review*.

Shirley Jackson, "My Life with R. H. Macy." Reprinted with the permission of Farrar, Straus & Giroux, Inc. from *The Lottery* by Shirley Jackson. Copyright 1948, 1949 by Shirley Jackson. Copyright renewed © 1967 by Laurence Hyman, Barry Hyman, Mrs. Sarah Webster, and Mrs. Joanne Schnurer.

Randall Jarrell, "The Death of the Ball Turret Gunner." Reprinted with the permission of Farrar, Straus & Giroux, Inc. from *The Complete Poems* by Randall Jarrell. Copyright 1945 by Randall Jarrell. Copyright renewed 1973 by Mary von Schrader Jarrell.

Robinson Jeffers, "Hurt Hawks." Copyright 1928 and renewed 1956 by Robinson Jeffers. Reprinted from *The Selected Poetry of Robinson Jeffers*, by permission of Random House, Inc.

Erica Jong, "Back to Africa." From *Half-Lives* by Erica Jong. Copyright © 1971, 1972, 1973 by Erica Mann Jong. Reprinted by permission of Holt, Rinehart and Winston, Publishers.

James Joyce, "The Boarding House." From *Dubliners* by James Joyce. Originally published by B. W. Huebsch, Inc. in 1916. Copyright © 1967 by the Estate of James Joyce. All rights reserved. Reprinted by permission of The Viking Press.

Barbara J. Katz, "A Quiet March for Liberation Begins." Reprinted with permission from the *National Observer*, December 29, 1973. Copyright Dow Jones & Company, Inc. 1973.

Daniel Keyes, "Flowers for Algernon." © 1959 by Mercury Press. Reprinted by permission of the author and the author's agent, Robert P. Mills, Ltd.

Martin Luther King, Jr., "I Have a Dream." Reprinted by permission of Joan Daves. Copyright © 1963 by Martin Luther King, Jr.

Etheridge Knight, "For Black Poets Who Think of Suicide." Reprinted by permission of Broadside Press.

Maxine Kumin, "For My Son on the Highways of His Mind." From *The Nightmare Factory* by Maxine Kumin. Copyright © 1970 by Maxine Kumin. Reprinted by permission of Harper & Row, Publishers.

Peter La Farge, "Vision of a Past Warrior." From *As Long as the Grass Shall Grow* by Peter La Farge. © 1964 United In-

Corporation. Copyright 1923 by Boni & Liveright. Copyright renewed 1951 by Jean Toomer.

Lionel Trilling, "Of This Time, Of That Place." Copyright 1943 by Lionel Trilling. Reprinted by permission of Diana Trilling.

Judith Viorst, "True Love." From *It's Hard to Be Hip Over Thirty* by Judith Viorst. Copyright © 1968 by Judith Viorst. Reprinted by arrangement with The New American Library, Inc., New York, N.Y.

E. B. White, "How to Tell a Major Poet from a Minor Poet." From *Quo Vadimus?* by E. B. White. Copyright 1930 by E. B. White. Originally appeared in the *New Yorker*. Reprinted by permission of Harper & Row, Publishers.

Nancy Willard, "The Graffiti Poet." Reprinted from *Carpenter of the Sun, Poems by Nancy Willard*. By permission of Liveright Publishing Corporation. Copyright © 1974 by Nancy Willard.

William Carlos Williams, "The Use of Force." From *The Farmers' Daughters* by William Carlos Williams. Copyright 1932, 1938 by William Carlos Williams. Reprinted by permission of New Directions Publishing Corporation.

Samuel T. Williamson, "How to Write Like a Social Scientist." Copyright 1947. Reprinted by permission of the *Saturday Review*.

Terrance Withers, "Corporate Flyer." Reprinted by permission of the author.

Jade Snow Wong, "A Measure of Freedom." From pp. 124–130 in *Fifth Chinese Daughter* by Jade Snow Wong. Copyright 1950 by Jade Snow Wong. Reprinted by permission of Harper & Row, Publishers.

Richard Wright, "Bright and Morning Star." From *Uncle Tom's Children* by Richard Wright. Copyright 1938 by Richard Wright, renewed 1964 by Ellen Wright. Reprinted by permission of Harper & Row, Publishers.

Kenneth Yasuda (Shosōn), "The Rainbow," "The Poppy-Field," "At Tacoma, Washington," "The Lizard," "The Mississippi River," and "Summer Shower." From *A Pepper Pod*. Reprinted by permission of Charles E. Tuttle Co., Inc.

William Butler Yeats, "The Folly of Being Comforted." Copyright 1903 by Macmillan Publishing Co., Inc., renewed 1931 by William Butler Yeats. "The Second Coming." Copyright 1924 by Macmillan Publishing Co., Inc., renewed 1952 by Bertha Georgie Yeats. "An Irish Airman Foresees His Death." Copyright 1919 by Macmillan Publishing Co., Inc., renewed 1947 by Bertha Georgie Yeats. Reprinted with permission of Macmillan Publishing Co., Inc. from *Collected Poems* by William Butler Yeats.

Chiang Yee, "Arrival at Boston." Reprinted from *The Silent Traveller in Boston* by Chiang Yee, by permission of W. W. Norton & Company, Inc. Copyright © 1959 by W. W. Norton & Company, Inc.

Contents

Love Is Not All   299

Man, Play, and Creativity   353

Choosing a Dream   447

Preface

Composition and Literary Form: An Anthology is designed primarily as a text for composition courses, though its contents and format are easily adaptable to writing courses at a higher level or to introduction to literature courses.

Many anthologies intended to be texts in composition classes provide the prospective writer with only a series of essays for study. Such books assume that the prose essay is an exotic phenomenon which may be adequately studied in isolation from other types of writing. We disagree. *Composition and Literary Form* assumes that the prose essay resembles other forms of writing more than it differs from them, and that the awareness gained from studying it along with other types of composition will make the student a better essayist than he would otherwise be.

The organization of our text, its contents, and the nature of the study questions reflect this basic orientation. *Composition and Literary Form* is organized thematically around six basic concepts: nature and science (*The Island Earth*), psychology and religion (*Desert Places*), sociology (*Of This Time, Of That Place*), interpersonal relationships (*Love Is Not All*), the arts (*Man, Play, and Creativity*), and minority group problems and attitudes (*Choosing a Dream*). Each of these units is composed of two or more subgroups whose selections exhibit even closer thematic parallels than those suggested by the general section title; for instance, *Desert Places* contains subgroups on individuals trying to find their place in the universe, misfits, the need to communicate, death, suicide, funerals, religious attitudes, and the magi. Within the thematic units a great variety of stylistic treatment is evident. For example, the hawk subsection in *The Island Earth* includes an essay ("The Bird and the Machine"), a short story ("Hook"), and two poems ("Hawk Roosting" and "Hurt Hawks"). Such an arrangement allows the student to see how the same topic may be treated through various techniques that work a multiplicity of effects on the reader. He learns that figurative language, logic, sentence structure, and many other elements occur in poems, stories, and essays, and that it is very difficult to draw hard and fast conclusions about how one goes about creating a successful composition of any type using these elements. By going beyond easy generalization he will have become sensitive to the manifold potential each word in a particular context has for affecting the reader; and this knowledge will make him a better writer.

Our study questions invite the student not only to understand the content and style of the composition at hand, but also to respond to the composition in terms of the questions it raises about his own private experiences and the world at large. We hope they will provoke him to write about not only the meaning and effect of the poem, story, or essay on him, but also about the areas of experience they exist in. For instance, a student might respond to a poem by writing an analysis of its metaphors, or by composing an essay on the issue it raises.

We wish to thank William C. Creasy, Sally Ann Drucker, Nicholas Diller Fratt, Kathryn Harris, David and Diane Hawkey, David Langness, Elizabeth Littin, Robert C. Lamm, Christine Marin, Dan and Karen Meyer, Margaret McCormack, Christi Miller, Jeff Morgan, R. Paul Murphy, Paul O'Connell, Nancy Potter, Stephen Rogers, Clifford Roth, Fran Salerno, Roger Schmidt, Patricia L. Smith, and Terrance Withers.

N.A.S.
N.J.H.

Composition & Literary Form

The Island Earth

When in the last act of *The Tempest,* Shakespeare's Miranda sees for the first time the group of men shipwrecked on her father's island, and exclaims: "O brave new world/That has such creatures in't," she speaks as sincerely and ingenuously as only a child can. But the phrase "brave new world" now carries negative connotations; Aldous Huxley's remarkably effective literary treatment of the world of the then-future—our present—has turned that phrase into a synonym for a mechanized, dehumanized universe. Today we find ourselves asking how long the world and the people who inhabit it can exist. If we don't blow ourselves to pieces in one last foolish display of fireworks, we may well achieve the same results by failing to recognize and cope successfully with our self-willed ecological crisis. We no longer hope for a return to paradise. We are willing to settle for survival in a reasonably healthy environment.

Recently, contemporary man has developed an ambivalent attitude to science. We seem to be bored with moon shots, and more concerned with solving sociological and psychological problems. We ask ourselves if science will save us before it destroys us. We revel in emotional reactions at the expense of objective detachment. The selections which follow reveal our changing attitudes toward science and nature, and our increasing concern with our environment.

The first subsection sets up the problem. Margaret Mead and Edgar Allan Poe suggest that objectivity and the scientific method have brought with them attendant losses; William Carlos Williams and John Steinbeck remind us that we may recognize an ideal but not be able to live up to it. Emily Dickinson and D. H. Lawrence offer counterpoint to the attitude of Steinbeck's scientist.

Modern man's increasing anonymity and the resultant perils are discussed in the second subsection by W. H. Auden and Shirley Jackson in prime examples of different literary genres. Then Jonathan Swift proposes a solution; how "modest" his proposal is is for the reader to judge.

The pollution problem is the theme of the third subsection. Jean Toomer, Sylvia Plath, and Robert Bridges rejoice in the beauty of the natural world. William Wordsworth looks at a city and finds it a vision of purity; the more contemporary Carl Sandburg focuses his attention on some white curtains to reveal our contamination of that purity. Joni Mitchell and Richard Brautigan align them-

1

selves with Sandburg, while Gerard Manley Hopkins encourages us with the thought that "nature is never spent."

Daniel Keyes's remarkable short story, "Flowers for Algernon," introduces a section on the sacredness of life. Few of us would conclude after reading Charlie's journal that he should not have submitted to the experiment. We are probably unwilling to deny Charlie the opportunity to shine in use rather than rust unburnished. Yet once again the best laid schemes of mice and men went astray. Of course, "Flowers for Algernon" has implications beyond those mentioned here, but man's treatment of man in the interests of science does figure prominently in this tale. Jon Silkin, Emily Dickinson, Theodore Roethke, and Jim Morrison continue the theme of this subsection with poems on our relationships with other living creatures, and the need to determine our own place in God's scheme of things.

Finally, a section on hawks is included, not for the significance of its subject but for its usefulness in demonstrating how different writers approach the same subject. Walter Van Tilburg Clark, a creative writer, gives us a seemingly objective study of a hawk while Loren Eiseley, a scientist, takes a very unscientific approach to the same creature. Robinson Jeffers and Ted Hughes turn hawks into animals endowed with very human traits.

The Island Earth

Margaret Mead

1   In 1940 Edna St. Vincent Millay wrote a poem called "There Are No Islands, Any More," which moved those who were involved in World War II very deeply. The theme, that nowhere on this planet could man flee from man and be safe, that war and its aftermath reached to the most remote islands, tugged at the imagination of those of us who were living through the most widespread war in history, a war that culminated in the horrors of Hiroshima. People stopped talking about finding themselves an island where life could be lived out in peace with nature, and those who were fond of quoting added, from Donne, "No man is an island, entire of itself. . . ." Islands as a daydream of escape went out, and casual acquaintances stopped asking to be taken along on my field trips. When islands were mentioned, it was their vulnerabilities that were spoken of: population growth in Mauritius and Samoa; Japan's awareness of the need for population control; the devastating volcanic eruption in Bali that destroyed a third of the arable land; the unwillingness of Java's population to leave their crowded island for a less crowded one. The emphasis continued to be on the theme, "no place to go, no hiding place down here." Islands pointed out the interconnectedness of men on earth and their mutual vulnerability to each others' homicidal and genocidal aims.

2   The emergence of Indonesia as a new nation—the fifth largest in the world—was all the more striking because this is a nation made up of 80 million people living on 3,000 islands, and people raised their eyebrows when Indonesia tried to extend the limits of sovereignty to include the inland waterways of her watery empire. Buckminster Fuller designed a map—a diomaxion map—which showed the continents of the earth as an interconnected land mass. Islands were definitely out, a handicap in some way or other to full-scale continental living.

3   Then came NASA and the moon program, and finally the first breathtaking photographs of the earth from the moon. Mankind joined the astronauts in their willowy, eerie, unweighted walks on the moon and saw the earth in all its isolated diversity. Earth became an island in space. The earth seen from the moon was a whole in a new sense, no longer simulated by a globe, but seen whole. Scientist fathers conversing with their small sons found themselves confused because they were still earthbound looking toward the moon, while the children were on the moon looking back toward earth.

4   Besides these major transforming events—the sense of political and
military vulnerability that grew up after World War II, and the specific
change in perspective that has grown with the space program as the earth
has become planet Earth—something else has been happening. Men
everywhere are becoming conscious that this planet, like any small
island, is interconnected in ways other than war and rumors of war. The
spread of radioactive dust; the long journey of DDT from someone's rose
garden to the shell-less eggs of unborn birds and the bones of unborn
children; the new, resistant strains of venereal disease and malaria,
which are robbing us of our recent conquest of these dangers; the
knowledge that man's activities can alter the temperature of the earth,
create storms of inestimable strength, pollute the oceans as well as the
small lakes and streams that are dying throughout the civilized world: all
have brought home to us that the earth is an island. Interconnected the
peoples of the earth are—vulnerable to each other's weapons and no
longer able to defend their frontiers and their children; vulnerable also
to the acts of people half a world away, as they casually dump tanks of
nuclear by-products into the sea depths, which no one has yet properly
explored, or send clouds of pollution through the air. As those who love
and protect the wilderness and try to save a part of it for man, and as
those who see their main crop destroyed by the by-products of human
intervention in agriculture or animal husbandry, so now the whole world
is coming to realize the interconnectedness between the way men live
and whether or not their children and their children's children will have
a habitable world. Not war, but a plethora of man-made things—
disposable, indestructible beer cans; too much industrial waste in the
lakes and streams, from antibiotics designed to protect egg-laying fowls
to pesticides designed to protect the orange crop—is threatening to
strangle us, suffocate us, bury us in the debris and by-products of our
technologically inventive and irresponsible age.

5   With this new realization, which is expressing itself in a hundred
different ways, from government commissions and antipollution groups,
to the American Association for the Advancement of Science's Committee on Science in the Promotion of Human Welfare, to the Scientists
Institute for Public Information, to small committees in small New England towns, the debate goes on. (A large number of these new
movements were discussed in "The New Conservation," by Richard L.
Means, *Natural History*, August-September, 1969.) With this prolif-
eration of public interest, those who have been fighting these battles for
conservation, for protection, for soil rehabilitation, for reforestation, and
those who have become more recently aware of the dangers of pollution,
overpopulation, and overload of every facility are meeting and looking
for new ways of stating their common interests. Words like *ecosystem*,
the whole interacting system in which a change in any one variable—
temperature, the number of fish or of fishermen, a factory built on the
banks of a stream, or a florist's seed field five miles away—may change

the whole system, and *biosphere*, the whole natural living system of the planet and its surrounding atmosphere, are coming into the vocabulary of the concerned all over the world. These terms come from the science of ecology, a science that, on the whole, took as its model a pond, a lake, or a marsh and, while allowing for interaction among every natural component, took little cognizance of man himself, except as an interfering factor. If we wanted to teach our children about ecosystems, the model we used was an aquarium, in which the delicate relationships between water, plants, and aquatic creatures had to be watched over and kept in balance.

6   Aquariums are indeed a fine teaching aid and will give children an idea of the balance of the natural world, especially the great mass of urban children who meet nature either in the form of a pet who has to be walked in the streets or provided with "kitty litter." But it is becoming increasingly clear that this model, over which the aquarium owner stands, like a god, presiding over a small glass tank heated by electricity (itself vulnerable to a power failure) is only a very partial model of what is happening to us. The child's aquarium is a model of a world almost totally dependent on man, but of which he is a spectator and protector, not an integral part.

7   If, from the science of ecology, we try to develop a new profession of those who stand guard over the environment, we stand in danger of still leaving man outside, to become an "environmental manager," a significant factor, but not a true part of the natural world. To the core subject of ecology, it is suggested that we add the human sciences to train aspirant young environmental managers to deal with the problem. As new subject matters develop in the field of urbanization—ekistics, urban planning, urban design—there is an attempt to patch together from a number of disciplines a new whole, a science of the total ecosystem, into which man, somewhat grudgingly, is to be admitted.

8   I do not think this is the way to do it. We have had many decades of various interdisciplinary projects. Either they represent a coalition of different disciplinary interests, in which each defends his own territory, or we get new incorporative fields, like economics or public health, which manufacture their own psychology and educational theory to suit themselves and, in turn, become little empires defending their domains against contenders.

9   I believe that there is another way to develop the kind of specialists that we will need as public concern for our endangered planet and for our starving millions mounts. And this is where islands come back again. What students need to learn if they are to think about environmental protection and development is about whole inhabited ecosystems: ecosystems in which man himself, the way he plants and reaps and disposes of waste, multiplies or stabilizes his population, is a *conscious* factor. Man has molded and changed his environment since he learned to make tools and control fire. But in those days, perhaps a million years

ago, he was not conscious of what he did, of how population was related to food supply, of how killing the young or eating all the eggs or gathering plants before they seeded would limit his future. It was on islands that man first began to learn these things. If there were too many people, either some would be driven out into the uncharted seas or there would be civil war. Some method of population control had to be adopted. Younger sons were forbidden to marry and infants exposed to die. Islanders knew when the birds came to nest, when the fish came to spawn, how periodic hurricanes affected their harvests. On many small islands today, the harsh realities of a rapidly changing world are forcing the men away to work, leaving only women and children at home. It was on islands that men first learned that they themselves were part of an ecosystem, so it is perhaps not surprising that the religious system of the ancient Polynesians emphasized taboo, that things were forbidden in the nature of the system itself. Under taboo, if men made no missteps they lived safely, but they had to be continuously alert to the consequences of infringement of the order of nature and the order of social life.

10   We need to find ways to understand, to teach children, and to prepare young men and women for careers in our interconnected and endangered world. The forces of public opinion are being marshalled nationally and internationally. A great international conference, conspicuous for its level of cooperation among usually rivalrous United Nations specialized agencies, was held in Paris in 1968. A conference on biology as the history of the future, sponsored by the International Union of Biological Sciences, was held in Chichén Itzá, Mexico, in January, 1969. At the initiative of Sweden, a great United Nations conference is being prepared for 1972. We need to have a model that will make man—always active, seldom conscious, irresponsible throughout most of history—a conscious participant in the development of planet Earth.

11   The smallest islands of the earth are almost all in trouble, whether it be the islands of the Hebrides, fighting the British Parliament and paying no income taxes; the burgeoning population of Mauritius; the belligerent population of Anguilla; or the small Greek islands whose men must all go away to sea. Such islands, grievously resourceless, overpopulated, and dependent upon distant and outside money, can become our models and our training grounds for the new professions that are needed. As small children were once asked to build a model of Solomon's Temple in Sunday School, or of Egyptian pyramids in day school to understand ancient civilizations centered on man alone and reflecting his natural environment, we now need materials so that each child in a class may have an island to think about: its size, its shape, its location, its weather, its resources, the habits and skills and despairs and hopes of its inhabitants, and its dependence upon world markets and diplomatic decisions in which its people have no part. And for those older students who wish to make a career of the protection and development of the whole of man's environment, a year on an island, learning

the language, mastering the intricacies of the interrelationships of its living population and all its plants and creatures, would be perfect preparation for thinking about wholes. We would not need to patch disciplines together in an uneasy truce: members of various specialized disciplines could first obtain a firm grounding in their own fields and then—with a year's field work on an island—learn to articulate that speciality into a whole.

12   Following in Darwin's footsteps, Harold Coolidge began the trek back to islands for inspiration when he took a whole group of scientists to Galápagos in January, 1964. But the Galápagos have no human beings on them. It is the inclusion of people and their purposes that is now our problem. Nor need we ask islands—often in dire straits—to contribute, yet gain nothing from what they teach us about our planet Earth. Each student could be asked to work on some real problem, urgent to the people themselves, and thus prepare himself for the kind of world role when, in the 1970's and 1980's man's survival will hang in the balance—and the generation now growing up will have the task of saving this planet as a habitable spot for their children and their children's children.

Study Questions

1. Mead's extended introduction leads to the thesis statement in paragraph 4: ". . . all have brought home to us that the earth is an island." How does Mead use restatement in subsequent sentences to broaden the scope of her thesis?
2. Identify the transitional words and phrases at the beginning of each paragraph.
3. The aquarium serves as a limited model for Mead's explanation of balance. What are the limits or the insufficiencies of this model? What model might be more accurate?
4. The most important part of a *periodic sentence* is postponed by the appearance of cumulative phrases, clauses, or parenthetical remarks: the subject-verb completion is delayed until the end of the sentence. What is the effect of the periodic sentences that make up paragraph 4?

Sonnet—To Science

Edgar Allan Poe

Science! true daughter of Old Time thou art!
  Who alterest all things with thy peering eyes.
Why preyest thou thus upon the poet's heart,
  Vulture, whose wings are dull realities?
How should he love thee? or how deem thee wise?
  Who wouldst not leave him in his wandering
To seek for treasure in the jewelled skies,
  Albeit he soared with an undaunted wing?
Hast thou not dragged Diana from her car?
  And driven the Hamadryad from the wood   10
To seek a shelter in some happier star?
  Hast thou not torn the Naiad from her flood,
The Elfin from the green grass, and from me
The summer dream beneath the tamarind tree?

Study Questions

1. What contrast does the sonnet present between the world evoked by science and that evoked by poetry? In one or two sentences, what is the theme of Poe's sonnet?
2. *Apostrophe* is the rhetorical term for the words used to address a person or personified object or concept, whether present or absent, in literary writing. Who or what is addressed in this poem? By what two metaphors is it personified?
3. Explain the statement-question structure of this sonnet. Are the structure and the rhyme scheme related in any regular fashion?
4. The poet asks a series of rhetorical questions which imply that science has altered or destroyed a good many of humanity's pleasurable myths. Explain the references to Diana, the Hamadryad, the Naiad, and the Elfin. Are the questions ever answered?
5. Is *elfin* a plural noun? Comment on Poe's use of *undaunted* and *happier*.

The Use of Force

William Carlos Williams

1   They were new patients to me, all I had was the name, Olson. Please come down as soon as you can, my daughter is very sick.

2   When I arrived I was met by the mother, a big startled looking woman, very clean and apologetic who merely said, Is this the doctor? and let me in. In the back, she added. You must excuse us, doctor, we have her in the kitchen where it is warm. It is very damp here sometimes.

3   The child was fully dressed and sitting on her father's lap near the kitchen table. He tried to get up, but I motioned for him not to bother, took off my overcoat and started to look things over. I could see that they were all very nervous, eyeing me up and down distrustfully. As often, in such cases, they weren't telling me more than they had to, it was up to me to tell them; that's why they were spending three dollars on me.

4   The child was fairly eating me up with her cold, steady eyes, and no expression to her face whatever. She did not move and seemed, inwardly, quiet; an unusually attractive little thing, and as strong as a heifer in appearance. But her face was flushed, she was breathing rapidly, and I realized that she had a high fever. She had magnificent blonde hair, in profusion. One of those picture children often reproduced in advertising leaflets and the photogravure sections of the Sunday papers.

5   She's had a fever for three days, began the father, and we don't know what it comes from. My wife has given her things, you know, like people do, but it don't do no good. And there's been a lot of sickness around. So we tho't you'd better look her over and tell us what is the matter.

6   As doctors often do I took a trial shot at it as a point of departure. Has she had a sore throat?

7   Both parents answered me together, No . . . No, she says her throat don't hurt her.

8   Does your throat hurt you? added the mother to the child. But the little girl's expression didn't change nor did she move her eyes from my face.

9   Have you looked?

10   I tried to, said the mother, but I couldn't see.

11   As it happens we had been having a number of cases of diphtheria in the school to which this child went during that month and we were all, quite apparently, thinking of that, though no one had as yet spoken of the thing.

12   Well, I said, suppose we take a look at the throat first. I smiled in my best professional manner and asking for the child's first name I said, come on, Mathilda, open your mouth and let's take a look at your throat.

13   Nothing doing.

14   Aw, come on, I coaxed, just open your mouth wide and let me take a look. Look, I said opening both hands wide, I haven't anything in my hands. Just open up and let me see.

15   Such a nice man, put in the mother. Look how kind he is to you. Come on, do what he tells you to. He won't hurt you.

16   At that I ground my teeth in disgust. If only they wouldn't use the word "hurt" I might be able to get somewhere. But I did not allow myself to be hurried or disturbed but speaking quietly and slowly I approached the child again.

17   As I moved my chair a little nearer suddenly with one cat-like movement both her hands clawed instinctively for my eyes and she almost reached them too. In fact she knocked my glasses flying and they fell, though unbroken, several feet away from me on the kitchen floor.

18   Both the mother and father almost turned themselves inside out in embarrassment and apology. You bad girl, said the mother, taking her and shaking her by one arm. Look what you've done. The nice man . . .

19   For heaven's sake, I broke in. Don't call me a nice man to her. I'm here to look at her throat on the chance that she might have diphtheria and possibly die of it. But that's nothing to her. Look here, I said to the child, we're going to look at your throat. You're old enough to understand what I'm saying. Will you open it now by yourself or shall we have to open it for you?

20   Not a move. Even her expression hadn't changed. Her breaths however were coming faster and faster. Then the battle began. I had to do it. I had to have a throat culture for her own protection. But first I told the parents that it was entirely up to them. I explained the danger but said that I would not insist on a throat examination so long as they would take the responsibility.

21   If you don't do what the doctor says you'll have to go to the hospital, the mother admonished her severely.

22   Oh yeah? I had to smile to myself. After all, I had already fallen in love with the savage brat, the parents were contemptible to me. In the ensuing struggle they grew more and more abject, crushed, exhausted while she surely rose to magnificent heights of insane fury of effort bred of her terror of me.

23   The father tried his best, and he was a big man but the fact that she was his daughter, his shame at her behavior and his dread of hurting her made him release her just at the critical moment several times when I had almost achieved success, till I wanted to kill him. But his dread also that she might have diphtheria made him tell me to go on, go on though he himself was almost fainting, while the mother moved back and forth

behind us raising and lowering her hands in an agony of apprehension.

24   Put her in front of you on your lap, I ordered, and hold both her wrists.

25   But as soon as he did the child let out a scream. Don't, you're hurting me. Let go of my hands. Let them go I tell you. Then she shrieked terrifyingly, hysterically. Stop it! Stop it! You're killing me!

26   Do you think she can stand it, doctor! said the mother.

27   You get out, said the husband to his wife. Do you want her to die of diphtheria?

28   Come on now, hold her, I said.

29   Then I grasped the child's head with my left hand and tried to get the wooden tongue depressor between her teeth. She fought, with clenched teeth, desperately! But now I also had grown furious—at a child. I tried to hold myself down but I couldn't. I know how to expose a throat for inspection. And I did my best. When finally I got the wooden spatula behind the last teeth and just the point of it into the mouth cavity, she opened up for an instant but before I could see anything she came down again and gripping the wooden blade between her molars she reduced it to splinters before I could get it out again.

30   Aren't you ashamed, the mother yelled at her. Aren't you ashamed to act like that in front of the doctor?

31   Get me a smooth-handled spoon of some sort, I told the mother. We're going through with this. The child's mouth was already bleeding. Her tongue was cut and she was screaming in wild hysterical shrieks. Perhaps I should have desisted and come back in an hour or more. No doubt it would have been better. But I have seen at least two children lying dead in bed of neglect in such cases, and feeling that I must get a diagnosis now or never I went at it again. But the worst of it was that I too had got beyond reason. I could have torn the child apart in my own fury and enjoyed it. It was a pleasure to attack her. My face was burning with it.

32   The damned little brat must be protected against her own idiocy, one says to one's self at such times. Others must be protected against her. It is social necessity. And all these things are true. But a blind fury, a feeling of adult shame, bred of a longing for muscular release are the operatives. One goes on to the end.

33   In a final unreasoning assault I overpowered the child's neck and jaws. I forced the heavy silver spoon back of her teeth and down her throat till she gagged. And there it was—both tonsils covered with membrane. She had fought valiantly to keep me from knowing her secret. She had been hiding that sore throat for three days at least and lying to her parents in order to escape just such an outcome as this.

34   Now truly she *was* furious. She had been on the defensive before but now she attacked. Tried to get off her father's lap and fly at me while tears of defeat blinded her eyes.

Study Questions

1. What is the point of view in "The Use of Force"? How might changing the point of view alter the reader's reaction to the doctor's behavior? Why does Williams choose not to use quotation marks?
2. Does the narrator's professional approach to problems affect his perceptions of people and his handling of events? Is the adversary situation described in this story compatible with medical ethics?
3. What is Williams telling us about the *use* of force? What does the story say about the degrading, irrational nature of force? What is the theme of the story?
4. On what level of diction is the story told?
5. Why does Williams italicize *was* in his final paragraph? How would the meaning of the sentence in which *was* appears be affected if *now* were italicized? *Truly*? *She*? *Furious*?

The Snake

John Steinbeck

1   It was almost dark when young Dr. Phillips swung his sack to his shoulder and left the tide pool. He climbed up over the rocks and squashed along the street in his rubber boots. The street lights were on by the time he arrived at his little commercial laboratory on the cannery street of Monterey. It was a tight little building, standing partly on piers over the bay water and partly on the land. On both sides the big corrugated-iron sardine canneries crowded in on it.

2   Dr. Phillips climbed the wooden steps and opened the door. The white rats in their cages scampered up and down the wire, and the captive cats in their pens mewed for milk. Dr. Phillips turned on the glaring light over the dissection table and dumped his clammy sack on the floor. He walked to the glass cages by the window where the rattlesnakes lived, leaned over and looked in.

3   The snakes were bunched and resting in the corners of the cage, but every head was clear; the dusty eyes seemed to look at nothing, but as the young man leaned over the cage the forked tongues, black on the

ends and pink behind, twittered out and waved slowly up and down. Then the snakes recognized the man and pulled in their tongues.

4   Dr. Phillips threw off his leather coat and built a fire in the tin stove; he set a kettle of water on the stove and dropped a can of beans into the water. Then he stood staring down at the sack on the floor. He was a slight young man with the mild, preoccupied eyes of one who looks through a microscope a great deal. He wore a short blond beard.

5   The draft ran breathily up the chimney and a glow of warmth came from the stove. The little waves washed quietly about the piles under the building. Arranged on shelves about the room were tier above tier of museum jars containing the mounted marine specimens the laboratory dealt in.

6   Dr. Phillips opened a side door and went into his bedroom, a booklined cell containing an army cot, a reading light and an uncomfortable wooden chair. He pulled off his rubber boots and put on a pair of sheepskin slippers. When he went back to the other room the water in the kettle was already beginning to hum.

7   He lifted his sack to the table under the white light and emptied out two dozen common starfish. These he laid out side by side on the table. His preoccupied eyes turned to the busy rats in the wire cages. Taking grain from a paper sack, he poured it into the feeding troughs. Instantly the rats scrambled down from the wire and fell upon the food. A bottle of milk stood on a glass shelf between a small mounted octopus and a jellyfish. Dr. Phillips lifted down the milk and walked to the cat cage, but before he filled the containers he reached in the cage and gently picked out a big rangy alley tabby. He stroked her for a moment and then dropped her in a small black painted box, closed the lid and bolted it and then turned on a petcock which admitted gas into the killing chamber. While the short soft struggle went on in the black box he filled the saucers with milk. One of the cats arched against his hand and he smiled and petted her neck.

8   The box was quiet now. He turned off the petcock, for the airtight box would be full of gas.

9   On the stove the pan of water was bubbling furiously about the can of beans. Dr. Phillips lifted out the can with a big pair of forceps, opened it, and emptied the beans into a glass dish. While he ate he watched the starfish on the table. From between the rays little drops of milky fluid were exuding. He bolted his beans and when they were gone he put the dish in the sink and stepped to the equipment cupboard. From this he took a microscope and a pile of little glass dishes. He filled the dishes one by one with sea water from a tap and arranged them in a line beside the starfish. He took out his watch and laid it on the table under the pouring white light. The waves washed with little sighs against the piles under the floor. He took an eyedropper from a drawer and bent over the starfish.

10   At that moment there were quick soft steps on the wooden stairs and a strong knocking at the door. A slight grimace of annoyance crossed the young man's face as he went to open. A tall, lean woman stood in the doorway. She was dressed in a severe dark suit—her straight black hair, growing low on a flat forehead, was mussed as though the wind had been blowing it. Her black eyes glittered in the strong light.

11   She spoke in a soft throaty voice, "May I come in? I want to talk to you."

12   "I'm very busy just now," he said half-heartedly. "I have to do things at times." But he stood away from the door. The tall woman slipped in.

13   "I'll be quiet until you can talk to me."

14   He closed the door and brought the uncomfortable chair from the bedroom. "You see," he apologized, "the process is started and I must get to it." So many people wandered in and asked questions. He had little routines of explanations for the commoner processes. He could say them without thinking. "Sit here. In a few minutes I'll be able to listen to you."

15   The tall woman leaned over the table. With the eye-dropper the young man gathered fluid from between the rays of the starfish and squirted it into a bowl of water, and then he drew some milky fluid and squirted it in the same bowl and stirred the water gently with the eyedropper. He began his little patter of explanation.

16   "When starfish are sexually mature they release sperm and ova when they are exposed at low tide. By choosing mature specimens and taking them out of the water, I give them a condition of low tide. Now I've mixed the sperm and eggs. Now I put some of the mixture in each one of these ten watch glasses. In ten minutes I will kill those in the first glass with menthol, twenty minutes later I will kill the second group and then a new group every twenty minutes. Then I will have arrested the process in stages, and I will mount the series on microscope slides for biologic study." He paused. "Would you like to look at this first group under the microscope?"

17   "No, thank you."

18   He turned quickly to her. People always wanted to look through the glass. She was not looking at the table at all, but at him. Her black eyes were on him, but they did not seem to see him. He realized why—the irises were as dark as the pupils, there was no color line between the two. Dr. Phillips was piqued at her answer. Although answering questions bored him, a lack of interest in what he was doing irritated him. A desire to arouse her grew in him.

19   "While I'm waiting the first ten minutes I have something to do. Some people don't like to see it. Maybe you'd better step into that room until I finish."

20   "No," she said in her soft flat tone. "Do what you wish. I will wait until you can talk to me." Her hands rested side by side on her lap. She

was completely at rest. Her eyes were bright but the rest of her was almost in a state of suspended animation. He thought, "Low metabolic rate, almost as low as a frog's, from the looks." The desire to shock her out of her inanition possessed him again.

21   He brought a little wooden cradle to the table, laid out scalpels and scissors and rigged a big hollow needle to a pressure tube. Then from the killing chamber he brought the limp dead cat and laid it in the cradle and tied its legs to hooks in the sides. He glanced sidewise at the woman. She had not moved. She was still at rest.

22   The cat grinned up into the light, its pink tongue stuck out between its needle teeth. Dr. Phillips deftly snipped open the skin at the throat; with a scalpel he slit through and found an artery. With flawless technique he put the needle in the vessel and tied it with gut. "Embalming fluid," he explained. "Later I'll inject yellow mass into the venous system and red mass into the arterial system—for bloodstream dissection—biology classes."

23   He looked around at her again. Her dark eyes seemed veiled with dust. She looked without expression at the cat's open throat. Not a drop of blood had escaped. The incision was clean. Dr. Phillips looked at his watch. "Time for the first group." He shook a few crystals of menthol into the first watch glass.

24   The woman was making him nervous. The rats climbed about on the wire of their cage again and squeaked softly. The waves under the building beat with little shocks on the piles.

25   The young man shivered. He put a few lumps of coal in the stove and sat down. "Now," he said. "I haven't anything to do for twenty minutes." He noticed how short her chin was between lower lip and point. She seemed to awaken slowly, to come up out of some deep pool of consciousness. Her head raised and her dark dusty eyes moved about the room and then came back to him.

26   "I was waiting," she said. Her hands remained side by side on her lap. "You have snakes?"

27   "Why, yes," he said rather loudly. "I have about two dozen rattlesnakes. I milk out the venom and send it to the anti-venom laboratories."

28   She continued to look at him but her eyes did not center on him, rather they covered him and seemed to see in a big circle all around him. "Have you a male snake, a male rattlesnake?"

29   "Well, it just happens I know I have. I came in one morning and found a big snake in—in coition with a smaller one. That's very rare in captivity. You see, I do know I have a male snake."

30   "Where is he?"

31   "Why, right in the glass cage by the window there."

32   Her head swung slowly around but her two quiet hands did not move. She turned back toward him. "May I see?"

33   He got up and walked to the case by the window. On the sand bottom the knot of rattlesnakes lay entwined, but their heads were clear.

The tongues came out and flickered a moment and then waved up and down feeling the air for vibrations. Dr. Phillips nervously turned his head. The woman was standing beside him. He had not heard her get up from the chair. He had heard only the splash of water among the piles and the scampering of the rats on the wire screen.

34   She said softly. "Which is the male you spoke of?"

35   He pointed to a thick, dusty gray snake lying by itself in one corner of the cage. "That one. He's nearly five feet long. He comes from Texas. Our Pacific coast snakes are usually smaller. He's been taking all the rats, too. When I want the others to eat I have to take him out."

36   The woman stared down at the blunt dry head. The forked tongue slipped out and hung quivering for a long moment. "And you're sure he's a male."

37   "Rattlesnakes are funny," he said glibly. "Nearly every generalization proves wrong. I don't like to say anything definite about rattlesnakes, but—yes—I can assure you he's a male."

38   Her eyes did not move from the flat head. "Will you sell him to me?"

39   "Sell him?" he cried. "Sell him to you?"

40   "You do sell specimens, don't you?"

41   "Oh—yes. Of course I do. Of course I do."

42   "How much? Five dollars? Ten?"

43   "Oh! Not more than five. But—do you know anything about rattlesnakes? You might be bitten."

44   She looked at him for a moment. "I don't intend to take him. I want to leave him here, but—I want him to be mine. I want to come here and look at him and feed him and to know he's mine." She opened a little purse and took out a five-dollar bill. "Here! Now he is mine."

45   Dr. Phillips began to be afraid. "You could come to look at him without owning him."

46   "I want him to be mine."

47   "Oh, Lord!" he cried. "I've forgotten the time." He ran to the table. "Three minutes over. It won't matter much." He shook menthol crystals into the second watch glass. And then he was drawn back to the cage where the woman still stared at the snake.

48   She asked, "What does he eat?"

49   "I feed them white rats, rats from the cage over there."

50   "Will you put him in the other cage? I want to feed him."

51   "But he doesn't need food. He's had a rat already this week. Sometimes they don't eat for three or four months. I had one that didn't eat for over a year."

52   In her low monotone she asked, "Will you sell me a rat?"

53   He shrugged his shoulders. "I see. You want to watch how rattlesnakes eat. All right. I'll show you. The rat will cost twenty-five cents. It's better than a bullfight if you look at it one way, and it's simply a snake eating his dinner if you look at it another." His tone had become acid. He hated people who made sport of natural processes. He was not a

sportsman but a biologist. He could kill a thousand animals for knowledge, but not an insect for pleasure. He'd been over this in his mind
before.

54   She turned her head slowly toward him and the beginning of a
smile formed on her thin lips. "I want to feed my snake," she said. "I'll
put him in the other cage." She had opened the top of the cage and
dipped her hand in before he knew what she was doing. He leaped
forward and pulled her back. The lid banged shut.

55   "Haven't you any sense," he asked fiercely. "Maybe he wouldn't
kill you, but he'd make you damned sick in spite of what I could do for
you."

56   "You put him in the other cage then," she said quietly.

57   Dr. Phillips was shaken. He found that he was avoiding the dark
eyes that didn't seem to look at anything. He felt that it was profoundly
wrong to put a rat into the cage, deeply sinful; and he didn't know why.
Often he had put rats in the cage when someone or other had wanted to
see it, but this desire tonight sickened him. He tried to explain himself
out of it.

58   "It's a good thing to see," he said. "It shows you how a snake can
work. It makes you have a respect for a rattlesnake. Then, too, lots of
people have dreams about the terror of snakes making the kill. I think
because it is a subjective rat. The person is the rat. Once you see it the
whole matter is objective. The rat is only a rat and the terror is removed."

59   He took a long stick equipped with a leather noose from the wall.
Opening the trap he dropped the noose over the big snake's head and
tightened the thong. A piercing dry rattle filled the room. The thick body
writhed and slashed about the handle of the stick as he lifted the snake
out and dropped it in the feeding cage. It stood ready to strike for a time,
but the buzzing gradually ceased. The snake crawled into a corner, made
a big figure eight with its body and lay still.

60   "You see," the young man explained, "these snakes are quite tame.
I've had them a long time. I suppose I could handle them if I wanted to,
but everyone who does handle rattlesnakes gets bitten sooner or later. I
just don't want to take the chance." He glanced at the woman. He hated
to put in the rat. She had moved over in front of the new cage; her black
eyes were on the stony head of the snake again.

61   She said, "Put in a rat."

62   Reluctantly he went to the rat cage. For some reason he was sorry
for the rat, and such a feeling had never come to him before. His eyes
went over the mass of swarming white bodies climbing up the screen
toward him. "Which one?" he thought. "Which one shall it be?" Suddenly he turned angrily to the woman. "Wouldn't you rather I put in a
cat? Then you'd see a real fight. The cat might even win, but if it did it
might kill the snake. I'll sell you a cat if you like."

63   She didn't look at him. "Put in a rat," she said. "I want him to eat."

64   He opened the rat cage and thrust his hand in. His fingers found a
tail and he lifted a plump, red-eyed rat out of the cage. It struggled up to

try to bite his fingers and, failing, hung spread out and motionless from its tail. He walked quickly across the room, opened the feeding cage and dropped the rat in on the sand floor. "Now, watch it," he cried.

65   The woman did not answer him. Her eyes were on the snake where it lay still. Its tongue flicking in and out rapidly, tasted the air of the cage.

66   The rat landed on its feet, turned around and sniffed at its pink naked tail and then unconcernedly trotted across the sand, smelling as it went. The room was silent. Dr. Phillips did not know whether the water sighed among the piles or whether the woman sighed. Out of the corner of his eye he saw her body crouch and stiffen.

67   The snake moved out smoothly, slowly. The tongue flicked in and out. The motion was so gradual, so smooth that it didn't seem to be motion at all. In the other end of the cage the rat perked up in a sitting position and began to lick down the fine white hair on its chest. The snake moved on, keeping always a deep S curve in its neck.

68   The silence beat on the young man. He felt the blood drifting up in his body. He said loudly, "See! He keeps the striking curve ready. Rattlesnakes are cautious, almost cowardly animals. The mechanism is so delicate. The snake's dinner is to be got by an operation as deft as a surgeon's job. He takes no chances with his instruments."

69   The snake had flowed to the middle of the cage by now. The rat looked up, saw the snake and then unconcernedly went back to licking its chest.

70   "It's the most beautiful thing in the world," the young man said. His veins were throbbing. "It's the most terrible thing in the world."

71   The snake was close now. Its head lifted a few inches from the sand. The head weaved slowly back and forth, aiming, getting distance, aiming. Dr. Phillips glanced again at the woman. He turned sick. She was weaving too, not much, just a suggestion.

72   The rat looked up and saw the snake. It dropped to four feet and back up, and then—the stroke. It was impossible to see, simply a flash. The rat jarred as though under an invisible blow. The snaked backed hurriedly into the corner from which it had come, and settled down, its tongue working constantly.

73   "Perfect!" Dr. Phillips cried. "Right between the shoulder blades. The fangs must almost have reached the heart."

74   The rat stood still, breathing like a little white bellows. Suddenly it leaped in the air and landed on its side. Its legs kicked spasmodically for a second and it was dead.

75   The woman relaxed, relaxed sleepily.

76   "Well," the young man demanded, "it was an emotional bath, wasn't it?"

77   She turned her misty eyes to him. "Will he eat it now?" she asked.

78   "Of course he'll eat it. He didn't kill it for a thrill. He killed it because he was hungry."

79   The corners of the woman's mouth turned up a trifle again. She looked back at the snake. "I want to see him eat it."

80   Now the snake came out of its corner again. There was no striking curve in its neck, but it approached the rat gingerly, ready to jump back in case it attacked. It nudged the body gently with its blunt nose, and drew away. Satisfied that it was dead, the snake touched the body all over with its chin, from head to tail. It seemed to measure the body and to kiss it. Finally it opened its mouth and unhinged its jaws at the corners.

81   Dr. Phillips put his will against his head to keep it from turning toward the woman. He thought, "If she's opening her mouth, I'll be sick. I'll be afraid." He succeeded in keeping his eyes away.

82   The snake fitted its jaws over the rat's head and then with a slow peristaltic pulsing, began to engulf the rat. The jaws gripped and the whole throat crawled up, and the jaws gripped again.

83   Dr. Phillips turned away and went to his work table. "You've made me miss one of the series," he said bitterly. "The set won't be complete." He put one of the watch glasses under a low-power microscope and looked at it, and then angrily he poured the contents of all the dishes into the sink. The waves had fallen so that only a wet whisper came up through the floor. The young man lifted a trapdoor at his feet and dropped the starfish down into the black water. He paused at the cat, crucified in the cradle and grinning comically into the light. Its body was puffed with embalming fluid. He shut off the pressure, withdrew the needle and tied the vein.

84   "Would you like some coffee?" he asked.

85   "No, thank you. I shall be going pretty soon."

86   He walked to her where she stood in front of the snake cage. The rat was swallowed, all except an inch of pink tail that stuck out of the snake's mouth like a sardonic tongue. The throat heaved again and the tail disappeared. The jaws snapped back into their sockets, and the big snake crawled heavily to the corner, made a big eight and dropped its head on the sand.

87   "He's asleep now," the woman said. "I'm going now. But I'll come back and feed my snake every little while. I'll pay for the rats. I want him to have plenty. And sometime—I'll take him away with me." Her eyes came out of their dusty dream for a moment. "Remember, he's mine. Don't take his poison. I want him to have it. Goodnight." She walked swiftly to the door and went out. He heard her footsteps on the stairs, but he could not hear her walk away on the pavement.

88   Dr. Phillips turned a chair around and sat down in front of the snake cage. He tried to comb out his thought as he looked at the torpid snake. "I've read so much about psychological sex symbols," he thought. "It doesn't seem to explain. Maybe I'm too much alone. Maybe I should kill the snake. If I knew—no, I can't pray to anything."

89   For weeks he expected her to return. "I will go out and leave her alone here when she comes," he decided. "I won't see the damned thing again."

90   She never came again. For months he looked for her when he walked about in the town. Several times he ran after some tall woman thinking it might be she. But he never saw her again—ever.

Study Questions

1. This story is told from the limited omniscient point of view and reflects the young biologist's reactions to events. How do the woman's presence and behavior in his laboratory violate the impersonality of his research?
2. What conventional explanations of the woman's behavior fail him? Is Dr. Phillips attracted or repulsed by her behavior?
3. What physical characteristics of the woman are reminiscent of the snake? What physical movement?
4. What explanation is there for Dr. Phillips's irrational behavior months after his single meeting with the woman?

A Narrow Fellow in the Grass

Emily Dickinson

A narrow Fellow in the Grass
Occasionally rides—
You may have met Him—did you not
His notice sudden is—

The Grass divides as with a Comb—
A spotted shaft is seen—
And then it closes at your feet
And opens further on—

He likes a Boggy Acre
A Floor too cool for Corn—   10
Yet when a Boy, and Barefoot—
I more than once at Noon
Have passed, I thought, a Whip lash
Unbraiding in the Sun
When stooping to secure it
It wrinkled, and was gone—

Several of Nature's People
I know, and they know me—
I feel for them a transport
Of cordiality—   20

But never met this Fellow
Attended, or alone
Without a tighter breathing
And Zero at the Bone—

Study Questions

1. Although the word *snake* does not occur in this poem, the subject is a snake and the persona's reactions to it. What metaphors and physical details describe a snake?
2. Are the metaphors and simile leading to the last line threatening? "Tighter breathing" clearly refers to the anxiety of the narrator. What might "Zero at the Bone" signify?
3. How does the pleasurable phrase, "transport/Of cordiality," contrast with the terse "Zero at the Bone"?

Snake

D. H. Lawrence

A snake came to my water-trough
On a hot, hot day, and I in pajamas for the heat,
To drink there.

In the deep, strange-scented shade of the great dark carob-tree
I came down the steps with my pitcher
And must wait, must stand and wait, for there he was at the trough
        before me.

He reached down from a fissure in the earth-wall in the gloom
And trailed his yellow-brown slackness soft-bellied down, over the
        edge of the stone trough
And rested his throat upon the stone bottom,
And where the water had dripped from the tap, in a small clearness,   10
He sipped with his straight mouth,
Softly drank through his straight gums, into his slack long body,
Silently.

Someone was before me at my water-trough,
And I, like a second comer, waiting.

He lifted his head from his drinking, as cattle do,
And looked at me vaguely, as drinking cattle do,
And flickered his two-forked tongue from his lips, and mused a
        moment,
And stooped and drank a little more,
Being earth-brown, earth-golden from the burning bowels of the
        earth   20
On the day of Sicilian July, with Etna smoking.

The voice of my education said to me
He must be killed,
For in Sicily the black, black snakes are innocent, the gold are
        venomous.

And voices in me said, If you were a man
You would take a stick and break him now, and finish him off.

But must I confess how I liked him,
How glad I was he had come like a guest in quiet, to drink at my
      water-trough
And depart peaceful, pacified, and thankless,
Into the burning bowels of this earth?   30

Was it cowardice, that I dared not kill him?
Was it perversity, that I longed to talk to him?
Was it humility, to feel so honored?
I felt so honored.

And yet those voices:
If you were not afraid, you would kill him!

And truly I was afraid, I was most afraid,
But even so, honored still more
That he should seek my hospitality
From out the dark door of the secret earth.   40

He drank enough
And lifted his head, dreamily, as one who has drunken,
And flickered his tongue like a forked night on the air, so black,
Seeming to lick his lips,
And looked round like a god, unseeing, into the air,
And slowly turned his head,
And slowly, very slowly, as if thrice adream,
Proceeded to draw his slow length curving round
And climb again the broken bank of my wall-face.

And as he put his head into that dreadful hole,   50
And as he slowly drew up, snake-easing his shoulders, and entered
      farther,
A sort of horror, a sort of protest against his withdrawing into that
      horrid black hole,
Deliberately going into the blackness, and slowly drawing himself
      after,
Overcame me now his back was turned.

I looked round, I put down my pitcher,
I picked up a clumsy log
And threw it at the water-trough with a clatter.

I think it did not hit him,
But suddenly that part of him that was left behind convulsed in
      undignified haste
Writhed like lightning, and was gone   60

Into the black hole, the earth-lipped fissure in the wall-front,
At which, in the intense still noon, I stared with fascination.

And immediately I regretted it.
I thought how paltry, how vulgar, what a mean act!
I despised myself and the voices of my accursed human education.

And I thought of the albatross
And I wished he would come back, my snake.

For he seemed to me again like a king,
Like a king in exile, uncrowned in the underworld,
Now due to be crowned again.   70

And so, I missed my chance with one of the lords
Of life.
And I have something to expiate;
A pettiness.

Study Questions

1. Identify words and phrases which Lawrence repeats. What is the effect of this repetition?
2. Comment on the contrast between light and darkness in this poem.
3. What is the significance of the phrases "uncrowned in the underworld" and "one of the lords/Of life"?
4. When the persona is talking about himself the language is matter-of-fact, clipped, monosyllabic, and lacking in metaphor. The language describing the snake, however, embodies movement, color, contrasts, and metaphors. What is achieved by such variation?
5. Read Samuel Taylor Coleridge's "The Rime of the Ancient Mariner" and comment on Lawrence's use of *albatross* and *expiate*. Are there snakes in Coleridge's poem?

The Unknown Citizen

W. H. Auden

(To JS/07/M/378
This Marble Monument
Is Erected by the State)

He was found by the Bureau of Statistics to be
One against whom there was no official complaint,
And all the reports on his conduct agree
That, in the modern sense of an old-fashioned word, he was a saint,
For in everything he did he served the Greater Community.
Except for the War till the day he retired
He worked in a factory and never got fired,
But satisfied his employers, Fudge Motors Inc.
Yet he wasn't a scab or odd in his views,
For his Union reports that he paid his dues,   10
(Our report on his Union shows it was sound)
And our Social Psychology workers found
That he was popular with his mates and liked a drink.
The Press are convinced that he bought a paper every day
And that his reactions to advertisements were normal in every way.
Policies taken out in his name prove that he was fully insured,
And his Health-card shows he was once in hospital but left it cured.
Both Producers Research and High-Grade Living declare
He was fully sensible to the advantages of the Instalment Plan
And had everything necessary to the Modern Man,   20
A phonograph, a radio, a car and a frigidaire.
Our researchers into Public Opinion are content
That he held the proper opinions for the time of year;
When there was peace, he was for peace; when there was war, he
            went.
He was married and added five children to the population,
Which our Eugenist says was the right number for a parent of his
            generation,
And our teachers report that he never interfered with their educa-
            tion,
Was he free? Was he happy? The question is absurd:
Had anything been wrong, we should certainly have heard.

Study Questions

1. From whose point of view is the unknown citizen described?
2. What do you learn from the inscription on the citizen's marble monument?
3. How does the poet satirize bureaucratic language, public relations, and acquisitive consumerism? Why and how does Auden use capitalization?
4. Why might the State be so approving of this citizen?
5. What has the citizen left behind after his death? Why are the questions "Was he free? Was he happy?" placed near the end, as if by afterthought?

My Life with R. H. Macy

Shirley Jackson

1   And the first thing they did was segregate me. They segregated me from the only person in the place I had even a speaking acquaintance with; that was a girl I had met going down the hall who said to me: "Are you as scared as I am?" And when I said, "Yes," she said, "I'm in lingerie, what are you in?" and I thought for a while and then said, "Spun glass," which was as good an answer as I could think of, and she said, "Oh. Well, I'll meet you here in a sec." And she went away and was segregated and I never saw her again.

2   Then they kept calling my name and I kept trotting over to wherever they called it and they would say ("They" all this time being startlingly beautiful young women in tailored suits and with short-clipped hair), "Go with Miss Cooper, here. She'll tell you what to do." All the women I met my first day were named Miss Cooper. And Miss Cooper would say to me: "What are you in?" and I had learned by that time to say, "Books," and she would say, "Oh, well, then, you belong with Miss Cooper here," and then she would call "Miss Cooper?" and another young woman would come and the first one would say, "13–3138 here belongs with you," and Miss Cooper would say, "What is she in?" and Miss Cooper would answer, "Books," and I would go away and be segregated again.

3   Then they taught me. They finally got me segregated into a classroom, and I sat there for a while all by myself (that's how far

segregated I was) and then a few other girls came in, all wearing tailored suits (I was wearing a red velvet afternoon frock) and we sat down and they taught us. They gave us each a big book with R. H. Macy written on it, and inside this book were pads of little sheets saying (from left to right): "Comp. keep for ref. cust. d.a. no. or c.t. no. salesbook no. sales-check no. clerk no. dept. date M." After M there was a long line for Mr. or Mrs. and the name, and then it began again with "No. item. class. at price. total." And down at the bottom was written ORIGINAL and then again, "Comp. keep for ref.," and "Paste yellow gift stamp here." I read all this very carefully. Pretty soon a Miss Cooper came, who talked for a little while on the advantages we had in working at Macy's, and she talked about the salesbooks, which it seems came apart into a sort of road map and carbons and things. I listened for a while, and when Miss Cooper wanted us to write on the little pieces of paper, I copied from the girl next to me. That was training.

4   Finally someone said we were going on the floor, and we descended from the sixteenth floor to the first. We were in groups of six by then, all following Miss Cooper doggedly and wearing little tags saying BOOK INFORMATION. I never did find out what that meant. Miss Cooper said I had to work on the special sale counter, and showed me a little book called *The Stage-Struck Seal*, which it seemed I would be selling. I had gotten about halfway through it before she came back to tell me I had to stay with my unit.

5   I enjoyed meeting the time clock, and spent a pleasant half-hour punching various cards standing around, and then someone came in and said I couldn't punch the clock with my hat on. So I had to leave, bowing timidly at the time clock and its prophet, and I went and found out my locker number, which was 1773, and my time clock number, which was 712, and my cash-box number, which was 1336, and my cash-register number, which was 253, and my cash-register-drawer number, which was K, and my cash-register-drawer-key number, which was 872, and my department number, which was 13. I wrote all these numbers down. And that was my first day.

6   My second day was better. I was officially on the floor. I stood in a corner of a counter, with one hand possessively on *The Stage-Struck Seal*, waiting for customers. The counter head was named 13–2246, and she was very kind to me. She sent me to lunch three times, because she got me confused with 13–6454 and 13–3141. It was after lunch that a customer came. She came over and took one of my stage-struck seals, and said "How much is this?" I opened my mouth and the customer said "I have a D. A. and I will have this sent to my aunt in Ohio. Part of that D.A. I will pay for with a book dividend of 32 cents, and the rest of course will be on my account. Is this book price-fixed?" That's as near as I can remember what she said. I smiled confidently, and said "Certainly; will you wait just one moment?" I found a little piece of paper in a drawer under the counter: it had "Duplicate Triplicate" printed across the front

in big letters. I took down the customer's name and address, her aunt's name and address, and wrote carefully across the front of the duplicate triplicate "1 Stg. Strk. Sl." Then I smiled at the customer again and said carelessly: "That will be seventy-five cents." She said "But I have a D.A." I told her that all D. A.'s were suspended for the Christmas rush, and she gave me seventy-five cents, which I kept. Then I rang up a "No Sale" on the cash register and I tore up the duplicate triplicate because I didn't know what else to do with it.

7   Later on another customer came and said "Where would I find a copy of Ann Rutherford Gwynn's *He Came Like Thunder?*" and I said "In medical books, right across the way," but 13-2246 came and said "That's philosophy, isn't it?" and the customer said it was, and 13-2246 said "Right down this aisle, in dictionaries." The customer went away, and I said to 13-2246 that her guess was as good as mine, anyway, and she stared at me and explained that philosophy, social sciences and Bertrand Russell were all kept in dictionaries.

8   So far I haven't been back to Macy's for my third day, because that night when I started to leave the store, I fell down the stairs and tore my stockings and the doorman said that if I went to my department head Macy's would give me a new pair of stockings and I went back and I found Miss Cooper and she said, "Go to the adjuster on the seventh floor and give him this," and she handed me a little slip of pink paper and on the bottom of it was printed "Comp. keep for ref. cust. d.a. no. or c.t. no. salesbook no. salescheck no. clerk no. dept. date M." And after M, instead of a name, she had written 13-3138. I took the little pink slip and threw it away and went up to the fourth floor and bought myself a pair of stockings for $.69 and then I came down and went out the customers' entrance.

9   I wrote Macy's a long letter, and I signed it with all my numbers added together and divided by 11,700, which is the number of employees in Macy's. I wonder if they miss me.

Study Questions

1. What satirical devices are used to describe the experience in this story?
2. How does the point of view contribute to the tone of "My Life with R. H. Macy"?
3. At what point in the story does efficiency fail? Why?
4. Why is *segregated* used so often? Why do so many sentences begin with *and*, and so many paragraphs with words indicating time (such as *then, finally,* and *later*)?
5. Comment on the variations in sentence structure and length.

A Modest Proposal

Jonathan Swift

1   It is a melancholly Object to those, who walk through this great Town or travel in the Country, when they see the Streets, the Roads and Cabbin-doors crowded with Beggers of the Female Sex, followed by three, four, or six Children, all in Rags, and importuning every Passenger for an Alms. These Mothers instead of being able to work for their honest livelyhood, are forced to employ all their time in Stroling to beg Sustenance for their helpless Infants, who, as they grow up, either turn Thieves for want of Work, or leave their dear Native Country, to fight for the Pretender in Spain, or sell themselves to the Barbadoes.

2   I think it is agreed by all Parties, that this prodigious number of Children in the Arms, or on the Backs, or at the Heels of their Mothers, and frequently of their Fathers, is in the present deplorable state of the Kingdom, a very great additional grievance; and therefore whoever could find out a fair, cheap and easy method of making these Children sound and useful Members of the Common-wealth, would deserve so well of the publick, as to have his Statue set up for a Preserver of the Nation.

3   But my Intention is very far from being confined to provide only for the Children of professed Beggers, it is of a much greater Extent, and shall take in the whole Number of Infants at a certain Age, who are born of Parents in effect as little able to support them, as those who demand our Charity in the Streets.

4   As to my own part, having turned my Thoughts, for many Years, upon this important Subject, and maturely weighed the several Schemes of other Projectors, I have always found them grossly mistaken in their computation. It is true, a Child just dropt from its Dam, may be supported by her Milk, for a Solar Year with little other Nourishment, at most not above the Value of two Shillings, which the Mother may certainly get, or the Value in Scraps, by her lawful Occupation of Begging; and it is exactly at one Year Old that I propose to provide for them in such a manner, as, instead of being a Charge upon their Parents, or the Parish, or wanting Food and Raiment for the rest of their Lives, they shall, on the Contrary, contribute to the Feeding and partly to the Cloathing of many Thousands.

5   There is likewise another great Advantage in my Scheme, that it will prevent those voluntary Abortions, and that horrid practice of Women murdering their Bastard Children, alas! too frequent among us,

Sacrificing the poor innocent Babes, I doubt, more to avoid the Expense than the Shame, which would move Tears and Pity in the most Savage and inhuman breast.

6   The number of Souls in this Kingdom being usually reckoned one Million and a half, Of these I calculate there may be about two hundred thousand Couples whose Wives are Breeders; from which number I substract thirty Thousand Couples, who are able to maintain their own Children, although I apprehend there cannot be so many, under the present Distresses of the Kingdom; but this being granted, there will remain an hundred and seventy thousand Breeders. I again Substract fifty Thousand, for those Women who miscarry, or whose Children die by accident, or disease within the Year. There only remain an hundred and twenty thousand Children of poor Parents annually born: The question therefore is, How this number shall be reared, and provided for? which, as I have already said, under the present Situation of Affairs, is utterly impossible by all the Methods hitherto proposed; for we can neither employ them in Handicraft or Agriculture; we neither build Houses, (I mean in the Country) nor cultivate Land: They can very seldom pick up a Livelihood by Stealing till they arrive at six years Old; except where they are of towardly parts; although, I confess, they learn the Rudiments much earlier; during which time they can however be properly looked upon only as Probationers; as I have been informed by a principal Gentleman in the County of Cavan, who protested to me, that he never knew above one or two Instances under the Age of six, even in a part of the Kingdom so renowned for the quickest proficiency in that Art.

7   I am assured by our Merchants, that a Boy or a Girl before twelve years Old, is no saleable Commodity, and even when they come to this Age, they will not yield above three Pounds, or three Pounds and half a Crown at most, on the Exchange; which cannot turn to Account either to the Parents or Kingdom, the Charge of Nutriment and Rags having been at least four times that Value.

8   I shall now therefore humbly propose my own Thoughts, which I hope will not be liable to the least Objection.

9   I have been assured by a very knowing American of my acquaintance in London, that a young healthy Child well Nursed is at a year Old a most delicious nourishing and wholesome Food, whether Stewed, Roasted, Baked, or Boiled; and I make no doubt that it will equally serve in a Fricasie, or a Ragout.

10   I do therefore humbly offer it to publick consideration, that of the Hundred and twenty thousand Children, already computed, twenty thousand may be reserved for Breed, whereof only one fourth part to be Males; which is more than we allow to Sheep, black Cattle, or Swine, and my Reason is, that these Children are seldom the Fruits of Marriage, a Circumstance not much regarded by our Savages, therefore, one Male will be sufficient to serve four Females. That the remaining Hundred thousand may at a year Old be offered in Sale to the Persons of Quality

and Fortune, through the Kingdom, always advising the Mother to let them Suck plentifully in the last Month, so as to render them Plump, and Fat for a good Table. A Child will make two Dishes at an Entertainment for Friends, and when the Family dines alone, the fore or hind Quarter will make a reasonable Dish, and seasoned with a little Pepper or Salt will be very good Boiled on the fourth Day, especially in Winter.

11   I have reckoned upon a Medium, that a Child just born will weigh 12 pounds, and in a solar Year, if tolerably nursed, encreaseth to 28 Pounds.

12   I grant this food will be somewhat dear, and therefore very proper for Landlords, who, as they have already devoured most of the Parents seem to have the best Title of the Children.

13   Infant's flesh will be in Season throughout the Year, but more plentiful in March, and a little before and after; for we are told by a grave Author an eminent French Physician, that Fish being a prolifick Dyet, there are more Children born in Roman Catholic Countries about nine Months after Lent, than at any other Season; therefore reckoning a Year after Lent, the Markets will be more glutted than usual, because the Number of Popish Infants, is at least three to one in this Kingdom, and therefore it will have one other Collateral advantage, by lessening the Number of Papists among us.

14   I have already computed the Charge of nursing a Begger's Child (in which List I reckon all Cottagers, Labourers, and four fifths of the Farmers) to be about two Shillings per Annum, Rags included; and I believe no Gentleman would repine to give Ten Shillings for the Carcass of a good fat Child, which, as I have said will make four Dishes of excellent Nutritive Meat, when he hath only some particular Friend, or his own Family to dine with him. Thus the Squire will learn to be a good Landlord, and grow popular among his Tenants, the Mother will have Eight Shillings neat Profit, and be fit for Work till she produces another Child.

15   Those who are more thrifty (as I must confess the Times require) may flay the Carcass; the Skin of which, Artificially dressed, will make admirable Gloves for Ladies, and Summer Boots for fine Gentlemen.

16   As to our City of Dublin, Shambles may be appointed for this purpose, in the most convenient parts of it, and Butchers we may be assured will not be wanting; although I rather recommend buying the Children alive, and dressing them hot from the Knife, as we do roasting Pigs.

17   A very worthy Person, a true Lover of his Country, and whose Virtues I highly esteem, was lately pleased, in discoursing on this matter, to offer a refinement upon my Scheme. He said, that many Gentlemen of this Kingdom, having of late destroyed their Deer, he conceived that the Want of Venison might be well supply'd by the Bodies of young Lads and Maidens, not exceeding fourteen Years of Age, nor under twelve; so great a Number of both Sexes in every Country being now

ready to Starve, for want of Work and Service: And these to be disposed of by their Parents if alive, or otherwise by their nearest Relations. But with due deference to so excellent a Friend, and so deserving a Patriot, I cannot be altogether in his Sentiments; for as to the Males, my American acquaintance assured me from frequent Experience, that their Flesh was generally Tough and Lean, like that of our Schoolboys, by continual exercise, and their Taste disagreeable, and to fatten them would not answer the Charge. Then as to the Females, it would, I think with humble Submission, be a Loss to the Publick, because they soon would become Breeders themselves: And besides it is not improbable that some scrupulous People might be apt to Censure such a Practice, (although indeed very unjustly) as a little bordering upon Cruelty, which, I confess, hath always been with me the strongest Objection against any Project, how well soever intended.

18   But in order to justify my Friend, he confessed, that this expedient was put into his Head by the famous Sallmanaazor, a Native of the Island Formosa, who came from thence to London, above twenty Years ago, and in Conversation told my Friend, that in his Country when any young Person happened to be put to Death, the Executioner sold the Carcass to Persons of Quality, as a prime Dainty, and that, in his Time, the Body of a plump Girl of fifteen, who was crucified for an attempt to poison the Emperor, was sold to his Imperial Majesty's prime Minister of State, and other great Mandarins of the Court, in Joints from the Gibbet, at four hundred Crowns. Neither indeed can I deny, that if the same Use were made of several plump young Girls in this Town, who, without single Groat to their Fortunes, cannot stir abroad without a Chair, and appear at a Play-house, and Assemblies in Foreign fineries, which they never will pay for; the Kingdom would not be the worse.

19   Some Persons of a desponding Spirit are in great concern about that vast Number of poor People, who are Aged, Diseased, or Maimed, and I have been desired to imploy my Thoughts what Course may be taken, to ease the Nation of so grevious an Incumbrance. But I am not in the least Pain upon that matter, because it is very well known, that they are every Day dying, and rotting, by cold and famine, and filth, and vermin, as fast as can be reasonably expected. And as to the younger Labourers, they are now in almost as hopeful a Condition. They cannot get Work, and consequently pine away for want of Nourishment, to a degree, that if at any Time they are accidentally hired to common Labour, they have not Strength to perform it, and thus the Country and themselves are happily delivered from the Evils to come.

20   I have too long digressed, and therefore shall return to my Subject. I think the Advantages by the Proposal which I have made are obvious and many, as well as of the highest Importance.

21   For *First*, as I have already observed, it would greatly lessen the Number of Papists, with whom we are Yearly over-run, being the princi-

pal Breeders of the Nation, as well as our most dangerous Enemies, and who stay at home on purpose with a Design to deliver the Kingdom to the Pretender, hoping to take their Advantage by the Absence of so many good Protestants, who have chosen rather to leave their Country, than stay at home, and pay Tithes against their conscience, to an Episcopal Curate.

22

Secondly, The poorer Tenants will have something valuable of their own which by Law may be made lyable to Distress, and help to pay their Landlord's Rent, their Corn and Cattle being already seized, and Money a Thing unknown.

23

Thirdly, Whereas the Maintenance of an hundred thousand Children, from two Years old, and upwards, cannot be computed at less than Ten Shillings a Piece per Annum, the Nation's Stock will be thereby increased fifty thousand Pounds per Annum, beside the Profit of a new Dish, introduced to the Tables of all Gentlemen of Fortune in the Kingdom, who have any Refinement in Taste, and the Money will circulate among our Selves, the Goods being entirely of our own Growth and Manufacture.

24

Fourthly, The constant Breeders besides the gain of eight Shillings Sterling per Annum, by the Sale of their Children, will be rid of the Charge of maintaining them after the first Year.

25

Fifthly, This Food would likewise bring great Custom to Taverns, where the Vintners will certainly be so prudent as to procure the best Receipts for dressing it to Perfection; and consequently have their Houses frequented by all the fine Gentlemen, who justly value themselves upon their Knowledge in good Eating; and a skilful Cook, who understands how to oblige his Guests, will contrive to make it as expensive as they please.

26

Sixthly, This would be a great Inducement to Marriage, which all wise Nations have either encouraged by Rewards, or enforced by Laws and Penalties. It would encrease the Care and Tenderness of Mothers towards their Children, when they were sure of a Settlement for Life, to the poor Babes, provided in some Sort by the Publick, to their annual Profit instead of Expence; we should soon see an honest Emulation among the married Women, which of them could bring the fattest Child to the Market. Men would become as fond of their Wives, during the Time of their Pregnancy, as they are now of their Mares in Foal, their Cows in Calf, or Sows when they are ready to farrow, nor offer to beat or kick them (as is too frequent a Practice) for fear of a Miscarriage.

27

Many other Advantages might be enumerated. For Instance, the Addition of some thousand Carcasses in our Exportation of Barrel'd Beef: The Propagation of Swine's Flesh, and Improvement in the Art of making good Bacon, so much wanted among us by the great Destruction of Pigs, too frequent at our Tables, which are no way comparable in Taste, or Magnificence to a well grown, fat yearling Child, which roasted whole will make a considerable Figure at a Lord Mayor's Feast, or any other Publick Entertainment. But this, and many others, I omit, being studious of Brevity.

28   Supposing that one thousand Families in this City, would be constant Customers for Infant's Flesh, besides others who might have it at merry Meetings, particularly at Weddings and Christenings, I compute that Dublin would take off Annually about twenty thousand Carcasses, and the rest of the Kingdom (where probably they will be sold somewhat cheaper) the remaining eighty Thousand.

29   I can think of no one Objection, that will possibly be raised against this Proposal, unless it should be urged, that the Number of People will be thereby much lessened in the Kingdom. This I freely own, and 'twas indeed one principal Design in offering it to the World. I desire the Reader will observe, that I calculate my Remedy for this one individual Kingdom of Ireland, and for no Other that ever was, is, or, I think, ever can be upon Earth. Therefore let no man talk to me of other Expedients: Of taxing our Absentees at five Shillings a Pound: Of using neither Cloaths, nor Household Furniture, except what is of our own Growth and Manufacture: Of utterly rejecting the Materials and Instruments that promote Foreign Luxury: Of curing the Expensiveness of Pride, Vanity, Idleness, and Gaming in our Women: Of introducing a Vein of Parcimony, Prudence and Temperance: Of learning to love our Country, wherein we differ even from Laplanders, and the Inhabitants of Topinamboo: Of quitting our Animosities, and Factions, nor act any longer like the Jews, who were murdering one another at the very Moment their City was taken: Of being a little cautious not to sell our Country and Consciences for nothing: Of teaching Landlords to have at least one Degree of Mercy towards their Tenants. Lastly, Of putting a Spirit of Honesty, Industry, and Skill into our Shop-keepers, who, if a Resolution could now be taken to buy only our Native Goods, would immediately unite to cheat and exact upon us in the Price, the Measure, and the Goodness, nor could ever yet be brought to make one fair Proposal of just Dealing, though often and earnestly invited to it.

30   Therefore I repeat, let no Man talk to me of these and the like Expedients, till he hath at least some Glimpse of Hope, that there will ever be some hearty and sincere Attempt to put them in Practice.

31   But as to my self, having been wearied out for many Years with offering vain, idle, visionary Thoughts, and at length utterly despairing of Success, I fortunately fell upon this Proposal, which as it is wholly new, so it hath something Solid and Real, of no Expence and little Trouble, full in our own Power, and whereby we can incur no Danger in disobliging England. For this kind of Commodity will not bear Exportation, the Flesh being of too tender a Consistence, to admit a long Continuance in Salt, although perhaps I cou'd name a Country, which wou'd be glad to eat up our whole Nation without it.

32   After all, I am not so violently bent upon my own Opinion, as to reject any Offer, proposed by wise Men, which shall be found equally Innocent, Cheap, Easy, and Effectual. But before something of that Kind shall be advanced in Contradiction to my Scheme, and offering a better, I desire the Author or Authors, will be pleased maturely to consider two Points. *First,* As Things now stand, how they will be able to find Food and Raiment for a hundred Thousand useless Mouths and Backs. And *Secondly,* There being a round Million of Creatures in Human Figure, throughout this Kingdom, whose whole Subsistence put into a common Stock, would leave them in Debt two Millions of Pounds Sterling, adding those, who are Beggers by Profession, to the Bulk of Farmers, Cottagers and Labourers, with their Wives and Children, who are Beggers in Effect; I desire those Politicians, who dislike my Overture, and may perhaps be so bold to attempt an Answer, that they will first ask the Parents of these Mortals, Whether they would not at this Day think it a great Happiness to have been sold for Food at a Year Old, in the manner I prescribe, and thereby have avoided such a perpetual Scene of Misfortunes, as they have since gone through, by the Oppression of Landlords, the Impossibility of paying Rent without Money or Trade, the Want of common Sustenance, with neither House nor Cloaths to cover them from the Inclemencies of the Weather, and the most inevitable Prospect of intailing the like, or greater Miseries, upon their Breed for ever.

33   I profess in the Sincerity of my Heart, that I have not the least Personal Interest in endeavouring to promote this Necessary Work, having no other Motive than the Publick Good of my Country, by advancing our Trade, providing for infants, relieving the Poor, and giving some Pleasure to the Rich. I have no Children, by which I can propose to get a single Penny; the youngest being nine Years Old, and my Wife past Child-bearing.

Study Questions

1. Why did Swift assume the persona of a philanthropist in writing "A Modest Proposal"? What irony is there in the essay's title?
2. What elements of practicality and thrift accompany the proposal? What tone do these elements contribute?
3. Explain the contrast between "Souls" and "Breeders" in paragraph 6.
4. What is the function of paragraph 29? Is this paragraph satirical?

November Cotton Flower

Jean Toomer

Boll-weevil's coming, and the winter's cold,
Made cotton-stalks look rusty, seasons old,
And cotton, scarce as any southern snow,
Was vanishing; the branch, so pinched and slow,
Failed in its function as the autumn rake;
Drought fighting soil has caused the soil to take
All water from the streams; dead birds were found
In wells a hundred feet below the ground—
Such was the season when the flower bloomed.
Old folks were startled, and it soon assumed   10
Significance. Superstition saw
Something it had never seen before:
Brown eyes that loved without a trace of fear,
Beauty so sudden for that time of year.

Study Questions

1. Structurally, this poem has two major sections. Where does the division occur? Does the rhyme scheme correspond to it? Why?
2. What does the simile in line 5 mean? Reconstruct the entire sentence in order to explain it.
3. What is the figurative meaning of "snow"? With what elements in the poem is the color "brown" rhetorically consistent?
4. What, specifically, did Superstition see in the blossoming of the flower?

Blackberrying

Sylvia Plath

Nobody in the lane, and nothing, nothing but blackberries,
Blackberries on either side, though on the right mainly,
A blackberry alley, going down in hooks, and a sea
Somewhere at the end of it, heaving. Blackberries
Big as the ball of my thumb, and dumb as eyes
Ebon in the hedges, fat
With blue-red juices. These they squander on my fingers.
I had not asked for such a blood sisterhood; they must love me.
They accommodate themselves to my milkbottle, flattening their
        sides.

Overhead go the choughs in black, cacophonous flocks—   10
Bits of burnt paper wheeling in a blown sky.
Theirs is the only voice, protesting, protesting.
I do not think the sea will appear at all.
The high, green meadows are glowing, as if lit from within.
I come to one bush of berries so ripe it is a bush of flies,
Hanging their blue-green bellies and their wing panes in a Chinese
        screen.
The honey-feast of the berries has stunned them; they believe in
        heaven.
One more hook, and the berries and bushes end.

The only thing to come now is the sea.
From between two hills a sudden wind funnels at me,   20
Slapping its phantom laundry in my face.
These hills are too green and sweet to have tasted salt.
I follow the sheep path between them. A last hook brings me
To the hills' northern face, and the face is orange rock
That looks out on nothing, nothing but a great space
Of white and pewter lights, and a din like silversmiths
Beating and beating at an intractable metal.

Study Questions

1. What experience is the poet *really* celebrating?
2. Identify the spatial progression in the poem.
3. Comment on Plath's use of repetition, sound effects, and color imagery. Which images contribute to the lushness of the scene?
4. What two associations does "a din like silversmiths/Beating and beating at an intractable metal" bring together?

London Snow

Robert Bridges

When men were all asleep the snow came flying,
In large white flakes falling on the city brown,
Stealthily and perpetually settling and loosely lying,
   Hushing the latest traffic of the drowsy town;
Deadening, muffling, stifling its murmurs failing;
Lazily and incessantly floating down and down:
   Silently sifting and veiling road, roof and railing;
Hiding difference, making unevenness even,
Into angles and crevices softly drifting and sailing.
   All night it fell, and when full inches seven   10
It lay in the depth of its uncompacted lightness,
The clouds blew off from a high and frosty heaven;
   And all woke earlier for the unaccustomed brightness
Of the winter dawning, the strange unheavenly glare:
The eye marvelled—marvelled at the dazzling whiteness;
   The ear hearkened to the stillness of the solemn air;
No sound of wheel rumbling nor of foot falling,
And the busy morning cries came thin and spare.
   Then boys I heard, as they went to school, calling,
They gathered up the crystal manna to freeze   20
Their tongues with tasting, their hands with snowballing;
   Or rioted in a drift, plunging up to the knees;
Or peering up from under the white-mossed wonder,

'O look at the trees!' they cried, 'O look at the trees!'
  With lessened load a few carts creak and blunder,
Following along the white deserted way,
A country company long dispersed asunder:
  When now already the sun, in pale display
Standing by Paul's high dome, spread forth below
His sparkling beams, and awoke the stir of the day.   30
  For now doors open, and war is waged with the snow;
And trains of sombre men, past tale of number,
Tread long brown paths, as toward their toil they go:
  But even for them awhile no cares encumber
Their minds diverted; the daily word is unspoken,
The daily thoughts of labour and sorrow slumber
At the sight of the beauty that greets them, for the charm they have
      broken.

Study Questions

1. What grammatical form conveys the movement of the snow in the first nine lines? The next fifteen lines are written in the past tense, and the last ten in the present indicative. What meaning can you derive from the poet's handling of tense?
2. What are some functions of the snow?
3. What contrasts in ways of perceiving the beauty of the snow does Bridges present?
4. Which words in the poem are primarily aural images? Which words are associated with light or brightness?

Composed upon Westminster Bridge, September 3, 1802

William Wordsworth

Earth has not anything to show more fair:
Dull would he be of soul who could pass by
A sight so touching in its majesty;
This City now doth, like a garment, wear
The beauty of the morning; silent, bare,
Ships, towers, domes, theaters, and temples lie
Open unto the fields, and to the sky;
All bright and glittering in the smokeless air.
Never did sun more beautifully steep
In his first splendor, valley, rock, or hill;   10
Ne'er saw I, never felt, a calm so deep!
The river glideth at his own sweet will:
Dear God! the very houses seem asleep;
And all that mighty heart is lying still!

Study Questions

1. What is the rhyme scheme of this sonnet? Does the rhyme scheme indicate a structural division in the poem?
2. Is Wordsworth inconsistent? Does he create a problem in logic by first stating that London wears the beauty of the morning "like a garment" and then stating that the city lies "bare" and "open"? In other words, can something be both clothed and bare at the same time?
3. Does Wordsworth invert any of the traditional adjective-noun or subject-verb relationships? Where? Why? Are these inversions effective?
4. What does the poet mean by "at his own sweet will"?
5. Is the metaphor of the last line ("that mighty heart") consistent with the other metaphors that Wordsworth applies to London?

Clean Curtains

Carl Sandburg

New neighbors came to the corner house at Congress and Green
      Streets.

The look of their clean white curtains was the same as the rim of a
      nun's bonnet.

One way was an oyster-pail factory, one way they made candy, one
      way paper boxes, strawboard cartons.

The warehouse trucks shook the dust of the ways loose and the
      wheels whirled dust—there was dust of hoof and wagon
      wheel and rubber tire—dust of police and fire wagons—
      dust of the winds that circled at midnight and noon lis-   10
      tening to no prayers.

"O mother, I know the heart of you," I sang passing the rim of a
      nun's bonnet—O white curtains—and people clean as
      the prayers of Jesus here in the faded ramshackle at
      Congress and Green.

Dust and the thundering trucks won—the barrages of the street
      wheels and the lawless wind took their way—was it five
      weeks or six the little mother, the new neighbors, battled
      and then took away the white prayers in the windows?

Study Questions

1. How does Sandburg objectify or make vivid the problem of polluted city air? What are the opposing forces and what battles are lost in this poem?
2. Explain the meaning of the simile "as the rim of a nun's bonnet" and "the white prayers in the windows."
3. What purpose does the persona—the "I"—serve in this poem? Is this first-person point of view necessary?

Big Yellow Taxi

Joni Mitchell

They paved paradise
And put up a parking lot
With a pink hotel, a boutique,
And a swinging hot spot.
Don't it always seem to go
That you don't know what you've got
Till it's gone?
They paved paradise
And put up a parking lot.

They took all the trees   10
And put them in a tree museum
And they charged all the people
A dollar and a half just to see 'em.
Don't it always seem to go
That you don't know what you've got
Till it's gone?
They paved paradise
And put up a parking lot.

Hey, farmer, farmer,
Put away that DDT now,   20
Give me spots on my apples,
But leave me the birds and the bees,
Please!
Don't it always seem to go
That you don't know what you've got
Till it's gone?
They paved paradise
And put up a parking lot.

Late last night
I heard the screen door slam   30
And a big yellow taxi
Took away my old man.
Don't it always seem to go
That you don't know what you've got

Till it's gone?
They paved paradise
And put up a parking lot.

Study Questions

1. Is there any humor in these lyrics? Any satire?
2. What is the figurative meaning of *paradise*?
3. What is the meaning of the refrain? Could it be the thesis of the song? Do poems ordinarily have refrains?
4. What is the final depredation in the last verse? Does this verse seem tacked on or gratuitous? Is this depredation analogous to the others?

The Cleveland Wrecking Yard

Richard Brautigan

1   Until recently my knowledge about the Cleveland Wrecking Yard had come from a couple of friends who'd bought things there. One of them bought a huge window: the frame, glass and everything for just a few dollars. It was a fine-looking window.

2   Then he chopped a hole in the side of his house up on Potrero Hill and put the window in. Now he has a panoramic view of the San Francisco County Hospital.

3   He can practically look right down into the wards and see old magazines eroded like the Grand Canyon from endless readings. He can practically hear the patients thinking about breakfast: *I hate milk,* and thinking about dinner: *I hate peas,* and then he can watch the hospital slowly drown at night, hopelessly entangled in huge bunches of brick seaweed.

4   He bought that window at the Cleveland Wrecking Yard.

5   My other friend bought an iron roof at the Cleveland Wrecking Yard and took the roof down to Big Sur in an old station wagon and then he

carried the iron roof on his back up the side of a mountain. He carried up half the roof on his back. It was no picnic. Then he bought a mule, George, from Pleasanton. George carried up the other half of the roof.

6   The mule didn't like what was happening at all. He lost a lot of weight because of the ticks, and the smell of the wildcats up on the plateau made him too nervous to graze there. My friend said jokingly that George had lost around two hundred pounds. The good wine country around Pleasanton in the Livermore Valley probably had looked a lot better to George than the wild side of the Santa Lucia Mountains.

7   My friend's place was a shack right beside a huge fireplace where there had once been a great mansion during the 1920s, built by a famous movie actor. The mansion was built before there was even a road down at Big Sur. The mansion had been brought over the mountains on the backs of mules, strung out like ants, bringing visions of the good life to the poison oak, the ticks, and the salmon.

8   The mansion was on a promontory, high over the Pacific. Money could see farther in the 1920s, and one could look out and see whales and the Hawaiian Islands and the Kuomintang in China.

9   The mansion burned down years ago.

10   The actor died.

11   His mules were made into soap.

12   His mistresses became bird nests of wrinkles.

13   Now only the fireplace remains as a sort of Carthaginian homage to Hollywood.

14   I was down there a few weeks ago to see my friend's roof. I wouldn't have passed up the chance for a million dollars, as they say. The roof looked like a colander to me. If that roof and the rain were running against each other at Bay Meadows, I'd bet on the rain and plan to spend my winnings at the World's Fair in Seattle.

15   My own experience with the Cleveland Wrecking Yard began two days ago when I heard about a used trout stream they had on sale out at the Yard. So I caught the Number 15 bus on Columbus Avenue and went out there for the first time.

16   There were two Negro boys sitting behind me on the bus. They were talking about Chubby Checker and the Twist. They thought that Chubby Checker was only fifteen years old because he didn't have a mustache. Then they talked about some other guy who did the twist forty-four hours in a row until he saw George Washington crossing the Delaware.

17   "Man, that's what I call twisting," one of the kids said.

18   "I don't think I could twist no forty-four hours in a row," the other kid said. "That's a lot of twisting."

19   I got off the bus right next to an abandoned Time Gasoline filling station and an abandoned fifty-cent self-service car wash. There was a long field on one side of the filling station. The field had once been covered with a housing project during the war, put there for the shipyard workers.

20 On the other side of the Time filling station was the Cleveland Wrecking Yard. I walked down there to have a look at the used trout stream. The Cleveland Wrecking Yard has a very long front window filled with signs and merchandise.

21 There was a sign in the window advertising a laundry marking machine for $65.00. The original cost of the machine was $175.00. Quite a saving.

22 There was another sign advertising new and used two and three ton hoists. I wondered how many hoists it would take to move a trout stream.

23 There was another sign that said:

The Family Gift Center, Gift Suggestions for the Entire Family

24 The window was filled with hundreds of items for the entire family. *Daddy, do you know what I want for Christmas? What, son? A bathroom. Mommy, do you know what I want for Christmas? What, Patricia? Some roofing material.*

25 There were jungle hammocks in the window for distant relatives and dollar-ten-cent gallons of earth-brown enamel paint for other loved ones.

26 There was also a big sign that said:

Used Trout Stream For Sale. Must be Seen to be Appreciated.

I went inside and looked at some ship's lanterns that were for sale next to the door. Then a salesman came up to me and said in a pleasant voice, "Can I help you?"

27 "Yes," I said. "I'm curious about the trout stream you have for sale. Can you tell me something about it? How are you selling it?"

28 "We're selling it by the foot length. You can buy as little as you want or you can buy all we've got left. A man came in here this morning and bought 563 feet. He's going to give it to his niece for a birthday present," the salesman said.

29 "We're selling the waterfalls separately of course, and the trees and birds, flowers, grass and ferns we're also selling extra. The insects we're giving away free with a minimum purchase of ten feet of stream."

30 "How much are you selling the stream for?" I asked.

31 "Six dollars and fifty-cents a foot," he said. "That's for the first hundred feet. After that it's five dollars a foot."

32 "How much are the birds?" I asked.

33 "Thirty-five cents apiece," he said. "But of course they're used. We can't guarantee anything."

34 "How wide is the stream?" I asked. "You said you were selling it by the length, didn't you?"

35   "Yes," he said. "We're selling it by the length. Its width runs between five and eleven feet. You don't have to pay anything extra for width. It's not a big stream, but it's very pleasant."

36   "What kinds of animals do you have?" I asked.

37   "We only have three deer left," he said.

38   "Oh . . . What about flowers?"

39   "By the dozen," he said.

40   "Is the stream clear?" I asked.

41   "Sir," the salesman said. "I wouldn't want you to think that we would ever sell a murky trout stream here. We always make sure they're running crystal clear before we even think about moving them."

42   "Where did the stream come from?" I asked.

43   "Colorado," he said. "We moved it with loving care. We've never damaged a trout stream yet. We treat them all as if they were china."

44   "You're probably asked this all the time, but how's fishing in the stream?" I asked.

45   "Very good," he said. "Mostly German browns, but there are a few rainbows."

46   "What do the trout cost?" I asked.

47   "They come with the stream," he said. "Of course it's all luck. You never know how many you're going to get or how big they are. But the fishing's very good, you might say it's excellent. Both bait and dry fly," he said smiling.

48   "Where's the stream at?" I asked. "I'd like to take a look at it."

49   "It's around in back," he said. "You go straight through that door and then turn right until you're outside. It's stacked in lengths. You can't miss it. The waterfalls are upstairs in the used plumbing department."

50   "What about the animals?"

51   "Well, what's left of the animals are straight back from the stream. You'll see a bunch of our trucks parked on a road by the railroad tracks. Turn right on the road and follow it down past the piles of lumber. The animal shed's right at the end of the lot."

52   "Thanks," I said. "I think I'll look at the waterfalls first. You don't have to come with me. Just tell me how to get there and I'll find my own way."

53   "All right," he said. "Go up those stairs. You'll see a bunch of doors and windows, turn left and you'll find the used plumbing department. Here's my card if you need any help."

54   "Okay," I said. "You've been a great help already. Thanks a lot. I'll take a look around."

55   "Good luck," he said.

56   I went upstairs and there were thousands of doors there, I'd never seen so many doors before in my life. You could have built an entire city out of those doors. Doorstown. And there were enough windows up there to build a little suburb entirely out of windows. Windowville.

57   I turned left and went back and saw the faint glow of pearl-colored light. The light got stronger and stronger as I went farther back, and then I was in the used plumbing department, surrounded by hundreds of toilets.

58   The toilets were stacked on shelves. They were stacked five toilets high. There was a skylight above the toilets that made them glow like the Great Taboo Pearl of the South Sea movies.

59   Stacked over against the wall were the waterfalls. There were about a dozen of them, ranging from a drop of a few feet to a drop of ten or fifteen feet.

60   There was one waterfall that was over sixty feet long. There were tags on the pieces of the big falls describing the correct order for putting the falls back together again.

61   The waterfalls all had price tags on them. They were more expensive than the stream. The waterfalls were selling for $19.00 a foot.

62   I went into another room where there were piles of sweet-smelling lumber, glowing a soft yellow from a different color skylight above the lumber. In the shadows at the edge of the room under the sloping roof of the building were many sinks and urinals covered with dust, and there was also another waterfall about seventeen feet long, lying there in two lengths and already beginning to gather dust.

63   I had seen all I wanted of the waterfalls, and now I was very curious about the trout stream, so I followed the salesman's directions and ended up outside the building.

64   O I had never in my life seen anything like that trout stream. It was stacked in piles of various lengths: ten, fifteen, twenty feet, etc. There was one pile of hundred-foot lengths. There was also a box of scraps. The scraps were in odd sizes ranging from six inches to a couple of feet.

65   There was a loudspeaker on the side of the building and soft music was coming out. It was a cloudy day and seagulls were circling high overhead.

66   Behind the stream were big bundles of trees and bushes. They were covered with sheets of patched canvas. You could see the tops and roots sticking out the ends of the bundles.

67   I went up close and looked at the lengths of stream. I could see some trout in them. I saw one good fish. I saw some crawdads crawling around the rocks at the bottom.

68   It looked like a fine stream. I put my hand in the water. It was cold and felt good.

69   I decided to go around to the side and look at the animals. I saw where the trucks were parked beside the railroad tracks. I followed the road down past the piles of lumber, back to the shed where the animals were.

70   The salesman had been right. They were practically out of animals. About the only thing they had left in any abundance were mice. There were hundreds of mice.

71   Beside the shed was a huge wire birdcage, maybe fifty feet high, filled with many kinds of birds. The top of the cage had a piece of canvas over it, so the birds wouldn't get wet when it rained. There were woodpeckers and wild canaries and sparrows.

72   On my way back to where the trout stream was piled, I found the insects. They were inside a prefabricated steel building that was selling for eighty-cents a square foot. There was a sign over the door. It said

Insects

Study Questions

1. What practices in the commercial world does this sketch satirize? How does Brautigan contrast the natural world with the demands of business?
2. Is Brautigan's paragraphing conventional? How does he achieve variation in sentence structure?
3. What is the effect of the five single-sentence paragraphs on page 44, beginning, "The mansion burned down years ago"?
4. What is the range of subjects from which Brautigan draws his allusions? Does he always use these allusions for humorous effect?

God's Grandeur

Gerard Manley Hopkins

The world is charged with the grandeur of God.
  It will flame out, like shining from shook foil;
  It gathers to a greatness, like the ooze of oil
Crushed. Why do men then now not reck his rod?
Generations have trod, have trod, have trod;
  And all is seared with trade; bleared, smeared with toil;
  And wears man's smudge and shares man's smell: the soil
Is bare now, nor can foot feel, being shod.

And for all this, nature is never spent;
   There lives the dearest freshness deep down things;   10
And though the last lights off the black West went
   Oh, morning, at the brown brink eastward, springs—
Because the Holy Ghost over the bent
   World broods with warm breast and with ah! bright wings.

Study Questions

1. What is the theme of this poem? The thematic structure? Do the thematic and stanzaic structures correspond?
2. What is the purpose of the internal rhyme? The alliteration? The repetition?
3. How does color figure in this poem?
4. What metaphor describes the Holy Ghost? Is this traditional?

Flowers for Algernon

Daniel Keyes

progris riport 1—martch 5 1965

1   Dr. Strauss says I shud rite down what I think and evrey thing that happins to me from now on. I dont know why but he says its importint so they will see if they will use me. I hope they use me. Miss Kinnian says maybe they can make me smart. I want to be smart. My name is Charlie Gordon. I am 37 years old and 2 weeks ago was my birthday. I have nuthing more to rite now so I will close for today.

progris riport 2—martch 6

2   I had a test today. I think I faled it. and I think that maybe now they wont use me. What happind is a nice young man was in the room and he

had some white cards with ink spillled all over them. He sed Charlie what do you see on this card. I was very skared even tho I had my rabits foot in my pockit because when I was a kid I always faled tests in school and I spillled ink to.

3   I told him I saw a inkblot. He said yes and it made me feel good. I thot that was all but when I got up to go he stopped me. He said now sit down Charlie we are not thru yet. Then I dont remember so good but he wantid me to say what was in the ink. I dint see nuthing in the ink but he said there was picturs there other pepul saw some picturs I couldnt see any picturs. I reely tryed to see. I held the card close up and then far away. Then I said if I had my glases I could see better I usally only ware my glases in the movies or TV but I said they are in the closit in the hall. I got them. Then I said let me see that card agen I bet I ll find it now.

4   I tryed hard but I still couldnt find the picturs I only saw the ink. I told him maybe I need new glases. He rote somthing down on a paper and I got skared of faling the test. I told him it was a very nice inkblot with littel points all around the eges. He looked very sad so that wasnt it. I said please let me try agen. I ll get it in a few minits becaus Im not so fast somtimes. Im a slow reeder too in Miss Kinnians class for slow adults but I'm trying very hard.

5   He gave me a chance with another card that had 2 kinds of ink spillled on it red and blue.

6   He was very nice and talked slow like Miss Kinnian does and he explaned it to me that it was a *raw shok*. He said pepul see things in the ink. I said show me where. He said think. I told him I think a inkblot but that wasnt rite eather. He said what does it remind you—pretend something. I closd my eyes for a long time to pretend. I told him I pretned a fowntan pen with ink leeking all over a table cloth. Then he got up and went out.

7   I dont think I passed the *raw shok* test.

progris report 3—martch 7

8   Dr Strauss and Dr Nemur say it dont matter about the inkblots. I told them I dint spill the ink on the cards and I couldn't see anything in the ink. They said that maybe they will still use me. I said Miss Kinnian never gave me tests like that one only spellin and reading. They said Miss Kinnian told that I was her bestist pupil in the adult nite scool becaus I tryed the hardist and I reely wantid to lern. They said how come you went to the adult nite scool all by yourself Charlie. How did you find it. I said I askd pepul and sumbody told me where I shud go to lern to read and spell good. They said why did you want to. I told them becaus all my life I wantid to be smart and not dumb. But its very hard to be smart. They said you know it will probly be tempirery. I said yes. Miss Kinnian told me. I dont care if it herts.

9   Later I had more crazy tests today. The nice lady who gave it me told me the name and I asked her how do you spellit so I can rite it in my progris riport. THEMATIC APPERCEPTION TEST. I dont know the frist 2 words but I know what *test* means. You got to pass it or you get bad marks. This test lookd easy becaus I coud see the picturs. Only this time she dint want me to tell her the picturs. That mixd me up. I said the man yesterday said I shoud tell him what I saw in the ink she said that dont make no difrence. She said make up storys about the pepul in the picturs.

10   I told her how can you tell storys about pepul you never met. I said why shud I make up lies. I never tell lies any more becaus I always get caut.

11   She told me this test and the other one the raw-shok was for getting personalty. I laffed so hard. I said how can you get that thing from inkblots and fotos. She got sore and put her picturs away. I dont care. It was sily. I gess I faled that test too.

12   Later some men in white coats took me to a difernt part of the hospitil and gave me a game to play. It was like a race with a white mouse. They called the mouse Algernon. Algernon was in a box with a lot of twists and turns like all kinds of walls and they gave me a pencil and a paper with lines and lots of boxes. On one side it said START and on the other end it said FINISH. They said it was *amazed* and that Algernon and me had the same *amazed* to do. I dint see how we could have the same *amazed* if Algernon had a box and I had a paper but I dint say nothing. Anyway there wasnt time because the race started.

13   One of the men had a watch he was trying to hide so I wouldnt see it so I tryed not to look and that made me nervus.

14   Anyway that test made me feel worser than all the others because they did it over 10 times with a difernt *amazeds* and Algernon won every time. I dint know that mice were so smart. Maybe thats because Algernon is a white mouse. Maybe white mice are smarter then other mice.

progis riport 4—Mar 8

15   Their going to use me! Im so excited I can hardly write. Dr Nemur and Dr Strauss had a argament about it first. Dr Nemur was in the office when Dr Strauss brot me in. Dr Nemur was worryed about using me but Dr Strauss told him Miss Kinnian rekemmended me the best from all the people who she was teaching. I like Miss Kinnian becaus shes a very smart teacher. And she said Charlie your going to have a second chance. If you volenteer for this experament you mite get smart. They dont know if it will be perminint but theirs a chance. Thats why I said ok even when I was scared because she said it was an operashun. She said dont be scared Charlie you done so much with so little I think you deserv it most of all.

16   So I got scaird when Dr Nemur and Dr Strauss argud about it. Dr Strauss said I had something that was very good. He said I had a good *motor-vation*. I never even knew I had that. I felt proud when he said that not every body with an eye-q of 68 had that thing. I dont know what it is or where I got it but he said Algernon had it too. Algernons *motor-vation* is the cheese they put in his box. But it cant be that because I didnt eat any cheese this week.

17   Then he told Dr Nemur something I dint understand so while they were talking I wrote down some of the words.

18   He said Dr Nemur I know Charlie is not what you had in mind as the first of your new brede of intelek** (coudnt get the word) superman. But most people of his low ment** are host** and uncoop** they are usualy dull apath** and hard to reach. He has a good natcher hes intristed and eager to please.

19   Dr Nemur said remember he will be the first human beeng ever to have his intelijence trippled by surgicle meens.

20   Dr Strauss said exakly. Look at how well hes lerned to read and write for his low mentel age its as grate an acheve** as you and I lerning einstines therey of **vity without help. That shows the intenss motor-vation. Its comparat** a tremen** achev** I say we use Charlie.

21   I dint get all the words and they were talking to fast but it sounded like Dr Strauss was on my side and like the other one wasnt.

22   Then Dr Nemur nodded he said all right maybe your right. We will use Charlie. When he said that I got so exited I jumped up and shook his hand for being so good to me. I told him thank you doc you wont be sorry for giving me a second chance. And I mean it like I told him. After the operashun Im gonna try to be smart. Im gonna try awful hard.

progris ript 5—Mar 10

23   Im skared. Lots of people who work here and the nurses and the people who gave me the tests came to bring me candy and wish me luck. I hope I have luck. I got my rabits foot and my lucky penny and my horse shoe. Only a black cat crossed me when I was comming to the hospitil. Dr Strauss says dont be supersitis Charlie this is sience. Anyway Im keeping my rabits foot with me.

24   I asked Dr. Strauss if I ll beat Algernon in the race after the operashun and he said maybe. If the operashun works I ll show that mouse I can be as smart as he is. Maybe smarter. Then I ll be abel to read better and spell the words good and know lots of things and be like other people. I want to be smart like other people. If it works perminint they will make everybody smart all over the wurld.

25   They dint give me anything to eat this morning. I dont know what that eating has to do with getting smart. Im very hungry and Dr Nemur took away my box of candy. That Dr Nemur is a grouch. Dr Strauss says I can have it back after the operashun. You cant eat befor a operashun . . .

Progress Report 6—Mar 15

26   The operashun dint hurt. He did it while I was sleeping. They took off the bandijis from my eyes and my head today so I can make a PROGRESS REPORT. Dr Nemur who looked at some of my other ones says I spell PROGRESS wrong and he told me how to spell it and REPORT too. I got to try and remember that.

27   I have a very bad memary for spelling. Dr Strauss says its ok to tell about all the things that happin to me but he says I shoud tell more about what I feel and what I think. When I told him I dont know how to think he said try. All the time when the bandijis were on my eyes I tryed to think. Nothing happened. I dont know what to think about. Maybe if I ask him he will tell me how I can think now that Im suppose to get smart. What do smart people think about. Fancy things I suppos. I wish I knew some fancy things alredy.

Progress Report 7—mar 19

28   Nothing is happining. I had lots of test and different kinds of races with Algernon. I hate that mouse. He always beats me. Dr Strauss said I got to play those games. And he said some time I got to take those tests over again. Thse inkblots are stupid. And those pictures are stupid too. I like to draw a picture of a man and a woman but I wont make up lies about people.

29   I got a headache from trying to think so much. I thot Dr Strauss was my frend but he dont help me. He dont tell me what to think or when I ll get smart. Miss Kinnian dint come to see me. I think writing these progress reports are stupid too.

Progress Report 8—Mar 23

30   Im going back to work at the factery. They said it was better I shud go back to work but I cant tell anyone what the operashun was for and I have to come to the hospitil for an hour evry night after work. They are gonna pay me mony every month for lerning to be smart.

31   Im glad Im going back to work because I miss my job and all my frends and all the fun we have there.

32   Dr Strauss says I shud keep writing things down but I dont have to do it every day just when I think of something or something speshul happins. He says dont get discoridged because it takes time and it happins slow. He says it took a long time with Algernon before he got 3 times smarter then he was before. Thats why Algernon beats me all the time because he had that operashun too. That makes me feel better. I could probly do that *amazed* faster than a reglar mouse. Maybe some day

I ll beat Algernon. Boy that would be something. So far Algernon looks like he mite be smart perminent.

33　**Mar 25**　(I dont have to write PROGRESS REPORT on top any more just when I hand it in once a week for Dr Nemur to read. I just have to put the date on. That saves time)

34　We had a lot of fun at the factery today. Joe Carp said hey look where Charlie had his operashun what did they do Charlie put some brains in. I was going to tell him but I remembered Dr Strauss said no. Then Frank Reilly said what did you do Charlie forget your key and open your door the hard way. That made me laff. Their really my friends and they like me.

35　Sometimes somebody will say hey look at Joe or Frank or George he really pulled a Charlie Gordon. I don't know why they say that but they always laff. This morning Amos Borg who is the 4 man at Donnegans used my name when he shouted at Ernie the office boy. Ernie lost a packige. He said Ernie for godsake what are you trying to be a Charlie Gordon. I dont understand why he said that. I never lost any packiges.

36　**Mar 28**　Dr. Strauss came to my room tonight to see why I dint come in like I was suppose to. I told him I dont like to race with Algernon any more. He said I dont have to for a while but I shud come in. He had a present for me only it wasnt a present but just for lend. I thot it was a little television but it wasnt. He said I got to turn it on when I go to sleep. I said your kidding why shud I turn it on when Im going to sleep. Who ever herd of a thing like that. But he said if I want to get smart I got to do what he says. I told him I dint think I was going to get smart and he put his hand on my sholder and said Charlie you dont know it yet but your getting smarter all the time. You wont notice for a while. I think he was just being nice to make me feel good because I dont look any smarter.

37　Oh yes I almost forgot. I asked him when I can go back to the class at Miss Kinnians school. He said I wont go their. He said that soon Miss Kinnian will come to the hospitil to start and teach me speshul. I was mad at her for not comming to see me when I got the operashun but I like her so maybe we will be frends again.

38　**Mar 29**　That crazy TV kept me up all night. How can I sleep with something yelling crazy things all night in my ears. And the nutty pictures. Wow. I dont know what it says when Im up so how am I going to know when Im sleeping.

39　Dr Strauss says its ok. He says my brains are lerning when I sleep and that will help me when Miss Kinnian starts my lessons in the hospitl (only I found out it isnt a hospitil its a labatory). I think its all crazy. If you can get smart when your sleeping why do people go to school. That thing I dont think will work. I use to watch the late show and the late late show on TV all the time and it never made me smart. Maybe you have to sleep while you watch it.

PROGRESS REPORT 9—April 3

40   Dr Strauss showed me how to keep the TV turned low so now I can sleep. I dont hear a thing. And I still dont understand what it says. A few times I play it over in the morning to find out what I lerned when I was sleeping and I dont think so. Miss Kinnian says Maybe its another langwidge or something. But most times its sounds american. It talks so fast faster than even Miss Gold who was my teacher in 6 grade and I remember she talked so fast I coudnt understand her.

41   I told Dr Strauss what good is it to get smart in my sleep. I want to be smart when Im awake. He says its the same thing and I have two minds. Theres the *subconscious* and the *conscious* (thats how you spell it). And one dont tell the other one what its doing. They dont even talk to each other. Thats why I dream. And boy have I been having crazy dreams. Wow. Ever since that night TV. The late late late late late show.

42   I forgot to ask him if it was only me or if everybody had those two minds.

43   (I just looked up the word in the dictionary Dr Strauss gave me. The word is *subconscious. adj. Of the nature of mental operations yet not present in consciousness; as, subconscious conflict of desires.*) Theres more but I still dont know what it means. This isnt a very good dictionary for dumb people like me.

44   Anyway the headache is from the party. My frends from the factery Joe Carp and Frank Reilly invited me to go with them to Muggsys Saloon for some drinks. I dont like to drink but they said we will have lots of fun. I had a good time.

45   Joe Carp said I should show the girls how I mop out the toilet in the factory and he got me a mop. I showed them and everyone laffed when I told that Mr Donnegan said I was the best janiter he ever had because I like my job and do it good and never come late or miss a day except for my operashun.

46   I said Miss Kinnian always said Charlie be proud of your job because you do it good.

47   Everybody laffed and we had a good time and they gave me lots of drinks and Joe said Charlie is a card when hes potted. I dont know what that means but everybody likes me and we have fun. I cant wait to be smart like my best frends Joe Carp and Frank Reilly.

48   I dont remember how the party was over but I think I went out to buy a newspaper and coffe for Joe and Frank and when I came back there was no one their. I looked for them all over till late. Then I dont remember so good but I think I got sleepy or sick. A nice cop brot me back home. Thats what my landlady Mrs Flynn says.

49   But I got a headache and a big lump on my head and black and blue all over. I think maybe I fell but Joe Carp says it was the cop they beat up drunks some times. I don't think so. Miss Kinnian says cops are to help people. Anyway I got a bad headache and Im sick and hurt all over. I dont think I ll drink anymore.

50   **April 6**   I beat Algernon! I dint even know I beat him until Burt the tester told me. Then the second time I lost because I got so exited I fell off the chair before I finished. But after that I beat him 8 more times. I must be getting smart to beat a smart mouse like Algernon. But I dont *feel* smarter.

51   I wanted to race Algernon some more but Burt said thats enough for one day. They let me hold him for a minit. Hes not so bad. Hes soft like a ball of cotton. He blinks and when he opens his eyes their black and pink on the eges.

52   I said can I feed him because I felt bad to beat him and I wanted to be nice and make frends. Burt said no Algernon is a very specshul mouse with an operashun like mine, and he was the first of all the animals to stay smart so long. He told me Algernon is so smart that every day he has to solve a test to get his food. Its a thing like a lock on a door that changes every time Algernon goes in to eat so he has to lern something new to get his food. That made me sad because if he couldnt lern he would be hungry.

53   I dont think its right to make you pass a test to eat. How woud Dr Nemur like it to have to pass a test every time he wants to eat. I think I ll be frends with Algernon.

54   **April 9**   Tonight after work Miss Kinnian was at the laboratory. She looked like she was glad to see me but scared. I told her dont worry Miss Kinnian Im not smart yet and she laffed. She said I have confidence in you Charlie the way you struggled so hard to read and right better than all the others. At werst you will have it for a little wile and your doing something for sience.

55   We are reading a very hard book. I never read such a hard book before. Its called *Robinson Crusoe* about a man who gets merooned on a dessert I land. Hes smart and figers out all kinds of things so he can have a house and food and hes a good swimmer. Only I feel sorry because hes all alone and has no frends. But I think their must be somebody else on the iland because theres a picture with his funny umbrella looking at footprints. I hope he gets a frend and not be lonely.

56   **April 10**   Miss Kinnian teaches me to spell better. She says look at a word and close your eyes and say it over and over until you remember. I have lots of truble with *through* that you say *threw* and *enough* and *tough* that you dont say *enew* and *tew*. You got to say *enuff* and *tuff*.

Thats how I use to write it before I started to get smart. Im confused but Miss Kinnian says theres no reason in spelling.

57   **Apr 14**   Finished *Robinson Crusoe.* I want to find out more about what happens to him but Miss Kinnian says thats all there is *Why*

58   **Apr 15**   Miss Kinnian says Im lerning fast. She read some of the Progress Reports and she looked at me kind of funny. Say says Im a fine person and I ll show them all. I asked her why. She said never mind but I shoudnt feel bad if I find out that everybody isnt nice like I think. She said for a person who god gave so little to you done more then a lot of people with brains they never even used. I said all my frends are smart people but there good. They like me and they never did anything that wasnt nice. Then she got something in her eye and she had to run out to the ladys room.

59   **Apr 16**   Today, I lerned, the *comma,* this is a comma (,) a period, with a tail, Miss Kinnian, says its importent, because, it makes writing better, she said, sombeody, coud lose, a lot of money, if a comma, isnt, in the, right place, I dont have, any money, and I dont see, how a comma, keeps you from losing it,
60   But she says, everybody, uses commas, so I ll use, them too,

61   **Apr 17**   I used the comma wrong. Its punctuation. Miss Kinnian told me to look up long words in the dictionary to lern to spell them. I said whats the difference if you can read it anyway. She said its part of your education so now on I'll look up all the words Im not sure how to spell. It takes a long time to write that way but I think Im remembering. I only have to look up once and after that I get it right. Anyway thats how come I got the word *punctuation* right. (Its that way in the dictionary). Miss Kinnian says a period is punctuation too, and there are lots of other marks to lern. I told her I thot all the periods had to have tails but she said no.

62   You got to mix them up, she showed? me" how. to mix! them(up,. and now; I can! mix up all kinds" of punctuation, in! my writing? There, are lots! of rules? to lern; but Im gettin'g them in my head.
63   One thing I? like about, Dear Miss Kinnian: (thats the way it goes in a business letter if I ever go into business) is she, always gives me' a reason" when—I ask. She's a gen'ius! I wish! I cou'd be smart' like, her;
64   (Punctuation, is; fun!)

65   **April 18**   What a dope I am! I didn't even understand what she was talking about. I read the grammar book last night and it explanes the whole thing. Then I saw it was the same way as Miss Kinnian was trying

to tell me, but I didn't get it. I got up in the middle of the night, and the whole thing straightened out in my mind.

66   Miss Kinnian said that the TV working in my sleep helped out. She said I reached a plateau. Thats like the flat top of a hill.

67   After I figgered out how punctuation worked, I read over all my old Progress Reports from the beginning. Boy, did I have crazy spelling and punctuation! I told Miss Kinnian I ought to go over the pages and fix all the mistakes but she said, "No, Charlie, Dr. Nemur wants them just as they are. That's why he let you keep them after they were photostated, to see your own progress. You're coming along fast, Charlie."

68   That made me feel good. After the lesson I went down and played with Algernon. We don't race any more.

69   **April 20**   I feel sick inside. Not sick like for a doctor, but inside my chest it feels empty like getting punched and a heartburn at the same time.

70   I wasn't going to write about it, but I guess I got to, because it's important. Today was the first time I ever stayed home from work.

71   Last night Joe Carp and Frank Reilly invited me to a party. There were lots of girls and some men from the factory. I remembered how sick I got last time I drank too much, so I told Joe I didn't want anything to drink. He gave me a plain Coke instead. It tasted funny, but I thought it was just a bad taste in my mouth.

72   We had a lot of fun for a while. Joe said I should dance with Ellen and she would teach me the steps. I fell a few times and I couldn't understand why because no one else was dancing besides Ellen and me. And all the time I was tripping because somebody's foot was always sticking out.

73   Then when I got up I saw the look on Joe's face and it gave me a funny feeling in my stomack. "He's a scream," one of the girls said. Everbody was laughing.

74   Frank said, "I ain't laughed so much since we sent him off for the newspaper that night at Muggsy's and ditched him."

75   "Look at him. His face is red."

76   "He's blushing. Charlie is blushing."

77   "Hey, Ellen, what'd you do to Charlie? I never saw him act like that before."

78   I didn't know what to do or where to turn. Everyone was looking at me and laughing and I felt naked. I wanted to hide myself. I ran out into the street and I threw up. Then I walked home. It's a funny thing I never knew that Joe and Frank and the others liked to have me around all the time to make fun of me.

79   Now I know what it means when they say "to pull a Charlie Gordon."

80   I'm ashamed.

Progress Report 11

81   **April 21**   Still didn't go into the factory. I told Mrs. Flynn my landlady to call and tell Mr. Donnegan I was sick. Mrs. Flynn looks at me very funny lately like she's scared of me.

82   I think it's a good thing about finding out how everybody laughs at me. I thought about it a lot. It's because I'm so dumb and I don't even know when I'm doing something dumb. People think it's funny when a dumb person can't do things the same way they can.

83   Anyway, now I know I'm getting smarter every day. I know punctuation and I can spell good. I like to look up all the hard words in the dictionary and I remember them. I'm reading a lot now, and Miss Kinnian says I read very fast. Sometimes I even understand what I'm reading about, and it stays in my mind. There are times when I can close my eyes and think of a page and it all comes back like a picture.

84   Besides history, geography, and arithmetic, Miss Kinnian said I should start to learn a few foreign languages. Dr. Strauss gave me some more tapes to play while I sleep. I still don't understand how that conscious and unconscious mind works, but Dr. Strauss says not to worry yet. He asked me to promise that when I start learning college subjects next week I wouldn't read any books on psychology—that is, until he gives me permission.

85   I feel a lot better today, but I guess I'm still a little angry that all the time people were laughing and making fun of me because I wasn't so smart. When I become intelligent like Dr. Strauss says, with three times my I.Q. of 68, then maybe I'll be like everyone else and people will like me and be friendly.

86   I'm not sure what an I.Q. is. Dr. Nemur said it was something that measured how intelligent you were—like a scale in the drug-store weighs pounds. But Dr. Strauss had a big argument with him and said an I.Q. didn't weigh intelligence at all. He said an I.Q. showed how much intelligence you could get, like the numbers on the outside of a measuring cup. You still had to fill the cup up with stuff.

87   Then when I asked Burt, who gives me my intelligence tests and works with Algernon, he said that both of them were wrong (only I had to promise not to tell them he said so). Burt says that the I.Q. measures a lot of different things including some of the things you learned already, and it really isn't any good at all.

88   So I still don't know what I.Q. is except that mine is going to be over 200 soon. I didn't want to say anything, but I don't see how if they don't know *what* it is, or *where* it is—I don't see how they know *how much* of it you've got.

89   Dr. Nemur says I have to take a *Rorshach Test* tomorrow. I wonder what *that* is.

90   **April 22**   I found out what a *Rorshach* is. It's the test I took before the operation—the one with the inkblots on the pieces of cardboard. The man who gave me the test was the same one.

91   I was scared to death of those inkblots. I knew he was going to ask me to find the pictures and I knew I wouldn't be able to. I was thinking to myself, if only there was some way of knowing what kind of pictures were hidden there. Maybe there weren't any pictures at all. Maybe it was just a trick to see if I was dumb enough to look for something that wasn't there. Just thinking about that made me sore at him.

92   "All right, Charlie," he said, "you've seen these cards before, remember?"

93   "Of course I remember."

94   The way I said it, he knew I was angry, and he looked surprised. "Yes, of course. Now I want you to look at this one. What might this be? What do you see on this card? People see all sorts of things in these inkblots. Tell me what it might be for you—what it makes you think of."

95   I was shocked. That wasn't what I had expected him to say at all. "You mean there are no pictures hidden in those inkblots?"

96   He frowned and took off his glasses. "What?"

97   "Pictures. Hidden in the inkblots. Last time you told me that everyone could see them and you wanted me to find them too."

98   He explained to me that the last time he had used almost the exact same words he was using now. I didn't believe it, and I still have the suspicion that he misled me at the time just for the fun of it. Unless—I don't know any more—could I have been *that* feebleminded?

99   We went through the cards slowly. One of them looked like a pair of bats tugging at something. Another one looked like two men fencing with swords. I imagined all sorts of things. I guess I got carried away. But I didn't trust him any more, and I kept turning them around and even looking on the back to see if there was anything there I was supposed to catch. While he was making his notes, I peeked out of the corner of my eye to read it. But it was all in code that looked like this:

WF + A DdF-Ad orig. WF-A SF + obj

100   The test still doesn't make sense to me. It seems to me that anyone could make up lies about things that they didn't really see. How could he know I wasn't making a fool of him by mentioning things that I didn't really imagine? Maybe I'll understand it when Dr. Strauss lets me read up on psychology.

101   **April 25**   I figured out a new way to line up the machines in the factory, and Mr. Donnegan says it will save him ten thousand dollars a year in labor and increased production. He gave me a twenty-five-dollar bonus.

102   I wanted to take Joe Carp and Frank Reilly out to lunch to cele-brate, but Joe said he had to buy some things for his wife, and Frank said he was meeting his cousin for lunch. I guess it'll take a little time for them to get used to the changes in me. Everybody seems to be frightened of me. When I went over to Amos Borg and tapped him on the shoulder, he jumped up in the air.

103   People don't talk to me much any more or kid around the way they used to. It makes the job kind of lonely.

104   **April 27**   I got up the nerve today to ask Miss Kinnian to have dinner with me tomorrow night to celebrate my bonus.

105   At first she wasn't sure it was right, but I asked Dr. Strauss and he said it was okay. Dr. Strauss and Dr. Nemur don't seem to be getting along so well. They're arguing all the time. This evening when I came in to ask Dr. Strauss about having dinner with Miss Kinnian, I heard them shouting. Dr. Nemur was saying that it was *his* experiment and *his* research, and Dr. Strauss was shouting back that he contributed just as much, because he found me through Miss Kinnian and he performed the operation. Dr. Strauss said that someday thousands of neurosurgeons might be using his technique all over the world.

106   Dr. Nemur wanted to publish the results of the experiment at the end of this month. Dr. Strauss wanted to wait a while longer to be sure. Dr. Strauss said that Dr. Nemur was more interested in the Chair of Psychology at Princeton than he was in the experiment. Dr. Nemur said that Dr. Strauss was nothing but an opportunist who was trying to ride to glory on *his* coattails.

107   When I left afterwards, I found myself trembling. I don't know why for sure, but it was as if I'd seen both men clearly for the first time. I remember hearing Burt say that Dr. Nemur had a shrew of a wife who was pushing him all the time to get things published so that he could become famous. Burt said that the dream of her life was to have a big-shot husband.

108   Was Dr. Strauss really trying to ride on his coattails?

109   **April 28**   I don't understand why I never noticed how beautiful Miss Kinnian really is. She has brown eyes and feathery brown hair that comes to the top of her neck. She's only thirty-four! I think from the beginning I had the feeling that she was an unreachable genius—and very, very old. Now, every time I see her she grows younger and more lovely.

110   We had dinner and a long talk. When she said that I was coming along so fast that soon I'd be leaving her behind, I laughed.

111   "It's true, Charlie. You're already a better reader than I am. You can read a whole page at a glance while I can take in only a few lines at a

time. And you remember every single thing you read. I'm lucky if I can recall the main thoughts and the general meaning."

112   "I don't feel intelligent. There are so many things I don't understand."

113   She took out a cigarette and I lit it for her. "You've got to be a *little* patient. You're accomplishing in days and weeks what it takes normal people to do in half a lifetime. That's what makes it so amazing. You're like a giant sponge now, soaking things in. Facts, figures, general knowledge. And soon you'll begin to connect them, too. You'll see how the different branches of learning are related. There are many levels, Charlie, like steps on a giant ladder that take you up higher and higher to see more and more of the world around you.

114   "I can see only a little bit of that, Charlie, and I won't go much higher than I am now, but you'll keep climbing up and up, and see more and more, and each step will open new worlds that you never even knew existed." She frowned. "I hope . . . I just hope to God—"

115   "What?"

116   "Never mind, Charles. I just hope I wasn't wrong to advise you to go into this in the first place."

117   I laughed. "How could that be? It worked, didn't it? Even Algernon is still smart."

118   We sat there silently for a while and I knew what she was thinking about as she watched me toying with the chain of my rabbit's foot and my keys. I didn't want to think of that possibility any more than elderly people want to think of death. I *knew* that this was only the beginning, I knew what she meant about levels because I'd seen some of them already. The thought of leaving her behind made me sad.

119   I'm in love with Miss Kinnian.

Progress Report 12

120   **April 30**   I've quit my job with Donnegan's Plastic Box Company. Mr. Donnegan insisted that it would be better for all concerned if I left. What did I do to make them hate me so?

121   The first I knew of it was when Mr. Donnegan showed me the petition. Eight hundred and forty names, everyone connected with the factory, except Fanny Girden. Scanning the list quickly, I saw at once that hers was the only missing name. All the rest demanded that I be fired.

122   Joe Carp and Frank Reilly wouldn't talk to me about it. No one else would either, except Fanny. She was one of the few people I'd known who set her mind to something and believed it no matter what the rest of the world proved, said, or did—and Fanny did not believe that I should have been fired. She had been against the petition on principle and despite the pressure and threats she'd held out.

123   "Which don't mean to say," she remarked, "that I don't think there's something mighty strange about you, Charlie. Them changes. I don't know. You used to be a good, dependable, ordinary man—not too bright maybe, but honest. Who knows what you done to yourself to get so smart all of a sudden. Like everybody around here's been saying, Charlie, it's not right."

124   "But how can you say that, Fanny? What's wrong with a man becoming intelligent and wanting to acquire knowledge and understanding of the world around him?"

125   She stared down at her work and I turned to leave. Without looking at me, she said: "It was evil when Eve listened to the snake and ate from the tree of knowledge. It was evil when she saw that she was naked. If not for that none of us would ever have to grow old and sick, and die."

126   Once again now I have the feeling of shame burning inside me. This intelligence has driven a wedge between me and all the people I once knew and loved. Before, they laughed at me and despised me for my ignorance and dullness; now, they hate me for my knowledge and understanding. What in God's name do they want of me?

127   They've driven me out of the factory. Now I'm more alone than ever before . . .

128   **May 15**   Dr. Strauss is very angry at me for not having written any progress reports in two weeks. He's justified because the lab is now paying me a regular salary. I told him I was too busy thinking and reading. When I pointed out that writing was such a slow process that it made me impatient with my poor handwriting, he suggested that I learn to type. It's much easier to write now because I can type nearly seventy-five words a minute. Dr. Strauss continually reminds me of the need to speak and write simply so that people will be able to understand me.

129   I'll try to review all the things that happened to me during the last two weeks. Algernon and I were presented to the American Psychological Association sitting in convention with the World Psychological Association last Tuesday. We created quite a sensation. Dr. Nemur and Dr. Strauss were proud of us.

130   I suspect that Dr. Nemur, who is sixty—ten years older than Dr. Strauss—finds it necessary to see tangible results of his work. Undoubtedly the result of pressure by Mrs. Nemur.

131   Contrary to my earlier impressions of him, I realize that Dr. Nemur is not at all a genius. He has a very good mind, but it struggles under the specter of self-doubt. He wants people to take him for a genius. Therefore, it is important for him to feel that his work is accepted by the world. I believe that Dr. Nemur was afraid of further delay because he worried that someone else might make a discovery along these lines and take the credit from him.

132   Dr. Strauss on the other hand might be called a genius, although I feel that his areas of knowledge are too limited. He was educated in the tradition of narrow specialization; the broader aspects of background were neglected far more than necessary—even for a neurosurgeon.

133   I was shocked to learn that the only ancient languages he could read were Latin, Greek, and Hebrew, and that he knows almost nothing of mathematics beyond the elementary levels of the calculus of variations. When he admitted this to me, I found myself almost annoyed. It was as if he'd hidden this part of himself in order to deceive me, pretending—as do many people I've discovered—to be what he is not. No one I've ever known is what he appears to be on the surface.

134   Dr. Nemur appears to be uncomfortable around me. Sometimes when I try to talk to him, he just looks at me strangely and turns away. I was angry at first when Dr. Strauss told me I was giving Dr. Nemur an inferiority complex. I thought he was mocking me and I'm oversensitive at being made fun of.

135   How was I to know that a highly respected psychoexperimentalist like Nemur was unacquainted with Hindustani and Chinese? It's absurd when you consider the work that is being done in India and China today in the very field of his study.

136   I asked Dr. Strauss how Nemur could refute Rahajamati's attack on his method and results if Nemur couldn't even read them in the first place. That strange look on Dr. Strauss' face can mean only one of two things. Either he doesn't want to tell Nemur what they're saying in India, or else—and this worries me—Dr. Strauss doesn't know either. I must be careful to speak and write clearly and simply so that people won't laugh.

137   **May 18**   I am very disturbed. I saw Miss Kinnian last night for the first time in over a week. I tried to avoid all discussions of intellectual concepts and to keep the conversation on a simple, everyday level, but she just stared at me blankly and asked me what I meant about the mathematical variance equivalent in Dobermann's *Fifth Concerto*.

138   When I tried to explain she stopped me and laughed. I guess I got angry, but I suspect I'm approaching her on the wrong level. No matter what I try to discuss with her, I am unable to communicate. I must review Vrostadt's equations on *Levels of Semantic Progression*. I find that I don't communicate with people much any more. Thank God for books and music and things I can think about. I am alone in my apartment at Mrs. Flynn's boardinghouse most of the time and seldom speak to anyone.

139   **May 20**   I would not have noticed the new dishwasher, a boy of about sixteen, at the corner diner where I take my evening meals if not for the incident of the broken dishes.

140   They crashed to the floor, shattering and sending bits of white china under the tables. The boy stood there, dazed and frightened, holding the

empty tray in his hand. The whistles and catcalls from the customers (the cries of "hey, there go the profits!" ... "*Mazeltov!*" ... and "well, *he* didn't work here very long ..." which invariably seems to follow the breaking of glass or dishware in a public restaurant) all seemed to confuse him.

141   When the owner came to see what the excitement was about, the boy cowered as if he expected to be struck and threw up his arms as if to ward off the blow.

142   "All right! All right, you dope," shouted the owner, "don't just stand there! Get the broom and sweep that mess up. A broom ... a broom, you idiot! It's in the kitchen. Sweep up all the pieces."

143   The boy saw that he was not going to be punished. His frightened expression disappeared and he smiled and hummed as he came back with the broom to sweep the floor. A few of the rowdier customers kept up the remarks, amusing themselves at his expense.

144   "Here, sonny, over here there's a nice piece behind you ..."

145   "C'mon, do it again ..."

146   "He's not so dumb. It's easier to break 'em than to wash 'em ..."

147   As his vacant eyes moved across the crowd of amused onlookers, he slowly mirrored their smiles and finally broke into an uncertain grin at the joke which he obviously did not understand.

148   I felt sick inside as I looked at his dull, vacuous smile, the wide, bright eyes of a child, uncertain but eager to please. They were laughing at him because he was mentally retarded.

149   And I had been laughing at him too.

150   Suddenly, I was furious at myself and all those who were smirking at him. I jumped up and shouted, "Shut up! Leave him alone! It's not his fault he can't understand! He can't help what he is! But for God's sake ... he's still a human being!"

151   The room grew silent. I cursed myself for losing control and creating a scene. I tried not to look at the boy as I paid my check and walked out without touching my food. I felt ashamed for both of us.

152   How strange it is that people of honest feelings and sensibility, who would not take advantage of a man born without arms or legs or eyes— how such people think nothing of abusing a man born with low intelligence. It infuriated me to think that not too long ago I, like this boy, had foolishly played the clown.

153   And I had almost forgotten.

154   I'd hidden the picture of the old Charlie Gordon from myself because now that I was intelligent it was something that had to be pushed out of my mind. But today in looking at that boy, for the first time I saw what I had been. *I was just like him!*

155   Only a short time ago, I learned that people laughed at me. Now I can see that unknowingly I joined with them in laughing at myself. That hurts most of all.

156   I have often reread my progress reports and seen the illiteracy, the childish naïveté, the mind of low intelligence peering from a dark room,

through the keyhole, at the dazzling light outside. I see that even in my dullness I knew that I was inferior, and that other people had something I lacked—something denied me. In my mental blindness, I thought that it was somehow connected with the ability to read and write, and I was sure that if I could get those skills I would automatically have intelligence too.

157   Even a feeble-minded man wants to be like other men.

158   A child may not know how to feed itself, or what to eat, yet it knows of hunger.

159   This then is what I was like, I never knew. Even with my gift of intellectual awareness, I never really knew.

160   This day was good for me. Seeing the past more clearly, I have decided to use my knowledge and skills to work in the field of increasing human intelligence levels. Who is better equipped for this work? Who else has lived in both worlds? These are my people. Let me use my gift to do something for them.

161   Tomorrow, I will discuss with Dr. Strauss the manner in which I can work in this area. I may be able to help him work out the problems of widespread use of the technique which was used on me. I have several good ideas of my own.

162   There is so much that might be done with this technique. If I could be made into a genius, what about thousands of others like myself? What fantastic levels might be achieved by using this technique on normal people? On *geniuses?*

163   There are so many doors to open. I am impatient to begin.

Progress Report 13

164   **May 23**   It happened today. Algernon bit me. I visited the lab to see him as I do occasionally, and when I took him out of his cage, he snapped at my hand. I put him back and watched him for a while. He was unusually disturbed and vicious.

165   **May 24**   Burt, who is in charge of the experimental animals, tells me that Algernon is changing. He is less co-operative, he refuses to run the maze any more; general motivation has decreased. And he hasn't been eating. Everyone is upset about what this may mean.

166   **May 25**   They've been feeding Algernon, who now refuses to work the shifting-lock problem. Everyone identifies me with Algernon. In a way we're both the first of our kind. They're all pretending that Algernon's behavior is not necessarily significant for me. But it's hard to hide the fact that some of the other animals who were used in this experiment are showing strange behavior.

167   Dr. Strauss and Dr. Nemur have asked me not to come to the lab any more. I know what they're thinking but I can't accept it. I am going

ahead with my plans to carry their research forward. With all due respect to both of these fine scientists, I am well aware of their limitations. If there is an answer, I'll have to find it out for myself. Suddenly, time has become very important to me.

168   **May 29**   I have been given a lab of my own and permission to go ahead with the research. I'm on to something. Working day and night. I've had a cot moved into the lab. Most of my writing time is spent on the notes which I keep in a separate folder, but from time to time I feel it necessary to put down my moods and my thoughts out of sheer habit.

169   I find the *calculus of intelligence* to be a fascinating study. Here is the place for the application of all the knowledge I have acquired. In a sense it's the problem I've been concerned with all my life.

170   **May 31**   Dr. Strauss thinks I'm working too hard. Dr. Nemur says I'm trying to cram a lifetime of research and thought into a few weeks. I know I should rest, but I'm driven on by something inside that won't let me stop. I've got to find the reason for the sharp regression in Algernon. I've got to know *if* and *when* it will happen to me.

June 4

Letter to Dr. Strauss (copy)
Dear Dr. Strauss:

171   *Under separate cover I am sending you a copy of my report entitled, "The Algernon-Gordon Effect: A Study of Structure and Function of Increased Intelligence," which I would like to have you read and have published.*

172   *As you see, my experiments are completed. I have included in my report all of my formulae, as well as mathematical analysis in the appendix. Of course, these should be verified.*

173   *Because of its importance to both you and Dr. Nemur (and need I say to myself, too?) I have checked and rechecked my results a dozen times in the hope of finding an error. I am sorry to say the results must stand. Yet for the sake of science, I am grateful for the little bit that I here add to the knowledge of the function of the human mind and of the laws governing the artificial increase of human intelligence.*

174   *I recall your once saying to me that an experimental failure or the disproving of a theory was as important to the advancement of learning as a success would be. I know now that this is true. I am sorry, however, that my own contribution to the field must rest upon the ashes of the work of two men I regard so highly.*

Yours truly,
Charles Gordon

encl.: rept.

175   **June 5**   I must not become emotional. The facts and the results of my experiments are clear, and the more sensational aspects of my own rapid climb cannot obscure the fact that the tripling of intelligence by the surgical technique developed by Drs. Strauss and Nemur must be viewed as having little or no practical applicability (at the present time) to the increase of human intelligence.

176   As I review the records and data on Algernon, I see that although he is still in his physical infancy, he has regressed mentally. Motor activity is impaired; there is a general reduction of glandular activity; there is an accelerated loss of co-ordination.

177   There are also strong indications of progressive amnesia.

178   As will be seen by my report, these and other physical and mental deterioration syndromes can be predicted with statistically significant results by the application of my formula.

179   The surgical stimulus to which we were both subjected has resulted in an intensification and acceleration of all mental processes. The unforeseen development, which I have taken the liberty of calling the *Algernon-Gordon Effect,* is the logical extension of the entire intelligence speed-up. The hypothesis here proven may be described simply in the following terms: Artificially increased intelligence deteriorates at a rate of time directly proportional to the quantity of the increase.

180   I feel that this, in itself, is an important discovery.

181   As long as I am able to write, I will continue to record my thoughts in these progress reports. It is one of my few pleasures. However, by all indications, my own mental deterioration will be very rapid.

182   I have already begun to notice signs of emotional instability and forgetfulness, the first symptoms of the burnout.

183   **June 10**   Deterioration progressing. I have become absentminded. Algernon died two days ago. Dissection shows my predictions were right. His brain had decreased in weight and there was a general smoothing out of cerebral convolutions as well as a deepening and broadening of brain fissures.

184   I guess the same thing is or will soon be happening to me. Now that it's definite, I don't want it to happen.

185   I put Algernon's body in a cheese box and buried him in the back yard. I cried.

186   **June 15**   Dr. Strauss came to see me again. I wouldn't open the door and I told him to go away. I want to be left to myself. I have become touchy and irritable. I feel the darkness closing in. It's hard to throw off thoughts of suicide. I keep telling myself how important this introspective journal will be.

187   It's a strange sensation to pick up a book that you've read and enjoyed just a few months ago and discover that you don't remember it. I

remembered how great I thought John Milton was, but when I picked up *Paradise Lost* I couldn't understand it at all. I got so angry I threw the book across the room.

188   I've got to try to hold on to some of it. Some of the things I've learned. Oh, God, please don't take it all away.

189   **June 19**   Sometimes, at night, I go out for a walk. Last night I couldn't remember where I lived. A policeman took me home. I have the strange feeling that this has all happened to me before—a long time ago. I keep telling myself I'm the only person in the world who can describe what's happening to me.

190   **June 21**   Why can't I remember? I've got to fight. I lie in bed for days and I don't know who or where I am. Then it all comes back to me in a flash. Fugues of amnesia. Symptoms of senility—second childhood. I can watch them coming on. It's so cruelly logical. I learned so much and so fast. Now my mind is deteriorating rapidly. I won't let it happen. I'll fight it. I can't help thinking of the boy in the restaurant, the blank expression, the silly smile, the people laughing at him. No—please—not that again . . .

191   **June 22**   I'm forgetting things that I learned recently. It seems to be following the classic pattern—the last things learned are the first things forgotten. Or is that the pattern? I'd better look it up again. . . .

192   I reread my paper on the *Algernon-Gordon Effect* and I get the strange feeling that it was written by someone else. There are parts I don't even understand.

193   Motor activity impaired. I keep tripping over things, and it becomes increasingly difficult to type.

194   **June 23**   I've given up using the typewriter completely. My coordination is bad. I feel that I'm moving slower and slower. Had a terrible shock today. I picked up a copy of an article I used in my research, Krueger's *Uber psychische Ganzheit,* to see if it would help me understand what I had done. First I thought there was something wrong with my eyes. Then I realized I could no longer read German. I tested myself in other languages. All gone.

195   **June 30**   A week since I dare to write again. It's slipping away like sand through my fingers. Most of the books I have are too hard for me now. I get angry with them because I know that I read and understood them just a few weeks ago.

196   I keep telling myself I must keep writing these reports so that somebody will know what is happening to me. But it gets harder to form the words and remember spellings. I have to look up even simple words in the dictionary now and it makes me impatient with myself.

197   Dr. Strauss comes around almost every day, but I told him I wouldn't see or speak to anybody. He feels guilty. They all do. But I don't blame anyone. I knew what might happen. But how it hurts.

198   **July 7** I don't know where the week went. Todays Sunday I know because I can see through my window people going to church. I think I stayed in bed all week but I remember Mrs. Flynn bringing food to me a few times. I keep saying over and over I've got to do something but then I forget or maybe its just easier not to do what I say Im going to do.

199   I think of my mother and father a lot these days. I found a picture of them with me taken at a beach. My father has a big ball under his arm and my mother is holding me by the hand. I don't remember them the way they are in the picture. All I remember is my father drunk most of the time and arguing with mom about money.

200   He never shaved much and he used to scratch my face when he hugged me. My mother said he died but Cousin Miltie said he heard his mom and dad say that my father ran away with another woman. When I asked my mother she slapped my face and said my father was dead. I dont think I ever found out which was true but I don't care much. (He said he was going to take me to see cows on a farm once but he never did. He never kept his promises . . .)

201   **July 10** My landlady Mrs. Flynn is very worried about me. She says the way I lay around all day and dont do anything I remind her of her son before she threw him out of the house. She said she doesn't like loafers. If Im sick its one thing, but if Im a loafer thats another thing and she wont have it. I told her I think Im sick.

202   I try to read a little bit every day, mostly stories, but sometimes I have to read the same thing over and over again because I dont know what it means. And its hard to write. I know I should look up all the words in the dictionary but its so hard and Im so tired all the time.

203   Then I got the idea that I would only use the easy words instead of the long hard ones. That saves time. I put flowers on Algernons grave about once a week. Mrs. Flynn thinks Im crazy to put flowers on a mouses grave but I told her that Algernon was special.

204   **July 14** Its sunday again. I dont have anything to do to keep me busy now because my television set is broke and I don't have any money to get it fixed. (I think I lost this months check from the lab. I dont remember)

205   I get awful headaches and asperin doesnt help me much. Mrs Flynn knows Im really sick and she feels very sorry for me. Shes a wonderful woman whenever someone is sick.

206   **July 22** Mrs. Flynn called a strange doctor to see me. She was afraid I was going to die. I told the doctor I wasnt too sick and that I only

forget sometimes. He asked me did I have any friends or relatives and I said no I dont have any. I told him I had a friend called Algernon once but he was a mouse and we used to run races together. He looked at me kind of funny like he thought I was crazy.

207   He smiled when I told him I used to be a genius. He talked to me like I was a baby and he winked at Mrs. Flynn. I got mad and chased him out because he was making fun of me the way they all used to.

208   **July 24**   I have no more money and Mrs Flynn says I got to go to work somewhere and pay the rent because I havent paid for over two months. I dont know any work but the job I used to have at Donnegans Plastic Box Company. I dont want to go back there because they all knew me when I was smart and maybe theyll laugh at me. But I don't know what else to do to get money.

209   **July 25**   I was looking at some of my old progress reports and its very funny but I cant read what I wrote. I can make out some of the words but they dont make sense.

210   Miss Kinnian came to the door but I said go away I dont want to see you. She cried and I cried too but I wouldn't let her in because I didn't want her to laugh at me. I told her I didn't like her any more. I told her I didnt want to be smart any more. Thats not true. I still love her and I still want to be smart but I had to say that so shed go away. She gave Mrs Flynn money to pay the rent. I dont want that. I got to get a job.

211   Please . . . please let me not forget how to read and write . . .

212   **July 27**   Mr Donnegan was very nice when I came back and asked him for my old job of janitor. First he was very suspicious but I told him what happened to me then he looked very sad and put his hand on my shoulder and said Charlie Gordon you got guts.

213   Everybody looked at me when I came downstairs and started working in the toilet sweeping it out like I used to. I told myself Charlie if they make fun of you dont get sore because you remember their not so smart as you once thot they were. And besides they were once your friends and if they laughed at you that doesnt mean anything because they liked you too.

214   One of the new men who came to work there after I went away made a nasty crack he said hey Charlie I hear your a very smart fella a real quiz kid. Say something intelligent. I felt bad but Joe Carp came over and grabbed him by the shirt and said leave him alone you lousy cracker or I ll break your neck. I didn't expect Joe to take my part so I guess hes really my friend.

215   Later Frank Reilly came over and said Charlie if anybody bothers you or trys to take advantage you call me or Joe and we will set em straight. I said thanks Frank and I got choked up so I had to turn around and go into the supply room so he wouldn't see me cry. Its good to have friends.

216   **July 28** I did a dumb thing today I forgot I wasnt in Miss Kinnians class at the adult center any more like I use to be. I went in and sat down in my old seat in the back of the room and she looked at me funny and she said Charles. I dint remember she ever called me that before only Charlie so I said hello Miss Kinnian Im redy for my lesin today only I lost my reader that we was using. She startid to cry and run out of the room and everybody looked at me and I saw they wasnt the same pepul who used to be in my class.

217   Then all of a suddin I remembered some things about the operashun and me getting smart and I said holy smoke I reely pulled a Charlie Gordon that time. I went away before she come back to the room.

218   Thats why Im going away from New York for good. I dont want to do nothing like that agen. I dont want Miss Kinnian to feel sorry for me. Evry body feels sorry at the factery and I dont want that eather so Im going someplace where nobody knows that Charlie Gordon was once a genus and now he cant even reed a book or rite good.

219   Im taking a cuple of books along and even if I cant reed them Ill practise hard and maybe I wont forget every thing I lerned. If I try reel hard maybe I ll be a littel bit smarter then I was before the operashun. I got my rabits foot and my luky penny and maybe they will help me.

220   If you ever reed this Miss Kinnian dont be sorry for me Im glad I got a second chanse to be smart becaus I lerned a lot of things that I never even new were in this world and Im grateful that I saw it all for a littel bit. I dont know why Im dumb agen or what I did wrong maybe its becaus I dint try hard enuff. But if I try and practis very hard maybe I ll get a littl smarter and know what all the words are. I remember a littel bit how nice I had a feeling with the blue book that has the torn cover when I red it. That why Im gonna keep trying to get smart so I can have that feeling agen. Its a good feeling to know things and be smart. I wish I had it rite now if I did I would sit down and reed all the time. Anyway I bet Im the first dumb person in the world who ever found out something importent for sience. I remember I did somthing but I dont remember what. So I gess its like I did it for all the dumb pepul like me.

221   Good-by Miss Kinnian and Dr Strauss and evreybody. And P.S. please tell Dr Nemur not to be such a grouch when pepul laff at him and he would have more frends. Its easy to make frends it you let pepul laff at you. Im going to have lots of frends where I go.

222   P.P.S. Please if you get a chanse put some flowrs on Algernons grave in the bak yard . . .

Study Questions

1. What is the time span covered by the journal entries that constitute this short story?
2. From what point of view is this story narrated? Is the point of view consistent? What devices (such as word choice, levels of usage, grammatical skill, spelling, and punctuation) alter the narration?
3. At what point does the narrator's analytical skill increase? How do you know?
4. How does Algernon's fate mirror the narrator's probable fate? What are the implications of the title? In short, what function does Algernon serve in this story?
5. How does this story comment on the morality of scientific experimentation on human beings? Is this comment overt or implied?

Caring for Animals

Jon Silkin

I ask sometimes why these small animals
With bitter eyes, why we should care for them.

I question the sky, the serene blue water,
But it cannot say. It gives no answer.

And no answer releases in my head
A procession of grey shades patched and whimpering,

Dogs with clipped ears, wheezing cart horses
A fly without shadow and without thought.

Is it with these menaces to our vision
With this procession led by a man carrying wood   10

We must be concerned? The holy land, the rearing
Green island should be kindlier than this.

Yet the animals, our ghosts, need tending to.
Take in the whipped cat and the blinded owl;

Take up the man-trapped squirrel upon your shoulder.
Attend to the unnecessary beasts.

From growing mercy and a moderate love
Great love for the human animal occurs.

And your love grows. Your great love grows and grows.

Study Questions

1. What images in this poem suggest the pain of animals? In what way is the pain of animals related to human morality?
2. What is "the holy land, the rearing/Green island"?
3. What proportionate relationship exists between mercy for animals and a great love for human beings? How does Silkin use *animal* in line 18?
4. Is this poem rhymed? What sorts of inversions does Silkin use? Why?
5. How are *shades, shadow,* and *ghosts* related? Which word in the poem takes on increasing significance with each repetition?

A Bird Came Down the Walk

Emily Dickinson

A bird came down the walk:
He did not know I saw;
He bit an angle-worm in halves
And ate the fellow, raw.

And then he drank a dew
From a convenient grass,

And then hopped sidewise to the wall
To let a bettle pass.

He glanced with rapid eyes
That hurried all around—   10
They looked like frightened beads, I thought
He stirred his velvet head

Like one in danger, cautious,
I offered him a crumb,
And he unrolled his feathers
And rowed him softer home

Than oars divide the ocean,
Too silver for a seam,
Or butterflies, off banks of noon,
Leap, plashless, as they swim.   20

Study Questions

1. What is the tone of this poem? How do words like *fellow* help create that tone?
2. What is the effect of the comma between *fellow* and *raw*?
3. What is achieved by Dickinson's use of *a* before *dew* and *grass*?
4. What does Dickinson mean by "*stirred* his velvet head"? Can you stir *your* head?
5. What metaphors are used to describe the bird's flight? Are these metaphors unusual? Appropriate?

The Meadow Mouse

Theodore Roethke

1

In a shoe box stuffed in an old nylon stocking
Sleeps the baby mouse I found in the meadow,
Where he trembled and shook beneath a stick
Till I caught him up by the tail and brought him in,
Cradled in my hand,
A little quaker, the whole body of him trembling,
His absurd whiskers sticking out like a cartoon-mouse,
His feet like small leaves,
Little lizard-feet,
Whitish and spread wide when he tried to struggle away,   10
Wriggling like a miniscule puppy.

Now he's eaten his three kinds of cheese and drunk from his bottle
          cap watering-trough—
So much he just lies in one corner,
His tail curled under him, his belly big
As his head; his bat-like ears
Twitching, tilting toward the least sound.

Do I imagine he no longer trembles
When I come close to him?
He seems no longer to tremble.

2

But this morning the shoe-box house on the back porch is empty.   20
Where has he gone, my meadow mouse,
My thumb of a child that nuzzled in my palm?—
To run under the hawk's wing,
Under the eye of the great owl watching from the elm-tree,
To live by courtesy of the shrike, the snake, the tom-cat.

I think of the nestling fallen into the deep grass,
The turtle gasping in the dusty rubble of the highway,
The paralytic stunned in the tub, and the water rising,—
All things innocent, hapless, forsaken.

Study Questions

1. How does the disappearance of the meadow mouse broaden into a larger area of concern for Roethke? Which comparisons help make the mouse stand for something more than a mouse—for all animals?
2. Is there any humor in this poem? In the phrase "a little quaker"?
3. What does "my thumb of a child" signify?

Horse Latitudes

Jim Morrison

When the still sea conspires an armor
And her sullen and aborted
Currents breed tiny monsters,
True sailing is dead.

Awkward instant
And the first animal is jettisoned,
Legs furiously pumping
Their stiff green gallop,
And heads bob up
Poise   10
Delicate

Pause
Consent
In mute nostril agony
Carefully refined
And sealed over.

Study Questions

1. What and where are the horse latitudes? How do they get their name?
2. Listen to the Doors' recording of this song. Are the lyrics enhanced when they are sung?
3. What do *armor, sullen,* and *sealed over* mean in context?
4. Can you suggest any reasons for Morrison's use of four single-word lines?

Hook

Walter Van Tilburg Clark

1   Hook, the hawks' child, was hatched in a dry spring among the oaks, beside the seasonal river, and was struck from the nest early. In the drouth his single-willed parents had to extend their hunting ground by more than twice, for the ground creatures upon which they fed died and dried by the hundreds. The range became too great for them to wish to return and feed Hook, and when they had lost interest in each other they drove Hook down into the sand and brush and went back to solitary courses over the bleaching hills.

2   Unable to fly yet, Hook crept over the ground, challenging all large movements with recoiled head, erected, rudimentary wings, and the small rasp of his clattering beak. It was during this time of abysmal ignorance and continual fear that his eyes took on the first quality of a hawk, that of being wide, alert and challenging. He dwelt, because of his helplessness, among the rattling brush which grew between the oaks and the river. Even in his thickets and near the water, the white sun was the dominant presence. Except in the dawn, when the land wind stirred, or in the late afternoon, when the sea wind became strong enough to penetrate the half-mile inland to this turn in the river, the sun was the major force, and everything was dry and motionless under it. The brush, small plants and trees alike husbanded the little moisture at their hearts; the moving creatures waited for dark, when sometimes the sea fog came over and made a fine, soundless rain which relieved them.

3   The two spacious sounds of his life environed Hook at this time. One was the great rustle of the slopes of yellowed wild wheat, with over

it the chattering rustle of the leaves of the California oaks, already as harsh and individually tremulous as in autumn. The other was the distant whisper of the foaming edge of the Pacific, punctuated by the hollow shoring of the waves. But these Hook did not yet hear, for he was attuned by fear and hunger to the small, spasmodic rustlings of live things. Dry, shrunken, and nearly starved, and with his plumage delayed, he snatched at beetles, dragging in the sand to catch them. When swifter and stronger birds and animals did not reach them first, which was seldom, he ate the small, silver fish left in the mud by the failing river. He watched, with nearly chattering beak, the quick, thin lizards pause, very alert, and raise and lower themselves, but could not catch them because he had to raise his wings to move rapidly, which startled them.

4   Only one sight and sound not of his world of microscopic necessity was forced upon Hook. That was the flight of the big gulls from the beaches, which sometimes, in quealing play, came spinning back over the foothills and the river bed. For some inherited reason, the big, shipbodied birds did not frighten Hook, but angered him. Small and chewed-looking, with his wide, already yellowing eyes glaring up at them, he would stand in an open place on the sand in the sun and spread his shaping wings and clatter his bill like shaken dice. Hook was furious about the swift, easy passage of gulls.

5   His first opportunity to leave off living like a ground owl came accidentally. He was standing in the late afternoon in the red light under the thicket, his eyes half-filmed with drowse and the stupefaction of starvation, when suddenly something beside him moved, and he struck, and killed a field mouse driven out of the wheat by thirst. It was a poor mouse, shriveled and lice ridden, but in striking, Hook had tasted blood, which raised nest memories and restored his nature. With started neck plumage and shining eyes, he tore and fed. When the mouse was devoured, Hook had entered hoarse adolescence. He began to seek with a conscious appetite, and to move more readily out of shelter. Impelled by the blood appetite, so glorious after his long preservation upon the flaky and bitter stuff of bugs, he ventured even into the wheat in the open sun beyond the oaks, and discovered the small trails and holes among the roots. With his belly often partially filled with flesh, he grew rapidly in strength and will. His eyes were taking on their final change, their yellow growing deeper and more opaque, their stare more constant, their challenge less desperate. Once during this transformation, he surprised a ground squirrel, and although he was ripped and wing-bitten and could not hold his prey, he was not dismayed by the conflict, but exalted. Even while the wing was still drooping and the pinions not grown back, he was excited by other ground squirrels and pursued them futilely, and was angered by their dusty escapes. He realized that his world was a great arena for killing, and felt the magnificence of it.

6   The two major events of Hook's young life occurred in the same day. A little after dawn he made the customary essay and succeeded in

flight. A little before sunset, he made his first sustained flight of over two hundred yards, and at its termination struck and slew a great buck squirrel whose thrashing and terrified gnawing and squealing gave him a wild delight. When he had gorged on the strong meat, Hook stood upright, and in his eyes was the stare of the hawk, never flagging in intensity but never swelling beyond containment. After that the stare had only to grow more deeply challenging and more sternly controlled as his range and deadliness increased. There was no change in kind. Hook had mastered the first of the three hungers which are fused into the single, flaming will of a hawk, and he had experienced the second.

7   The third and consummating hunger did not awaken in Hook until the following spring, when the exultation of space had grown slow and steady in him, so that he swept freely with the wind over the miles of coastal foothills, circling, and ever in sight of the sea, and used without struggle the warm currents lifting from the slopes, and no longer desired to scream at the range of his vision, but intently sailed above his shadow swiftly climbing to meet him on the hillsides, sinking away and rippling across the brush-grown canyons.

8   That spring the rains were long, and Hook sat for hours, hunched and angry under their pelting, glaring into the fogs of the river valley, and killed only small, drenched things flooded up from their tunnels. But when the rains had dissipated, and there were sun and sea wind again, the game ran plentiful, the hills were thick and shining green, and the new river flooded about the boulders where battered turtles climbed up to shrink and sleep. Hook then was scorched by the third hunger. Ranging farther, often forgetting to kill and eat, he sailed for days with growing rage, and woke at night clattering on his dead tree limb, and struck and struck and struck at the porous wood of the trunk, tearing it away. After days, in the draft of a coastal canyon miles below his own hills, he came upon the acrid taint he did not know but had expected, and sailing down it, felt his neck plumes rise and his wings quiver so that he swerved unsteadily. He saw the unmated female perched upon the tall and jagged stump of a tree that had been shorn by storm, and he stooped, as if upon game. But she was older than he, and wary of the gripe of his importunity, and banked off screaming, and he screamed also at the intolerable delay.

9   At the head of the canyon, the screaming pursuit was crossed by another male with a great wing-spread, and the light golden in the fringe of his plumage. But his more skillful opening played him false against the ferocity of the twice-balked Hook. His rising maneuver for position was cut short by Hook's wild, upward swoop, and at the blow he raked desperately and tumbled off to the side. Dropping, Hook struck him again, struggled to clutch, but only raked and could not hold, and diving, struck once more in passage, and then beat up, yelling triumph, and saw the crippled antagonist side-slip away, half-tumble once, as the ripped

wing failed to balance, then steady and glide obliquely into the cover of brush on the canyon side. Beating hard and stationary in the wind above the bush that covered his competitor, Hook waited an instant, but when the bush was still, screamed again, and let himself go off with the current, reseeking, infuriated by the burn of his own wounds, the thin choke-thread of the acrid taint.

10   On a hilltop projection of stone two miles inland, he struck her down, gripping her rustling body with his talons, beating her wings down with his wings, belting her head when she whimpered or thrashed, and at last clutching her neck with his hook and, when her coy struggles had given way to stillness, succeeded.

11   In the early summer, Hook drove the three young ones from their nest, and went back to lone circling above his own range. He was complete.

12   Throughout that summer and the cool, growthless weather of the winter, when the gales blew in the river canyon and the ocean piled upon the shore, Hook was master of the sky and the hills of his range. His flight became a lovely and certain thing, so that he played with the treacherous currents of the air with a delicate ease surpassing that of the gulls. He could sail for hours, searching the blanched grasses below him with telescopic eyes, gaining height against the wind, descending in mile-long gently declining swoops when he curved and rode back, and never beating either wing. At the swift passage of his shadow within their vision, gophers, ground squirrels and rabbits froze, or plunged gibbering into their tunnels beneath matted turf. Now, when he struck, he killed easily in one hard-knuckled blow. Occasionally, in sport, he soared up over the river and drove the heavy and weaponless gulls downstream again, until they would no longer venture inland.

13   There was nothing which Hook feared now, and his spirit was wholly belligerent, swift and sharp, like his gaze. Only the mixed smells and incomprehensible activities of the people at the Japanese farmer's home, inland of the coastwise highway and south of the bridge across Hook's river, troubled him. The smells were strong, unsatisfactory and never clear, and the people, though they behaved foolishly, constantly running in and out of their built-up holes, were large, and appeared capable, with fearless eyes looking up at him, so that he instinctively swerved aside from them. He cruised over their yard, their gardens, and their bean fields, but he would not alight close to their buildings.

14   But this one area of doubt did not interfere with his life. He ignored it, save to look upon it curiously as he crossed, his afternoon shadow sliding in an instant over the chicken-and-crate-cluttered yard, up the side of the unpainted barn, and then out again smoothly, just faintly, liquidly rippling over the furrows and then over the stubble of the grazing slopes. When the season was dry, and the dead earth blew on the

fields, he extended his range to satisfy his great hunger, and again narrowed it when the fields were once more alive with the minute movements he could not only see but anticipate.

15   Four times that year he was challenged by other hawks blowing up from behind the coastal hills to scud down his slopes, but two of these he slew in mid-air, and saw hurtle down to thump on the ground and lie still while he circled, and a third, whose wing he tore, he followed closely to earth and beat to death in the grass, making the crimson jet out from its breast and neck into the pale wheat. The fourth was a strong flier and experienced fighter, and theirs was a long, running battle, with brief, rising flurries of striking and screaming, from which down and plumage soared off.

16   Here, for the first time, Hook felt doubts, and at moments wanted to drop away from the scoring, burning talons and the twisted hammer strokes of the strong beak, drop away shrieking, and take cover and be still. In the end, when Hook, having outmaneuvered his enemy and come above him, wholly in control, and going with the wind, tilted and plunged for the death rap, the other, in desperation, threw over on his back and struck up. Talons locked, beaks raking, they dived earthward. The earth grew and spread under them amazingly, and they were not fifty feet above it when Hook, feeling himself turning toward the underside, tore free and beat up again on heavy, wrenched wings. The other, stroking swiftly, and so close to down that he lost wing plumes to a bush, righted himself and planed up, but flew on lumberingly between the hills and did not return. Hook screamed the triumph, and made a brief pretense of pursuit, but was glad to return, slow and victorious, to his dead tree.

17   In all these encounters Hook was injured, but experienced only the fighter's pride and exultation from the sting of wounds received in successful combat. And in each of them he learned new skill. Each time the wounds healed quickly, and left him a more dangerous bird.

18   In the next spring, when the rains and the night chants of the little frogs were past, the third hunger returned upon Hood with a new violence. In this quest, he came into the taint of a young hen. Others too were drawn by the unnerving perfume, but only one of them, the same with which Hook had fought his great battle, was a worthy competitor. This hunter drove off two, while two others, game but neophytes, were glad enough that Hook's impatience would not permit him to follow and kill. Then the battle between the two champions fled inland, and was a tactical marvel, but Hook lodged the neck-breaking blow, and struck again as they dropped past the treetops. The blood had already begun to pool on the gray, fallen foliage as Hook flapped up between branches, too spent to cry his victory. Yet his hunger would not let him rest until, late in the second day, he drove the female to ground among the laurels of a strange river canyon.

19   When the two fledglings of this second brood had been driven from the nest, and Hook had returned to his own range, he was not only complete, but supreme. He slept without concealment on his bare limb, and did not open his eyes when, in the night, the heavy-billed cranes coughed in the shallows below him.

20   The turning point of Hook's career came that autumn, when the brush in the canyons rustled dryly and the hills, mowed close by the cattle, smoked under the wind as if burning. One midafternoon, when the black clouds were torn on the rim of the sea and the surf flowered white and high on the rocks, raining in over the low cliffs, Hook rode the wind diagonally across the river mouth. His great eyes, focused for small things, stirring in the dust and leaves, overlooked so large and slow a movement as that of the Japanese farmer rising from the brush and lifting the two black eyes of his shotgun. Too late Hook saw and, startled, swerved, but wrongly. The surf muffled the reports, and nearly without sound, Hook felt the minute whips of the first shot, and the astounding, breath-taking blow of the second.

21   Beating his good wing, tasting the blood that quickly swelled into his beak, he tumbled off with the wind and struck into the thickets on the far side of the river mouth. The branches tore him. Wild with rage, he thrust up and clattered his beak, challenging, but when he had fallen over twice, he knew that the trailing wing would not carry, and then heard the boots of the hunter among the stones in the river bed and, seeing him loom at the edge of the bushes, crept back among the thickest brush and was still. When he saw the boots stand before him, he reared back, lifting his good wing and cocking his head for the serpent-like blow, his beak open but soundless, his great eyes hard and very shining. The boots passed on. The Japanese farmer, who believed that he had lost chickens, and who had cunningly observed Hook's flight for many afternoons, until he could plot it, did not greatly want a dead hawk.

22   When Hook could hear nothing but the surf and the wind in the thicket, he let the sickness and shock overcome him. The fine film of the inner lid dropped over his big eyes. His heart beat frantically, so that it made the plumage of his shot-aching breast throb. His own blood throttled his breathing. But these things were nothing compared to the lightning of pain in his left shoulder, where the shot had bunched, shattering the airy bones so the pinions trailed on the ground and could not be lifted. Yet, when a sparrow lit in the bush over him, Hook's eyes flew open again, hard and challenging, his good wing was lifted and his beak strained open. The startled sparrow darted piping out over the river.

23   Throughout that night, while the long clouds blew across the stars and the wind shook the bushes about him, and throughout the next day, while the clouds still blew and massed until there was no gleam of sunlight on the sand bar, Hook remained stationary, enduring his sick-

ness. In the second evening, the rains began. First there was a long, running patter of drops upon the beach and over the dry trees and bushes. At dusk there came a heavier squall, which did not die entirely, but slacked off to a continual, spaced splashing of big drops, and then returned with the front of the storm. In long, misty curtains, gust by gust, the rain swept over the sea, beating down its heaving, and coursed up the beach. The little jets of dust ceased to rise about the drops in the fields, and the mud began to gleam. Among the boulders of the river bed, darkling pools grew slowly.

24   Still Hook stood behind his tree from the wind, only gentle drops reaching him, falling from the upper branches and then again from the brush. His eyes remained closed, and he could still taste his own blood in his mouth, though it had ceased to come up freshly. Out beyond him, he heard the storm changing. As rain conquered the sea, the heave of the surf became a hushed sound, often lost in the crying of the wind. Then gradually, as the night turned toward morning, the wind also was broken by the rain. The crying became fainter, the rain settled toward steadiness, and the creep of the waves could be heard again, quiet and regular upon the beach.

25   At dawn there was no wind and no sun, but everywhere the roaring of the vertical, relentless rain. Hook then crept among the rapid drippings of the bushes, dragging his torn sail, seeking better shelter. He stopped often and stood with the shutters of film drawn over his eyes. At midmorning he found a little cave under a ledge at the base of the sea cliff. Here, lost without branches and leaves about him, he settled to await improvement.

26   When, at midday of the third day, the rain stopped altogether, and the sky opened before a small, fresh wind, letting light through to glitter upon a tremulous sea, Hook was so weak that his good wing trailed also to prop him upright, and his open eyes were lusterless. But his wounds were hardened, and he felt the return of hunger. Beyond his shelter, he heard the gulls flying in great numbers and crying their joy at the cleared air. He could even hear, from the fringe of the river, the ecstatic and unstinted bubblings and chirpings of the small birds. The grassland, he felt, would be full of the stirring anew of the close-bound life, the undrowned insects clicking as they dried out, the snakes slithering down, heads half erect, into the grasses where the mice, gophers and ground squirrels ran and stopped and chewed and licked themselves smoother and drier.

27   With the aid of this hunger, and on the crutches of his wings, Hook came down to stand in the sun beside his cave, whence he could watch the beach. Before him, in ellipses on tilting planes, the gulls flew. The surf was rearing again, and beginning to shelve and hiss on the sand. Through the white foam-writing it left, the long-billed pipers twinkled in bevies, escaping each wave, then racing down after it to plunge their fine drills into the minute double holes where the sand crabs bubbled.

In the third row of breakers two seals lifted sleek, streaming heads and barked, and over them, trailing his spider legs, a great crane flew south. Among the stones at the foot of the cliff, small red and green crabs made a little, continuous rattling and knocking. The cliff swallows glittered and twanged on aerial forays.

28   The afternoon began auspiciously for Hook also. One of the two gulls which came squabbling above him dropped a freshly caught fish to the sand. Quickly Hook was upon it. Gripping it, he raised his good wing and cocked his head with open beak at the many gulls which had circled and come down at once toward the fall of the fish. The gulls sheered off, cursing raucously. Left alone on the sand, Hook devoured the fish and, after resting in the sun, withdrew again to his shelter.

29   In the succeeding days, between rains, he foraged on the beach. He learned to kill and crack the small green crabs. Along the edge of the river mouth, he found the drowned bodies of mice and squirrels and even sparrows. Twice he managed to drive feeding gulls from their catch, charging upon them with buffeting wing and clattering beak. He grew stronger slowly, but the shot sail continued to drag. Often, at the choking thought of soaring and striking and the good, hot-blood kill, he strove to take off, but only the one wing came up, winnowing with a hiss, and drove him over onto his side in the sand. After these futile trials, he would rage and clatter. But gradually he learned to believe that he could not fly, that his life must now be that of the discharged nestling again. Denied the joy of space, without which the joy of loneliness was lost, the joy of battle and killing, the blood lust, became his whole concentration. It was his hope, as he charged feeding gulls, that they would turn and offer battle, but they never did. The sandpipers, at his approach, fled peeping, or, like a quiver of arrows shot together, streamed out over the surf in a long curve. Once, pent beyond bearing, he disgraced himself by shrieking challenge at the businesslike heron which flew south every evening at the same time. The heron did not even turn his head, but flapped and glided on.

30   Hook's shame and anger became such that he stood awake at night. Hunger kept him awake also, for these little leavings of the gulls could not sustain his great body in its renewed violence. He became aware that the gulls slept at night in flocks on the sand, each with one leg tucked under him. He discovered also that the curlews and the pipers, often mingling, likewise slept, on the higher remnant of the bar. A sensation of evil delight filled him in the consideration of protracted striking among them.

31   There was only half of a sick moon in a sky of running but far-separated clouds on the night when he managed to stalk into the center of the sleeping gulls. This was light enough, but so great was his vengeful pleasure that there broke from him a shrill scream of challenge as he first struck. Without the power of flight behind it, the blow was not

murderous, and this newly discovered impotence made Hook crazy, so that he screamed again and again as he struck and tore at the felled gull. He slew the one, but was twice knocked over by its heavy flounderings, and all the others rose above him, weaving and screaming, protesting in the thin moonlight. Wakened by their clamor, the wading birds also took wing, startled and plaintive. When the beach was quiet again, the flocks had settled elsewhere, beyond his pitiful range, and he was left alone beside the single kill. It was a disappointing victory. He fed with lowering spirit.

32   Thereafter, he stalked silently. At sunset he would watch where the gulls settled along the miles of beach, and after dark he would come like a sharp shadow among them, and drive with his hook on all sides of him, till the beatings of a poorly struck victim sent the flock up. Then he would turn vindictively upon the fallen and finish them. In his best night, he killed five from one flock. But he ate only a little from one, for the vigor resulting from occasional repletion strengthened only his ire, which became so great at such a time that food revolted him. It was not the joyous, swift, controlled hunting anger of a sane hawk, but something quite different, which made him dizzy if it continued too long, and left him unsatisfied with any kill.

33   Then one day, when he had very nearly struck a gull while driving it from a gasping yellowfin, the gull's wing rapped against him as it broke for its running start, and, the trailing wing failing to support him, he was knocked over. He flurried awkwardly in the sand to regain his feet, but his mastery of the beach was ended. Seeing him, in clear sunlight, struggling after the chance blow, the gulls returned about him in a flashing cloud, circling and pecking on the wing. Hook's plumage showed quick little jets of irregularity here and there. He reared back, clattering and erecting the good wing, spreading the great, rusty tail for balance. His eyes shone with a little of the old pleasure. But it died, for he could reach none of them. He was forced to turn and dance awkwardly on the sand, trying to clash bills with each tormentor. They banked up quealing and returned, weaving about him in concentric and overlapping circles. His scream was lost in their clamor, and he appeared merely to be hopping clumsily with his mouth open. Again he fell sideways. Before he could right himself, he was bowled over, and a second time, and lay on his side, twisting his neck to reach them and clappering in blind fury, and was struck three times by three successive gulls, shrieking their flock triumph.

34   Finally he managed to roll to his breast, and to crouch with his good wing spread wide and the other stretched nearly as far, so that he extended like a gigantic moth, only his snake head, with its now silent scimitar, erect. One great eye blazed under its level brow, but where the other had been was a shallow hole from which thin blood trickled to his russet gap.

35   In this crouch, by short stages, stopping repeatedly to turn and drive the gulls up, Hook dragged into the river canyon and under the stiff cover of the bitter-leafed laurel. There the gulls left him, soaring up with great clatter of their valor. Till nearly sunset Hook, broken spirited and enduring his hardening eye socket, heard them celebrating over the waves.

36   When his will was somewhat replenished, and his empty eye socket had stopped the twitching and vague aching which had forced him often to roll ignominiously to rub it in the dust, Hook ventured from the protective lacings of his thicket. He knew fear again, and the challenge of his remaining eye was once more strident, as in adolescence. He dared not return to the beaches, and with a new, weak hunger, the home hunger, enticing him, made his way by short hunting journeys back to the wild wheat slopes and the crisp oaks. There was in Hook an unwonted sensation now, that of the ever-neighboring possibility of death. This sensation was beginning, after his period as a mad bird on the beach, to solidify him into his last stage of life. When, during his slow homeward passage, the gulls wafted inland over him, watching the earth with curious, miserish eyes, he did not cower, but neither did he challenge, either by opened beak or by raised shoulder. He merely watched carefully, learning his first lessons in observing the world with one eye.

37   At first the familiar surroundings of the bend in the river and the tree with the dead limb to which he could not ascend, aggravated his humiliation, but in time, forced to live cunningly and half-starved, he lost much of his savage pride. At the first flight of a strange hawk over his realm, he was wild at his helplessness, and kept twisting his head like an owl, or spinning in the grass like a small and feathered dervish, to keep the hateful beauty of the wind-rider in sight. But in the succeeding weeks, as one after another coasted his beat, his resentment declined, and when one of the raiders, a haughty yearling, sighted his upstaring eye, and plunged and struck him dreadfully, and failed to kill him only because he dragged under a thicket in time, the second of his great hungers was gone. He had no longer the true lust to kill, no joy of battle, but only the poor desire to fill his belly.

38   Then truly he lived in the wheat and the brush like a ground owl, ridden with ground lice, dusty or muddy, ever half-starved, forced to sit for hours by small holes for petty and unsatisfying kills. Only once during the final months before his end did he make a kill where the breath of danger recalled his valor, and then the danger was such as a hawk with wings and eyes would scorn. Waiting beside a gopher hole, surrounded by the high, yellow grass, he saw the head emerge, and struck, and was amazed that there writhed in his clutch the neck and dusty coffin-skull of a rattlesnake. Holding his grip, Hook saw the great, thick body slither up after, the tip an erect, strident blur, and writhe on the dirt of the gopher's mound. The weight of the snake pushed Hook

about, and once threw him down, and the rising and falling whine of the rattles made the moment terrible, but the vaulted mouth, gaping from the closeness of Hook's grip, so that the pale, envenomed sabers stood out free, could not reach him. When Hook replaced the grip of his beak with the grip of his talons, and was free to strike again and again at the base of the head, the struggle was over. Hook tore and fed on the fine, watery flesh, and left the tattered armor and the long, jointed bone for the marching ants.

39   When the heavy rains returned, he ate well during the period of the first escapes from flooded burrows, and then well enough, in a vulture's way, on the drowned creatures. But as the rains lingered, and the burrows hung full of water, and there were no insects in the grass and no small birds sleeping in the thickets, he was constantly hungry, and finally unbearably hungry. His sodden and ground-broken plumage stood out raggedly about him, so that he looked fat, even bloated, but underneath it his skin clung to his bones. Save for his great talons and clappers, and the rain in his down, he would have been like a handful of air. He often stood for a long time under some bush or ledge, heedless of the drip, his one eye filmed over, his mind neither asleep or awake, but between. The gurgle and swirl of the brimming river, and the sound of chunks of the bank cut away to splash and dissolve in the already muddy flood, became familiar to him, and yet a torment, as if that great, ceaselessly working power of water ridiculed his frailty, within which only the faintest spark of valor still glimmered. The last two nights before the rain ended, he huddled under the floor of the bridge on the coastal highway, and heard the palpitant thunder of motors swell and roar over him. The trucks shook the bridge so that Hook, even in his famished lassitude, would sometimes open his one great eye wide and startled.

40   After the rains, when things became full again, bursting with growth and sound, the trees swelling, the thickets full of song and chatter, the fields, turning green in the sun, alive with rustling passages, and the moonlit nights strained with the song of the peepers all up and down the river and in the pools in the fields, Hook had to bear the return of the one hunger left him. At times this made him so wild that he forgot himself and screamed challenge from the open ground. The fretfulness of it spoiled his hunting, which was not entirely a matter of patience. Once he was in despair, and lashed himself through the grass and thickets, trying to rise when that virgin scent drifted for a few moments above the current of his own river. Then, breathless, his beak agape, he saw the strong suitor ride swiftly down on the wind over him, and heard afar the screaming fuss of the harsh wooing in the alders. For that moment even the battle heart beat in him again. The rim of his good eye was scarlet, and a little bead of new blood stood in the socket of the other. With beak and talon, he ripped at a fallen log, and made loam and leaves fly from about it.

41   But the season of love passed over to the nesting season, and Hook's love hunger, unused, shriveled in him with the others, and there remained in him only one stern quality befitting a hawk, and that the negative one, the remnant, the will to endure. He resumed his patient, plotted hunting, now along a field of the Japanese farmer, but ever within reach of the river thickets.

42   Growing tough and dry again as the summer advanced, inured to the family of the farmer, whom he saw daily, stooping and scraping with sticks in the ugly, open rows of their fields, where no lovely grass rustled and no life stirred save the shameless gulls, which walked at the heels of the workers, gobbling the worms and grubs they turned up, Hook became nearly content with his shard of life. The only longing or resentment to pierce him was that which he suffered occasionally when forced to hide at the edge of the mile-long bean field from the wafted cruising and the restive, down-bent gaze of one of his own kind. For the rest, he was without flame, a snappish, dust-colored creature, fading into the grasses he trailed through, and suited to his petty ways.

43   At the end of that summer, for the second time in his four years, Hook underwent a drouth. The equinoctial period passed without a rain. The laurel and the rabbit-brush dropped dry leaves. The foliage of the oaks shriveled and curled. Even the night fogs in the river canyon failed. The farmer's red cattle on the hillside lowed constantly, and could not feed on the dusty stubble. Grass fires broke out along the highways, and ate fast in the wind, filling the hollows with the smell of smoke, and died in the dirt of the shorn hills. The river made no sound. Scum grew on its vestigial pools, and turtles died and stank among the rocks. The dust, rode before the wind, and ascended and flowered to nothing between the hills, and every sunset was red with the dust in the air. The people in the farmer's house quarreled, and even struck one another. Birds were silent, and only the hawks flew much. The animals lay breathing hard for very long spells, and ran and crept jerkily. Their flanks were fallen in, and their eyes were red.

44   At first Hook gorged at the fringe of the grass fires on the multitudes of tiny things that came running and squeaking. But thereafter there were the blackened strips on the hills, and little more in the thin, crackling grass. He found mice and rats, gophers and ground-squirrels, and even rabbits, dead in the stubble and under the thickets, but so dry and fleshless that only a faint smell rose from them, even on the sunny days. He starved on them. By early December he had wearily stalked the length of the eastern foothills, hunting at night to escape the voracity of his own kind, resting often upon his wings. The queer trail of his short steps and great horned toes zigzagged in the dust and was erased by the wind at dawn. He was nearly dead, and could make no sound through the horn funnels of his clappers.

45   Then one night the dry wind brought him, with the familiar, lifeless dust, another familiar scent, troublesome, mingled and unclear. In his vision-dominated brain he remembered the swift circle of his flight a

year past, crossing in one segment, his shadow beneath him, a yard cluttered with crates and chickens, a gray barn and then again the plowed land and the stubble. Traveling faster than he had for days, impatient of his shrunken sweep, Hook came down to the farm. In the dark wisps of cloud blown among the stars over him, but no moon, he stood outside the wire of the chicken run. The scent of fat and blooded birds reached him from the shelter, and also within the enclosure was water. At the breath of the water, Hook's gorge contracted, and his tongue quivered and clove in its groove of horn. But there was the wire. He stalked its perimeter and found no opening. He beat it with his good wing, and felt it cut but not give. He wrenched at it with his beak in many places, but could not tear it. Finally, in a fury which drove the thin blood through him, he leaped repeatedly against it, beating and clawing. He was thrown back from the last leap as from the first, but in it he had risen so high as to clutch with his beak at the top wire. While he lay on his breast on the ground, the significance of this came upon him.

46   Again he leapt, clawed up the wire, and, as he would have fallen, made even the dead wing bear a little. He grasped the top and tumbled within. There again he rested flat, searching the dark with quick-turning head. There was no sound or motion but the throb of his own body. First he drank at the chill metal trough hung for the chickens. The water was cold, and loosened his tongue and his tight throat, but it also made him drunk and dizzy, so that he had to rest again, his claws spread wide to brace him. Then he walked stiffly, to stalk down the scent. He trailed it up the runway. Then there was the stuffy, body-warm air, acrid with droppings, full of soft rustlings as his talons clicked on the board floor. The thick, white shapes showed faintly in the darkness. Hook struck quickly, driving a hen to the floor with one blow, its neck broken and stretched out stringily. He leaped the still pulsing body, and tore it. The rich, streaming blood was overpowering to his dried senses, his starved, leathery body. After a few swallows, the flesh choked him. In his rage, he struck down another hen. The urge to kill took him again, as in those nights on the beach. He could let nothing go. Balked of feeding, he was compelled to slaughter. Clattering, he struck again and again. The henhouse was suddenly filled with the squawking and helpless rushing and buffeting of the terrified, brainless fowls.

47   Hook reveled in mastery. Here was game big enough to offer weight against a strike, and yet unable to soar away from his blows. Turning in the midst of the turmoil, cannily, his fury caught at the perfect pitch, he struck unceasingly. When the hens finally discovered the outlet, and streamed into the yard, to run around the fence, beating and squawking, Hook followed them, scraping down the incline, clumsy and joyous. In the yard, the cock, a bird as large as he, and much heavier, found him out and gave valiant battle. In the dark, and both earthbound, there was little skill, but blow upon blow, and only chance parry. The still squawking hens pressed into one corner of the yard. While the duel

went on, a dog, excited by the sustained scuffling, began to bark. He continued to bark, running back and forth along the fence on one side. A light flashed on in an uncurtained window of the farmhouse, and streamed whitely over the crates littering the ground.

48   Enthralled by his old battle joy, Hook knew only the burly cock before him. Now, in the farthest reach of the window light, they could see each other dimly. The Japanese farmer, with his gun and lantern, was already at the gate when the finish came. The great cock leapt to jab with his spurs and, toppling forward with extended neck as he fell, was struck and extinguished. Blood had loosened Hook's throat. Shrilly he cried his triumph. It was a thin and exhausted cry, but within him as good as when he shrilled in mid-air over the plummeting descent of a fine foe in his best spring.

49   The light from the lantern partially blinded Hook. He first turned and ran directly from it, into the corner where the hens were huddled. They fled apart before his charge. He essayed the fence, and on the second try, in his desperation, was out. But in the open dust, the dog was on him, circling, dashing in, snapping. The farmer, who at first had not fired because of the chickens, now did not fire because of the dog, and, when he saw that the hawk was unable to fly, relinquished the sport to the dog, holding the lantern up in order to see better. The light showed his own flat, broad, dark face as sunken also, the cheekbones very prominent, and showed the torn-off sleeves of his shirt and the holes in the knees of his overalls. His wife, in a stained wrapper, and barefooted, heavy black hair hanging around a young, passionless face, joined him hesitantly, but watched, fascinated and a little horrified. His son joined them too, encouraging the dog, but quickly grew silent. Courageous and cruel death, however it may afterward sicken the one who has watched it, is impossible to look away from.

50   In the circle of the light, Hook turned to keep the dog in front of him. His one eye gleamed with malevolence. The dog was an Airedale, and large. Each time he pounced, Hook stood ground, raising his good wing, the pinions newly torn by the fence, opening his beak soundlessly, and, at the closest approach, hissed furiously, and at once struck. Hit and ripped twice by the whetted horn, the dog recoiled more quickly from several subsequent jumps and, infuriated by his own cowardice, began to bark wildly. Hook maneuvered to watch him, keeping his head turned to avoid losing the foe on the blind side. When the dog paused, safely away, Hook watched him quietly, wing partially lowered, beak closed, but at the first move again lifted the wing and gaped. The dog whined, and the man spoke to him encouragingly. The awful sound of his voice made Hook for an instant twist his head to stare up at the immense figures behind the light. The dog again sallied, barking, and Hook's head spun back. His wing was bitten this time, and with a furious sideblow, he caught the dog's nose. The dog dropped him with a yelp, and then, smarting, came on more warily, as Hook propped himself up from the

ground again between his wings. Hook's artificial strength was waning, but his heart still stood to the battle, sustained by a fear of such dimension as he had never known before, but only anticipated when the arrogant young hawk had driven him to cover. The dog, unable to find any point at which the merciless, unwinking eye was not watching him, the parted beak waiting, paused and whimpered again.

51   "Oh, kill the poor thing," the woman begged.

52   The man, though, encouraged the dog again, saying, "Sick him; sick him."

53   The dog rushed bodily. Unable to avoid him, Hook was bowled down, snapping and raking. He left long slashes, as from the blade of a knife, on the dog's flank, but before he could right himself and assume guard again, was caught by the good wing and dragged, clattering, and seeking to make a good stroke from his back. The man followed them to keep the light on them, and the boy went with him, wetting his lips with his tongue and keeping his fists closed tightly. The woman remained behind, but could not help watching the diminished conclusion.

54   In the little, palely shining arena, the dog repeated his successful maneuver three times, growling but not barking, and when Hook thrashed up from the third blow, both wings were trailing, and dark, shining streams crept on his black-fretted breast from the shoulders. The great eye flashed more furiously than it ever had in victorious battle, and the beak still gaped, but there was no more clatter. He faltered when turning to keep front; the broken wings played him false even as props. He could not rise to use his talons.

55   The man had tired of holding the lantern up, and put it down to rub his arm. In the low, horizontal light, the dog charged again, this time throwing the weight of his forepaws against Hook's shoulder, so that Hook was crushed as he struck. With his talons up, Hook raked at the dog's belly, but the dog conceived the finish, and furiously worried the feathered bulk. Hook's neck went limp, and between his gaping clappers came only a faint chittering, as from some small kill of his own in the grasses.

56   In this last conflict, however, there had been some minutes of the supreme fire of the hawk whose three hungers are perfectly fused in the one will; enough to burn off a year of shame.

57   Between the great sails the light body lay caved and perfectly still. The dog, smarting from his cuts, came to the master and was praised. The woman, joining them slowly, looked at the great wingspread, her husband raising the lantern that she might see it better.

58   "Oh, the brave bird," she said.

Study Questions

1. Rarely does a reader fail to like and even sympathize with Hook, the bird. By what means does Clark elicit this response?
2. Does Hook demonstrate nobility? Is he ever ignoble? Can we legitimately attribute nobility to animals, or is nobility merely a word by which people describe how they feel about animals?
3. In what way is the man identified with the dog and the woman with the hawk in the last scene?
4. Is there any pattern in the way Clark constructs his paragraphs?
5. Why does Clark divide his story into sections? What happens in each section? How are the first and fourth sections related?

The Bird and the Machine

Loren Eiseley

1   I suppose their little bones have years ago been lost among the stones and winds of those high glacial pastures. I suppose their feathers blew eventually into the piles of tumbleweed beneath the straggling cattle fences and rotted there in the mountain snows, along with dead steers and all the other things that drift to an end in the corners of the wire. I do not quite know why I should be thinking of birds over the *New York Times* at breakfast, particularly the birds of my youth half a continent away. It is a funny thing what the brain will do with memories and how it will treasure them and finally bring them into odd juxtapositions with other things, as though it wanted to make a design, or get some meaning out of them, whether you want it or not, or even see it.

2   It used to seem marvelous to me, but I read now that there are machines that can do these things in a small way, machines that can crawl about like animals, and that it may not be long now until they do more things—maybe even make themselves—I saw that piece in the *Times* just now. And then they will, maybe—well, who knows—but you read about it more and more with no one making any protest, and already they can add better than we and reach up and hear things through the dark and finger the guns over the night sky.

3   This is the new world that I read about at breakfast. This is the world that confronts me in my biological books and journals, until there are times when I sit quietly in my chair and try to hear the little purr of the cogs in my head and the tubes flaring and dying as the messages go through them and the circuits snap shut or open. This is the great age, make no mistake about it; the robot has been born somewhat appropriately along with the atom bomb, and the brain they say now is just another type of more complicated feedback system. The engineers have its basic principles worked out; it's mechanical, you know; nothing to get superstitious about; and man can always improve on nature once he gets the idea. Well, he's got it all right and that's why, I guess, that I sit here in my chair, with the article crunched in my hand, remembering those two birds and that blue mountain sunlight. There is another magazine article on my desk that reads "Machines Are Getting Smarter Every Day." I don't deny it, but I'll still stick with the birds. It's life I believe in, not machines.

4   Maybe you don't believe there is any difference. A skeleton is all joints and pulleys, I'll admit. And when man was in his simpler stages of machine building in the eighteenth century, he quickly saw the resemblances. "What," wrote Hobbes, "is the heart but a spring, and the nerves but so many strings, and the joints but so many wheels, giving motion to the whole body?" Tinkering about in their shops it was inevitable in the end that men would see the world as a huge machine "subdivided into an infinite number of lesser machines."

5   The idea took on with a vengeance. Little automatons toured the country—dolls controlled by clockwork. Clocks described as little worlds were taken on tours by their designers. They were made up of moving figures, shifting scenes and other remarkable devices. The life of the cell was unknown. Man, whether he was conceived as possessing a soul or not, moved and jerked about like these tiny puppets. A human being thought of himself in terms of his own tools and implements. He had been fashioned like the puppets he produced and was only a more clever model made by a greater designer.

6   Then in the nineteenth century, the cell was discovered, and the single machine in its turn was found to be the product of millions of infinitesimal machines—the cells. Now, finally, the cell itself dissolves away into an abstract chemical machine—and that into some intangible, inexpressible flow of energy. The secret seems to lurk all about, the wheels get smaller and smaller, and they turn more rapidly, but when you try to seize it the life is gone—and so, by popular definition, some would say that life was never there in the first place. The wheels and the cogs are the secret and we can make them better in time—machines that will run faster and more accurately than real mice to real cheese.

7   I have no doubt it can be done, though a mouse harvesting seeds on an autumn thistle is to me a fine sight and more complicated, I think, in his multiform activity, than a machine "mouse" running a maze. Also, I

like to think of the possible shape of the future brooding in mice, just as it brooded once in a rather ordinary mousy insectivore who became a man. It leaves a nice fine indeterminate sense of wonder that even an electronic brain hasn't got, because you know perfectly well that if the electronic brain changes, it will be because of something man has done to it. But what man will do to himself he doesn't really know. A certain scale of time and a ghostly intangible thing called change are ticking in him. Powers and potentialities like the oak in the seed, or a red and awful ruin. Either way, it's impressive; and the mouse has it, too. Or those birds, I'll never forget those birds—yet before I measured their significance, I learned the lesson of time first of all. I was young then and left alone in a great desert—part of an expedition that had scattered its men over several hundred miles in order to carry on research more effectively. I learned there that time is a series of planes existing superficially in the same universe. The tempo is a human illusion, a subjective clock ticking in our own kind of protoplasm.

8   As the long months passed, I began to live on the slower planes and to observe more readily what passed for life there. I sauntered, I passed more and more slowly up and down the canyons in the dry baking heat of midsummer. I slumbered for long hours in the shade of huge brown boulders that had gathered in tilted companies out on the flats. I had forgotten the world of men and the world had forgotten me. Now and then I found a skull in the canyons, and these justified my remaining there. I took a serene cold interest in these discoveries. I had come, like many a naturalist before me, to view life with a wary and subdued attention. I had grown to take pleasure in the divested bone.

9   I sat once on a high ridge that fell away before me into a waste of sand dunes. I sat through hours of a long afternoon. Finally, as I glanced beside my boot an indistinct configuration caught my eye. It was a coiled rattlesnake, a big one. How long he had sat with me I do not know. I had not frightened him. We were both locked in the sleep-walking tempo of the earlier world, baking in the same high air and sunshine. Perhaps he had been there when I came. He slept on as I left, his coils, so ill discerned by me, dissolving once more among the stones and gravel from which I had barely made him out.

10   Another time I got on a higher ridge, among some tough little wind-warped pines half covered over with sand in a basin-like depression that caught everything carried by the air up to those heights. There were a few thin bones of birds, some cracked shells of indeterminable age, and the knotty fingers of pine roots bulged out of shape from their long and agonizing grasp upon the crevices of the rock. I lay under the pines in the sparse shade and went to sleep once more.

11   It grew cold finally, for autumn was in the air by then, and the few things that lived thereabouts were sinking down into an even chillier scale of time. In the moments between sleeping and waking I saw the

roots about me and slowly, slowly, a foot in what seemed many centuries, I moved my sleep-stiffened hands over the scaling bark and lifted my numbed face after the vanishing sun. I was a great awkward thing of knots and aching limbs, trapped up there in some long, patient endurance that involved the necessity of putting living fingers into rock and by slow, aching expansion bursting those rocks asunder. I suppose, so thin and slow was the time of my pulse by then, that I might have stayed on to drift still deeper into the lower cadences of the frost, or the crystalline life that glistens pebbles, or shines in a snowflake, or dreams in the meteoric iron between the worlds.

12   It was a dim descent, but time was present in it. Somewhere far down in that scale the notion struck me that one might come the other way. Not many months thereafter I joined some colleagues heading higher into a remote windy tableland where huge bones were reputed to protrude like boulders from the turf. I had drowsed with reptiles and moved with the century-long pulse of trees; now, lethargically, I was climbing back up some invisible ladder of quickening hours. There had been talk of birds in connection with my duties. Birds are intense, fast-living creatures—reptiles, I suppose one might say, that have escaped out of the heavy sleep of time, transformed fairy creatures dancing over sunlit meadows. It is a youthful fancy, no doubt, but because of something that happened up there among the escarpments of that range, it remains with me a lifelong impression. I can never bear to see a bird imprisoned.

13   We came into that valley through the trailing mists of a spring night. It was a place that looked as though it might never have known the foot of man, but our scouts had been ahead of us and we knew all about the abandoned cabin of stone that lay far up on one hillside. It had been built in the land rush of the last century and then lost to the cattlemen again as the marginal soils failed to take to the plow.

14   There were spots like this all over that country. Lost graves marked by unlettered stones and old corroding rim-fire cartridge cases lying where somebody had made a stand among the boulders that rimmed the valley. They are all that remain of the range wars; the men are under the stones now. I could see our cavalcade winding in and out through the mist below us: torches, the reflection of the truck lights on our collecting tins, and the far-off bumping of a loose dinosaur thigh bone in the bottom of a trailer. I stood on a rock a moment looking down and thinking what it cost in money and equipment to capture the past.

15   We had, in addition, instructions to lay hands on the present. The word had come through to get them alive—birds, reptiles, anything. A zoo somewhere abroad needed restocking. It was one of those reciprocal matters in which science involves itself. Maybe our museum needed a stray ostrich egg and this was the payoff. Anyhow, my job was to help capture some birds and that was why I was there before the trucks.

16   The cabin had not been occupied for years. We intended to clean it out and live in it, but there were holes in the roof and the birds had come in and were roosting in the rafters. You could depend on it in a place like this where everything blew away, and even a bird needed some place out of the weather and away from coyotes. A cabin going back to nature in a wild place draws them till they come in, listening at the eaves, I imagine, pecking softly among the shingles till they find a hole and then suddenly the place is theirs and man is forgotten.

17   Sometimes of late years I find myself thinking the most beautiful sight in the world might be the birds taking over New York after the last man has run away to the hills. I will never live to see it, of course, but I know just how it will sound because I've lived up high and I know the sort of watch birds keep on us. I've listened to sparrows tapping tentatively on the outside of air conditioners when they thought no one was listening, and I know how other birds test the vibrations that come up to them through the television aerials.

18   "Is he gone?" they ask, and the vibrations come up from below, "Not yet, not yet."

19   Well, to come back, I got the door open softly and I had the spotlight all ready to turn on and blind whatever birds there were so they couldn't see to get out through the roof. I had a short piece of ladder to put against the far wall where there was a shelf on which I expected to make the biggest haul. I had all the information I needed just like any skilled assassin. I pushed the door open, the hinges squeaking only a little. A bird or two stirred—I could hear them—but nothing flew and there was a faint starlight through the holes in the roof.

20   I padded across the floor, got the ladder up and the light ready, and slithered up the ladder till my head and arms were over the shelf. Everything was dark as pitch except for the starlight at the little place back of the shelf near the eaves. With the light to blind them, they'd never make it. I had them. I reached my arm carefully over in order to be ready to seize whatever was there and I put the flash on the edge of the shelf where it would stand by itself when I turned it on. That way I'd be able to use both hands.

21   Everything worked perfectly except for one detail—I didn't know what kind of birds were there. I never thought about it at all, and it wouldn't have mattered if I had. My orders were to get something interesting. I snapped on the flash and sure enough there was a great beating and feathers flying, but instead of my having them, they, or rather he, had me. He had my hand, that is, and for a small hawk not much bigger than my fist he was doing all right. I heard him give one short metallic cry when the light went on and my hand descended on the bird beside him; after that he was busy with his claws and his beak was sunk in my thumb. In the struggle I knocked the lamp over on the shelf, and his mate got her sight back and whisked neatly through the hole in

the roof and off among the stars outside. It all happened in fifteen seconds and you might think I would have fallen down the ladder, but no, I had a professional assassin's reputation to keep up, and the bird, of course, made the mistake of thinking the hand was the enemy and not the eyes behind it. He chewed my thumb up pretty effectively and lacerated my hand with his claws, but in the end I got him, having two hands to work with.

22   He was a sparrow hawk and a fine young male in the prime of life. I was sorry not to catch the pair of them, but as I dripped blood and folded his wings carefully, holding him by the back so that he couldn't strike again, I had to admit the two of them might have been more than I could have handled under the circumstances. The little fellow had saved his mate by diverting me, and that was that. He was born to it, and made no outcry now, resting in my hand hopelessly, but peering toward me in the shadows behind the lamp with a fierce, almost indifferent glance. He neither gave nor expected mercy and something out of the high air passed from him to me, stirring a faint embarrassment.

23   I quit looking into that eye and managed to get my huge carcass with its fist full of prey back down the ladder. I put the bird in a box too small to allow him to injure himself by struggle and walked out to welcome the arriving trucks. It had been a long day, and camp still to make in the darkness. In the morning that bird would be just another episode. He would go back with the bones in the truck to a small cage in a city where he would spend the rest of his life. And a good thing, too. I sucked my aching thumb and spat out some blood. An assassin has to get used to these things. I had a professional reputation to keep up.

24   In the morning, with the change that comes on suddenly in that high country, the mist that had hovered below us in the valley was gone. The sky was a deep blue, and one could see for miles over the high outcroppings of stone. I was up early and brought the box in which the little hawk was imprisoned out onto the grass where I was building a cage. A wind as cool as a mountain spring ran over the grass and stirred my hair. It was a fine day to be alive. I looked up and all around and at the hole in the cabin roof out of which the other little hawk had fled. There was no sign of her anywhere that I could see.

25   "Probably in the next county by now," I thought cynically, but before beginning work I decided I'd have a look at my last night's capture.

26   Secretively, I looked again all around the camp and up and down and opened the box. I got him right out in my hand with his wings folded properly and I was careful not to startle him. He lay limp in my grasp and I could feel his heart pound under the feathers but he only looked beyond me and up.

27   I saw him look that last look away beyond me into a sky so full of light that I could not follow his gaze. The little breeze flowed over me again, and nearby a mountain aspen shook all its tiny leaves. I suppose I

must have had an idea then of what I was going to do, but I never let it come up into consciousness. I just reached over and laid the hawk on the grass.

28   He lay there a long minute without hope, unmoving, his eyes still fixed on that blue vault above him. It must have been that he was already so far away in heart that he never felt the release from my hand. He never even stood. He just lay with his breast against the grass.

29   In the next second after that long minute he was gone. Like a flicker of light, he had vanished with my eyes full on him, but without actually seeing even a premonitory wing beat. He was gone straight into that towering emptiness of light and crystal that my eyes could scarcely bear to penetrate. For another long moment there was silence. I could not see. The light was too intense. Then from far up somewhere a cry came ringing down.

30   I was young then and had seen little of the world, but when I heard that cry my heart turned over. It was not the cry of the hawk I had captured; for, by shifting my position against the sun, I was now seeing further up. Straight out of the sun's eye, where she must have been soaring restlessly above us for untold hours, hurtled his mate. And from far up, ringing from peak to peak of the summits over us, came a cry of such unutterable and ecstatic joy that it sounds down across the years and tingles among the cups on my quiet breakfast table.

31   I saw them both now. He was rising fast to meet her. They met in a great soaring gyre that turned to a whirling circle and a dance of wings. Once more, just once, their two voices, joined in a harsh wild medley of question and response, struck and echoed against the pinnacles of the valley. Then they were gone forever somewhere into those upper regions beyond the eyes of men.

32   I am older now, and sleep less, and have seen most of what there is to see and am not very much impressed any more, I suppose, by anything. "What Next in the Attributes of Machines?" my morning headline runs. "It Might Be the Power to Reproduce Themselves."

33   I lay the paper down and across my mind a phrase floats insinuatingly: "It does not seem that there is anything in the construction, constituents, or behavior of the human being which it is essentially impossible for science to duplicate and synthesize. On the other hand . . ."

34   All over the city the cogs in the hard, bright mechanisms have begun to turn. Figures move through computers, names are spelled out, a thoughtful machine selects the fingerprints of a wanted criminal from an array of thousands. In the laboratory an electronic mouse runs swiftly through a maze toward the cheese it can neither taste not enjoy. On the second run it does better than a living mouse.

35   "On the other hand . . ." Ah, my mind takes up, on the other hand the machine does not bleed, ache, hang for hours in the empty sky in a torment of hope to learn the fate of another machine, nor does it cry out

with joy nor dance in the air with the fierce passion of a bird. Far off, over a distance greater than space, that remote cry from the heart of heaven makes a faint buzzing among my breakfast dishes and passes on and away.

Study Questions

1. Which is the thesis sentence of this essay? How effective is the transition between that sentence and the paragraph that follows?
2. Does this essay compare birds with machines? Contrast them? Compare *and* contrast them? What is the relationship between the thesis sentence and the episode of the bird?
3. Explain how time and a sense of the future figure in the essay. The introduction to the essay is set off from the body by extra spacing. Why isn't the conclusion similarly set off?
4. What is your reaction to the conversation between the sparrows and the vibrations? Is it too "cute"?
5. Why is Eiseley slightly embarrassed by the bird's glance? Why does he say he quit looking into "that eye" instead of "those eyes" (paragraph 23)?

Hurt Hawks

Robinson Jeffers

I

The broken pillar of the wing jags from the clotted shoulder,
The wing trails like a banner in defeat,
No more to use the sky forever but live with famine
And pain a few days: cat nor coyote
Will shorten the week of waiting for death, there is game without
      talons.

He stands under the oak-bush and waits
The lame feet of salvation; at night he remembers freedom
And flies in a dream, the dawns ruin it.
He is strong and pain is worse to the strong, incapacity is worse.
The curs of the day come and torment him   10
At distance, no one but death the redeemer will humble that head,
The intrepid readiness, the terrible eyes.
The wild God of the world is sometimes merciful to those
That ask mercy, not often to the arrogant.
You do not know him, you communal people, or you have forgotten
        him;
Intemperate and savage, the hawk remembers him;
Beautiful and wild, the hawks, and men that are dying, remember
        him.

II

I'd sooner, except the penalties, kill a man than a hawk; but the
        great redtail
Had nothing left but unable misery
From the bone too shattered for mending, the wing that trailed
        under his talons when he moved.   20
We had fed him six weeks, I gave him freedom,
He wandered over the foreland hill and returned in the evening,
        asking for death,
Not like a beggar, still eyed with the old
Implacable arrogance. I gave him the lead gift in the twilight. What
        fell was relaxed,

Owl-downy, soft feminine feathers; but what
Soared: the fierce rush: the night-herons by the flooded river cried
        fear at its rising
Before it was quite unsheathed from reality.

___

Study Questions

1. After reading "Hurt Hawks," would you conclude that Jeffers is both a misanthrope and a bird lover? If not, how would you characterize the attitude expressed here?
2. What adjectives does Jeffers use to describe the hawk before and after its death? How does the phrase "Owl-downy, soft feminine feathers" contrast with the rest of the poem?

3. What is the basis for Jeffers's division of the poem into two parts? How does he make the transition between them?
4. What does "unsheathed from reality" mean? Does it mean more than than merely "died"?
5. Jeffers seems to leave out words which are ordinarily considered aids to understanding—prepositions and conjunctions, especially. Where and why does he do this?

Hawk Roosting

Ted Hughes

I sit in the top of the wood, my eyes closed.
Inaction, no falsifying dream
Between my hooked head and hooked feet:
Or in sleep rehearse perfect kills and eat.

The convenience of the high trees!
The air's buoyancy and the sun's ray
Are of advantage to me;
And the earth's face upward for my inspection.

My feet are locked upon the rough bark.
It took the whole of Creation   10
To produce my foot, my each feather:
Now I hold Creation in my foot

Or fly up, and revolve it all slowly—
I kill where I please because it is all mine.
There is no sophistry in my body:
My manners are tearing off heads—

The allotment of death.
For the one path of my flight is direct
Through the bones of the living.
No arguments assert my right: 20

The sun is behind me.
Nothing has changed since I began.
My eye has permitted no change.
I am going to keep things like this.

Study Questions

1. It is neither easy nor usual to write in the first person from an animal's point of view. How successfully does Hughes do it?
2. How does the hawk reveal its confidence—or is it arrogance?
3. What does the hawk mean by "sophistry," and how does it contrast with "tearing off heads"?
4. How does the meaning of *Creation* differ the two times the hawk uses it?
5. To what avail are arguments against the hawk's perfect instincts?

Desert Places

Sigmund Freud published his *Interpretation of Dreams* in 1899, and the world has not been the same since. Some contemporary critics consider Freud and our acceptance—conscious or unconscious (to use some Freudian terms)—of the implications of his work as the most important force in the life of twentieth-century man. Nearly every aspect of our life is touched, if not controlled, by psychological considerations. The cars we drive, the foods we eat (when we're not dieting), the clothes we wear, the lovers and strangers that we meet—all and each are determined, so we are told, by psychological needs. Each of us seems to be "psyching out" everyone else, and doing so almost as if we had the *right* to know what made Sammy and Elaine run.

And so we take pep pills to stay awake and tranquilizers to fall asleep. We riot in the name of peace. We insist that we don't want to get involved while preaching the ideal of commitment. The paradoxes of modern life are undeniable, unavoidable, and bewildering. Life is indeed a puzzlement. In an attempt to solve the puzzle and discover who and what we are, some of us grit our teeth and face the world boldly; others find solace where we can, often within ourselves; and still others cope with reality by escaping from it.

The selections in *Desert Places* are all concerned with our exploration of the self, or our avoidance of it. Conrad Aiken, James Thurber, Katherine Anne Porter, Frank O'Connor, T. S. Eliot, Terrance Withers, and Robert Browning all explore the world of misfits, of the neurotic and the psychotic. Thurber and Withers write of those who find temporary surcease from their problems, while Aiken and Browning depict characters unlikely ever to face the world again. On the other hand, Frank O'Connor's character adjusts and finds his self. Next, Walt Whitman, Sara Teasdale, Robert Frost, and Alfred, Lord Tennyson bring us face to face with the desert places within ourselves, and suggest alternative ways to fill those spaces.

With Percy Bysshe Shelley's "Ozymandias" we begin a subsection on the need to communicate. Shelley's king writes his own obituary and attempts to communicate with future generations. Nancy Willard and Paul Simon present us with individuals seeking auditors, while Richard Rhodes shows us how greeting cards paradoxically both ask for and cut off meaningful dialogue.

105

Dylan Thomas's "Do Not Go Gentle into That Good Night" introduces a group of essays and poems about men and women who face death with different degrees of willingness. This subsection offers comparisons concerned with the death of children, of parents' reactions when their children die, and of children's reactions when their parents die. One voice seemingly addresses us from the grave in "I Heard a Fly Buzz When I Died."

The high suicide rate on college campuses has led us to include the four selections on suicide, or rather on the reactions of the living to death by suicide. The topic is treated in the poem, the short story, and the song. Then Robert Frost and Jessica Mitford explore modern man's attitudes toward burial and funerals.

Finally, we include a provocative section on various religious viewpoints. John Milton, Nathaniel Hawthorne, and Bernard Malamud provide traditional views of man's relationships to God, while Zitkala-Ša (Gertrude Bonnin) happily tells us why she is a pagan, if that is indeed the right word to describe her. The section closes with two poets and a science-oriented essayist taking on the Nativity and its implication for the Wise Men and humanity in general. These selections provide the capstone to the discussion of the themes which inform *Desert Places*.

Silent Snow, Secret Snow

Conrad Aiken

1   Just why it should have happened, or why it should have happened just when it did, he could not, of course, possibly have said; nor perhaps would it even have occurred to him to ask. The thing was above all a secret, something to be preciously concealed from Mother and Father; and to that very fact it owed an enormous part of its deliciousness. It was like a peculiarly beautiful trinket to be carried unmentioned in one's trouser pocket—a rare stamp, an old coin, a few tiny gold links found trodden out of shape on the path in the park, a pebble of carnelian, a seashell distinguishable from all others by an unusual spot or stripe— and, as if it were any one of these, he carried around with him everywhere a warm and persistent and increasingly beautiful sense of possession. Nor was it only a sense of possession—it was also a sense of protection. It was as if, in some delightful way, his secret gave him a fortress, a wall behind which he could retreat into heavenly seclusion. This was almost the first thing he had noticed about it—apart from the oddness of the thing itself—and it was this that now again, for the fiftieth time, occurred to him, as he sat in the little schoolroom. It was the half hour for geography. Miss Buell was revolving with one finger, slowly, a huge terrestrial globe which had been placed on her desk. The green and yellow continents passed and repassed, questions were asked and answered, and now the little girl in front of him, Deirdre, who had a funny little constellation of freckles on the back of her neck, exactly like the Big Dipper, was standing up and telling Miss Buell that the equator was the line that ran round the middle.

2   Miss Buell's face, which was old and grayish and kindly, with gray stiff curls beside the cheeks, and eyes that swam very brightly, like little minnows, behind thick glasses, wrinkled itself into a complication of amusements.

3   "Ah! I see. The earth is wearing a belt, or a sash. Or someone drew a line round it!"

4   "Oh no—not that —I mean—"

5   In the general laughter, he did not share, or only a very little. He was thinking about the Arctic and Antarctic regions, which of course, on the globe, were white. Miss Buell was now telling them about the tropics, the jungles, the steamy heat of equatorial swamps, where the birds and butterflies, and even the snakes, were like living jewels. As he listened to these things, he was already, with a pleasant sense of half-

effort, putting his secret between himself and the words. Was it really an effort at all? For effort implied something voluntary, and perhaps even something one did not especially want; whereas this was distinctly pleasant, and came almost of its own accord. All he needed to do was to think of that morning, the first one, and then of all the others—

6   But it was all so absurdly simple! It had amounted to so little. It was nothing, just an idea—and just why it should have become so wonderful, so permanent, was a mystery—a very pleasant one, to be sure, but also, in an amusing way, foolish. However, without ceasing to listen to Miss Buell, who had now moved up to the north temperate zones, he deliberately invited his memory of the first morning. It was only a moment or two after he had waked up—or perhaps the moment itself. But was there, to be exact, an exact moment? Was one awake all at once? or was it gradual? Anyway, it was after he had stretched a lazy hand up toward the headrail, and yawned, and then relaxed again among his warm covers, all the more grateful on a December morning, that the thing had happened. Suddenly, for no reason, he had thought of the postman, he remembered the postman. Perhaps there was nothing so odd in that. After all, he heard the postman almost every morning in his life—his heavy boots could be heard clumping round the corner at the top of the little cobbled hill-street, and then, progressively nearer, progressively louder, the double knock at each door, the crossings and recrossings of the street, till finally the clumsy steps came stumbling across to the very door, and the tremendous knock came which shook the house itself.

7   (Miss Buell was saying, "Vast wheat-growing areas in North America and Siberia."

8   Deirdre had for the moment placed her left hand across the back of her neck.)

9   But on this particular morning, the first morning, as he lay there with his eyes closed, he had for some reason *waited* for the postman. He wanted to hear him come round the corner. And that was precisely the joke—he never did. He never came. He never had come—*round the corner*—again. For when at last the steps *were* heard, they had already, he was quite sure, come a little down the hill, to the first house; and even so, the steps were curiously different—they were softer, they had a new secrecy about them, they were muffled and indistinct; and while the rhythm of them was the same, it now said a new thing—it said peace, it said remoteness, it said cold, it said sleep. And he had understood the situation at once—nothing could have seemed simpler—there had been snow in the night, such as all winter he had been longing for; and it was this which had rendered the postman's first footsteps inaudible, and the later ones faint. Of course! How lovely! And even now it must be snowing—it was going to be a snowy day—the long white ragged lines were drifting and sifting across the street, across the faces of the old houses, whispering and hushing, making little triangles of white in the corners between cobblestones, seething a little when the wind blew

them over the ground to a drifted corner; and so it would be all day, getting deeper and deeper and silenter and silenter.

10   (Miss Buell was saying, "Land of perpetual snow.")

11   All this time, of course (while he lay in bed), he had kept his eyes closed, listening to the nearer progress of the postman, the muffled footsteps thumping and slipping on the snow-sheathed cobbles; and all the other sounds—the double knocks, a frosty far-off voice or two, a bell ringing thinly and softly as if under a sheet of ice—had the same slightly abstracted quality, as if removed by one degree from actuality—as if everything in the world had been insulated by snow. But when at last, pleased, he opened his eyes, and turned them toward the window, to see for himself this long-desired and now so clearly imagined miracle—what he saw instead was brilliant sunlight on a roof; and when, astonished, he jumped out of bed and stared down into the street, expecting to see the cobbles obliterated by the snow, he saw nothing but the bare bright cobbles themselves.

12   Queer, the effect this extraordinary surprise had had upon him—all the following morning he had kept with him a sense as of snow falling about him, a secret screen of new snow between himself and the world. If he had not dreamed such a thing—and how could he have dreamed it while awake?—how else could one explain it? In any case, the delusion had been so vivid as to affect his entire behavior. He could not now remember whether it was on the first or the second morning—or was it even the third?—that his mother had drawn attention to some oddness in his manner.

13   "But my darling"—she had said at the breakfast table—"what has come over you? You don't seem to be listening. . . ."

14   And how often that very thing had happened since!

15   (Miss Buell was now asking if anyone knew the difference between the North Pole and the Magnetic Pole. Deirdre was holding up her flickering brown hand, and he could see the four white dimples that marked the knuckles.)

16   Perhaps it hadn't been either the second or third morning—or even the fourth or fifth. How could he be sure? How could he be sure just when the delicious *progress* had become clear? Just when it had really *begun*? The intervals weren't very precise. . . . All he now knew was, that at some point or other—perhaps the second day, perhaps the sixth—he had noticed that the presence of the snow was a little more insistent, the sound of it clearer; and, conversely, the sound of the postman's footsteps more indistinct. Not only could he not hear the steps come round the corner, he could not even hear them at the first house. It was below the first house that he heard them; and then, a few days later, it was below the second house that he heard them; and a few days later again, below the third. Gradually, gradually, the snow was becoming heavier, the sound of its seething louder, the cobblestones more and more muffled. When he found, each morning, on going to the window,

after the ritual of listening, that the roofs and cobbles were as bare as ever, it made no difference. This was, after all, only what he had expected. It was even what pleased him, what rewarded him: the thing was his own, belonged to no one else. No one else knew about it, not even his mother and father. There, outside, were the bare cobbles; and here, inside, was the snow. Snow growing heavier each day, muffling the world, hiding the ugly, and deadening increasingly—above all—the steps of the postman.

17   "But, my darling"—she had said at the luncheon table—"what has come over you? You don't seem to listen when people speak to you. That's the third time I've asked you to pass your plate. . . ."

18   How was one to explain this to Mother? or to Father? There was, of course, nothing to be done about it: nothing. All one could do was to laugh embarrassedly, pretend to be a little ashamed, apologize, and take a sudden and somewhat disingenuous interest in what was being done or said. The cat had stayed out all night. He had a curious swelling on his left cheek—perhaps somebody had kicked him, or a stone had struck him. Mrs. Kempton was or was not coming to tea. The house was going to be housecleaned, or "turned out," on Wednesday instead of Friday. A new lamp was provided for his evening work—perhaps it was eyestrain which accounted for this new and so peculiar vagueness of his—Mother was looking at him with amusement as she said this, but with something else as well. A new lamp? A new lamp. Yes, Mother, No, Mother, Yes, Mother. School is going very well. The geometry is very easy. The history is very dull. The geography is very interesting—particularly when it takes one to the North Pole. Why the North Pole? Oh, well, it would be fun to be an explorer. Another Peary or Scott or Shackleton. And then abruptly he found his interest in the talk at an end, stared at the pudding on his plate, listened, waited, and began once more—ah, how heavenly, too, the first beginnings—to hear or feel—for could he actually hear it?—the silent snow, the secret snow.

19   (Miss Buell was telling them about the search for the Northwest Passage, about Hendrik Hudson, the *Half Moon*.)

20   This had been, indeed, the only distressing feature of the new experience; the fact that it so increasingly had brought him into a kind of mute misunderstanding, or even conflict, with his father and mother. It was as if he were trying to lead a double life. On the one hand, he had to be Paul Hasleman, and keep up the appearance of being that person—dress, wash, and answer intelligently when spoken to—; on the other, he had to explore this new world which had been opened to him. Nor could there be the slightest doubt—not the slightest—that the new world was the profounder and more wonderful of the two. It was irresistible. It was miraculous. Its beauty was simply beyond anything—beyond speech as beyond thought—utterly incommunicable. But how then, between the two worlds, of which he was thus constantly aware, was he to keep a balance? One must get up, one must go to breakfast, one must talk with Mother, go to school, do one's lessons—and, in all this, try not to appear

too much of a fool. But if all the while one was also trying to extract the full deliciousness of another and quite separate existence, one which could not easily (if at all) be spoken of—how was one to manage? How was one to explain? Would it be safe to explain? Would it be absurd? Would it merely mean that he would get into some obscure kind of trouble?

21   These thoughts came and went, came and went, as softly and secretly as the snow; they were not precisely a disturbance, perhaps they were even a pleasure; he liked to have them; their presence was something almost palpable, something he could stroke with his hand, without closing his eyes, and without ceasing to see Miss Buell and the school-room and the globe and the freckles on Deirdre's neck; nevertheless he did in a sense cease to see, or to see the obvious external world, and substituted for this vision the vision of snow, the sound of snow, and the slow, almost soundless, approach of the postman. Yesterday, it had been only at the sixth house that the postman had become audible; the snow was much deeper now, it was falling more swiftly and heavily, the sound of its seething was more distinct, more soothing, more persistent. And this morning, it had been—as nearly as he could figure—just above the seventh house—perhaps only a step or two above; at most, he had heard two or three footsteps before the knock had sounded. . . . And with each such narrowing of the sphere, each nearer approach of the limit at which the postman was first audible, it was odd how sharply was increased the amount of illusion which had to be carried into the ordinary business of daily life. Each day, it was harder to get out of bed, to go to the window, to look out at the—as always—perfectly empty and snowless street. Each day it was more difficult to go through the perfunctory motions of greeting Mother and Father at breakfast, to reply to their questions, to put his books together and go to school. And at school, how extraordinarily hard to conduct with success simultaneously the public life and the life that was secret! There were times when he longed—positively ached—to tell everyone about it—to burst out with it—only to be checked almost at once by a far-off feeling as of some faint absurdity which was inherent in it—but *was* it absurd?—and more importantly by a sense of mysterious power in his very secrecy. Yes; it must be kept secret. That, more and more, became clear. At whatever cost to himself, whatever pain to others—

22   (Miss Buell looked straight at him, smiling, and said, "Perhaps we'll ask Paul. I'm sure Paul will come out of his daydream long enough to be able to tell us. Won't you, Paul?" He rose slowly from his chair, resting one hand on the brightly varnished desk, and deliberately stared through the snow toward the blackboard. It was an effort, but it was amusing to make it. "Yes," he said slowly, "it was what we now call the Hudson River. This he thought to be the Northwest Passage. He was disappointed." He sat down again, and as he did so Deirdre half turned in her chair and gave him a shy smile, of approval and admiration.)

23   At whatever pain to others.

24   This part of it was very puzzling, very puzzling, Mother was very nice, and so was Father. Yes, that was all true enough. He wanted to be nice to them, to tell them everything—and yet, was it really wrong of him to want to have a secret place of his own?

25   At bedtime, the night before, Mother had said, "If this goes on, my lad, we'll have to see a doctor, we will! We can't have our boy—" But what was it she had said? "Live in another world"? "Live so far away"? The word "far" had been in it, he was sure, and then Mother had taken up a magazine again and laughed a little, but with an expression which wasn't mirthful. He had felt sorry for her . . .

26   The bell rang for dismissal. The sound came to him through long curved parallels of falling snow. He saw Deirdre rise, and had himself risen almost as soon—but not quite as soon—as she.

27   On the walk homeward, which was timeless, it pleased him to see through the accompaniment, or counterpoint, of snow, the items of mere externality on his way. There were many kinds of brick in the sidewalks, and laid in many kinds of pattern. The garden walls, too, were various, some of wooden palings, some of plaster, some of stone. Twigs of bushes leaned over the walls: the little hard green winter-buds of lilac, on gray stems, sheathed and fat; other branches very thin and fine and black and desiccated. Dirty sparrows huddled in the bushes, as dull in color as dead fruit left in leafless trees. A single starling creaked on a weather vane. In the gutter, beside a drain, was a scrap of torn and dirty newspaper, caught in a little delta of filth; the word ECZEMA appeared in large capitals, and below it was a letter from Mrs. Amelia D. Cravath, 2100 Pine Street, Fort Worth, Texas, to the effect that after being a sufferer for years she had been cured by Caley's Ointment. In the little delta, beside the fanshaped and deeply runneled continent of brown mud, were lost twigs, descended from their parent trees, dead matches, a rusty horse chestnut burr, a small concentration of eggshell, a streak of yellow sawdust which had been wet and now was dry and congealed, a brown pebble, and a broken feather. Farther on was a cement sidewalk, ruled into geometrical parallelograms, with a brass inlay at one end commemorating the contractors who had laid it, and, halfway across, an irregular and random series of dog tracks, immortalized in synthetic stone. He knew these well, and always stepped on them; to cover the little hollows with his own foot had always been a queer pleasure; today he did it once more, but perfunctorily and detachedly, all the while thinking of something else. That was a dog, a long time ago, who had made a mistake and walked on the cement while it was still wet. He had probably wagged his tail, but that hadn't been recorded. Now, Paul Hasleman, aged twelve, on his way home from school, crossed the same river, which in the meantime had frozen into rock. Homeward through the snow, the snow falling in bright sunshine. Homeward?

28   Then came the gateway with the two posts surmounted by egg-shaped stones which had been cunningly balanced on their ends, as if by Columbus, and mortared in the very act of balance; a source of perpetual wonder. On the brick wall just beyond, the letter H had been stenciled, presumably for some purpose. H? H.

29   The green hydrant, with a little green-painted chain attached to the brass screw-cap.

30   The elm tree, with the great gray wound in the bark, kidneyshaped, into which he always put his hand—to feel the cold but living wood. The injury, he had been sure, was due to the gnawings of a tethered horse. But now it deserved only a passing palm, a merely tolerant eye. There were more important things. Miracles. Beyond the thoughts of trees, mere elms. Beyond the thoughts of sidewalks, mere stone, mere brick, mere cement. Beyond the thoughts even of his own shoes, which trod these sidewalks obediently, bearing a burden—far above—of elaborate mystery. He watched them. They were not very well polished; he had neglected them, for a very good reason: they were one of the many parts of the increasing difficulty of the daily return to daily life, the morning struggle. To get up, having at last opened one's eyes, to go to the window, and discover no snow, to wash, to dress, to descend the curving stairs to breakfast—

31   At whatever pain to others, nevertheless, one must persevere in severance, since the incommunicability of the experience demanded it. It was desirable, of course, to be kind to Mother and Father, especially as they seemed to be worried, but it was also desirable to be resolute. If they should decide—as appeared likely—to consult the doctor, Doctor Howells, and have Paul inspected, his heart listened to through a kind of dictaphone, his lungs, his stomach—well, that was all right. He would go through with it. He would give them answer for question, too—perhaps such answers as they hadn't expected? No. That would never do. For the secret world must, at all costs, be preserved.

32   The birdhouse in the apple tree was empty—it was the wrong time of year for wrens. The little round black door had lost its pleasure. The wrens were enjoying other houses, other nests, remoter trees. But this too was a notion which he only vaguely and grazingly entertained—as if, for the moment, he merely touched an edge of it; there was something further on, which was already assuming a sharper importance; something which already teased at the corners of his eyes, teasing also at the corner of his mind. It was funny to think that he so wanted this, so awaited it—and yet found himself enjoying this momentary dalliance with the birdhouse, as if for a quite deliberate postponement and enhancement of the approaching pleasure. He was aware of his delay, of his smiling and detached and now almost uncomprehending gaze at the little birdhouse; he knew what he was going to look at next: it was his own little cobbled hill-street, his own house, the little river at the bottom

of the hill, the grocer's shop with the cardboard man in the window—and now, thinking of all this, he turned his head, still smiling, and looking quickly right and left through the snow-laden sunlight.

33   And the mist of snow, as he had foreseen, was still on it—a ghost of snow falling in the bright sunlight, softly and steadily floating and turning and pausing, soundlessly meeting the snow that covered, as with a transparent mirage, the bare bright cobbles. He loved it—he stood still and loved it. Its beauty was paralyzing—beyond all words, all experience, all dream. No fairy story he had ever read could be compared with it—none had ever given him this extraordinary combination of ethereal loveliness with a something else, unnameable, which was just faintly and deliciously terrifying. What was this thing? As he thought of it, he looked upward toward his own bedroom window, which was open—and it was as if he looked straight into the room and saw himself lying half awake in his bed. There he was—at this very instant he was still perhaps actually there—more truly there than standing here at the edge of the cobbled hill-street, with one hand lifted to shade his eyes against the snow-sun. Had he indeed ever left his room, in all this time? since that very first morning? Was the whole progress still being enacted there, was it still the same morning, and himself not yet wholly awake? And even now, had the postman not yet come round the corner? . . .

34   This idea amused him, and automatically, as he thought of it, he turned his head and looked toward the top of the hill. There was, of course, nothing there—nothing and no one. The street was empty and quiet. And all the more because of its emptiness it occurred to him to count the houses—a thing which, oddly enough, he hadn't before thought of doing. Of course, he had known there weren't many—many, that is, on his own side of the street, which were the ones that figured in the postman's progress—but nevertheless it came as something of a shock to find that there were precisely *six*, above his own house—his own house was the seventh.

35   Six!

36   Astonished, he looked at his own house—looked at the door, on which was the number thirteen—and then realized that the whole thing was exactly and logically and absurdly what he ought to have known. Just the same, the realization gave him abruptly, and even a little frighteningly, a sense of hurry. He was being hurried—he was being rushed. For—he knit his brow—he couldn't be mistaken—it was just above the *seventh* house, his *own* house, that the postman had first been audible this very morning. But in that case—in that case—did it mean that tomorrow he would hear nothing? The knock he had heard must have been the knock of their own door. Did it mean—and this was an idea which gave him a really extraordinary feeling of surprise—that he would never hear the postman again?—that tomorrow morning the postman would already have passed the house, in a snow so deep as to render his footsteps completely inaudible? That he would have made his

approach down the snow-filled street so soundlessly, so secretly, that he, Paul Hasleman, there lying in bed, would not have waked in time, or waking, would have heard nothing?

37   But how could that be? Unless even the knocker should be muffled in the snow—frozen tight, perhaps? . . . But in that case—

38   A vague feeling of disappointment came over him; a vague sadness as if he felt himself deprived of something which he had long looked forward to, something much prized. After all this, all this beautiful progress, the slow delicious advance of the postman through the silent and secret snow, the knock creeping closer each day, and the footsteps nearer, the audible compass of the world thus daily narrowed, narrowed, narrowed, as the snow soothingly and beautifully encroached and deepened, after all this, was he to be defrauded of the one thing he had so wanted—to be able to count, as it were, the last two or three solemn footsteps, as they finally approached his own door? Was it all going to happen, at the end, so suddenly? or indeed, had it already happened? with no slow and subtle gradations of menace, in which he could luxuriate?

39   He gazed upward again, toward his own window which flashed in the sun; and this time almost with a feeling that it would be better if he *were* still in bed, in that room; for in that case this must still be the first morning, and there would be six more mornings to come—or, for that matter, seven or eight or nine—how could he be sure?—or even more.

40   After supper, the inquisition began. He stood before the doctor, under the lamp, and submitted silently to the usual thumpings and tappings.

41   "Now will you please say 'Ah!'?"

42   "Ah!"

43   "Now again, please, if you don't mind."

44   "Ah."

45   "Say it slowly, and hold it if you can—"

46   "Ah-h-h-h-h-h—"

47   "Good."

48   How silly all this was. As if it had anything to do with his throat! Or his heart, or lungs!

49   Relaxing his mouth, of which the corners, after all this absurd stretching, felt uncomfortable, he avoided the doctor's eyes, and stared toward the fireplace, past his mother's feet (in gray slippers) which projected from the green chair, and his father's feet (in brown slippers) which stood neatly side by side on the hearth rug.

50   "Hm. There is certainly nothing wrong there . . . ?"

51   He felt the doctor's eyes fixed upon him, and, as if merely to be polite, returned the look, but with a feeling of justifiable evasiveness.

52   "Now, young man, tell me—do you feel all right?"

53   "Yes, sir, quite all right."

54   "No headaches? no dizziness?"

55   "No, I don't think so."

56   "Let me see. Let's get a book, if you don't mind—yes, thank you, that will do splendidly—and now, Paul, if you'll just read it, holding it as you would normally hold it—"

57   He took the book and read:

58   "And another praise have I to tell for this the city our mother, the gift of a great god, a glory of the land most high; the might of horses, the might of young horses, the might of the sea. . . . For thou, son of Cronus, our lord Poseidon, hath throned herein this pride, since in these roads first thou didst show forth the curb that cures the rage of steeds. And the shapely oar, apt to men's hands, hath a wondrous speed on the brine, following the hundred-footed Nereids. . . . O land that art praised above all lands, now is it for thee to make those bright praises seen in deeds."

59   He stopped, tentatively, and lowered the heavy book.

60   "No—as I thought—there is certainly no superficial sign of eye-strain."

61   Silence thronged the room, and he was aware of the focused scrutiny of the three people who confronted him. . . .

62   "We could have his eyes examined—but I believe it is something else."

63   "What could it be?" That was his father's voice.

64   "It's only this curious absent mindedness—" This was his mother's voice.

65   In the presence of the doctor, they both seemed irritatingly apologetic.

66   "I believe it is something else. Now Paul—I would like very much to ask you a question or two. You will answer them, won't you—you know I'm an old, old friend of yours, eh? That's right! . . ."

67   His back was thumped twice by the doctor's fat fist—then the doctor was grinning at him with false amiability, while with one finger-nail he was scratching the top button of his waistcoat. Beyond the doctor's shoulder was the fire, the fingers of flame making light prestidigitation against the sooty fireback, the soft sound of their random flutter the only sound.

68   "I would like to know—is there anything that worries you?"

69   The doctor was again smiling, his eyelids low against the little black pupils, in each of which was a tiny white bead of light. Why answer him? why answer him at all? "At whatever pain to others"—but it was all a nuisance, this necessity for resistance, this necessity for attention; it was as if one had been stood up on a brilliantly lighted stage, under a great round blaze of spotlight; as if one were merely a trained seal, or a performing dog, or a fish, dipped out of an aquarium and held up by the tail. It would serve them right if he were merely to bark or growl. And meanwhile, to miss these last few precious hours, these hours of which each minute was more beautiful than the last, more menacing—! He still

looked, as if from a great distance, at the beads of light in the doctor's eyes, at the fixed false smile, and then, beyond, once more at his mother's slippers, his father's slippers, the soft flutter of the fire. Even here, even amongst these hostile presences, and in this arranged light, he could see the snow, he could hear it—it was in the corners of the room, where the shadow was deepest, under the sofa, behind the half-opened door which led to the dining room. It was gentler here, softer, its seethe the quietest of whispers, as if, in deference to a drawing room, it had quite deliberately put on its "manners"; it kept itself out of sight, obliterated itself, but distinctly with an air of saying, "Ah, but just wait! Wait till we are alone together! Then I will begin to tell you something new! Something white! something cold! something sleepy! something of cease, and peace, and the long bright curve of space! Tell them to go away. Banish them. Refuse to speak. Leave them, go upstairs to your room, turn out the light and get into bed—I will go with you, I will be waiting for you, I will tell you a better story than Little Kay of the Skates, or The Snow Ghost—I will surround your bed, I will close the windows, pile a deep drift against the door, so that none will ever again be able to enter. Speak to them! . . ." It seemed as if the little hissing voice came from a slow white spiral of falling flakes in the corner by the front window—but he could not be sure. He felt himself smiling, then, and said to the doctor, but without looking at him, looking beyond him still—

70   "Oh no, I think not—"

71   "But are you sure, my boy?"

72   His father's voice came softly and coldly then—the familiar voice of silken warning.

73   "You needn't answer at once, Paul—remember we're trying to help you—think it over and be quite sure, won't you?"

74   He felt himself smiling again, at the notion of being quite sure. What a joke! As if he weren't so sure that reassurance was no longer necessary, and all this cross-examination a ridiculous farce, a grotesque parody! What could they know about it? these gross intelligences, these humdrum minds so bound to the usual, the ordinary? Impossible to tell them about it! Why, even now, even now, with the proof so abundant, so formidable, so imminent, so appallingly present here in this very room, could they believe it?—could even his mother believe it? No—it was only too plain that if anything were said about it, the merest hint given, they would be incredulous—they would laugh—they would say "Absurd!"—think things about him which weren't true. . . .

75   "Why no, I'm not worried—why should I be?"

76   He looked then straight at the doctor's low-lidded eyes, looked from one of them to the other, from one bead of light to the other, and gave a little laugh.

77   The doctor seemed to be disconcerted by this. He drew back in his chair, resting a fat white hand on either knee. The smile faded slowly from his face.

78   "Well, Paul!" he said, and paused gravely, "I'm afraid you don't take this quite seriously enough. I think you perhaps don't quite realize—don't quite realize—" He took a deep quick breath and turned, as if helplessly, at a loss for words, to the others. But Mother and Father were both silent—no help was forthcoming.

79   "You must surely know, be aware, that you have not been quite yourself, of late? Don't you know that? . . ."

80   It was amusing to watch the doctor's renewed attempt at a smile, a queer disorganized look, as of confidential embarrassment.

81   "I feel all right, sir," he said, and again gave the little laugh.

82   "And we're trying to help you." The doctor's tone sharpened.

83   "Yes, sir, I know. But why? I'm all right. I'm just *thinking*, that's all."

84   His mother made a quick movement forward, resting a hand on the back of the doctor's chair.

85   "Thinking?" she said. "But my dear, about what?"

86   This was a direct challenge—and would have to be directly met. But before he met it, he looked again into the corner by the door, as if for reassurance. He smiled again at what he saw, at what he heard. The little spiral was still there, still softly whirling, like the ghost of a white kitten chasing the ghost of a white tail, and making as it did so the faintest of whispers. It was all right! If only he could remain firm, everything was going to be all right.

87   "Oh, about anything, about nothing—*you* know the way you do!"

88   "You mean—daydreaming?"

89   "Oh, no—thinking!"

90   "But thinking about *what*?"

91   "Anything."

92   He laughed a third time—but this time, happening to glance upward toward his mother's face, he was appalled at the effect his laughter seemed to have upon her. Her mouth had opened in an expression of horror. . . . This was too bad! Unfortunate! He had known it would cause pain, of course—but he hadn't expected it to be quite so bad as this. Perhaps—perhaps if he just gave them a tiny gleaming hint—?

93   "About the snow," he said.

94   "What on earth?" This was his father's voice. The brown slippers came a step nearer on the hearthrug.

95   "But my dear, what do you mean?" This was his mother's voice.

96   The doctor merely stared.

97   "Just *snow*, that's all. I like to think about it."

98   "Tell us about it, my boy."

99   "But that's all it is. There's nothing to tell. *You* know what snow is?"

100   This he said almost angrily, for he felt that they were trying to corner him. He turned sideways so as no longer to face the doctor, and the better to see the inch of blackness between the windowsill and the

lowered curtain—the cold inch of beckoning and delicious night. At once he felt better, more assured.

101   "Mother—can I go to bed, now, please? I've got a headache."

102   "But I thought you said—"

103   "It's just come. It's all these questions—! Can I, mother?"

104   "You can go as soon as the doctor has finished."

105   "Don't you think this thing ought to be gone into thoroughly, and *now*?" This was Father's voice. The brown slippers again came a step nearer, the voice was the well-known "punishment" voice, resonant and cruel.

106   "Oh, what's the use, Norman—"

107   Quite suddenly, everyone was silent. And without precisely facing them, nevertheless he was aware that all three of them were watching him with an extraordinary intensity—staring hard at him—as if he had done something monstrous, or was himself some kind of monster. He could hear the soft irregular flutter of the flames; the cluck-click-cluck-click of the clock; far and faint, two sudden spurts of laughter from the kitchen, as quickly cut off as begun; a murmur of water in the pipes; and then, the silence seemed to deepen, to spread out, to become world-long and world-wide, to become timeless and shapeless, and to center inevitably and rightly, with a slow and sleepy but enormous concentration of all power, on the beginning of a new sound. What this new sound was going to be, he knew perfectly well. It might begin with a hiss, but it would end with a roar—there was no time to lose—he must escape. It mustn't happen here—

108   Without another word, he turned and ran up the stairs.

109   Not a moment too soon. The darkness was coming in long white waves. A prolonged sibilance filled the night—a great seamless seethe of wild influence went abruptly across it—a cold low humming shook the windows. He shut the door and flung off his clothes in the dark. The bare black floor was like a little raft tossed in waves of snow, almost overwhelmed, washed under whitely, up again, smothered in curled billows of feather. The snow was laughing; it spoke from all sides at once; it pressed closer to him as he ran and jumped exulting into his bed.

110   "Listen to us!" it said. "Listen! We have come to tell you the story we told you about. You remember? Lie down. Shut your eyes, now—you will no longer see much—in this white darkness who could see, or want to see? We will take the place of everything. . . . Listen—"

111   A beautiful varying dance of snow began at the front of the room, came forward and then retreated, flattened out toward the floor, then rose fountain-like to the ceiling, swayed, recruited itself from a new stream of flakes which poured laughing in through the humming window, advanced again, lifted long white arms. It said peace, it said remoteness, it said cold—it said—

112   But then a gash of horrible light fell brutally across the room from

the opening door—the snow drew back hissing—something alien had come into the room—something hostile. This thing rushed at him, clutched at him, shook him—and he was not merely horrified, he was filled with such a loathing as he had never known. What was this? this cruel disturbance? this act of anger and hate? It was as if he had to reach up a hand toward another world for any understanding of it—an effort of which he was only barely capable. But of that other world he still remembered just enough to know the exorcising words. They tore themselves from his other life suddenly—

113   "Mother! Mother! Go away! I hate you!"

114   And with that effort, everything was solved, everything became all right: the seamless hiss advanced once more, the long white wavering lines rose and fell like enormous whispering sea-waves, the whisper becoming louder, the laughter more numerous.

115   "Listen!" it said. "We'll tell you the last, the most beautiful and secret story—shut your eyes—it is a very small story—a story that gets smaller and smaller—it comes inward instead of opening like a flower—it is a flower becoming a seed—a little cold seed—do you hear? we are leaning closer to you—"

116   The hiss was now becoming a roar—the whole world was a vast moving screen of snow—but even now it said peace, it said remoteness, it said cold, it said sleep.

Study Questions

1. What is *schizophrenia?* What sort of behavior typifies the schizoid personality? Is Paul a classic case of this mental disorder?

2. Comment on the relationship between Paul and his parents. Why is it significant that Paul notices only parts of his father (such as his voice and his feet)? Why does Paul's last statement make everything "all right"? If Paul's parents asked for your advice, what would you tell them?

3. What special qualities does Paul find in snow? Are these qualities generally attributed to snow? How can you account for the difference? How are the snow and the geography lesson related?

4. What sort of material does Aiken include within parentheses? Aside from dialogue, why does he sometimes use one-sentence paragraphs?

5. Are the similes which Aiken permits Paul to use—the stage and the seed—indicative of the boy's state of mind? What other similes seem appropriate? Inappropriate?

The Secret Life of Walter Mitty

James Thurber

1   "We're going through!" The Commander's voice was like thin ice breaking. He wore his full-dress uniform, with the heavily braided white cap pulled down rakishly over one cold gray eye. "We can't make it, sir. It's spoiling for a hurricane, if you ask me." "I'm not asking you, Lieutenant Berg," said the Commander. "Throw on the power light! Rev her up to 8,500! We're going through!" The pounding of the cylinders increased: ta pocketa-pocketa-pocketa-*pocketa-pocketa*. The Commander stared at the ice forming on the pilot window. He walked over and twisted a row of complicated dials. "Switch on No. 8 auxiliary!" he shouted. "Switch on No. 8 auxiliary!" repeated Lieutenant Berg. "Full strength in No. 3 turret!" shouted the Commander. "Full strength in No. 3 turret!" The crew, bending to their various tasks in the huge, hurtling eight-engined Navy hydroplane, looked at each other and grinned. "The Old Man'll get us through," they said to one another. "The Old Man ain't afraid of Hell!" . . .

2   "Not so fast! You're driving too fast!" said Mrs. Mitty. "What are you driving so fast for?"

3   "Hmm?" said Walter Mitty. He looked at his wife, in the seat beside him, with shocked astonishment. She seemed grossly unfamiliar, like a strange woman who had yelled at him in a crowd. "You were up to fifty-five," she said. "You know I don't like to go more than forty. You were up to fifty-five." Walter Mitty drove on toward Waterbury in silence, the roaring of the SN202 through the worst storm in twenty years of Navy flying fading in the remote, intimate airways of his mind. "You're tensed up again," said Mrs. Mitty. "It's one of your days. I wish you'd let Dr. Renshaw look you over."

4   Walter Mitty stopped the car in front of the building where his wife went to have her hair done. "Remember to get those overshoes while I'm having my hair done," she said. "I don't need overshoes," said Mitty. She put her mirror back into her bag. "We've been all through that," she said, getting out of the car. "You're not a young man any longer." He raced the engine a little. "Why don't you wear your gloves? Have you lost your gloves?" Walter Mitty reached in a pocket and brought out the gloves. He put them on, but after she had turned and gone into the building and he had driven on to a red light, he took them off again. "Pick it up, brother!" snapped a cop as the light changed, and Mitty hastily pulled on his gloves and lurched ahead. He drove around the

streets aimlessly for a time, and then he drove past the hospital on his way to the parking lot.

5   . . . "It's the millionaire banker, Wellington McMillan," said the pretty nurse. "Yes?" said Walter Mitty, removing his gloves slowly. "Who has the case?" "Dr. Renshaw and Dr. Benbow, but there are two specialists here, Dr. Remington from New York and Mr. Pritchard-Mitford from London. He flew over." A door opened down a long, cool corridor and Dr. Renshaw came out. He looked distraught and haggard. "Hello, Mitty," he said. "We're having the devil's own time with McMillan, the millionaire banker and close personal friend of Roosevelt. Obstreosis of the ductal tract. Tertiary. Wish you'd take a look at him." "Glad to," said Mitty.

6   In the operating room there were whispered introductions: "Dr. Remington, Dr. Mitty. Mr. Pritchard-Mitford, Dr. Mitty." "I've read your book on streptothricosis," said Pritchard-Mitford, shaking hands. "A brilliant performance, sir." "Thank you," said Walter Mitty. "Didn't know you were in the States, Mitty," grumbled Remington. "Coals to Newcastle, bringing Mitford and me up here for a tertiary." "You are very kind," said Mitty. A huge, complicated machine, connected to the operating table, with many tubes and wires, began at this moment to go pocketa-pocketa-pocketa. "The new anesthetizer is giving way!" shouted an interne. "There is no one in the East who knows how to fix it!" "Quiet man!" said Mitty, in a low, cool voice. He sprang to the machine, which was now going pocketa-pocketa-queep-pocketa-queep. He began fingering delicately a row of glistening dials.

7   "Give me a fountain pen!" he snapped. Someone handed him a fountain pen. He pulled a faulty piston out of the machine and inserted the pen in its place. "That will hold for ten minutes," he said. "Get on with the operation." A nurse hurried over and whispered to Renshaw, and Mitty saw the man turn pale. "Coreopsis has set in," said Renshaw nervously. "If you would take over, Mitty?" Mitty looked at him and at the craven figure of Benbow, who drank, and at the grave, uncertain faces of the two great specialists. "If you wish," he said. They slipped a white gown on him; adjusted a mask and drew on thin gloves; nurses handed him shining . . .

8   "Back it up, Mac! Look out for that Buick!" Walter Mitty jammed on the brakes. "Wrong lane, Mac," said the parking lot attendant, looking at Mitty closely. "Gee. Yeh," muttered Mitty. He began cautiously to back out of the lane marked "Exit Only." "Leave her sit there," said the attendant. "I'll put her away." Mitty got out of the car. "Hey, better leave the key." "Oh," said Mitty, handing the man the ignition key. The attendant vaulted into the car, backed it up with insolent skill, and put it where it belonged.

9   They're so damn cocky, thought Walter Mitty, walking along Main Street; they think they know everything. Once he had tried to take his chains off, outside New Milford, and he had got them wound around the

axles. A man had had to come out in a wrecking car and unwind them, a young, grinning garageman. Since then Mrs. Mitty always made him drive to a garage to have the chains taken off. The next time, he thought, I'll wear my right arm in a sling; they won't grin at me then. I'll have my right arm in a sling and they'll see I couldn't possibly take the chains off myself. He kicked at the slush on the sidewalk. "Overshoes," he said to himself, and he began looking for a shoe store.

10   When he came out into the street again, with the overshoes in a box under his arm, Walter Mitty began to wonder what the other thing was his wife had told him to get. She had told him twice, before they set out from their house for Waterbury. In a way he hated these weekly trips to town—he was always getting something wrong. Kleenex, he thought, Squibb's, razor blades? No. Toothpaste, toothbrush, bicarbonate, carborundum, initiative and referendum? He gave it up. But she would remember it. "Where's the what's-its-name?" she would ask. "Don't tell me you forgot the what's-its-name." A newsboy went by shouting something about the Waterbury trial.

11   . . . "Perhaps this will refresh your memory." The District Attorney suddenly thrust a heavy automatic at the quiet figure on the witness stand. "Have you seen this before?" Walter Mitty took the gun and examined it expertly. "This is my Webley-Vickers 50.80," he said calmly. An excited buzz ran around the courtroom. The judge rapped for order. "You are a crack shot with any sort of firearms, I believe?" said the District Attorney, insinuatingly. "Objection!" shouted Mitty's attorney. "We have shown that the defendant could not have fired the shot. We have shown that he wore his right arm in a sling on the night of the fourteenth of July." Walter Mitty raised his hand briefly and the bickering attorneys were stilled. "With any known make of gun," he said evenly, "I could have killed Gregory Fitzhurst at three hundred feet *with my left hand.*" Pandemonium broke loose in the courtroom. A woman's scream rose above the bedlam and suddenly a lovely, dark-haired girl was in Walter Mitty's arms. The District Attorney struck at her savagely. Without rising from his chair, Mitty let the man have it on the point of the chin. "You miserable cur!" . . .

12   "Puppy biscuit," said Walter Mitty. He stopped walking and the buildings of Waterbury rose up out of the misty courtroom and surrounded him again. A woman who was passing laughed. "He said 'Puppy biscuit,'" she said to her companion. "That man said 'Puppy biscuit' to himself." Walter Mitty hurried on. He went into an A. & P., not the first one he came to but a smaller one farther up the street. "I want some biscuit for small, young dogs," he said to the clerk. "Any special brand, sir?" The greatest pistol shot in the world thought a moment. "It says 'Puppies Bark for It' on the box," said Walter Mitty.

13   His wife would be through at the hairdresser's in fifteen minutes, Mitty saw in looking at his watch, unless they had trouble drying it;

sometimes they had trouble drying it. She didn't like to get to the hotel first; she would want him to be there waiting for her as usual. He found a big leather chair in the lobby, facing a window, and he put the overshoes and the puppy biscuit on the floor beside it. He picked up an old copy of *Liberty* and sank down into the chair. "Can Germany Conquer the World Through the Air?" Walter Mitty looked at the pictures of bombing planes and of ruined streets.

14   . . . "The cannonading has got the wind up in young Raleigh, sir," said the sergeant. Captain Mitty looked up at him through tousled hair. "Get him to bed," he said wearily. "With the others. I'll fly alone." "But you can't, sir," said the sergeant anxiously. "It takes two men to handle that bomber and the Archies are pounding hell out of the air. Von Richtman's circus is between here and Saulier." "Somebody's got to get that ammunition dump," said Mitty. "I'm going over. Spot of brandy?" He poured a drink for the sergeant and one for himself. War thundered and whined around the dugout and battered at the door. There was a rending of wood and splinters flew through the room. "A bit of a near thing," said Captain Mitty carelessly. "The box barrage is closing in," said the sergeant. "We only live once, Sergeant," said Mitty, with his faint, fleeting smile. "Or do we?" He poured another brandy and tossed it off. "I never see a man could hold his brandy like you, sir," said the sergeant. "Begging your pardon, sir." Captain Mitty stood up and strapped on his huge Webley-Vickers automatic. "It's forty kilometers through hell, sir," said the sergeant. Mitty finished one last brandy. "After all," he said softly, "what isn't?" The pounding of the cannon increased; there was the rat-tat-tatting of machine guns, and from somewhere came the menacing pocketa-pocketa-pocketa of the new flame-throwers. Walter Mitty walked to the door of the dugout humming "Auprès de Ma Blonde." He turned and waved to the sergeant. "Cheerio!" he said. . . .

15   Something struck his shoulder. "I've been looking all over this hotel for you," said Mrs. Mitty. "Why do you have to hide in this old chair? How did you expect me to find you?" "Things close in," said Walter Mitty vaguely. "What?" Mrs. Mitty said. "Did you get the what's-its-name? The puppy biscuit? What's in that box?" "Overshoes," said Mitty. "Couldn't you have put them on in the store?" "I was thinking," said Walter Mitty. "Does it ever occur to you that I am sometimes thinking?" She looked at him. "I'm going to take your temperature when I get you home," she said.

16   They went out through the revolving doors that made a faintly derisive whistling sound when you pushed them. It was two blocks to the parking lot. At the drugstore on the corner she said, "Wait here for me. I forgot something. I won't be a minute." She was more than a minute. Walter Mitty lighted a cigarette. It began to rain, rain with sleet in it. He stood up against the wall of the drugstore, smoking. . . . He put his shoulders back and his heels together. "To hell with the handker-

chief," said Walter Mitty scornfully. He took one last drag on his cigarette and snapped it away. Then, with that faint, fleeting smile playing about his lips, he faced the firing squad; erect and motionless, proud and disdainful, Walter Mitty the Undefeated, inscrutable to the last.

Study Questions

1. What is a *romantic*? A *realist*? Which is Mitty? Mrs. Mitty?
2. Is this story funny? Is Mitty a good example of contemporary humanity? Is he a distinctly American type?
3. Mrs. Mitty is at least partially responsible for driving Mitty into his fantasy world. Does he ever stand up to her? How does Mitty react to other authority figures?
4. Mitty seems to think of mechanical objects as complicated gadgets that go pocketa-pocketa-pocketa. What incidents in his real life might have helped him form such a conclusion?
5. What associative words or ideas carry Mitty from reality to fantasy and back again? Does any one line provide the key to Mitty's problem?
6. What is significant about the language that Mitty uses in his fantasies? Was Mitty "thinking" when his wife struck his shoulder?
7. The crew of the hydroplane calls Mitty the "Old Man." His wife says that he's no longer a young man. Is there a difference?

Theft

Katherine Anne Porter

1   She had the purse in her hand when she came in. Standing in the middle of the floor, holding her bathrobe around her and trailing a damp towel in one hand, she surveyed the immediate past and remembered everything clearly. Yes, she had opened the flap and spread it out on the bench after she had dried the purse with her handkerchief.

2   She had intended to take the Elevated, and naturally she looked in her purse to make certain she had the fare, and was pleased to find forty cents in the coin envelope. She was going to pay her own fare, too, even

if Camilo did have the habit of seeing her up the steps and dropping a nickel in the machine before he gave the turnstile a little push and sent her through it with a bow. Camilo by a series of compromises had managed to make effective a fairly complete set of smaller courtesies, ignoring the larger and more troublesome ones. She had walked with him to the station in a pouring rain, because she knew he was almost as poor as she was, and when he insisted on a taxi, she was firm and said, "You know it simply will not do." He was wearing a new hat of a pretty biscuit shade, for it never occurred to him to buy anything of a practical color; he had put it on for the first time and the rain was spoiling it. She kept thinking, "But this is dreadful, where will he get another?" She compared it with Eddie's hats that always seemed to be precisely seven years old and as if they had been quite purposely left out in the rain, and yet they sat with a careless and incidental rightness on Eddie. But Camilo was far different; if he wore a shabby hat it would be merely shabby on him, and he would lose his spirits over it. If she had not feared Camilo would take it badly, for he insisted on the practice of his little ceremonies up to the point he had fixed for them, she would have said to him as they left Thora's house, "Do go home. I can surely reach the station by myself."

3   "It is written that we must be rained upon tonight," said Camilo, "so let it be together."

4   At the foot of the platform stairway she staggered slightly—they were both nicely set up on Thora's cocktails—and said: "At least, Camilo, do me the favor not to climb these stairs in your present state, since for you it is only a matter of coming down again at once, and you'll certainly break your neck."

5   He made three quick bows, he was Spanish, and leaped off through the rainy darkness. She stood watching him, for he was a very graceful young man, thinking that tomorrow morning he would gaze soberly at his spoiled hat and soggy shoes and possibly associate her with his misery. As she watched, he stopped at the far corner and took off his hat and hid it under his overcoat. She felt she had betrayed him by seeing, because he would have been humiliated if he thought she even suspected him of trying to save his hat.

6   Roger's voice sounded over her shoulder above the clang of the rain falling on the stairway shed, wanting to know what she was doing out in the rain at this time of night, and did she take herself for a duck? His long, imperturbable face was streaming with water, and he tapped a bulging spot on the breast of his buttoned-up overcoat: "Hat," he said. "Come on, let's take a taxi."

7   She settled back against Roger's arm which he laid around her shoulders, and with the gesture they exchanged a glance full of long amiable associations, then she looked through the window at the rain changing the shapes of everything, and the colors. The taxi dodged in

and out between the pillars of the Elevated, skidding slightly on every curve, and she said: "The more it skids the calmer I feel, so I really must be drunk."

8   "You must be," said Roger. "This bird is a homicidal maniac, and I could do with a cocktail myself this minute."

9   They waited on the traffic at Fortieth Street and Sixth Avenue, and three boys walked before the nose of the taxi. Under the globes of light they were cheerful scarecrows, all very thin and all wearing very seedy snappy-cut suits and gay neckties. They were not very sober either, and they stood for a moment wobbling in front of the car, and there was an argument going on among them. They leaned toward each other as if they were getting ready to sing, and the first one said: "When I get married it won't be jus' for getting married, I'm gonna marry for *love*, see?" and the second one said, "Aw, gwan and tell that stuff to *her*, why n't yuh?" and the third one gave a kind of hoot, and said, "Hell, dis guy? Wot the hell's he got?" and the first one said: "Aaah, shurrup yuh mush, I got plenty." Then they all squealed and scrambled across the street beating the first one on the back and pushing him around.

10   "Nuts," commented Roger, "pure nuts."

11   Two girls went skittering by in short transparent raincoats, one green, one red, their heads tucked against the drive of the rain. One of them was saying to the other, "Yes, I know all about *that*. But what about me? You're always so sorry for *him* . . ." and they ran on with their little pelican legs flashing back and forth.

12   The taxi backed up suddenly and leaped forward again, and after a while Roger said: "I had a letter from Stella today, and she'll be home on the twenty-sixth, so I suppose she's made up her mind and it's all settled."

13   "I had a sort of letter today too," she said, "making up my mind for me. I think it is time for you and Stella to do something definite."

14   When the taxi stopped on the corner of West Fifty-third Street, Roger said, "I've just enough if you'll add ten cents," so she opened her purse and gave him a dime, and he said, "That's beautiful, that purse."

15   "It's a birthday present," she told him, "and I like it. How's your show coming?"

16   "Oh, still hanging on, I guess. I don't go near the place. Nothing sold yet. I mean to keep right on the way I'm going and they can take it or leave it. I'm through with the argument."

17   "It's absolutely a matter of holding out, isn't it?"

18   "Holding out's the tough part."

19   "Good night, Roger."

20   "Good night, you should take aspirin and push yourself into a tub of hot water, you look as though you're catching cold."

21   "I will."

22   With the purse under her arm she went upstairs, and on the first

landing Bill heard her step and poked his head out with his hair tumbled and his eyes red, and he said: "For Christ's sake, come in and have a drink with me. I've had some bad news."

23   "You're perfectly sopping," said Bill, looking at her drenched feet. They had two drinks, while Bill told how the director had thrown his play out after the cast had been picked over twice, and had gone through three rehearsals. "I said to him, 'I didn't say it was a masterpiece, I said it would make a good show.' And he said, 'It just doesn't *play*, do you see? It needs a doctor.' So I'm stuck, absolutely stuck," said Bill, on the edge of weeping again. "I've been crying," he told her, "in my cups." And he went on to ask her if she realized his wife was ruining him with her extravagance. "I send her ten dollars every week of my unhappy life, and I don't really have to. She threatens to jail me if I don't, but she can't do it. God, let her try it after the way she treated me! She's no right to alimony and she knows it. She keeps on saying she's got to have it for the baby and I keep on sending it because I can't bear to see anybody suffer. So I'm way behind on the piano and the victrola, both—"

24   "Well, this is a pretty rug, anyhow," she said.

25   Bill stared at it and blew his nose. "I got it at Ricci's for ninety-five dollars," he said. "Ricci told me it once belonged to Marie Dressler, and cost fifteen hundred dollars, but there's a burnt place on it, under the divan. Can you beat that?"

26   "No," she said. She was thinking about her empty purse and that she could not possibly expect a check for her latest review for another three days, and her arrangement with the basement restaurant could not last much longer if she did not pay something on account. "It's no time to speak of it," she said, "but I've been hoping you would have by now that fifty dollars you promised for my scene in the third act. Even if it doesn't play. You were to pay me for the work anyhow out of your advance."

27   "Weeping Jesus," said Bill, "you, too?" He gave a loud sob, or hiccough, in his moist handkerchief. "Your stuff was no better than mine, after all. Think of that."

28   "But you got something for it," she said. "Seven hundred dollars."

29   Bill said, "Do me a favor, will you? Have another drink and forget about it. I can't, you know I can't, I would if I could, but you know the fix I'm in."

30   "Let it go, then," she found herself saying almost in spite of herself. She had meant to be quite firm about it. They drank again without speaking, and she went to her apartment on the floor above.

31   There, she now remembered distinctly, she had taken the letter out of the purse before she spread the purse out to dry.

32   She had sat down and read the letter over again: but there were phrases that insisted on being read many times, they had a life of their own separate from the others, and when she tried to read past and around them, they moved with the movement of her eyes, and she could not escape them . . . "thinking about you more than I mean to . . . yes, I

even talk about you . . . why were you so anxious to destroy . . . even if I could see you now I would not . . . not worth all this abominable . . . the end . . ."

33   Carefully she tore the letter into narrow strips and touched a lighted match to them in the coal grate.

34   Early the next morning she was in the bathtub when the janitress knocked and then came in, calling out that she wished to examine the radiators before she started the furnace going for the winter. After moving about the room for a few minutes, the janitress went out, closing the door very sharply.

35   She came out of the bathroom to get a cigarette from the package in the purse. The purse was gone. She dressed and made coffee, and sat by the window while she drank it. Certainly the janitress had taken the purse, and certainly it would be impossible to get it back without a great deal of ridiculous excitement. Then let it go. With this decision of her mind, there rose coincidentally in her blood a deep almost murderous anger. She set the cup carefully in the center of the table, and walked steadily downstairs, three long flights and a short hall and a steep short flight into the basement, where the janitress, her face streaked with coal dust, was shaking up the furnace. "Will you please give me back my purse? There isn't any money in it. It was a present, and I don't want to lose it."

36   The janitress turned without straightening up and peered at her with hot flickering eyes, a red light from the furnace reflected in them. "What do you mean, your purse?"

37   "The gold cloth purse you took from the wooden bench in my room," she said. "I must have it back."

38   "Before God I never laid eyes on your purse, and that's the holy truth," said the janitress.

39   "Oh, well then, keep it," she said, but in a very bitter voice; "keep it if you want it so much." And she walked away.

40   She remembered how she had never locked a door in her life, on some principle of rejection in her that made her uncomfortable in the ownership of things, and her paradoxical boast before the warnings of her friends, that she had never lost a penny by theft; and she had been pleased with the bleak humility of this concrete example designed to illustrate and justify a certain fixed, otherwise baseless and general faith which ordered the movements of her life without regard to her will in the matter.

41   In this moment she felt that she had been robbed of an enormous number of valuable things, whether material or intangible: things lost or broken by her own fault, things she had forgotten and left in houses when she moved: books borrowed from her and not returned, journeys she had planned and had not made, words she had waited to hear spoken to her and had not heard, and the words she had meant to answer with; bitter alternatives and intolerable substitutes worse than nothing, and

yet inescapable: the long patient suffering of dying friendships and the dark inexplicable death of love—all that she had had, and all that she had missed, were lost together, and were twice lost in this landslide of remembered losses.

42   The janitress was following her upstairs with the purse in her hand and the same deep red fire flickering in her eyes. The janitress thrust the purse towards her while they were still a half dozen steps apart, and said: "Don't never tell on me. I musta been crazy. I get crazy in the head sometimes, I swear I do. My son can tell you."

43   She took the purse after a moment, and the janitress went on: "I got a niece who is going on seventeen, and she's a nice girl and I thought I'd give it to her. She needs a pretty purse. I musta been crazy; I thought maybe you wouldn't mind, you leave things around and don't seem to notice much."

44   She said: "I missed this because it was a present to me from someone . . ."

45   The janitress said: "He'd get you another if you lost this one. My niece is young and needs pretty things, we oughta give the young ones a chance. She's got young men after her maybe will want to marry her. She ought have nice things. She needs them bad right now. You're a grown woman, you've had your chance, you ought to know how it is!"

46   She held the purse out to the janitress saying: "You don't know what you're talking about. Here, take it, I've changed my mind. I really don't want it."

47   The janitress looked up at her with hatred and said: "I don't want it either now. My niece is young and pretty, she don't need fixin' up to be pretty, she's young and pretty anyhow! I guess you need it worse than she does!"

48   "It wasn't really yours in the first place," she said, turning away. "You mustn't talk as if I had stolen it from you."

49   "It's not from me, it's from her you're stealing it," said the janitress, and went back downstairs.

50   She laid the purse on the table and sat down with the cup of chilled coffee, and thought: I was right not to be afraid of any thief but myself, who will end by leaving me nothing.

Study Questions

1. From what point of view is this story told?
2. What values and attitudes does the main character live by? What compromises does she make in her relationships with the other characters? How can these be considered a series of robberies? Explain the possible meanings of *theft* in this story.
3. What is the theme of "Theft"? Is it presented in any succinct statement?
4. Much of "Theft" is a flashback. Where does the flashback begin and end? How does Porter make these transitions?
5. What purpose do the wobbling boys and skittering girls serve?

My Oedipus Complex

Frank O'Connor

1   Father was in the army all through the war—the first war, I mean—so, up to the age of five, I never saw much of him, and what I saw did not worry me. Sometimes I woke and there was a big figure in khaki peering down at me in the candlelight. Sometimes in the early morning I heard the slamming of the front door and the clatter of nailed boots down the cobbles of the lane. These were Father's entrances and exits. Like Santa Claus he came and went mysteriously.

2   In fact, I rather liked his visits, though it was an uncomfortable squeeze between Mother and him when I got into the big bed in the early morning. He smoked, which gave him a pleasant musty smell, and shaved, an operation of astounding interest. Each time he left a trail of souvenirs—model tanks and Gurkha knives with handles made of bullet cases, and German helmets and cap badges and button-sticks, and all sorts of military equipment—carefully stowed away in a long box on top of the wardrobe, in case they ever came in handy. There was a bit of the magpie about Father; he expected everything to come in handy. When his back was turned, Mother let me get a chair and rummage through his treasures. She didn't seem to think so highly of them as he did.

3   The war was the most peaceful period of my life. The window of my attic faced southeast. My mother had curtained it, but that had small

effect. I always woke with the first light and, with all the responsibilities of the previous day melted, feeling myself rather like the sun, ready to illumine and rejoice. Life never seemed so simple and clear and full of possibilities as then. I put my feet out from under the clothes—I called them Mrs. Left and Mrs. Right—and invented dramatic situations for them in which they discussed the problems of the day. At least Mrs. Right did; she was very demonstrative, but I hadn't the same control of Mrs. Left, so she mostly contented herself with nodding agreement.

4   They discussed what Mother and I should do during the day, what Santa Claus should give a fellow for Christmas, and what steps should be taken to brighten the home. There was that little matter of the baby, for instance. Mother and I could never agree about that. Ours was the only house in the terrace without a new baby, and Mother said we couldn't afford one till Father came back from the war because they cost seventeen and six. That showed how simple she was. The Geneys up the road had a baby, and everyone knew they couldn't afford seventeen and six. It was probably a cheap baby, and Mother wanted something really good, but I felt she was too exclusive. The Geneys' baby would have done us fine.

5   Having settled my plans for the day, I got up, put a chair under the attic window, and lifted the frame high enough to stick out my head. The window overlooked the front gardens of the terrace behind ours, and beyond these it looked over a deep valley to the tall, red-brick houses terraced up the opposite hillside, which were all still in shadow, while those at our side of the valley were all lit up, though with long strange shadows that made them seem unfamiliar; rigid and painted.

6   After that I went into Mother's room and climbed into the big bed. She woke and I began to tell her of my schemes. By this time, though I never seem to have noticed it, I was petrified in my nightshirt, and I thawed as I talked until, the last frost melted, I fell asleep beside her and woke again only when I heard her below in the kitchen, making the breakfast.

7   After breakfast we went into town; heard Mass at St. Augustine's and said a prayer for Father, and did the shopping. If the afternoon was fine we either went for a walk in the country or a visit to Mother's great friend in the convent, Mother St. Dominic. Mother had them all praying for Father, and every night, going to bed, I asked God to send him back safe from the war to us. Little, indeed, did I know what I was praying for!

8   One morning, I got into the big bed, and there, sure enough, was Father in his usual Santa Claus manner, but later, instead of uniform, he put on his best blue suit, and Mother was as pleased as anything. I saw nothing to be pleased about, because, out of uniform, Father was altogether less interesting, but she only beamed, and explained that our prayers had been answered, and off we went to Mass to thank God for having brought Father safely home.

9   The irony of it! That very day when he came in to dinner he took off his boots and put on his slippers, donned the dirty old cap he wore about

the house to save him from colds, crossed his legs and began to talk gravely to Mother, who looked anxious. Naturally, I disliked her looking anxious, because it destroyed her good looks, so I interrupted him.

10   "Just a moment, Larry!" she said gently.

11   This was only what she said when we had boring visitors, so I attached no importance to it and went on talking.

12   "Do be quiet, Larry!" she said impatiently. "Don't you hear me talking to Daddy?"

13   This was the first time I had heard those ominous words, "talking to Daddy," and I couldn't help feeling that if this was how God answered prayers, he couldn't listen to them very attentively.

14   "Why are you talking to Daddy?" I asked with as great a show of indifference as I could muster.

15   "Because Daddy and I have business to discuss. Now, don't interrupt again!"

16   In the afternoon, at Mother's request, Father took me for a walk. This time we went into town instead of out the country, and I thought at first, in my usual optimistic way, that it might be an improvement. It was nothing of the sort. Father and I had quite different notions of a walk in town. He had no proper interest in trams, ships, and horses, and the only thing that seemed to divert him was talking to fellows as old as himself. When I wanted to stop he simply went on, dragging me behind him by the hand; when he wanted to stop I had no alternative but to do the same. I noticed that it seemed to be a sign that he wanted to stop for a long time whenever he leaned against a wall. The second time I saw him do it I got wild. He seemed to be settling himself forever. I pulled him by the coat and trousers, but, unlike Mother who, if you were too persistent, got into a wax and said: "Larry, if you don't behave yourself, I'll give you a good slap," Father had an extraordinary capacity for amiable inattention. I sized him up and wondered would I cry, but he seemed to be too remote to be annoyed even by that. Really, it was like going for a walk with a mountain! He either ignored the wrenching and pummeling entirely, or else glanced down with a grin of amusement from his peak. I had never met anyone so absorbed in himself as he seemed.

17   At teatime, "talking to Daddy" began again, complicated this time by the fact that he had an evening paper, and every few minutes he put it down and told Mother something new out of it. I felt this was foul play. Man for man, I was prepared to compete with him any time for Mother's attention, but when he had it all made up for him by other people it left me no chance. Several times I tried to change the subject without success.

18   "You must be quiet while Daddy is reading, Larry," Mother said impatiently.

19   It was clear that she either genuinely liked talking to Father better than talking to me, or else that he had some terrible hold on her which made her afraid to admit the truth.

20   "Mummy," I said that night when she was tucking me up, "do you think if I prayed hard God would send Daddy back to the war?"

21   She seemed to think about that for a moment.

22   "No, dear," she said with a smile. "I don't think he would."

23   "Why wouldn't he, Mummy?"

24   "Because there isn't a war any longer, dear."

25   "But, Mummy, couldn't God make another war, if He liked?"

26   "He wouldn't like to, dear. It's not God who makes wars, but bad people."

27   "Oh!" I said.

28   I was disappointed about that. I began to think that God wasn't quite what he was cracked up to be.

29   Next morning I woke at my usual hour, feeling like a bottle of champagne. I put out my feet and invented a long conversation in which Mrs. Right talked of the trouble she had with her own father till she put him in the Home. I didn't quite know what the Home was but it sounded the right place for Father. Then I got my chair and stuck my head out of the attic window. Dawn was just breaking, with a guilty air that made me feel I had caught it in the act. My head bursting with stories and schemes, I stumbled in next door, and in the half-darkness scrambled into the big bed. There was no room at Mother's side so I had to get between her and Father. For the time being I had forgotten about him, and for several minutes I sat bolt upright, racking my brains to know what I could do with him. He was taking up more than his fair share of the bed, and I couldn't get comfortable, so I gave him several kicks that made him grunt and stretch. He made room all right, though. Mother waked and felt for me. I settled back comfortably in the warmth of the bed with my thumb in my mouth.

30   "Mummy!" I hummed, loudly and contentedly.

31   "Sssh! dear," she whispered. "Don't wake Daddy!"

32   This was a new development, which threatened to be even more serious than "talking to Daddy." Life without my early-morning conferences was unthinkable.

33   "Why?" I asked severely.

34   "Because poor Daddy is tired."

35   This seemed to me a quite inadequate reason, and I was sickened by the sentimentality of her "poor Daddy." I never liked that sort of gush; it always struck me as insincere.

36   "Oh!" I said lightly. Then in my most winning tone: "Do you know where I want to go with you today, Mummy?"

37   "No, dear," she sighed.

38   "I want to go down the Glen and fish for thornybacks with my new net, and then I want to go out to the Fox and Hounds, and—"

39   "Don't-wake-Daddy!" she hissed angrily, clapping her hand across my mouth.

40   But it was too late. He was awake, or nearly so. He grunted and reached for the matches. Then he stared incredulously at his watch.

41   "Like a cup of tea, dear?" asked Mother in a meek, hushed voice I had never heard her use before. It sounded almost as though she were afraid.

42   "Tea?" he exclaimed indignantly. "Do you know what the time is?"

43   "And after that I want to go up the Rathcooney Road," I said loudly, afraid I'd forget something in all those interruptions.

44   "Go to sleep at once, Larry!" she said sharply.

45   I began to snivel. I couldn't concentrate, the way that pair went on, and smothering my early-morning schemes was like burying a family from the cradle.

46   Father said nothing, but lit his pipe and sucked it, looking out into the shadows without minding Mother or me. I knew he was mad. Every time I made a remark Mother hushed me irritably. I was moritfied. I felt it wasn't fair; there was even something sinister in it. Every time I had pointed out to her the waste of making two beds when we could both sleep in one, she had told me it was healthier like that, and now here was this man, this stranger, sleeping with her without the least regard for her health!

47   He got up early and made tea, but though he brought Mother a cup he brought none for me.

48   "Mummy," I shouted, "I want a cup of tea, too."

49   "Yes, dear," she said patiently. "You can drink from Mummy's saucer."

50   That settled it. Either Father or I would have to leave the house. I didn't want to drink from Mother's saucer; I wanted to be treated as an equal in my own home, so, just to spite her, I drank it all and left none for her. She took that quietly, too.

51   But that night when she was putting me to bed she said gently:

52   "Larry, I want you to promise me something."

53   "What is it?" I asked.

54   "Not to come in and disturb poor Daddy in the morning. Promise?"

55   "Poor Daddy" again! I was becoming suspicious of everything involving that quite impossible man.

56   "Why?" I asked.

57   "Because poor Daddy is worried and tired and he doesn't sleep well."

58   "Why doesn't he, Mummy?"

59   "Well, you know, don't you, that while he was at the war Mummy got the pennies from the Post Office?"

60   "From Miss MacCarthy?"

61   "That's right. But now, you see, Miss MacCarthy hasn't any more pennies, so Daddy must go out and find us some. You know what would happen if he couldn't?"

62   "No," I said, "tell us."

63   "Well, I think we might have to go out and beg for them like the poor old woman on Fridays. We wouldn't like that, would we?"

64   "No," I agreed. "We wouldn't."

65   "So you'll promise not to come in and wake him?"

66   "Promise."

67   Mind you, I meant that. I knew pennies were a serious matter, and I was all against having to go out and beg like the old woman on Fridays. Mother laid out all my toys in a complete ring round the bed so that, whatever way I got out, I was bound to fall over one of them.

68   When I woke I remembered my promise all right. I got up and sat on the floor and played—for hours, it seemed to me. Then I got my chair and looked out the attic window for more hours. I wished it was time for Father to wake; I wished someone would make me a cup of tea. I didn't feel in the least like the sun; instead, I was bored and so very, very cold! I simply longed for the warmth and depth of the big featherbed.

69   At last I could stand it no longer. I went into the next room. As there was still no room at Mother's side I climbed over her and she woke with a start.

70   "Larry," she whispered, gripping my arm very tightly, "what did you promise?"

71   "But I did, Mummy," I wailed, caught in the very act. "I was quiet for ever so long."

72   "Oh, dear, and you're perished!" she said sadly, feeling me all over. "Now, if I let you stay will you promise not to talk?"

73   "But I want to talk, Mummy," I wailed.

74   "That has nothing to do with it," she said with a firmness that was new to me. "Daddy wants to sleep. Now, do you understand that?"

75   I understood it only too well. I wanted to talk, he wanted to sleep—whose house was it, anyway?

76   "Mummy," I said with equal firmness, "I think it would be healthier for Daddy to sleep in his own bed."

77   That seemed to stagger her, because she said nothing for a while.

78   "Now, once for all," she went on, "you're to be perfectly quiet or go back to your own bed. Which is it to be?"

79   The injustice of it got me down. I had convicted her out of her own mouth of inconsistency and unreasonableness, and she hadn't even attempted to reply. Full of spite, I gave Father a kick, which she didn't notice but which made him grunt and open his eyes in alarm.

80   "What time it is?" he asked in a panic-stricken voice, not looking at Mother but at the door, as if he saw someone there.

81   "It's early yet," she replied soothingly. "It's only the child. Go to sleep again. . . . Now, Larry," she added, getting out of bed, "you've wakened Daddy and you must go back."

82   This time, for all her quiet air, I knew she meant it, and knew that my principal rights and privileges were as good as lost unless I asserted them at once. As she lifted me, I gave a screech, enough to wake the dead, not to mind Father. He groaned.

83   "That damn child! Doesn't he ever sleep?"

84   "It's only a habit, dear," she said quietly, though I could see she was vexed.

85   "Well, it's time he got out of it," shouted Father, beginning to heave in the bed. He suddenly gathered all the bedclothes about him, turned to the wall, and then looked back over his shoulder with nothing showing only two small, spiteful, dark eyes. The man looked very wicked.

86   To open the bedroom door, Mother had to let me down, and I broke free and dashed for the farthest corner, screeching. Father sat bolt up-right in bed.

87   "Shut up, you little puppy!" he said in a choking voice.

88   I was so astonished that I stopped screeching. Never, never had anyone spoken to me in that tone before. I looked at him incredulously and saw his face convulsed with rage. It was only then that I fully realized how God had codded me, listening to my prayers for the safe return of this monster.

89   "Shut up, you!" I bawled, beside myself.

90   "What's that you said?" shouted Father, making a wild leap out of the bed.

91   "Mick, Mick!" cried Mother. "Don't you see the child isn't used to you?"

92   "I see he's better fed than taught," snarled Father, waving his arms wildly. "He wants his bottom smacked."

93   All his previous shouting was as nothing to these obscene words referring to my person. They really made my blood boil.

94   "Smack your own!" I screamed hysterically. "Smack your own! Shut up! Shut up!"

95   At this he lost his patience and let fly at me. He did it with the lack of conviction you'd expect of a man under Mother's horrified eyes, and it ended up as a mere tap, but the sheer indignity of being struck at all by a stranger, a total stranger who had cajoled his way back from the war into our big bed as a result of my innocent intercession, made me completely dotty. I shrieked and shrieked, and danced in my bare feet, and Father, looking awkward and hairy in nothing but a short grey army shirt, glared down at me like a mountain out for murder. I think it must have been then that I realized he was jealous too. And there stood Mother in her nightdress, looking as if her heart was broken between us. I hoped she felt as she looked. It seemed to me that she deserved it all.

96   From that morning out my life was a hell. Father and I were enemies, open and avowed. We conducted a series of skirmishes against one another, he trying to steal my time with Mother and I his. When she was sitting on my bed, telling me a story, he took to looking for some pair of old boots which he alleged he had left behind him at the beginning of the war. While he talked to Mother I played loudly with my toys to show my total lack of concern. He created a terrible scene one evening when

he came in from work and found me at his box, playing with his regimental badges, Gurkha knives and button-sticks. Mother got up and took the box from me.

97   "You mustn't play with Daddy's toys unless he lets you, Larry," she said severely. "Daddy doesn't play with yours."

98   For some reason Father looked at her as if she had struck him and then turned away with a scowl.

99   "Those are not toys," he growled, taking down the box again to see had I lifted anything. "Some of those curios are very rare and valuable."

100   But as time went on I saw more and more how he managed to alienate Mother and me. What made it worse was that I couldn't grasp his method or see what attraction he had for Mother. In every possible way he was less winning than I. He had a common accent and made noises at his tea. I thought for a while that it might be the newspapers she was interested in, so I made up bits of news of my own to read to her. Then I thought it might be the smoking, which I personally thought attractive, and took his pipes and went round the house dribbling into them till he caught me. I even made noises at my tea, but Mother only told me I was disgusting. It all seemed to hinge round that unhealthy habit of sleeping together, so I made a point of dropping into their bedroom and nosing round, talking to myself, so that they wouldn't know I was watching them, but they were never up to anything that I could see. In the end it beat me. It seemed to depend on being grown-up and giving people rings, and I realized I'd have to wait.

101   But at the same time I wanted him to see that I was only waiting, not giving up the fight. One evening when he was being particularly obnoxious, chattering away well above my head, I let him have it.

102   "Mummy," I said, "do you know what I'm going to do when I grow up?"

103   "No, dear," she replied. "What?"

104   "I'm going to marry you," I said quietly.

105   Father gave a great guffaw out of him, but he didn't take me in. I knew it must only be pretence. And Mother, in spite of everything, was pleased. I felt she was probably relieved to know that one day Father's hold on her would be broken.

106   "Won't that be nice?" she said with a smile.

107   "It'll be very nice," I said confidently. "Because we're going to have lots and lots of babies."

108   "That's right, dear," she said placidly. "I think we'll have one soon, and then you'll have plenty of company."

109   I was no end pleased about that because it showed that in spite of the way she gave in to Father she still considered my wishes. Besides, it would put the Geneys in their place.

110   It didn't turn out like that, though. To begin with, she was very preoccupied—I supposed about where she would get the seventeen and six—and though Father took to staying out late in the evenings it did me

no particular good. She stopped taking me for walks, became as touchy as blazes, and smacked me for nothing at all. Sometimes I wished I'd never mentioned the confounded baby—I seemed to have a genius for bringing calamity on myself.

111 And calamity it was! Sonny arrived in the most appalling hullabaloo—even that much he couldn't do without a fuss—and from the first moment I disliked him. He was a difficult child—so far as I was concerned he was always difficult—and demanded far too much attention. Mother was simply silly about him, and couldn't see when he was only showing off. As company he was worse than useless. He slept all day, and I had to go round the house on tiptoe to avoid waking him. It wasn't any longer a question of not waking Father. The slogan now was "Don't-wake-Sonny!" I couldn't understand why the child wouldn't sleep at the proper time, so whenever Mother's back was turned I woke him. Sometimes to keep him awake I pinched him as well. Mother caught me at it one day and gave me a most unmerciful flaking.

112 One evening, when Father was coming in from work, I was playing trains in the front garden. I let on not to notice him; instead, I pretended to be talking to myself, and said in a loud voice: "If another bloody baby comes into this house, I'm going out."

113 Father stopped dead and looked at me over his shoulder.

114 "What's that you said?" he asked sternly.

115 "I was only talking to myself," I replied, trying to conceal my panic. "It's private."

116 He turned and went in without a word. Mind you, I intended it as a solemn warning, but its effect was quite different. Father started being quite nice to me. I could understand that, of course. Mother was quite sickening about Sonny. Even at mealtimes she's get up and gawk at him in the cradle with an idiotic smile, and tell Father to do the same. He was always polite about it, but he looked so puzzled you could see he didn't know what she was talking about. He complained of the way Sonny cried at night, but she only got cross and said that Sonny never cried except when there was something up with him—which was a flaming lie, because Sonny never had anything up with him, and only cried for attention. It was really painful to see how simple-minded she was. Father wasn't attractive, but he had a fine intelligence. He saw through Sonny, and now he knew that I saw through him as well.

117 One night I woke with a start. There was someone beside me in the bed. For one wild moment I felt sure it must be Mother, having come to her senses and left Father for good, but then I heard Sonny in convulsions in the next room, and Mother saying: "There! There! There!" and I knew it wasn't she. It was Father. He was lying beside me, wide awake, breathing hard and apparently as mad as hell.

118 After a while it came to me what he was mad about. It was his turn now. After turning me out of the big bed, he had been turned out himself. Mother had no consideration now for anyone but that poisonous

pup, Sonny. I couldn't help feeling sorry for Father. I had been through it all myself, and even at that age I was magnanimous. I began to stroke him down and say: "There! There!" He wasn't exactly responsive.

119   "Aren't you asleep either?" he snarled.

120   "Ah, come on and put your arm around us, can't you?" I said, and he did, in a sort of way. Gingerly, I suppose, is how you'd describe it. He was very bony but better than nothing.

121   At Christmas he went out of his way to buy me a really nice model railway.

Study Questions

1. What is an *Oedipus complex*? What are its classic symptoms? Is the title of the story literal or figurative?
2. How old is Larry at the time he tells this story? How do you know? Why is innocence, such as Larry's at five years of age, the source of humor?
3. How severely is point of view limited?
4. What does Larry's creation of Mrs. Left and Mrs. Right tell you about his life? What event turns Larry and his father into allies?
5. Comment on Larry's statement, "The war was the most peaceful period of my life."

The Love Song of J. Alfred Prufrock

T. S. Eliot

S'io credesse che mia risposta fosse
A persona che mai tornasse al mondo,
Questa fiamma staria senza piu scosse.
Ma perciocche giammai di questo fondo
Non torno vivo alcun, s'i'odo il vero,
Senza tema d'infamia ti rispondo.

Let us go then, you and I,
When the evening is spread out against the sky
Like a patient etherised upon a table;
Let us go, through certain half-deserted streets,
The muttering retreats
Of restless nights in one-night cheap hotels
And sawdust restaurants with oyster-shells:
Streets that follow like a tedious argument
Of insidious intent
To lead you to an overwhelming question . . .   10
Oh, do not ask, "What is it?"
Let us go and make our visit.

    In the room the women come and go
Talking of Michelangelo.

    The yellow fog that rubs its back upon the window-panes,
The yellow smoke that rubs its muzzle on the window-panes
Licked its tongue into the corners of the evening,
Lingered upon the pools that stand in drains,
Let fall upon its back the soot that falls from chimneys,
Slipped by the terrace, made a sudden leap,   20
And seeing that it was a soft October night,
Curled once about the house, and fell asleep.

    And indeed there will be time
For the yellow smoke that slides along the street,
Rubbing its back upon the window-panes;
There will be time, there will be time
To prepare a face to meet the faces that you meet;
There will be time to murder and create,
And time for all the works and days of hands
That lift and drop a question on your plate;   30
Time for you and time for me,
And time yet for a hundred indecisions,
And for a hundred visions and revisions,
Before the taking of a toast and tea.

    In the room the women come and go
Talking of Michelangelo.

    And indeed there will be time
To wonder, "Do I dare?" and, "Do I dare?"
Time to turn back and descend the stair,
With a bald spot in the middle of my hair—   40
[They will say: "How his hair is growing thin!"]

My morning coat, my collar mounting firmly to the chin,
My necktie rich and modest, but asserted by a simple pin—
[They will say: "But how his arms and legs are thin!"]
Do I dare
Disturb the universe?
In a minute there is time
For decisions and revisions which a minute will reverse.

For I have known them all already, known them all:—
Have known the evenings, mornings, afternoons,   50
I have measured out my life with coffee spoons;
I know the voices dying with a dying fall
Beneath the music from a farther room.
    So how should I presume?

And I have known the eyes already, known them all—
The eyes that fix you in a formulated phrase,
And when I am formulated, sprawling on a pin,
When I am pinned and wriggling on the wall,
Then how should I begin
To spit out all the butt-ends of my days and ways?   60
    And how should I presume?

And I have known the arms already, known them all—
Arms that are braceleted and white and bare
[But in the lamplight, downed with light brown hair!]
Is it perfume from a dress
That makes me so digress?
Arms that lie along a table, or wrap about a shawl.
    And should I then presume?
    And how should I begin?
                    .   .   .   .   .
Shall I say, I have gone at dusk through narrow streets   70
And watched the smoke that rises from the pipes
Of lonely men in shirt-sleeves, leaning out of windows? . . .

    I should have been a pair of ragged claws
Scuttling across the floors of silent seas.
                    .   .   .   .   .
And the afternoon, the evening, sleeps so peacefully!
Smoothed by long fingers,
Asleep . . . tired . . . or it malingers,
Stretched on the floor, here beside you and me.
Should I, after tea and cakes and ices,
Have the strength to force the moment to its crisis?   80
But though I have wept and fasted, wept and prayed,

Though I have seen my head [grown slightly bald] brought in upon
      a platter,
I am no prophet—and here's no great matter;
I have seen the moment of my greatness flicker,
And I have seen the eternal Footman hold my coat, and snicker,
And in short, I was afraid.

And would it have been worth it, after all,
After the cups, the marmalade, the tea,
Among the porcelain, among some talk of you and me,
Would it have been worth while,   90
To have bitten off the matter with a smile,
To have squeezed the universe into a ball
To roll it toward some overwhelming question,
To say: "I am Lazarus, come from the dead,
Come back to tell you all, I shall tell you all"—
If one, settling a pillow by her head,
    Should say: "That is not what I meant at all.
    That is not it, at all."

And would it have been worth it, after all,
Would it have been worth while,   100
After the sunsets and the dooryards and the sprinkled streets,
After the novels, after the teacups, after the skirts that trail along the
      floor—
And this, and so much more?—
It is impossible to say just what I mean!
But as if a magic lantern threw the nerves in patterns on a screen:
Would it have been worth while
If one, settling a pillow or throwing off a shawl,
And turning toward the window, should say:
    "That is not it at all,
    That is not what I meant, at all."   110
         . . . . .
No! I am not Prince Hamlet, nor was meant to be;
Am an attendant lord, one that will do
To swell a progress, start a scene or two,
Advise the prince; no doubt, an easy tool,
Deferential, glad to be of use,
Politic, cautious, and meticulous;
Full of high sentence, but a bit obtuse;
At times, indeed, almost ridiculous—
Almost, at times, the Fool.

    I grow old . . . I grow old . . .   120
I shall wear the bottoms of my trousers rolled.

Shall I part my hair behind? Do I dare to eat a peach?
I shall wear white flannel trousers, and walk upon the beach.
I have heard the mermaids singing, each to each.

I do not think that they will sing to me.

I have seen them riding seaward on the waves
Combing the white hair of the waves blown back
When the wind blows the water white and black.

We have lingered in the chambers of the sea
By sea-girls wreathed with seaweed red and brown   130
Till human voices wake us, and we drown.

Study Questions

1. This poem is considered one of the central documents of contemporary literature. Do you think it makes a significant statement about man's fate? Is Prufrock's problem a common one today?
2. Is Prufrock thinking or actually speaking? Is this a soliloquy or a monologue?
   Who are the "us," "you," and "I" of the first line? The "we" of the last line?
3. Where is Prufrock at the beginning of the poem? Is he there throughout the
   poem?
4. What is the "overwhelming question" Prufrock wants to ask? Is it a specific
   question, or merely a general matter he wants to discuss?
5. How old is Prufrock?
6. Prufrock alludes to numerous Biblical and literary characters. How do these
   allusions help characterize him? Do these allusions employ comparison or
   contrast? What do the figures of speech Prufrock uses tell us about his frame of
   mind or his view of the world? Do they have anything in common?
7. What animals figure in Prufrock's thoughts? Do these animals carry traditional
   symbolic values?
8. Prufrock has been called super–hair-conscious. Do you agree?
9. How is the epigraph from Dante related to the poem?

Corporate Flyer

Terrance Withers

Reality Finance Corporation
to its employees
Proudly Announces

CHEAP
SUNDAY
EXCURSIONS

Departing from Reality
at the morning hour
of nine
Returning Promptly   10
from exotic perimeters
at five p.m.

Study Questions

1. "Corporate Flyer" is a commentary on our often feeble attempts to escape the humdrum in our lives. How does the title help focus your attention? Why is it appropriate?
2. How does the physical appearance of the poem on the page—lines, spacing, capitalization, and so on—contribute to its general meaning?
3. Which word is the most important in terms of the two levels of meaning on which the poem operates?
4. Why is "exotic perimeters" a particularly effective phrase?
5. Why are nine a.m. and five p.m. the hours chosen for the departure and return of the Sunday excursions?

Soliloquy of the Spanish Cloister

Robert Browning

Gr-r-r—there go, my heart's abhorrence!
  Water your damned flowerpots, do!
If hate killed men, Brother Lawrence,
  God's blood, would not mine kill you!
What? your myrtle bush wants trimming?
  Oh, that rose has prior claims—
Needs its leaden vase filled brimming
  Hell dry you up with its flames!

At the meal we sit together:
  Salve tibi! I must hear   10
Wise talk of the kind of weather,
  Sort of season, time of year:
Not a plenteous cork crop; scarcely
  Dare we hope oak galls, I doubt;
What's the Latin name for "parsley"?
  What's the Greek name for "swine's snout"?

Whew! We'll have our platter burnished,
  Laid with care on our own shelf!
With a fire-new spoon we're furnished,
  And a goblet for ourself,   20
Rinsed like something sacrificial
  Ere 'tis fit to touch our chaps—
Marked with L for our initial!
  (He-he! There his lily snaps!)

Saint, forsooth! While brown Dolores
  Squats outside the Convent bank
With Sanchicha, telling stories,
  Steeping tresses in the tank,
Blue-black, lustrous, thick like horsehairs
  —Can't I see his dead eye glow,   30
Bright as 'twere a Barbary corsair's?
  (That is, if he'd let it show!)

When he finishes refection,
  Knife and fork he never lays

Crosswise, to my recollection,
   As do I, in Jesu's praise.
I the Trinity illustrate,
   Drinking watered orange pulp—
In three sips the Arian frustrate;
   While he drains his at one gulp.   40

Oh, those melons! If he's able
   We're to have a feast! so nice!
One goes to the Abbot's table,
   All of us get each a slice.
How go on your flowers? None double?
   Not one fruit-sort can you spy?
Strange!—And I, too, at such trouble
   Keep them close-nipped on the sly!

There's a great text in Galatians,
   Once you trip on it, entails   50
Twenty-nine distinct damnations,
   One sure, if another fails;
If I trip him just a-dying,
   Sure of heaven as sure can be,
Spin him round and send him flying
   Off to hell, a Manichee?

Or, my scrofulous French novel
   On gray paper with blunt type!
Simply glance at it, you grovel
   Hand and foot in Belial's gripe;   60

If I double down its pages
   At the woeful sixteenth print,
When he gathers his greengages,
   Ope a sieve and slip in 't?

Or, there's Satan!—one might venture
   Pledge one's soul to him, yet leave
Such a flaw in the indenture
   As he'd miss till, past retrieve,
Blasted lay that rose acacia
   We're so proud of! *Hy, Zy, Hine* . . .   70
'St, there's Vespers! *Plena gratia,*
   Ave, Virgo! Gr-r-r—you swine!

Study Questions

1. What is a *soliloquy*? Should this poem be spoken aloud, *in toto* or in part? By whom?
2. What kind of life do people in monasteries lead? What is Browning satirizing? On the basis of this poem, would you call Browning anti-Catholic?
3. What are the terms of the pledge that the monk contemplates making with Satan?
4. Why are certain words italicized? Why are some sentences in parentheses?
5. How does the rhythm either increase or decrease the poem's effectiveness? How successful are Browning's onomatopoetic words?
6. Which stanzas are particularly ironic in view of the monk's seeming unawareness of the full import of his words?

A Noiseless Patient Spider

Walt Whitman

A noiseless patient spider,
I mark'd where on a little promontory it stood isolated,
Mark'd how to explore the vacant vast surrounding,
It launch'd forth filament, filament, filament, out of itself,
Ever unreeling them, ever tirelessly speeding them.

And you O my soul where you stand,
Surrounded, detached, in measureless oceans of space,
Ceaselessly musing, venturing, throwing, seeking the spheres to
            connect them,
Till the bridge you will need be form'd, till the ductile anchor hold,
Till the gossamer thread you fling catch somewhere, O my soul.   10

Study Questions

1. What is the connection between the spider and the soul? The spider stands on a little promontory. Where does the soul stand?
2. What grammatical form imparts a feeling of continuous movement to the poem?
3. Comment on the meaning of "spheres," "bridge," "anchor," and "thread."
4. What is the antecedent of *them* in line 5, and of *them* in line 8?

Barter

Sara Teasdale

Life has loveliness to sell,
All beautiful and splendid things,
Blue waves whitened on a cliff,
Soaring fire that sways and sings,
And children's faces looking up
Holding wonder like a cup.

Life has loveliness to sell,
Music like a curve of gold,
Scent of pine trees in the rain,
Eyes that love you, arms that hold,   10
And for your spirit's still delight,
Holy thoughts that star the night.

Spend all you have for loveliness,
Buy it and never count the cost;
For one white singing hour of peace
Count many a year of strife well lost,
And for a breath of ecstasy
Give all you have been, or could be.

Study Questions

1. How does Teasdale make the transitions between stanzas, and thus help unify her poem?
2. What is accomplished by the parallelism in the three stanzas? Besides through the verb forms, how is the parallelism achieved?
3. Does life's loveliness, as presented here, include appeals to all five senses?
4. Is the title of the poem appropriate?
5. Comment on Teasdale's use of *still* and *star*. Which words are repeated either exactly or with variations? Why?

Desert Places

Robert Frost

Snow falling and night falling fast, oh, fast
In a field I looked into going past,
And the ground almost covered smooth in snow,
But a few weeds and stubble showing last.

The woods around it have it—it is theirs.
All animals are smothered in their lairs.
I am too absent-spirited to count;
The loneliness includes me unawares.

And lonely as it is, that loneliness
Will be more lonely ere it will be less—   10
A blanker whiteness of benighted snow
With no expression, nothing to express.

They cannot scare me with their empty spaces
Between stars—on stars where no human race is.
I have it in me so much nearer home
To scare myself with my own desert places.

Study Questions

1. What does Frost mean by "desert places"? Is his meaning specific?
2. Identify the rhyme scheme of the poem. Is it regular throughout? What is the function of the third line in each stanza?
3. Comment on the antecedents of the pronouns in this poem—the various *it*s and *theirs,* and *they.*
4. What single word could be substituted for "showing last"? How does Frost use *smothered* and *benighted*?
5. How does the poet prepare you for his remarks in the last stanza? Does he make an analogy?

Ulysses

Alfred, Lord Tennyson

It little profits that an idle king,
By this still hearth, among these barren crags,
Match'd with an aged wife, I mete and dole
Unequal laws unto a savage race,
That hoard, and sleep, and feed, and know not me.
I cannot rest from travel; I will drink
Life to the lees. All times I have enjoy'd
Greatly, have suffer'd greatly, both with those
That loved me, and alone; on shore, and when
Thro' scudding drifts the rainy Hyades   10
Vext the dim sea. I am become a name;
For always roaming with a hungry heart
Much have I seen and known,—cities of men
And manners, climates, councils, governments,
Myself not least, but honor'd of them all,—
And drunk delight of battle with my peers,
Far on the ringing plains of windy Troy.
I am a part of all that I have met;

Yet all experience is an arch wherethro'
Gleams that untravel'd world whose margin fades   20
For ever and for ever when I move.
How dull it is to pause, to make an end,
To rust unburnish'd, not to shine in use!
As tho' to breathe were life! Life piled on life
Were all too little, and of one to me
Little remains; but every hour is saved
From that eternal silence, something more,
A bringer of new things; and vile it were
For some three suns to store and hoard myself,
And this gray spirit yearning in desire   30
To follow knowledge like a sinking star,
Beyond the utmost bound of human thought.
    This is my son, mine own Telemachus,
To whom I leave the scepter and the isle,—
Well-loved of me, discerning to fulfil
This labor, by slow prudence to make mild
A rugged people, and thro' soft degrees
Subdue them to the useful and the good.
Most blameless is he, centered in the sphere
Of common duties, decent not to fail   40
In offices of tenderness, and pay
Meet adoration to my household gods,
When I am gone. He works his work, I mine.
    There lies the port; the vessel puffs her sail;
There gloom the dark, broad seas. My mariners,
Souls that have toil'd, and wrought, and thought with me,—
That ever with a frolic welcome took
The thunder and the sunshine, and opposed
Free hearts, free foreheads,—you and I are old;
Old age hath yet his honor and his toil.   50
Death closes all; but something ere the end,
Some work of noble note, may yet be done,
Not unbecoming men that strove with Gods.
The lights begin to twinkle from the rocks;
The long day wanes; the slow moon climbs; the deep
Moans round with many voices. Come, my friends,
'Tis not too late to seek a newer world.
Push off, and sitting well in order smite
The sounding furrows; for my purpose holds
To sail beyond the sunset, and the baths   60
Of all the western stars, until I die.
It may be that the gulfs will wash us down;
It may be we shall touch the Happy Isles,
And see the great Achilles, whom we knew.

Tho' much is taken, much abides; and tho'
We are not now that strength which in old days
Moved earth and heaven, that which we are, we are,—
One equal temper of heroic hearts,
Made weak by time and fate, but strong in will
To strive, to seek, to find, and not to yield.   70

Study Questions

1. Most critics view Ulysses' words as the praiseworthy sentiments of a mature and courageous individual. But at least one critic feels that Ulysses is irresponsible and childish, that he fails to "act his age." What do you feel is a reasonable interpretation?
2. What is Ulysses' attitude toward his son? His wife? His people? Knowledge?
3. What does Ulysses hope to accomplish by his proposed voyage?
4. The poem seems to have three structural units of thought. Thematically and structurally, what happens at each point of division (lines 33 and 44)?
5. Is "Ulysses" a soliloquy? A monologue? Both?

Ozymandias

Percy Bysshe Shelley

I met a traveler from an antique land
Who said: Two vast and trunkless legs of stone
Stand in the desert . . . Near them, on the sand,
Half sunk, a shattered visage lies, whose frown,
And wrinkled lip, and sneer of cold command,
Tell that its sculptor well those passions read
Which yet survive, stamped on these lifeless things,
The hand that mocked them, and the heart that fed:

And on the pedestal these words appear:
"My name is Ozymandias, king of kings: 10
Look on my works, ye Mighty, and despair!"
Nothing beside remains. Round the decay
Of that colossal wreck, boundless and bare
The lone and level sands stretch far away.

Study Questions

1. What is the point of Shelley's poem? Is it stated or implied?
2. How would the effect of the poem be different if it began with "Two vast and trunkless legs . . ."?
3. Some critics feel that the last three lines of Shelley's sonnet are a detriment, that they restate weakly the point which the poem has already made strongly. Do you agree?
4. How does this poem work within the sonnet form?
5. Rephrase into conventional English word order lines 6–8.

The Graffiti Poet

Nancy Willard

I grew up in the schoolrooms of the Dakotas,
I sat by the wood stove and longed for spring.
My desk leaned like a clavichord, stripped of its hammers,
and on it I carved my name, forever and ever,
so the seed of that place should never forget me.
Outside, in their beehive tombs, I could hear
the dead spinning extravagant honey.
I remembered their names and wanted only
that the living remember mine.

I am the invisible student, dead end   10
of a crowded class. I write and nobody answers.
On the Brooklyn Bridge, I wrote a poem:
the rain washed it away.
On the walls of the Pentagon, I made
My sign; a workman blasted me off like dung.
From the halls of Newark to the shores
of Detroit, I engrave my presence with fire
so the lords of those places may never forget me.

Save me. I can hardly speak. So we pass,
not speaking. In bars where your dreams drink,   20
I scrawl your name, my name, in a heart
that the morning daily erases.
At Dachau, at Belsen I blazoned my cell
with voices and saw my poem sucked
into a single cry:
throw me a fistful of stars.
I died writing, as the walls fell.

I am lonely. More than any monument,
I want you to see me writing: *I love*
you (or someone), *I live* (or you live).   30
Canny with rancour, with love, I teach you
to spell, to remember your name
and your epitaphs which are always changing.
Listen to me stranger, keep me alive.
                    I am you.

Study Questions

1. What are graffiti? Where are they usually found? In what locations and situations do they occur in this poem?
2. What is the sign on the walls of the Pentagon? What is the allusion in "From the halls of Newark to the shores/of Detroit"?
3. What does this poem say about the function of language? What psychological value do graffiti have?
4. Comment on the single cry of the graffiti poet in the cells at Dachau and Belsen.

The Sound of Silence

Paul Simon

Hello darkness my old friend,
I've come to talk with you again,
Because a vision softly creeping,
Left its seeds while I was sleeping
And the vision that was planted in my brain
Still remains within the sound of silence.

In restless dreams I walked alone,
Narrow streets of cobble stone
'Neath the halo of a street lamp,
I turned my collar to the cold and damp   10
When my eyes were stabbed by the flash of a neon light
That split the night, and touched the sound of silence.

And in the naked light I saw
Ten thousand people maybe more,
People talking without speaking,
People hearing without listening,
People writing songs that voices never share
And no one dares disturb the sound of silence.

"Fools!" said I, "You do not know
Silence like a cancer grows.   20
Hear my words that I might teach you
Take my arms that I might reach you."
But my words like silent raindrops fell
And echoed, in the wells of silence.

And the people bowed and prayed
To the neon God they made,
And the sign flashed out its warning
In the words that it was forming.
And the sign said:
        "The words of the prophets are written   30
        on the subway walls and tenement halls"
And whispered in the sounds of silence.

Study Questions

1. The title states a paradox. How is its meaning clarified by the lyrics of this song?
2. Is the metaphor supported by the flower imagery in the first stanza fully developed? Is the degree of its development significant?
3. Who are the prophets? Is the location of their scribbles important?
4. What kind of religious experience is parodied in this song?
5. To what extent do you feel that the parallel structuring in the third and fourth stanzas, for instance, is dictated by the fact that this is a song to be sung?

Packaged Sentiment

Richard Rhodes

1   Christmas is come, the holiday season, and with it our annual deluge of cards, whose successful dispersal across the land the Postal Service heralds to justify failing us for the rest of the year. "By God, we moved the Christmas cards!" Well, half of all the personal mail moved annually in the United States is greeting cards. Cards for Christmas but also cards for New Year's, Valentine's Day, Easter, Mother's Day, Father's Day, Independence Day and Thanksgiving and Halloween, the official holidays of the American year. And for the occasions greeting-card people call "Everyday," though they are not, births and birthdays, graduations, weddings, anniversaries, showers, vacations, friendship, promotion, hello, love, thanks, goodbye, illness and bereavement, and even to have Thought O' You and for a Secret Pal. We are a nation not of letter writers but of card signers. If the personal letter is long dead, maimed by the penny post and murdered by the telephone, the mass-produced card thrives, picturing what we haven't skill to picture, saying what we haven't words to say. Cards knot the ties that bind in a land where a fourth of us change residence with every change of calendar and where grown children no longer live at home. They show us at our best, if in borrowed finery. You may buy a card made of pansies and doggerel or you may buy a card made of da Vinci and the Sermon on the Mount. Whoever receives it will understand what you meant, and that you meant well.

2   The Christmas card was an English invention, but the greeting card an American one. One hundred twenty-eight years ago this season, an Englishman distracted by business matters failed to get his Christmas cards written. Boldly he turned an embarrassment into an opportunity, commissioned a paper tableau of Pickwickians, their glasses raised in toast, and inside each engraved and colored folio he printed a verse. His friends' reactions were not recorded. No doubt some found the idea distastefully impersonal and lamented the decline of manners in a declining age. Others, alert for new twists, thought it charming. The sensible saw its efficiency. It met the first requirement of all mechanical inventions: it saved time.

3   We have taken the idea and made it ours. The English send few cards today, and Europeans fewer still. We send cards for everything, mechanizing and standardizing the complex relationships we maintain with one another, to give us time to breathe. We needn't be ashamed of our custom. Elegant mechanizing is what we do best. It is the form our national character has taken. Look at our office buildings raised on narrow pillars ten feet off the ground as if someone had dared us to float a fifty-story building in the air. Compare our white and graceful moon rockets to the Soviet Union's drab boiler plate. Look at our cards, little shuttles of sentiment weaving across the land.

4   Some of the old cards, the nineteenth-century cards that borrowed the Englishman's invention, were masterpieces of reproduction, printed in as many as twelve colors with verses selected in national contests with cash prizes, verses no better than they should be for all the fanfare. The Victorian Age produced German cards that opened up into three-dimensional sleighing scenes of marvelous intricacy, cards with moving parts, cards fringed like a love-seat pillow with gaudy silks, cards as ornate as any gingerbread house. Cards, one presumes, for the wealthy, because the rest of us hadn't begun sending them in today's incredible numbers, today's fifteen or twenty *billion* cards a year. Now that we do, the special effects that delicate handwork once supplied have had to be scaled down, though the cards we send today carry their weight of handwork too, and with it their weight of amusing stories, cautionary tales of American ingenuity gone berserk. I remember a humorous card that required for its gag a small plastic sack of what it called "belly-button fuzz" stapled below its punch line. No supplier could thumb out enough of the authentic material to meet the demand, so the manufacturer turned to the clothes dryers of a nearby college town, bought up the lint franchise, sterlized the lint to meet health regulations, and bagged it and stapled it on, by hand, and got the effect it was seeking and probably, college towns being college towns, got some belly-button fuzz too. "Attachments," such devices are called—plastic tears, toy scissors, miniature boxes of crayons, feathers, spring-and-paper jumping jacks, pencils, beans, the detritus of industrial civilization shrunk to card size. An attachment will sell a humorous card all by itself if it isn't stolen first, a

problem for greeting-card manufacturers as surely as it is a problem for the sellers of screws and beads and hair ribbons in dime stores. Like children we lust to get our hands on little things, finding magic in tiny representations of the lumbering world.

Nuggets of Emotion

5   The business of greeting cards began in the ambitions of hungry men, and they improvised as they went. There are schools of nursing and schools of nuclear physics, but there are no schools for the makers of greeting cards, only apprenticeships. When Joyce Hall of country Nebraska began his enterprise in Kansas City, Missouri, more than sixty years ago, there weren't even many kinds of cards. Christmas, Easter, birthdays, and weddings were about the only occasions we announced. Hall, Fred Rust of Rust Craft, and a few people like them had to teach us to send cards by making cards we wanted to send. In that work, Hall's career strikingly parallels the career of another Midwesterner, Walt Disney, for both men learned to parse our emotions and recast them in visual and verbal form. Disney, for example, took some shadowy figures from a fairy tale, clothed them in universals, and gave us the Seven Dwarfs. Hall and his people took our need to signal our degrees of social familiarity and our various notions of good taste and gave us a choice among greeting cards.

6   For any given social occasion, depending on how well you know someone and what you want him to think of you, you may select a card for him that is Formal, Traditional, Humorous, Floral, Cute, Contemporary, or some other among Hallmark's many categories of mood. Two cards for a friend who is hospitalized give the flavor. One, an embossed vase of flowers, says, "Glad your Operation's Over" on the cover, and inside:

> *You're thought of so often*
> *As days come and go*
> *That this card comes to tell you,*
> *And then let you know*
> *How much you are wished*
> *A recovery that's quick—*
> *For someone like you*
> *Is too nice to be sick!*

The other card, a photograph of a cotton bunny in a flower-bedecked four-poster, opens with, "Hope you'll soon be out of that *blooming bed*!" and carries the flower pun through:

Sure like to see you back in the pink,
So just take it easy, 'cause then
You'll soon be in clover,
Feeling just rosy,
And fresh as a daisy *again!*

Moods and tones and levels, you see. You are not likely to send a Contemporary card to your maiden aunt nor a Formal card to your spouse. The greeting-card people give you a range of choices. It may be a narrower range than you would prefer, but if you are a sender of cards at all, the choices will not be so narrow that you turn away in disgust and write a letter. You may choose frank sentiment; humor ranging from the modestly ethnic (hillbillies, Indians, Dead End Kids—blacks, Italians, and Eastern Europeans are out today, though they used to be a staple) to the heavily punned to the backward compliment to the gentle slap; simple statement, favored for Christmas and sympathy cards, both occasions being to some people matters serious enough for prose; and a number of alternatives between. Visually, you may choose flowers, cartoons, arabesque gilding, photographs, even reproductions of fine art, though few enough of those because few people buy them. Or stylized little children with ink-drop eyes, or encrustations of plastic jewels, or velvet flocking, or metallic glitter. Variations in texture and surface are legion—and the pride of the older generation of greeting-card men, who believed in making a quality product, who learned what would sell by selling, and who relied for their judgment in such matters on what Joyce Hall once called "the vapors of past experience."

7   Even if you have never given thought to such matters as categories of emotion and levels of taste, greeting-card people know you operate by them, and know how many cards to make to meet your needs. Such is the variety, of cards and of needs, that the largest of the manufacturers, Hallmark Cards, would have collapsed a decade ago if the computer hadn't come along to speed their sorting. The company claims 12,000 products, counting each separate design a product, and the figure is certainly conservative. Twelve thousand different products in quantities of six to perhaps 20,000 different stores: you can do the multiplication yourself, but count in the envelopes; count in as many as ten or twenty different manufacturing operations on every card; count in all the designs being prepared for future publication, designs that pass through hundreds of hands at drawing boards and typewriters and approval committees and lithographic cameras and printing plants; count in all these different bits of information and many more besides, and you arrive at a total that demands the kind of machines that track astronauts to the moon.

8   And count in one thing more: every display in every store is a modest computer of its own, each of its pockets filled with designs that favor the social and cultural biases of the neighborhood around the store,

and among those favored designs the best sellers of the day. "Tailoring," Hallmark calls it—loading the display to favor the preferences of the young or old or black or white or Catholic or Jewish or rich or poor who regularly shop there. The salesman sets up the display with the help of the owner; after that the computer in Kansas City keeps track. The point, of course, is to give you a maximum range of choice among the choices available. Tucked away in the stock drawer below the display, quietly humming, an IBM card meters every design.

9   Despite appearances, then, greeting-card manufacture is no work of hand coloring performed by elderly ladies in lace. The Hallmark plant in Kansas City occupies two city blocks, and the company doesn't even do its own printing. Times Square would fit nicely inside the new distribution center Hallmark is building on a railroad spur outside of town. More than one printing firm in the United States owes its giant color presses to Hallmark orders, which is why the company gets the kind of quality it is known for—because it has the heft to stop the presses and pull a proof. It claims 400 artists in residence, the largest art department in the world, and if you include the girls who separate out the colors of a design by hand, a procedure that still costs less for certain designs than separating the colors by machine, the claim is fair.

10   So many different operations go into the production of greeting cards that even a glimpse of them boggles the mind, serene and simple as the cards look when they finally reach the store. Hallmark buys paper by the boxcar, paper of every imaginable texture and weight, parchment, deckle, bond, pebble-grained, leather-grained, cloth-grained, board, brown wrapping, hard-finished, soft-finished, smooth. Special committees earnestly debate the future popularity of roses or ragamuffins. An artist conceives a group of cards that feature cartoon mice, and the cards sell and the artist is rewarded with a trip to San Francisco. Down in the bowels of the building, behind a secret door, a master photographer labors as he has labored for most of a decade to perfect flat three-dimensional photography using a camera on which Hallmark owns the license, a camera that rolls around in a semicircle on model railroad tracks, its prisms awhirr. In California a contract artist makes dolls of old socks and ships them to Kansas City to be photographed for children's cards. Market-research girls carry cards mounted on black panels to meetings of women's clubs, where the ladies, at a charitable fifty cents a head, choose among different designs with the same verses, or different verses with the same design, helping Hallmark determine the very best that you might care to send. An engineer, a stack of handmade designs before him on his desk, struggles to arrange them on a lithography sheet to get the maximum number of designs per sheet so that they can be printed all at once with minimum waste of paper—"nesting," the process is called. Artists roam the streets of major cities at Christmastime, studying shop windows and the offerings of art galleries to discover new trends in visual design. A deputation of sales managers retreats to an

Ozark resort for a multimedia presentation of next year's line. A mechanical genius grown old in the service of the firm remembers the tricks he has taught mere paper cards to do: walking, talking, sticking out their tongues, growling, snoring, squeaking, issuing forth perfume at the scratch of a fingernail across microscopic beads. An engineer sits down at a handwork table and conducts a motion study and designs a system and lines and lines of young girls in gray smocks follow the system to assemble a complicated card by hand, their hands making the memorized motions while they dream of boyfriends or listen to the rhythm of the gluing machines interweaving fugally along the line. A master engraver puts the finishing touches on a die that will punch a dotted line around a paper puppet on a get-well card. A commmittee of executives meets and decides that the pink of a card isn't cheerful enough and the cartoon figure on another card not sufficiently neuter to appeal both to men and to women. A shipment of paper for a line of children's books is frozen into a harbor in Finland when it should be steaming its way to a printing plant in Singapore. A baby leopard runs loose in the photography department while an editor upstairs sorts through another shipment of amateur verse mailed in by the card lovers of America. He has not found a writer worth encouraging in three years. Greeting cards aren't simply manufactured, like soap or breakfast cereal. They are rescued from the confusing crosscurrents of American life, every one of them a difficult recovery. John Donne found the King's likeness on a coin: greeting-card manufacturers must discover Everyman's likeness and somehow fix it on paper with all its idiosyncrasies smoothed away.

11   Hallmark employs far fewer writers than artists, about fifteen or twenty. Unlike designs, verses enjoy a long half-life if they are adjusted for minor changes in the language along the way. These days they are often selected—selected entire, not written—by computer from a stock of the most popular verses of the past. The writers try to think up new words, and from time to time they do. Greeting-card verse has come in for its share of ridicule, which perhaps it deserves, but before it is ridiculed its distinction ought to be explained. Most song lyrics look equally ridiculous when printed bald, because the rhetoric of a song lyric, the source of its emotional impact, is the music that accompanies it. The rhetoric of greeting-card verse is the card, the physical and visual accompaniment to the verse. A few greeting-card makers have caught on to the similarity between song lyrics and greeting-card verse and have begun to borrow effects they can use, as in this verse from one of American Greetings' new "Soft Touch" cards, cards for young people that feature soft-focus photography:

> untold the times i've kissed you
> in the moments i have missed you
> and our love goes on forever . . .
> with you softly on my mind

If that doesn't quite make sense, well, neither do most lyrics away from their music, or greeting-card verses away from their cards. A poem, a real poem, the thing itself, works no better on a greeting card or in a song, because it contains its own orchestration and goes dissonant when larded with the scrapings of Mantovani strings.

12   Modern young people don't like eight-line rhymed verses, preferring song words or evocative sentences. One card on my desk is captioned merely "Peace," which makes it appropriate to almost every occasion except Halloween. Finding the right words for a card is harder today than it used to be because a generation trained on the film expects the words and images to subtly interlock. Getting new words approved by management is harder still. Like most American corporations of healthy middle age, Hallmark has discovered the benefits of redundant personnel and of a certain resistance to fad. Good ideas don't come along every morning, and they must always be weighed against the success of the old: there are only so many pockets in a greeting-card display. Joyce Hall, a tall, spare man with a W. C. Fields nose and a lifetime of practical experience, used to approve every card Hallmark made, words, music, and all; and his son, Donald Hall, who is now president of the firm, still approves every Contemporary card that gets past his secretary, or did when I worked there. A friend of mine who free-lanced for Hallmark once earned that secretary's enmity with a design she thought in questionable taste. "It's nice, Bill," she told him, "but it's not Hallmark." You cannot be too careful, and who is to say she wasn't right?

13   If the process of selection was once a matter of subjective judgment, it is today at least outwardly scientific. For reasons that only statisticians understand, Kansas City is a superb test market. If products sell in Kansas City, they will sell to the nation, a fact that city sophisticates might soberly consider the next time they buy a card. The formula doesn't always work—the East Coast prefers the word "Pop" to the word "Dad" on its Father cards, for example—but it works often enough to keep Hallmark researchers close to home. Yet market research is often discounted at Hallmark. The vapors of past experience still blow through the halls, and men whose only business experience has been with greeting cards still ignore the information of market tests if it conflicts with the information of the gut.

14   Daring subjectivity was Joyce Hall's genius, and remains a legacy of sorts in the hands of less remarkable men now that he has reluctantly relinquished command. Like every successful self-made man he has found retirement difficult. He is a man of quirks and crotchets and always was, but the enterprise he began out of a suitcase stashed under his bed at the Kansas City YMCA now ranks high on *Fortune* magazine's list of the 500 leading privately owned American corporations. The Hall family still owns the place lock, stock, and barrel. It is one of the few privately owned companies of any size left in Kansas City, where wealthy sons of fathers who sweated their way up from poverty tend to sell

out to national conglomerations and pass their time at Martha's Vineyard or Harbor Point or Cannes. "You can teach your children everything but poverty," Hall once said, but he taught his son to care about the family firm; and today Hallmark thrives, branching out into gift books, stationery, party goods, calendars and albums, puzzles, candy, pens, urban redevelopment, retail stores on the Neiman-Marcus model, and whatever other enterprises it can find that fit its broad conception of its business, which it calls, modestly enough, "social expression."

Green Cards Don't Sell

15   I could complain against greeting cards. It isn't difficult to do in a world where more people feel pain than feel pleasure. There is even the risk that if I don't complain you will take me for a patsy. The greeting card's contribution to literacy will not be decisive, but I don't believe it does us that much harm. By definition, popular art can only be defended numerically, and to those who equate numbers with mediocrity, to the antipopulists, a numerical defense amounts to a certain conviction. Television is mediocre because it caters to popular taste, and greeting cards too. No. If either of them has a glaring weakness, it is that among their plethora of choices they do not give us all the choices we might want, or need. That is the effect of the marketplace, lopping off the ends of the bell curve, but the marketplace pays our bills. And if you would like to consider an opposing view, consider Joyce Hall's, who remembers this nation when it was largely rural and uneducated, and who believed that one of Hallmark's responsibilities was the elevation of American taste, a view that might seem didactic of him, but I was a country boy too, and the first play I ever saw, chills running down my back, was *Macbeth*, on television's *Hallmark Hall of Fame*.

16   Hallmark established its considerable reputation with thought and care, spending far less on advertising than most companies that make consumer products do. It sponsors television specials and between the acts simply shows its cards. Can you remember a year when the *Hall of Fame* didn't come in for at least one Emmy? Do you know how many Americans traipsed through art galleries they had never visited before to see the collection of paintings by Winston Churchill that Hallmark shipped around the land? No breath of public scandal has ever blown through the organization. It does not make napalm and until very recently was old-fashioned enough to pay its bills in cash. One of its best men, now retired, a German Jew named Hans Archenhold whose printing plant was seized by the Nazis, came to Kansas City in its gangster years and found the printing industry there a sty of kickbacks and corruption. With the leverage of Hallmark printing orders he helped to clean it up. Hall himself switched his employees from coffee to milk breaks during the Depression, reasoning, in memory of his own hungry years,

that they probably ate no breakfast and might not be sure of lunch, and I doubt that many complained of paternalism. By all means rail against the size and impersonality of American corporations—your arguments will be well taken—but remember also that most are little Swedens now, dispensing profits and medical care and life insurance and retirement funds with a cheerful hand.

17   Today Hallmark's brand identity, an elusive commodity in a competitive society, approaches 100 per cent. Schoolchildren, asked to make cards in class, often draw a crown on the back of their productions or attempt the famous slogan, "When you care enough to send the very best," in sturdy Big Chief print. There are other greeting-card companies, American, Buzza-Cardozo, Rust Craft, and Hallmark's own poor cousin, Ambassador Cards, to name only the biggest, but the one giant has come to stand for them all.

18   Strangely, 80 per cent of the buyers of greeting cards are women. That is why cards are tested at women's clubs. Even cards for men are designed with a woman buyer in mind, featuring scenes so romantically masculine that only the coldest feminine heart would not be touched: pipes and slippers, a red-capped hunter knocking down a brace of ducks, a fleet of galleons in harbor unaccountably full-sailed, knightly shields and lordly crests, racy automobiles, workshop tools, or smiling Dad (Pop) himself. Why do women buy most of the cards? The answer may be simpler than it seems. Men think themselves too busy running the nation to find time for the smaller amenities, but they rationalize. The truth is that they are locked into an office or on a production line all day. Running an office, doing a job, no more takes all day than housework— few of us have brains that run so uniformly by the clock—but when the housework is done the woman who does it is free to go visiting or wander through the shops, while the man must shuffle papers and watch the clock. The woman may feel uncomfortable with her freedom, may feel she buys it at too high a price. It is hers nonetheless, and she uses it, among other good works, to buy cards. The new cards, by the way, the cards for young people, don't draw such sharp distinctions between masculine and feminine roles. They are androgynous. We all are, underneath: the kids have found us out.

19   I suspect we send each other cards partly from guilt, believing we haven't kept our friendships in good repair. If we are gregarious, we are also shy, uneasy as only a people raised in a society straining toward egalitarianism can be. Most of us were never rich and never desperately poor. We never learned our place: we started this country so we wouldn't have to, but our mobility leaves us unsure of where our elbows belong. We are known for our humor, but not for our wit; for our ability, but not for our style; for our strength, but not for our grace. We find ourselves harried and we fumble, or think we do.

20   Our guilt is misplaced. Thoreau's three chairs for company and two for friendship nicely defines our human limits. They are no longer limits

to which we can comfortably adhere. We would hurt too many feelings if we did, the feelings of the people we work with, of our relatives and our neighbors and the neighbors we left behind. Anyone who has moved recently knows how much sheer matter we accumulate in our houses, but imagine also the long list of acquaintances we have accumulated, back to our earliest years. If we are fond of people at all, we have met thousands in our lives. Perhaps that is why so few of us read. Perhaps our culture is really oral, despite the science fiction of our media, satellites above and wires and presses below and the air itself in fervent vibration. One recalls the theory that ghetto children have difficulty in school not because of deprivation but because of excess, of overstimulation by the teeming world in which they live. It is true to some degree of us all. With China and the Soviet Union, and for much of the same reasons of origin and purpose, we are a national people far more than we are local. Our traditions and our associations extend from ocean to ocean, and our burden of communication too. The Communist nations, not having finished their first industrial revolution, turn to party meetings and rallies to stay in touch; with a more ritualized social structure, we send cards.

21   Making greeting cards to suit us isn't easy. Try to imagine a card that would please both your grandmother and your revolutionary son— and yet your Christmas card probably did. For reasons no one knows, green cards don't sell. Writers of greeting cards must search their verses for unintentional double entendres, and because of that danger, the word "it" used as a direct object is taboo. "Today's your day to get *it*!" It won't do. St. Patrick's Day cards that kid Irish drinking habits elicit indignant letters from Hibernian Societies, a sign that the Irish are ready to melt the rest of the way into the pot. A card is two years in the making: what if hemlines change? Superman cards reached the stores the day the Superman fad collapsed. And what do you say, in a card, in mere words, to a widow whose world has emptied of the life she loved? (You say, in rhymed verse, that words can't express your sympathy.)

22   When I worked at Hallmark I sometimes thought of cards as pretty packages with nothing inside, but I am a year older now and I wonder. Perhaps, ephemeral though they are, they carry a greater weight of emotion to a greater number of people than we can bear to carry ourselves. They are tactful, discreet; they strike the right tone. Their designers sweat blood, believe me, to make them so. Even when they fail we forgive the sender and blame the card, as we forgive a caller a bad connection on the phone. Greeting cards have inertia. Like Santa's bag they hang a little behind. They are innately conservative because the occasions of our lives are too important for fads, of style or of spirit. Hallmark has discovered that the young people who buy its breezily pessimistic Contemporary cards return to more traditional forms when they acquire families and careers. Pessimism becomes a luxury they can no longer afford.

23   We grow older; the cards for our stops along the way await us in the
store. They are not dangerous or subversive or mean; they espouse no
causes except the old mute causes of life itself, birth and marriage and
begetting and death, and these gently. I celebrate them as E. M. Forster
celebrated democracy, with a hearty two cheers Merry Christmas.

Study Questions

1. How does mass-produced doggerel contrast with graffiti?
2. What is the thesis statement of Rhodes's essay?
3. What is the effect of the numerous lists that Rhodes uses?
4. Considering paragraphs 10 and 12, comment on the construction of the paragraphs in this essay.
5. What is the tone of this essay?
6. The schoolchildren example in paragraph 17 does not seem like something discovered by careful research; rather it seems invented for effect. Can you find other similar examples where Rhodes seems carried away by his own enthusiasm?

Do Not Go Gentle into That Good Night

Dylan Thomas

Do not go gentle into that good night,
Old age should burn and rave at close of day;
Rage, rage against the dying of the light.

Though wise men at their end know dark is right,
Because their words had forked no lightning they
Do not go gentle into that good night.

Good men, the last wave by, crying how bright
Their frail deeds might have danced in a green bay,
Rage, rage against the dying of the light.

Wild men who caught and sang the sun in flight,   10
And learn, too late, they grieved it on its way,
Do not go gentle into that good night.

Grave men, near death, who see with blinding sight
Blind eyes could blaze like meteors and be gay,
Rage, rage against the dying of the light.

And you, my father, there on the sad height,
Curse, bless, me now with your fierce tears, I pray.
Do not go gentle into that good night.
Rage, rage against the dying of the light.

Study Questions

1. What is the rhyme scheme of this poem? How is it varied in the final stanza? How is this variation connected to the two oft-repeated lines?
2. Which words and images in the poem are evocative of light? Why should light figure so prominently here?
3. Comment on Thomas's use of *gentle* and *grieved,* and on the paradox in "blinding sight."

Little Boy Blue

Eugene Field

The little toy dog is covered with dust,
   But sturdy and stanch he stands;
And the little toy soldier is red with rust,
   And his musket molds in his hands.
Time was when the little toy dog was new
   And the soldier was passing fair,
And that was the time when our Little Boy Blue
   Kissed them and put them there.

"Now, don't you go till I come," he said,
   "And don't you make any noise!"   10
So toddling off to his trundle-bed
   He dreamed of the pretty toys.
And as he was dreaming, an angel song
   Awakened our Little Boy Blue,—
Oh, the years are many, the years are long,
   But the little toy friends are true.

Ay, faithful to Little Boy Blue they stand,
   Each in the same old place,
Awaiting the touch of a little hand,
   The smile of a little face.   20
And they wonder, as waiting these long years through,
   In the dust of that little chair,
What has become of our Little Boy Blue
   Since he kissed them and put them there.

Study Questions

1. Is pathos present in "Little Boy Blue"? Bathos? Is the poem sentimental? What are the connotations of *sentiment* and *sentimental*?
2. Field personifies the little boy's toys. What reaction is he trying to provoke in his audience? Is he successful?
3. Does Field ever vary the rhythm of the poem? Does he demonstrate any subtlety in his rhyme scheme?
4. What is the effect of the repetition of *little*?

Bells for John Whiteside's Daughter

John Crowe Ransom

There was such speed in her little body,
And such lightness in her footfall,
It is no wonder her brown study
Astonishes us all.

Her wars were bruited in our high window.
We looked among orchard trees and beyond
Where she took arms against her shadow,
Or harried unto the pond

The lazy geese, like a snow cloud
Dripping their snow on the green grass,
Tricking and stopping, sleepy and proud,
Who cried in goose, Alas,

For the tireless heart within the little
Lady with rod that made them rise

10

From their noon apple-dreams and scuttle
Goose fashion under the skies!

But now go the bells, and we are ready,
In one house we are sternly stopped
To say we are vexed at her brown study,
Lying so primly propped.   20

Study Questions

1. What is a "brown study"? Why couldn't it have been a "red study"?
2. Is the snow image in the third stanza a good vehicle for describing, physically and emotively, the flight of geese?
3. The adverb *primly* has an extraordinary effect on the reader. What is it which precedes *primly* in the poem which makes it so powerful?
4. What practice of good essay writing does this poem exemplify?
5. Contrast "Little Boy Blue" with "Bells for John Whiteside's Daughter."

I Heard a Fly Buzz When I Died

Emily Dickinson

I heard a fly buzz when I died;
    The stillness round my form
Was like the stillness in the air
    Between the heaves of storm.

The eyes beside had wrung them dry,
    And breaths were gathering sure
For that last onset, when the king
    Be witnessed in his power.

I willed my keepsakes, signed away
   What portion of me I
Could make assignable,—and then
   There interposed a fly,   10

With blue, uncertain, stumbling buzz,
   Between the light and me;
And then the windows failed, and then
   I could not see to see.

Study Questions

1. What point in time does the fly's presence mark?
2. How many physical dimensions does the fly add to the scene? Figurative dimensions?
3. Are we to assume that these lines are addressed to someone? If so, to whom? Are they the persona's thoughts?
4. What is the predominant tense of the verb forms in this poem? Has the persona died even before the first line? What word suggests movement in time?
5. How regular is Dickinson's rhyme scheme? How does her punctuation affect the rhythm of the poem?

Dirge without Music

Edna St. Vincent Millay

I am not resigned to the shutting away of loving hearts in the hard
          ground.
So it is, and so it will be, for so it has been, time out of mind:
Into the darkness they go, the wise and the lovely. Crowned
With lilies and with laurel they go; but I am not resigned.

Lovers and thinkers, into the earth with you.
Be one with the dull, the indiscriminate dust.
A fragment of what you felt, of what you knew,
A formula, a phrase remains,—but the best is lost.

The answers quick and keen, the honest look, the laughter, the
          love,
They are gone. They have gone to feed the roses. Elegant and
          curled   10
Is the blossom. Fragrant is the blossom. I know. But I do not
          approve.
More precious was the light in your eyes than all the roses in the
          world.

Down, down, down into the darkness of the grave
Gently they go, the beautiful, the tender, the kind;
Quietly they go, the intelligent, the witty, the brave.
I know. But I do not approve. And I am not resigned.

Study Questions

1. What is a *dirge?* Why is this a dirge without music? What is there to indicate that a specific death, rather than death in general, is the impetus for this dirge?
2. What is the thesis of this poem? How emphatic is it?
3. Which does the persona of this poem prefer—the physical presence of objects or symbols and memories? Does symbol in this poem ever turn to cliché?
4. Comment on the variations in Millay's sentence structure.
5. Many words in this poem are grouped in twos and threes: for example, "lilies and laurel," and "So it is, and so it will be, for so it has been. . . ." Why?

All My Pretty Ones

Anne Sexton

> All my pretty ones?
> Did you say all? O hell-kite! All?
> What! all my pretty chickens and their dam
> At one fell swoop? . . .
> I cannot but remember such things were,
> That were most precious to me.
> MACBETH

Father, this year's jinx rides us apart
where you followed our mother to her cold slumber,
a second shock boiling its stone to your heart,
leaving me here to shuffle and disencumber
you from the residence you could not afford:
a gold key, your half of a woollen mill,
twenty suits from Dunne's, an English Ford,
the love and legal verbiage of another will,
boxes of pictures of people I do not know.
I touch their carboard faces. They must go.   10

But the eyes, as thick as wood in this album,
hold me. I stop here, where a small boy
waits in a ruffled dress for someone to come . . .
for this soldier who holds his bugle like a toy
or for this velvet lady who cannot smile.
Is this your father's father, this commodore
in a mailman suit? My father, time meanwhile
has made it unimportant who you are looking for.
I'll never know what these faces are all about.
I lock them into their book and throw them out.   20

This is the yellow scrapbook that you began
the year I was born; as crackling now and wrinkly
as tobacco leaves: clippings where Hoover outran
the Democrats, wiggling his dry finger at me
and Prohibition; news where the *Hindenburg* went
down and recent years where you went flush
on war. This year, solvent but sick, you meant
to marry that pretty widow in a one-month rush.

But before you had that second chance, I cried
on your fat shoulder. Three days later you died.   30

These are the snapshots of marriage, stopped in places.
Side by side at the rail toward Nassau now;
here, with the winner's cup at the speedboat races,
here, in tails at the Cotillion, you take a bow,
here, by our kennel of dogs with their pink eyes,
running like show-bred pigs in their chain-link pen;
here, at the horseshow where my sister wins a prize;
and here, standing like a duke among groups of men.
Now I fold you down, my drunkard, my navigator,
my first lost keeper, to love or look at later.   40

I hold a five-year diary that my mother kept
for three years, telling all she does not say
of your alcoholic tendency. You overslept,
she writes. My God, father, each Christmas Day
with your blood, will I drink down your glass
of wine? The diary of your hurly-burly years
goes to my shelf to wait for my age to pass.
Only in this hoarded span will love persevere.
Whether you are pretty or not, I outlive you,
bend down my strange face to yours and forgive you.   50

Study Questions

1. What is the relevance of the epigraph from *Macbeth?* Who are the "pretty ones" of the poem? In what activity is the persona engaged?
2. The rhyme scheme of the five stanzas is identical except for one variation. Why does that variation occur?
3. How does each of the stanzas in the poem resemble a paragraph in an essay?
4. Is this poem merely an address to a dead father, or is it equally concerned with someone else? Who?

Richard Cory

Edwin Arlington Robinson

Whenever Richard Cory went down town,
We people on the pavement looked at him:
He was a gentleman from sole to crown,
Clean favored, and imperially slim.

And he was always quietly arrayed,
And he was always human when he talked;
But still he fluttered pulses when he said,
'Good-morning,' and he glittered when he walked.

And he was rich—yes, richer than a king—
And admirably schooled in every grace: 10
In fine, we thought that he was everything
To make us wish that we were in his place.

So on we worked, and waited for the light,
And went without the meat, and cursed the bread;
And Richard Cory, one calm summer night,
Went home and put a bullet through his head.

Study Questions

1. What is the theme of this poem?
2. Does the name of Robinson's titular hero have any particular significance? Is there irony in this choice of a name?
3. Richard Cory was "richer than a king." How does the poem's diction contribute to the picture of a regal man?
4. Which words carry double meanings?
5. Where and why does Robinson vary his basic rhythmical pattern?

Richard Cory

Paul Simon

They say that Richard Cory owns one half of this whole town,
With political connections to spread his wealth around.
Born into society, a banker's only child,
He had ev'rything a man could want: power, grace and style.

Chorus:
But I work in his factory
And I curse the life I'm livin'
And I curse my poverty
And I wish that I could be,
Oh, I wish that I could be,
Oh, I wish that I could be Richard Cory.   10

The papers print his picture almost ev'rywhere he goes;
Richard Cory at the op'ra, Richard Cory at a show.
And the rumor of his parties and the orgies on his yacht!
Oh, he surely must be happy with ev'rything he's got.

Chorus

He freely gave to charity, he had the common touch,
And they were grateful for his patronage and they thanked him very
          much,
So my mind was filled with wonder when the evening headlines
          read:
"Richard Cory went home last night and put a bullet through his
          head."

Chorus

Study Questions

1. Which "Richard Cory" do you think is better—Robinson's or Simon's?
2. Do you know why Cory committed suicide? How does your answer affect your reaction to that suicide?
3. How does the diction of Simon's persona help to characterize him? What kind of man is he? How much of Cory's life has he seen first-hand?
4. How does the fact that these lyrics are meant to be sung influence their content and structure?
5. Which version is more rhetorically economical?

Lady Lazarus

Sylvia Plath

I have done it again.
One year in every ten
I manage it—

A sort of walking miracle, my skin
Bright as a Nazi lampshade,
My right foot

A paperweight,
My face a featureless, fine
Jew linen.

Peel off the napkin   10
O my enemy.
Do I terrify?—

The nose, the eye pits, the full set of teeth?
The sour breath
Will vanish in a day.

Soon, soon the flesh
The grave cave ate will be
At home on me

And I a smiling woman.
I am only thirty.   20
And like the cat I have nine times to die.

This is Number Three.
What a trash
To annihilate each decade.

What a million filaments.
The peanut-crunching crowd
Shoves in to see

Them unwrap me hand and foot—
The big strip tease.
Gentlemen, ladies   30

These are my hands
My knees.
I may be skin and bone,

Nevertheless, I am the same, identical woman.
The first time it happened I was ten.
It was an accident.

The second time I meant
To last it out and not come back at all.
I rocked shut

As a seashell.   40
They had to call and call
And pick the worms off me like sticky pearls.

Dying
Is an art, like everything else.
I do it exceptionally well.

I do it so it feels like hell.
I do it so it feels real.
I guess you could say I've a call.

It's easy enough to do it in a cell.
It's easy enough to do it and stay put.   50
It's the theatrical

Comeback in broad day
To the same place, the same face, the same brute
Amused shout:

'A miracle!'
That knocks me out.
There is a charge

For the eyeing of my scars, there is a charge
For the hearing of my heart—
It really goes.   60

And there is a charge, a very large charge
For a word or a touch
Or a bit of blood

Or a piece of my hair or my clothes.
So, so, Herr Doktor.
So, Herr Enemy.

I am your opus,
I am your valuable,
The pure gold baby

That melts to a shriek.   70
I turn and burn.
Do not think I underestimate your great concern.

Ash, ash—
You poke and stir.
Flesh, bone, there is nothing there—

A cake of soap,
A wedding ring,
A gold filling.

Herr God, Herr Lucifer
Beware   80
Beware.

Out of the ash
I rise with my red hair
And I eat men like air.

Study Questions

1. Who was Lazarus? How was his experience similar to that described in this poem?
2. When do you learn, specifically, that the persona attempted suicide? How is suicide an art? A theatrical? A miracle?
3. Explain the allusions to the Nazi lampshade and rising from the ashes.
4. Does "Lady Lazarus" contain black humor?

On Saturday Afternoon

Alan Sillitoe

1   I once saw a bloke try to kill himself. I'll never forget the day because I was sitting in the house one Saturday afternoon, feeling black and fed up because everybody in the family had gone to the pictures, except me who'd for some reason been left out of it. 'Course, I didn't know then that I would soon see something you can never see in the same way on the pictures, a real bloke stringing himself up. I was only a kid at the time, so you can imagine how much I enjoyed it.

2   I've never known a family to look as black as our family when they're fed up. I've seen the old man with his face so dark and full of murder because he ain't got no fags or was having to use saccharine to sweeten his tea, or even for nothing at all, that I've backed out of the house in case he got up from his fireside chair and came for me. He just sits, almost on top of the fire, his oil-stained Sunday-joint maulers opened out in front of him and facing inwards to each other, his thick shoulders scrunched forward, and his dark brown eyes staring into the fire. Now and again he'd say a dirty word, for no reason at all, the worst word you can think of, and when he starts saying this you know it's time to clear out. If mam's in it gets worse than ever, because she says sharp to him: "What are yo' looking so bleddy black for?" as if it might be because of something she's done, and before you know what's happening he's tipped up a tableful of pots and mam's gone out of the house crying. Dad hunches back over the fire and goes on swearing. All because of a packet of fags.

3   I once saw him broodier than I'd ever seen him, so that I thought

he'd gone crackers in a quiet sort of way—until a fly flew to within a yard of him. Then his hand shot out, got it, and slung it crippled into the roaring fire. After that he cheered up a bit and mashed some tea.

4   Well, that's where the rest of us get our black looks from. It stands to reason we'd have them with a dad who carries on like that, don't it? Black looks run in the family. Some families have them and some don't. Our family has them right enough, and that's certain, so when we're fed up we're really fed up. Nobody knows why we get as fed up as we do or why it gives us these black looks when we are. Some people get fed up and don't look bad at all: they seem happy in a funny sort of way, as if they've just been set free from clink after being in there for something they didn't do, or come out of the pictures after sitting plugged for eight hours at a bad film, or just missed a bus they ran half a mile for and seen it was the wrong one just after they'd stopped running—but in our family it's murder for the others if one of us is fed up. I've asked myself lots of times what it is, but I can never get any sort of answer even if I sit and think for hours, which I must admit I don't do, though it looks good when I say I do. But I sit and think for long enough, until mam says to me, at seeing me scrunched up over the fire like dad: "What are yo' looking so black for?" So I've just got to stop thinking about it in case I get really black and fed up and go the same way as dad, tipping up a tableful of pots and all.

5   Mostly I suppose there's nothing to look so black for: though it's nobody's fault and you can't blame anyone for looking black because I'm sure it's summat in the blood. But on this Saturday afternoon I was looking so black that when dad came in from the bookie's he said to me: "What's up wi' yo'?"

6   "I feel badly," I fibbed. He'd have had a fit if I'd said I was only black because I hadn't gone to the pictures.

7   "Well have a wash," he told me.

8   "I don't want a wash," I said, and that was a fact.

9   "Well, get outside and get some fresh air then," he shouted.

10   I did as I was told, double quick, because if ever dad goes as far as to tell me to get some fresh air I know it's time to get away from him. But outside the air wasn't so fresh, what with that bloody great bike factory bashing away at the yard-end. I didn't know where to go, so I walked up the yard a bit and sat down near somebody's back gate.

11   Then I saw this bloke who hadn't lived long in our yard. He was tall and thin and had a face like a parson except that he wore a flat cap and had a mustache that drooped, and looked as though he hadn't had a square meal for a year. I didn't think much o' this at the time: but I remember that as he turned in by the yard-end one of the nosy gossiping women who stood there every minute of the day except when she trudged to the pawnshop with her husband's bike or best suit, shouted to him: "What's that rope for, mate?"

12   He called back: "It's to 'ang messen wi', missis," and she cackled at

his bloody good joke so loud and long you'd think she never heard such a good 'un, though the next day she cackled on the other side of her fat face.

13   He walked by me puffing a fag and carrying his coil of brand-new rope, and he had to step over me to get past. His boot nearly took my shoulder off, and when I told him to watch where he was going I don't think he heard me because he didn't even look round. Hardly anybody was about. All the kids were still at the pictures, and most of their mams and dads were downtown doing the shopping.

14   The bloke walked down the yard to his back door, and having nothing better to do because I hadn't gone to the pictures I followed him. You see, he left his back door open a bit, so I gave it a push and went in. I stood there, just watching him, sucking my thumb, the other hand in my pocket. I suppose he knew I was there, because his eyes were moving more natural now, but he didn't seem to mind. "What are yer going to do wi' that rope, mate?" I asked him.

15   "I'm going ter 'ang messen, lad," he told me, as though he'd done it a time or two already, and people had usually asked him questions like this beforehand.

16   "What for, mate?" He must have thought I was a nosy young bogger.

17   "'Cause I want to, that's what for," he said, clearing all the pots off the table and pulling it to the middle of the room. Then he stood on it to fasten the rope to the light fitting. The table creaked and didn't look very safe, but it did him for what he wanted.

18   "It wain't hold up, mate," I said to him, thinking how much better it was being here than sitting in the pictures and seeing the Jungle Jim serial.

19   But he got nettled now and turned on me. "Mind yer own business."

20   I thought he was going to tell me to scram, but he didn't. He made ever such a fancy knot with that rope, as though he'd been a sailor or summat, and as he tied it he was whistling a fancy tune to himself. Then he got down from the table and pushed it back to the wall, and put a chair in its place. He wasn't looking black at all, nowhere near as black as anybody in our family when they're feeling fed up. If ever he'd looked only half as black as our dad looked twice a week he'd have hanged himself years ago, I couldn't help thinking. But he was making a good job of that rope all right, as though he'd thought about it a lot anyway, and as though it was going to be the last thing he'd ever do. But I knew something he didn't know, because he wasn't standing where I was, I knew the rope wouldn't hold up, and I told him so, again.

21   "Shut yer gob," he said, but quiet-like, "or I'll kick yer out."

22   I didn't want to miss it, so I said nothing. He took his cap off and put it on the dresser, then he took his coat off, and his scarf, and spread them out on the sofa. I wasn't a bit frightened, like I might be now at sixteen,

because it was interesting. And being only ten I'd never had a chance to see a bloke hang himself before. We got pally, the two of us, before he slipped the rope around his neck.

23   "Shut the door," he asked me, and I did as I was told. "Ye're a good lad for your age," he said to me while I sucked my thumb, and he felt in his pockets and pulled out all that was inside, throwing the handful of bits and bobs on the table: fag-packet and peppermints, a pawn ticket, an old comb, and a few coppers. He picked out a penny and gave it to me, saying: "Now listen ter me, young 'un. I'm going to 'ang messen, and when I'm swinging I want you to gi' this chair a bloody good kick and push it away. All right?"

24   I nodded.

25   He put the rope around his neck, and then took it off like it was a tie that didn't fit. "What are yer going to do it for, mate?" I asked again.

26   "Because I'm fed up," he said, looking very unhappy. "And because I want to. My missus left me, and I'm out o' work."

27   I didn't want to argue, because the way he said it, I knew he couldn't do anything else except hang himself. Also there was a funny look in his face: even when he talked to me I swear he couldn't see me. It was different to the black looks my old man puts on, and I suppose that's why my old man would never hang himself, worse luck, because he never gets a look into his clock like this bloke had. My old man's look stares *at* you, so that you have to back down and fly out of the house: this bloke's look looked *through* you, so that you could face it and know it wouldn't do you any harm. So I saw now that dad would never hang himself because he could never get the right sort of look into his face, in spite of the fact that he'd been out of work often enough. Maybe mam would have to leave him first, and then he might do it; but no—I shook my head—there wasn't much chance of that even though he did lead her a dog's life.

28   "Yer wain't forget to kick that chair away?" he reminded me, and I swung my head to say I wouldn't. So my eyes were popping and I watched every move he made. He stood on the chair and put the rope around his neck so that it fitted this time, still whistling his fancy tune. I wanted to get a better goz at the knot, because my pal was in the scouts, and would ask to know how it was done, and if I told him later he'd let me know what happened at the pictures in the Jungle Jim serial, so's I could have my cake and eat it as well, as mam says, tit for tat. But I thought I'd better not ask the bloke to tell me, and I stayed back in my corner. The last thing he did was take the wet dirty butt end from his lips and sling it into the empty firegrate, following it with his eyes to the black fireback where it landed—as if he was then going to mend a fault in the lighting like any electrician.

29   Suddenly his long legs wriggled and his feet tried to kick the chair, so I helped him as I'd promised I would and took a runner at it as if I was playing center forward for Notts Forest, and the chair went scooting back

against the sofa, dragging his muffler to the floor as it tipped over. He swung for a bit, his arms chafing like he was a scarecrow flapping birds away, and he made a noise in his throat as if he'd just took a dose of salts and was trying to make them stay down.

30   Then there was another sound, and I looked up and saw a big crack come in the ceiling, like you see on the pictures when an earthquake's happening, and the bulb began circling round and round as though it was a space ship. I was just beginning to get dizzy when, thank Christ, he fell down with such a horrible thump on the floor that I thought he'd broke every bone he'd got. He kicked around for a bit, like a dog that's got colic bad. Then he lay still.

31   I didn't stay to look at him. "I told him that rope wouldn't hold up," I kept saying to myself as I went out of the house, tut-tutting because he hadn't done the job right, hands stuffed deep into my pockets and nearly crying at the balls-up he'd made of everything. I slammed his gate so hard with disappointment that it nearly dropped off its hinges.

32   Just as I was going back up the yard to get my tea at home, hoping the others had come back from the pictures so's I wouldn't have anything to keep on being black about, a copper passed me and headed for the bloke's door. He was striding quickly with his head bent forward, and I knew that somebody had narked. They must have seen him buy the rope and then tipped off the cop. Or happen the old hen at the yard-end had finally caught on. Or perhaps he'd even told somebody himself, because I supposed that the bloke who'd strung himself up hadn't much known what he was doing, especially with the look I'd seen in his eyes. But that's how it is, I said to myself, as I followed the copper back to the bloke's house, a poor bloke can't even hang himself these days.

33   When I got back the copper was slitting the rope from his neck with a penknife, then he gave him a drink of water, and the bloke opened his peepers. I didn't like the copper, because he'd got a couple of my mates sent to approved school for pinching lead piping from lavatories.

34   "What did you want to hang yourself for?" he asked the bloke, trying to make him sit up. He could hardly talk, and one of his hands was bleeding from where the light bulb had smashed. I knew that rope wouldn't hold up, but he hadn't listened to me. I'll never hang myself anyway, but if I want to I'll make sure I do it from a tree or something like that, not a light fitting. "Well, what did you do it for?"

35   "Because I wanted to," the bloke croaked.

36   "You'll get five years for this," the copper told him. I'd crept back into the house and was sucking my thumb in the same corner.

37   "That's what yo' think," the bloke said, a normal frightened look in his eyes now. "I only wanted to hang myself."

38   "Well," the copper said, taking out his book, "it's against the law, you know."

39   "Nay," the bloke said, "it can't be. It's my life, ain't it?"

40   "You might think so," the copper said, "but it ain't."

41   He began to suck the blood from his hand. It was such a little scratch though that you couldn't see it. "That's the first thing I knew," he said.

42   "Well I'm telling you," the copper told him.

43   'Course, I didn't let on to the copper that I'd helped the bloke to hang himself. I wasn't born yesterday, nor the day before yesterday either.

44   "It's a fine thing if a bloke can't tek his own life," the bloke said, seeing he was in for it.

45   "Well he can't," the copper said, as if reading out of his book and enjoying it. "It ain't your life. And it's a crime to take your own life. It's killing yourself. It's suicide."

46   The bloke looked hard, as if every one of the copper's words meant six months cold. I felt sorry for him, and that's a fact, but if only he'd listened to what I'd said and not depended on that light fitting. He should have done it from a tree, or something like that.

47   He went up the yard with the copper like a peaceful lamb, and we all thought that that was the end of that.

48   But a couple of days later the news was flashed through to us—even before it got to the *Post* because a woman in our yard worked at the hospital of an evening dishing grub out and tidying up. I heard her spilling it to somebody at the yard-end. "I'd never 'ave thought it. I thought he'd got that daft idea out of his head when they took him away. But no. Wonders'll never cease. Chucked 'issen from the hospital window when the copper who sat near his bed went off for a pee. Would you believe it? Dead? Not much 'e ain't."

49   He'd heaved himself at the glass, and fallen like a stone on to the road. In one way I was sorry he'd done it, but in another I was glad, because he'd proved to the coppers and everybody whether it was his life or not all right. It was marvellous though, the way the brainless bastards had put him in a ward six floors up, which finished him off, proper, even better than a tree.

50   All of which will make me think twice about how black I sometimes feel. The black coal bag locked inside you, and the black look it puts on your face, doesn't mean you're going to string yourself up or sling yourself under a double-decker or chuck yourself out of a window or cut your throat with a sardine tin or put your head in the gas oven or drop your rotten sack-bag of a body on to a railway line, because when you're feeling that black you can't even move from your chair. Anyhow, I know I'll never get so black as to hang myself, because hanging don't look very nice to me, and never will, the more I remember old what's-his-name swinging from the light fitting.

51   More than anything else, I'm glad now I didn't go to the pictures that Saturday afternoon when I was feeling black and ready to do myself in. Because you know, I shan't ever kill myself. Trust me. I'll stay alive half barmy till I'm a hundred and five, and then go out screaming blue murder because I want to stay where I am.

Study Questions

1. What moral issue does "On Saturday Afternoon" raise?
2. Explain the contrast between "black" and "blue" in the story.
3. What elements in Sillitoe's story contribute to its matter-of-fact tone?
4. What does the boy feel that the attempted suicide and its aftermath have taught him? Is he being funny? Is there black humor in "On Saturday Afternoon"?
5. Are there any words or expressions that you don't understand? Are these words merely common in British usage or are they dialect as well? How does his language help characterize the boy?

Departmental

Robert Frost

An ant on the tablecloth
Ran into a dormant moth
Of many times his size.
He showed not the least surprise.
His business wasn't with such.
He gave it scarcely a touch,
And was off on his duty run.
Yet if he encountered one
Of the hive's enquiry squad
Whose work is to find out God   10
And the nature of time and space,
He would put him onto the case.
Ants are a curious race;
One crossing with hurried tread
The body of one of their dead
Isn't given a moment's arrest—
Seems not even impressed.
But he no doubt reports to any
With whom he crosses antennae,
And they no doubt report   20
To the higher-up at court.

Then word goes forth in Formic:
"Death's come to Jerry McCormic,
Our selfless forager Jerry.
Will the special Janizary
Whose office it is to bury
The dead of the commissary
Go bring him home to his people.
Lay him in state on a sepal.
Wrap him for shroud in a petal.   30
Embalm him with ichor of nettle.
This is the word of your Queen."
And presently on the scene
Appears a solemn mortician;
And taking formal position
With feelers calmly atwiddle,
Seizes the dead by the middle,
And heaving him high in air,
Carries him out of there.
No one stands round to stare.   40
It is nobody else's affair.

It couldn't be called ungentle.
But how thoroughly departmental.

Study Questions

1. What effect might you expect from an unrelieved series of couplets such as Frost uses here? How does the punctuation in "Departmental" prevent your worst expectations from being realized?
2. What are the connotations of *departmental* as it is used here? Are the ants in their attitude toward death callous or realistic?
3. Clearly this poem is humorous, but the humor derives from something other than the situation. From what then?
4. Comment on the diction of this poem as it relates to the subject.
5. How do you suppose Frost came up with Jerry McCormic for the name of the dead ant?

The Menace of P.O.

Jessica Mitford

WISCONSIN FLORISTS, MORTICIANS COOPERATE TO FIGHT P.O.
—Headline in *Florists' Review*, June 1, 1961

1   What is P.O.? Your best friend won't tell you, because he won't know. It has nothing to do with perspiration and it does not stand for Petal Odor. It stands for the words "Please Omit," as in Please Omit Flowers, which is in turn a phrase people sometimes wish to have inserted in the newspaper notice of a funeral.

2   P.O. is denounced as a Menace, a Peril, a Threat, a Problem and sometimes even a Specter in florists' trade journals, perhaps because 65 to 70 per cent* of the flower industry's revenue, or $414 million a year, derives from the sale of funeral flowers. This comes to a nationwide *average* of over $246 for flowers per funeral. It sounds like an incredibly high figure; yet the florists themselves give it, and funeral directors have told me that it does not sound out of line to them. After all, if an ordinary citizen dies, his foreman, his union, some of his co-workers will likely send flowers, and so will his relatives and perhaps a few neighbors; and these offerings may cost from $10 up. If he was a sociable fellow, a churchgoer or a clubman, he will get proportionately more flowers from his cronies; and if he was a person of any prominence in the community, he will be deluged. This will all be in addition to the casket spray, "scarf" or blanket, etc., that his widow has purchased for anywhere from $25 to $250.

3   The funeral director sometimes gets rather fed up with all these flowers. To him falls the task of their care and supervision: receiving them, arranging them in the slumber room, setting them on racks in the funeral chapel, compiling a list of those who sent them, and eventually carting them off and disposing of them. There is little or no profit in this for him, for he is not supposed to receive a kickback from the florist, and in some states he is barred by law from owning his own flower shop.

4   A writer in *Canadian Funeral Service* comments: "I believe the funeral profession provides the largest single outlet for retail sales they [the florists] have, bar none. Yet it is the funeral director who hears all the remarks about 'paganism,' 'lavishness' and the like. I don't know any

---

* 65% figure: "Sympathy flowers were estimated at 65% of all flower orders." *Florists' Review*, May 12, 1960. 70% figure: *Casket and Sunnyside*, June, 1961.

other situation where one business displays the products of another the way we are expected to do . . . receiving rooms for flowers . . . photos . . . attendant to set them up . . . $1,000 in stands, etc.—just to accommodate someone else's product. And you should hear them scream if they come in and find the flowers not too well set up. . . ."

5   Besides the chores involved, there are other disadvantages: the florist, betting on the fact that the bereaved family will hardly glance at the flowers, may send some very moribund specimens to the funeral. This practice has often been commented on by funeralgoers, and is evidently widespread enough to call for some criticism within the flower industry: "The greatest fault of some florists is that of selling wilted, old blooms in funeral pieces, because they feel that they will not be noticed or returned. Yet these unethical florists are often loudest in asking florists organizations to assist them in preventing Please Omit Flowers notices." These unethical florists are a problem for the funeral director since their festering flowers can hardly fail to detract from the Beautiful Memory Picture which he has worked so hard to create.

6   Equally distressing is the possibility that the widow might decide on a full floral blanket. This, from the undertaker's point of view, is as bad as the traditional funeral pall required by some churches, for it hides the lovely casket completely, and at the very moment when there is a maximum audience on hand to drink in its beauty and note its enduring qualities.

7   These minor irritations between funeral directors and florists have begun to fade in the face of a common danger, the Menace of P.O. The custodians of the fragile spring bloom, the tenders of the lily of the valley, the summer rose, the winter snowdrop, can be most bellicose on the subject of P.O. The anti-P.O. campaign is most often discussed in military terms: "combatting current attacks," "deploying our forces in the field," "massive breakthrough," "crusade," etc. It gets more than a little bloodthirsty; *Business Week*, commenting on a 1954 business slump in flowers, reported, "The wholesaler who found business 'lousy' gave as his unhesitating explanation, 'Nobody's dying.' The slowed-up death rate makes a big difference to an industry that gets nearly 85 per cent of its $1.25 billion retail business from funerals and weddings. Worse still, funeral notices in the newspapers increasingly carry the message, 'Please Omit Flowers.'"

8   The funeral directors are key allies in the blitzkrieg against P.O. because they control the wording of obituary notices; according to a florists' survey, 92 per cent of the death notices published in newspapers are given to the papers by funeral directors. Florists spend a good deal of time and money cementing the alliance by speaking at conclaves of funeral directors, advertising in their journals, and contributing articles to the funeral trade press. There is a certain amount of buttering up, as in an article addressed to funeral directors by the President of the Florists' Telegraph Delivery Association: "Your highest duty is creation. It is

surely a function that is guided by the Great Creator, for in your hands has been placed the responsibility of creating a living Memory Picture." He warns of a common danger: "the attitude in some places that the present high standards of funeral service are unnecessary. Being close to the funeral directors in their daily work, F.T.D. florists feel that this attitude is dangerous and strikes at the very roots of our civilization." He lists "11 Ways To Meet 'Please Omit' Trend," the first way being "Say they may unthinkably offend sincere friends."

9   An appeal for the formation of a common front against the foe is contained in a full-page advertisement sponsored by F.T.D. which appears regularly (possibly, to some constant readers like myself, monotonously) in the pages of a number of funeral and cemetery trade magazines. It marshals the arguments to be used against P.O. and contains the hint of a threat of what can happen to the funeral director himself should he prove to be a deserter from the cause. An illustration designed to strike fear in the heart of a funeral director shows a completely bare chapel—pews, but no mourners; casket bier but no casket; flower vases but no flowers. The text:

PLEASE OMIT . . . WHAT?

10   What will they want to omit next? Ministers? Music? All but the plainest caskets? When does a funeral service stop comforting the bereaved—and become merely the mechanical fulfillment of an obligation? Once you start subtracting warmth and human feeling, where do you end—and what do you have left?

11   *Think it over.*

12   And the next time a client asks you about "Please Omit," remember that you and your florist friends serve the bereaved best by understanding their needs better, perhaps, than they may do themselves.

13   Your experience, your common sense and any good psychologist will tell you that most grieving people should have the extra warmth and comfort of living flowers. At an emotional moment, 'please omit' may seem like a simple solution to a torturing problem. It does not and cannot, however, serve the memory through the years.

14   That's why you're so right to recommend sympathy flowers and a full funeral service. They pay tribute to the life accomplishment of the deceased, and bring comfort to the bereaved when they need it most.

15   This solicitous concern for the psychological well-being of the bereaved family is considered a winning card by florists. "Softness comes back to her face as sorrow begins to slip away" is the caption for a picture of a young widow receiving some chrysanthemums; and the text continues, "Psychologists agree that funeral flowers comfort as almost nothing else can. . . . So you're on firm psychological ground when you recommend flowers." What psychologists? Psychologists like the proprietor of the Drive-In Floral Mart, who in a lecture to students at the Indiana College of Mortuary Science "stressed the importance of floral

tributes in the therapy of grief for the mourners and in providing an outlet for the expressions of sympathy for friends of the deceased."

16   Spokesmen for the florists also express great solicitude for family friends who may be caused to suffer embarrassment by the publication of a Please Omit request. Such notices, they warn, may even rupture lifelong friendships; but an alert funeral director can help to prevent these dread consequences. Mr. Cecil Brown, Society of American Florists public relations representative, suggested an approach to the problem in a talk on "Sense in Sentiment": "The best place to combat this trend is in the counseling room. There the family places its faith in the funeral director, counting on his experience to arrange the funeral with dignity and good taste and in a way that creates a beautiful memory picture. Flowers, of course, are an integral part of this. When a client suggests omitting them, it is the duty of the funeral director to alert him to some of the unpleasantness which can follow in the wake of a 'Please Omit' notice. . . . The end result may well be a deterioration of relations between friends, who object to capitalizing on death in order to raise funds for charity. . . . A further unpleasant aspect is the embarrassment of friends who heed the admonition to omit flowers, only to find that others have not."

17   Not only are the mental health of the bereaved family, the peace of mind of their friends, and relations between family and friends all imperiled by the Please Omit notice—the very foundation of our country is at stake. As Mr. Brown went on to say, "It is to the benefit of all funeral directors to cooperate with florists in eliminating P.O., in order to preserve the sentiment now attached to funeral customs. Sentiment is one of the foundations upon which we have built our country, and history shows what happens when countries abandon it. It is our responsibility to preserve sentiment in order to protect our traditional American burial customs. Once they are gone, they can never be replaced."

18   The flower industry, shouldering this weighty responsibility to homeland and tradition for some three decades, has recorded some spectacular victories. True, in the early years of the fight against P.O., methods were a little crude, and sometimes brought down unseemly ridicule on the campaigners. *The New Yorker* reprinted an anti-P.O. letter from a florist to the St. Louis *Post-Dispatch* as an end-of-column filler under the heading O DEATH, WHERE IS THY ADVERTISING APPROPRIATION?:

19   We wish to express an objection to the reporting of an article concerning the death of ——— as it appeared in a recent issue of your paper.

20   At the close of this article you reported, "The family has asked that flowers be omitted and any tribute be given to the Red Cross or to the Mary Endowment Fund." We feel it is not clean business or necessary in reporting a situation, for one business to express the opinion that another business can afford to be penalized in the light of charity. We do not believe in

doing a good job of reporting it was necessary to include this paragraph, and the omission of this request would not have changed your ability of reporting his passing.

21   As a member of the Allied Florists of St. Louis publicity committee, I know the *Post-Dispatch* has a generous share of our advertising funds, and the encouragement by your paper to "kindly omit flowers" can hasten the day when the funds available for advertising can be so restricted that the newspapers of this community can lose that source of revenue they have been receiving.

22   It is not of my mind to question the wishes of any person or family. I naturally am puzzled as to why we florists have been selected as a business which can afford to do without a portion of their business at the expense of charity. I have yet to see a newspaper article or a paid obituary notice suggesting the omission of candy, liquor, cosmetics or tobacco, with funds to be forwarded to charity. It is only in the light of what I consider good business that I draw this to your attention. D. S. Geddes, Jr.

23   The point made about advertising funds and good business was perhaps too starkly stated, and was perhaps a little too revealing. Clearly, a subtler approach, and one less likely to make the pages of humor magazines, was needed. A campaign was launched in the late fifties, backed by a $2-million-a-year advertising budget, to erase P.O. forever from the public prints. It is described by Marc Williams in *Flowers-by-Wire, The Story of The Florists' Telegraph Delivery Association:* "Before the end of 1957, Sales and Advertising conducted a national survey on the 'Please Omit' problem, which covered all the newspapers, radio and television stations in the United States. . . . Between 75 per cent and 85 per cent of the country's newspapers accepted such obituary notices." Armed with this information, the Florists' Information Council "was able to send its field men into the affected areas, to hold meetings with the advertising departments of the papers and also with the funeral directors to arrive at a solution."

24   The field men in their sorties into the affected areas wielded both clubs and carrots, the latter consisting of "a series of 85-line ads on the obituary pages of 70 newspapers . . . for obvious reasons, *The American Funeral Director* was listed for six insertions." Success was almost instantaneous: by 1959, the executive secretary of the Society of American Florists was able to report that "because of Florists' Telegraph Delivery's financial aid, 241 cities had been visited by field men and 199 newspapers had agreed to refrain from using 'Please Omit' phrases."

25   This was followed up by another survey, results of which were reported to industry leaders in November, 1960, in a two-day session held "to give the committee members and guests ample time to scrutinize the many 'Please Omit' problem areas in which the Florists' Information Council is working." F.I.C.'s public relations representatives had called on 151 newspaper executives between July 1, 1959 and

June 30, 1960 to discuss policies regarding obituary notices. "The survey also revealed which newspapers are keeping their word as to policy on flowers," the report says darkly, information essential to the continuing success of the campaign because editors of delinquent papers can often be brought back into line with a "return call" from the field men.

26   The San Francisco papers, I had observed, never use "Please omit flowers" or "In lieu of flowers" in funeral notices, although they do publish requests for donations to worthy causes, usually in the words "Memorial contributions to the ——— fund preferred." I was curious to know how the advertising department of a newspaper that has given its word to the florists would handle a request from an individual to print the forbidden phrase in a death notice.

27   I telephoned one of the large San Francisco dailies, and was connected with Miss Black. ("Miss Black" is, I learned, a fictitious name assigned to the employee who handles this department; I was struck with the passing thought that, to be up with the times in the changing funereal color scheme, the newspaper might consider changing her name to Miss Honey Beige, or Miss Peach Pink.) I explained to Miss Black that I was telephoning on behalf of a friend whose mother had just died and who had asked me to arrange for newspaper notices of the funeral. She briskly told me that the proper person to take care of the notice is the funeral director. "There is no funeral director," I answered. "My friend's mother was cremated, and there will be a memorial service." Miss Black said she could not accept the notice from anybody other than a funeral director; I said I bet she could, and in this case she would have to. Miss Black excused herself to go and consult her supervisor. She returned to the phone several minutes later to report that the supervisor said the notice could be accepted in this case, subject only to later confirmation of the death by the crematorium, a routine precaution against practical jokers.

28   Now we got to the point. "The notice is to read 'Please omit flowers,'" I said.

29   "Well, we never put it that way. How about 'Memorial Contributions Preferred,' or 'Memorial gifts . . .'"? suggested Miss Black.

30   "No, I don't think that will do. The family wouldn't like to ask for charitable contributions on an occasion like this. Besides, my friend's mother left exact instructions in her will about the wording of the notice, and she specified that it should say, 'Please omit flowers.'"

31   Sounds of Miss Black being in deep water. "I'm sorry, ma'am, that would be against our policy. We are not allowed to accept ads that are derogatory about anyone, or about any*thing*."

32   "But this isn't derogatory about anyone."

33   "It's derogatory about flowers."

34   "There is nothing unkind about flowers in that notice. As a matter of fact, my friend's mother adored flowers. She just doesn't want them cluttering up her funeral, that's all."

35   Miss Black was firm; she spoke about newspaper policy, she said she had her instructions. I was firm; I spoke about freedom of the press and the rights of the individual, but to no avail. Later, I telephoned the head of the department; he was firm, too. "We couldn't publish a notice like that," he said. "Why, the florists would be right on our necks!"

36   I called the other newspapers in the area, and got the same reaction.

37   While major accomplishments are being chalked up, there are nevertheless occasional setbacks. When President Eisenhower's mother-in-law died in September, 1960, the only funeral flowers were a white carnation cross sent by the President and one spray from members of the immediate family. The Washington *Post* carried this announcement: "The President and Mrs. Eisenhower requested that no flowers be sent and that contributions to charities be made instead." (For some reason *The New York Times* did not, in its story, see fit to print this portion of the President's statement.)* The florists were stung to the quick. Association executives rushed into action to get newspapers, television and radio stations to suppress the President's request. The *Florists' Review* says, "This was most important because many newspapers and TV and radio stations have already set their policy to not include 'In lieu of flowers' requests in their obituary notices. It was felt that such policies should be called to their attention. . . . The Society of American Florists is still doing everything within its power to remedy the dangerous effects which the President's unintentional bombshell exploded within the industry." Gratitude was expressed "to all industry members who immediately took action to support the florists' industry at this critical time." But efforts to obtain a retraction from the White House were in vain, and in fact brought down criticism from that arbiter of good taste, *Mortuary Management:* "Sending a wire to the White House over a matter that could have rank commercial overtones was, in our opinion, very bad taste. A breach of good manners will be remembered long after the public has forgotten this one 'Please Omit' notice."

38   On the whole, though, continued vigilance pays off. The least hint that a criticism of overspending on funeral flowers may be publicly voiced brings squadrons of florists' field men on the double to the affected area. Fortunately for the occasional library browser, they sometimes allow themselves to boast in print about the results of their successful forays into potentially hostile territory. Thus the *Florists' Review:*

39   It is a rare occurrence when florists can be grateful that funeral flowers are omitted. But such was the case when an article titled 'Can You Afford to Die?' appeared in the June 17 (1961) issue of the *Saturday*

---

* However, the *Times* is among the major newspapers that are holding out and that will accept "Please Omit" notices. Among others are the New York *Herald Tribune* and the Washington *Post.*

Evening Post, a popular consumer magazine with a circulation running into the millions. . . .

40   The important point here is that this omission of funeral flowers did not just happen. Derogatory references to flowers did not appear in the article because of intensive behind-the-scenes efforts of the Florists' Information Committee of the Society of American Florists. By working closely with the magazine's advertising department, the F.I.C. successfully headed off statements which would have been extremely damaging to the industry.

41   The article goes on, rather unkindly, to report that in spite of the fact that the florists' committee had tried its best to include Howard C. Raether, executive secretary of the National Funeral Directors Association, in the behind-the-scenes meetings, the latter was unsuccessful:

42   Despite all his efforts, the magazine went ahead with its original plans and refused to eliminate the article or to make changes suggested by him.

43   There is a moral to it all:

44   The article definitely illustrates a point that florists have been bringing to the attention of funeral directors—that the P.O. problem can easily spread from flowers to the services offered by funeral directors.

45   This war of the roses, like its earlier counterpart, was more than a little embellished in the telling. Having been the lucky recipient of a manuscript copy of the beleaguered *Saturday Evening Post* article, I checked this against the published version, and found but three deletions:

46   1) "Not long ago the flowers in the bill of one far from wealthy man in Washington. D.C. came to $1,000 alone. . . ."

47   2) "Furthermore they [ministers] urged that flowers on such occasions be kept to a minimum and that friends express their sympathy by gifts to favorite causes that benefit the whole community. . . ."

48   3) "'We wanted a few flowers but not the elaborate set pieces which were impossible to give away to hospitals after the ceremony.' . . ."

49   Just how the florists engineered these clever little changes remains a mystery. The editor of the *Post* told me he was completely flabbergasted by the article in *Florists' Review*, and had turned the magazine upside down to find out what happened. He added that during his seven years at the *Post* he had never heard of anything happening to an article which remotely resembled the tampering indicated by the florists.

Study Questions

1. How can you tell that this article is well researched despite the absence of traditional footnotes?
2. Speculate on the evidence that provided the material for paragraph 3.
3. Is it clear that Mitford has an opinion on her topic here? Does she maintain her objectivity? What is the tone of her discussion?

When I Consider How My Light Is Spent

John Milton

When I consider how my light is spent,
    Ere half my days, in this dark world and wide,
    And that one talent which is death to hide
    Lodged with me useless, though my soul more bent
To serve therewith my Maker, and present
    My true account, lest he returning chide,
    "Doth God exact day-labor, light denied?"
    I fondly ask. But Patience, to prevent
That murmur, soon replies: "God doth not need
    Either man's work or his own gifts; who best   10
    Bear his mild yoke, they serve him best. His state
Is kingly: thousands at his bidding speed,
    And post o'er land and ocean without rest;
    They also serve who only stand and wait."

Study Questions

1. An *ellipsis* occurs in a sentence when a word that would normally be present in the sentence is left out. In the first sentence of this poem there are several ellipses. Is the sentence more easily understood when the missing words are supplied? Why would the poet create ellipses in his sentences?
2. What tone does the verb *consider* establish? Is this tone maintained throughout the poem?
3. What two meanings for the adjective *spent* in line 1 are relevant?
4. In line 8 the poet personifies Patience. Is this personification effective?
5. Who is the poet's audience? Of what is he attempting to persuade his audience? Explain the form of his argument.

Young Goodman Brown

Nathaniel Hawthorne

1   Young Goodman Brown came forth at sunset into the street at Salem village; but put his head back, after crossing the threshold, to exchange a parting kiss with his young wife. And Faith, as the wife was aptly named, thrust her own pretty head into the street, letting the wind play with the pink ribbons of her cap while she called to Goodman Brown.

2   "Dearest heart," whispered she, softly and rather sadly, when her lips were close to his ear, "prithee put off your journey until sunrise and sleep in your own bed to-night. A lone woman is troubled with such dreams and such thoughts that she's afeared of herself sometimes. Pray tarry with me this night, dear husband, of all nights in the year."

3   "My love and my Faith," replied young Goodman Brown, "of all nights in the year, this one night must I tarry away from thee. My journey, as thou callest it, forth and back again, must needs be done 'twixt now and sunrise. What, my sweet, pretty wife, dost thou doubt me already, and we but three months married?"

4   "Then God bless you!" said Faith, with the pink ribbons; "and may you find all well when you come back."

5   "Amen!" cried Goodman Brown. "Say thy prayers, dear Faith, and go to bed at dusk, and no harm will come to thee."

6   So they parted; and the young man pursued his way until, being about to turn the corner by the meeting-house, he looked back and saw the head of Faith still peeping after him with a melancholy air, in spite of her pink ribbons.

7   "Poor little Faith!" thought he, for his heart smote him. "What a wretch am I to leave her on such an errand! She talks of dreams, too. Methought as she spoke there was trouble in her face, as if a dream had warned her what work is to be done to-night. But no, no; 'twould kill her to think it. Well, she's a blessed angel on earth; and after this one night I'll cling to her skirts and follow her to heaven."

8   With this excellent resolve for the future, Goodman Brown felt himself justified in making more haste on his present evil purpose. He had taken a dreary road, darkened by all the gloomiest trees of the forest, which barely stood aside to let the narrow path creep through, and closed immediately behind. It was all as lonely as could be; and there is this peculiarity in such a solitude, that the traveller knows not who may be concealed by the innumerable trunks and the thick boughs overhead; so that with lonely footsteps he may yet be passing through an unseen multitude.

9   "There may be a devilish Indian behind every tree," said Goodman Brown to himself; and he glanced fearfully behind him as he added, "What if the devil himself should be at my very elbow!"

10   His head being turned back, he passed a crook of the road, and, looking forward again, beheld the figure of a man, in grave and decent attire, seated at the foot of an old tree. He arose at Goodman Brown's approach and walked onward side by side with him.

11   "You are late, Goodman Brown," said he. "The clock of the Old South was striking as I came through Boston, and that is full fifteen minutes agone."

12   "Faith kept me back a while," replied the young man, with a tremor in his voice, caused by the sudden appearance of his companion, though not wholly unexpected.

13   It was now deep dusk in the forest, and deepest in that part of it where these two were journeying. As nearly as could be discerned, the second traveller was about fifty years old, apparently in the same rank of life as Goodman Brown, and bearing a considerable resemblance to him, though perhaps more in expression than features. Still they might have been taken for father and son. And yet, though the elder person was as simply clad as the younger, and as simple in manner too, he had an indescribable air of one who knew the world, and who would not have felt abashed at the governor's dinner table or in King William's court, were it possible that his affairs should call him thither. But the only thing about him that could be fixed upon as remarkable was his staff, which bore the likeness of a great black snake, so curiously wrought that it

might almost be seen to twist and wriggle itself like a living serpent. This, of course, must have been an ocular deception, assisted by the uncertain light.

14   "Come, Goodman Brown," cried his fellow-traveller, "this is a dull pace for the beginning of a journey. Take my staff, if you are so soon weary."

15   "Friend," said the other, exchanging his slow pace for a full stop, "having kept covenant by meeting thee here, it is my purpose now to return whence I came. I have scruples touching the matter thou wot'st of."

16   "Sayest thou so?" replied he of the serpent, smiling apart. "Let us walk on, nevertheless, reasoning as we go; and if I convince thee not thou shalt turn back. We are but a little way in the forest yet."

17   "Too far! too far!" exclaimed the goodman, unconsciously resuming his walk. "My father never went into the woods on such an errand, nor his father before him. We have been a race of honest men and good Christians since the days of the martyrs; and shall I be the first of the name of Brown that ever took this path and kept"—

18   "Such company, thou wouldst say," observed the elder person, interpreting his pause. "Well said, Goodman Brown! I have been as well acquainted with your family as with ever a one among the Puritans; and that's no trifle to say. I helped your grandfather, the constable, when he lashed the Quaker woman so smartly through the streets of Salem; and it was I that brought your father a pitch-pine knot, kindled at my own hearth, to set fire to an Indian village, in King Philip's war. They were my good friends, both; and many a pleasant walk have we had along this path, and returned merrily after midnight. I would fain be friends with you for their sake."

19   "If it be as thou sayest," replied Goodman Brown, "I marvel they never spoke of these matters; or, verily, I marvel not, seeing that the least rumor of the sort would have driven them from New England. We are a people of prayer, and good works to boot, and abide no such wicked-ness."

20   "Wickedness or not," said the traveller with the twisted staff, "I have a very general acquaintance here in New England. The deacons of many a church have drunk the communion wine with me; the selectmen of divers towns make me their chairman; and a majority of the Great and General Court are firm supporters of my interest. The governor and I, too—But these are state secrets."

21   "Can this be so?" cried Goodman Brown, with a stare of amazement at his undisturbed companion. "Howbeit, I have nothing to do with the governor and council; they have their own ways, and are no rule for a simple husbandman like me. But, were I to go on with thee, how should I meet the eye of that good old man, our minister, at Salem village? Oh, his voice would make me tremble both Sabbath day and lecture day."

22   Thus far the elder traveller had listened with due gravity; but now

burst into a fit of irrepressible mirth, shaking himself so violently that his snakelike staff actually seemed to wriggle in sympathy.

23   "Ha! ha! ha!" shouted he again and again; then composing himself, "Well, go on, Goodman Brown, go on; but, prithee, don't kill me with laughing."

24   "Well, then, to end the matter at once," said Goodman Brown, considerably nettled, "there is my wife, Faith. It would break her dear little heart: and I'd rather break my own."

25   "Nay, if that be the case," answered the other, "e'en go thy ways, Goodman Brown. I would not for twenty old women like the one hobbling before us that Faith should come to any harm."

26   As he spoke he pointed his staff at a female figure on the path, in whom Goodman Brown recognized a very pious and exemplary dame, who had taught him his catechism in youth, and was still his moral and spiritual adviser, jointly with the minister and Deacon Gookin.

27   "A marvel, truly, that Goody Cloyse should be so far in the wilderness at nightfall," said he. "But with your leave, friend, I shall take a cut through the woods until we have left this Christian woman behind. Being a stranger to you, she might ask whom I was consorting with and whither I was going."

28   "Be it so," said his fellow-traveller. "Betake you to the woods, and let me keep the path."

29   Accordingly the young man turned aside, but took care to watch his companion, who advanced softly along the road until he had come within a staff's length of the old dame. She, meanwhile, was making the best of her way, with singular speed for so aged a woman, and mumbling some indistinct words—a prayer, doubtless—as she went. The traveller put forth his staff and touched her withered neck with what seemed the serpent's tail.

30   "The devil!" screamed the pious old lady.

31   "Then Goody Cloyse knows her old friend?" observed the traveller, confronting her and leaning on his writhing stick.

32   "Ah, forsooth, and is it your worship indeed?" cried the good dame. "Yea, truly is it, and in the very image of my old gossip, Goodman Brown, the grandfather of the silly fellow that now is. But—would your worship believe it?—my broomstick hath strangely disappeared, stolen, as I suspect, by that unhanged witch, Goody Cory, and that, too, when I was all anointed with the juice of smallage, and cinquefoil, and wolf's bane"—

33   "Mingled with fine wheat and the fat of a new-born babe," said the shape of old Goodman Brown.

34   "Ah, your worship knows the recipe," cried the old lady, cackling aloud. "So, as I was saying, being all ready for the meeting, and no horse to ride on, I made up my mind to foot it; for they tell me there is a nice young man to be taken into communion to-night. But now your good worship will lend me your arm, and we shall be there in a twinkling."

35   "That can hardly be," answered her friend. "I may not spare you my arm, Goody Cloyse; but here is my staff, if you will."

36   So saying, he threw it down at her feet, where, perhaps, it assumed life, being one of the rods which its owner had formerly lent to the Egyptian magi. Of this fact, however, Goodman Brown could not take cognizance. He had cast up his eyes in astonishment, and, looking down again, beheld neither Goody Cloyse nor the serpentine staff, but his fellow-traveller alone, who waited for him as calmly as if nothing had happened.

37   "That old woman taught me my catechism," said the young man; and there was a world of meaning in this simple comment.

38   They continued to walk onward, while the elder traveller exhorted his companion to make good speed and persevere in the path, discoursing so aptly that his arguments seemed rather to spring up in the bosom of his auditor than to be suggested by himself. As they went, he plucked a branch of maple to serve for a walking stick, and began to strip it of the twigs and little boughs, which were wet with evening dew. The moment his fingers touched them they became strangely withered and dried up as with a week's sunshine. Thus the pair proceeded, at a good free pace, until suddenly, in a gloomy hollow of the road, Goodman Brown sat himself down on the stump of a tree and refused to go any farther.

39   "Friend," said he, stubbornly, "my mind is made up. Not another step will I budge on this errand. What if a wretched old woman do choose to go to the devil when I thought she was going to heaven: is that any reason why I should quit my dear Faith and go after her?"

40   "You will think better of this by and by," said his acquaintance, composedly. "Sit here and rest yourself a while; and when you feel like moving again, there is my staff to help you along."

41   Without more words, he threw his companion the maple stick, and was as speedily out of sight as if he had vanished into the deepening gloom. The young man sat a few moments by the roadside, applauding himself greatly, and thinking with how clear a conscience he should meet the minister in his morning walk, nor shrink from the eye of good old Deacon Gookin. And what calm sleep would be his that very night, which was to have been spent so wickedly, but so purely and sweetly now, in the arms of Faith! Amidst these pleasant and praiseworthy meditations, Goodman Brown heard the tramp of horses along the road, and deemed it advisable to conceal himself within the verge of the forest, conscious of the guilty purpose that had brought him thither, though now so happily turned from it.

42   On came the hoof tramps and the voices of the riders, two grave old voices, conversing soberly as they drew near. These mingled sounds appeared to pass along the road, within a few yards of the young man's hiding-place; but, owing doubtless to the depth of the gloom at that particular spot, neither the travellers nor their steeds were visible.

Though their figures brushed the small boughs by the wayside, it could not be seen that they intercepted, even for a moment, the faint gleam from the strip of bright sky athwart which they must have passed. Goodman Brown alternately crouched and stood on tiptoe, pulling aside the branches and thrusting forth his head as far as he durst without discerning so much as a shadow. It vexed him the more, because he could have sworn, were such a thing possible, that he recognized the voices of the minister and Deacon Gookin, jogging along quietly, as they were wont to do, when bound to some ordination or ecclesiastical council. While yet within hearing, one of the riders stopped to pluck a switch.

43   "Of the two, reverend sir," said the voice like the deacon's, "I had rather miss an ordination dinner than to-night's meeting. They tell me that some of our community are to be here from Falmouth and beyond, and others from Connecticut and Rhode Island, besides several of the Indian powwows, who, after their fashion, know almost as much deviltry as the best of us. Moreover, there is a goodly young woman to be taken into communion."

44   "Mighty well, Deacon Gookin!" replied the solemn old tones of the minister. "Spur up, or we shall be late. Nothing can be done, you know, until I get on the ground."

45   The hoofs clattered again; and the voices, talking so strangely in the empty air, passed on through the forest, where no church had ever been gathered or solitary Christian prayed. Whither, then, could these holy men be journeying so deep into the heathen wilderness? Young Goodman Brown caught hold of a tree for support, being ready to sink down on the ground, faint and overburdened with the heavy sickness of his heart. He looked up to the sky, doubting whether there really was a heaven above him. Yet there was the blue arch, and the stars brightening in it.

46   "With heaven above and Faith below, I will yet stand firm against the devil!" cried Goodman Brown.

47   While he still gazed upward into the deep arch of the firmament and had lifted his hands to pray, a cloud, though no wind was stirring, hurried across the zenith and hid the brightening stars. The blue sky was still visible, except directly overhead, where this black mass of cloud was sweeping swiftly northward. Aloft in the air, as if from the depths of the cloud, came a confused and doubtful sound of voices. Once the listener fancied that he could distinguish the accents of towns-people of his own, men and women, both pious and ungodly, many of whom he had met at the communion table, and had seen others rioting at the tavern. The next moment, so indistinct were the sounds, he doubted whether he had heard aught but the murmur of the old forest, whispering without a wind. Then came a stronger swell of those familiar tones, heard daily in the sunshine at Salem village, but never until now from a cloud of night. There was one voice, of a young woman, uttering lamen-

tations, yet with an uncertain sorrow, and entreating for some favor, which, perhaps, it would grieve her to obtain; and all the unseen multitude, both saints and sinners, seemed to encourage her onward.

48   "Faith!" shouted Goodman Brown, in a voice of agony and desperation; and the echoes of the forest mocked him, crying, "Faith! Faith!" as if bewildered wretches were seeking her all through the wilderness.

49   The cry of grief, rage, and terror was yet piercing the night, when the unhappy husband held his breath for a response. There was a scream, drowned immediately in a louder murmur of voices, fading into far-off laughter, as the dark cloud swept away, leaving the clear and silent sky above Goodman Brown. But something fluttered lightly down through the air and caught on the branch of a tree. The young man seized it, and beheld a pink ribbon.

50   "My Faith is gone!" cried he, after one stupefied moment. "There is no good on earth; and sin is but a name. Come, devil; for to thee is this world given."

51   And, maddened with despair, so that he laughed loud and long, did Goodman Brown grasp his staff and set forth again, at such a rate that he seemed to fly along the forest path rather than to walk or run. The road grew wilder and drearier and more faintly traced, and vanished at length, leaving him in the heart of the dark wilderness, still rushing onward with the instinct that guides mortal man to evil. The whole forest was peopled with frightful sounds—the creaking of the trees, the howling of wild beasts, and the yell of Indians; while sometimes the wind tolled like a distant church bell, and sometimes gave a broad roar around the traveller, as if all Nature were laughing him to scorn. But he was himself the chief horror of the scene, and shrank not from its other horrors.

52   "Ha! ha! ha!" roared Goodman Brown when the wind laughed at him. "Let us hear which will laugh loudest. Think not to frighten me with your deviltry. Come witch, come wizard, come Indian powwow, come devil himself, and here comes Goodman Brown. You may as well fear him as he fear you."

53   In truth, all through the haunted forest there could be nothing more frightful than the figure of Goodman Brown. On he flew among the black pines, brandishing his staff with frenzied gestures, now giving vent to an inspiration of horrid blasphemy, and now shouting forth such laughter as set all the echoes of the forest laughing like demons around him. The fiend in his own shape is less hideous than when he rages in the breast of man. Thus sped the demoniac on his course, until, quivering among the trees, he saw a red light before him, as when the felled trunks and branches of a clearing have been set on fire, and throw up their lurid blaze against the sky, at the hour of midnight. He paused, in a lull of the tempest that had driven him onward, and heard the swell of what seemed a hymn, rolling solemnly from a distance with the weight of many voices. He knew the tune; it was a familiar one in the choir of the village meeting-house. The verse died heavily away, and was

lengthened by a chorus, not of human voices, but of all the sounds of the benighted wilderness pealing in awful harmony together. Goodman Brown cried out, and his cry was lost to his own ear by its unison with the cry of the desert.

54   In the interval of silence he stole forward until the light glared full upon his eyes. At one extremity of an open space, hemmed in by the dark wall of the forest, arose a rock, bearing some rude, natural resemblance either to an altar or a pulpit, and surrounded by four blazing pines, their tops aflame, their stems untouched, like candles at an evening meeting. The mass of foliage that had overgrown the summit of the rock was all on fire, blazing high into the night and fitfully illuminating the whole field. Each pendent twig and leafy festoon was in a blaze. As the red light arose and fell, a numerous congregation alternately shone forth, then disappeared in shadow, and again grew, as it were, out of the darkness, peopling the heart of the solitary woods at once.

55   "A grave and dark-clad company," quoth Goodman Brown.

56   In truth they were such. Among them, quivering to and fro between gloom and splendor, appeared faces that would be seen next day at the council board of the province, and others which, Sabbath after Sabbath, looked devoutly heavenward, and benignantly over the crowded pews, from the holiest pulpits in the land. Some affirm that the lady of the governor was there. At least there were high dames well known to her, and wives of honored husbands, and widows, a great multitude, and ancient maidens, all of excellent repute, and fair young girls, who trembled lest their mothers should espy them. Either the sudden gleams of light flashing over the obscure field bedazzled Goodman Brown, or he recognized a score of the church members of Salem village famous for their especial sanctity. Good old Deacon Gookin had arrived, and waited at the skirts of that venerable saint, his revered pastor. But, irreverently consorting with these grave, reputable, and pious people, these elders of the church, these chaste dames and dewy virgins, there were men of dissolute lives and women of spotted fame, wretches given over to all mean and filthy vice, and suspected even of horrid crimes. It was strange to see that the good shrank not from the wicked, nor were the sinners abashed by the saints. Scattered also among their pale-faced enemies were the Indian priests, or powwows, who had often scared their native forest with more hideous incantations than any known to English witch-craft.

57   "But where is Faith?" thought Goodman Brown; and, as hope came into his heart, he trembled.

58   Another verse of the hymn arose, a slow and mournful strain, such as the pious love, but joined to words which expressed all that our nature can conceive of sin, and darkly hinted at far more. Unfathomable to mere mortals is the lore of fiends. Verse after verse was sung; and still the chorus of the desert swelled between like the deepest tone of a mighty organ; and with the final peal of that dreadful anthem there came a

sound, as if the roaring wind, the rushing streams, the howling beasts, and every other voice of the unconcerted wilderness were mingling and according with the voice of guilty man in homage to the prince of all. The four blazing pines threw up a loftier flame, and obscurely discovered shapes and visages of horror on the smoke wreaths above the impious assembly. At the same moment the fire on the rock shot redly forth and formed a glowing arch above its base, where now appeared a figure. With reverence be it spoken, the figure bore no slight similitude, both in garb and manner, to some grave divine of the New England churches.

59   "Bring forth the converts!" cried a voice that echoed through the field and rolled into the forest.

60   At the word, Goodman Brown stepped forth from the shadow of the trees and approached the congregation, with whom he felt a loathful brotherhood by the sympathy of all that was wicked in his heart. He could have well-nigh sworn that the shape of his own dead father beckoned him to advance, looking downward from a smoke wreath, while a woman, with dim features of despair, threw out her hand to warn him back. Was it his mother? But he had no power to retreat one step, nor to resist, even in thought, when the minister and good old Deacon Gookin seized his arms and led him to the blazing rock. Thither came also the slender form of a veiled female, led between Goody Cloyse, that pious teacher of the catechism, and Martha Carrier, who had received the devil's promise to be queen of hell. A rampant hag was she. And there stood the proselytes beneath the canopy of fire.

61   "Welcome, my children," said the dark figure, "to the communion of your race. Ye have found thus young your nature and your destiny. My children, look behind you!"

62   They turned; and flashing forth, as it were, in a sheet of flame, the fiend worshippers were seen; the smile of welcome gleamed darkly on every visage.

63   "There," resumed the sable form, "are all whom ye have reverenced from youth. Ye deemed them holier than yourselves and shrank from your own sin, contrasting it with their lives of righteousness and prayerful aspirations heavenward. Yet here are they all in my worshipping assembly. This night it shall be granted you to know their secret deeds: how hoary-bearded elders of the church have whispered wanton words to the young maids of their households; how many a woman, eager for widows' weeds, has given her husband a drink at bedtime and let him sleep his last sleep in her bosom; how beardless youths have made haste to inherit their fathers' wealth; and how fair damsels—blush not, sweet ones—have dug little graves in the garden, and bidden me, the sole guest, to an infant's funeral. By the sympathy of your human hearts for sin ye shall scent out all the places—whether in church, bedchamber, street, field, or forest—where crime has been committed, and shall exult to behold the whole earth one stain of guilt, one mighty blood spot. Far more than this. It shall be yours to penetrate, in every bosom, the deep

mystery of sin, the fountain of all wicked arts, and which inexhaustibly supplies more evil impulses than human power—than my power at its utmost—can make manifest in deeds. And now, my children, look upon each other."

64   They did so; and, by the blaze of the hell-kindled torches, the wretched man beheld his Faith, and the wife her husband, trembling before that unhallowed altar.

65   "Lo, there ye stand, my children," said the figure, in a deep and solemn tone, almost sad with its despairing awfulness, as if his once angelic nature could yet mourn for our miserable race. "Depending upon one another's hearts, ye had still hoped that virtue were not all a dream. Now are ye undeceived. Evil is the nature of mankind. Evil must be your only happiness. Welcome again, my children, to the communion of your race."

66   "Welcome," repeated the fiend worshippers, in one cry of despair and triumph.

67   And there they stood, the only pair, as it seemed, who were yet hesitating on the verge of wickedness in this dark world. A basin was hollowed, naturally, in the rock. Did it contain water, reddened by the lurid light? or was it blood? or, perchance, a liquid flame? Herein did the shape of evil dip his hand and prepare to lay the mark of baptism upon their foreheads, that they might be partakers of the mystery of sin, more conscious of the secret guilt of others, both in deed and thought, than they could now be of their own. The husband cast one look at his pale wife, and Faith at him. What polluted wretches would the next glance show them to each other, shuddering alike at what they disclosed and what they saw!

68   "Faith! Faith!" cried the husband, "look up to heaven, and resist the wicked one."

69   Whether Faith obeyed he knew not. Hardly had he spoken when he found himself amid calm night and solitude, listening to a roar of the wind which died heavily away through the forest. He staggered against the rock, and felt it chill and damp; while a hanging twig, that had been all on fire, besprinkled his cheek with the coldest dew.

70   The next morning young Goodman Brown came slowly into the street of Salem village, staring around him like a bewildered man. The good old minister was taking a walk along the graveyard to get an appetite for breakfast and meditate his sermon, and bestowed a blessing, as he passed, on Goodman Brown. He shrank from the venerable saint as if to avoid an anathema. Old Deacon Gookin was at domestic worship, and the holy words of his prayer were heard through the open window. "What God doth the wizard pray to?" quoth Goodman Brown. Goody Cloyse, that excellent old Christian, stood in the early sunshine at her own lattice, catechizing a little girl who had brought her a pint of morning's milk. Goodman Brown snatched away the child as from the grasp of the fiend himself. Turning the corner by the meeting-house, he

spied the head of Faith, with the pink ribbons, gazing anxiously forth, and bursting into such joy at sight of him that she skipped along the street and almost kissed her husband before the whole village. But Goodman Brown looked sternly and sadly into her face, and passed on without a greeting.

71   Had Goodman Brown fallen asleep in the forest and only dreamed a wild dream of a witch-meeting?

72   Be it so if you will; but, alas! it was a dream of evil omen for young Goodman Brown. A stern, a sad, a darkly meditative, a distrustful, if not a desperate man did he become from the night of that fearful dream. On the Sabbath day, when the congregation were singing a holy psalm, he could not listen because an anthem of sin rushed loudly upon his ear and drowned all the blessed strain. When the minister spoke from the pulpit with power and fervid eloquence, and, with his hand on the open Bible, of the sacred truths of our religion, and of saint-like lives and triumphant deaths, and of future bliss or misery unutterable, then did Goodman Brown turn pale, dreading lest the roof should thunder down upon the gray blasphemer and his hearers. Often, awaking suddenly at midnight, he shrank from the bosom of Faith; and at morning or eventide, when the family knelt down at prayer, he scowled and muttered to himself, and gazed sternly at his wife, and turned away. And when he had lived long, and was borne to his grave a hoary corpse, followed by Faith, an aged woman, and children and grandchildren, a goodly procession, besides neighbors not a few, they carved no hopeful verse upon his tombstone, for his dying hour was gloom.

Study Questions

1. Define *allegory*. How is this short story allegorical?
2. What is the relationship between ambiguity and the supernatural in this short story? How does the narration maintain this relationship?
3. How is Goodman Brown's youth significant in terms of his experience in the forest? Why does he feel that he can make his journey into the forest, with impunity, but that his wife should remain behind?
4. Comment on the names of the characters in Hawthorne's tale.
5. What does the forest symbolize? The road? The pink ribbons?

The Magic Barrel

Bernard Malamud

1   Not long ago there lived in uptown New York, in a small, almost meager room, though crowded with books, Leo Finkle, a rabbinical student in the Yeshivah University. Finkle, after six years of study, was to be ordained in June and had been advised by an acquaintance that he might find it easier to win himself a congregation if he were married. Since he had no present prospects of marriage, after two tormented days of turning it over in his mind, he called in Pinye Salzman, a marriage broker whose two-line advertisement he had read in the *Forward*.

2   The matchmaker appeared one night out of the dark fourth-floor hallway of the graystone rooming house where Finkle lived, grasping a black, strapped portfolio that had been worn thin with use. Salzman, who had been long in the business, was of slight but dignified build, wearing an old hat, and an overcoat too short and tight for him. He smelled frankly of fish, which he loved to eat, and although he was missing a few teeth, his presence was not displeasing, because of an amiable manner curiously contrasted with mournful eyes. His voice, his lips, his wisp of beard, his bony fingers were animated, but give him a moment of repose and his mild blue eyes revealed a depth of sadness, a characteristic that put Leo a little at ease although the situation, for him, was inherently tense.

3   He at once informed Salzman why he had asked him to come, explaining that his home was in Cleveland, and that but for his parents, who had married comparatively late in life, he was alone in the world. He had for six years devoted himself almost entirely to his studies, as a result of which, understandably, he had found himself without time for a social life and the company of young women. Therefore he thought it the better part of trial and error—of embarrassing fumbling—to call in an experienced person to advise him on these matters. He remarked in passing that the function of the marriage broker was ancient and honorable, highly approved in the Jewish community, because it made practical the necessary without hindering joy. Moreover, his own parents had been brought together by a matchmaker. They had made, if not a financially profitable marriage—since neither had possessed any worldly goods to speak of—at least a successful one in the sense of their everlasting devotion to each other. Salzman listened in embarrassed surprise, sensing a sort of apology. Later, however, he experienced a glow of pride in his work, an emotion that had left him years ago, and he heartily approved of Finkle.

209

4   The two went to their business. Leo had led Salzman to the only clear place in the room, a table near a window that overlooked the lamp-lit city. He seated himself at the matchmaker's side but facing him, attempting by an act of will to suppress the unpleasant tickle in his throat. Salzman eagerly unstrapped his portfolio and removed a loose rubber band from a thin packet of much-handled cards. As he flipped through them, a gesture and sound that physically hurt Leo, the student pretended not to see and gazed steadfastly out the window. Although it was still February, winter was on its last legs, signs of which he had for the first time in years begun to notice. He now observed the round white moon, moving high in the sky through a cloud menagerie, and watched with half-open mouth as it penetrated a huge hen, and dropped out of her like an egg laying itself. Salzman, though pretending through eyeglasses he had just slipped on, to be engaged in scanning the writing on the cards, stole occasional glances at the young man's distinguished face, noting with pleasure the long, severe scholar's nose, brown eyes heavy with learning, sensitive yet ascetic lips, and a certain, almost hollow quality of the dark cheeks. He gazed around at shelves upon shelves of books and let out a soft, contented sigh.

5   When Leo's eyes fell upon the cards, he counted six spread out in Salzman's hand.

6   "So few?" he asked in disappointment.

7   "You wouldn't believe me how much cards I got in my office," Salzman replied. "The drawers are already filled to the top, so I keep them now in a barrel, but is every girl good for a new rabbi?"

8   Leo blushed at this, regretting all he had revealed of himself in a curriculum vitae he had sent to Salzman. He had thought it best to acquaint him with his strict standards and specifications, but in having done so, felt he had told the marriage broker more than was absolutely necessary.

9   He hesitantly inquired, "Do you keep photographs of your clients on file?"

10   "First comes family, amount of dowry, also what kind promises," Salzman replied, unbuttoning his tight coat and settling himself in the chair. "After comes pictures, rabbi."

11   "Call me Mr. Finkle. I'm not yet a rabbi."

12   Salzman said he would, but instead called him doctor, which he changed to rabbi when Leo was not listening too attentively.

13   Salzman adjusted his horn-rimmed spectacles, gently cleared his throat and read in an eager voice the contents of the top card:

14   "Sophie P. Twenty four years. Widow one year. No children. Educated high school and two years college. Father promises eight thousand dollars. Has wonderful wholesale business. Also real estate. On the mother's side comes teachers, also one actor. Well known on Second Avenue."

15   Leo gazed up in surprise. "Did you say a widow?"

16   "A widow don't mean spoiled, rabbi. She lived with her husband

maybe four months. He was a sick boy she made a mistake to marry him."

17   "Marrying a widow has never entered my mind."

18   "This is because you have no experience. A widow, especially if she is young and healthy like this girl, is a wonderful person to marry. She will be thankful to you the rest of her life. Believe me, if I was looking now for a bride, I would marry a widow."

19   Leo reflected, then shook his head.

20   Salzman hunched his shoulders in an almost imperceptible gesture of disappointment. He placed the card down on the wooden table and began to read another:

21   "Lily H. High school teacher. Regular. Not a substitute. Has savings and new Dodge car. Lived in Paris one year. Father is successful dentist thirty-five years. Interested in professional man. Well Americanized family. Wonderful opportunity."

22   "I knew her personally," said Salzman. "I wish you could see this girl. She is a doll. Also very intelligent. All day you could talk to her about books and theyater and what not. She also knows current events."

23   "I don't believe you mentioned her age?"

24   "Her age?" Salzman said, raising his brows. "Her age is thirty-two years."

25   Leo said after a while, "I'm afraid that seems a little too old."

26   Salzman let out a laugh. "So how old are you, rabbi?"

27   "Twenty-seven."

28   "So what is the difference, tell me, between twenty-seven and thirty-two? My own wife is seven years older than me. So what did I suffer?—Nothing. If Rothschild's daughter wants to marry you, would you say on account her age, no?"

29   "Yes," Leo said dryly.

30   Salzman shook off the no in the yes. "Five years don't mean a thing. I give you my word that when you will live with her for one week you will forget her age. What does it mean five years—that she lived more and knows more than somebody who is younger? On this girl, God bless her, years are not wasted. Each one that it comes makes better the bargain."

31   "What subject does she teach in high school?"

32   "Languages. If you heard the way she speaks French, you will think it is music. I am in the business twenty-five years, and I recommend her with my whole heart. Believe me, I know what I'm talking, rabbi."

33   "What's on the next card?" Leo said abruptly.

34   Salzman reluctantly turned up the third card:

35   "Ruth K. Nineteen years. Honor student. Father offers thirteen thousand cash to the right bridegroom. He is a medical doctor. Stomach specialist with marvelous practice. Brother in law owns own garment business. Particular people."

36   Salzman looked as if he had read his trump card.

37   "Did you say nineteen?" Leo asked with interest.

38   "On the dot."

39   "Is she attractive?" He blushed. "Pretty?"

40   Salzman kissed his finger tips. "A little doll. On this I give you my word. Let me call the father tonight and you will see what means pretty."

41   But Leo was troubled. "You're sure she's that young?"

42   "This I am positive. The father will show you the birth certificate."

43   "Are you positive there isn't something wrong with her?" Leo insisted.

44   "Who says there is wrong?"

45   "I don't understand why an American girl her age should go to a marriage broker."

46   A smile spread over Salzman's face.

47   "So for the same reason you went, she comes."

48   Leo flushed. "I am pressed for time."

49   Salzman, realizing he had been tactless, quickly explained. "The father came, not her. He wants she should have the best, so he looks around himself. When we will locate the right boy he will introduce him and encourage. This makes a better marriage than if a young girl without experience takes for herself. I don't have to tell you this."

50   "But don't you think this young girl believes in love?" Leo spoke uneasily.

51   Salzman was about to guffaw but caught himself and said soberly, "Love comes with the right person, not before."

52   Leo parted dry lips but did not speak. Noticing that Salzman had snatched a glance at the next card, he cleverly asked, "How is her health?"

53   "Perfect," Salzman said, breathing with difficulty. "Of course, she is a little lame on her right foot from an auto accident that it happened to her when she was twelve years, but nobody notices on account she is so brilliant and also beautiful."

54   Leo got up heavily and went to the window. He felt curiously bitter and upbraided himself for having called in the marriage broker. Finally, he shook his head.

55   "Why not?" Salzman persisted, the pitch of his voice rising.

56   "Because I detest stomach specialists."

57   "So what do you care what is his business? After you marry her do you need him? Who says he must come every Friday night in your house?"

58   Ashamed of the way the talk was going, Leo dismissed Salzman, who went home with heavy, melancholy eyes.

59   Though he had felt only relief at the marriage broker's departure, Leo was in low spirits the next day. He explained it as arising from Salzman's failure to produce a suitable bride for him. He did not care for his type of clientele. But when Leo found himself hesitating whether to seek out another matchmaker, one more polished than Pinye, he won-

dered if it could be—his protestations to the contrary, and although he honored his father and mother—that he did not, in essence, care for the matchmaking institution? This thought he quickly put out of mind yet found himself still upset. All day he ran around in the woods—missed an important appointment, forgot to give out his laundry, walked out of a Broadway cafeteria without paying and had to run back with the ticket in his hand; had even not recognized his landlady in the street when she passed with a friend and courteously called out, "A good evening to you, Doctor Finkle." By nightfall, however, he had regained sufficient calm to sink his nose into a book and there found peace from his thoughts.

60   Almost at once there came a knock on the door. Before Leo could say enter, Salzman, commercial cupid, was standing in the room. His face was gray and meager, his expression hungry, and he looked as if he would expire on his feet. Yet the marriage broker managed, by some trick of the muscles, to display a broad smile.

61   "So good evening. I am invited?"

62   Leo nodded, disturbed to see him again, yet unwilling to ask the man to leave.

63   Beaming still, Salzman laid his portfolio on the table. "Rabbi, I got for you tonight good news."

64   "I've asked you not to call me rabbi. I'm still a student."

65   "Your worries are finished. I have for you a first-class bride."

66   "Leave me in peace concerning this subject." Leo pretended lack of interest.

67   "The world will dance at your wedding."

68   "Please, Mr. Salzman, no more."

69   "But first must come back my strength," Salzman said weakly. He fumbled with the portfolio straps and took out of the leather case an oily paper bag, from which he extracted a hard, seeded roll and a small, smoked white fish. With a quick motion of his hand he stripped the fish out of its skin and began ravenously to chew. "All day in a rush," he muttered.

70   Leo watched him eat.

71   "A sliced tomato you have maybe?" Salzman hesitantly inquired.

72   "No."

73   The marriage broker shut his eyes and ate. When he had finished he carefully cleaned up the crumbs and rolled up the remains of the fish, in the paper bag. His spectacled eyes roamed the room until he discovered, amid some piles of books, a one-burner gas stove. Lifting his hat he humbly asked, "A glass tea you got, rabbi?"

74   Conscience-stricken, Leo rose and brewed the tea. He served it with a chunk of lemon and two cubes of lump sugar, delighting Salzman.

75   After he had drunk his tea, Salzman's strength and good spirits were restored.

76   "So tell me, rabbi," he said amiably, "you considered some more the three clients I mentioned yesterday?"

77   "There was no need to consider."

78   "Why not?"

79   "None of them suits me."

80   "What then suits you?"

81   Leo let it pass because he could give only a confused answer.

82   Without waiting for a reply, Salzman asked, "You remember this girl I talked to you—the high school teacher?"

83   "Age thirty-two?"

84   But, surprisingly, Salzman's face lit in a smile. "Age twenty-nine."

85   Leo shot him a look. "Reduced from thirty-two?"

86   "A mistake," Salzman avowed. "I talked today with the dentist. He took me to his safety deposit box and showed me the birth certificate. She was twenty-nine years last August. They made her a party in the mountains where she went for her vacation. When her father spoke to me the first time I forgot to write the age and I told you thirty-two, but now I remember this was a different client, a widow."

87   "The same one you told me about? I thought she was twenty-four?"

88   "A different. Am I responsible that the world is filled with widows?"

89   "No, but I'm not interested in them, nor for that matter, in school teachers."

90   Salzman pulled his clasped hands to his breast. Looking at the ceiling he devoutly exclaimed, "Yiddishe kinder, what can I say to somebody that he is not interested in high school teachers? So what then you are interested?"

91   Leo flushed but controlled himself.

92   "In what else will you be interested." Salzman went on, "if you not interested in this fine girl that she speaks four languages and has personally in the bank ten thousand dollars? Also her father guarantees further twelve thousand. Also she has a new car, wonderful clothes, talks on all subjects, and she will give you a first-class home and children. How near do we come in our life to paradise?"

93   "If she's so wonderful, why wasn't she married ten years ago?"

94   "Why?" said Salzman with a heavy laugh. "—Why? Because she is *partikiler*. This is why. She wants the *best*."

95   Leo was silent, amused at how he had entangled himself. But Salzman had aroused his interest in Lily H., and he began seriously to consider calling on her. When the marriage broker observed how intently Leo's mind was at work on the facts he had supplied, he felt certain they would soon come to an agreement.

96   Late Saturday afternoon, conscious of Salzman, Leo Finkle walked with Lily Hirschorn along Riverside Drive. He walked briskly and erectly, wearing with distinction the black fedora he had that morning taken with trepidation out of the dusty hat box on his closet shelf, and the heavy black Saturday coat he had thoroughly whisked clean. Leo also

owned a walking stick, a present from a distant relative, but quickly put temptation aside and did not use it. Lily, petite and not unpretty, had on something signifying the approach of spring. She was au courant, animatedly, with all sorts of subjects, and he weighed her words and found her surprisingly sound—score another for Salzman, whom he uneasily sensed to be somewhere around, hiding perhaps high in a tree along the street, flashing the lady signals with a pocket mirror; or perhaps a cloven-hoofed Pan, piping nuptial ditties as he danced his invisible way before them, strewing wild buds on the walk and purple grapes in their path, symbolizing fruit of a union, though there was of course still none.

97   Lily startled Leo by remarking, "I was thinking of Mr. Salzman, a curious figure, wouldn't you say?"

98   Not certain what to answer, he nodded.

99   She bravely went on, blushing, "I for one am grateful for his introducing us. Aren't you?"

100   He courteously replied, "I am."

101   "I mean," she said with a little laugh—and it was all in good taste, or at least gave the effect of being not in bad—"do you mind that we came together so?"

102   He was not displeased with her honesty, recognizing that she meant to set the relationship aright, and understanding that it took a certain amount of experience in life, and courage, to want to do it quite that way. One had to have some sort of past to make that kind of beginning.

103   He said that he did not mind. Salzman's function was traditional and honorable—valuable for what it might achieve, which, he pointed out, was frequently nothing.

104   Lily agreed with a sigh. They walked on for a while and she said after a long silence, again with a nervous laugh, "Would you mind if I asked you something a little bit personal? Frankly, I find the subject fascinating." Although Leo shrugged, she went on half embarrassedly, "How was it that you came to your calling? I mean was it a sudden passionate inspiration?"

105   Leo, after a time, slowly replied, "I was always interested in the Law."

106   "You saw revealed in it the presence of the Highest?"

107   He nodded and changed the subject. "I understand that you spent a little time in Paris, Miss Hirschorn?"

108   "Oh, did Mr. Salzman tell you, Rabbi Finkle?" Leo winced but she went on, "It was ages ago and almost forgotten. I remember I had to return for my sister's wedding."

109   And Lily would not be put off. "When," she asked in a trembly voice, "did you become enamored of God?"

110   He stared at her. Then it came to him that she was talking not about Leo Finkle, but of a total stranger, some mystical figure, perhaps even

passionate prophet that Salzman had dreamed up for her—no relation to the living or dead. Leo trembled with rage and weakness. The trickster had obviously sold her a bill of goods, just as he had him, who'd expected to become acquainted with a young lady of twenty-nine, only to behold, the moment he laid eyes upon her strained and anxious face, a woman past thirty-five and aging rapidly. Only his self control had kept him this long in her presence.

111   "I am not," he said gravely, "a talented religious person," and in seeking words to go on, found himself possessed by shame and fear. "I think," he said in a strained manner, "that I came to God not because I loved Him, but because I did not."

112   This confession he spoke harshly because its unexpectedness shook him.

113   Lily wilted. Leo saw a profusion of loaves of bread go flying like ducks high over his head, not unlike the winged loaves by which he had counted himself to sleep last night. Mercifully, then, it snowed, which he would not put past Salzman's machinations.

114   He was infuriated with the marriage broker and swore he would throw him out of the room the minute he reappeared. But Salzman did not come that night, and when Leo's anger had subsided, an unaccountable despair grew in its place. At first he thought this was caused by his disappointment in Lily, but before long it became evident that he had involved himself with Salzman without a true knowledge of his own intent. He gradually realized—with an emptiness that seized him with six hands—that he had called in the broker to find him a bride because he was incapable of doing it himself. This terrifying insight he had derived as a result of his meeting and conversation with Lily Hirschorn. Her probing questions had somehow irritated him into revealing—to himself more than her—the true nature of his relationship to God, and from that it had come upon him, with shocking force, that apart from his parents, he had never loved anyone. Or perhaps it went the other way, that he did not love God so well as he might, because he had not loved man. It seemed to Leo that his whole life stood starkly revealed and he saw himself for the first time as he truly was—unloved and loveless. This bitter but somehow not fully unexpected revelation brought him to a point of panic, controlled only by extraordinary effort. He covered his face with his hands and cried.

115   The week that followed was the worst of his life. He did not eat and lost weight. His beard darkened and grew ragged. He stopped attending seminars and almost never opened a book. He seriously considered leaving the Yeshivah, although he was deeply troubled at the thought of the loss of all his years of study—saw them like pages torn from a book, strewn over the city—and at the devastating effect of this decision upon his parents. But he had lived without knowledge of himself, and never in

the Five Books and all the Commentaries—mea culpa—had the truth been revealed to him. He did not know where to turn, and in all this desolating loneliness there was no *to whom,* although he often thought of Lily but not once could bring himself to go downstairs and make the call. He became touchy and irritable, especially with his landlady, who asked him all manner of personal questions; on the other hand, sensing his own disagreeableness, he waylaid her on the stairs and apologized abjectly, until mortified, she ran from him. Out of this, however, he drew the consolation that he was a Jew and that a Jew suffered. But gradually, as the long and terrible week drew to a close, he regained his composure and some idea of purpose in life: to go on as planned. Although he was imperfect, the ideal was not. As for his quest of a bride, the thought of continuing afflicted him with anxiety and heartburn, yet perhaps with this new knowledge of himself he would be more successful than in the past. Perhaps love would now come to him and a bride to that love. And for this sanctified seeking who needed a Salzman?

116   The marriage broker, a skeleton with haunted eyes, returned that very night. He looked, withal, the picture of frustrated expectancy—as if he had steadfastly waited the week at Miss Lily Hirschorn's side for a telephone call that never came.

117   Casually coughing, Salzman came immediately to the point: "So how did you like her?"

118   Leo's anger rose and he could not refrain from chiding the matchmaker: "Why did you lie to me, Salzman?"

119   Salzman's pale face went dead white, the world had snowed on him.

120   "Did you not state that she was twenty-nine?" Leo insisted.

121   "I give you my word—"

122   "She was thirty-five, if a day. *At least* thirty-five."

123   "Of this don't be too sure. Her father told me—"

124   "Never mind. The worst of it was that you lied to her."

125   "How did I lie to her, tell me?"

126   "You told her things about me that weren't true. You made me out to be more, consequently less than I am. She had in mind a totally different person, a sort of semi-mystical Wonder Rabbi."

127   "All I said, you was a religious man."

128   "I can imagine."

129   Salzman sighed. "This is my weakness that I have," he confessed. "My wife says to me I shouldn't be a salesman, but when I have two fine people that they would be wonderful to be married, I am so happy that I talk too much." He smiled wanly. "This is why Salzman is a poor man."

130   Leo's anger left him. "Well, Salzman, I'm afraid that's all."

131   The marriage broker fastened hungry eyes on him.

132   "You don't want any more a bride?"

133   "I do," said Leo, "but I have decided to seek her in a different way.

I am no longer interested in an arranged marriage. To be frank, I now admit the necessity of premarital love. That is, I want to be in love with the one I marry."

134   "Love?" said Salzman, astounded. After a moment he remarked, "For us, our love is our life, not for the ladies. In the ghetto they—"

135   "I know, I know," said Leo. "I've thought of it often. Love, I have said to myself, should be a by-product of living and worship rather than its own end. Yet for myself I find it necessary to establish the level of my need and fulfill it."

136   Salzman shrugged but answered, "Listen, rabbi, if you want love, this I can find for you also. I have such beautiful clients that you will love them the minute your eyes will see them."

137   Leo smiled unhappily. "I'm afraid you don't understand."

138   But Salzman hastily unstrapped his portfolio and withdrew a manila packet from it.

139   "Pictures," he said, quickly laying the envelope on the table.

140   Leo called after him to take the pictures away, but as if on the wings of the wind, Salzman had disappeared.

141   March came. Leo had returned to his regular routine. Although he felt not quite himself yet—lacked energy—he was making plans for a more active social life. Of course it would cost something, but he was an expert in cutting corners; and when there were no corners left he would make circles rounder. All the while Salzman's pictures had lain on the table, gathering dust. Occasionally as Leo sat studying, or enjoying a cup of tea, his eyes fell on the manila envelope, but he never opened it.

142   The days went by and no social life to speak of developed with a member of the opposite sex—it was difficult, given the circumstances of his situation. One morning Leo toiled up the stairs to his room and stared out the window at the city. Although the day was bright his view of it was dark. For some time he watched the people in the street below hurrying along and then turned with a heavy heart to his little room. On the table was the packet. With a sudden relentless gesture he tore it open. For a half-hour he stood by the table in a state of excitement, examining the photographs of the ladies Salzman had included. Finally, with a deep sigh he put them down. There were six, of varying degrees of attractiveness, but look at them long enough and they all became Lily Hirschorn: all past their prime, all starved behind bright smiles, not a true personality in the lot. Life, despite their frantic yoohooings, had passed them by; they were pictures in a briefcase that stank of fish. After a while, however, as Leo attempted to return the photographs into the envelope, he found in it another, a snapshot of the type taken by a machine for a quarter. He gazed at it a moment and let out a cry.

143   Her face deeply moved him. Why, he could at first not say. It gave him the impression of youth—spring flowers, yet age—a sense of having been used to the bone, wasted; this came from the eys, which were

hauntingly familiar, yet absolutely strange. He had a vivid impression that he had met her before, but try as he might he could not place her although he could almost recall her name, as if he had read it in her own handwriting. No, this couldn't be; he would have remembered her. It was not, he affirmed, that she had an extraordinary beauty—no, though her face was attractive enough; it was that *something* about her moved him. Feature for feature, even some of the ladies of the photographs could do better; but she leaped forth to his heart—had *lived,* or wanted to—more than just wanted, perhaps regretted how she had lived—had somehow deeply suffered: it could be seen in the depths of those reluctant eyes, and from the way the light enclosed and shone from her, and within her, opening realms of possibility: this was her own. Her he desired. His head ached and eyes narrowed with the intensity of his gazing, then as if an obscure fog had blown up in the mind, he experienced fear of her and was aware that he had received an impression, somehow, of evil. He shuddered, saying softly, it is thus with us all. Leo brewed some tea in a small pot and sat sipping it without sugar, to calm himself. But before he had finished drinking, again with excitement he examined the face and found it good: good for Leo Finkle. Only such a one could understand him and help him seek whatever he was seeking. She might, perhaps, love him. How she had happened to be among the discards in Salzman's barrel he could never guess, but he knew he must urgently go find her.

144   Leo rushed downstairs, grabbed up the Bronx telephone book, and searched for Salzman's home address. He was not listed, nor was his office. Neither was he in the Manhattan book. But Leo remembered having written down the address on a slip of paper after he had read Salzman's advertisement in the "personals" column of the *Forward.* He ran up to his room and tore through his papers, without luck. It was exasperating. Just when he needed the matchmaker he was nowhere to be found. Fortunately Leo remembered to look in his wallet. There on a card he found his name written and a Bronx address. No phone number was listed. the reason—Leo now recalled—he had originally communicated with Salzman by letter. He got on his coat, put a hat on over his skull cap and hurried to the subway station. All the way to the far end of the Bronx he sat on the edge of his seat. He was more than once tempted to take out the picture and see if the girl's face was as he remembered it, but he refrained, allowing the snapshot to remain in his inside coat pocket, content to have her so close. When the train pulled into the station he was waiting at the door and bolted out. He quickly located the street Salzman had advertised.

145   The building he sought was less than a block from the subway, but it was not an office building, nor even a loft, nor a store in which one could rent office space. It was a very old tenement house. Leo found Salzman's name in pencil on a soiled tag under the bell and climbed

three dark flights to his apartment. When he knocked, the door was opened by a thin, asthmatic, gray-haired woman, in felt slippers.

146   "Yes?" she said, expecting nothing. She listened without listening. He could have sworn he had seen her, too, before but knew it was an illusion.

147   "Salzman—does he live here? Pinye Salzman," he said, "the matchmaker?"

148   She stared at him a long minute. "Of course."

149   He felt embarrassed. "Is he in?"

150   "No." Her mouth, though left open, offered nothing more.

151   "The matter is urgent. Can you tell me where his office is?"

152   "In the air." She pointed upward.

153   "You mean he has no office?" Leo asked.

154   "In his socks."

155   He peered into the apartment. It was sunless and dingy, one large room divided by a half-open curtain, beyond which he could see a sagging metal bed. The near side of a room was crowded with rickety chairs, old bureaus, a three-legged table, racks of cooking utensils, and all the apparatus of a kitchen. But there was no sign of Salzman or his magic barrel, probably also a figment of the imagination. An odor of frying fish made Leo weak to the knees.

156   "Where is he?" he insisted. "I've got to see your husband."

157   At length she answered, "So who knows where he is? Every time he thinks a new thought he runs to a different place. Go home, he will find you."

158   "Tell him Leo Finkle."

159   She gave no sign she had heard.

160   He walked downstairs, depressed.

161   But Salzman, breathless, stood waiting at his door.

162   Leo was astounded and overjoyed. "How did you get here before me?"

163   "I rushed."

164   "Come inside."

165   They entered. Leo fixed tea, and a sardine sandwich for Salzman. As they were drinking he reached behind him for the packet of pictures and handed them to the marriage broker.

166   Salzman put down his glass and said expectantly, "You found somebody you like?"

167   "Not among these."

168   The marriage broker turned away.

169   "Here is the one I want." Leo held forth the snapshot.

170   Salzman slipped on his glasses and took the picture into his trembling hand. He turned ghastly and let out a groan.

171   "What's the matter?" cried Leo.

172   "Excuse me. Was an accident this picture. She isn't for you."

173   Salzman frantically shoved the manila packet into his portfolio. He thrust the snapshot into his pocket and fled down the stairs.

174   Leo, after momentary paralysis, gave chase and cornered the marriage broker in the vestibule. The landlady made hysterical outcries but neither of them listened.

175   "Give me back the picture, Salzman."

176   "No." The pain in his eyes was terrible.

177   "Tell me who she is then."

178   "This I can't tell you. Excuse me."

179   He made to depart, but Leo, forgetting himself, seized the matchmaker by his tight coat and shook him frenziedly.

180   "Please," sighed Salzman. *"Please."*

181   Leo ashamedly let him go. "Tell me who she is," he begged. "It's very important for me to know."

182   "She is not for you. She is a wild one—wild, without shame. This is not a bride for a rabbi."

183   "What do you mean wild?"

184   "Like an animal. Like a dog. For her to be poor was a sin. This is why to me she is dead now."

185   "In God's name, what do you mean?"

186   "Her I can't introduce to you," Salzman cried.

187   "Why are you so excited?"

188   "Why, he asks," Salzman said, bursting into tears. "This is my baby, my Stella, she should burn in hell."

189   Leo hurried up to bed and hid under the covers. Under the covers he thought his life through. Although he soon fell asleep he could not sleep her out of his mind. He woke, beating his breast. Though he prayed to be rid of her, his prayers went unanswered. Through days of torment he endlessly struggled not to love her; fearing success, he escaped it. He then concluded to convert her to goodness, himself to God. The idea alternately nauseated and exalted him.

190   He perhaps did not know that he had come to a final decision until he encountered Salzman in a Broadway cafeteria. He was sitting alone at a rear table, sucking the bony remains of a fish. The marraige broker appeared haggard, and transparent to the point of vanishing.

191   Salzman looked up at first without recognizing him. Leo had grown a pointed beard and his eyes were weighted with wisdom.

192   "Salzman," he said, "love has at last come to my heart."

193   "Who can love from a picture?" mocked the marriage broker.

194   "It is not impossible."

195   "If you can love her, then you can love anybody. Let me show you some new clients that they just sent me their photographs. One is a little doll."

196   "Just her I want," Leo murmured.

197   "Don't be a fool, doctor. Don't bother with her."

198   "Put me in touch with her, Salzman," Leo said humbly. "Perhaps I can be of service."

199   Salzman had stopped eating and Leo understood with emotion that it was now arranged.

200   Leaving the cafeteria, he was, however, afflicted by a tormenting suspicion that Salzman had planned it all to happen this way.

201   Leo was informed by letter that she would meet him on a certain corner, and she was there one spring night, waiting under a street lamp. He appeared, carrying a small bouquet of violets and rosebuds. Stella stood by the lamp post, smoking. She wore white with red shoes, which fitted his expectations, although in a troubled moment he had imagined the dress red, and only the shoes white. She waited uneasily and shyly. From afar he saw that her eyes—clearly her father's—were filled with desperate innocence. He pictured, in her, his own redemption. Violins and lit candles revolved in the sky. Leo ran forward with flowers out-thrust.

202   Around the corner, Salzman, leaning against a wall, chanted prayers for the dead.

Study Questions

1. How do the syntax and diction of the story's opening sentence combine to create what might be called a fairy-tale atmosphere? Is this ambience maintained throughout the story?
2. What word choices establish a buyer-seller relationship in this story?
3. What is the relationship between the rational and the irrational in the events of "The Magic Barrel"? How is the title relevant to the relationship?
4. Are we meant to sympathize with Finkle, to laugh at him, or to condemn him?
5. Explain the paradox in Leo's statement, "I think that I came to God not because I loved Him, but because I did not."
6. To what extent is knowledge of Jewish or Hebrew traditions necessary to understanding Malamud's story?

Why I Am a Pagan

Zitkala-Sä (Gertrude Bonnin)

1   When the spirit swells my breast I love to roam leisurely among the green hills; or sometimes, sitting on the brink of the murmuring Missouri, I marvel at the great blue overhead. With half closed eyes I watch the huge cloud shadows in their noiseless play upon the high bluffs opposite me, while into my ear ripple the sweet, soft cadences of the river's song. Folded hands lie in my lap, for the time forgot. My heart and I lie small upon the earth like a grain of throbbing sand. Drifting clouds and tinkling waters, together with the warmth of a genial summer day, bespeak with eloquence the loving Mystery round about us. During the idle while I sat upon the sunny river brink, I grew somewhat, though my response be not so clearly manifest as in the green grass fringing the edge of the high bluff back of me.

2   At length retracing the uncertain footpath scaling the precipitous embankment, I seek the level lands where grow the wild prairie flowers. And they, the lovely little folk, soothe my soul with their perfumed breath.

3   Their quaint round faces of varied hue convince the heart which leaps with glad surprise that they, too, are living symbols of omnipotent thought. With a child's eager eye I drink in the myriad star shapes wrought in luxuriant color upon the green. Beautiful is the spiritual essence they embody.

4   I leave them nodding in the breeze, but take along with me their impress upon my heart. I pause to rest me upon a rock embedded on the side of a foothill facing the low river bottom. Here the Stone-Boy, of whom the American aborigine tells, frolics about, shooting his baby arrows and shouting aloud with glee at the tiny shafts of lightning that flash from the flying arrow-beaks. What an ideal warrior he became, baffling the siege of the pests of all the land till he triumphed over their united attack. And here he lay,—Inyan our great-great-grandfather, older than the hill he rested on, older than the race of men who love to tell of his wonderful career.

5   Interwoven with the thread of this Indian legend of the rock, I fain would trace a subtle knowledge of the native folk which enabled them to recognize a kinship to any and all parts of this vast universe. By the leading of an ancient trail I move toward the Indian village.

6   With the strong, happy sense that both great and small are so surely enfolded in His magnitude that, without a miss, each has his allotted individual ground of opportunities, I am buoyant with good nature.

7   Yellow Breast, swaying upon the slender stem of a wild sunflower, warbles a sweet assurance of this as I pass near by. Breaking off the clear crystal song, he turns his wee head from side to side eyeing me wisely as slowly I plod with moccasined feet. Then again he yields himself to his song of joy. Flit, flit hither and yon, he fills the summer sky with his swift, sweet melody. And truly does it seem his vigorous freedom lies more in his little spirit than in his wing.

8   With these thoughts I reach the log cabin whither I am strongly drawn by the tie of a child to an aged mother. Out bounds my four-footed friend to meet me, frisking about my path with unmistakable delight. Chän is a black shaggy dog, "a thorough bred little mongrel" of whom I am very fond. Chän seems to understand many words in Sioux, and will go to her mat even when I whisper the word, though generally I think she is guided by the tone of the voice. Often she tries to imitate the sliding inflection and long drawn out voice to the amusement of our guests, but her articulation is quite beyond any ear. In both my hands I hold her shaggy head and gaze into her large brown eyes. At once the dilated pupils contract into tiny black dots, as if the roguish spirit within would evade my questioning.

9   Finally resuming the chair at my desk I feel in keen sympathy with my fellow creatures, for I seem to see clearly again that all are akin.

10   The racial lines, which once were bitterly real, now serve nothing more than marking out a living mosaic of human beings. And even here men of the same color are like the ivory keys of one instrument where each resembles all the rest, yet varies from them in pitch and quality of voice. And those creatures who are for a time mere echoes of another's note are not unlike the fable of the thin sick man whose distorted shadow, dressed like a real creature, came to the old master to make him follow as a shadow. Thus with a compassion for all echoes in human guise, I greet the solemn-faced "native preacher" whom I find awaiting me. I listen with respect for God's creature, though he mouth most strangely the jangling phrases of a bigoted creed.

11   As our tribe is one large family, where every person is related to all the others, he addressed me:—

12   "Cousin, I came from the morning church service to talk with you."

13   "Yes?" I said interrogatively, as he paused for some word from me.

14   Shifting uneasily about in the straight-backed chair he sat upon, he began: "Every holy day (Sunday) I look about our little God's house, and not seeing you there, I am disappointed. This is why I come to-day. Cousin, as I watch you from afar, I see no unbecoming behavior and hear only good reports of you, which all the more burns me with the wish that you were a church member. Cousin, I was taught long years ago by kind missionaries to read the holy book. These godly men taught me also the folly of our old beliefs.

15   "There is one God who gives reward or punishment to the race of dead men. In the upper region the Christian dead are gathered in

unceasing song and prayer. In the deep pit below, the sinful ones dance in torturing flames.

16   "Think upon these things, my cousin, and choose now to avoid the after-doom of hell fire!" Then followed a long silence in which he clasped tighter and unclasped again his interlocked fingers.

17   Like instantaneous lightning flashes came pictures of my own mother's making, for she, too, is now a follower of the new superstition.

18   "Knocking out the chinking of our log cabin, some evil hand thrust in a burning taper of braided dry grass, but failed of his intent, for the fire died out and the half burned brand fell inward to the floor. Directly above it, on a shelf, lay the holy book. This is what we found after our return from a several days' visit. Surely some great power is hid in the sacred book!"

19   Brushing away from my eyes many like pictures, I offered midday meal to the converted Indian sitting wordless and with downcast face. No sooner had he risen from the table with "Cousin, I have relished it," than the church bell rang.

20   Thither he hurried forth with his afternoon sermon. I watched him as he hastened along, his eyes bent fast upon the dusty road till he disappeared at the end of a quarter of a mile.

21   The little incident recalled to mind the copy of a missionary paper brought to my notice a few days ago, in which a "Christian" pugilist commented upon a recent article of mine, grossly perverting the spirit of my pen. Still I would not forget that the pale-faced missionary and the hoodooed aborigine are both God's creatures, though small indeed their own conceptions of Infinite Love. A wee child toddling in a wonder world, I prefer to their dogma my excursions into the natural gardens where the voice of the Great Spirit is heard in the twittering of birds, the rippling of mighty waters, and the sweet breathing of flowers. If this is Paganism, then at present, at least, I am a Pagan.

Study Questions

1.   What personfications do you find in this essay?
2.   What simile helps the author explain the "mosaic of human beings"?
3.   What is a *stipulative definition*? How is "Why I Am a Pagan" an example of such a definition?

The Journey of the Magi

T. S. Eliot

'A cold coming we had of it,
Just the worst time of the year
For a journey, and such a long journey:
The ways deep and the weather sharp,
The very dead of winter.'
And the camels galled, sore-footed, refractory,
Lying down in the melting snow.
There were times we regretted
The summer palaces on slopes, the terraces,
And the silken girls bringing sherbet.   10
Then the camel men cursing and grumbling
And running away, and wanting their liquor and women,
And the night-fires going out, and the lack of shelters,
And the cities hostile and the towns unfriendly
And the villages dirty and charging high prices:
A hard time we had of it.
At the end we preferred to travel all night,
Sleeping in snatches,
With the voices singing in our ears, saying
That this was all folly.   20

   Then at dawn we came down to a temperate valley,
Wet, below the snow line, smelling of vegetation;
With a running stream and a water-mill beating the darkness,
And three trees on the low sky,
And an old white horse galloped away in the meadow.

Then we came to a tavern with vine-leaves over the lintel,
Six hands at an open door dicing for pieces of silver,
And feet kicking the empty wine-skins.
But there was no information, and so we continued
And arrived at evening, not a moment too soon   30
Finding the place; it was (you may say) satisfactory.

   All this was a long time ago, I remember,
And I would do it again, but set down
This set down

This: were we led all that way for
Birth or Death? There was a Birth, certainly,
We had evidence and no doubt. I had seen birth and death,
But had thought they were different; this Birth was
Hard and bitter agony for us, like Death, our death.
We returned to our places, these Kingdoms,   40
But no longer at ease here, in the old dispensation,
With an alien people clutching their gods.
I should be glad of another death.

Study Questions

1. From what temporal perspective is this poem presented? Why is time important in terms of the poem's climax?
2. How do the various Biblical allusions in stanzas 2 and 3 create irony at the speaker's expense?
3. Why weren't the Magi "at ease" after witnessing the Birth? What was "the old dispensation" and how is it connected to their alienation?
4. Does the poem's ending seem forced, in that no convincing context is created for the speaker's rejection of his culture?

The Second Coming

William Butler Yeats

Turning and turning in the widening gyre
The falcon cannot hear the falconer;
Things fall apart; the centre cannot hold;
Mere anarchy is loosed upon the world,
The blood-dimmed tide is loosed, and everywhere
The ceremony of innocence is drowned;
The best lack all conviction, while the worst
Are full of passionate intensity.

Surely some revelation is at hand;
Surely the Second Coming is at hand.   10
The Second Coming! Hardly are those words out
When a vast image out of *Spiritus Mundi*
Troubles my sight: somewhere in sands of the desert.
A shape with lion body and the head of a man,
A gaze blank and pitiless as the sun,
Is moving its slow thighs, while all about it
Reel shadows of the indignant desert birds.
The darkness drops again; but now I know
That twenty centuries of stony sleep
Were vexed to nightmare by a rocking cradle,   20
And what rough beast, its hour come round at last,
Slouches towards Bethlehem to be born?

Study Questions

1. How does the poem's animal imagery ("falcon," "lion body," "desert birds," and "rough beast") function figuratively?
2. Why is the word *mere* so precise and striking in line 4?
3. Where does the persona's personality become apparent? Is the point of his entrance significant?
4. Is this poem ambiguous? Is ambiguity a virtue here?

The Star of the Magi

Arthur C. Clarke

1   Go out of doors any morning this December and look up at the eastern sky an hour or so before dawn. You will see there one of the most beautiful sights in all the heavens—a blazing, blue-white beacon, many times brighter than Sirius, the most brilliant of the stars. Apart from the

Moon itself, it will be the brightest object you will ever see in the night sky. It will still be visible even when the Sun rises; you will even be able to find it at midday if you know exactly where to look.

2   It is the planet Venus, our sister world, reflecting across the gulfs of space the sunlight glancing from her unbroken cloud shield. Every nineteen months she appears in the morning sky, rising shortly before the Sun, and all who see this brilliant herald of the Christmas dawn will inevitably be reminded of the star that led the Magi to Bethlehem.

3   What was that star, assuming that it had some natural explanation? Could it, in fact, have been Venus? At least one book has been written to prove this theory, but it will not stand up to serious examination. To all the people of the Eastern world, Venus was one of the most familiar objects in the sky. Even today, she serves as a kind of alarm clock to the Arab nomads. When she rises, it is time to start moving, to make as much progress as possible before the Sun begins to blast the desert with its heat. For thousands of years, shining more brilliantly than we ever see her in our cloudy northern skies, she has watched the camps struck and the caravans begin to move.

4   Even to the ordinary, uneducated Jews of Herod's kingdom, there could have been nothing in the least remarkable about Venus. And the Magi were no ordinary men; they were certainly experts on astronomy, and must have known the movements of the planets better than do ninety-nine people out of a hundred today. To explain the Star of Bethlehem we must look elsewhere.

5   The Bible gives us very few clues; all that we can do is to consider some possibilities which at this distance in time can be neither proved nor disproved. One of these possibilities—the most spectacular and awe-inspiring of all—has been discovered only in the last few years, but let us first look at some of the earlier theories.

6   In addition to Venus, there are four other planets visible to the naked eye—Mercury, Mars, Jupiter, and Saturn. During their movements across the sky, two planets may sometimes appear to pass very close to one another—though in reality, of course, they are actually millions of miles apart.

7   Such occurrences are called "conjunctions"; on occasion they may be so close that the planets cannot be separated by the naked eye. This happened for Mars and Venus on October 4, 1953, when for a short while the two planets appeared to be fused together to give a single star. Such a spectacle is rare enough to be very striking, and the great astronomer Johannes Kepler devoted much time to proving that the Star of Bethlehem was a special conjunction of Jupiter and Saturn. The planets passed very close together (once again, remember, this was purely from the Earth's point of view—in reality they were half a billion miles apart!) in May, 7 B.C. This is quite near the date of Christ's birth, which probably took place in the spring of 7 or 6 B.C. (This still surprises most people, but as Herod is known to have died early in 4 B.C., Christ must

have been born before 5 B.C. We should add six years to the calendar for A.D. to mean what it says.)

8   Kepler's proposal, however, is as unconvincing as the Venus theory. Better calculations than those he was able to make in the seventeenth century have shown that this particular conjunction was not a very close one, and the planets were always far enough apart to be easily separated by the eye. Moreover, there was a closer conjunction in 66 B.C., which on Kepler's theory should have brought a delegation of wise men to Bethlehem sixty years too soon!

9   In any case, the Magi could be expected to be as familiar with such events as with all other planetary movements, and the Biblical account also indicates that the Star of Bethlehem was visible over a period of weeks (it must have taken the Magi a considerable time to reach Judea, have their interview with Herod, and then go on to Bethlehem). The conjunction of two planets lasts only a very few days, since they soon separate in the sky and go once more upon their individual ways.

10   We can get over the difficulty if we assume that the Magi were astrologers ("Magi" and "magician" have a common root) and had somehow deduced the birth of the Messiah from a particular configuration of the planets, which to them, if to no one else, had a unique significance. It is an interesting fact that the Jupiter-Saturn conjunction of 7 B.C. occurred in the constellation Pisces, the Fish. Now though the ancient Jews were too sensible to believe in astrology, the constellation Pisces was supposed to be connected with them. Anything peculiar happening in Pisces would, naturally, direct the attention of Oriental astrologers toward Jerusalem.

11   This theory is simple and plausible, but a little disappointing. One would like to think that the Star of Bethlehem was something more dramatic and not anything to do with the familiar planets whose behavior had been perfectly well known for thousands of years before the birth of Christ. Of course, if one accepts as *literally* true the statement that "the star, which they saw in the east, *went before them, till it came and stood over where the young Child was*," no natural explanation is possible. Any heavenly body—star, planet, comet, or whatever—must share in the normal movement of the sky, rising in the east and setting some hours later in the west. Only the Pole Star, because it lies on the invisible axis of the turning Earth, appears unmoving in the sky and can act as a fixed and constant guide.

12   But the phrase, "went before them," like so much else in the Bible, can be interpreted in many ways. It may be that the star—whatever it might have been—was so close to the Sun that it could be seen only for a short period near dawn, and so would never have been visible except in the eastern sky. Like Venus when she is a morning star, it might have risen shortly before the Sun, then been lost in the glare of the new day before it could climb very far up the sky. The wise men would thus have seen it ahead of them at the beginning of each day, and then lost it in the

dawn before it had veered around to the south. Many other readings are also possible.

13   Very well, then, can we discover some astronomical phenomenon sufficiently startling to surprise men completely familiar with the movements of the stars and planets and which fits the Biblical text?

14   Let's see if a comet would answer the specification. There have been no really spectacular comets in this century—though there were several in the 1800s—and most people do not know what they look like or how they behave. They even confuse them with meteors, which any observer is bound to see if he goes out on a clear night and watches the sky for half an hour.

15   No two classes of object could be more different. A meteor is a speck of matter, usually smaller than a grain of sand, which burns itself up by friction as it tears through the outer layers of Earth's atmosphere. But a comet may be millions of times larger than the entire Earth, and may dominate the night sky for weeks on end. A really great comet may look like a searchlight shining across the stars, and it is not surprising that such a portentous object always caused alarm when it appeard in the heavens. As Calpurnia said to Caesar:

When beggars die, there are no comets seen;
The heavens themselves blaze forth the death of princes.

16   Most comets have a bright, starlike core, or nucleus, which is completely dwarfed by their enormous tail—a luminous appendage which may be in the shape of a narrow beam or a broad, diffuse fan. At first sight it would seem very unlikely that anyone would call such an object a star, but as a matter of fact in old records comets are sometimes referred to, not inaptly, as "hairy stars."

17   Comets are unpredictable: the great ones appear without warning, come racing in through the planets, bank sharply around the Sun, and then head out toward the stars, not to be seen again for hundreds or even millions of years. Only a few large comets—such as Halley's—have relatively short periods and have been observed on many occasions. Halley's comet, which takes seventy-five years to go around its orbit, has managed to put in an appearance at several historic events. It was visible just before the sack of Jerusalem in A.D. 66, and before the Norman invasion of England in A.D. 1066. Of course, in ancient times (or modern ones, for that matter) it was never very difficult to find a suitable disaster to attribute to any given comet. It is not surprising, therefore, that their reputation as portents of evil lasted for so long.

18   It is perfectly possible that a comet appeared just before the birth of Christ. Attempts have been made, without success, to see if any of the known comets were visible around that date. (Halley's, as will be seen from the figures above, was just a few years too early on its last appearance before the fall of Jerusalem.) But the number of comets whose paths

and periods we do know is very small compared with the colossal number that undoubtedly exists. If a comet did shine over Bethlehem, it may not be seen again from Earth for a hundred thousand years.

19   We can picture it in that Oriental dawn—a band of light streaming up from the eastern horizon, perhaps stretching vertically toward the zenith. The tail of a comet always points away from the Sun; the comet would appear, therefore, like a great arrow, aimed at the east. As the Sun rose, it would fade into invisibility; but the next morning, it would be in almost the same place, still directing the travelers to their goal. It might be visible for weeks before it disappeared once more into the depths of space.

20   The picture is a dramatic and attractive one. It may even be the correct explanation; one day, perhaps, we shall know.

21   But there is yet another theory, and this is the one which most astronomers would probably accept today. It makes the other explanations look very trivial and commonplace indeed, for it leads us to contemplate one of the most astonishing—and terrifying—events yet discovered in the whole realm of nature.

22   We will forget now about planets and comets and the other denizens of our own tight little Solar System. Let us go out across *real* space, right out to the stars—those other suns, many far greater than our own, which sheer distance has dwarfed to dimensionless points of light.

23   Most of the stars shine with unwavering brilliance, century after century. Sirius appears now exactly as it did to Moses, as it did to Neanderthal man, as it did to the dinosaurs—if they ever bothered to look at the night sky. Its brilliance has changed little during the entire history of our Earth and will be the same a billion years from now.

24   But there are some stars—the so-called "novae," or new stars— which through internal causes suddenly become celestial atomic bombs. Such a star may explode so violently that it leaps a hundred-thousand-fold in brilliance within a few hours. One night it may be invisible to the naked eye; on the next, it may dominate the sky. If our Sun became such a nova, Earth would melt to slag and puff into vapor in a matter of minutes, and only the outermost of the planets would survive.

25   Novae are not uncommon; many are observed every year, though few are near enough to be visible except through telescopes. They are the routine, everyday disasters of the Universe.

26   Two or three times in every thousand years, however, there occurs something which makes a mere nova about as inconspicuous as a firefly at noon. When a star becomes a *super*nova, its brilliance may increase not by a hundred thousand but by a *billion* in the course of a few hours. The last time such an event was witnessed by human eyes was in A.D. 1604; there was another supernova in A.D. 1572 (so brilliant that it was visible in broad daylight); and the Chinese astronomers recorded one in A.D. 1054. It is quite possible that the Bethlehem star was such a supernova, and if so one can draw some very surprising conclusions.

27   We'll assume that Supernova Bethlehem was about as bright as the supernova of A.D. 1572—often called "Tycho's star," after the great astronomer who observed it at the time. Since this star could be seen by day, it must have been as brilliant as Venus. As we also know that a supernova is, in reality, at least a hundred million times more brilliant than our own Sun, a very simple calculation tells us how far away it must have been for its *apparent* brightness to equal that of Venus.

28   It turns out that Supernova Bethlehem was more than three thousand light years—or, if you prefer, 18 quadrillion miles—away. That means that its light had been traveling for at least three thousand years before it reached Earth and Bethlehem, so that the awesome catastrophe of which it was the symbol took place five thousand years ago, when the Great Pyramid was still fresh from the builders.

29   Let us, in imagination, cross the gulfs of space and time and go back to the moment of the catastrophe. We might find ourselves watching an ordinary star—a sun, perhaps, no different from our own. There may have been planets circling it; we do not know how common planets are in the scheme of the Universe, and how many suns have these small companions. But there is no reason to think that they are rare, and many novae must be the funeral pyres of worlds, and perhaps races, greater than ours.

30   There is no warning at all—only a steadily rising intensity of the sun's light. Within minutes the change is noticeable; within an hour, the nearer worlds are burning. The star is expanding like a balloon, blasting off shells of gas at a million miles an hour as it blows its outer layers into space. Within a day, it is shining with such supernal brilliance that it gives off more light than *all the other suns in the Universe combined.* If it had planets, they are now no more than flecks of flame in the still-expanding shells of fire. The conflagration will burn for weeks before the dying star collapses back into quiescence.

31   But let us consider what happens to the light of the nova, which moves a thousand times more swiftly than the blast wave of the explosion. It will spread out into space, and after four or five years it will reach the next star. If there are planets circling that star, they will suddenly be illuminated by a second sun. It will give them no appreciable heat, but will be bright enough to banish night completely, for it will be more than a thousand times more luminous than our full Moon. All that light will come from a single blazing point, since even from its nearest neighbor Supernova Bethlehem would appear too small to show a disk.

32   Century after century, the shell of light will continue to expand around its source. It will flash past countless suns and flare briefly in the skies of their planets. Indeed, on the most conservative estimate, this great new star must have shone over thousands of worlds before its light reached Earth—and to all those worlds it appeared far, far brighter than it did to the men it led to Judea.

33   For as the shell of light expanded, it faded also. Remember, by the

time it reached Bethlehem it was spread over the surface of a sphere six thousand light-years across. A thousand years earlier, when Homer was singing the song of Troy, the nova would have appeared twice as brilliant to any watchers further upstream, as it were, to the time and place of the explosion.

34   That is a strange thought; there is a stranger one to come. For the light of Supernova Bethlehem is still flooding out through space; it has left Earth far behind in the twenty centuries that have elapsed since men saw it for the first and last time. Now that light is spread over a sphere ten thousand light-years across and must be correspondingly fainter. It is simple to calculate how bright the supernova must be to any beings who may be seeing it now as a new star in *their* skies. To them, it will still be far more brilliant than any other star in the entire heavens, for its brightness will have fallen only by 50 per cent on its extra two thousand years of travel.

35   At this very moment, therefore, the Star of Bethlehem may still be shining in the skies of countless worlds, circling far suns. Any watchers on those worlds will see its sudden appearance and its slow fading, just as the Magi did two thousand years ago when the expanding shell of light swept past the Earth. And for thousands of years to come, as its radiance ebbs out toward the frontiers of the Universe, Supernova Bethlehem will still have power to startle all who see it, wherever—and whatever—they may be.

36   Astronomy, as nothing else can do, teaches men humility. We know now that our Sun is merely one undistinguished member of a vast family of stars, and no longer think of ourselves as being at the center of creation. Yet it is strange to think that before its light fades away below the limits of vision, we may have shared the Star of Bethlehem with the beings of perhaps a million worlds—and that to many of them, nearer to the source of the explosion, it must have been a far more wonderful sight than ever it was to any eyes on earth.

37   What did they make of it—and did it bring them good tidings, or ill?

Study Questions

1. Is Clarke's essay exposition? Argument? Persuasion?
2. How does he organize the facts he presents? What is scientific about his method?
3. What does Clarke accomplish by using the personal pronouns?
4. How far beyond the validation of the star of the Magi, in terms of other aspects of the Nativity, does Clarke's discussion extend?

Of This Time, Of That Place

Of This Time, Of That Place is a collection of writings about what might be termed social concepts. More specifically, each subsection is concerned with a topic that is pertinent and of interest to the college student. In choosing selections for this section we have drawn on our experiences as teachers of freshman English and have included material we feel will speak directly to you—if not to your experience, then to your sensibilities. The authors represent a wide span of periods, from Francis Bacon in the 1600s to a whole handful of people in the 1970s. Many viewpoints are presented on issues that have been very much alive for centuries and promise to remain so.

The first group is concerned with patriotism and war. Most of us have had occasion, at one time or another, to question the abstract word *patriotism*. What exactly does it mean? Is patriotism joining the army? Or is it refusing to fight in a war seen as morally wrong? Is it more patriotic to vote for somebody—anybody—than to stay away from the polls because there seems to be no viable choice between candidates? Is saluting the flag more patriotic than marching to support a cause? Henry David Thoreau articulates the traditional and basic concept of civil disobedience, while Woody Allen takes a light, humorous look at civil disobedience today.

War has been included in this subsection because the subject is so closely allied with patriotism in today's philosophical viewpoints. The selections about war are predominantly poems which present opposing views of the same topic. John McCrae's "In Flanders' Fields" is the World War I veteran's message about war, tending to glorify the deaths of the thousands of Americans who are buried beneath the poppy fields in Belgium. Carl Sandburg takes quite a different approach in depicting the dead warrior. Opposing views are also presented by William Butler Yeats and Randall Jarrell in two poems on air warfare. Yeats glorifies flying, whether or not it is for the purpose of doing battle and possibly dying, while Jarrell finds that the dead airman never really lived at all. Margaret Mead, finally, calls on the science of anthropology to support her postulation that war is not really necessary to human survival at all—that there are alternatives.

Education is the topic of the second subsection. Marianne Moore and Robert Hogan open the section with descriptions of students; their viewpoints differ somewhat. Any freshman who has ever had a beautifully worded, artistic, creative theme returned by an instructor covered with red comments and graded C– will understand what Hogan is saying. So will the teacher who graded that theme. Hogan does see the possibility of communication; W. H. Auden denies that any is possible. He holds out little hope for teachers *or* students; all are trying, he thinks, but their efforts are mutually futile. Lionel Trilling looks at the college classroom from the professor's point of view; most students will recognize their peers, although rarely themselves, sitting in one of Professor Howe's classes. Walt Whitman closes this subsection with a poem similar to Hogan's. He wants to see the actuality, not the abstraction.

In closing *Of This Time, Of That Place,* we consider several different treatments of the generation gap. Bacon, who in the early 1600s had definite ideas about the proper role of children in the family, opens the section. Arthur Hoppe pursues the question of growing old, a topic that is gaining more prominence in our society every year. The remaining four authors deal with specific relationships between the generations. Both Cat Stevens and Dabney Stuart present fathers and sons. Stevens's song lyrics constitute a dialogue that might more realistically be described as two monologues, while Stuart's short poem speaks, beyond its actual words, on the same theme: neither generation hears the other. Maxine Kumin, conversely, while writing to her son, "They take you as you are," seems to be feeling, "I will accept you as you are."

A careful analysis of the material presented here may lead to an awareness on the reader's part that questions thought by each generation to be unique to its own time and place are in actuality universal; only the methods for dealing with the questions undergo change. It is very likely that our grandchildren will seek their own definitions of patriotism, form their own moral standards to deal with war, have their own interpretations for the word *student,* and experience the generation gap according to their society's expectations and demands. The concepts themselves, however, will not be much altered.

From *Civil Disobedience*

Henry David Thoreau

1   Under a government which imprisons any unjustly, the true place for a just man is also a prison. The proper place to-day, the only place which Massachusetts has provided for her freer and less desponding spirits, is in her own prisons, to be put out and locked out of the State by her own act, as they have already put themselves out by their principles. It is there that the fugitive slave, and the Mexican prisoner on parole, and the Indian come to plead the wrongs of his race, should find them; on that separate, but more free and honorable ground, where the State places those who are not *with* her but *against* her,—the only house in a slave-state in which a free man can abide with honor. If any think that their influence would be lost there, and their voices no longer afflict the ear of the State, that they would not be as an enemy within its walls, they do not know by how much truth is stronger than error, nor how much more eloquently and effectively he can combat injustice who has experienced a little in his own person. Cast your whole vote, not a strip of paper merely, but your whole influence. A minority is powerless while it conforms to the majority; it is not even a minority then; but it is irresistible when it clogs by its whole weight. If the alternative is to keep all just men in prison, or give up war and slavery, the State will not hesitate which to choose. If a thousand men were not to pay their tax-bills this year, that would not be a violent and bloody measure, as it would be to pay them, and enable the State to commit violence and shed innocent blood. This is, in fact, the definition of a peaceable revolution, if any such is possible. If the tax-gatherer, or any other public officer, asks me, as one has done, "But what shall I do?" my answer is, "If you really wish to do any thing, resign your office." When the subject has refused allegiance, and the officer has resigned his office, then the revolution is accomplished. But even suppose blood should flow. Is there not a sort of blood shed when the conscience is wounded? Through this wound a man's real manhood and immortality flow out, and he bleeds to an everlasting death. I see this blood flowing now.

2   I have contemplated the imprisonment of the offender, rather than the seizure of his goods,—though both will serve the same purpose,—because they who assert the purest right, and consequently are most dangerous to a corrupt State, commonly have not spent much time in accumulating property. To such the State renders comparatively small service, and a slight tax is wont to appear exorbitant, particularly if they

237

are obliged to earn it by special labor with their hands. If there were one who lived wholly without the use of money, the State itself would hesitate to demand it of him. But the rich man—not to make any invidious comparison—is always sold to the institution which makes him rich. Absolutely speaking, the more money, the less virtue; for money comes between a man and his objects, and obtains them for him; and it was certainly no great virtue to obtain it. It puts to rest many questions which he would otherwise be taxed to answer; while the only new question which it puts is the hard but superfluous one, how to spend it. Thus his moral ground is taken from under his feet. The opportunities of living are diminished in proportion as what are called the "means" are increased. The best thing a man can do for his culture when he is rich is to endeavour to carry out those schemes which he entertained when he was poor. Christ answered the Herodians according to their condition. "Show me the tribute-money," said he;—and one took a penny out of his pocket;—If you use money which has the image of Cæsar on it, and which he has made current and valuable, that is, *if you are men of the State,* and gladly enjoy the advantages of Cæsar's government, then pay him back some of his own when he demands it; "Render therefore to Cæsar that which is Cæsar's, and to God those things which are God's,"— leaving them no wiser than before as to which was which; for they did not wish to know.

3   When I converse with the freest of my neighbors, I perceive that, whatever they may say about the magnitude and seriousness of the question, and their regard for the public tranquillity, the long and the short of the matter is, that they cannot spare the protection of the existing government, and they dread the consequences of disobedience to it to their property and families. For my own part, I should not like to think that I ever rely on the protection of the State. But, if I deny the authority of the State when it presents its tax-bill, it will soon take and waste all my property, and so harass me and my children without end. This is hard. This makes it impossible for a man to live honestly and at the same time comfortably in outward respects. It will not be worth the while to accumulate property; that would be sure to go again. You must hire or squat somewhere, and raise but a small crop, and eat that soon. You must live within yourself, and depend upon yourself, always tucked up and ready for a start, and not have many affairs. A man may grow rich in Turkey even, if he will be in all respects a good subject of the Turkish government. Confucius said,—"If a State is governed by the principles of reason, poverty and misery are subjects of shame; if a State is not governed by the principles of reason, riches and honors are the subjects of shame." No: until I want the protection of Massachusetts to be extended to me in some distant southern port, where my liberty is endangered, or until I am bent solely on building up an estate at home by peaceful enterprise, I can afford to refuse allegiance to Massachusetts, and her right to my property and life. It costs me less in every sense to

incur the penalty of disobedience to the State, than it would to obey. I should feel as if I were worth less in that case.

Study Questions

1. What is the thesis of this essay? Is this thesis valid today?
2. Explain the logic in the statements from Confucius. How is this logic extended in Thoreau's essay?
3. Explain the use of paradox in paragraph 2.
4. Does Thoreau use sufficient examples and details in presenting his case? Are they helpful to you in understanding the essay?

A Brief, Yet Helpful, Guide to Civil Disobedience

Woody Allen

1   In perpetrating a revolution, there are two requirements: someone or something to revolt against and someone to actually show up and do the revolting. Dress is usually casual and both parties may be flexible about time and place but if either faction fails to attend, the whole enterprise is likely to come off badly. In the Chinese Revolution of 1650 neither party showed up and the deposit on the hall was forfeited.

2   The people or parties revolted against are called the "oppressors" and are easily recognized as they seem to be the ones having all the fun. The "oppressors" generally get to wear suits, own land, and play their radios late at night without being yelled at. Their job is to maintain the "status quo," a condition where everything remains the same although they may be willing to paint every two years.

3   When the "oppressors" become too strict, we have what is known as a police state wherein all dissent is forbidden as is chuckling, showing up in a bow tie, or referring to the mayor as "Fats." Civil liberties are greatly curtailed in a police state and freedom of speech is unheard of although one is allowed to mime to a record. Opinions critical of the government are not tolerated, particularly about their dancing. Freedom of the press is also curtailed and the ruling party "manages" the news, permitting the citizens to hear only acceptable political ideas and ball scores that will not cause unrest.

4   The groups who revolt are called the "oppressed" and can generally be seen milling about and grumbling or claiming to have headaches. (It should be noted that the oppressors never revolt and attempt to become the oppressed as that would entail a change of underwear.)

5   Some famous examples of revolutions are:

6   *The French Revolution,* in which the peasants seized power by force and quickly changed all locks on the palace doors so the nobles could not get back in. Then they had a large party and gorged themselves. When the nobles finally recaptured the palace they were forced to clean up and found many stains and cigarette burns.

7   *The Russian Revolution,* which simmered for years and suddenly erupted when the serfs finally realized that the Czar and the Tsar were the same person.

8   It should be noted that after a revolution is over, the "oppressed" frequently take over and begin acting like the "oppressors." Of course by then it is very hard to get them on the phone and money lent for cigarettes and gum during the fighting may as well be forgotten about.

Methods of Civil Disobedience:

9   *Hunger Strike.* Here the oppressed goes without food until his demands are met. Insidious politicians will often leave biscuits within easy reach or perhaps some cheddar cheese but they must be resisted. If the party in power can get the striker to eat, they usually have little trouble putting down the insurrection. If they can get him to eat and also lift the check, they have won for sure. In Pakistan, a hunger strike was broken when the Government produced an exceptionally fine veal cordon bleu which the masses found was too appealing to turn down but such gourmet dishes are rare.

10   The problem with the hunger strike is that after several days one can get quite hungry, particularly since sound-trucks are paid to go through the street saying, "Um . . . what nice chicken—umm . . . some peas . . . umm. . . ."

11   A modified form of the Hunger Strike for those whose political convictions are not quite so radical is giving up chives. This small gesture, when used properly, can greatly influence a government and it

is well known that Mahatma Gandhi's insistence on eating his salads untossed shamed the British Government into many concessions. Other things besides food one can give up are: whist, smiling, and standing on one foot and imitating a crane.

12   *Sit-down Strike.* Proceed to a designated spot and then sit down, but sit all the way down. Otherwise you are squatting, a position that makes no political point unless the government is also squatting. (This is rare, although a government will occasionally crouch in cold weather.) The trick is to remain seated until concessions are made but as in the Hunger Strike, the government will try subtle means of making the striker rise. They may say, "Okay, everybody up, we're closing." Or, "Can you get up for a minute, we'd just like to see how tall you are?"

13   *Demonstration and Marches.* The key point about a demonstration is that it must be seen. Hence the term, "demonstration." If a person demonstrates privately in his own home, this is not technically a demonstration but merely "acting silly," or "behaving like an ass."

14   A fine example of demonstration was The Boston Tea Party where outraged Americans disguised as Indians dumped British tea into the harbor. Later, Indians disguised as outraged Americans dumped actual British into the harbor. Following that, the British disguised as tea, dumped each other into the harbor. Finally, German mercenaries clad only in costumes from "The Trojan Women" leapt into the harbor for no apparent reason.

15   When demonstrating, it is good to carry a placard stating one's position. Some suggested positions are: (1) lower taxes, (2) raise taxes, and (3) stop grinning at Persians.

Miscellaneous Methods of Civil Disobedience:

16   Standing in front of City Hall and chanting the word "pudding" until one's demands are met.

17   Tying up traffic by leading a flock of sheep into the shopping area.

18   Phoning members of "the establishment" and singing "Bess, You Is My Woman, Now" into the phone.

19   Dressing as a policeman and then skipping.

20   Pretending to be an artichoke but punching people as they pass.

Study Questions

1. Is this guide brief? Is it helpful?
2. What attitudes toward food and luxury appear in this essay? How do they contribute humor?
3. Compare this essay with Thoreau's "guide." Would Thoreau agree with Allen?
4. What is *incongruity*? How does it figure in this essay?

In Flanders' Fields

John McCrae

In Flanders' fields the poppies blow
Between the crosses, row on row,
That mark our place, and in the sky
The larks, still bravely singing, fly
Scarce heard amid the guns below.

We are the Dead! Short days ago
We lived, felt dawn, saw sunset glow,
Loved and were loved, and now we lie
In Flanders' fields.

Take up our quarrel with the foe!   10
To you from failing hands we throw
The Torch. Be yours to hold it high!
If ye break faith with us who die
We shall not sleep, though poppies grow,
In Flanders' fields.

Study Questions

1. Does stanza 3 consistently develop the tone of stanzas 1 and 2?
2. Is the imagery in lines 11–12 consistent temporally with the rest of the poem?
3. What connection does the poet see between the "sleep" of the dead and the growth of the poppies?
4. Notice the pattern of sentence structure used in the poem. Do changes in sentence structure signal changes in tone?
5. McCrae argues that once a certain number of men have been killed in a war, only victory (with no consideration of its consequences) can justify their deaths. Evaluate the logic of this assertion.

Grass

Carl Sandburg

Pile the bodies high at Austerlitz and Waterloo.
Shovel them under and let me work—
            I am the grass; I cover all.

And pile them high at Gettysburg
And pile them high at Ypres and Verdun.
Shovel them under and let me work.
Two years, ten years, and passengers ask the conductor:
            What place is this?
            Where are we now?

            I am the grass.   10
            Let me work.

Study Questions

1. Who "speaks" in this poem? What is the effect of the personification?
2. What is the "work" of the grass?
3. By what means is the human quality of the dead diminished in this poem?
4. What is the function of time in this poem?

An Irish Airman Foresees His Death

William Butler Yeats

I know that I shall meet my fate
Somewhere among the clouds above;
Those that I fight I do not hate,
Those that I guard I do not love;
My country is Kiltartan Cross,
My countrymen Kiltartan's poor,
No likely end could bring them less
Or leave them happier than before.
Nor law, nor duty bade me fight,
Nor public men, nor cheering crowds,   10
A lonely impulse of delight
Drove to this tumult in the clouds;
I balanced all, brought all to mind,
The years to come seemed waste of breath,
A waste of breath the years behind
In balance with this life, this death.

Study Questions

1. Was the airman's decision deliberate? Does the poem's form (meter and rhyme scheme) present data relevant to this question?
2. Explain how parallelism works in the poem's sentence structure.
3. Explain the paradox stated in lines 3–4.
4. How does line 11 represent a contradiction to and a culmination of the preceding ten lines?

The Death of the Ball Turret Gunner

Randall Jarrell

From my mother's sleep I fell into the State,
And I hunched in its belly till my wet fur froze.
Six miles from earth, loosed from its dream of life,
I woke to black flak and the nightmare fighters.
When I died they washed me out of the turret with a hose.

Study Questions

1. How many "wombs" does the speaker occupy? Does he ever achieve a satisfactory birth?
2. What does the image of "wet fur" imply about the speaker? To what literal image does it refer?
3. What was the speaker's conception of the State? Were his expectations violated?
4. How would the poem be changed if the last three lines were in the passive voice? Would it be a better poem for the change?

Warfare Is Only an Invention—
Not a Biological Necessity

Margaret Mead

1   Is war a biological necessity, a sociological inevitability, or just a bad invention? Those who argue for the first view endow man with such pugnacious instincts that some outlet in aggressive behavior is necessary if man is to reach full human stature. It was this point of view which lay back of William James's famous essay, "The Moral Equivalent of War" (*supra*), in which he tried to retain the warlike virtues and channel them in new directions. A similar point of view has lain back of the Soviet Union's attempt to make competition between groups rather than between individuals. A basic, competitive, aggressive, warring human nature is assumed, and those who wish to outlaw war or outlaw competitiveness merely try to find new and less socially destructive ways in which these biologically given aspects of man's nature can find expression. Then there are those who take the second view: warfare is the inevitable concomitant of the development of the state, the struggle for land and natural resources of class societies springing not from the nature of man, but from the nature of history. War is nevertheless inevitable unless we change our social system and outlaw classes, the struggle for power, and possessions; and in the event of our success warfare would disappear, as a symptom vanishes when the disease is cured.

2   One may hold a sort of compromise position between these two extremes; one may claim that all aggression springs from the frustration of man's biologically determined drives and that, since all forms of culture are frustrating, it is certain each new generation will be aggressive and the aggression will find its natural and inevitable expression in race war, class war, nationalistic war, and so on. All three of these positions are very popular today among those who think seriously about the problems of war and its possible prevention, but I wish to urge another point of view, less defeatist, perhaps, than the first and third and more accurate than the second: that is, that warfare, by which I mean recognized conflict between two groups *as groups*, in which each group puts an army (even if the army is only fifteen pygmies) into the field to fight and kill, if possible, some of the members of the army of the other group—that warfare of this sort is an invention like any other of the inventions in terms of which we order our lives, such as writing, marriage, cooking our food instead of eating it raw, trial by jury, or burial of

the dead, and so on. Some of this list anyone will grant are inventions: trial by jury is confined to very limited portions of the globe; we know that there are tribes that do not bury their dead but instead expose or cremate them; and we know that only part of the human race has had the knowledge of writing as its cultural inheritance. But, whenever a way of doing things is found universally, such as the use of fire or the practice of some form of marriage, we tend to think at once that it is not an invention at all but an attribute of humanity itself. And yet even such universals as marriage and the use of fire are inventions like the rest, very basic ones, inventions which were, perhaps, necessary if human history was to take the turn that it has taken, but nevertheless inventions. At some point in his social development man was undoubtedly without the institution of marriage or the knowledge of the use of fire.

3   The case for warfare is much clearer because there are peoples even today who have no warfare. Of these the Eskimos are perhaps the most conspicuous examples, but the Lepchas of Sikkim described by Geoffrey Gorer in *Himalayan Village* are as good. Neither of these peoples understands war, not even defensive warfare. The idea of warfare is lacking, and this idea is as essential to really carrying on war as an alphabet or a syllabary is to writing. But, whereas the Lepchas are a gentle, unquarrelsome people, and the advocates of other points of view might argue that they are not full human beings or that they had never been frustrated and so had no aggression to expand in warfare, the Eskimo case gives no such possibility of interpretation. The Eskimos are not a mild and meek people; many of them are turbulent and troublesome. Fights, theft of wives, murder, cannibalism, occur among them— all outbursts of passionate men goaded by desire or intolerable circumstance. Here are men faced with hunger, men faced with loss of their wives, men faced with the threat of extermination by other men, and here are orphan children, growing up miserably with no one to care for them, mocked and neglected by those about them. The personality necessary for war, the circumstances necessary to goad men to desperation are present, but there is no war. When a traveling Eskimo entered a settlement, he might have to fight the strongest man in the settlement to establish his position among them, but this was a test of strength and bravery, not war. The idea of warfare, of one *group* organizing against another *group* to maim and wound and kill them was absent. And, without that idea, passions might rage but there was no war.

4   But, it may be argued, is not this because the Eskimos have such a low and undeveloped form of social organization? They own no land, they move from place to place, camping, it is true, season after season on the same site, but this is not something to fight for as the modern nations of the world fight for land and raw materials. They have no permanent possessions that can be looted, no towns that can be burned. They have no social classes to produce stress and strains within the society which might force it to go to war outside. Does not the absence of war among

the Eskimos, while disproving the biological necessity of war, just go to confirm the point that it is the state of development of the society which accounts for war and nothing else?

5   We find the answer among the pygmy peoples of the Andaman Islands in the Bay of Bengal. The Andamans also represent an exceedingly low level of society; they are a hunting and food-gathering people; they live in tiny hordes without any class stratification; their houses are simpler than the snow houses of the Eskimo. But they knew about warfare. The army might contain only fifteen determined pygmies marching in a straight line, but it was the real thing none the less. Tiny army met tiny army in open battle, blows were exchanged, casualties suffered, and the state of warfare could only be concluded by a peace-making ceremony.

6   Similarly, among the Australian aborigines, who built no permanent dwellings but wandered from water hole to water hole over their almost desert country, warfare—and rules of "international law"—were highly developed. The student of social evolution will seek in vain for his obvious causes of war, struggle for lands, struggle for power of one group over another, expansion of population, need to divert the minds of a populace restive under tyranny, or even the ambition of a successful leader to enhance his own prestige. All are absent, but warfare as a practice remained, and men engaged in it and killed one another in the course of a war because killing is what is done in wars.

7   From instances like these it becomes apparent that an inquiry into the causes of war misses the fundamental point as completely as does an insistence upon the biological necessity of war. If a people have an idea of going to war and the idea that war is the way in which certain situations, defined within their society, are to be handled, they will sometimes go to war. If they are a mild and unaggressive people, like the Pueblo Indians, they may limit themselves to defensive warfare, but they will be forced to think in terms of war because there are peoples near them who have warfare as a pattern, and offensive, raiding, pillaging warfare at that. When the pattern of warfare is known, people like the Pueblo Indians will defend themselves, taking advantage of their natural defenses, the mesa village site, and people like the Lepchas, having no natural defenses and no idea of warfare, will merely submit to the invader. But the essential point remains the same. There is a way of behaving which is known to a given people and labeled as an appropriate form of behavior; a bold and warlike people like the Sioux or the Maori may label warfare as desirable as well as possible, a mild people like the Pueblo Indians may label warfare as undesirable, but to the minds of both peoples the possibility of warfare is present. Their thoughts, their hopes, their plans are oriented about this idea—that warfare may be selected as the way to meet some situation.

8   So simple peoples and civilized peoples, mild peoples and violent, assertive peoples, will all go to war if they have the invention, just as

those peoples who have the custom of dueling will have duels and peoples who have the pattern of vendetta will indulge in vendetta. And, conversely, peoples who do not know of dueling will not fight duels, even though their wives are seduced and their daughters ravished; they may on occasion commit murder but they will not fight duels. Cultures which lack the idea of the vendetta will not meet every quarrel in this way. A people can use only the forms it has. So the Balinese have their special way of dealing with a quarrel between two individuals: if the two feel that the causes of quarrel are heavy, they may go and register their quarrel in the temple before the gods, and, making offerings, they may swear never to have anything to do with each other again. . . . But in other societies, although individuals might feel as full of animosity and as unwilling to have any further contact as do the Balinese, they cannot register their quarrel with the gods and go on quietly about their business because registering quarrels with the gods is not an invention of which they know.

9   Yet, if it be granted that warfare is, after all, an invention, it may nevertheless be an invention that lends itself to certain types of personality, to the exigent needs of autocrats, to the expansionist desires of crowded peoples, to the desire for plunder and rape and loot which is engendered by a dull and frustrating life. What, then, can we say of this congruence between warfare and its uses? If it is a form which fits so well, is not this congruence the essential point? But even here the primitive material causes us to wonder, because there are tribes who go to war merely for glory, having no quarrel with the enemy, suffering from no tyrant within their boundaries, anxious neither for land nor loot nor women, but merely anxious to win prestige which within that tribe has been declared obtainable only by war and without which no young man can hope to win his sweetheart's smile of approval. But if, as was the case with the Bush Negroes of Dutch Guiana, it is artistic ability which is necessary to win a girl's approval, the same young man would have to be carving rather than going out on a war party.

10   In many parts of the world, war is a game in which the individual can win counters—counters which bring him prestige in the eyes of his own sex or of the opposite sex; he plays for these counters as he might, in our society, strive for a tennis championship. Warfare is a frame for such prestige-seeking merely because it calls for the display of certain skills and certain virtues; all of these skills—riding straight, shooting straight, dodging the missiles of the enemy and sending one's own straight to the mark—can be equally well exercised in some other framework and, equally, the virtues—endurance, bravery, loyalty, steadfastness—can be displayed in other contexts. The tie-up between proving oneself a man and proving this by a success in organized killing is due to a definition which many societies have made of manliness. And often, even in those societies which counted success in warfare a proof of human worth, strange turns were given to the idea, as when the plains Indians gave

their highest awards to the man who touched a live enemy rather than to the man who brought in a scalp—from a dead enemy—because the latter was less risky. Warfare is just an invention known to the majority of human societies by which they permit their young men either to accumulate prestige or avenge their honor or acquire loot or wives or slaves or sago lands or cattle or appease the blood lust of their gods or the restless souls of the recently dead. It is just an invention, older and more widespread than the jury system, but none the less an invention.

11   But, once we have said this, have we said anything at all? Despite a few instances, dear to the hearts of controversialists, of the loss of the useful arts, once an invention is made which proves congruent with human needs or social forms, it tends to persist. Grant that war is an invention, that it is not a biological necessity nor the outcome of certain special types of social forms, still, once the invention is made, what are we to do about it? The Indian who had been subsisting on the buffalo for generations because with his primitive weapons he could slaughter only a limited number of buffalo did not return to his primitive weapons when he saw that the white man's more efficient weapons were exterminating the buffalo. A desire for the white man's cloth may mortgage the South Sea Islander to the white man's plantation, but he does not return to making bark cloth, which would have left him free. Once an invention is known and accepted, men do not easily relinquish it. The skilled workers may smash the first steam looms which they feel are to be their undoing, but they accept them in the end, and no movement which has insisted upon the mere abandonment of usable inventions has ever had much success. Warfare is here, as part of our thought; the deeds of warriors are immortalized in the words of our poets, the toys of our children are modeled upon the weapons of the soldier, the frame of reference within which our statesmen and our diplomats work always contains war. If we know that it is not inevitable, that it is due to historical accident that warfare is one of the ways in which we think of behaving, are we given any hope by that? What hope is there of persuading nations to abandon war, nations so thoroughly imbued with the idea that resort to war is, if not actually desirable and noble, at least inevitable whenever certain defined circumstances arise?

12   In answer to this question I think we might turn to the history of other social inventions, and inventions which must once have seemed as firmly entrenched as warfare. Take the methods of trial which preceded the jury system: ordeal and trial by combat. Unfair, capricious, alien as they are to our feeling today, they were once the only methods open to individuals accused of some offense. The invention of trial by jury gradually replaced these methods until only witches, and finally not even witches, had to resort to the ordeal. And for a long time the jury system seemed the one best and finest method of settling legal disputes, but today new inventions, trial before judges only or before commissions, are replacing the jury system. In each case the old method was

replaced by a new social invention. The ordeal did not go out because people thought it unjust or wrong; it went out because a method more congruent with the institutions and feelings of the period was invented. And, if we despair over the way in which war seems such an ingrained habit of most of the human race, we can take comfort from the fact that a poor invention will usually give place to a better invention.

13   For this, two conditions, at least, are necessary. The people must recognize the defects of the old invention, and someone must make a new one. Propaganda against warfare, documentation of its terrible cost in human suffering and social waste, these prepare the ground by teaching people to feel that warfare is a defective social institution. There is further needed a belief that social invention is possible and the invention of new methods which will render warfare as out of date as the tractor is making the plow, or the motor car the horse and buggy. A form of behavior becomes out of date only when something else takes its place, and, in order to invent forms of behavior which will make war obsolete, it is a first requirement to believe that an invention is possible.

Study Questions

1. At the beginning of the first paragraph, Mead presents three causes of war. She elaborates on two of them within that same paragraph but gives the last a paragraph of its own. Why?
2. Does the author acknowledge an opposing viewpoint? Does such an acknowledgment have a sound rhetorical purpose?
3. In the final paragraph, Mead says that we need "the invention of new methods which will render warfare as out of date as the tractor is making the plow, or the motor car the horse and buggy." Is this analogy valid?

The Student

Marianne Moore

"In America," began
the lecturer, "everyone must have a
degree. The French do not think that
all can have it, they don't say everyone
    must go to college." We
incline to feel
    that although it may be unnecessary

to know fifteen languages,
one degree is not too much. With us, a
school—like the singing tree of which
the leaves were mouths singing in concert—
    is both a tree of knowledge
and of liberty—
    seen in the unanimity of college

mottoes, *Lux et veritas,*
Christo et ecclesiae, Sapient
felici. It may be that we
have not knowledge, just opinions, that we
    are undergraduates,
not students; we know
    we have been told with smiles, by expatriates

of whom we had asked "When will
your experiment be finished?" "Science
is never finished." Secluded
from domestic strife, Jack Bookworm led a
    college life, says Goldsmith;
and here also as
    in France or Oxford, study is beset with
dangers,—with bookworms, mildews,
and complaisancies. But someone in New
England has known enough to say
the student is patience personified,
    is a variety
of hero, "patient
    of neglect and of reproach"—who can "hold by

himself." You can't beat hens to
make them lay. Wolf's wool is the best of wool,
but it cannot be sheared because
the wolf will not comply. With knowledge as
   with the wolf's surliness,
the student studies
   voluntarily, refusing to be less   30

than individual. He
"gives his opinion and then rests on it";
he renders service when there is
no reward, and is too reclusive for
   some things to seem to touch
him, not because he
   has no feeling but because he has so much.

Study Questions

1. What is the distinction between "undergraduates" and "students" and between "knowledge" and "opinions" implicit in this poem?
2. How do "expatriates" figure in this poem?
3. How is American education institutionalized? What examples in the poem relate to this question?

After Sending Freshmen to Describe a Tree

Robert Hogan

Twenty inglorious Miltons looked at a tree and saw God,
Noted its "clutching fingers groping in the sod,"
Heard "Zephyr's gentle breezes wafting through her hair,"

Saw "a solemn statue," heard "a growing woody prayer,"
Saw "dancing skirts" and "the Lord's design,"
"Green arrows to God" instead of pine,
Saw symbols in squirrels, heard musings in bees:
Not one of the Miltons saw any trees.

If you must see a tree, clean, clear, and bright,
For God's sake and mine, look *outside* your heart and write.   10

Study Questions

1. Compare the diction of the last stanza with that of the first. What is the poet satirizing?
2. What does this poem say about descriptive writing?
3. Is Hogan being fair to freshmen?
4. Why is Milton a particularly apt choice of poets for this poem?

How to Write Like a Social Scientist

Samuel T. Williamson

1   During my years as an editor, I have seen probably hundreds of job applicants who were either just out of college or in their senior year. All wanted "to write." Many brought letters from their teachers. But I do not recall one letter announcing that its bearer could write what he wished to say with clarity and directness, with economy of words, and with pleasing variety of sentence structure.

2   Most of these young men and women could not write plain English. Apparently their noses had not been rubbed in the drudgery of putting one simple well-chosen word behind the other. If this was true of teachers' pets, what about the rest? What about those going into business and industry? Or those going into professions? What about those who remain at college—first for a Master of Arts degree, then an instructorship combined with work for a Ph.D., then perhaps an assistant professorship, next a full professorship and finally, as an academic crown of laurel, appointment as head of a department or as dean of a faculty?

3   Certainly, faculty members of a front-rank university should be better able to express themselves than those they teach. Assume that those in the English department have this ability. Can the same be said of the social scientists—economists, sociologists, and authorities on government? We need today as we never needed so urgently before all the understanding they can give us of problems of earning a living, caring for our fellows, and governing ourselves. Too many of them, I find, can't write as well as their students.

4   I am still convalescing from overexposure some time ago to products of the academic mind. One of the foundations engaged me to edit manuscripts of a socio-economic research report designed for the thoughtful citizen as well as for the specialist. My expectations were not high—no deathless prose, merely a sturdy, no-nonsense report of explorers into the wilderness of statistics and half-known facts. I knew from experience that economic necessity compels many a professional writer to be a cream-skimmer and a gatherer of easily obtainable material; for unless his publishers will stand the extra cost, he cannot afford the exhaustive investigation which endowed research makes possible. Although I did not expect fine writing from a trained, professional researcher, I did assume that a careful fact-finder would write carefully.

5   And so, anticipating no literary treat, I plunged into the forest of words of my first manuscript. My weapons were a sturdy eraser and several batteries of sharpened pencils. My armor was a thesaurus. And if I should become lost, a near-by public library was a landmark, and the Encyclopedia of Social Sciences on its reference shelves was an ever-ready guide.

6   Instead of big trees, I found underbrush. Cutting through involved, lumbering sentences was bad enough, but the real chore was removal of the burdocks of excess verbiage which clung to the manuscript. Nothing was big or large; in my author's lexicon, it was "substantial." When he meant "much," he wrote "to a substantially high degree." If some event took place in the early 1920's, he put it "in the early part of the decade of the twenties." And instead of "that depends," my author wrote, "any answer to this question must bear in mind certain peculiar characteristics of the industry."

7   So it went for 30,000 words. The pile of verbal burdocks grew—sometimes twelve words from a twenty-word sentence. The shortened

version of 20,000 words was perhaps no more thrilling than the original report; but it was terser and crisper. It took less time to read and it could be understood quicker. That was all I could do. As S. S. McClure once said to me, "An editor can improve a manuscript, but he cannot put in what isn't there."

8   I did not know the author I was editing; after what I did to his copy it may be just as well that we have not met. Aside from his cat-chasing-its-own-tail verbosity, he was a competent enough workman. Apparently he is well thought of. He has his doctorate, he is a trained researcher and a pupil of an eminent professor. He has held a number of fellowships and he has performed competently several jobs of economic research. But, after this long academic preparation for what was to be a life work, it is a mystery why so little attention was given to acquiring use of simple English.

9   Later, when I encountered other manuscripts, I found I had been too hard on this promising Ph.D. Tone-deaf as he was to words, his report was a lighthouse of clarity among the chapters turned in by his so-called academic betters. These brethren—and sister'n—who contributed the remainder of the foundation's study were professors and assistant professors in our foremost colleges and universities. The names of one or two are occasionally in newspaper headlines. All of them had, as the professional term has it, "published."

10   Anyone who edits copy, regardless of whether it is good or bad, discovers in a manuscript certain pet phrases, little quirks of style and other individual traits of its author. But in the series I edited, all twenty reports read alike. Their words would be found in any English dictionary, grammar was beyond criticism, but long passages in these reports demanded not editing but actual translation. For hours at a time, I floundered in brier patches like this: "In eliminating wage changes due to purely transitory conditions, collective bargaining has eliminated one of the important causes of industrial conflict, for changes under such conditions are almost always followed by a reaction when normal conditions appear."

11   I am not picking on my little group of social scientists. They are merely members of a caste; they are so used to taking in each other's literary washing that it has become a habit for them to clothe their thoughts in the same smothering verbal garments. Nor are they any worse than most of their colleagues, for example:

> In the long run, developments in transportation, housing, optimum size of plant, etc., might tend to induce an industrial and demographic pattern similar to the one that consciousness of vulnerability would dictate. Such a tendency might be advanced by public persuasion and governmental inducement, and advanced more effectively if the causes of urbanization had been carefully studied.

12   Such pedantic Choctaw may be all right as a sort of code language or shorthand of social science to circulate among initiates, but its perpe-

trators have no right to impose it on others. The tragedy is that its users appear to be under the impression that it is good English usage.

13   Father, forgive them; for they know not what they do! There once was a time when everyday folk spoke one language, and learned men wrote another. It was called the Dark Ages. The world is in such a state that we may return to the Dark Ages if we do not acquire wisdom. If social scientists have answers to our problems yet feel under no obligation to make themselves understood, then we laymen must learn their language. This may take some practice, but practice should become perfect by following six simple rules of the guild of social science writers. Examples which I give are sound and well tested; they come from manuscripts I edited.

14   *Rule 1. Never use a short word when you can think of a long one.* Never say "now," but "currently." It is not "soon" but "presently." You did not have "enough" but a "sufficiency." Never do you come to the "end" but to the "termination." This rule is basic.

15   *Rule 2. Never use one word when you can use two or more.* Eschew "probably." Write, "it is improbable," and raise this to "it is not improbable." Then you'll be able to parlay "probably" into "available evidence would tend to indicate that it is not unreasonable to suppose."

16   *Rule 3. Put one-syllable thought into polysyllabic terms.* Instead of observing that a work force might be bigger and better, write, "In addition to quantitative enlargement, it is not improbable that there is need also for qualitative improvement in the personnel of the service." If you have discovered that musicians out of practice can't hold jobs, report that "the fact of rapid deterioration of musical skill when not in use soon converts the unemployed into the unemployable." Resist the impulse to say that much men's clothing is machine made. Put it thus: "Nearly all operations in the industry lend themselves to performance by machine, and all grades of men's clothing sold in significant quality involve a very substantial amount of machine work."

17   *Rule 4. Put the obvious in terms of the unintelligible.* When you write that "the product of the activity of janitors is expended in the identical locality in which that activity takes place," your lay reader is in for a time of it. After an hour's puzzlement, he may conclude that janitors' sweepings are thrown on the town dump. See what you can do with this: "Each article sent to the cleaner is handled separately." You become a member of the guild in good standing if you put it like this. "Within the cleaning plant proper the business of the industry involves several well-defined processes, which, from the economic point of view, may be characterized simply by saying that most of them require separate handling of each individual garment or piece of material to be cleaned."

18   *Rule 5. Announce what you are going to say before you say it.* This pitcher's wind-up technique before hurling towards—not at—home plate has two varieties. First in the quick wind-up: "In the following section the policies of the administration will be considered." Then you become strong enough for the contortionist wind-up: "Perhaps more

important, therefore, than the question of what standards are in a particular case, there are the questions of the extent of observance of these standards and the methods of their enforcement." Also you can play with reversing Rule 5 and *say what you have said after you have said it.*

19   *Rule 6. Defend your style as "scientific."* Look down on—not up to—clear simple English. Sneer at it as "popular." Scorn it as "journalistic." Explain your failure to put more mental sweat into your writing on the ground that "the social scientists who want to be scientific believe that we can have scientific description of human behavior and trustworthy predictions in the scientific sense only as we build adequate taxonomic systems for observable phenomena and symbolic systems for the manipulation of ideal and abstract entities."

20   For this explanation I am indebted to Lyman Bryson in the *Saturday Review of Literature* article (Oct. 13, 1945) "Writers: Enemies of Social Science." Standing on ground considerably of his own choosing, Mr. Bryson argued against judging social science writing by literary standards.

21   Social scientists are not criticized because they are not literary artists. The trouble with social science does not lie in its special vocabulary. Those words are doubtless chosen with great care. The trouble is that too few social scientists take enough care with words outside their special vocabularies.

22   It is not much to expect that teachers should be more competent in the art of explanation than those they teach. Teachers of social sciences diligently try to acquire knowledge; too few exert themselves enough to impart it intelligently.

23   Too long has this been excused as "the academic mind." It should be called by what it is: intellectual laziness and grubbymindedness.

Study Questions

1. Explain the metaphorical contrast between "big trees" and "underbrush" in this essay.
2. What is the target of this satirical essay?
3. Discuss the introduction and conclusion. Do they follow good rhetorical practice? Where is the thesis statement? Does Williamson restate the thesis in his conclusion?

Schoolchildren

W. H. Auden

Here are all the captives; the cells are as real:
But these are unlike the prisoners we know
Who are outraged or pining or wittily resigned
      Or just wish all away.

For they dissent so little, so nearly content
With the dumb play of the dog, the licking and rushing;
The bars of love are so strong, their conspiracies
      Weak like the vows of drunkards.

Indeed their strangeness is difficult to watch:
The condemned see only the fallacious angels of a vision;   10
So little effort lies behind their smiling,
      The beast of vocation is afraid.

But watch them, O, set against our size and timing
The almost neuter, the slightly awkward perfection;
For the sex is there, the broken bootlace is broken,
      The professor's dream is not true.

Yet the tyranny is so easy. The improper word
Scribbled upon the fountain, is that all the rebellion?
The storm of tears shed in the corner, are these
      The seeds of the new life?   20

Study Questions

1. Why does Auden cast the drunkard image in the last line of stanza 2 as a simile rather than as a metaphor?
2. What is there about his subject that compels the poet to use seemingly paradoxical images such as "the bars of love" and "the beast of vocation"?
3. What is the "professor's dream" in the last line of stanza 4?
4. Why does the poet shift his imagistic description of the children from animals

("dog," "beast") in the first three stanzas to sexuality ("neuter," "sex," "seeds")
in the final two stanzas?

5. What are the possible meanings of the word *strangeness* in line 9?

Of This Time, Of That Place

Lionel Trilling

1   It was a fine September day. By noon it would be summer again but
now it was true autumn with a touch of chill in the air. As Joseph Howe
stood on the porch of the house in which he lodged, ready to leave for his
first class of the year, he thought with pleasure of the long indoor days
that were coming. It was a moment when he could feel glad of his
profession.

2   On the lawn the peach tree was still in fruit and young Hilda Aiken
was taking a picture of it. She held the camera tight against her chest.
She wanted the sun behind her but she did not want her own long
morning shadow in the foreground. She raised the camera but that did
not help, and she lowered it but that made things worse. She twisted her
body to the left, then to the right. In the end she had to step out of the
direct line of the sun. At last she snapped the shutter and wound the film
with intense care.

3   Howe, watching her from the porch, waited for her to finish and
called good morning. She turned, startled, and almost sullenly lowered
her glance. In the year Howe had lived at the Aikens', Hilda had accepted him as one of her family, but since his absence of the summer she
had grown shy. Then suddenly she lifted her head and smiled at him,
and the humorous smile confirmed his pleasure in the day. She picked
up her bookbag and set off for school.

4   The handsome houses on the streets to the college were not yet
fully awake but they looked very friendly. Howe went by the Bradby
house where he would be a guest this evening at the first dinner-party of
the year. When he had gone the length of the picket fence, the whitest in
town, he turned back. Along the path there was a fine row of asters and

he went through the gate and picked one for his buttonhole. The Brad-bys would be pleased if they happened to see him invading their lawn and the knowledge of this made him even more comfortable.

5   He reached the campus as the hour was striking. The students were hurrying to their classes. He himself was in no hurry. He stopped at his dim cubicle of an office and lit a cigarette. The prospect of facing his class had suddenly presented itself to him and his hands were cold, the lawful seizure of power he was about to make seemed momentous. Waiting did not help. He put out his cigarette, picked up a pad of theme paper and went to his classroom.

6   As he entered, the rattle of voices ceased and the twenty-odd freshmen settled themselves and looked at him appraisingly. Their faces seemed gross, his heart sank at their massed impassivity, but he spoke briskly.

7   "My name is Howe," he said and turned and wrote it on the blackboard. The carelessness of the scrawl confirmed his authority. He went on: "My office is 412 Slemp Hall and my office hours are Monday, Wednesday, and Friday from eleven-thirty to twelve-thirty."

8   He wrote: "M., W., F., 11.30–12.30." He said: "I'll be very glad to see any of you at that time. Or if you can't come then, you can arrange with me for some other time."

9   He turned again to the blackboard and spoke over his shoulder. "The text for the course is Jarman's *Modern Plays*, revised edition. The Co-op has it in stock." He wrote the name, underlined "revised edition" and waited for it to be taken down in the new note-books.

10   When the bent heads were raised again he began his speech of prospectus. "It is hard to explain——" he said, and paused as they composed themselves. "It is hard to explain what a course like this is intended to do. We are going to try to learn something about modern literature and something about prose composition."

11   As he spoke, his hands warmed and he was able to look directly at the class. Last year on the first day the faces had seemed just as cloddish, but as the term wore on they became gradually alive and quite likeable. It did not seem possible that the same thing could happen again.

12   "I shall not lecture in this course," he continued. "Our work will be carried on by discussion and we will try to learn by an exchange of opinion. But you will soon recognize that my opinion is worth more than anyone else's here."

13   He remained grave as he said it, but two boys understood and laughed. The rest took permission from them and laughed too. All Howe's private ironies protested the vulgarity of the joke but the laugh-ter made him feel benign and powerful.

14   When the little speech was finished, Howe picked up the pad of paper he had brought. He announced that they would write an extem-poraneous theme. Its subject was traditional: "Who I am and why I came to Dwight College." By now the class was more at ease and it gave a

ritualistic groan of protest. Then there was a stir as fountain-pens were brought out and the writing arms of the chairs were cleared and the paper was passed about. At last all the heads bent to work and the room became still.

15   Howe sat idly at his desk. The sun shone through the tall clumsy windows. The cool of the morning was already passing. There was a scent of autumn and of varnish, and the stillness of the room was deep and oddly touching. Now and then a student's head was raised and scratched in the old elaborate students' pantomime that calls the teacher to witness honest intellectual effort.

16   Suddenly a tall boy stood within the frame of the open door. "Is this," he said, and thrust a large nose into a college catalogue, "is this the meeting place of English 1A? The section instructed by Dr. Joseph Howe?"

17   He stood on the very sill of the door, as if refusing to enter until he was perfectly sure of all his rights. The class looked up from work, found him absurd and gave a low mocking cheer.

18   The teacher and the new student, with equal pointedness, ignored the disturbance. Howe nodded to the boy, who pushed his head forward and then jerked it back in a wide elaborate arc to clear his brow of a heavy lock of hair. He advanced into the room and halted before Howe, almost at attention. In a loud clear voice he announced: "I am Tertan, Ferdinand R., reporting at the direction of Head of Department Vincent."

19   The heraldic formality of this statement brought forth another cheer. Howe looked at the class with a sternness he could not really feel, for there was indeed something ridiculous about this boy. Under his displeased regard the rows of heads dropped to work again. Then he touched Tertan's elbow, led him up to the desk and stood so as to shield their conversation from the class.

20   "We are writing an extemporaneous theme," he said. "The subject is 'Who I am and why I came to Dwight College.'"

21   He stripped a few sheets from the pad and offered them to the boy. Tertan hesitated and then took the paper, but he held it only tentatively. As if with the effort of making something clear, he gulped, and a slow smile fixed itself on his face. It was at once knowing and shy.

22   "Professor," he said, "to be perfectly fair to my classmates"—he made a large gesture over the room—"and to you"—he inclined his head to Howe—"this would not be for me an extemporaneous subject."

23   Howe tried to understand. "You mean you've already thought about it—you've heard we always give the same subject? That doesn't matter."

24   Again the boy ducked his head and gulped. It was the gesture of one who wishes to make a difficult explanation with perfect candor. "Sir," he said, and made the distinction with great care, "the topic I did not expect but I have given much ratiocination to the subject."

25   Howe smiled and said: "I don't think that's an unfair advantage. Just go ahead and write."

26   Tertan narrowed his eyes and glanced sidewise at Howe. His strange mouth smiled. Then in quizzical acceptance, he ducked his head, threw back the heavy dank lock, dropped into a seat with a great loose noise and began to write rapidly.

27   The room fell silent again and Howe resumed his idleness. When the bell rang, the students who had groaned when the task had been set now groaned again because they had not finished. Howe took up the papers and held the class while he made the first assignment. When he dismissed it, Tertan bore down on him, his slack mouth held ready for speech.

28   "Some professors," he said, "are pedants. They are Dryasdusts. However, some professors are free souls and creative spirits. Kant, Hegel, and Nietzsche were all professors." With this pronouncement he paused. "It is my opinion," he continued, "that you occupy the second category."

29   Howe looked at the boy in surprise and said with good-natured irony: "With Kant, Hegel, and Nietzsche?"

30   Not only Tertan's hand and head but his whole awkward body waved away the stupidity. "It is the kind and not the quantity of the kind," he said sternly.

31   Rebuked, Howe said as simply and seriously as he could: "It would be nice to think so." He added: "Of course, I am not a professor."

32   This was clearly a disappointment but Tertan met it. "In the French sense," he said with composure. "Generically, a teacher."

33   Suddenly he bowed. It was such a bow, Howe fancied, as a stage-director might teach an actor playing a medieval student who takes leave of Abelard—stiff, solemn, with elbows close to the body and feet together. Then, quite as suddenly, he turned and left.

34   A queer fish, and as soon as Howe reached his office he sifted through the batch of themes and drew out Tertan's. The boy had filled many sheets with his unformed headlong scrawl. "Who am I?" he had begun. "Here, in a mundane, not to say commercialized academe, is asked the question which from time long immemorably out of mind has accreted doubts and thoughts in the psyche of man to pester him as a nuisance. Whether in St. Augustine (or Austin as sometimes called) or Miss Bashkirtsieff or Frederic Amiel or Empedocles, or in less lights of the intellect than these, this posed question has been ineluctable."

35   Howe took out his pencil. He circled "academe" and wrote "vocab." in the margin. He underlined "time long immemorably out of mind" and wrote "Diction!" But this seemed inadequate for what was wrong. He put down his pencil and read ahead to discover the principle of error in the theme. "To-day as ever, in spite of gloomy prophets of the dismal science (economics) the question is uninvalidated. Out of the

starry depths of heaven hurtles this spear of query demanding to be caught on the shield of the mind ere it pierces the skull and the limbs be unstrung."

36   Baffled but quite caught, Howe read on. "Materialism, by which is meant the philosophic concept and not the moral idea, provides no aegis against the question which lies beyond the tangible (metaphysics). Existence without alloy is the question presented. Environment and heredity relegated aside, the rags and old clothes of practical life discarded, the name and the instrumentality of livelihood do not, as the prophets of the dismal science insist on in this connection, give solution to the interrogation which not from the professor merely but veritably from the cosmos is given. I think, therefore I am (cogito etc.) but who am I? Tertan I am, but what is Tertan? Of this time, of that place, of some parentage, what does it matter?"

37   Existence without alloy: the phrase established itself. Howe put aside Tertan's paper and at random picked up another. "I am Arthur J. Casebeer, Jr.," he read. "My father is Arthur J. Casebeer and my grandfather was Arthur J. Casebeer before him. My mother is Nina Wimble Casebeer. Both of them are college graduates and my father is in insurance. I was born in St. Louis eighteen years ago and we still make our residence there."

38   Arthur J. Casebeer, who knew who he was, was less interesting than Tertan, but more coherent. Howe picked up Tertan's paper again. It was clear that none of the routine marginal comments, no "sent. str." or "punct." or "vocab." could cope with this torrential rhetoric. He read ahead, contenting himself with underscoring the errors against the time when he should have the necessary "conference" with Tertan.

39   It was a busy and official day of cards and sheets, arrangements and small decisions, and it gave Howe pleasure. Even when it was time to attend the first of the weekly Convocations he felt the charm of the beginning of things when intention is still innocent and uncorrupted by effort. He sat among the young instructors on the platform and joined in their humorous complaints at having to assist at the ceremony, but actually he got a clear satisfaction from the ritual of prayer and prosy speech and even from wearing his academic gown. And when the Convocation was over the pleasure continued as he crossed the campus, exchanging greetings with men he had not seen since the spring. They were people who did not yet, and perhaps never would, mean much to him, but in a year they had grown amiably to be part of his life. They were his fellow-townsmen.

40   The day had cooled again at sunset and there was a bright chill in the September twilight. Howe carried his voluminous gown over his arm, he swung his doctoral hood by its purple neckpiece and on his head he wore his mortarboard with its heavy gold tassel bobbing just over his eye. These were the weighty and absurd symbols of his new profession and they pleased him. At twenty-six Joseph Howe had discovered that

he was neither so well off nor so bohemian as he had once thought. A small income, adequate when supplemented by a sizable cash legacy, was genteel poverty when the cash was all spent. And the literary life—the room at the Lafayette or the small apartment without a lease, the long summers on the Cape, the long afternoons and the social evenings—began to weary him. His writing filled his mornings and should perhaps have filled his life, yet it did not. To the amusement of his friends and with a certain sense that he was betraying his own freedom, he had used the last of his legacy for a year at Harvard. The small but respectable reputation of his two volumes of verse had proved useful—he continued at Harvard on a fellowship and when he emerged as Dr. Howe he received an excellent appointment, with prospects, at Dwight.

41   He had his moments of fear when all that had ever been said of the dangers of the academic life had occurred to him. But after a year in which he had tested every possibility of corruption and seduction he was ready to rest easy. His third volume of verse, most of it written in his first year of teaching, was not only ampler but, he thought, better than its predecessors.

42   There was a clear hour before the Bradby dinner-party and Howe looked forward to it. But he was not to enjoy it, for lying with his mail on the hall table was a copy of this quarter's issue of *Life and Letters*, to which his landlord subscribed. Its severe cover announced that its editor, Frederic Woolley, had this month contributed an essay called "Two Poets," and Howe, picking it up, curious to see who the two poets might be, felt his own name start out at him with cabalistic power— Joseph Howe. As he continued to turn the pages his hand trembled.

43   Standing in the dark hall, holding the neat little magazine, Howe knew that his literary contempt for Frederic Woolley meant nothing, for he suddenly understood how he respected Woolley in the way of the world. He knew this by the trembling of his hand. And of the little world as well as the great, for although the literary groups of New York might dismiss Woolley, his name carried high authority in the academic world. At Dwight it was even a revered name, for it had been here at the college that Frederic Woolley had made the distinguished scholarly career from which he had gone on to literary journalism. In middle life he had been induced to take the editorship of *Life and Letters*, a literary monthly not widely read but heavily endowed and in its pages he had carried on the defence of what he sometimes called the older values. He was not without wit, he had great knowledge and considerable taste and even in the full movement of the "new" literature he had won a certain respect for his refusal to accept it. In France, even in England, he would have been connected with a more robust tradition of conservatism, but America gave him an audience not much better than genteel. It was known in the college that to the subsidy of *Life and Letters* the Bradbys contributed a great part.

44   As Howe read, he saw that he was involved in nothing less than an event. When the Fifth Series of *Studies in Order and Value* came to be collected, this latest of Frederic Woolley's essays would not be merely another step in the old direction. Clearly and unmistakably, it was a turning-point. All his literary life Woolley had been concerned with the relation of literature to morality, religion, and the private and delicate pieties, and he had been unalterably opposed to all that he had called "inhuman humanitarianism." But here, suddenly, dramatically late, he had made an about-face, turning to the public life and to the humanitarian politics he had so long despised. This was the kind of incident the histories of literature make much of. Frederic Woolley was opening for himself a new career and winning a kind of new youth. He contrasted the two poets, Thomas Wormser who was admirable, Joseph Howe who was almost dangerous. He spoke of the "precious subjectivism" of Howe's verse. "In times like ours," he wrote, "with millions facing penury and want, one feels that the qualities of the *tour d'ivoire* are well-nigh inhuman, nearly insulting. The *tour d'ivoire* becomes the *tour d'ivresse* and it is not self-intoxicated poets that our people need." The essay said more: "The problem is one of meaning. I am not ignorant that the creed of the esoteric poets declares that a poem does not and should not *mean* anything, that it *is* something. But poetry is what the poet makes it, and if he is a true poet he makes what his society needs. And what is needed now is the tradition in which Mr. Wormser writes, the true tradition of poetry. The Howes do no harm, but they do no good when positive good is demanded of all responsible men. Or do the Howes indeed do no harm? Perhaps Plato would have said they do, that in some ways theirs is the Phrygian music that turns men's minds from the struggle. Certainly it is true that Thomas Wormser writes in the lucid Dorian mode which sends men into battle with evil."

45   It was easy to understand why Woolley had chosen to praise Thomas Wormser. The long, lilting lines of *Corn Under Willows* hymned, as Woolley put it, the struggle for wheat in the Iowa fields and expressed the real lives of real people. But why out of the dozen more notable examples he had chosen Howe's little volume as the example of "precious subjectivism" was hard to guess. In a way it was funny, this multiplication of himself into "the Howes." And yet this becoming the multiform political symbol by whose creation Frederic Woolley gave the sign of a sudden new life, this use of him as a sacrifice whose blood was necessary for the rites of rejuvenation, made him feel oddly unclean.

46   Nor could Howe get rid of a certain practical resentment. As a poet he had a special and respectable place in the college life. But it might be another thing to be marked as the poet of a wilful and selfish obscurity.

47   As he walked to the Bradbys' Howe was a little tense and defensive. It seemed to him that all the world knew of the "attack" and agreed with it. And indeed the Bradbys had read the essay, but Professor Bradby, a kind and pretentious man, said, "I see my old friend knocked you about a

bit, my boy," and his wife Eugenia looked at Howe with her child-like blue eyes and said: "I shall *scold* Frederic for the untrue things he wrote about you. You aren't the least obscure." They beamed at him. In their genial snobbery they seemed to feel that he had distinguished himself. He was the leader of Howeism. He enjoyed the dinner-party as much as he had thought he would.

48   And in the following days, as he was more preoccupied with his duties, the incident was forgotten. His classes had ceased to be mere groups. Student after student detached himself from the mass and required or claimed a place in Howe's awareness. Of them all it was Tertan who first and most violently signalled his separate existence. A week after classes had begun Howe saw his silhouette on the frosted glass of his office door. It was motionless for a long time, perhaps stopped by the problem of whether or not to knock before entering. Howe called, "Come in!" and Tertan entered with his shambling stride.

49   He stood beside the desk, silent and at attention. When Howe asked him to sit down, he responded with a gesture of head and hand as if to say that such amenities were beside the point. Nevertheless he did take the chair. He put his ragged crammed brief-case between his legs. His face, which Howe now observed fully for the first time, was confusing, for it was made up of florid curves, the nose arched in the bone and voluted in the nostril, the mouth loose and soft and rather moist. Yet the face was so thin and narrow as to seem the very type of asceticism. Lashes of unusual length veiled the eyes and, indeed, it seemed as if there were a veil over the whole countenance. Before the words actually came, the face screwed itself into an attitude of preparation for them.

50   "You can confer with me now?" Tertan said.

51   "Yes, I'd be glad to. There are several things in your two themes I want to talk to you about." Howe reached for the packet of themes on his desk and sought for Tertan's. But the boy was waving them away.

52   "These are done perforce," he said. "Under the pressure of your requirement. They are not significant, mere duties." Again his great hand flapped vaguely to dismiss his themes. He leaned forward and gazed at his teacher.

53   "You are," he said, "a man of letters? You are a poet?" It was more declaration than question.

54   "I should like to think so," Howe said.

55   At first Tertan accepted the answer with a show of appreciation, as though the understatement made a secret between himself and Howe. Then he chose to misunderstand. With his shrewd and disconcerting control of expression, he presented to Howe a puzzled grimace. "What does that mean?" he said.

56   Howe retracted the irony. "Yes. I am a poet." It sounded strange to say.

57   "That," Tertan said, "is a wonder." He corrected himself with his ducking head. "I mean that is wonderful."

58   Suddenly he dived at the miserable brief-case between his legs, put it on his knees and began to fumble with the catch, all intent on the difficulty it presented. Howe noted that his suit was worn thin, his shirt almost unclean. He became aware, even, of a vague and musty odor of garments worn too long in unaired rooms. Tertan conquered the lock and began to concentrate upon a search into the interior. At last he held in his hand what he was after, a torn and crumpled copy of *Life and Letters*.

59   "I learned it from here," he said, holding it out.

60   Howe looked at him sharply, his hackles a little up. But the boy's face was not only perfectly innocent, it even shone with a conscious admiration. Apparently nothing of the import of the essay had touched him except the wonderful fact that his teacher was a "man of letters." Yet this seemed too stupid and Howe, to test it, said: "The man who wrote that doesn't think it's wonderful."

61   Tertan made a moist hissing sound as he cleared his mouth of saliva. His head, oddly loose on his neck, wove a pattern of contempt in the air. "A critic," he said, "who admits *prima facie* that he does not understand." Then he said grandly: "It is the inevitable fate."

62   It was absurd, yet Howe was not only aware of the absurdity but of a tension suddenly and wonderfully relaxed. Now that the "attack" was on the table between himself and this strange boy and subject to the boy's funny and absolutely certain contempt, the hidden force of his feeling was revealed to him in the very moment that it vanished. All unsuspected, there had been a film over the world, a transparent but discoloring haze of danger. But he had no time to stop over the brightened aspect of things. Tertan was going on. "I also am a man of letters. Putative."

63   "You have written a good deal?" Howe meant to be no more than polite and he was surprised at the tenderness he heard in his words.

64   Solemnly the boy nodded, threw back the dank lock and sucked in a deep anticipatory breath. "First, a work of homiletics, which is a defense of the principles of religious optimism against the pessimism of Schopenhauer and the humanism of Nietzsche."

65   "Humanism? Why do you call it humanism?"

66   "It is my nomenclature for making a deity of man," Tertan replied negligently. "Then three fictional works, novels. And numerous essays in science, combating materialism. Is it your duty to read these if I bring them to you?"

67   Howe answered simply: "No, it isn't exactly my duty, but I shall be happy to read them."

68   Tertan stood up and remained silent. He rested his bag on the chair. With a certain compunction—for it did not seem entirely proper that, of two men of letters, one should have the right to blue-pencil the other, to grade him or to question the quality of his "sentence structure"—Howe reached for Tertan's papers. But before he could take them up, the boy suddenly made his bow-to-Abelard, the stiff inclination of the body with the hands seeming to emerge from the scholar's gown. Then he was gone.

69   But after his departure something was still left of him. The timbre of his curious sentences, the downright finality of so quaint a phrase as "It is the inevitable fate" still rang in the air. Howe gave the warmth of his feeling to the new visitor who stood at the door announcing himself with a genteel clearing of the throat.

70   "Dr. Howe, I believe?" the student said. A large hand advanced into the room and grasped Howe's hand. "Blackburn, sir, Theodore Blackburn, vice-president of the Student Council. A great pleasure, sir."

71   Out of a pair of ruddy cheeks a pair of small eyes twinkled good-naturedly. The large face, the large body were not so much fat as beefy and suggested something "typical," monk, politician, or innkeeper.

72   Blackburn took the seat beside Howe's desk. "I may have seemed to introduce myself in my public capacity, sir," he said. "But it is really as an individual that I came to see you. That is to say, as one of your students to be."

73   He spoke with an "English" intonation and he went on: "I was once an English major, sir."

74   For a moment Howe was startled, for the roast-beef look of the boy and the manner of his speech gave a second's credibility to one sense of his statement. Then the collegiate meaning of the phrase asserted itself, but some perversity made Howe say what was not really in good taste even with so forward a student: "Indeed? What regiment?"

75   Blackburn stared and then gave a little pouf-pouf of laughter. He waved the misapprehension away. "*Very* good, sir. It certainly is an ambiguous term." He chuckled in appreciation of Howe's joke, then cleared his throat to put it aside. "I look forward to taking your course in the romantic poets, sir," he said earnestly. "To me the romantic poets are the very crown of English literature."

76   Howe made a dry sound, and the boy, catching some meaning in it, said: "Little as I know them, of course. But even Shakespeare who is so dear to us of the Anglo-Saxon tradition is in a sense but the preparation for Shelley, Keats and Byron. And Wadsworth."

77   Almost sorry for him, Howe dropped his eyes. With some embarrassment, for the boy was not actually his student, he said softly: "Wordsworth."

78   "Sir?"

79   "Wordsworth, not Wadsworth. You said Wadsworth."

80   "Did I, sir?" Gravely he shook his head to rebuke himself for the error. "Wordsworth, of course—slip of the tongue." Then, quite in command again, he went on. "I have a favor to ask of you, Dr. Howe. You see, I began my college course as an English major"—he smiled—"as I said."

81   "Yes?"

82   "But after my first year I shifted. I shifted to the social sciences. Sociology and government—I find them stimulating and very *real.*" He paused, out of respect for reality. "But now I find that perhaps I have neglected the other side."

83   "The other side?" Howe said.

84   "Imagination, fancy, culture. A well-rounded man." He trailed off as if there were perfect understanding between them. "And so, sir, I have decided to end my senior year with your course in the romantic poets."

85   His voice was filled with an indulgence which Howe ignored as he said flatly and gravely: "But that course isn't given until the spring term."

86   "Yes, sir, and that is where the favor comes in. Would you let me take your romantic prose course? I can't take it for credit, sir, my program is full, but just for background it seems to me that I ought to take it. I do hope," he concluded in a manly way, "that you will consent."

87   "Well, it's no great favor, Mr. Blackburn. You can come if you wish, though there's not much point in it if you don't do the reading."

88   The bell rang for the hour and Howe got up.

89   "May I begin with this class, sir?" Blackburn's smile was candid and boyish.

90   Howe nodded carelessly and together, silently, they walked to the classroom down the hall. When they reached the door Howe stood back to let his student enter, but Blackburn moved adroitly behind him and grasped him by the arm to urge him over the threshold. They entered together with Blackburn's hand firmly on Howe's biceps, the student inducting the teacher into his own room. Howe felt a surge of temper rise in him and almost violently he disengaged his arm and walked to the desk, while Blackburn found a seat in the front row and smiled at him.

II

91   The question was: At whose door must the tragedy be laid?

92   All night the snow had fallen heavily and only now was abating in sparse little flurries. The windows were valanced high with white. It was very quiet, something of the quiet of the world had reached the class and Howe found that everyone was glad to talk or listen. In the room there was a comfortable sense of pleasure in being human.

93   Casebeer believed that the blame for the tragedy rested with heredity. Picking up the book he read: "The sins of the fathers are visited on their children." This opinion was received with general favor. Nevertheless Johnson ventured to say that the fault was all Pastor Manders' because the Pastor had made Mrs. Alving go back to her husband and was always hiding the truth. To this Hibbard objected with logic enough: "Well, then, it was really all her husband's fault. He *did* all the bad things." De Witt, his face bright with an impatient idea, said that the fault was all society's. "By society I don't mean upper-crust society," he said. He looked around a little defiantly, taking in any members of the class who might be members of upper-crust society. "Not in that sense. I mean the social unit."

94   Howe nodded and said: "Yes, of course."

95   "If the society of the time had progressed far enough in science," De Witt went on, "then there would be no problem for Mr. Ibsen to write about. Captain Alving plays around a little, gives way to perfectly natural biological urges, and he gets a social disease, a venereal disease. If the disease is cured, no problem. Invent salvarsan and the disease is cured. The problem of heredity disappears and li'l Oswald just doesn't get paresis. No paresis, no problem—no problem, no play."

96   This was carrying the ark into battle and the class looked at De Witt with respectful curiosity. It was his usual way and on the whole they were sympathetic with his struggle to prove to Howe that science was better than literature. Still, there was something in his reckless manner that alienated them a little.

97   "Or take birth-control, for instance," De Witt went on. "If Mrs. Alving had had some knowledge of contraception, she wouldn't have had to have li'l Oswald at all. No li'l Oswald, no play."

98   The class was suddenly quieter. In the back row Stettenhover swung his great football shoulders in a righteous sulking gesture, first to the right, then to the left. He puckered his mouth ostentatiously. Intellect was always ending up by talking dirty.

99   Tertan's hand went up and Howe said: "Mr. Tertan." The boy shambled to his feet and began his long characteristic gulp. Howe made a motion with his fingers, as small as possible, and Tertan ducked his head and smiled in apology. He sat down. The class laughed. With more than half the term gone, Tertan had not been able to remember that one did not rise to speak. He seemed unable to carry on the life of the intellect without this mark of respect for it. To Howe the boy's habit of rising seemed to accord with the formal shabbiness of his dress. He never wore the casual sweaters and jackets of his classmates. Into the free and comfortable air of the college classroom he brought the stuffy sordid strictness of some crowded metropolitan high school.

100 "Speaking from one sense," Tertan began slowly, "there is no blame ascribable. From the sense of determinism, who can say where the blame lies? The preordained is the preordained and it cannot be said without rebellion against the universe, a palpable absurdity."

101 In the back row Stettenhover slumped suddenly in his seat, his heels held out before him, making a loud dry disgusted sound. His body sank until his neck rested on the back of his chair. He folded his hands across his belly and looked significantly out of the window, exasperated not only with Tertan but with Howe, with the class, with the whole system designed to encourage this kind of thing. There was a certain insolence in the movement and Howe flushed. As Tertan continued to speak, Howe walked casually towards the window and placed himself in the line of Stettenhover's vision. He stared at the great fellow, who pretended not to see him. There was so much power in the big body, so much contempt in the Greek-athlete face under the crisp Greek-athlete

curls, that Howe felt almost physical fear. But at last Stettenhover admitted him to focus and under his disapproving gaze sat up with slow indifference. His eyebrows raised high in resignation, he began to examine his hands. Howe relaxed and turned his attention back to Tertan.

102   "Flux of existence," Tertan was saying, "produces all things, so that judgment wavers. Beyond the phenomena, what? But phenomena are adumbrated and to them we are limited."

103   Howe saw it for a moment as perhaps it existed in the boy's mind—the world of shadows which are cast by a great light upon a hidden reality as in the old myth of the Cave. But the little brush with Stettenhover had tired him and he said irritably: "But come to the point, Mr. Tertan."

104   He said it so sharply that some of the class looked at him curiously. For three months he had gently carried Tertan through his verbosities, to the vaguely respectful surprise of the other students, who seemed to conceive that there existed between this strange classmate and their teacher some special understanding from which they were content to be excluded. Tertan looked at him mildly and at once came brilliantly to the point. "This is the summation of the play," he said and took up his book and read: " 'Your poor father never found any outlet for the overmastering joy of life that was in him. And I brought no holiday into his home, either. Everything seemed to turn upon duty and I am afraid I made your poor father's home unbearable to him, Oswald.' Spoken by Mrs. Alving."

105   Yes, that was surely the "summation" of the play and Tertan had hit it, as he hit, deviously and eventually, the literary point of almost everything. But now, as always, he was wrapping it away from sight. "For most mortals," he said, "there are only joys of biological urgings, gross and crass, such as the sensuous Captain Alving. For certain few there are the transmutations beyond these to a contemplation of the utter whole."

106   Oh, the boy was mad. And suddenly the word, used in hyperbole, intended almost for the expression of exasperated admiration, became literal. Now that the word was used, it became simply apparent to Howe that Tertan was mad.

107   It was a monstrous word and stood like a bestial thing in the room. Yet it so completely comprehended everything that had puzzled Howe, it so arranged and explained what for three months had been perplexing him that almost at once its horror became domesticated. With this word Howe was able to understand why he had never been able to communicate to Tertan the value of a single criticism or correction of his wild, verbose themes. Their conferences had been frequent and long but had done nothing to reduce to order the splendid confusion of the boy's ideas. Yet, impossible though its expression was, Tertan's incandescent mind could always strike for a moment into some dark corner of thought.

108   And now it was suddenly apparent that it was not a faulty rhetoric that Howe had to contend with. With his new knowledge he looked at Tertan's face and wondered how he could have so long deceived him-

self. Tertan was still talking and the class had lapsed into a kind of patient unconsciousness, a coma of respect for words which, for all that most of them knew, might be profound. Almost with a suffusion of shame, Howe believed that in some dim way the class had long ago had some intimation of Tertan's madness. He reached out as decisively as he could to seize the thread of Tertan's discourse before it should be entangled further.

109   "Mr. Tertan says that the blame must be put upon whoever kills the joy of living in another. We have been assuming that Captain Alving was a wholly bad man, but what if we assume that he became bad only because Mrs. Alving, when they were first married, acted towards him in the prudish way she says she did?"

110   It was a ticklish idea to advance to freshmen and perhaps not profitable. Not all of them were following.

111   "That would put the blame on Mrs. Alving herself, whom most of you admire. And she herself seems to think so." He glanced at his watch. The hour was nearly over. "What do you think, Mr. De Witt?"

112   De Witt rose to the idea, wanted to know if society couldn't be blamed for educating Mrs. Alving's temperament in the wrong way. Casebeer was puzzled, Stettenhover continued to look at his hands until the bell rang.

113   Tertan, his brows louring in thought, was making as always for a private word. Howe gathered his books and papers to leave quickly. At this moment of his discovery and with the knowledge still raw, he could not engage himself with Tertan. Tertan sucked in his breath to prepare for speech and Howe made ready for the pain and confusion. But at that moment Casebeer detached himself from the group with which he had been conferring and which he seemed to represent. His constituency remained at a tactful distance. The mission involved the time of an assigned essay. Casebeer's presentation of the plea—it was based on the freshmen's heavy duties at the fraternities during Carnival Week—cut across Tertan's preparations for speech. "And so some of us fellows thought," Casebeer concluded with heavy solemnity, "that we could do a better job, give our minds to it more, if we had more time."

114   Tertan regarded Casebeer with mingled curiosity and revulsion. Howe not only said that he would postpone the assignment but went on to talk about the Carnival and even drew the waiting constituency into the conversation. He was conscious of Tertan's stern and astonished stare, then of his sudden departure.

115   Now that the fact was clear, Howe knew that he must act on it. His course was simple enough. He must lay the case before the Dean. Yet he hesitated. His feeling for Tertan must now, certainly, be in some way invalidated. Yet could he, because of a word, hurry to assign to official and reasonable solicitude what had been, until this moment, so various and warm? He could at least delay and, by moving slowly, lend a poor grace to the necessary, ugly act of making his report.

116   It was with some notion of keeping the matter in his own hands that he went to the Dean's office to look up Tertan's records. In the outer office the Dean's secretary greeted him brightly and at his request brought him the manila folder with the small identifying photograph pasted in the corner. She laughed. "He was looking for the birdie in the wrong place," she said.

117   Howe leaned over her shoulder to look at the picture. It was as bad as all the Dean's office photographs were, but it differed from all that Howe had ever seen. Tertan, instead of looking into the camera, as no doubt he had been bidden, had, at the moment of exposure, turned his eyes upward. His mouth, as though conscious of the trick played on the photographer, had the sly superior look that Howe knew.

118   The secretary was fascinated by the picture. "What a funny boy," she said. "He looks like Tartuffe!"

119   And so he did, with the absurd piety of the eyes and the conscious slyness of the mouth and the whole face bloated by the bad lens.

120   "Is he *like* that?" the secretary said.

121   "Like Tartuffe? No."

122   From the photograph there was little enough comfort to be had. The records themselves gave no clue to madness, though they suggested sadness enough. Howe read of a father, Stanislaus Tertan, born in Budapest and trained in engineering in Berlin, once employed by the Hercules Chemical Corporation—this was one of the factories that dominated the south end of the town—but now without employment. He read of a mother Erminie (Youngfellow) Tertan, born in Manchester, educated at a Normal School at Leeds, now housewife by profession. The family lived on Greenbriar Street, which Howe knew as a row of once elegant homes near what was now the factory district. The old mansions had long ago been divided into small and primitive apartments. Of Ferdinand himself there was little to learn. He lived with his parents, had attended a Detroit high school and had transferred to the local school in his last year. His rating for intelligence, as expressed in numbers, was high, his scholastic record was remarkable, he held a college scholarship for his tuition.

123   Howe laid the folder on the secretary's desk. "Did you find what you wanted to know?" she asked.

124   The phrases from Tertan's momentous first theme came back to him. "Tertan I am, but what is Tertan? Of this time, of that place, of some parentage, what does it matter?"

125   "No, I didn't find it," he said.

126   Now that he had consulted the sad half-meaningless record he knew all the more firmly that he must not give the matter out of his own hands. He must not release Tertan to authority. Not that he anticipated from the Dean anything but the greatest kindness for Tertan. The Dean would have the experience and skill which he himself could not have. One way or another the Dean could answer the question: "What is

Tertan?" Yet this was precisely what he feared. He alone could keep alive—not for ever but for a somehow important time—the question: "What is Tertan?" He alone could keep it still a question. Some sure instinct told him that he must not surrender the question to a clean official desk in a clear official light to be dealt with, settled and closed.

127   He heard himself saying: "Is the Dean busy at the moment? I'd like to see him."

128   His request came thus unbidden, even forbidden, and it was one of the surprising and startling incidents of his life. Later, when he reviewed the events, so disconnected in themselves or so merely odd, of the story that unfolded for him that year, it was over this moment, on its face the least notable, that he paused longest. It was frequently to be with fear and never without a certainty of its meaning in his own knowledge of himself that he would recall this simple, routine request and the feeling of shame and freedom it gave him as he sent everything down the official chute. In the end, of course, no matter what he did to "protect" Tertan, he would have had to make the same request and lay the matter on the Dean's clean desk. But it would always be a landmark of his life that, at the very moment when he was rejecting the official way, he had been, without will or intention, so gladly drawn to it.

129   After the storm's last delicate flurry, the sun had come out. Reflected by the new snow, it filled the office with a golden light which was almost musical in the way it made all the commonplace objects of efficiency shine with a sudden sad and noble significance. And the light, now that he noticed it, made the utterance of his perverse and unwanted request even more momentous.

130   The secretary consulted the engagement pad. "He'll be free any minute. Don't you want to wait in the parlor?"

131   She threw open the door of the large and pleasant room in which the Dean held his Committee meetings and in which his visitors waited. It was designed with a homely elegance on the masculine side of the eighteenth-century manner. There was a small coal fire in the grate and the handsome mahogany table was strewn with books and magazines. The large windows gave on the snowy lawn and there was such a fine width of window that the white casements and walls seemed at this moment but a continuation of the snow, the snow but an extension of casement and walls. The outdoors seemed taken in and made safe, the indoors seemed luxuriously freshened and expanded.

132   Howe sat down by the fire and lighted a cigarette. The room had its intended effect upon him. He felt comfortable and relaxed, yet nicely organized, some young diplomatic agent of the eighteenth century, the newly fledged Swift carrying out Sir William Temple's business. The rawness of Tertan's case quite vanished. He crossed his legs and reached for a magazine.

133   It was that famous issue of *Life and Letters* that his idle hand had found and his blood raced as he sifted through it and the shape of his

own name, Joseph Howe, sprang out at him, still cabalistic in its power. He tossed the magazine back on the table as the door of the Dean's office opened and the Dean ushered out Theodore Blackburn.

134   "Ah, Joseph!" the Dean said.

135   Blackburn said: "Good morning, Doctor." Howe winced at the title and caught the flicker of amusement over the Dean's face. The Dean stood with his hand high on the door-jamb and Blackburn, still in the doorway, remained standing almost under his long arm.

136   Howe nodded briefly to Blackburn, snubbing his eager deference. "Can you give me a few minutes?" he said to the Dean.

137   "All the time you want. Come in." Before the two men could enter the office, Blackburn claimed their attention with a long full "Er." As they turned to him, Blackburn said: "Can *you* give *me* a few minutes, Dr. Howe?" His eyes sparkled at the little audacity he had committed, the slightly impudent play with hierarchy. Of the three of them Blackburn kept himself the lowest, but he reminded Howe of his subaltern relation to the Dean.

138   "I mean, of course," Blackburn went on easily, "when you've finished with the Dean."

139   "I'll be in my office shortly," Howe said, turned his back on the ready "Thank you, sir," and followed the Dean into the inner room.

140   "Energetic boy," said the Dean. "A bit beyond himself but very energetic. Sit down."

141   The Dean lighted a cigarette, leaned back in his chair, sat easy and silent for a moment, giving Howe no signal to go ahead with business. He was a young Dean, not much beyond forty, a tall handsome man with sad, ambitious eyes. He had been a Rhodes scholar. His friends looked for great things from him and it was generally said that he had notions of education which he was not yet ready to try to put into practice.

142   His relaxed silence was meant as a compliment to Howe. He smiled and said: "What's the business, Joseph?"

143   "Do you know Tertan—Ferdinand Tertan, a freshman?"

144   The Dean's cigarette was in his mouth and his hands were clasped behind his head. He did not seem to search his memory for the name. He said: "What about him?"

145   Clearly the Dean knew something and he was waiting for Howe to tell him more. Howe moved only tentatively. Now that he was doing what he had resolved not to do, he felt more guilty at having been so long deceived by Tertan and more need to be loyal to his error.

146   "He's a strange fellow," he ventured. He said stubbornly: "In a strange way he's very brilliant." He concluded: "But very strange."

147   The springs of the Dean's swivel chair creaked as he came out of his sprawl and leaned forward to Howe. "Do you mean he's so strange that it's something you could give a name to?"

148   Howe looked at him stupidly. "What do you mean?" he said.

149   "What's his trouble?" the Dean said more neutrally.

150   "He's very brilliant, in a way. I looked him up and he has a top intelligence rating. But somehow, and it's hard to explain just how, what he says is always on the edge of sense and doesn't quite make it."

151   The Dean looked at him and Howe flushed up. The Dean had surely read Woolley on the subject of "the Howes" and the *tour d'iv-resse*. Was that quick glance ironical?

152   The Dean picked up some papers from his desk and Howe could see that they were in Tertan's impatient scrawl. Perhaps the little gleam in the Dean's glance had come only from putting facts together.

153   "He sent me this yesterday," the Dean said. "After an interview I had with him. I haven't been able to do more than glance at it. When you said what you did, I realized there was something wrong."

154   Twisting his mouth, the Dean looked over the letter. "You seem to be involved," he said without looking up. "By the way, what did you give him at mid-term?"

155   Flushing, setting his shoulders, Howe said firmly: "I gave him A-minus."

156   The Dean chuckled. "Might be a good idea if some of our nicer boys went crazy—just a little." He said, "Well," to conclude the matter and handed the papers to Howe. "See if this is the same thing you've been finding. Then we can go into the matter again."

157   Before the fire in the parlor, in the chair that Howe had been occupying, sat Blackburn. He sprang to his feet as Howe entered.

158   "I said my office, Mr. Blackburn." Howe's voice was sharp. Then he was almost sorry for the rebuke, so clearly and naïvely did Blackburn seem to relish his stay in the parlor, close to authority.

159   "I'm in a bit of a hurry, sir," he said, "and I did want to be sure to speak to you, sir."

160   He was really absurd, yet fifteen years from now he would have grown up to himself, to the assurance and mature beefiness. In banks, in consular offices, in brokerage firms, on the bench, more seriously affable, a little sterner, he would make use of his ability to be administered by his job. It was almost reassuring. Now he was exercising his too-great skill on Howe. "I owe you an apology, sir," he said.

161   Howe knew that he did but he showed surprise.

162   "I mean, Doctor, after your having been so kind about letting me attend your class, I stopped coming." He smiled in depreciation. "Extra-curricular activities take up so much of my time. I'm afraid I undertook more than I could perform."

163   Howe had noticed the absence and had been a little irritated by it after Blackburn's elaborate plea. It was an absence that might be interpreted as a comment on the teacher. But there was only one way for him to answer. "You've no need to apologize," he said. "It's wholly your affair."

164   Blackburn beamed. "I'm so glad you feel that way about it, sir. I was worried you might think I had stayed away because I was influenced by—" He stopped and lowered his eyes.

165   Astonished, Howe said: "Influenced by what?"

166   "Well, by—" Blackburn hesitated and for answer pointed to the table on which lay the copy of *Life and Letters*. Without looking at it, he knew where to direct his hand. "By the unfavorable publicity, sir." He hurried on. "And that brings me to another point, sir. I am secretary of Quill and Scroll, sir, the student literary society, and I wonder if you would address us. You could read your own poetry, sir, and defend your own point of view. It would be very interesting."

167   It was truly amazing. Howe looked long and cruelly into Blackburn's face, trying to catch the secret of the mind that could have conceived this way of manipulating him, this way so daring and inept— but not entirely inept—with its malice so without malignity. The face did not yield its secret. Howe smiled broadly and said: "Of course I don't think you were influenced by the unfavorable publicity."

168   "I'm still going to take—regularly, for credit—your romantic poets course next term," Blackburn said.

169   "Don't worry, my dear fellow, don't worry about it."

170   Howe started to leave and Blackburn stopped him with: "But about Quill, sir?"

171   "Suppose we wait until next term? I'll be less busy then."

172   And Blackburn said: "Very good, sir, and thank you."

173   In his office the little encounter seemed less funny to Howe, was even in some indeterminate way disturbing. He made an effort to put it from his mind by turning to what was sure to disturb him more, the Tertan letter read in the new interpretation. He found what he had always found, the same florid leaps beyond fact and meaning, the same headlong certainty. But as his eye passed over the familiar scrawl it caught his own name and for the second time that hour he felt the race of his blood.

174   "The Paraclete," Tertan had written to the Dean, "from a Greek word meaning to stand in place of, but going beyond the primitive idea to mean traditionally the helper, the one who comforts and assists, cannot without fundamental loss be jettisoned. Even if taken no longer in the supernatural sense, the concept remains deeply in the human consciousness inevitably. Humanitarianism is no reply, for not every man stands in the place of every other man for this other's comrade comfort. But certain are chosen out of the human race to be the consoler of some other. Of these, for example, is Joseph Barker Howe, Ph.D. Of intellects not the first yet of true intellect and lambent instructions, given to that which is intuitive and irrational, not to what is logical in the strict word, what is judged by him is of the heart and not the head. Here is one chosen, in that he chooses himself to stand in the place of another for comfort and consolation. To him more than another I give my gratitude,

with all respect to our Dean who reads this, a noble man, but merely dedicated, not consecrated. But not in the aspect of the Paraclete only is Dr. Joseph Barker Howe established, for he must be the Paraclete to another aspect of himself, that which is driven and persecuted by the lack of understanding in the world at large, so that he in himself embodies the full history of man's tribulations and, overflowing upon others, notably the present writer, is the ultimate end."

175   This was love. There was no escape from it. Try as Howe might to remember that Tertan was mad and all his emotions invalidated, he could not destroy the effect upon him of his student's stern, affectionate regard. He had betrayed not only a power of mind but a power of love. And however firmly he held before his attention the fact of Tertan's madness, he could do nothing to banish the physical sensation of gratitude he felt. He had never thought of himself as "driven and persecuted" and he did not now. But still he could not make meaningless his sensation of gratitude. The pitiable Tertan sternly pitied him, and comfort came from Tertan's never-to-be-comforted mind.

III

176   In an academic community, even an efficient one, official matters move slowly. The term drew to a close with no action in the case of Tertan, and Joseph Howe had to confront a curious problem. How should he grade his strange student, Tertan?

177   Tertan's final examination had been no different from all his other writing, and what did one "give" such a student? De Witt must have his A, that was clear. Johnson would get a B. With Casebeer it was a question of a B-Minus or a C-plus, and Stettenhover, who had been crammed by the team tutor to fill half a blue-book with his thin feminine scrawl, would have his C-minus which he would accept with mingled indifference and resentment. But with Tertan it was not so easy.

178   The boy was still in the college process and his name could not be omitted from the grade sheet. Yet what should a mind under suspicion of madness be graded? Until the medical verdict was given, it was for Howe to continue as Tertan's teacher and to keep his judgment pedagogical. Impossible to give him an F: he had not failed. B was for Johnson's stolid mediocrity. He could not be put on the edge of passing with Stettenhover, for he exactly did not pass. In energy and richness of intellect he was perhaps even De Witt's superior, and Howe toyed grimly with the notion of giving him an A, but that would lower the value of the A De Witt had won with his beautiful and clear, if still arrogant, mind. There was a notation which the Registrar recognized—Inc. for Incomplete and in the horrible comedy of the situation, Howe considered that. But really only a mark of M for Mad would serve.

179   In his perplexity, Howe sought the Dean, but the Dean was out of

town. In the end, he decided to maintain the A-minus he had given Tertan at mid-term. After all, there had been no falling away from that quality. He entered it on the grade sheet with something like bravado.

180   Academic time moves quickly. A college year is not really a year, lacking as it does three months. And it is endlessly divided into units which, at their beginning, appear larger than they are—terms, half-terms, months, weeks. And the ultimate unit, the hour, is not really an hour, lacking as it does ten minutes. And so the new term advanced rapidly and one day the fields about the town were all brown, cleared of even the few thin patches of snow which had lingered so long.

181   Howe, as he lectured on the romantic poets, became conscious of Blackburn emanating wrath. Blackburn did it well, did it with enormous dignity. He did not stir in his seat, he kept his eyes fixed on Howe in perfect attention, but he abstained from using his notebook, there was no mistaking what he proposed to himself as an attitude. His elbow on the writing-wing of the chair, his chin on the curled fingers of his hand, he was the embodiment of intellectual indignation. He was thinking his own thoughts, would give no public offence, yet would claim his due, was not to be intimidated. Howe knew that he would present himself at the end of the hour.

182   Blackburn entered the office without invitation. He did not smile, there was no cajolery about him. Without invitation he sat down beside Howe's desk. He did not speak until he had taken the blue-book from his pocket. He said: "What does this mean, sir?"

183   It was a sound and conservative student tactic. Said in the usual way it meant: "How could you have so misunderstood me?" or "What does this mean for my future in the course?" But there were none of the humbler tones in Blackburn's way of saying it.

184   Howe made the established reply: "I think that's for you to tell me."

185   Blackburn continued icy. "I'm sure I can't, sir."

186   There was a silence between them. Both dropped their eyes to the blue-book on the desk. On its cover Howe had penciled: "F. This is very poor work."

187   Howe picked up the blue-book. There was always the possibility of injustice. The teacher may be bored by the mass of papers and not wholly attentive. A phrase, even the student's handwriting, may irritate him unreasonably. "Well," said Howe, "let's go through it."

188   He opened the first page. "Now here: you write: 'In *The Ancient Mariner,* Coleridge lives in and transports us to a honey-sweet world where all is rich and strange, a world of charm to which we can escape from the humdrum existence of our daily lives, the world of romance. Here, in this warm and honey-sweet land of charming dreams we can relax and enjoy ourselves.'"

189   Howe lowered the paper and waited with a neutral look for Blackburn to speak. Blackburn returned the look boldly, did not speak,

sat stolid and lofty. At last Howe said, speaking gently: "Did you mean that, or were you just at a loss for something to say?"

190   "You imply that I was just 'bluffing'?" The quotation marks hung palpable in the air about the word.

191   "I'd like to know. I'd prefer believing that you were bluffing to believing that you really thought this."

192   Blackburn's eyebrows went up. From the height of a great and firm-based idea he looked at his teacher. He clasped the crags for a moment and then pounced, craftily, suavely. "Do you mean, Dr. Howe, that there aren't two opinions possible?"

193   It was superbly done in its air of putting all of Howe's intellectual life into the balance. Howe remained patient and simple. "Yes, many opinions are possible, but not this one. Whatever anyone believes of *The Ancient Mariner*, no one can in reason believe that it represents a—a honey-sweet world in which we can relax."

194   "But that is what I *feel*, sir."

195   This was well done too. Howe said: "Look, Mr. Blackburn. Do you really relax with hunger and thirst, the heat and the sea-serpents, the dead men with staring eyes, Life in Death and the skeletons? Come now, Mr. Blackburn."

196   Blackburn made no answer and Howe pressed forward. "Now you say of Wordsworth: 'Of peasant stock himself, he turned from the effete life of the salons and found in the peasant the hope of a flaming revolution which would sweep away all the old ideas. This is the subject of his best poems.'"

197   Beaming at his teacher with youthful eagerness, Blackburn said: "Yes, sir, a rebel, a bringer of light to suffering mankind. I see him as a kind of Prothemeus."

198   "A kind of what?"

199   "Prothemeus, sir."

200   "Think, Mr. Blackburn. We were talking about him only today and I mentioned his name a dozen times. You don't mean Prothemeus. You mean—" Howe waited but there was no response.

201   "You mean Prometheus."

202   Blackburn gave no assent and Howe took the reins. "You've done a bad job here, Mr. Blackburn, about as bad as could be done." He saw Blackburn stiffen and his genial face harden again. "It shows either a lack of preparation or a complete lack of understanding." He saw Blackburn's face begin to go to pieces and he stopped.

203   "Oh, sir," Blackburn burst out. "I've never had a mark like this before, never anything below a B, never. A thing like this has never happened to me before."

204   It must be true, it was a statement too easily verified. Could it be that other instructors accepted such flaunting nonsense? Howe wanted to end the interview. "I'll set it down to lack of preparation," he said. "I know you're busy. That's not an excuse but it's an explanation. Now

suppose you really prepare and then take another quiz in two weeks. We'll forget this one and count the other."

205   Blackburn squirmed with pleasure and gratitude. "Thank you, sir. You're really very kind, very kind."

206   Howe rose to conclude the visit. "All right then—in two weeks."

207   It was that day that the Dean imparted to Howe the conclusion of the case of Tertan. It was simple and a little anticlimactic. A physician had been called in, and had said the word, given the name.

208   "A classic case, he called it," the Dean said. "Not a doubt in the world," he said. His eyes were full of miserable pity and he clutched at a word. "A classic case, a classic case." To his aid and to Howe's there came the Parthenon and the form of the Greek drama, the Aristotelian logic, Racine and the Well-Tempered Clavichord, the blueness of the Aegean and its clear sky. Classic—that is to say, without a doubt, perfect in its way, a veritable model, and, as the Dean had been told, sure to take a perfectly predictable and inevitable course to a foreknown conclusion.

209   It was not only pity that stood in the Dean's eyes. For a moment there was fear too. "Terrible," he said, "it is simply terrible."

210   Then he went on briskly. "Naturally we've told the boy nothing. And naturally we won't. His tuition's paid by his scholarship and we'll continue him on the rolls until the end of the year. That will be kindest. After that the matter will be out of our control. We'll see, of course, that he gets into the proper hands. I'm told there will be no change, he'll go on like this, be as good as this, for four to six months. And so we'll just go along as usual."

211   So Tertan continued to sit in Section 5 of English 1A, to his classmates still a figure of curiously dignified fun, symbol to most of them of the respectable but absurd intellectual life. But to his teacher he was now very different. He had not changed—he was still the greyhound casting for the scent of ideas and Howe could see that he was still the same Tertan, but he could not feel it. What he felt as he looked at the boy sitting in his accustomed place was the hard blank of a fact. The fact itself was formidable and depressing. But what Howe was chiefly aware of was that he had permitted the metamorphosis of Tertan from person to fact.

212   As much as possible he avoided seeing Tertan's upraised hand and eager eye. But the fact did not know of its mere factuality, it continued its existence as if it were Tertan, hand up and eye questioning, and one day it appeared in Howe's office with a document.

213   "Even the spirit who lives egregiously, above the herd, must have its relations with the fellow-man," Tertan declared. He laid the document on Howe's desk. It was headed "Quill and Scroll Society of Dwight College. Application for Membership."

214   "In most ways these are crass minds," Tertan said, touching the paper. "Yet as a whole, bound together in their common love of letters, they transcend their intellectual lacks, since it is not a paradox that the whole is greater than the sum of its parts."

215 "When are the elections?" Howe asked.

216 "They take place to-morrow."

217 "I certainly hope you will be successful."

218 "Thank you. Would you wish to implement that hope?" A rather dirty finger pointed to the bottom of the sheet. "A faculty recommender is necessary," Tertan said stiffly, and waited.

219 "And you wish me to recommend you?"

220 "It would be an honor."

221 "You may use my name."

222 Tertan's finger pointed again. "It must be a written sponsorship, signed by the sponsor." There was a large blank space on the form under the heading: "Opinion of Faculty Sponsor."

223 This was almost another thing and Howe hesitated. Yet there was nothing else to do and he took out his fountain-pen. He wrote: "Mr. Ferdinand Tertan is marked by his intense devotion to letters and by his exceptional love of all things of the mind." To this he signed his name which looked bold and assertive on the white page. It disturbed him, the strange affirming power of a name. With a business-like air, Tertan whipped up the paper, folded it with decision and put it into his pocket. He bowed and took his departure, leaving Howe with the sense of having done something oddly momentous.

224 And so much now seemed odd and momentous to Howe that should not have seemed so. It was odd and momentous, he felt, when he sat with Blackburn's second quiz before him and wrote in an excessively firm hand the grade of C-minus. The paper was a clear, an indisputable failure. He was carefully and consciously committing a cowardice. Blackburn had told the truth when he had pleaded his past record. Howe had consulted it in the Dean's office. It showed no grade lower than a B-minus. A canvass of some of Blackburn's previous instructors had brought vague attestations to the adequate powers of a student imperfectly remembered and sometimes surprise that his abilities could be questioned at all.

225 As he wrote the grade, Howe told himself that this cowardice sprang from an unwillingness to have more dealings with a student he disliked. He knew it was simpler than that. He knew he feared Blackburn: that was the absurd truth. And cowardice did not solve the matter after all. Blackburn, flushed with a first success, attacked at once. The minimal passing grade had not assuaged his feelings, and he sat at Howe's desk and again the blue-book lay between them. Blackburn said nothing. With an enormous impudence, he was waiting for Howe to speak and explain himself.

226 At last Howe said sharply and rudely: "Well?" His throat was tense and the blood was hammering in his head. His mouth was tight with anger at himself for his disturbance.

227 Blackburn's glance was almost baleful. "This is impossible, sir."

228 "But there it is," Howe answered.

229   "Sir?" Blackburn had not caught the meaning but his tone was still haughty.

230   Impatiently Howe said: "There it is, plain as day. Are you here to complain again?"

231   "Indeed I am, sir." There was surprise in Blackburn's voice that Howe should ask the question.

232   "I shouldn't complain if I were you. You did a thoroughly bad job on your first quiz. This one is a little, only a very little, better." This was not true. If anything, it was worse.

233   "That might be a matter of opinion, sir."

234   "It is a matter of opinion. Of my opinion."

235   "Another opinion might be different, sir."

236   "You really believe that?" Howe said.

237   "Yes." The omission of the "sir" was monumental.

238   "Whose, for example?"

239   "The Dean's, for example." Then the fleshy jaw came forward a little. "Or a certain literary critic's, for example."

240   It was colossal and almost too much for Blackburn himself to handle. The solidity of his face almost crumpled under it. But he withstood his own audacity and went on. "And the Dean's opinion might be guided by the knowledge that the person who gave me this mark is the man whom a famous critic, the most eminent judge of literature in this country, called a drunken man. The Dean might think twice about whether such a man is fit to teach Dwight students."

241   Howe said in quiet admonition, "Blackburn, you're mad," meaning no more than to check the boy's extravagance.

242   But Blackburn paid no heed. He had another shot in the locker. "And the Dean might be guided by the information, of which I have evidence, documentary evidence"—he slapped his breast-pocket twice—"that this same person personally recommended to the college literary society, the oldest in the country, that he personally recommended a student who is crazy, who threw the meeting into an uproar, a psychiatric case. The Dean might take that into account."

243   Howe was never to learn the details of that "uproar." He had always to content himself with the dim but passionate picture which at that moment sprang into his mind, of Tertan standing on some abstract height and madly denouncing the multitude of Quill and Scroll who howled him down.

244   He sat quiet a moment and looked at Blackburn. The ferocity had entirely gone from the student's face. He sat regarding his teacher almost benevolently. He had played a good card and now, scarcely at all unfriendly, he was waiting to see the effect. Howe took up the blue-book and negligently sifted through it. He read a page, closed the book, struck out the C-minus and wrote an F.

245   "Now you may take the paper to the Dean," he said. "You may tell him that after reconsidering it, I lowered the grade."

246   The gasp was audible. "Oh, sir!" Blackburn cried. "Please!" His

face was agonized. "It means my graduation, my livelihood, my future. Don't do this to me."

247   "It's done already."

248   Blackburn stood up. "I spoke rashly, sir, hastily. I had no intention, no real intention, of seeing the Dean. It rests with you—entirely, entirely. I *hope* you will restore the first mark."

249   "Take the matter to the Dean or not, just as you choose. The grade is what you deserve and it stands."

250   Blackburn's head dropped. "And will I be failed at mid-term, sir?"

251   "Of course."

252   From deep out of Blackburn's great chest rose a cry of anguish. "Oh, sir, if you want me to go down on my knees to you, I will, I will."

253   Howe looked at him in amazement.

254   "I will, I will. On my knees, sir. This mustn't, mustn't happen."

255   He spoke so literally, meaning so very truly that his knees and exactly his knees were involved and seeming to think that he was offering something of tangible value to his teacher, that Howe, whose head had become icy clear in the nonsensical drama, thought, "The boy is mad," and began to speculate fantastically whether something in himself attracted or developed aberration. He could see himself standing absurdly before the Dean and saying: "I've found another. This time it's the vice-president of the Council, the manager of the debating team, and secretary of Quill and Scroll."

256   One more such discovery, he thought, and he himself would be discovered! And there, suddenly, Blackburn was on his knees with a thump, his huge thighs straining his trousers, his hands outstretched in a great gesture of supplication.

257   With a cry, Howe shoved back his swivel chair and it rolled away on its casters half across the little room. Blackburn knelt for a moment to nothing at all, then got to his feet.

258   Howe rose abruptly. He said: "Blackburn, you will stop acting like an idiot. Dust your knees off, take your paper and get out. You've behaved like a fool and a malicious person. You have half a term to do a decent job. Keep your silly mouth shut and try to do it. Now get out."

259   Blackburn's head was low. He raised it and there was a pious light in his eyes. "Will you shake hands, sir?" he said. He thrust out his hand.

260   "I will not," Howe said.

261   Head and hand sank together. Blackburn picked up his blue-book and walked to the door. He turned and said: "Thank you, sir." His back, as he departed, was heavy with tragedy and stateliness.

IV

262   After years of bad luck with the weather, the College had a perfect day for Commencement. It was wonderfully bright, the air so transparent, the wind so brisk that no one could resist talking about it.

263   As Howe set out for the campus he heard Hilda calling from the back yard. She called, "Professor, professor," and came running to him.

264   Howe said: "What's this 'professor' business?"

265   "Mother told me," Hilda said. "You've been promoted. And I want to take your picture."

266   "Next year," said Howe. "I won't be a professor until next year. And you know better than to call anybody 'professor.'"

267   "It was just in fun," Hilda said. She seemed disappointed.

268   "But you can take my picture if you want. I won't look much different next year." Still, it was frightening. It might mean that he was to stay in this town all his life.

269   Hilda brightened. "Can I take it in this?" she said, and touched the gown he carried over his arm.

270   Howe laughed. "Yes, you can take it in this."

271   "I'll get my things and meet you in front of Otis," Hilda said. "I have the background all picked out."

272   On the campus the Commencement crowd was already large. It stood about in eager, nervous little family groups. As he crossed, Howe was greeted by a student, capped and gowned, glad of the chance to make an event for his parents by introducing one of his teachers. It was while Howe stood there chatting that he saw Tertan.

273   He had never seen anyone quite so alone, as though a circle had been woven about him to separate him from the gay crowd on the campus. Not that Tertan was not gay—he was the gayest of all. Three weeks had passed since Howe had last seen him, the weeks of examination, the lazy week before Commencement, and this was now a different Tertan. On his head he wore a panama hat, broad-brimmed and fine, of the shape associated with South American planters. He wore a suit of raw silk, luxurious but yellowed with age and much too tight, and he sported a whangee cane. He walked sedately, the hat tilted at a devastating angle, the stick coming up and down in time to his measured tread. He had, Howe guessed, outfitted himself to greet the day in the clothes of that ruined father whose existence was on record in the Dean's office. Gravely and arrogantly he surveyed the scene—in it, his whole bearing seemed to say, but not of it. With his haughty step, with his flashing eye, Tertan was coming nearer. Howe did not wish to be seen. He shifted his position slightly. When he looked again, Tertan was not in sight.

274   The chapel clock struck the quarter hour. Howe detached himself from his chat and hurried to Otis Hall at the far end of the campus. Hilda had not yet come. He went up into the high portico and, using the glass of the door for a mirror, put on his gown, adjusted the hood on his shoulders and set the mortar-board on his head. When he came down the steps Hilda had arrived.

275   Nothing could have told him more forcibly that a year had passed than the development of Hilda's photographic possessions from the box camera of the previous fall. By a strap about her neck was hung a leather case, so thick and strong, so carefully stitched and so moulded to its

contents that it could only hold a costly camera. The appearance was deceptive, Howe knew, for he had been present at the Aikens' pre-Christmas conference about its purchase. It was only a fairly good domestic camera. Still, it looked very impressive. Hilda carried another leather case from which she drew a collapsible tripod. Decisively she extended each of its gleaming legs and set it up on the path. She removed the camera from its case and fixed it to the tripod. In its compact efficiency the camera almost had a life of its own, but Hilda treated it with easy familiarity, looked into its eye, glanced casually at its gauges. Then from a pocket she took still another leather case and drew from it a small instrument through which she looked first at Howe, who began to feel inanimate and lost, and then at the sky. She made some adjustment on the instrument, then some adjustment on the camera. She swept the scene with her eye, found a spot and pointed the camera in its direction. She walked to the spot, stood on it and beckoned to Howe. With each new leather case, with each new instrument and with each new adjustment she had grown in ease and now she said: "Joe, will you stand here?"

276   Obediently Howe stood where he was bidden. She had yet another instrument. She took out a tape-measure on a mechanical spool. Kneeling down before Howe, she put the little metal ring of the tape under the tip of his shoe. At her request, Howe pressed it with his toe. When she had measured her distance, she nodded to Howe who released the tape. At a touch, it sprang back into the spool. "You have to be careful if you're going to get what you want," Hilda said. "I don't believe in all this snap-snap-snapping," she remarked loftily. Howe nodded in agreement, although he was beginning to think Hilda's care excessive.

277   Now at last the moment had come. Hilda squinted into the camera, moved the tripod slightly. She stood to the side, holding the plunger of the shutter-cable. "Ready," she said. "Will you relax, Joseph, please?" Howe realized that he was standing frozen. Hilda stood poised and precise as a setter, one hand holding the little cable, the other extended with curled dainty fingers like a dancer's, as if expressing to her subject the precarious delicacy of the moment. She pressed the plunger and there was the click. At once she stirred to action, got behind the camera, turned a new exposure. "Thank you," she said. "Would you stand under that tree and let me do a character study with light and shade?"

278   The childish absurdity of the remark restored Howe's ease. He went to the little tree. The pattern the leaves made on his gown was what Hilda was after. He had just taken a satisfactory position when he heard in the unmistakable voice: "Ah, Doctor! Having your picture taken?"

279   Howe gave up the pose and turned to Blackburn who stood on the walk, his hands behind his back, a little too large for his bachelor's gown. Annoyed that Blackburn should see him posing for a character study in light and shade, Howe said irritably: "Yes, having my picture taken."

280   Blackburn beamed at Hilda. "And the little photographer," he said.

Hilda fixed her eyes on the ground and stood closer to her brilliant and aggressive camera. Blackburn, teetering on his heels, his hands behind his back, wholly prelatical and benignly patient, was not abashed at the silence. At last Howe said: "If you'll excuse us, Mr. Blackburn, we'll go on with the picture."

281   "Go right ahead, sir. I'm running along." But he only came closer. "Dr. Howe," he said fervently, "I want to tell you how glad I am that I was able to satisfy your standards at last."

282   Howe was surprised at the hard insulting brightness of his own voice and even Hilda looked up curiously as he said: "Nothing you have ever done has satisfied me and nothing you could ever do would satisfy me, Blackburn."

283   With a glance at Hilda, Blackburn made a gesture as if to hush Howe—as though all his former bold malice had taken for granted a kind of understanding between himself and his teacher, a secret which must not be betrayed to a third person. "I only meant, sir," he said, "that I was able to pass your course after all."

284   Howe said: "You didn't pass my course. I passed you out of my course. I passed you without even reading your paper. I wanted to be sure the college would be rid of you. And when all the grades were in and I did read your paper, I saw I was right not to have read it first."

285   Blackburn presented a stricken face. "It was very bad, sir?"

286   But Howe had turned away. The paper had been fantastic. The paper had been, if he wished to see it so, mad. It was at this moment that the Dean came up behind Howe and caught his arm. "Hello, Joseph," he said. "We'd better be getting along, it's almost late."

287   He was not a familiar man, but when he saw Blackburn, who approached to greet him, he took Blackburn's arm too. "Hello, Theodore," he said. Leaning forward on Howe's arm and on Blackburn's, he said: "Hello, Hilda dear." Hilda replied quietly: "Hello, Uncle George."

288   Still clinging to their arms, still linking Howe and Blackburn, the Dean said: "Another year gone, Joe, and we've turned out another crop. After you've been here a few years, you'll find it reasonably upsetting— you wonder how there can be so many graduating classes while you stay the same. But, of course, you don't stay the same." Then he said, "Well," sharply, to dismiss the thought. He pulled Blackburn's arm and swung him around to Howe. "Have you heard about Teddy Blackburn?" he asked. "He has a job already, before graduation, the first man of his class to be placed." Expectant of congratulations, Blackburn beamed at Howe. Howe remained silent.

289   "Isn't that good?" the Dean said. Still Howe did not answer and the Dean, puzzled and put out, turned to Hilda. "That's a very fine-looking camera, Hilda." She touched it with affectionate pride.

290   "Instruments of precision," said a voice. "Instruments of precision." Of the three with joined arms, Howe was the nearest to Tertan, whose gaze took in all the scene except the smile and the nod which

Howe gave him. The boy leaned on his cane. The broad-brimmed hat, canting jauntily over his eyes, confused the image of his face that Howe had established, suppressed the rigid lines of the ascetic and brought out the baroque curves. It made an effect of perverse majesty.

291

"Instruments of precision," said Tertan for the last time, addressing no one, making a casual comment to the universe. And it occurred to Howe that Tertan might not be referring to Hilda's equipment. The sense of the thrice-woven circle of the boy's loneliness smote him fiercely. Tertan stood in majestic jauntiness, superior to all the scene, but his isolation made Howe ache with a pity of which Tertan was more the cause than the object, so general and indiscriminate was it.

292

Whether in his sorrow he made some unintended movement towards Tertan which the Dean checked or whether the suddenly tightened grip on his arm was the Dean's own sorrow and fear, he did not know. Tertan watched them in the incurious way people watch a photograph being taken and suddenly the thought that, to the boy, it must seem that the three were posing for a picture together made Howe detach himself almost rudely from the Dean's grasp.

293

"I promised Hilda another picture," he announced—needlessly, for Tertan was no longer there, he had vanished in the last sudden flux of visitors who, now that the band had struck up, were rushing nervously to find seats.

294

"You'd better hurry," the Dean said. "I'll go along, it's getting late for me." He departed and Blackburn walked stately by his side.

295

Howe again took his position under the little tree which cast its shadow over his face and gown. "Just hurry, Hilda, won't you?" he said. Hilda held the cable at arm's-length, her other arm crooked and her fingers crisped. She rose on her toes and said "Ready," and pressed the release. "Thank you," she said gravely and began to dismantle her camera as he hurried off to join the procession.

Study Questions

1. How do Howe's attitudes toward himself and toward the educational process of which he is a part change during the course of the story?
2. How does the author use medieval imagery and allusion?
3. Is Trilling's presentation of classroom activity realistic?
4. Do you believe that Trilling's suggestion in this story—that people of inferior intelligence and ethical standards most often rise to the top of American political and economic life—is accurate?

When I Heard the Learn'd Astronomer

Walt Whitman

When I heard the learn'd astronomer;
When the proofs, the figures, were ranged in columns before me;
When I was shown the charts and the diagrams, to add, divide, and
      measure them;
When I, sitting, heard the astronomer, where he lectured with
      much applause in the lecture-room,
How soon, unaccountable, I became tired and sick;
Till rising and gliding out, I wander'd off by myself,
In the mystical moist night-air, and from time to time,
Look'd up in perfect silence at the stars.

Study Questions

1. What is the point of this poem? Can you state it in one declarative sentence?
2. Explain the grammatical structure of the first five lines. How does parallelism work in these lines?
3. How does "silence" in the last line contrast with the tone of the rest of the poem?

Of Parents and Children

Francis Bacon

1
The joys of parents are secret; and so are their griefs and fears. They cannot utter the one, nor they will not utter the other. Children sweeten labours, but they make misfortunes more bitter. They increase the cares of life, but they mitigate the remembrance of death. The perpetuity by generation is common to beasts, but memory, merit, and noble works are proper to men. And surely a man shall see the noblest works and foundations have proceeded from childless men, which have sought to express the images of their minds, where those of their bodies have failed. So the care of posterity is most in them that have no posterity. They that are the first raisers of their houses are most indulgent towards their children, beholding them as the continuance not only of their kind but of their work; and so both children and creatures.

2
The difference in affection of parents towards their several children is many times unequal and sometimes unworthy, especially in the mother; as Salomon saith, *A wise son rejoiceth the father, but an ungracious son shames the mother.* A man shall see, where there is a house full of children, one or two of the eldest respected, and the youngest made wantons, but in the midst some that are as it were forgotten, who many times nevertheless prove the best. The illiberality of parents in allowance towards their children is an harmful error; makes them base; acquaints them with shifts; makes them sort with mean company; and makes them surfeit more when they come to plenty. And therefore the proof is best, when men keep their authority towards their children, but not their purse. Men have a foolish manner (both parents and schoolmasters and servants) in creating and breeding an emulation between brothers during childhood, which many times sorteth to discord when they are men, and disturbeth families. The Italians make little difference between children and nephews or near kinsfolks; but so they be of the lump, they care not though they pass not through their own body. And, to say truth, in nature it is much a like matter; insomuch that we see a nephew sometimes resembleth an uncle or a kinsman more than his own parent, as the blood happens. Let parents choose betimes the vocations and courses they mean their children should take, for then they are most flexible; and let them not too much apply themselves to the disposition of their children, as thinking they will take best to that which they have most mind to. It is true that if the affection or aptness of the children be extraordinary, then it is good not to cross it; but generally the precept is

291

good, *optimum elige, suave et facile illud faciet consuetudo.* Younger brothers are commonly fortunate but seldom or never where the elder are disinherited.

Study Questions

1. How does *antithesis* work in this essay?
2. Discuss sentence structure. Consider parallelism, use of coordination and subordination, and punctuation.
3. This essay was written in the early seventeenth century and may be difficult to understand, Consider Bacon's diction. Are there any archaic words in the essay? Any whose meaning has changed?
4. Looking beyond its actual structure, is this a timely essay? Is it valid or pertinent today?

The Greatest Generation

Arthur Hoppe

1. Once upon a time there was a man named Ben Adam, who, like most members of The Older Generation, had little hair and overwhelming guilt feelings.

2. He also had a son named Irwin, who, like most members of The Younger Generation, had lots of hair and an overwhelming contempt for anybody over 30.

3. "Man, what a mess your generation made of things," Irwin was fond of saying, several times daily. "Because of your bumbling, we face a society that's racist, militaristic, polluted, overpopulated and terrorized by the hydrogen bomb. Thanks a lot."

4. "I guess we're about the worst generation that ever lived," Ben Adam would say, nodding guiltily. "I'm sorry, Irwin." And Irwin would shrug and go off with his friends to smoke pot.

5   Ben Adam couldn't help feeling that he was in for a bit of divine wrath in return for his sins. And he was therefore somewhat shaken on awakening one night to find an Angel at the foot of his bed writing in a Golden Book.

6   "I have come, Ben Adam," said the Angel, "to grant you one wish."

7   "Me?" said Ben Adam with surprise. "Why me?"

8   "You have been selected by the Heavenly Computer as typical of your generation," said the Angel "And your generation is to be rewarded for its magnificence."

9   "There must be some mistake," said Ben Adam with a frown. "We've been awful. We created a racist society . . ."

10   "Mankind has always been racist," said the Angel gently. "You were the first to admit it and attempt a remedy."

11   "And we militarized our democracy. Why, when I was a boy, we only had an Army of 134,000 men."

12   "You built an Army of four million men in hopes of bringing freedom and democracy to all the world," said the Angel. "Truly, a noble goal."

13   "Well, maybe," said Ben Adam. "But you can't deny that we polluted the water and the air and scattered garbage far and wide."

14   "That is so," said the Angel. "But the environment is polluted solely because you constructed the most affluent society the world has ever seen."

15   "I guess that's right," said Ben Adam. "Yet look at the Population Explosion. Famine and pestilence threaten mankind."

16   "Only because your generation cured diseases, increased the food supply and thereby lengthened man's life span," said the Angel. "A tremendous achievement."

17   "And we live in the terror of the hydrogen bomb," said Ben Adam gloomily. "What a legacy."

18   "Only because your generation unlocked the secrets of the atom in its search for wisdom," said the Angel. "What a glorious triumph."

19   "You really think so?" said Ben Adam, sitting straighter and smiling tentatively.

20   "Your motives were excellent, your goals ideal, your energies boundless and your achievements tremendous," said the Angel, reading from the Golden Book. "In the eons of mankind, the names of your generation, Ben Adam, lead all the rest. And therefore, by the authority vested in me, I am empowered to grant you one wish. What shall it be?"

21   "I wish," said Ben Adam, the heavenly-chosen representative of The Older Generation, with a sigh, "that you'd have a little talk with Irwin."

Study Questions

1. How does Irwin oversimplify the basis of his contempt for his father's generation?
2. What function does the Angel serve?
3. What seems to be the theme of this sketch?
4. How does the structure of paragraph 4 determine subsequent development in this sketch?

Father and Son

Cat Stevens

FATHER   It's not time to make a change, just relax take it easy, you're still young that's your fault there's so much you have to know. Find a girl settle down. If you want you can marry, look at me. I am old but I'm happy. I was once like you are now, and I know that it's not easy to be calm when you've found something going on, but take your time, think a lot, why think of everything you've got, For you will still be here tomorrow but your dreams may not.

SON   How can I try to explain, 'cause when I do he turns away again. It's always been the same same old story. From the moment I could talk I was ordered to listen, now there's a way and I know that I have to go. Away, I know I have to go.

FATHER   It's not time to make a change, just sit down take it slowly, you're still young that's your fault there's so much you have to go through. Find a girl settle down if you want you can marry, look at me I am old but I'm happy.

SON   Away away away, I know I have to make this decision alone—no.

SON   All the times that I've cried keeping all the things I knew inside it's hard, but it's harder to ignore it. If they were right I'd agree but it's them they know not me now there's a way, and I know that I have to go away, I know I have to go.

FATHER   Stay stay stay, why must you go and make this decision alone?

Study Questions

1.   What classic conflicts does this interchange between father and son relate?
2.   Is the conflict one of point of view alone or one of objective truth?
3.   What is the effect of the simultaneous refrains?

Ties

Dabney Stuart

When I faded back to pass
Late in the game, as one
Who has been away some time
Fades back into memory,
My father, who had been nodding
At home by the radio,
Would wake, asking
My mother, who had not
Been listening, "What's the score?"
And she would answer, "Tied,"   10
While the pass I threw
Hung high in the brilliant air
Beneath the dark, like a star.

Study Questions

1. What are the multiple meanings of *ties* in this poem?
2. How does the simile in lines 2–4 corroborate the meanings of *ties*?
3. What is the function of the imagery of fading, sleeping, and waking in this poem?

For My Son on the Highways of His Mind

Maxine Kumin

for Dan

Today the jailbird maple in the yard
sends down a thousand red hands in the rain.
Trussed at the upstairs window I
watch the great drenched leaves flap by
knowing that on the comely boulevard
incessant in your head you stand again
at the cloverleaf, thumb crooked outward.

Dreaming you travel light
guitar pick and guitar
bedroll sausage-tight
they take you as you are.   10

They take you as you are
there's nothing left behind
guitar pick and guitar
on the highways of your mind.

Instead you come home with two cops, your bike
lashed to the back of the cruiser because

an old lady, afraid of blacks and boys
with hair like yours, is simon-sure you took
her purse. They search you and of course you're clean.   20
Later we make it into a family joke,
a poor sort of catharsis. It wasn't the scene
they made—that part you rather enjoyed—
and not the old woman whose money turned up next day
in its usual lunatic place under a platter
but the principle of the thing, to be toyed
with cat and mouse, be one mouse who got away
somehow under the baseboard or radiator
and expect to be caught again sooner or later.

Dreaming you travel light   30
guitar pick and guitar
bedroll sausage-tight
they take you as you are.

Collar up, your discontent goes wrapped
at all times in the flannel army shirt
your father mustered out in, wars ago,
the ruptured duck still pinned to the pocket flap
and the golden toilet seat—the award his unit
won for making the bomb that killed the Japs—
now rubbed to its earliest threads, an old trousseau.   40

Meanwhile the posters on your bedroom wall
give up their glue. The corners start to fray.
Belmondo, Brando, Uncle Ho and Che,
last year's giants, hang lop-eared but hang on.
The merit badges, the model airplanes, all
the paraphernalia of a simpler day
gather dust on the shelf. That boy is gone.

They take you as you are
there's nothing left behind
guitar pick and guitar   50
on the highways of your mind.

How it will be tomorrow is anyone's guess.
The *Rand McNally* opens at a nudge
to forty-eight contiguous states, easy
as a compliant girl. In Minneapolis
I see you drinking wine under a bridge.
I see you turning on in Washington, D.C.,
panhandling in New Orleans, friendless

in Kansas City in an all-night beanery
and mugged on the beach in Venice outside L.A.   60
They take your watch and wallet and crack your head
as carelessly as an egg. The yolk runs red.
All this I see, or say it's what I see
in leaf fall, in rain, from the top of the stairs today
while your maps, those sweet pastels, lie flat and ready.

Dreaming you travel light
guitar pick and guitar
bedroll sausage-tight
they take you as you are.

They take you as you are   70
there's nothing left behind
guitar pick and guitar
on the highways of your mind.

Study Questions

1. What physical image and what season of the year evoke this narrator's musing on her son?
2. What is the figurative meaning of the title of this poem?
3. How does the narrator empathize with her son's discontent? With his wander-lust?
4. What fears does the narrator have for her son's physical safety?
5. What is the play on words in "simon-sure"?

Love Is Not All

There have been, especially in the past two decades, notable changes in the views articulated by women—and men—about their own identity, function, and place in the general scheme of things. Not surprisingly, these changes have been reflected in literature. We have chosen, in *Love Is Not All,* to concern ourselves with attitudes toward love past and present. Both men and women speak here. Some support tradition; some discuss alternatives; each offers his or her own comments on love.

The first group of writers in *Love Is Not All* are committed—in varying degrees—to love and loving. They don't have all the answers; some of them are not quite sure of the questions. Edna St. Vincent Millay, while suggesting that many negative aspects of life are beyond love's provenance to redeem, nevertheless says she'll take her chances with love. William Shakespeare recognizes that lovers are fallible human beings, that all is not moonlight and roses. He postulates the need for lovers to view one another realistically, and shows us that there are variations on the "Sleeping Beauty–Handsome Prince" theme. Robert Browning's persona wonders what she has missed by turning away from love, and Judy Collins sings of what is in store for those who accept it. Finally, James Joyce depicts love as a game, albeit a serious one with high stakes.

In the second subsection of *Love Is Not All* we find our lovers past the first romantic bloom of young love and discovering, in one way or another, that living with another person is not easy. Emily Dickinson's persona has turned her back on her own "requirements" to meet those of her husband, and if she feels less than fulfilled, nevertheless she has accepted her life. James Thurber's hero, too, accepted his fortune—or misfortune—for awhile. But the worm can turn, and we are inclined to cheer at this man's ultimate and fitting victory in the battle of the sexes. George Meredith's husband and wife, in spite of outward appearances, have come to an impasse that cannot be resolved; only "Love's corpse-light" remains. And the couple in Erica Jong's poem seem to be discovering, painfully, that it is difficult for the "new woman" and the "male chauvinist" to identify a common meeting ground.

The selections in the third subsection (except for a demurer from Anthony Hecht) deal with what Judith Viorst calls "true love." In Viorst's poem acceptance is the foundation of a relationship that has fulfilled an earlier potential for durability. The speaker knows that both she and her husband are less than perfect; each has been able to accept the other's frailties. Anthony Burgess seems to have arrived at a relationship with his wife that most of us would agree works very well. The lines of communication are open; the relationship flourishes. John Donne and William Butler Yeats both give us poems demonstrating the durability of relationships based on a deep awareness of the support each partner can give to the other. Matthew Arnold carries on this theme, and Denise Levertov brings it full circle, suggesting the possibility that mutual support can redeem an apparently crumbling relationship.

There are, of course, many alternatives today to the age-old dream of marrying and living happily ever after. Some of these alternatives are presented in the final subsection of *Love Is Not All*. The first selection, "Dwellers in Silence" by Ray Bradbury, depicts a man who is able to survive in a completely alien situation through his ability to find an alternative. Gloria Steinem and Barbara Katz discuss the modern liberation movement as it concerns both women and men. Gail Sheehy, Gerard Manley Hopkins, and Adrian Henri all present women who have identified their alternatives; from streetwalker to nun, all are experiencing, in varying degrees, success. How viable are these alternatives? Where among all these writings of and by men and women can the reader find the one particular selection that speaks, either through its theme, its subject, or its words, to him or her? That's for you to answer.

Love Is Not All

Edna St. Vincent Millay

Love is not all; it is not meat nor drink
Nor slumber nor a roof against the rain,
Nor yet a floating spar to men that sink
And rise and sink and rise and sink again;
Love can not fill the thickened lung with breath,
Nor clean the blood, nor set the fractured bone;
Yet many a man is making friends with death
Even as I speak, for lack of love alone.
It well may be that in a difficult hour,
Pinned down by pain and moaning for release,   10
Or nagged by want past resolution's power,
I might be driven to sell your love for peace,
Or trade the memory of this night for food.
It well may be. I do not think I would.

Study Questions

1. What is the thesis statement of this poem?
2. Is the sonnet form compatible with the content of this particular poem? Explain.
3. What stylistic devices does this poem display? To what end?
4. Of the spiritual and physical needs of the speaker, which is the most important? Has the speaker put physical needs in their proper perspective?
5. What is the effect of the negatives in the first six lines? Of the conditional verb form in the last eight lines?

My Mistress' Eyes Are Nothing Like the Sun

William Shakespeare

My mistress' eyes are nothing like the sun;
Coral is far more red than her lips' red;
If snow be white, why then her breasts are dun;
If hairs be wires, black wires grow on her head.
I have seen roses damasked, red and white,
But no such roses see I in her cheeks;
And in some perfumes is there more delight
Than in the breath that from my mistress reeks.
I love to hear her speak, yet well I know
That music hath a far more pleasing sound;   10
I grant I never saw a goddess go;
My mistress, when she walks, treads on the ground.
And yet, by heaven, I think my love as rare
As any she belied with false compare.

Study Questions

1. What is the source of the humor in this sonnet?
2. To be truly complimentary today, to what would you compare each of this woman's features?
3. On what connective does the concluding couplet pivot?
4. Shakespeare has used parallel construction in many of the clauses and sentences of this sonnet. Note examples.

Youth and Art

Robert Browning

It once might have been, once only:
    We lodged in a street together,
You, a sparrow on the housetop lonely,
    I, a lone she-bird of his feather.

Your trade was with sticks and clay,
    You thumbed, thrust, patted, and polished,
Then laughed "They will see some day
    Smith made, and Gibson demolished."

My business was song, song, song;
    I chirped, cheeped, trilled, and twittered,   10
"Kate Brown's on the boards ere long,
    And Grisi's existence embittered!"

I earned no more by a warble
    Than you by a sketch in plaster;
You wanted a piece of marble,
    I needed a music-master.

We studied hard in our styles,
    Chipped each at a crust like Hindus,
For air, looked out on the tiles,
    For fun, watched each other's windows.   20

You lounged, like a boy of the South,
    Cap and blouse—nay, a bit of beard too;
Or you got it, rubbing your mouth
    With fingers the clay adhered to.

And I—soon managed to find
    Weak points in the flower-fence facing,
Was forced to put up a blind
    And be safe in my corset-lacing.

No harm! It was not my fault
    If you never turned your eye's tail up   30

As I shook upon E *in alt.*,
   Or ran the chromatic scale up;

For spring bade the sparrows pair,
   And the boys and girls gave guesses,
And stalls in our street looked rare
   With bulrush and watercresses.

Why did not you pinch a flower
   In a pellet of clay and fling it?
Why did not I put a power
   Of thanks in a look, or sing it?   40

I did look, sharp as a lynx
   (And yet the memory rankles),
When models arrived, some minx
   Tripped upstairs, she and her ankles.

But I think I gave you as good!
   "That foreign fellow—who can know
How she pays, in a playful mood,
   For his tuning her that piano?"

Could you say so, and never say,
   "Suppose we join hands and fortunes,   50
And I fetch her from over the way,
   Her, piano, and long tunes and short tunes"?

No, no; you would not be rash,
   Nor I rasher and something over.
You've to settle yet Gibson's hash,
   And Grisi yet lives in clover.

But you meet the Prince at the Board,
   I'm queen myself at *bals-paré,*
I've married a rich old lord,
   And you're dubbed knight and an R. A.   60

Each life unfulfilled, you see;
   It hangs still, patchy and scrappy.
We have not sighed deep, laughed free,
   Starved, feasted, despaired—been happy.

And nobody calls you a dunce,
   And people suppose me clever;
This could but have happened once,
   And we missed it, lost it forever.

Study Questions

1. What is the theme of "Youth and Art"? Can you suggest a more appropriate title? To what degree is the theme of this poem still a vital issue?
2. Is "Youth and Art" a soliloquy or a dramatic monologue?
3. What is the "it" of the first and last lines?
4. Identify the rhyme scheme of the stanzas and its function.
5. What is the tone of the poem?

Since You've Asked

Judy Collins

What I'll give you, since you've asked,
Is all my time together
Take the rugged sunny days
The warm and rocky weather
Take the roads that I have walked along
Looking for tomorrow's time, peace of mind

As my life spills into yours
Changing with the hours
Filling up the world with time
Turning time to flowers   10
I can show you all the songs
That I never sang to one man before

We have seen a million stones
Lying by the water
You have climbed the hills with me
To the mountain shelter
Taken off the days one by one
Setting them to breathe in the sun

Take the lilies and the lace
From the days of childhood   20
All the willow winding paths

Leading up and outward
This is what I give
This is what I ask you for, nothing more

Study Questions

1. The most striking poetic feature of this song is the metaphorical language. What are the metaphors for time, life, and days of childhood?
2. What does "Taken off the days one by one/Setting them to breathe in the sun" signify?
3. To what question could this song be a thoughtful rejoinder?

The Boarding House

James Joyce

1   Mrs. Mooney was a butcher's daughter. She was a woman who was quite able to keep things to herself: a determined woman. She had married her father's foreman and opened a butcher's shop near Spring Gardens. But as soon as his father-in-law was dead Mr. Mooney began to go to the devil. He drank, plundered the till, ran headlong into debt. It was no use making him take the pledge: he was sure to break out again a few days after. By fighting his wife in the presence of customers and by buying bad meat he ruined his business. One night he went for his wife with the cleaver and she had to sleep in a neighbour's house.

2   After that they lived apart. She went to the priest and got a separation from him with care of the children. She would give him neither money nor food nor house-room; and so he was obliged to enlist himself as a sheriff's man. He was a shabby stooped little drunkard with a white face and a white moustache and white eyebrows, pencilled above his little eyes, which were pink-veined and raw; and all day long he sat in the bailiff's room, waiting to be put on a job. Mrs. Mooney, who had

taken what remained of her money out of the butcher business and set up a boarding house in Hardwicke Street, was a big imposing woman. Her house had a floating population made up of tourists from Liverpool and the Isle of Man and, occasionally, *artistes* from the music halls. Its resident population was made up of clerks from the city. She governed her house cunningly and firmly, knew when to give credit, when to be stern and when to let things pass. All the resident young men spoke of her as *The Madam*.

3   Mrs. Mooney's young men paid fifteen shillings a week for board and lodgings (beer or stout at dinner excluded). They shared in common tastes and occupations and for this reason they were very chummy with one another. They discussed with one another the chances of favourites and outsiders. Jack Mooney, the Madam's son, who was clerk to a commission agent in Fleet Street, had the reputation of being a hard case. He was fond of using soldiers' obscenities: usually he came home in the small hours. When he met his friends he had always a good one to tell them and he was always sure to be on to a good thing—that is to say, a likely horse or a likely *artiste*. He was also handy with the mits and sang comic songs. On Sunday nights there would often be a reunion in Mrs. Mooney's front drawing-room. The music-hall *artistes* would oblige; and Sheridan played waltzes and polkas and vamped accompaniments. Polly Mooney, the Madam's daughter, would also sing. She sang:

I'm a . . . naughty girl.
You needn't sham:
You know I am.

4   Polly was a slim girl of nineteen, she had light soft hair and a small full mouth. Her eyes, which were grey with a shade of green through them, had a habit of glancing upwards when she spoke with anyone, which made her look like a little perverse madonna. Mrs. Mooney had first sent her daughter to be a typist in a corn-factor's office but, as a disreputable sheriff's man used to come every other day to the office, asking to be allowed to say a word to his daughter, she had taken her daughter home again and set her to do housework. As Polly was very lively the intention was to give her the run of the young men. Besides, young men like to feel that there is a young woman not very far away. Polly, of course, flirted with the young men but Mrs. Mooney, who was a shrewd judge, knew that the young men were only passing the time away: none of them meant business. Things went on so for a long time and Mrs. Mooney began to think of sending Polly back to typewriting when she noticed that something was going on between Polly and one of the young men. She watched the pair and kept her own counsel.

5   Polly knew that she was being watched, but still her mother's persistent silence could not be misunderstood. There had been no open complicity between mother and daughter, no open understanding but,

though people in the house began to talk of the affair, still Mrs. Mooney did not intervene. Polly began to grow a little strange in her manner and the young man was evidently perturbed. At last, when she judged it to be the right moment, Mrs. Mooney intervened. She dealt with moral problems as a cleaver deals with meat: and in this case she had made up her mind.

6   It was a bright Sunday morning of early summer, promising heat, but with a fresh breeze blowing. All the windows of the boarding house were open and the lace curtains ballooned gently towards the street beneath the raised sashes. The belfry of George's Church sent out constant peals and worshippers, singly or in groups, traversed the little circus before the church, revealing their purpose by their self-contained demeanour no less than by the little volumes in their gloved hands. Breakfast was over in the boarding house and the table of the breakfast-room was covered with plates on which lay yellow streaks of eggs with morsels of bacon-fat and bacon-rind. Mrs. Mooney sat in the straw arm-chair and watched the servant Mary remove the breakfast things. She made Mary collect the crusts and pieces of broken bread to help to make Tuesday's bread-pudding. When the table was cleared, the broken bread collected, the sugar and butter safe under lock and key, she began to reconstruct the interview which she had had the night before with Polly. Things were as she had suspected: she had been frank in her questions and Polly had been frank in her answers. Both had been somewhat awkward, of course. She had been made awkward by her not wishing to receive the news in too cavalier a fashion or to seem to have connived and Polly had been made awkward not merely because allusions of that kind always made her awkward but also because she did not wish it to be thought that in her wise innocence she had divined the intention behind her mother's tolerance.

7   Mrs. Mooney glanced instinctively at the little gilt clock on the mantelpiece as soon as she had become aware through her revery that the bells of George's Church had stopped ringing. It was seventeen minutes past eleven: she would have lots of time to have the matter out with Mr. Doran and then catch short twelve at Marlborough Street. She was sure she would win. To begin with she had all the weight of social opinion on her side: she was an outraged mother. She had allowed him to live beneath her roof, assuming that he was a man of honour, and he had simply abused her hospitality. He was thirty-four or thirty-five years of age, so that youth could not be pleaded as his excuse; nor could ignorance be his excuse since he was a man who had seen something of the world. He had simply taken advantage of Polly's youth and inexperience: that was evident. The question was: What reparation would he make?

8   There must be reparation made in such cases. It is all very well for the man: he can go his ways as if nothing had happened, having had his moment of pleasure, but the girl has to bear the brunt. Some mothers

would be content to patch up such an affair for a sum of money; she had known cases of it. But she would not do so. For her only one reparation could make up for the loss of her daughter's honour: marriage.

9 She counted all her cards again before sending Mary up to Mr. Doran's room to say that she wished to speak with him. She felt sure she would win. He was a serious young man, not rakish or loud-voiced like the others. If it had been Mr. Sheridan or Mr. Meade or Bantam Lyons her task would have been much harder. She did not think he would face publicity. All the lodgers in the house knew something of the affair; details had been invented by some. Besides, he had been employed for thirteen years in a great Catholic wine-merchant's office and publicity would mean for him, perhaps, the loss of his sit. Whereas if he agreed all might be well. She knew he had a good screw for one thing and she suspected he had a bit of stuff put by.

10 Nearly the half-hour! She stood up and surveyed herself in the pier-glass. The decisive expression of her great florid face satisfied her and she thought of some mothers she knew who could not get their daughters off their hands.

11 Mr. Doran was very anxious indeed this Sunday morning. He had made two attempts to shave but his hand had been so unsteady that he had been obliged to desist. Three days' reddish beard fringed his jaws and every two or three minutes a mist gathered on his glasses so that he had to take them off and polish them with his pocket-handkerchief. The recollection of his confession of the night before was a cause of acute pain to him; the priest had drawn out every ridiculous detail of the affair and in the end had so magnified his sin that he was almost thankful at being afforded a loophole of reparation. The harm was done. What could he do now but marry her or run away? He could not brazen it out. The affair would be sure to be talked of and his employer would be certain to hear of it. Dublin is such a small city: everyone knows everyone else's business. He felt his heart leap warmly in his throat as he heard in his excited imagination old Mr. Leonard calling out in his rasping voice: *Send Mr. Doran here, please.*

12 All his long years of service gone for nothing! All his industry and diligence thrown away! As a young man he had sown his wild oats, of course; he had boasted of his free-thinking and denied the existence of God to his companions in public-houses. But that was all passed and done with . . . nearly. He still bought a copy of *Reynolds's Newspaper* every week but he attended to his religious duties and for nine-tenths of the year lived a regular life. He had money enough to settle down on; it was not that. But the family would look down on her. First of all there was her disreputable father and then her mother's boarding house was beginning to get a certain fame. He had a notion that he was being had. He could imagine his friends talking of the affair and laughing. She *was* a little vulgar; sometimes she said *I seen* and *If I had've known.* But what would grammar matter if he really loved her? He could not make up his

mind whether to like her or despise her for what she had done. Of course, he had done it too. His instinct urged him to remain free, not to marry. Once you are married you are done for, it said.

13   While he was sitting helplessly on the side of the bed in shirt and trousers she tapped lightly at his door and entered. She told him all, that she had made a clean breast of it to her mother and that her mother would speak with him that morning. She cried and threw her arms round his neck, saying:

14   —O, Bob! Bob! What am I to do? What am I to do at all?

15   She would put an end to herself, she said.

16   He comforted her feebly, telling her not to cry, that it would be all right, never fear. He felt against his shirt the agitation of her bosom.

17   It was not altogether his fault that it had happened. He remembered well, with the curious patient memory of the celibate, the first casual caresses her dress, her breath, her fingers had given him. Then late one night as he was undressing for bed she had tapped at his door, timidly. She wanted to relight her candle at his for hers had been blown out by a gust. It was her bath night. She wore a loose open combing-jacket of printed flannel. Her white instep shone in the opening of her furry slippers and the blood glowed warmly behind her perfumed skin. From her hands and wrists too as she lit and steadied her candle a faint perfume arose.

18   On nights when he came in very late it was she who warmed up his dinner. He scarcely knew what he was eating, feeling her beside him alone, at night, in the sleeping house. And her thoughtfulness! If the night was anyway cold or wet or windy there was sure to be a little tumbler of punch ready for him. Perhaps they could be happy together. . . .

19   They used to go upstairs together on tiptoe, each with a candle, and on the third landing exchange reluctant goodnights. They used to kiss. He remembered well her eyes, the touch of her hand and his delirium. . . .

20   But delirium passes. He echoed her phrase, applying it to himself: *What am I to do?* The instinct of the celibate warned him to hold back. But the sin was there; even his sense of honour told him that reparation must be made for such a sin.

21   While he was sitting with her on the side of the bed Mary came to the door and said that the missus wanted to see him in the parlour. He stood up to put on his coat and waistcoat, more helpless than ever. When he was dressed he went over to her to comfort her. It would be all right, never fear. He left her crying on the bed and moaning softly: *O my God!*

22   Going down the stairs his glasses became so dimmed with moisture that he had to take them off and polish them. He longed to ascend through the roof and fly away to another country where he would never hear again of his trouble, and yet a force pushed him downstairs step by step. The implacable faces of his employer and of the Madam stared

upon his discomfiture. On the last flight of stairs he passed Jack Mooney who was coming up from the pantry nursing two bottles of *Bass*. They saluted coldly; and the lover's eyes rested for a second or two on a thick bulldog face and a pair of thick short arms. When he reached the foot of the staircase he glanced up and saw Jack regarding him from the door of the return-room.

23   Suddenly he remembered the night when one of the music-hall *artistes*, a little blond Londoner, had made a rather free allusion to Polly. The reunion had been almost broken up on account of Jack's violence. Everyone tried to quiet him. The music-hall *artiste*, a little paler than usual, kept smiling and saying that there was no harm meant: but Jack kept shouting at him that if any fellow tried that sort of a game on with *his* sister he'd bloody well put his teeth down his throat, so he would.

. . . .

24   Polly sat for a little time on the side of the bed, crying. Then she dried her eyes and went over to the looking-glass. She dipped the end of the towel in the water-jug and refreshed her eyes with the cool water. She looked at herself in profile and readjusted a hairpin above her ear. Then she went back to the bed again and sat at the foot. She regarded the pillows for a long time and the sight of them awakened in her mind secret amiable memories. She rested the nape of her neck against the cool iron bed-rail and fell into a revery. There was no longer any perturbation visible on her face.

25   She waited on patiently, almost cheerfully, without alarm, her memories gradually giving place to hopes and visions of the future. Her hopes and visions were so intricate that she no longer saw the white pillows on which her gaze was fixed or remembered that she was waiting for anything.

26   At last she heard her mother calling. She started to her feet and ran to the banister.

27   —Polly! Polly!

28   —Yes, mamma?

29   —Come down, dear. Mr. Doran wants to speak to you.

30   Then she remembered what she had been waiting for.

Study Questions

1. Clearly, Mr. Doran has been had. Are you at all amused by his plight?
2. Polly's brother threatened to drub "any fellow who tried that sort of a game on with *his* sister." What indications are there that Mrs. Mooney was playing a game? Who are the players? What are the stakes? Is there a consolation prize?

3. What are some possible connotations for "The Madam"? Which of these connotations are applicable?
4. Why does Joyce include the lyrics of Polly's song? Does the song help advance the action? Provide an ironic commentary on the action? Add depth to characterization?
5. What is especially appropriate about the statement that Mrs. Mooney "dealt with moral problems as a cleaver deals with meat"? What figure of speech does this exemplify?
6. What is the effect of the paradoxical juxtaposition of words in such phrases as "perverse madonna" and "wise innocence"?

She Rose to His Requirement

Emily Dickinson

She rose to his requirement, dropped
The playthings of her life
To take the honorable work
Of woman and of wife.

If aught she missed in her new day
Of amplitude, or awe,
Or first prospective, or the gold
In using wore away,

It lay unmentioned, as the sea
Develops pearl and weed,
But only to himself is known   10
The fathoms they abide.

Study Questions

1. What are the "playthings" Dickinson refers to? Is the subject of this poem a child bride?

2. What is "gold" in "the gold/In using wore away"?
3. The second and third stanzas form one lengthy complex sentence, the grammatical analysis of which can yield a deeper understanding of this poem. Explain.
4. The first stanza is written in the language of ordinary discourse, while the second and third are written almost entirely in metaphor. What is the significance of this shift in language?

The Unicorn in the Garden

James Thurber

1   Once upon a sunny morning a man who sat in a breakfast nook looked up from his scrambled eggs to see a white unicorn with a gold horn quietly cropping the roses in the garden. The man went up to the bedroom where his wife was still asleep and woke her. "There's a unicorn in the garden," he said. "Eating roses." She opened one unfriendly eye and looked at him. "The unicorn is a mythical beast," she said, and turned her back on him. The man walked slowly downstairs and out into the garden. The unicorn was still there; he was now browsing among the tulips. "Here, unicorn," said the man, and he pulled up a lily and gave it to him. The unicorn ate it gravely. With a high heart, because there was a unicorn in his garden, the man went upstairs and roused his wife again. "The unicorn," he said, "ate a lily." His wife sat up in bed and looked at him, coldly. "You are a booby," she said, "and I am going to have you put in the booby-hatch." The man, who had never liked the words "booby" and "booby-hatch," and who liked them even less on a shining morning when there was a unicorn in the garden, thought for a moment. "We'll see about that," he said. He walked over to the door. "He has a golden horn in the middle of his forehead," he told her. Then he went back to the garden to watch the unicorn; but the unicorn had gone away. The man sat down among the roses and went to sleep.

2   As soon as the husband had gone out of the house, the wife got up and dressed as fast as she could. She was very excited and there was a gloat in her eye. She telephoned the police and she telephoned a psychiatrist; she told them to hurry to her house and bring a strait-jacket.

When the police and the psychiatrist arrived they sat down in chairs and looked at her, with great interest. "My husband," she said, "saw a unicorn this morning." The police looked at the psychiatrist and the psychiatrist looked at the police. "He told me it ate a lily," she said. The psychiatrist looked at the police and the police looked at the psychiatrist. "He told me it had a golden horn in the middle of its forehead," she said. At a solemn signal from the psychiatrist, the police leaped from their chairs and seized the wife. They had a hard time subduing her, for she put up a terrific struggle, but they finally subdued her. Just as they got her into the strait-jacket, the husband came back into the house.

3   "Did you tell your wife you saw a unicorn?" asked the police. "Of course not," said the husband. "The unicorn is a mythical beast." "That's all I wanted to know," said the psychiatrist. "Take her away. I'm sorry, sir, but your wife is as crazy as a jay bird." So they took her away, cursing and screaming, and shut her up in an institution. The husband lived happily ever after.

4   *Moral: Don't count your boobies until they are hatched.*

Study Questions

1. "The Unicorn in the Garden" is one of Thurber's collected *Fables for Our Time*, written in 1939–1940. What is a fable?
2. What is the effect of the juxtaposition of "scrambled eggs" and "a white unicorn with a gold horn"?
3. The unicorn browses among the tulips but eats the roses and a lily. What do the rose and lily traditionally symbolize?
4. Why is there a comma between *him* and *coldly* in the first paragraph?

From *Modern Love*

George Meredith

No. 17

At dinner, she is hostess, I am host.
Went the feast ever cheerfuller? She keeps
The Topic over intellectual deeps
In buoyancy afloat. They see no ghost.
With sparkling surface-eyes we ply the ball:
It is in truth a most contagious game:
Hiding the Skeleton, shall be its name.
Such play as this the devils might appal!
But here's the greater wonder: in that we,
Enamored of an acting naught can tire,   10
Each other, like true hypocrites, admire;
Warm-lighted looks, Love's ephemeridæ,
Shoot gayly o'er the dishes and the wine.
We waken envy of our happy lot.
Fast, sweet, and golden, shows the marriage-knot.
Dear guests, you now have seen Love's corpse-light shine.

Study Questions

1. Who is the speaker in this poem? What do you know about him?
2. What event dramatizes the situation?
3. Why has Meredith capitalized *Topic* and italicized *Hiding the Skeleton*?
4. What does *ephemeridæ* mean? How does this word contribute to the tone?
5. *Modern Love* was published in 1862. In spite of its date, does this seem like a modern poem? Comment.

Back to Africa

Erica Jong

"Among the Gallas, when a woman grows tired of the cares of housekeeping, she begins to talk incoherently and demean herself extravagantly. This is a sign of the descent of the holy spirit Callo upon her. Immediately, her husband prostrates himself and adores her; she ceases to bear the humble title of wife and is called 'Lord'; domestic duties have no further claim on her, and her will is a divine law."

—Sir James George Frazer, *The Golden Bough*

Seeing me weary
      of patching the thatch
      of pounding the bread
      of pacing the floor nightly
      with the baby in my arms,

my tall black husband
      (with eyes like coconuts)
      has fallen down on the floor to adore me!
      I curse myself for being born a woman.
      He thinks I'm God!   10

      I mutter incoherently of Friedan, Millet, Greer . . .
      He thinks the spirit
      has descended.
      He calls me "Lord."

               *

Lord, lord, he's weary in his castle now.
      It's no fun living with a God.
      He rocks the baby, patches the thatch
      & pounds the bread.
      I stay out all night with the Spirit.

Towards morning when the Spirit brings me home,   20
      he's almost too pooped to adore me.
      I lecture him on the nature
      & duties of men.
      "Biology is destiny," I say.

Already I hear stirrings of dissent.
    He says he could have been a movie star.
    He says he needs a full-time maid.
    He says he never *meant*
    to marry God.

Study Questions

1. Jong has applied the events of a domestic situation of an African couple to the events of her own married life. Describe the humor in such a juxtaposition.
2. Identify the irony in the fifth and sixth stanzas.
3. What is "the Spirit"? What does "patching the thatch" signify? Why does the speaker mutter of Friedan, Millet, and Greer?

True Love

Judith Viorst

It's true love because
I put on eyeliner and a concerto and make pungent
  observations about the great issues of the day
Even when there's no one here but him,
And because
I do not resent watching the Green Bay Packers
Even though I am philosophically opposed to football,
And because
When he is late for dinner and I know he must be
  either having an affair or lying dead in the
   middle of the street,
I always hope he's dead.

10

It's true love because
If he said quit drinking martinis but I kept drinking
    them and the next morning I couldn't get out of
    bed,
He wouldn't tell me he told me,
And because
He is willing to wear unironed undershorts
Out of respect for the fact that I am philosophically   20
    opposed to ironing,
And because
If his mother was drowning and I was drowning and
    he had to choose one of us to save,
He says he'd save me.

It's true love because
When he went to San Francisco on business while I
    had to stay home with the painters and the
    exterminator and the baby who was getting the
    chicken pox,   30
He understood why I hated him,
And because
When I said that playing the stock market was
    juvenile and irresponsible and then the stock I
    wouldn't let him buy went up twenty-six points,
I understood why he hated me,
And because
Despite cigarette cough, tooth decay, acid indigestion,
    dandruff, and other features of married life that
    tend to dampen the fires of passion,   40
We still feel something
We can call
True love.

Study Questions

1. How would you describe the speaker of this poem? Where does she live? What kind of life role is hers? Is she resentful of her position in life?
2. Is this poem easy to read? What features of structure aid continuity? What are the sources of diction and images?
3. Does the poem reveal more about the character of the husband or of the wife? Explain.

The Private Dialect of Husbands and Wives

Anthony Burgess

1   I remember an old film about Alcatraz or Sing Sing or somewhere, in which Wallace Beery, having organized the killing of several wardens, broken up the prison hospital, and kicked the deputy governor in the guts, said in his defense: "I was only kiddin'." I've never gone so far, but I fear that my own kind of kidding may be the death of me. Like giving a college lecture on a purely fictitious Elizabethan dramatist called Grasmere Tadworth (1578–1621). Like writing a pseudonymous review of one of my own books. Like, when asked by the editors of *Who's Who* to give the names of my clubs, answering with Toby's Gym, the Nudorama Strip Club, the Naked City and so on. This is not really funny. When the same editors asked me for hobbies, I gave *wife* as one of them, and they let that go through. There it is now, perpetuated from edition to edition, waiting for *Who Was Who,* and sooner or later I was bound to be asked what the hell I meant, mean.

2   It's tempting to retreat into that high-school thicket of evasiveness, the dictionary. Thus, my wife is a small species of falcon, *falco subbuteo.* My wife is a horse of middle size, a pacing horse, a stick or figure of a horse on which boys ride. My wife is (Old French *hobin*) a stupid fellow. All right, all right, stop fooling about; try the definition "favourite pursuit" and don't, for God's sake, say: "Ha, ha, I stopped pursuing her a long time ago."

3   I recognize a number of horrible possibilities, most of them appropriate to the evenings and weekends after the honeymoon, but those are not really applicable. The other possibilities are sentimental, so I reject those too. Popular songs used to approach the woman-in-one's-life as something of either gold or silver—nubile nymph or fulfilled mother—but they never hymned her in middle age. In middle age she has none of the properties of a cult. Not being an icon, she is not a thing. She resists being used and she resists being worshipped; she is at her most human.

4   My wife and I have now been married over twenty-six years, and I recognize that by the standards of our milieu—an artistic one—we have not played quite fair. We should have changed partners at least once before now, and there was a time, just after World War Two, when we tried. That was a period of almost mandatory disruption, and there was no shortage of new marital opportunities. But things went wrong; she

319

and I found it more interesting to discuss what we proposed doing than actually to do it. The prospect of learning somebody else's language, of building up new mythologies from scratch, seemed shamefully wasteful. So we just carried on as we were, carry on as we are.

5   The lure of a fresh young body seems to me quite irrelevant to questions of marriage; the desire to regenerate one's glands is only a valid excuse for divorce in communities where adultery is a civil crime. A marriage is really a civilization in miniature, and one breaks up a civilization at the peril of one's soul. The vital element in any civilized community is language, and without language there can be no marriage. By language I mean something more subtle, and much less useful, than the signals of commerce and the directives of the law: I mean sounds, noises, grunts, idioms, jokes, bits of silliness, inconsequential stupidities which affirm that a special *closed* community exists. They are a sort of shorthand way of summing up a whole complex of feelings; time (history, if you like) has given them a meaning; they totally resist translation.

6   They can be explained, but then their significance disappears. Explain a joke, and there is no laughter. Explain a poem, and the poem dissolves into nonsense. If, at a party, I am asked to play the piano, and if I play the piano for too long, my wife has only to call "Mary!" for me to stop playing. The reference is to the scene in *Pride and Predjudice* where Mr. Bennet says, to his piano-playing daughter, "Mary, you have delighted us long enough." This is a fairly public example of marital shorthand; the private ones tend to wither in the air of disclosure. "Blue, honey?" doesn't mean what it says. It's a common memory from some old trashy woman's magazine story, invoked in mockery during a needless posture of depression. A reversion to dialect (the Lancashire *aye*, for instance, instead of the Southern English *yes*) denotes an instinctive testing of a metropolitan pretension (our own or someone else's) against the earthier standards of my, or her, regional background.

7   I needn't labour this point about the marital language, or about the marital mythology which contains characters from literature or films, real relatives, the fat Birmingham woman who said "I down't eat enough to keep a baird aloive," the man who comes into the pub belching, dead cats, living dogs, the Holy Ghost. Every married man or woman knows what I mean, but may not be willing to see the importance of it. It can only be built up over a long tract of time, and after a quarter of a century it can become rich, subtle and allusive as Shakespeare's English, though less long-winded. But, unlike literature, it is relaxed, and it promotes relaxation. It can even encompass long silences broken by noises, rude gestures, lines of filthy doggerel, rows of isolated vowel-sounds, bursts of *bel canto*, exaggerated tooth-picking.

8   I seem to derive as much spare-time fulfillment from this sort of unproductive communion as other men get from boats, golf, stamp collecting, and drilling holes in the kitchen wall. Working at home as I do, I'm prepared to waste a whole morning on it; it's a two-way communica-

tive process, which is more than can be said for hammering at a typewriter. It can be helped along with games of Scrabble, gin, doing the crossword in the morning paper, kicking the dog's flank with one's bare foot, seeing how long one can hold one's breath. It ends with guilt and astonishment when the Angelus is tolled at midday from the nearby church; the shopping has not been done, lunch is unprepared (but does one deserve lunch?), not one word has been fired at the sheet in the typewriter. A hobby shouldn't get in the way of one's work.

9   Am I using this term *hobby* correctly? It probably denotes a sub-creative process, like constructing model cathedrals out of matches, and it goes more easily with plurals than with singulars. *Wives,* as with some notable serial polygamist, fits better than *wife,* and it connotes collection as well as sub-creation (very sub: a brief marriage is hardly worth the making). There's also a strong whiff of the impersonal, or depersonalized, about it. I see now that, hobbled by *hobby,* I've presented my wife as a very intricately programmed phatic communicatrix (or whatever the sociological jargon is). Let me straighten out my own usage.

10   We talk about our hobbies because we're shy of mentioning the word *vocation*—unless we earn money from a vocation, when it promptly turns into a profession. And yet a lot of hobbies are true vocations—the fugues composed by the nightclub pianist, the paintings of a customs officer called Rousseau, the house that the bank clerk builds on summer evenings. In this term *vocation,* creation and religion combine. If one has a vocation for writing lyric poetry when the shop is shut for the day, one may also have a vocation for the priesthood. I think I have a vocation for gaining the maximal social fulfillment, which means communicative fulfillment, which means even a kind of spiritual fulfillment, out of living with a particular woman. But, frightened of the big words, and also incurably facetious, I have to talk of my wife as a hobby—the culminating item in a list that contains piano-playing, musical composition, and language-learning. Yet the term *hobby* is not really inept, since it implies enjoyment and not just, like *vocation,* a sort of pretension to uplift. One of Kingsley Amis's characters talks about going to bed with his wife as being ennobling but also good fun—as though some stunning work of literature were also a good read. That will do pretty well for most levels of marital intercourse.

11   My *Who's Who* avowal has been taken by some people as a misprint. Once I had to give an after-dinner speech, and the chairman, introducing me, said that *wife* was undoubtedly meant to be *wine.* The right facetious response is to say that a wife transubstantiates life into wine. The right highbrow response would take in the new communication philosophers—Marshall McLuhan in America and Roland Barthes in France—and point out that the basis of living is semiological, which means concerned with all possible modes of human signalling—from vulgar lip-noises to sublime poetry. In a marriage, you have an opportunity to erect the most subtle and exact semiological system civilization is

capable of. It takes a long time, but it's worth it. So, apart from what else she is, my wife continues to be my non-professional vocation. Or, not to leave the fun out, my hobby. I hope to God I continue to be hers.

Study Questions

1. How does the word *dialect* figure literally and whimsically in this essay?
2. To what end does the series of anecdotes in the opening paragraph lead?
3. Identify the thesis statement of this essay.
4. How does the reversal of tone in the last sentence alter the by now firmly established tone of the essay?

A Valediction: Forbidding Mourning

John Donne

As virtuous men pass mildly away,
   And whisper to their souls to go,
Whilst some of their sad friends do say,
   "The breath goes now," and some say, "No,"

So let us melt and make no noise,
   No tear-floods nor sigh-tempests move;
'Twere profanation of our joys
   To tell the laity our love.

Moving of th' earth brings harms and fears;
   Men reckon what it did and meant,
But trepidation of the spheres,
   Though greater far, is innocent.

10

Dull sublunary lovers' love,
  Whose soul is sense, cannot admit
Absence, because it doth remove
  Those things which elemented it.

But we by a love so much refin'd
  That ourselves know not what it is,
Interassured of the mind,
  Care less eyes, lips, and hands to miss.   20

Our two souls, therefore, which are one,
  Though I must go, endure not yet
A breach, but an expansion,
  Like gold to airy thinness beat.

If they be two, they are two so
  As stiff twin compasses are two;
Thy soul, the fix'd foot, makes no show
  To move, but doth if th' other do.

And though it in the center sit,
  Yet when the other far doth roam,   30
It leans and hearkens after it,
  And grows erect as that comes home.

Such wilt thou be to me, who must,
  Like th' other foot, obliquely run;
Thy firmness makes my circle just,
  And makes me end where I begun.

Study Questions

1. This poem is generally considered one of Donne's best. It contains his most famous image—the compass—and has been the center of critical controversy for centuries. Does the emotion strike you as deeply felt?
2. Define *valediction.*
3. From which sciences does Donne cull his images?
4. What words cluster metaphorically around *profanation* and *gold*?
5. This poem is written in nine stanzas. What structural function does the fifth stanza serve?

The Folly of Being Comforted

William Butler Yeats

One that is ever kind said yesterday:
"Your well-beloved's hair has threads of grey,
And little shadows come about her eyes;
Time can but make it easier to be wise
Though now it seem impossible, and so
Patience is all that you have need of."
                                        No,
I have not a crumb of comfort, not a grain,
Time can but make her beauty over again:
Because of that great nobleness of hers
The fire that stirs about her, when she stirs   10
Burns but more clearly. O she had not these ways,
When all the wild summer was in her gaze.
O heart! O heart! if she'd but turn her head,
You'd know the folly of being comforted.

Study Questions

1. One critic has said that every woman ought to have this poem addressed to her at least once before she dies. Paraphrase Yeats. What is he saying that every woman should hear?
2. Who is the "one that is ever kind"?
3. What word marks a turning point in the poem? What images tie the two parts of the poem together?
4. What does Yeats mean by "fire" and "wild summer"?

Dover Beach

Matthew Arnold

    The sea is calm to-night,
The tide is full, the moon lies fair
Upon the Straits;—on the French coast, the light
Gleams, and is gone; the cliffs of England stand,
Glimmering and vast, out in the tranquil bay.
Come to the window, sweet is the night air!
 Only, from the long line of spray
Where the ebb meets the moon-blanched sand,
Listen! you hear the grating roar
Of pebbles which the waves suck back, and fling,   10
At their return, up the high strand,
Begin, and cease, and then again begin,
With tremulous cadence slow, and bring
The eternal note of sadness in.

    Sophocles long ago
Heard it on the Ægean, and it brought
Into his mind the turbid ebb and flow
    Of human misery; we
Find also in the sound a thought,
Hearing it by this distant northern sea.   20

    The sea of faith
Was once, too, at the full, and round earth's shore
Lay like the folds of a bright girdle furled;
    But now I only hear
Its melancholy, long, withdrawing roar,
    Retreating to the breath
Of the night-wind down the vast edges drear
And naked shingles of the world.

    Ah, love, let us be true
To one another! for the world, which seems   30
To lie before us like a land of dreams,
So various, so beautiful, so new,
Hath really neither joy, nor love, nor light,
Nor certitude, nor peace, nor help for pain;

And we are here as on a darkling plain
Swept with confused alarms of struggle and flight,
Where ignorant armies clash by night.

Study Questions

1. How strong a force does the poet seem to feel love is? Is his conclusion definitive or tentative? Could this love be generalized into something beyond that between men and women?
2. Besides providing the setting for the poem, what else does the first stanza accomplish?
3. Which clauses or phrases act as transitions between stanzas?
4. To whom does "we" refer?
5. What two metaphors express the theme? Are these metaphors logically related to one another?

The Novel

Denise Levertov

A wind is blowing. The book being written
shifts, halts, pages
yellow and white drawing apart
and inching together in
new tries. A single white half sheet
skims out under the door.

And cramped in their not yet
halfwritten lives, a man and a woman
grimace in pain. Their cat
yawning its animal secret,   10
stirs in the monstrous limbo of erasure.
They live (when they live) in fear

of blinding, of burning, of choking under a
mushroom cloud in the year of the roach.
And they want (like us) the eternity
of today, they want this fear to be
struck out at once by a thick black
magic marker, everywhere, every page,

the whole sheets of it crushed, crackling,
and tossed in the fire   20
      and when they were fine ashes
      the stove would cool and be cleaned
      and a jar of flowers would be put to stand
      on top of the stove in the spring light.

Meanwhile from page to page they
buy things, acquiring the look of a
full life; they argue, make silence bitter,
plan journeys, move house, implant
despair in each other
and then in the nick of time   30

they save one another with tears,
remorse, tenderness—
hooked on those wonder-drugs.
Yet they do have—
don't they—like us—
their days of grace, they

halt, stretch, a vision
breaks in on the cramped grimace,
inscape of transformation.
Something sundered begins to knit.   40
By scene, by sentence, something is rendered
Back into life, back to the gods.

Study Questions

1. What is the metaphorical relationship between life and letters described in this poem?
2. Explain the figurative meaning of "monstrous limbo of erasure."
3. What force in the poem threatens to completely obliterate civilization?
4. What kinds of grace are available to the man and woman of this poem? Can it be said that this poem argues for the necessity of art?

Dwellers in Silence

Ray Bradbury

1   When the wind came through the sky, he and his small family would sit in the stone hut and warm their hands over a small fire. The wind would stir the canal waters and almost blow the stars out of the sky, but Mr. Hathaway would sit contented and talk to his wife and his wife would talk back, and he would talk to his two daughters and his son about the old days on Earth, and they would all reply neatly.

2   It was the twentieth year after the Great War. Mars was a tomb planet. Whether or not Earth was the same was a matter for much silent debate for himself, or his family, on the long Martian nights. Then the dust storms came over the low hexagonal tomb buildings, whining past the great ancient gargoyles on the iron mountains, blowing between the last standing pillars of an old city, and tearing away the plastic walls of a newer, American-built city that was melting away into the sand, desolated.

3   Hathaway rose from the family circle from time to time and went out into the suddenly clear weather following the storm to look up and see Earth burning green there on the windy sky. He put his hand up for a moment, as one might reach up a hand to adjust a dimly burning light globe in the ceiling of a dark room. Then he said something, quietly, and looked across the long dead sea bottom not moving. Not another living thing on this entire planet, he thought. Just myself. And *them*. He looked back inside the stone hut.

4   What was happening on Earth now? He stared up until his eyes watered with strain. Had the atom bomb eaten everybody there? He had seen no visible sign of change in the aspect of Earth through his thirty-inch telescope. Well, he thought, he was good for another twenty years if he was careful. Someone might come. Either across the dead seas, or out of space in a rocket, on a little thread of red flame.

5   He peered into the hut. "I think I'll take a walk," he said.

6   His wife did not turn.

7   "I said," he cried, "I think I'll take a walk."

8   "All right," his wife said.

9   "That's better," said Hathaway.

10   He turned and walked quietly down through a series of low ruins. "Made in New York," he read from a piece of metal as he passed. "This will all be gone long before the old Martian ruins." He waved at a city ten thousand years old, intact, that lay on the rim of the dead sea twenty miles over, in a mist. "Did anything like that ever happen on Earth?

Well, the Egyptians, almost. They came nearest, because they took their time."

11   He quieted. He came to the Martian graveyard. It was a series of small hexagonal stones and buildings set in the top of a hill. The drifting sand had never covered them because the hill was too high and swept by the winds.

12   There were four graves with crude wooden crosses on them, and names. He stood for a moment looking down at them. He did nothing with his eyes, they would do nothing. They had dried up long ago.

13   "Do you forgive me for what I have done?" he asked of the crosses. "I had to do it. I was so lonely," he said. "You *do* forgive me, don't you? You don't mind. No. No, you don't mind. I'm glad."

14   He walked back down the hill, looking at the sea bottom. If only something would come; even a monster of some sort would be welcome. Something to run from, perhaps, would be a change.

15   He reached the stone hut and, once more, just before going inside, he shaded his eyes with his hands, searching the sky.

16   "You keep waiting and waiting and looking and looking," he said. "And one night, perhaps—"

17   There was a tiny point of red flame on the sky.

18   "And you keep looking," he said. "And you look," he said. He stopped. He looked down at the ground. Then he stepped away from the light of the stone hut. "—and you look *again*," he whispered.

19   The tiny flame point was still there.

20   "It wasn't there last night," he murmured.

21   "It *is* red," he said, finally.

22   And then his eyes were wet with pain.

23   "It is a rocket," he said. "My telescope." He stumbled and fell, picked himself up, got around back of the hut and swiveled the telescope so that it pointed into the sky.

24   A minute later, after a long wild staring, he appeared in the low doorway and he came in to sit by the fireplace. He looked at the fire. The wife and the two daughters and the son looked at him. Finally he said, "I have good news. A ship is coming to take us all home. It will be here in the early morning."

25   He put his hands down and put his head into his hands and began to cry, gently, with long waiting pain, like a child.

26   He burned what was left of New York that morning at three.

27   He took a torch and moved into the plastic and wood city and tapped the walls here or there and the city went up in great tosses of heat and light. When he walked back out of the city it was a square mile of illumination, big enough to be seen out in space. It would beckon the rocket down to him and his family.

28   His heart beating rapidly, he returned to the hut where the family waited. "See," he said. He held up an old bottle into the light. "Wine I saved. Just for tonight. I knew that perhaps one day someone would

come. And so I saved this. I hid it in the storage shed. We'll have a drink and celebrate!" And he popped the cork out and poured five glasses full. His wife and the three children picked up their glasses, smiling.

29   "It's been a long time," he said gravely, looking into his drink. "Remember the day the War broke? How long ago? Nineteen years and seven months, exactly. And all the rockets were called home from Mars, and you and I and the children were out in the mountains, doing archaeological work, doing research on the ancient methods of surgery used by the Martians; it helped me a lot in my own work. And we ran our horses, almost killing them, but got back here to the city a week late. Everyone was gone. America had been destroyed; every rocket had left without waiting for stragglers, remember, remember? And, it turned out, we were the only ones left? Lord, Lord, how the years pass. It seems only a day, now. I couldn't have stood it without you here, all of you. I couldn't have stood it at all. I'd have killed myself without you. But, with you, it was worth waiting. Here's to *us*, then." He raised his drink. "And to our long wait together. And here's to *them*." He gestured at the sky. "May they land safely and—" A troubled frown.

30   "—may they be friends to us when they land." He drank his wine.
31   The wife and the three children raised their glasses to their lips.
32   The wine ran down over the chins of all four of them.

33   By morning the city was blowing in great black soft flakes across the sea bottom. The fire was exhausted, but it had served its purpose; the red spot on the sky enlarged and came down.

34   From the stone hut came the rich brown smell of baked gingerbread. His wife stood over the table, setting down the hot pans of new bread as Hathaway entered. The two daughters were gently sweeping the bare stone floor with stiff brooms, and the son was polishing the silverware. "We will have a breakfast for them, for everyone in the crew," said Hathaway. "You must all put on your best clothes."

35   He walked across his land to the vast metal storage shed. Inside was the cold storage unit and power plant he had repaired and restored with his efficient, small, nervous fingers over the years, just as he had repaired clocks and telephones and spool recorders in his spare time. The shed was full of things he had built, some of them senseless mechanisms the functions of which were a mystery even to himself now as he looked at them. There were jars of liquid and jars of gelatin and other substances.

36   One day, just for a joke, he had laid telephone wires all the way from the hut to the dead city twenty miles away. He had installed a phone in an empty Martian tower room of the highest cupola in the city and come back, whistling quietly to a freshly fixed dinner of cold storage turnips and filet mignon. Many nights, for the hell of it, he dialed the dead city number, which, with a shine to his eye, he had fixed at 00-000-00.

37   It would have been interesting if someone had answered.

38   From the storage deep freeze compartment he now carried frozen cartons of beans and strawberries, twenty years old. Lazarus, come forth, he thought, as he pulled out a cool chicken.

39   Then the Rocket landed.

40   Hathaway ran down the hill like a young boy. He had to stop once, because of a sudden sickening pain in his chest. He sat on a rock and breathed out and in. Then he got up and ran all the rest of the way.

41   "Hello, hello!"

42   He stood in the hot air of summer that had been caused by the fiery heat of the rocket exhausts. A vent opened in the side of the rocket and a man stood in the round entrance looking down.

43   "You're an American!" the man shouted.

44   "So are you; hello!" cried Hathaway, pink-cheeked.

45   "Well, I'll be damned!" The man leaped down and walked across the sand swiftly, his hand out. "We expected nothing, and here *you* are!"

46   Their hands clasped and held, they looked into each other's faces.

47   "Why, you're Hathaway, I *know* you." The man was amazed. His grip tightened. His mouth was open and shut and open again, speechless. "Hathaway! When I was a kid, twenty years ago, I saw you in the television set at school. I watched you perform a difficult surgery for a cerebral tumor!"

48   "Thank you, thank you, I had almost forgotten."

49   The man from the rocket looked beyond Hathaway. "You're alone? Your wife, I remember her. And there were children—"

50   "My son, my daughters, my wife, they are at our hut."

51   "Good, good, splendid. You look *fine*, sir."

52   "Cold storage and a lot of work. I've kept myself busy. I've had time for my hobbies. I was always interested in machines as they relate to physiology and physiology as it relates to machines, you know. But, your name?"

53   "Captain Ernest Parsons of Joliet, Illinois, sir."

54   "Captain Parsons." They were not done with the handshaking yet. "How many in your crew?" "Twenty, sir." "Fine, there's a good breakfast waiting all of you up the hill. Will you come?" "Will we come?" asked the captain. He turned and looked at the rocket. "Abandon ship!" And it was done in half a minute.

55   They walked up the hill together, Hathaway and the captain, the men following dutifully and talkatively behind, taking in deep breaths of the thin Martian air. The sun rose and it was a good day. It would be warm later. Smoke lifted from the stone hut.

56   "I'm sorry." Hathaway sat down, his hand on his chest. "All the excitement. I'll have to wait." He felt his heart moving under his hand. He counted the beats. It was not good.

57 "We have a doctor with us," said Parsons. "I beg your pardon, sir, I know you *are* one, but we'd best check you with our own, and if you need anything—"

58 "I'll be all right, the excitement, the waiting." Hathaway could hardly breathe. His face was pale and wet, his lips blue. His hand trembled. "You know," he said, as the doctor came up and put a stethoscope against him, "it's as if I've kept alive just for this day, all those years, and now that you're here and I know Earth is still alive—well, I can lie down and quit."

59 "You can't do that, sir, there's the breakfast to eat," insisted Parsons, gently. "A fine host that would be."

60 "Here we are," and the doctor gave Hathaway a small yellow pellet. "I suggest this. You're badly overexcited. It might be a good idea if we carried you the rest of the way."

61 "Nonsense, just let me sit here a moment. It's good to see you all. It's good to hear your names. What were they again? You introduced me, but when you're excited you don't see or hear or do anything right. Parsons and Glasbow and Williamson and Hamilton and Spaulding and Ellison and Smith and someone named Brackett and that's all I remember." He smiled weakly, his eyes squinted. "See how good I am?"

62 "Splendid. Did the pellet work?"

63 "Well enough. Here we go."

64 They walked on up the hill.

65 "Alice, come out and see who we have here," Hathaway called into the hut. The men of the rocket stood waiting and smiling. Hathaway frowned slightly and bent into the doorway once more. "Alice, did you hear, come out now."

66 His wife appeared in the doorway. A moment later the two daughters, tall and gracious, came out, followed by an even taller son.

67 "Captain Parsons, my wife. Alice, this is Captain Parsons."

68 "Mrs. Hathaway, I remember you from a long time ago."

69 "Captain Parsons." She shook his hand and turned, still holding his hand. "My daughters, Marguerite and Susan. My son, John. Captain Parsons."

70 Hathaway stood smiling as hands were shaken all around.

71 "It's like coming home," said Parsons, simply.

72 "It's like home having you," said the wife.

73 Parsons sniffed the air. "Is that *gingerbread*?"

74 "Will you have a piece?"

75 Everybody laughed. And while folding tables were carried down and set up by the wide canal and hot foods were brought out and set down and plates were placed about with fine silverware and damask napkins, Captain Parsons looked first at Mrs. Hathaway and then at her son and then at her two tall, gracious daughters. He sat upon a folding chair which the son brought him and said, "How old are you, son?"

76 The son replied, "Twenty-three."

77   Parsons said nothing else. He looked down at his silverware but his face grew pale and sickly. Hathaway was helping his wife bring out more tureens of food. The man next to Parsons said, "Sir, that can't be right."

78   "What's that, Williamson? . . ." asked Parsons.

79   "I'm thirty-eight myself, sir. I was in school the same time as young John Hathaway there, twenty years ago. And he says he's only twenty-three. And, by God, he only *looks* twenty-three. But that can't be right. He should be thirty-eight."

80   "Yes, I know," said Parsons, quietly.

81   "What does it mean, sir?"

82   "I don't know."

83   "You don't look well, sir."

84   "I'm not feeling very well. Will you do me a favor?"

85   "Yes, sir."

86   "I want you to run a little errand for me. I'll tell you where to go and what to check. Late in the breakfast, slip away. It should take you only five minutes. The place is not far from here."

87   "Yes, sir."

88   "Here, what are you two talking so seriously about?" Mrs. Hathaway ladled quick ladles of soup into their bowls. "Smile now, we're all together, the trip's over, and it's like home!"

89   "Yes, ma'am," said Captain Parsons. "You look very young, Mrs. Hathaway, I hope you don't mind my saying."

90   "Isn't that like a man?" And she gave him an extra ladle of soup.

91   Parsons watched her move away. Her face was filled with warmth, it was smooth and unwrinkled. She moved around the tables and placed things neatly and laughed at every joke. She stopped never once to sit and take her breath. And the son and daughters were brilliant and witty as their father, telling of the long years and their quiet life.

92   The breakfast went through its courses. Midway, Williamson slipped quietly off and walked down the hill. "Where is *he* going so suddenly?" inquired Hathaway.

93   "He'll be right back. There's some stuff he's to check in the rocket," explained Parsons. "But, as I was saying sir, there wasn't much left of America. The grass country towns, was about all. New York was a wreck. It took twenty years to get things back on an even keel, what with the radio-activity and all. Europe wasn't any better off. But we finally have a World Government."

94   Parsons talked automatically, reading it off from memory, not listening to himself, thinking only of Williamson going down the hill and coming back to tell what he had found. "Ours is the only rocket now available," said Parsons. "There'll be more in about four years. We're here on a preliminary survey to see what's left of our colonies. Not much here. Perhaps more over at New Chicago. We'll check there this afternoon.

95   "Thanks," he said, as Marguerite Hathaway filled his water glass.

He touched her hand, suddenly. She did not even mind it. Her hand was warm. "Incredible," thought Parsons.

96   Hathaway, at the head of the table, paused long enough to press his hand to his chest. Then he went on, listening to the talk, looking now and then, with concern, at Parsons, who did not seem to be enjoying his meal.

97   Williamson returned up the hill, in a great hurry.

98   Williamson sat down beside Parsons. He was agitated and his cheeks were white. He could not keep his mind on his food, he kept picking at it until the captain whispered aside to him, "Well?"

99   "I found it, sir, what you sent me to find, sir."

100   "And?"

101   "I went down the hill and up that other hill until I came to the graveyard, as you directed." Williamson kept his eyes on the party. People were laughing. The daughters were smiling gravely and blinking and the son was telling a joke. Hathaway was smoking a cigarette, his first really fresh one in years. "And," said Williamson, "I went into the graveyard."

102   "The four crosses were there?" asked Parsons.

103   "The four crosses were there, sir. The names were still on them. I wrote them down to be sure." He produced a white paper and read from it. "Alice Hathaway, Marguerite, Susan and John Hathaway. All four died of the plague in July, 1997."

104   "Thank you, Williamson," said Parsons. He closed his eyes.

105   "Twenty years ago, sir," said Williamson, his hands trembling. He was afraid to look up at the people at the table.

106   "Yes, twenty years ago," said Parsons.

107   "Then, who are *these*?" And Williamson wide-eyed, nodded at the two daughters and the son and the wife of Hathaway, the last man on Mars.

108   "I don't know, Williamson."

109   "What are you going to do, sir?"

110   "I don't know that either," he said, slowly.

111   "Will we tell the other men?"

112   "No, not yet. Later. Go on with your food as if nothing had happened."

113   "I'm not very hungry now, sir."

114   They both began on their dessert.

115   The meal ended with wine brought from the rocket. Hathaway rose to his feet, holding his glass. "A toast to all of you, it is good to be with friends again." He moved his wine glass ever so little in the air. "And to my wife, and my children, without whom I could not have survived alone. It is only through their kindness in caring for me, that I have lived on, waiting for your arrival. Else, years ago, I would have put a bullet in my head." He moved his glass now to his wife, now to his children, who looked back self-consciously, lowering their eyes at last as everyone drank.

116   Parsons' eyelids were flickering nervously. His hands were moving uneasily on his lap.

117   Hathaway drank down his wine and fell forward onto the table and then slipped toward the ground. He did not cry out. Several of the men caught and eased him to the ground where the doctor felt of his chest, listened, and remained there, listening, until Parsons arrived with Williamson.

118   The doctor looked up and shook his head. Parsons knelt and took the old man's hand. "Parsons, is that you?" Hathaway's voice was barely audible. Parsons nodded. "I'm sorry," said Hathaway, gently grieved. "I had to spoil the breakfast." "Never you mind," said Parsons. "Say good-bye to Alice and the children for me," said the old man. "They're right here," said Parsons. "Just a moment, I'll call them." "No, no, don't; they wouldn't understand, I wouldn't *want* them to understand, no, don't," whispered Hathaway. Parsons did not move.

119   A moment later old Dr. Hathaway was dead.

120   Parsons waited for a long time. Then he arose and walked away from the small stunned group around Hathaway. He went to Alice Hathaway and looked into her face and said, "Do you know what has just happened?"

121   "It's something about my husband," she said.

122   "He's just passed away; his heart," said Parsons, watching her.

123   "I'm sorry," she said.

124   "How do you feel?" he asked.

125   "He didn't want us to feel badly, he told us it would happen one day, and he didn't want us to cry. He didn't teach us how, you know. He didn't want us to know, he said it was the worst thing that could happen to a man to know how to be lonely and to know how to be sad and then cry. So we're not to know what death is or what crying is or being sad."

126   Parsons looked off at the mountains. "Perhaps it's just as well." He glanced at her hands, the soft warm hands and the fine manicured nails and the tapered wrists. And he looked at the slender smooth white neck and the intelligent eyes. "I know all about you," he said, finally.

127   "But the others don't." She was confident of that.

128   "No, you're so perfect they haven't guessed. Mr. Hathaway did a fine job on you and your children."

129   "He would have liked to hear you say that. He was so very proud of us. After a while he even forgot that he had made us. At the end he loved and took us as his real wife and children. And, in a way, we *are*."

130   "You gave him a great deal of comfort," said Parsons.

131   "Yes, over the years we sat and talked and talked. He so much loved to talk. He liked the stone hut and the open fire. We could have lived in a regular house in the town, but he liked it up here, where he could be primitive if he liked, or modern if he liked. He told me all about his laboratory and the things he did in it. Once he wired the entire dead American town below with sound speakers and when he pressed a button the town lit up and made noises as if ten thousand people lived in

it. There were airplane noises and car noises and the sounds of people talking. He would sit and light a cigar and talk to us and the sounds would come up from the town and once in a while the phone would ring and a recorded voice, Mr. Hathaway himself, would ask Mr. Hathaway scientific and surgical questions and he would answer them, and then I'd make strawberry biscuits. Mr Hathaway took a transcription of his voice down into town each day, put in in an automatic telephone that called us every night. And with the phone ringing and us here and the sounds of the town and the cigar, I'm sure Mr. Hathaway was quite happy."

132   "Twenty years, the five of you living here," said Parsons.

133   "There's only one thing he couldn't make us do," she said. "And that was grow old. He got older every day but we stayed the same. I guess he didn't mind. I guess he wanted us that way."

134   "We'll bury him down in the yard where the other four crosses are. I think he would like that."

135   She put her hand on his wrist, lightly. "I'm sure he would."

136   Orders were given. The wife and the three children followed the little procession down the hill. Two men carried Hathaway on a covered stretcher. They passed the stone hut and the storage shed where Hathaway twenty years ago had begun his work. Parsons stepped from the procession a moment to stand within the doorway of the workshop.

137   How would it be to be alone on a planet with a wife and three children and then to have them die of the plague, leaving you alone in a world with nothing on it but wind and silence? What would you do? You would bury them with crosses in the graveyard and then come back up to your workshop and with all the power of mind and memory and accuracy of finger and genius, put together, bit by bit, all those things that were wife, son and daughter. With an entire American city below from which to draw needed supplies, a brilliant man might do anything.

138   Parsons returned to the procession. The sound of their footsteps was muffled in the sand. At the graveyard, as they turned in, two men were already spading out the earth.

139   The men came back to the rocket in the late afternoon. They stood in a circle around the captain.

140   Williamson nodded up at the stone hut. "What are you going to do about *them*?"

141   "I don't know," said the captain.

142   "Are you going to turn them off?"

143   "Off?" The captain looked faintly surprised. "It never entered my mind."

144   "You're not going to take them back with us?"

145   "No, we haven't space for them."

146   "You mean you're going to leave them here, like that, like they are? It's sort of ghastly, the thought of them being here."

147   The captain gave Williamson a gun. "If you can do something about this, you're a better man than I."

148   Five minutes later, Williamson returned from the hut, sweating. He handed the gun back. "Here. Take it. I know what you mean, now. I went in with the gun. One of the daughters looked up at me. She smiled. So did the others. The wife said something about sitting down for a cup of tea. That did it. God, God, it would be murder." He shook his head.

149   Parsons nodded. "After all the work he put in on them, it would be killing. There'll never be anything as fine as them again, ever. They're built to last; ten, fifty, two hundred years. Yes, they've as much right to live as you or I or any of us." He knocked out his pipe. "Well, get aboard. We're taking off. This city's done for, we'll not be using it."

150   It was getting late in the day. The wind was rising. All the men were aboard. The captain hesitated. Williamson looked at him and said, "Don't tell me you're going back to say—good-bye—to them?"

151   The captain looked at Williamson coldly. "None of your damn business."

152   Parsons walked up toward the hut through the darkening wind. The men in the rocket saw his shadow lingering inside the stone hut door. They saw a woman's shadow. They saw the captain put out his hand to shake her hand.

153   A minute later, he came running back to the rocket.

154   The rocket went up into the sky. It was only a red point, going away.

155   And now, on nights when the wind comes over the dead sea bottoms and through the hexagonal graveyard where there are four old crosses and one new fresh one, there is a light burning in the low stone hut on the edge of the burned New New ·York, and in that hut, as the wind roars by and the dust sifts down and the cold stars burn, are four figures, a woman, two daughters and a son, tending a low fire for no reason and talking and laughing, and this goes on night after night for every year and every year, and some nights, for no reason, the wife comes out and looks at the sky, her hands up, for a long moment, looking at the green burning of Earth, not knowing why she looks, knowing nothing, and then she goes back in and throws a stick on the fire and the wind comes up and the dead sea goes on being dead.

Study Questions

1. Do you feel that Hathaway's attempts to create a living environment are successful? If not, why not?
2. Identify the setting, and the perspective that this setting gives to events.
3. How does the allusion to Lazarus figure in the short story?

What It Would Be Like If Women Win

Gloria Steinem

1   Any change is fearful, especially one affecting both politics and sex roles, so let me begin these utopian speculations with a fact. To break the ice.

2   Women don't want to exchange places with men. Male chauvinists, science-fiction writers and comedians may favor that idea for its shock value, but psychologists say it is a fantasy based on ruling-class ego and guilt. Men assume that women want to imitate them, which is just what white people assumed about blacks. An assumption so strong that it may convince the second-class group of the need to imitate, but for both women and blacks that stage has passed. Guilt produces the question: What if they could treat us as we have treated them?

3   That is not our goal. But we do want to change the economic system to one more based on merit. In Women's Lib Utopia, there will be free access to good jobs—and decent pay for the bad ones women have been performing all along, including housework. Increased skilled labor might lead to a four-hour workday, and higher wages would encourage further mechanization of repetitive jobs now kept alive by cheap labor.

4   With women as half the country's elected representatives, and a woman President once in a while, the country's *machismo* problems would be greatly reduced. The old-fashioned idea that manhood depends on violence and victory is, after all, an important part of our troubles in the streets, and in Viet Nam. I'm not saying that women leaders would eliminate violence. We are not more moral than men; we are only uncorrupted by power so far. When we do acquire power, we might turn out to have an equal impulse toward aggression. Even now, Margaret Mead believes that women fight less often but more fiercely than men, because women are not taught the rules of the war game and fight only when cornered. But for the next 50 years or so, women in politics will be very valuable by tempering the idea of manhood into something less aggressive and better suited to this crowded, post-atomic planet. Consumer protection and children's rights, for instance, might get more legislative attention.

5   Men will have to give up ruling-class privileges, but in return they will no longer be the only ones to support the family, get drafted, bear the strain of power and responsibility. Freud to the contrary, anatomy is

not destiny, at least not for more than nine months at a time. In Israel, women are drafted, and some have gone to war. In England, more men type and run switchboards. In India and Israel, a woman rules. In Sweden, both parents take care of the children. In this country, come Utopia, men and women won't reverse roles; they will be free to choose according to individual talents and preferences.

6   If role reform sounds sexually unsettling, think how it will change the sexual hypocrisy we have now. No more sex arranged on the barter system, with women pretending interest, and men never sure whether they are loved for themselves or for the security few women can get any other way. (Married or not, for sexual reasons or social ones, most women still find it second nature to Uncle-Tom.) No more men who are encouraged to spend a lifetime living with inferiors; with housekeepers, or dependent creatures who are still children. No more domineering wives, emasculating women, and "Jewish mothers," all of whom are simply human beings with all their normal ambition and drive confined to the home. No more unequal partnerships that eventually doom love and sex.

7   In order to produce that kind of confidence and individuality, child rearing will train according to talent. Little girls will no longer be surrounded by air-tight, self-fulfilling prophecies of natural passivity, lack of ambition and objectivity, inability to exercise power, and dexterity (so long as special aptitude for jobs requiring patience and dexterity is confined to poorly paid jobs; brain surgery is for males).

8   Schools and universities will help to break down traditional sex roles, even when parents will not. Half the teachers will be men, a rarity now at preschool and elementary levels; girls will not necessarily serve cookies or boys hoist up the flag. Athletic teams will be picked only by strength and skill. Sexually segregated courses like auto mechanics and home economics will be taken by boys and girls together. New courses in sexual politics will explore female subjugation as the model for political oppression, and women's history will be an academic staple, along with black history, at least until the white-male-oriented textbooks are integrated and rewritten.

9   As for the American child's classic problem—too much mother, too little father—that would be cured by an equalization of parental responsibility. Free nurseries, school lunches, family cafeterias built into every housing complex, service companies that will do household cleaning chores in a regular, businesslike way, and more responsibility by the entire community for the children: all these will make it possible for both mother and father to work, and to have equal leisure time with the children at home. For parents of very young children, however, a special job category, created by Government and unions, would allow such parents a shorter work day.

10   The revolution would not take away the option of being a housewife. A woman who prefers to be her husband's housekeeper and/or hostess would receive a percentage of his pay determined by the domes-

tic relations courts. If divorced, she might be eligible for a pension fund, and for a job-training allowance. Or a divorce could be treated the same way that the dissolution of a business partnership is now.

11   If these proposals seem farfetched, consider Sweden, where most of them are already in effect. Sweden is not yet a working Women's Lib model; most of the role-reform programs began less than a decade ago, and are just beginning to take hold. But that country is so far ahead of us in recognizing the problem that Swedish statements on sex and equality sound like bulletins from the moon.

12   Our marriage laws, for instance, are so reactionary that Women's Lib groups want couples to take a compulsory written exam on the law, as for a driver's license, before going through with the wedding. A man has alimony and wifely debts to worry about, but a woman may lose so many of her civil rights that in the U.S. now, in important legal ways, she becomes a child again. In some states, she cannot sign credit agreements, use her maiden name, incorporate a business, or establish a legal residence of her own. Being a wife, according to most social and legal definitions, is still a 19th century thing.

13   Assuming, however, that these blatantly sexist laws are abolished or reformed, that job discrimination is forbidden, that parents share financial responsibility for each other and the children, and that sexual relationships become partnerships of equal adults (some pretty big assumptions), then marriage will probably go right on. Men and women are, after all, physically complementary. When society stops encouraging men to be exploiters and women to be parasites, they may turn out to be more complementary in emotion as well. Women's Lib is not trying to destroy the American family. A look at the statistics on divorce—plus the way in which old people are farmed out with strangers and young people flee the home—shows the destruction that has already been done. Liberated women are just trying to point out the disaster, and build compassionate and practical alternatives from the ruins.

14   What will exist is a variety of alternative life-styles. Since the population explosion dictates that childbearing be kept to a minimum, parents-and-children will be only one of many "families": couples, age groups, working groups, mixed communes, blood-related clans, class groups, creative groups. Single women will have the right to stay single without ridicule, without the attitudes now betrayed by "spinster" and "bachelor." Lesbians or homosexuals will no longer be denied legally binding marriages, complete with mutual-support agreements and inheritance rights. Paradoxically, the number of homosexuals may get smaller. With fewer overpossessive mothers and fewer fathers who hold up an impossibly cruel or perfectionist idea of manhood, boys will be less likely to be denied or reject their identity as males.

15   Changes that now seem small may get bigger:

16   *Men's Lib.* Men now suffer from more diseases due to stress, heart

attacks, ulcers, a higher suicide rate, greater difficulty living alone, less adaptability to change and, in general, a shorter life span than women. There is some scientific evidence that what produces physical problems is not work itself, but the inability to choose which work, and how much. With women bearing half the financial responsibility, and with the idea of "masculine" jobs gone, men might well feel freer and live longer.

17   *Religion.* Protestant women are already becoming ordained ministers; radical nuns are carrying out liturgical functions that were once the exclusive property of priests; Jewish women are rewriting prayers— particularly those that Orthodox Jews recite every morning thanking God they are not female. In the future, the church will become an area of equal participation by women. This means, of course, that organized religion will have to give up one of its great historical weapons: sexual repression. In most structured faiths, from Hinduism through Roman Catholicism, the status of women went down as the position of priests ascended. Male clergy implied, if they did not teach, that women were unclean, unworthy and sources of ungodly temptation, in order to remove them as rivals for the emotional forces of men. Full participation of women in ecclesiastical life might involve certain changes in theology, such as, for instance, a radical redefinition of sin.

18   *Literary Problems.* Revised sex roles will outdate more children's books than civil rights ever did. Only a few children had the problem of a *Little Black Sambo,* but most have the male-female stereotypes of "Dick and Jane." A boomlet of children's books about mothers who work has already begun, and liberated parents and editors are beginning to pressure for change in the textbook industry. Fiction writing will change more gradually, but romantic novels with wilting heroines and swashbuckling heroes will be reduced to historical value. Or perhaps to the sado-masochist trade. (*Marjorie Morningstar,* a romantic novel that took the '50s by storm, has already begun to seem as unreal as its '20s predecessor, *The Sheik.*) As for the literary plots that turn on forced marriages or horrific abortions, they will seem as dated as Prohibition stories. Free legal abortions and free birth control will force writers to give up pregnancy as the *deus ex machina.*

19   *Manners and Fashion.* Dress will be more androgynous, with class symbols becoming more important than sexual ones. Pro- or anti-Establishment styles may already be more vital than who is wearing them. Hardhats are just as likely to rough up antiwar girls as antiwar men in the street, and police understand that women are just as likely to be pushers or bombers. Dances haven't required that one partner lead the other for years, anyway. Chivalry will transfer itself to those who need it, or deserve respect: old people, admired people, anyone with an armload of packages. Women with normal work identities will be less likely to attach their whole sense of self to youth and appearance; thus there will be fewer nervous breakdowns when the first wrinkles appear.

Lighting cigarettes and other treasured niceties will become gestures of mutual affection. "I like to be helped on with my coat," says one Women's Lib worker, "but not if it costs me $2,000 a year in salary."

20   For those with nostalgia for a simpler past, here is word of comfort. Anthropologist Geoffrey Gorer studied the few peaceful human tribes and discovered one common characteristic: sex roles were not polarized. Differences of dress and occupation were at a minimum. Society, in other words, was not using sexual blackmail as a way of getting women to do cheap labor, or men to be aggressive.

21   Thus Women's Lib may achieve a more peaceful society on the way toward its other goals. That is why the Swedish government considers reform to bring about greater equality in the sex roles one of its most important concerns. As Prime Minister Olof Palme explained in a widely ignored speech delivered in Washington this spring: "It is *human beings* we shall emancipate. In Sweden today, if a politician should declare that the woman ought to have a different role from man's, he would be regarded as something from the Stone Age." In other words, the most radical goal of the movement is egalitarianism.

22   If Women's Lib wins, perhaps we all do.

Study Questions

1. Does the title of this essay accurately describe its content?
2. Define *utopia*. Would a "Women's Lib Utopia" eradicate the problems described in paragraph 6?
3. What rhetorical pattern does this essay most closely represent?
4. Steinem makes excellent use of the standard expository devices of transition and parallelism. Find and discuss examples of each throughout the essay.

A Quiet March for Liberation Begins

Barbara Katz

1   The men are on the march. But it's a quiet, decidedly uncoordinated march, so hidden from view that one must listen very carefully to hear its stirrings. It's the first, faltering footsteps of a men's liberation movement.

2   *Men's* liberation? That's right. In cities, suburbs, and small towns as diverse as Fresno, Calif., Lawrence, Kan., and Fort Lee, N.J., an estimated 300 men's groups now meet regularly to explore the ways in which sex-role stereotypes limit and inhibit them. In heart-of-the-country places like Oberlin, Ohio; Lansing, Mich.; and Iowa City, Iowa, conferences on such topics as "the new masculine consciousness" attract hundreds of participants. And once in a while, in sophisticated urban centers like New York City and Chicago, small groups of men demonstrate against the "crippling sex-role training" found in children's books and the "exploitation of the insecurities of men" practiced by Playboy king Hugh Hefner.

3   Some men put their new views into print in publications like Brother: A Forum for Men against Sexism, published in Berkeley, Calif. Some are writing books: At least five books on men's liberation are now in the works. Others form organizations, like Boston's Fathers for Equal Justice, to try to dispel what they regard as a widespread view of men—particularly divorced men—as bystanders unconcerned with the rearing of their children. Others act as individuals, like the teacher from New York City who has successfully challenged a school policy denying men the right to take child-care leaves.

4   Generally, though, the men taking part in this new movement—mostly white, middle-class, and in their mid-20s to mid-50s—are more introspective than political. Most have become involved in response to the women's movement: At first defensive under female questioning of accepted sex roles, they soon came to question these roles themselves.

5   Unlike the members of the women's movement, however, they have not yet formulated a widely accepted set of social and political goals, nor produced a highly visible structure to fight for these goals. Some would even deny they are members of a "movement." Eschewing rhetoric, they explore their concerns about the traditional male sex role on an intensely personal level, usually within groups of from 6 to 10 members.

343

6   *In a brightly lit, comfortable living room in North Arlington, Va., four men, one of them with his 3-month-old son on his knee, are "rapping." Jean, a 37-year-old sandy-haired, craggy-faced lawyer, is talking:*

7   I was brought up in a family where traditionally the males keep everything to themselves. You grin and bear it and never recognize that there are any problems. Or if there is a problem, you just take a deep breath, throw back your shoulders, and say, "I'm a big guy and I'm just gonna live through it and override it."

8   Competitive pressures are something else I've always felt strongly— "Get in there and compete and work your 10-hour days and work every week end." I've always done a lot of that, sort of following the road map that others have laid out, neglecting my family and my personal desires in the process. I'm trying to get out of both these binds now, but it's not that easy to change the rules after playing the game the old way for so long.

9   "'Getting ahead' and 'staying cool'—these have been the two main prescriptions of the male role in our society," says Joseph Pleck, a psychology instructor at the University of Michigan and a frequent speaker at men's conferences. "But it's becoming clear to many of us that many of our most important inner needs cannot be met by acting in the ways we have been expected to act as men."

10   Dr. Robert Gould, a psychiatrist at New York's Metropolitan General Hospital and speaker at a recent men's conference at Oberlin College, agrees: "It's more difficult to appreciate men's distress, since they have the dominant role in society, but their role is just as rigidly defined and stereotyped."

11   The idealized male sex-role, Gould explains, is to be tough, competitive, unfeeling, emotionally inexpressive, and masterful—"to come as close as possible to satisfying the John Wayne image." But trying to play that role exacts its price. Says Gould: "By striving to fulfill the role society sets forth for them, men repress many of their most basic human traits. They thus cut off about half their potential for living."

12   Men's consciousness-raising, or "rap," groups are one tool for increasing that potential. In these groups, men simply try to talk honestly about their lives to other men—a new experience for many—and to raise the questions that have begun to bother them.

13   Why, the men ask, aren't men supposed to express emotions? Why must men never reveal weakness? Why can't men be more than "buddies" with one another, sharing their feelings, not just their views on sports, women, and work? Why can't men touch one another, the way women do, without being thought homosexual?

14   Why must men be the sole or major breadwinner? Why must they always assume the dominant role with women? Why must they prove their "manliness" by "putting down" or "beating out" the next guy? Why must men always strive to "get ahead" instead of just enjoying their work? Why aren't men supposed to have too much to do with children, even their own?

15   Warren Farrell, who teaches "sexual politics" at American University and heads the National Organization for Women's task force on the "male mystique," believes that men's groups are "the basic instrument of the men's liberation movement." Farrell, whose book, *The Liberated Man,* will be published in the autumn, travels around the country lecturing on men's liberation and after each talk invites members of the audience to become the nucleus of a new group. "So far we've formed at least 50 groups this way," he says. So great is the demand for men's groups, he says, that he and other concerned men are now planning a national conference to train group "facilitators."

16   Why this sudden concern for men's liberation? Most men in the movement today credit the growing strength of the women's liberation movement. For every woman rethinking *her* role, they say, there's probably a man somewhere rethinking *his.*

17   *In a small, pleasant living room in Berwyn, Ill., a Chicago suburb, eight men, one with a 7-month-old daughter, and four cats of mixed descent sit in the overstuffed furniture and sprawl on the floor. Bowls of turkey soup—made by one of the men—and jugs of wine and apple juice are passed around. George, a tall gangly, 47-year-old Unitarian minister, is talking:*

18   When my wife got involved in the women's movement several years ago, her thinking and questioning about her role started having an effect on both our lives. I saw I had to start dealing with some of the issues she was raising.

19   When I first joined a group, about four years ago, we did some "guilt-tripping" at first—flagellating ourselves for the ways we were oppressing women—but we soon moved on to sharing other problems. We soon came to see that it wasn't just the women in our lives who were having problems and whom we were having problems relating to, but we also had problems within ourselves, and problems relating to each other. We discovered that in some way we had been dehumanized, and we came to want to find out what it means to be a male human being.

20   But is the move toward greater awareness only a process of raising questions? No, reply the men who've stayed with it. There are answers and gains.

21   For some men, it's meant their first close male friendships. For others, it's meant a lessening of competitive pressure and a greater recognition of the importance of personal and family desires.

22   For Jean, the Virginia lawyer trying to emerge from his double bind, it's meant "being able to show more emotion with our little daughter" and a willingness to take "an enormous amount of time off of work"—even at the risk of cutting his salary—to help his wife through a difficult pregnancy.

23   For George, the Chicago minister, it's meant a "net energy gain" from the support provided by "people I really dig." It's meant being able

to share the most personal of concerns with peers who understand and share his concerns—even his emotional struggle over the "finality" of the vasectomy he's considering.

24   For Mark, a 40-year-old burglar-alarm specialist in Chicago, it's meant being able to view his wife "more as an equal partner, a whole person, a friend. Before I saw her primarily as a mother and house-keeper, and I was always playing the big protector, the big man around the house. That's really a pretty crummy role, and besides, you can't have a really open relationship with a servant. It's been a lot nicer lately."

25   And for Jeff, a 26-year-old advertising executive in Deale, Md., it's meant the discovery that "vulnerability isn't necessarily a bad thing," and that "crying is a tremendous release." It's also enabled him to face the fact that, although successful at his job, he doesn't like what he's doing. "It's so easy to get caught up in simply doing what you're trained to do, what you're expected to do, even if you know it's not what you really want," he says. Jeff is planning to switch to an entirely different field—ecological architecture.

26   Liberation, these men say, does not mean that men will be "liber-ated" from the need to work or to share family responsibilities. It does mean becoming aware of what they see as the subtle ways they are forced into doing things because they must satisfy society's expectations of "what it takes to be a man."

27   Those who have given some thought to men's liberation say there are two major obstacles to overcome if one is to "unlearn" those expecta-tions: The first is recognizing and unlearning the underlying contempt they say most men feel for women; the second is questioning the male "hierarchy of values."

28   "Men learn from the time they're boys that the worst possible thing is to be considered feminine—a 'sissy,'" says Warren Farrell. "The male's fear that he might be thought of as a female—with all the negative implications that carries—has been the central basis of his need to prove himself 'masculine.' A more positive image of women frees a man to come in contact with the so-called feminine parts of his personality and allows him to start displaying human emotions without fear of being called feminine."

29   The male "hierarchy of values," with its emphasis on competition and "success," is so ingrained in our society that "it takes a revolution in one's thinking to see what it's about," says psychiatrist Robert Gould. "In American society, success has nothing to do with how you live your life," he says, "but with whether you satisfy American values of what success is—wealth, power, and status. One learns very early that if you're bigger and stronger and louder, you'll win all the marbles. One seldom questions whether what is given up in the process of winning the marbles—meaningful relationships with people, enjoyment of work for its own sake—is worth it."

30   The men taking part in the men's movement *are* doing that questioning. But their movement is small and, while growing, not yet at the pace of the women's movement. Some, like Jim, a 33-year-old reporter in Washington, D.C., believe "the real guts of this is in the children we bring up.

31   "Surely our impact, for good or ill, is going to have an impact on them," he says. "We're not going to find exact answers to all our questions immediately, but certainly we're setting a different example from what we had."

Study Questions

1. By what means is this essay developed?
2. How does the women's liberation movement relate to the events described in this essay?
3. In what ways does the "march" described differ from the women's movement?

$70,000 a Year, Tax Free

Gail Sheehy

1   How many women do you know who can take home seventy thousand dollars a year? A psychiatrist? She might take home half that. A congresswoman? Shirley Chisholm's salary is forty-two-five.

2   No, the quickest way for a woman to get ahead in this country is to take up the oldest profession: prostitution.

3   As one veteran streetwalker explained to a runaway she was breaking in: "You have no status, no power, and no way to get it except by using your body. Why give it away? You're sitting on a gold mine!"

4   And so, every summer, in New York City, the hue and cry goes up: Crack down on prostitution! Close the massage parlors! But why has New York become a boomtown for hustlers? Not because of the increased use of drugs, as most people assume. It began with a change in

New York's penal code four years ago. Loitering for the purpose of prostitution was reduced by former Police Commissioner Leary from a misdemeanor to a violation. Even girls found guilty on the more serious "pross collar" rarely go to jail. Most judges let them go for a twenty-five to fifty dollar fine—and a week to pay. It amounts to a license.

5   Word of this change spread with interest through the pimp grapevine around the country: New York was wide open. Today, you'd hardly guess which four states have the largest pipeline shipping prostitutes to New York: in order, they are Minnesota, Massachusetts, Michigan, and Ohio. There are lots of fair haired girls from Minnesota with street names like Little Tiffany, and Marion the Librarian. But why do they come? It couldn't be a more American phenomenon: The prostitute's dream is the most upward mobile, middle class, American pie dream of all.

6   Number one: she wants money—high-style clothes, a model apartment, candy color wigs and her teeth capped.

7   Number two: she's looking for a "family." Most of the girls have one or two children—illegitimate. On top of that, the girl is often white and her illegitimate child is black. Back home in Minneapolis, she was already a social pariah, and she couldn't make a go of living and working while dragging a baby from room to rented room. So she comes to New York, looking for a new kind of family—exactly what the pimp provides.

8   He puts up his stable of three or four girls in a high-rise apartment, pays their rent, buys their clothes, foots their doctor bills. Top woman in this "family"—the pimp's favorite, who brings in the most money—is called his "wife." The rest are known as "wife-in-laws." Remarkably enough, they all get along quite well. The tie that really binds is the baby sitter—the girls share one for seventy-five dollars a week and this is what frees them to work.

9   As a midtown hooker from Virginia put it to me: "Most of the girls are here doing it for their kids. I don't want my daughter to have the kind of childhood I had. She's going to have the best!"

10   So now the prostitute has money, a family, a baby sitter. The other things she craves is "glamour and excitement," things she probably dreamed of finding in a career as a model or actress. But those fields are fiercely competitive. Besides, as a prostitute sees it, models and actresses are treated like dress hangers or pieces of meat: they give their bodies away to advance their careers, while so-called straight women exchange sex for the financial security of marriage. A "working girl," as the prostitute refers to herself, is the only honest one: She sets the price, delivers the goods, and concludes her business within the hour—no romantic nonsense about it.

11   And finally, after she is on the street for a few months, the pace of peeping and hiding, the game of stinging johns and ducking police vans become a way of life. It gets into the blood like gambler's fever.

12   The hooker with the heart of gold? That's a male myth. Many of our street girls can be as vicious and money mad as any corporation president. Moreover, they can be less emotional than men in conducting acts of personal violence. The bulk of their business is not the dispensation of pleasure: it is to mug, rob, swindle, knife, and possibly, even murder their patrons. Police drags against them are about as effective as pacification programs in Vietnam. Apply police pressure to streetwalkers and robberies generally go up. If a girl doesn't bring in that fixed amount, two hundred and fifty a night, she'll go home to a beating from her pimp.

13   People are puzzled: why this boom in prostitution when young America is bursting with sexual freedom? They forget about men over forty, men who learned their sexual fantasies from nudie calendars in the gas station. To be fun, the bedmate must be a no-no. "You can't fantasize about your wife or girlfriend," one man explained. "The woman has to be an unknown." And where is this illicit thrill of forbidden flesh still to be found? On the black market of course. Furthermore, the prostitute makes no emotional demands. She would never call his office the next day. It is her stock in trade to encourage men's sexual fantasies and exploit them. How else can a girl make seventy thousand dollars a year, tax free!

Study Questions

1. Does this essay seem to be a thorough cause-effect analysis?
2. Note Sheehy's introduction and conclusion. Are they effective? Why?
3. Explain the author's use of simile.
4. What is the tone of the essay? What audience is Sheehy addressing? Consider paragraph length, dictation, and punctuation.

Heaven-Haven

Gerard Manley Hopkins

A nun takes the veil

I have desired to go
   Where springs not fail,
To fields where flies no sharp and sided hail
   And a few lilies below.

And I have asked to be
   Where no storms come,
Where the green swell is in the havens dumb,
   And out of the swing of the sea.

Study Questions

1. Why does the nun take the veil? How does she compare to contemporary nuns? Is this a poem of escapism?
2. Which of the things that the nun seeks to avoid are metaphors or symbols for something else?
3. Where does Hopkins invert standard noun-verb order?

Poem for Roger McGough

Adrian Henri

A nun in a supermarket
standing in the queue
Wondering what it's like
To buy groceries for two.

Study Questions

1. How does the poet know what the nun is wondering? Is this, then, a poem about a nun?
2. Henri's poem has no finite verb. Why is an awareness of this lack significant?
3. Can you explain the poem's title?

Man, Play, and Creativity

One of the means through which people have traditionally come to grips with their desert places, or have avoided thinking about them at all, is art. In *Man, Play, and Creativity* we explore the arts and modern humanity's attitudes toward them. Eric Hoffer's essay gives the section its title; he posits a theory about our need for art, past, and present.

Music, painting and sculpture, and literature are the topics of the three subsections which follow. In a variety of literary forms Donald Barthelme, James Baldwin, Imamu Amiri Baraka, and Gabriel Okara help us understand why music's charms soothe the savage breast. The selections by Baldwin and Baraka may be considered companion pieces in which two contemporary authors discuss jazz and the black American.

Then John Keats finds a beauty that transcends time and mortality on a Grecian urn, and Wallace Stevens discovers a jar that brings order to the surrounding wilderness. W. H. Auden's examination of the "Old Masters" leads him to a greater understanding of man's fate, of the place of suffering in the human condition.

Widely varied forms are used by the poets who consider the written word in the section which follows. Samuel Taylor Coleridge gives us the poet as prophet and seer in "Kubla Khan," while the more contemporary Etheridge Knight reminds black poets of their obligation to their people. The imaginative world of Chapman's Homer opens up entirely new realms of experience to a young John Keats. Alfred, Lord Tennyson's Lady of Shalott learns, alas, that the artist must live a life of isolation. Then Emily Dickinson in a few short lines convinces us that there are no limits to what the human imagination can produce. The section on literature concludes with Ogden Nash, in a poem, and Grace Paley, in a short story, examining reality and truth in writing.

Rose K. Goldsen's essay on how certain types of toys can encourage violence in children, and later in adults, begins a new subsection. Goldsen's concerns are echoed in "Saki's" amusing story of parents who fail to divert the attention of their children to educational toys; an experiment in antiviolence fails. Howard Nemerov's poem on the violence in children's television concludes this unit.

The last two selections in *Man, Play, and Creativity* are concerned with the media. Marya Mannes discusses the distorted images of the family and women created by television. And Stephen Crane voices our modern concern over the distortion of news.

Music, painting, sculpture, literature, toys, television, the newspaper—all are considered in this section about our attempts to enlighten and entertain ourselves through the arts and the media.

Man, Play, and Creativity

Eric Hoffer

1   It is a story worth retelling. In 1879, the Spanish amateur archaeologist the Marquis de Sautuola and his little daughter Maria discovered the breathtaking paintings of bison and other animals on the ceiling of the cave at Altamira. The Marquis recognized immediately the significance of the discovery. Moreover, he was 48 years old, and saw here a heaven-sent chance to make his mark as a prehistorian. He was going to write a monograph on the paintings, magnificently illustrated by a good painter.

2   Everything went swimmingly for a while. The Marquis wrote to his friend Professor Villanova of the University of Madrid. The professor came, saw the paintings, and was swept off his feet. The Madrid newspapers had front page stories and photographs of the momentous discovery. King Alphonso XII visited the cave and stayed at the Marquis' castle in Santillana del Mar. The Marquis also had a painter. He had some time earlier befriended a destitute French painter, afflicted with dumbness, who had been stranded in the neighborhood, and he now put him to make the sketches required for his treatise.

3   Then disaster struck out of the blue. At the congress of prehistory held in Lisbon in 1880, the assembled experts and scholars denied the authenticity of the Altamira paintings. Professor Emile Cartailhac of the University of Toulouse thought it was all a hoax perpetrated by the Marquis to obtain cheap renown and make fools of the experts. Anti-Altamira articles began to appear in the press. Professor Villanova eventually went over to the experts. The Marquis tried again at the next congress held in Algiers in 1882. No one would listen to him. The Marquis retired to his estates and died in 1888 at the relatively early age of 57.

4   The denouement is interesting. Eighteen years after the death of the Marquis, Professor Emile Cartailhac of the University of Toulouse published a beautifully illustrated monograph under the title *La Caverne d'Altamira.*

5   The story is told here not to demonstrate fallibility of the experts. Actually the experts could not help themselves. Think of it: these paintings which were supposedly done by Paleolithic savages who lived 15,000–30,000 years ago had nothing primitive, crude or awkward about them. They were masterpieces unsurpassed in any age, and closer to the feel and understanding of modern man than any ancient art. Moreover,

the oil colors, deep reds and the blackest black, were vivid and fresh, and felt damp to the touch. It was natural to suspect that the paintings were the work of a living painter—probably of the French painter in the Marquis' employ.

6   Equally crucial was the picture the experts had of the Paleolithic savage. He was more primitive than most of the global dropouts who make up the present-day primitive tribes in various parts of the world— at least as primitive as the Australian aborigines. Paleolithic man had only the most rudimentary tools. He could not make a pot, weave cloth or work metals. He had no domesticated animals, not even a dog. What connection could there be between such an utterly primitive creature and works of art which are among the greatest achievements of mankind?

7   We know that, eventually, around 1900, the experts changed their minds about the cave paintings. Was this due to a drastic revision of their thought on the life of early man? Not that you can notice it. Pick up an armful of books on prehistoric man and you still find the Paleolithic hunter depicted as wholly absorbed in a perpetual, cruel struggle for sheer survival—always only one step ahead of starvation; always facing the problem of how to eat without being eaten; never knowing when he fell asleep whether he would be there in the morning. How come, then, the paintings? They were, we are told, an aid in the eternal quest for food; they reflect the deep anxiety of the hunter community about the animals on whose meat they depended for very life; they were part of the magical rites connected with the capture and killing of game. The savage, we are told, had noticed that by imitating, by disguising himself as an animal, he could lure and kill his prey, which led him to believe that likeness was the key to mysterious powers by which to control other creatures. The more lifelike the likeness the greater the magic. Hence the marvelous realism of the paintings.

8   Now, one can admit the magical connotations of the cave paintings and yet reject the suggestion that Paleolithic art had its origin in magic. Giotto and Michelangelo painted for the church, and many of their paintings had a magical purpose, but no one would maintain that religion was at the root of the impulse, drive, preoccupation and aspiration which animated these artists. We know that the shaman, medicine man, and priest make use of the artist—they subsidize him and enable him to execute momentous works. But magic and religion do not bring forth the artist. The artist is there first. The Paleolithic artists engraved, carved, and modeled in clay long before they executed the animal frescoes in the caves. The artistic impulse is likely to emerge where there is leisure, a fascination with objects, and a delight in tinkering and playing with things.

9   The first thing I do when I get a book on prehistoric man is go to the index to see whether it has the word *play*. It is not there! You find Plato but not play. The experts take it for granted that man's ability to master

his environment has been the product of a grim, relentless struggle for existence. Man prevailed because he was more purposeful, determined and cunning than other creatures. Yet, whenever we try to trace the origin of a skill or a practice which played a crucial role in the ascent of man, we usually reach the realm of play.

10   Almost every utilitarian device had its ancestry in a nonutilitarian pursuit or pastime. The first domesticated animal—the dog puppy—was not the most useful but the most playful animal. The hunting dog is a rather late development. The first domesticated animals were children's pets. Planting and irrigating, too, were probably first attempted in the course of play. It is also plausible that the wheel, sail, brickmaking, etc. were invented in the course of play. The Aztecs did not have the wheel, but some of their animal toys had rollers for feet. Ornaments preceded clothing. The bow, we are told, was a musical instrument before it became a weapon.

11   Seen thus it is evident that play has been man's most useful occupation. It is imperative to keep in mind that man painted, engraved, carved and modeled long before he made a pot, wove cloth, worked metals or domesticated an animal. Man as an artist is infinitely more ancient than man as a worker. Play came before work; art before production for use. Pressing necessity often prompted man to make use of things which amuse. When grubbing for necessities man is still in the animal kingdom. He becomes uniquely human and is at his creative best when he expends his energies, and even risks his life, for that which is not essential for sheer survival. Hence it is reasonable to assume that the humanization of man took place in an environment where nature was bountiful, and man had the leisure and the inclination to tinker and play.

12   Let us return to the Paleolithic hunters who painted the cave masterpieces. Were their daily lives merely endless cruel struggles for sheer survival?

Actually they lived in a hunter's paradise, a crossroad of the seasonal migrations of huge herds of bison, reindeer, wild horses, musk-ox and deer. The animals filed past in their thousands along well-defined routes. Food was almost no problem. The hunters lived mostly in skin tents and were clad in sable, arctic fox and other fancy furs. Judged by their fine bone needles the Paleolithic hunters were expert tailors. They sported swagger sticks of mammoth ivory beautifully carved and engraved. They wore necklaces of shell and perforated animal teeth, and engraved pendants made of ivory, bone, horn or baked clay. They were sportsmen, their life rich with leisure yet not without tensions and passionate preoccupations. They had leisure to develop and exercise subtle skills not only in carving, engraving and painting but also in elaborating the sophisticated art of fishing with bone fishhooks and sinew lines. They probably had secret societies which met in cave hideouts adorned with engravings and paintings of animals. The shaman injected himself in these sporting activities and gradually endowed them with a pronounced magical connotation.

13   Almost all the engravings, carvings and paintings of Paleolithic man were of animals. What was his attitude toward animals? He adored and worshipped them. They were his betters. Man among the animals is an amateur among superbly skilled and equipped specialists, each with a built-in tool kit. Man has neither claws, nor fangs, nor horns to fight with; neither scales nor hide to shield him; no special adaptations for burrowing, swimming, climbing or running. He craved the strength, speed and skill of the superior animals around him. When he boasted he likened himself unto an elephant, a bull, a deer. He watched the adored animals with the total absorption of a lover, and could paint them in vivid detail, even on the ceiling of a dark cave.

14   Man's being an unfinished, defective animal has been the root of his uniqueness and creativeness. He is the only animal not satisfied with being what he is. His ideal was a combination of the perfections he saw in the animals around him. His art, dances, songs, rituals and inventions were born of his groping to compensate himself for what he lacked as an animal. His spirituality had its inception not in a craving to overcome his animality, but in a striving to become a superior animal. In the cave of *Les Trois Frères* the sorcerer, painted high on a ledge above the ground, seems to rule over the world of animals on the walls below, and this sorcerer, whose face is human, is a composite of animals.

15   The most crucial consequence of man's incurable unfinishedness is, of course, that he cannot truly grow up. Man is the only perpetually young thing in the world, and the playground is the ideal milieu for the unfolding of his capacities and talents. It is the child in man that is the source of his uniqueness and creativeness. Whom the Gods love, said the Greeks, die young—stay young till the day they die.

16   I have always felt that five is a golden age. We are all geniuses at the age of five. The trouble with the juvenile is not that he is not yet a man, but that he is no longer a child. If maturing is to have meaning it must be a recapturing of the capacity for total absorption and the avidity to master skills characteristic of a five-year-old. But it needs leisure to be a child. When we grow up the world steals our hours and the most it gives us in return is a sense of usefulness. Should automation rob us of our sense of usefulness, the world will no longer be able to steal our hours. Banned from the marketplace we shall return to the playground and resume the task of learning and growing. Thus, to me the coming of automation is the coming of a grand consummation; the completion of a magic circle. Man first became human in an Eden playground, and now we have a chance to attain our ultimate destiny, our fullest humanness, by returning to the playground.

17   When, at the age of 27, I first read how God drove man out of Eden, there flashed before my eyes a tableau: I saw my ancestor Adam get up

from the dust after he had been bounced out, shake his fist at the closed gates and the watching angels and mutter, "I shall return!" May it fall to this or the next generation to redeem the promise.

Study Questions

1. What is the thesis of Hoffer's essay? What logical inconsistency does he attempt to eradicate?
2. Why does this essay open with an anecdote?
3. What concrete examples amplify paragraph 10? How do they contribute to the thesis of the essay?
4. What is the figurative meaning of "returning to the playground" (paragraph 16)?
5. Can you find evidence that Hoffer has researched his subject?

The Police Band

Donald Barthelme

1   It was kind of the department to think up the Police Band. The original impulse, I believe, was creative and humanitarian. A better way of doing things. Unpleasant, bloody things required by the line of duty. Even if it didn't work out.

2   The Commissioner (the old Commissioner, not the one they have now) brought us up the river from Detroit. Where our members had been, typically, working the Sho Bar two nights a week. Sometimes the Glass Crutch. Friday and Saturday. And the rest of the time wandering the streets disguised as postal employees. Bitten by dogs and burdened with third-class mail.

3   What are our duties? we asked at the interview. Your duties are to wail, the Commissioner said. That only. We admired our new dark-blue uniforms as we came up the river in canoes like Indians. We plan to use you in certain situations, certain tense situations, to alleviate tensions,

the Commissioner said. I can visualize great success with this new method. And would you play "Entropy." He was pale, with a bad liver.

4   We are subtle, the Commissioner said, never forget that. Subtlety is what has previously been lacking in our line. Some of the old ones, the Commissioner said, all they know is the club. He took a little pill from a little box and swallowed it with his Scotch.

5   When we got to town we looked at those Steve Canyon recruiting posters and wondered if we resembled them. Henry Wang, the bass man, looks like a Chinese Steve Canyon, right? The other cops were friendly in a suspicious way. They liked to hear us wail, however.

6   The Police Band is a very sensitive highly trained and ruggedly anti-Communist unit whose efficacy will be demonstrated in due time, the Commissioner said to the Mayor (the old Mayor). The Mayor took a little pill from a little box and said, We'll see. He could tell we were musicians because we were holding our instruments, right? Emptying spit valves, giving the horn that little shake. Or coming in at letter E with some sly emotion stolen from another life.

7   The old Commissioner's idea was essentially that if there was a disturbance on the city's streets—some ethnic group cutting up some other ethnic group on a warm August evening—the Police Band would be sent in. The handsome dark-green band bus arriving with sirens singing, red lights whirling. Hard-pressed men on the beat in their white hats raising a grateful cheer. We stream out of the vehicle holding our instruments at high port. A skirmish line fronting the angry crowd. And play "Perdido." The crowd washed with new and true emotion. Startled, they listen. Our emotion stronger than their emotion. A triumph of art over good sense.

8   That was the idea. The old Commissioner's *musical* ideas were not very interesting, because after all he was a cop, right? But his police ideas were interesting.

9   We had drills. Poured out of that mother-loving bus onto vacant lots holding our instruments at high port like John Wayne. Felt we were heroes already. Playing "Perdido," "Stumblin'," "Gin Song," "Feebles." Laving the terrain with emotion stolen from old busted-up loves, broken marriages, the needle, economic deprivation. A few old ladies leaning out of high windows. Our emotion washing rusty Rheingold cans and parts of old doors.

10   This city is too much! We'd be walking down the street talking about our techniques and we'd see out of our eyes a woman standing in the gutter screaming to herself about what we could not imagine. A drunk trying to strangle a dog somebody'd left leashed to a parking meter. The drunk and the dog screaming at each other. This city is too much!

11   We had drills and drills. It is true that the best musicians come from Detroit but there is something here that you have to get in your playing and that is simply the scream. We got that. The Commissioner, a sixty-

three-year-old hippie with no doubt many graft qualities and unpleasant qualities, nevertheless understood that. When we'd play "ugly," he understood that. He understood the rising expectations of the world's peoples also. That our black members didn't feel like toting junk mail around Detroit forever until the ends of their lives. For some strange reason.

12   He said one of our functions would be to be sent out to play in places where people were trembling with fear inside their houses, right? To inspirit them in difficult times. This was the plan. We set up in the street. Henry Wang grabs hold of his instrument. He has a four-bar lead-in all by himself. Then the whole group. The iron shutters raised a few inches. Shorty Alanio holding his horn at his characteristic angle (sideways). The reeds dropping lacy little fill-ins behind him. We're cooking. The crowd roars.

13   The Police Band was an idea of a very romantic kind. The Police Band was an idea that didn't work. When they retired the old Commissioner (our Commissioner), who it turned out had a little drug problem of his own, they didn't let us even drill anymore. We have never been used. His idea was a romantic idea, they said (right?), which was not adequate to the rage currently around in the world. Rage must be met with rage, they said. (Not in so many words.) We sit around the precinct houses, under the filthy lights, talking about our techniques. But I thought it might be good if you knew that the Department still has us. We have a good group. We still have emotion to be used. We're still here.

Study Questions

1. What is the target of this satire—the commissioner's romantic ideas or the practical techniques of those who would fight rage with rage?
2. From what fields of study does Barthelme choose diction? From what levels of usage?
3. What is the tone of this short story? Is it resigned? Cynical?
4. Why doesn't Barthelme use quotation marks for the dialogue?
5. What effects are achieved by the use of sentence fragments?

Sonny's Blues

James Baldwin

1   I read about it in the paper, in the subway, on my way to work. I read it, and I couldn't believe it, and I read it again. Then perhaps I just stared at it, at the newsprint spelling out his name, spelling out the story. I stared at it in the swinging lights of the subway car, and in the faces and bodies of the people, and in my own face, trapped in the darkness which roared outside.

2   It was not to be believed, and I kept telling myself that as I walked from the subway station to the high school. And at the same time I couldn't doubt it. I was scared, scared for Sonny. He became real to me again. A great block of ice got settled in my belly and kept melting there slowly all day long, while I taught my classes algebra. It was a special kind of ice. It kept melting, sending trickles of ice water all up and down my veins, but it never got less. Sometimes it hardened and seemed to expand until I felt my guts were going to come spilling out or that I was going to choke or scream. This would always be at a moment when I was remembering some specific thing Sonny had once said or done.

3   When he was about as old as the boys in my classes, his face had been bright and open, there was a lot of copper in it; and he'd had wonderfully direct brown eyes, and great gentleness and privacy. I wondered what he looked like now. He had been picked up, the evening before, in a raid on an apartment downtown, for peddling and using heroin.

4   I couldn't believe it: but what I mean by that is that I couldn't find any room for it anywhere inside me. I had kept it outside me for a long time. I hadn't wanted to know. I had had suspicions, but I didn't name them, I kept putting them away. I told myself that Sonny was wild, but he wasn't crazy. And he'd always been a good boy, he hadn't even turned hard or evil or disrespectful, the way kids can, so quick, so quick, especially in Harlem. I didn't want to believe that I'd ever see my brother going down, coming to nothing, all that light in his face gone out, in the condition I'd already seen so many others. Yet it had happened and here I was, talking about algebra to a lot of boys who might, every one of them for all I knew, be popping off needles every time they went to the head. Maybe it did more for them than algebra could.

5   I was sure that the first time Sonny had ever had horse, he couldn't have been much older than these boys were now. These boys, now, were living as we'd been living then, they were growing up with a rush and

their heads bumped abruptly against the low ceiling of their actual possibilities. They were filled with rage. All they really knew were two darknesses, the darkness of their lives, which was now closing in on them, and the darkness of the movies, which had blinded them to that other darkness, and in which they now, vindictively, dreamed, at once more together than they were at any other time, and more alone.

6   When the last bell rang, the last class ended, I let out my breath. It seemed I'd been holding it for all that time. My clothes were set—I may have looked as though I'd been sitting in a steam bath, all dressed up, all afternoon. I sat alone in the classroom a long time. I listened to the boys outside, downstairs, shouting and cursing and laughing. Their laughter struck me for perhaps the first time. It was not the joyous laughter which—God knows why—one associates with children. It was mocking and insular, its intent was to denigrate. It was disenchanted, and in this, also, lay the authority of their curses. Perhaps I was listening to them because I was thinking about my brother and in them I heard my brother. And myself.

7   One boy was whistling a tune, at once very complicated and very simple, it seemed to be pouring out of him as though he were a bird, and it sounded very cool and moving through all that harsh, bright air, only just holding its own through all those other sounds.

8   I stood and walked over to the window and looked down into the courtyard. It was the beginning of the spring, and the sap was rising in the boys. A teacher passed through them every now and again, quickly, as though he or she couldn't wait to get out of that courtyard, to get those boys out of their sight and off their minds. I started collecting my stuff. I thought I'd better get home and talk to Isabel.

9   The courtyard was almost deserted by the time I got downstairs. I saw this boy standing in the shadow of a doorway, looking just like Sonny. I almost called his name. Then I saw that it wasn't Sonny, but somebody we used to know, a boy from around our block. He'd been Sonny's friend. He'd never been mine, having been too young for me, and, anyway, I'd never liked him. And now, even though he was a grown-up man, he still hung around that block, still spent hours on the street corner, was always high and raggy. I used to run into him from time to time, and he'd often work around to asking me for a quarter or fifty cents. He always had some real good excuse, too, and I always gave it to him, I don't know why.

10   But now, abruptly, I hated him. I couldn't stand the way he looked at me, partly like a dog, partly like a cunning child. I wanted to ask him what the hell he was doing in the school courtyard.

11   He sort of shuffled over to me, and he said, "I see you got the papers. So you already know about it."

12   "You mean about Sonny? Yes, I already know about it. How come they didn't get you?"

13   He grinned. It made him repulsive and it also brought to mind what he'd looked like as a kid. "I wasn't there. I stay away from them people."

14   "Good for you." I offered him a cigarette and I watched him through the smoke. "You come all the way down here just to tell me about Sonny?"

15   "That's right." He was sort of shaking his head and his eyes looked strange, as though they were about to cross. The bright sun deadened his damp dark brown skin and it made his eyes look yellow and showed up the dirt in his conked hair. He smelled funky. I moved a little away from him and I said, "Well, thanks. But I already know about it and I got to get home."

16   "I'll walk you a little ways," he said. We started walking. There were a couple of kids still loitering in the courtyard and one of them said good night to me and looked strangely at the boy beside me.

17   "What're you going to do?" he asked me. "I mean, about Sonny?"

18   "Look. I haven't seen Sonny for over a year, I'm not sure I'm going to do anything. Anyway, what the hell *can* I do?"

19   "That's right," he said quickly, "ain't nothing you can do. Can't much help old Sonny no more, I guess."

20   It was what I was thinking and so it seemed to me he had no right to say it.

21   "I'm surprised at Sonny, though," he went on—he had a funny way of talking, he looked straight ahead as though he were talking to himself—"I thought Sonny was a smart boy, I thought he was too smart to get hung."

22   "I guess he thought so, too," I said sharply, "and that's how he got hung. And how about you? You're pretty goddamn smart, I bet."

23   Then he looked directly at me, just for a minute. "I ain't smart," he said. "If I was smart, I'd have reached for a pistol a long time ago."

24   "Look. Don't tell *me* your sad story, if it was up to me, I'd give you one." Then I felt guilty—guilty probably for never having supposed that the poor bastard *had* a story of his own, much less a sad one, and I asked, quickly, "What's going to happen to him now?"

25   He didn't answer this. He was off by himself someplace. "Funny thing," he said, and from his tone we might have been discussing the quickest way to get to Brooklyn, "when I saw the papers this morning, the first thing I asked myself was if I had anything to do with it. I felt sort of responsible."

26   I began to listen more carefully. The subway station was on the corner, just before us, and I stopped. He stopped, too. We were in front of a bar and he ducked slightly, peering in, but whoever he was looking for didn't seem to be there. The juke box was blasting away with something black and bouncy, and I half watched the barmaid as she danced her way from the juke box to her place behind the bar. And I watched her face as she laughingly responded to something someone said to her, still keeping time to the music. When she smiled one saw the little girl, one sensed the doomed, still-struggling woman beneath the battered face of the semi-whore.

27   "I never *give* Sonny nothing," the boy said finally, "but a long time ago I come to school high and Sonny asked me how it felt." He paused, I couldn't bear to watch him, I watched the barmaid, and I listened to the music which seemed to be causing the pavement to shake. "I told him it felt great." The music stopped, the barmaid paused and watched the juke box until the music began again. "It did."

28   All this was carrying me someplace I didn't want to go. I certainly didn't want to know how it felt. It filled everything, the people, the houses, the music, the dark, quicksilver barmaid, with menace; and this menace was their reality.

29   "What's going to happen to him now?" I asked again.

30   "They'll send him away someplace and they'll try to cure him." He shook his head. "Maybe he'll even think he's kicked the habit. Then they'll turn him loose"—He gestured, throwing his cigarette into the gutter. "That's all."

31   "What do you mean, that's *all*?"

32   But I knew what he meant.

33   "I *mean*, that's *all*." He turned his head and looked at me pulling down the corners of his mouth. "Don't you know what I mean?" he asked softly.

34   "How the hell *would* I know what you mean?" I almost whispered it, I don't know why.

35   "That's right," he said to the air, "how would *he* know what I mean?" He turned toward me again, patient and calm, and yet I somehow felt him shaking, shaking as though he were going to fall apart. I felt that ice in my guts again, the dread I'd felt all afternoon; and again I watched the barmaid, moving about the bar, washing glasses, and singing. "Listen. They'll let him out and then it'll just start over again. That's what I mean."

36   "You mean—they'll let him out. And then he'll just start working his way back in again. You mean he'll never kick the habit. Is that what you mean?"

37   "That's right," he said, cheerfully. "*You* see what I mean."

38   "Tell me," I said at last, "why does he want to die? He must want to die, he's killing himself, why does he want to die?"

39   He looked at me in surprise. He licked his lips. "He don't want to die. He wants to live. Don't nobody want to die, ever."

40   Then I wanted to ask him—too many things. He could not have answered, or if he had, I could not have borne the answers. I started walking. "Well, I guess it's none of my business."

41   "It's going to be rough on old Sonny," he said. We reached the subway station. "This is your station?" he asked. I nodded. I took one step down. "Damn!" he said, suddenly. I looked up at him. He grinned again. "Damn if I didn't leave all my money home. You ain't got a dollar on you, have you? Just for a couple of days, is all."

42   All at once something inside gave and threatened to come pouring

out of me. I didn't hate him any more. I felt that in another moment I'd start crying like a child.

43   "Sure," I said, "Don't sweat." I looked in my wallet and didn't have a dollar, I only had a five. "Here," I said. "That hold you?"

44   He didn't look at it—he didn't want to look at it. A terrible, closed look came over his face, as though he were keeping the number on the bill a secret from him and me. "Thanks," he said, and now he was dying to see me go. "Don't worry about Sonny. Maybe I'll write him or something."

45   "Sure," I said. "You do that. So long."

46   "Be seeing you," he said. I went on down the steps.

47   And I didn't write Sonny or send him anything for a long time. When I finally did, it was just after my little girl died, he wrote me back a letter which made me feel like a bastard.

48   Here's what he said:

Dear brother,

    You don't know how much I needed to hear from you. I wanted to write you many a time but I dug how much I must have hurt you and so I didn't write. But now I feel like a man who's been trying to climb up out of some deep, real deep and funky hole and just saw the sun up there, outside. I got to get outside.

    I can't tell you much about how I got here. I mean I don't know how to tell you. I guess I was afraid of something or I was trying to escape from something and you know I have never been very strong in the head (smile). I'm glad Mama and Daddy are dead and can't see what's happened to their son and I swear if I'd known what I was doing I would never have hurt you so, you and a lot of other fine people who were nice to me and who believed in me.

    I don't want you to think it had anything to do with me being a musician. It's more than that. Or maybe less than that. I can't get anything straight in my head down here and I try not to think about what's going to happen to me when I get outside again. Sometime I think I'm going to flip and never get outside and sometime I think I'll come straight back. I tell you one thing, though, I'd rather blow my brains out than go through this again. But that's what they all say, so they tell me. If I tell you when I'm coming to New York and if you could meet me, I sure would appreciate it. Give my love to Isabel and the kids and I was sure sorry to hear about little Gracie. I wish I could be like Mama and say the Lord's will be done, but I don't know it seems to me that trouble is the one thing that never does get stopped and I don't know what good it does to blame it on the Lord. But maybe it does some good if you believe it.

Your brother,
Sonny

49   Then I kept in constant touch with him and I sent him whatever I could and I went to meet him when he came back to New York. When I saw him, many things I thought I had forgotten came flooding back to me. This was because I had begun, finally, to wonder about Sonny, about the life that Sonny lived inside. This life, whatever it was, had made him older and thinner and it had deepened the distant stillness in which he had always moved. He looked very unlike my baby brother. Yet, when he smiled, when we shook hands, the baby brother I'd never known looked out from the depths of his private life, like an animal waiting to be coaxed into the light.

50   "How you been keeping?" he asked me.

51   "All right. And you?"

52   "Just fine." He was smiling all over his face. "It's good to see you again."

53   "It's good to see you."

54   The seven years' difference in our ages lay between us like a chasm: I wondered if these years would ever operate between us as a bridge. I was remembering, and it made it hard to catch my breath, that I had been there when he was born; and I had heard the first words he had ever spoken. When he started to walk, he walked from our mother straight to me. I caught him just before he fell when he took the first steps he ever took in this world.

55   "How's Isabel?"

56   "Just fine. She's dying to see you."

57   "And the boys?"

58   "They're fine, too, They're anxious to see their uncle."

59   "Oh, come on. You know they don't remember me."

60   "Are you kidding? Of course they remember you."

61   He grinned again. We got into a taxi. We had a lot to say to each other, far too much to know how to begin.

62   As the taxi began to move, I asked, "You still want to go to India?"

63   He laughed. "You still remember that. Hell, no. This place is Indian enough for me."

64   "It used to belong to them," I said.

65   And he laughed again. "They damn sure knew what they were doing when they got rid of it."

66   Years ago, when he was around fourteen, he'd been all hipped on the idea of going to India. He read books about people sitting on rocks, naked, in all kinds of weather, but mostly bad, naturally, and walking barefoot through hot coals and arriving at wisdom. I used to say that it sounded to me as though they were getting away from wisdom as fast as they could. I think he sort of looked down on me for that.

67   "Do you mind," he asked, "if we have the driver drive alongside the park? On the west side—I haven't seen the city in so long."

68   "Of course not," I said. I was afraid that I might sound as though I were humoring him, but I hoped he wouldn't take it that way.

69   So we drove along, between the green of the park and the stony, lifeless elegance of hotels and apartment buildings, toward the vivid, killing streets of our childhood. These streets hadn't changed, though housing projects jutted up out of them now like rocks in the middle of a boiling sea. Most of the houses in which we had grown up had vanished, as had the stores from which we had stolen, the basements in which we had first tried sex, the rooftops from which we had hurled tin cans and bricks. But houses exactly like the houses of our past yet dominated the landscape, boys exactly like the boys we once had been found themselves smothering in these houses, came down into the streets for light and air and found themselves encircled by disaster. Some escaped the trap, most didn't. Those who got out always left something of themselves behind, as some animals amputate a leg and leave it in the trap. It might be said, perhaps, that I had escaped, after all, I was a schoolteacher; or that Sonny had, he hadn't lived in Harlem for years. Yet, as the cab moved uptown through streets which seemed, with a rush, to darken with dark people, and as I covertly studied Sonny's face, it came to me that what we both were seeking through our separate cab windows was that part of ourselves which had been left behind. It's always at the hour of trouble and confrontation that the missing member aches.

70   We hit 110th Street and started rolling up Lenox Avenue. And I'd known this avenue all my life, but it seemed to me again, as it had seemed on the day I'd first heard about Sonny's trouble, filled with a hidden menace which was its very breath of life.

71   "We almost there," said Sonny.

72   "Almost." We were both too nervous to say anything more.

73   We live in a housing project. It hasn't been up long. A few days after it was up it seemed uninhabitably new, now, of course, it's already run-down. It looked like a parody of the good, clean, faceless life—God knows the people who live in it do their best to make it a parody. The beat-looking grass lying around isn't enough to make their lives green, the hedges will never hold out the streets, and they know it. The big windows fool no one, they aren't big enough to make space out of no space. They don't bother with the windows, they watch the TV screen instead. The playground is most popular with the children who don't play at jacks, or skip rope, or roller skate, or swing, and they can be found in it after dark. We moved in partly because it's not too far from where I teach, and partly for the kids; but it's really just like the houses in which Sonny and I grew up. The same things happen, they'll have the same things to remember. The moment Sonny and I started into the house I had the feeling that I was simply bringing him back into the danger he had almost died trying to escape.

74   Sonny has never been talkative. So I don't know why I was sure he'd be dying to talk to me when supper was over the first night. Everything went fine, the oldest boy remembered him, and the youngest

boy liked him, and Sonny had remembered to bring something for each of them; and Isabel, who is really much nicer than I am, more open and giving, had gone to a lot of trouble about dinner and was genuinely glad to see him. And she'd always been able to tease Sonny in a way that I haven't. It was nice to see her face so vivid again and to hear her laugh and watch her make Sonny laugh. She wasn't, or, anyway, she didn't seem to be, at all uneasy or embarrassed. She chatted as though there were no subject which had to be avoided and she got Sonny past his first, faint stiffness. And thank God she was there, for I was filled with that icy dread again. Everything I did seemed awkward to me, and everything I said sounded freighted with hidden meaning. I was trying to remember everything I'd heard about dope addiction and I couldn't help watching Sonny for signs. I wasn't doing it out of malice. I was trying to find out something about my brother. I was dying to hear him tell me he was safe.

75   "Safe!" my father grunted, whenever Mama suggested trying to move to a neighborhood which might be safer for children. "Safe, hell! Ain't no place safe for kids, nor nobody."

76   He always went on like this, but he wasn't, ever, really as bad as he sounded, not even on weekends, when he got drunk. As a matter of fact, he was always on the lookout for "something a little better," but he died before he found it. He died suddenly, during a drunken weekend in the middle of the war, when Sonny was fifteen. He and Sonny hadn't ever got on too well. And this was partly because Sonny was the apple of his father's eye. It was because he loved Sonny so much and was frightened for him, that he was always fighting with him. It doesn't do any good to fight with Sonny. Sonny just moves back, inside himself, where he can't be reached. But the principal reason that they never hit it off is that they were so much alike. Daddy was big and rough and loud-talking, just the opposite of Sonny, but they both had—that same privacy.

77   Mama tried to tell me something about this, just after Daddy died. I was home on leave from the army.

78   This was the last time I ever saw my mother alive. Just the same, this picture gets all mixed up in my mind with pictures I had of her when she was younger. The way I always see her is the way she used to be on a Sunday afternoon, say, when the old folks were talking after the big Sunday dinner. I always see her wearing pale blue. She'd be sitting on the sofa. And my father would be sitting in the easy chair, not far from her. And the living room would be full of church folks and relatives. There they sit, in chairs all around the living room, and the night is creeping up outside, but nobody knows it yet. You can see the darkness growing against the windowpanes and you hear the street noises every now and again, or maybe the jangling beat of a tambourine from one of the churches close by, but it's real quiet in the room. For a moment nobody's talking, but every face looks darkening, like the sky outside. And my mother rocks a little from the waist, and my father's eyes are

closed. Everyone is looking at something a child can't see. For a minute they've forgotten the children. Maybe a kid is lying on the rug, half asleep. Maybe somebody's got a kid in his lap and is absent-mindedly stroking the kid's head. Maybe there's a kid, quiet and big-eyed, curled up in a big chair in the corner. The silence, the darkness coming, and the darkness in the faces frighten the child obscurely. He hopes that the hand which strokes his forehead will never stop—will never die. He hopes that there will never come a time when the old folks won't be sitting around the living room, talking about where they've come from, and what they've seen, and what's happened to them and their kinfolk.

79   But something deep and watchful in the child knows that this is bound to end, is already ending. In a moment someone will get up and turn on the light. Then the old folks will remember the children and they won't talk any more that day. And when light fills the room, the child is filled with darkness. He knows that every time this happens he's moved just a little closer to that darkness outside. The darkness outside is what the old folks have been talking about. It's what they've come from. It's what they endure. The child knows that they won't talk any more be-cause if he knows too much about what's happened to *them,* he'll know too much too soon, about what's going to happen to *him.*

80   The last time I talked to my mother, I remember I was restless. I wanted to get out and see Isabel. We weren't married then and we had a lot to straighten out between us.

81   There Mama sat, in black, by the window. She was humming an old church song, *Lord, you brought me from a long ways off.* Sonny was out somewhere. Mama kept watching the streets.

82   "I don't know," she said, "if I'll ever see you again, after you go off from here. But I hope you'll remember the things I tried to teach you."

83   "Don't talk like that," I said, and smiled. "You'll be here a long time yet."

84   She smiled, too, but she said nothing. She was quiet for a long time. And I said, "Mama, don't you worry about nothing. I'll be writing all the time, and you be getting the checks. . . ."

85   "I want to talk to you about your brother," she said, suddenly. "If anything happens to me, he ain't going to have nobody to look out for him."

86   "Mama," I said, "ain't nothing going to happen to you *or* Sonny, Sonny's all right. He's a good boy and he's got good sense."

87   "It ain't a question of his being a good boy," Mama said, "nor of his having good sense. It ain't only the bad ones, nor yet the dumb ones that gets sucked under." She stopped, looking at me. "Your Daddy once had a brother," she said, and smiled in a way that made me feel she was in pain. "You didn't never know that, did you?"

88   "No," I said. "I never knew that," and I watched her face.

89   "Oh, yes," she said, "your Daddy had a brother." She looked out of the window again. "I know you never saw your Daddy cry. But *I* did— many a time, through all these years."

90   I asked her, "What happened to his brother? How come nobody's ever talked about him?"

91   This was the first time I ever saw my mother look old.

92   "His brother got killed," she said, "when he was just a little younger than you are now. I knew him. He was a fine boy. He was maybe a little full of the devil, but he didn't mean nobody no harm."

93   Then she stopped, and the room was silent, exactly as it had sometimes been on those Sunday afternoons. Mama kept looking out into the streets.

94   "He used to have a job in the mill," she said, "and, like all young folks, he just liked to perform on Saturday nights. Saturday nights, him and your father would drift around to different places, go to dances and things like that, or just sit around with people they knew, and your father's brother would sing, he had a fine voice, and play along with himself on his guitar. Well, this particular Saturday night, him and your father was coming home from some place, and they were both a little drunk and there was a moon that night, it was bright like day. Your father's brother was feeling kind of good, and he was whistling to himself, and he had his guitar slung over his shoulder. They was coming down a hill, and beneath them was a road that turned off from the highway. Well, your father's brother, being always kind of frisky, decided to run down this hill, and he did, with that guitar banging and clanging behind him, and he ran across the road, and he was making water behind a tree. And your father was sort of amused at him and he was still coming down the hill, kind of slow. Then he heard a car motor and that same minute his brother stepped from behind the tree, into the road, in the moonlight. And he started to cross the road. And your father started to run down the hill, he says he don't know why. This car was full of white men. They was all drunk, and when they seen your father's brother they let out a great whoop and holler and they aimed the car straight at him. They was having fun, they just wanted to scare him, the way they do sometimes, you know. But they was drunk. And I guess the boy, being drunk, too, and scared, kind of lost his head. By the time he jumped it was too late. Your father says he heard his brother scream when the car rolled over him, and he heard the wood of that guitar when it give, and he heard them strings go flying, and he heard them white men shouting, and the car kept on a-going and it ain't stopped till this day. And, time your father got down the hill, his brother weren't nothing but blood and pulp."

95   Tears were gleaming on my mother's face. There wasn't anything I could say.

96   "He never mentioned it," she said, "because I never let him mention it before you children. Your Daddy was like a crazy man that night and for many a night thereafter. He says he never in his life seen anything as dark as that road after the lights of that car had gone away. Weren't nothing, weren't nobody on that road, just your Daddy and his brother and that busted guitar. Oh, yes. Your Daddy never did really get

right again. Till the day he died he weren't sure but that every white man he saw was the man that killed his brother."

97   She stopped and took out her handkerchief and dried her eyes and looked at me.

98   "I ain't telling you all this," she said, "to make you scared or bitter or to make you hate nobody. I'm telling you this because you got a brother. And the world ain't changed."

99   I guess I didn't want to believe this. I guess she saw this in my face. She turned away from me, toward the window again, searching those streets.

100   "But I praise my Redeemer," she said at last, "that he called your Daddy home before me. I ain't saying it to throw no flowers at myself, but, I declare, it keeps me from feeling too cast down to know I helped your father get safely through this world. Your father always acted like he was the roughest, strongest man on earth. And everybody took him to be like that. But if he hadn't had *me* there—to see his tears!"

101   She was crying again. Still, I couldn't move. I said, "Lord, Lord, Mama, I didn't know it was like that."

102   "Oh, honey," she said, "there's a lot that you don't know. But you are going to find it out." She stood up from the window and came over to me. "You got to hold on to your brother," she said, "and don't let him fall, no matter what it looks like is happening to him and no matter how evil you gets with him. You going to be evil with him many a time. But don't you forget what I told you, you hear?"

103   "I won't forget," I said. "Don't you worry, I won't forget. I won't let nothing happen to Sonny."

104   My mother smiled as though she were amused at something she saw in my face. Then, "You may not be able to stop nothing from happening. But you got to let him know you's *there*."

105   Two days later I was married, and then I was gone. And I had a lot of things on my mind and I pretty well forgot my promise to Mama until I got shipped home on a special furlough for her funeral.

106   And, after the funeral, with just Sonny and me alone in the empty kitchen, I tried to find out something about him.

107   "What do you want to do?" I asked him.

108   "I'm going to be a musician," he said.

109   For he had graduated, in the time I had been away, from dancing to the juke box to finding out who was playing what, and what they were doing with it, and he had bought himself a set of drums.

110   "You mean, you want to be a drummer?" I somehow had the feeling that being a drummer might be all right for other people but not for my brother Sonny.

111   "I don't think," he said, looking at me very gravely, " that I'll ever be a good drummer. But I think I can play a piano."

112   I frowned. I'd never played the role of the older brother quite so seriously before, had scarcely ever, in fact, *asked* Sonny a damn thing. I sensed myself in the presence of something I didn't really know how to

handle, didn't understand. So I made my frown a little deeper as I asked: "What kind of musician do you want to be?"

113   He grinned. "How many kinds do you think there are?"

114   "Be *serious*," I said.

115   He laughed, throwing his head back, and then looked at me. "I *am* serious."

116   "Well, then, for Christ's sake, stop kidding around and answer a serious question. I mean, do you want to be a concert pianist, you want to play classical music and all that, or—or, what?" Long before I finished he was laughing again. "For Christ's *sake*, Sonny!"

117   He sobered, but with difficulty. "I'm sorry. But you sound so—*scared!*" And he was off again.

118   "Well, you may think it's funny now, baby, but it's not going to be so funny when you have to make your living at it, let me tell you *that*." I was furious because I knew he was laughing at me and I didn't know why.

119   "No," he said, very sober now, and afraid, perhaps, that he'd hurt me, "I don't want to be a classical pianist. That isn't what interests me. I mean"—he paused, looking hard at me, as though his eyes would help me to understand, and then gestured helplessly, as though perhaps his hand would help—"I mean, I'll have a lot of studying to do, and I'll have to study *everything*, but, I mean, I want to play *with*—jazz musicians." He stopped. "I want to play jazz," he said.

120   Well, the word had never before sounded as heavy, as real, as it sounded that afternoon in Sonny's mouth. I just looked at him and I was probably frowning a real frown by this time. I simply couldn't see why on earth he'd want to spend his time hanging around night clubs, clowning around on bandstands, while people pushed each other around a dance floor. It seemed—beneath him, somehow. I had never thought about it before, had never been forced to, but I suppose I had always put jazz musicians in a class with what Daddy called "good-time people."

121   "Are you *serious*?"

122   "Hell, *yes*, I'm serious."

123   He looked more helpless than ever, and annoyed, and deeply hurt.

124   I suggested, helpfully: "You mean—like Louis Armstrong?"

125   His face closed as though I'd struck him. "No. I'm not talking about none of that old-time, down home crap."

126   "Well, look, Sonny, I'm sorry, don't get mad. I just don't altogether get it, that's all. Name somebody—you know, a jazz musician you admire."

127   "Bird."

128   "Who?"

129   "Bird! Charlie Parker! Don't they teach you nothing in the goddam army?"

130   I lit a cigarette. I was surprised and then a little amused to discover that I was trembling. "I've been out of touch," I said. "You'll have to be patient with me. Now. Who's this Parker character?"

131   "He's just one of the greatest jazz musicians alive," said Sonny, sullenly, his hands in his pockets, his back to me. "Maybe *the* greatest," he added bitterly, "that's probably why *you* never heard of him."

132   "All right," I said, "I'm ignorant. I'm sorry. I'll go out and buy all the cat's records right away, all right?"

133   "It don't," said Sonny, with dignity, "make any difference to me. I don't care what you listen to. Don't do me no favors."

134   I was beginning to realize that I'd never seen him so upset before. With another part of my mind I was thinking that this would probably turn out to be one of those things kids go through and that I shouldn't make it seem important by pushing it too hard. Still, I didn't think it would do any harm to ask: "Doesn't all this take a lot of time? Can you make a living at it?"

135   He turned back to me and half leaned, half-sat, on the kitchen table. "Everything takes time," he said, "and—well, yes, sure, I can make a living at it. But what I don't seem to be able to make you understand is that it's the only thing I want to do."

136   "Well, Sonny," I said gently, "you know people can't always do exactly what they want to do—"

137   "*No,* I don't know that," said Sonny, surprising me. "I think people *ought* to do what they want to do, what else are they alive for?"

138   "You getting to be a big boy," I said desperately, "it's time you started thinking about your future."

139   "I'm thinking about my future," said Sonny, grimly. "I think about it all the time."

140   I gave up. I decided, if he didn't change his mind, that we could always talk about it later. "In the meantime," I said, "you got to finish school." We had already decided that he'd have to move in with Isabel and her folks. I knew this wasn't the ideal arrangement because Isabel's folks are inclined to be dirty and they hadn't especially wanted Isabel to marry me. But I didn't know what else to do. "And we have to get you fixed up at Isabel's."

141   There was a long silence. He moved from the kitchen table to the window. "That's a terrible idea. You know it yourself."

142   "Do you have a *better* idea?"

143   He just walked up and down the kitchen for a minute. He was as tall as I was. He had started to shave. I suddenly had the feeling that I didn't know him at all.

144   He stopped at the kitchen table and picked up my cigarettes. Looking at me with a kind of mocking, amused defiance, he put one between his lips. "You mind?"

145   "You smoking already?"

146   He lit the cigarette and nodded, watching me through the smoke. "I just wanted to see if I'd have the courage to smoke in front of you." He grinned and blew a great cloud of smoke to the ceiling. "It was easy." He looked at my face. "Come on, now. I bet you was smoking at my age, tell the truth."

147   I didn't say anything but the truth was on my face, and he laughed. But now there was something very strained in his laugh. "Sure. And I bet that ain't all you was doing."

148   He was frightening me a little. "Cut the crap," I said. "We already decided that you was going to go and live at Isabel's. Now what's got into you all of a sudden?"

149   "*You* decided it," he pointed out. "*I* didn't decide nothing." He stopped in front of me, leaning against the stove, arms loosely folded. "Look, brother. I don't want to stay in Harlem no more, I really don't." He was very earnest. He looked at me, then over toward the kitchen window. There was something in his eyes I'd never seen before, some thoughtfulness, some worry all his own. He rubbed the muscle of one arm. "It's time I was getting out of here."

150   "Where do you want to *go*, Sonny?"

151   "I want to join the army. Or the navy, I don't care. If I say I'm old enough, they'll believe me."

152   Then I got mad. It was because I was so scared. "You must be crazy. You goddamn fool, what the hell do you want to go and join the *army* for?"

153   "I just told you. To get out of Harlem."

154   "Sonny, you haven't even finished *school.* And if you really want to be a musician, how do you expect to study if you're in the *army?*"

155   He looked at me, trapped, and in anguish. "There's ways. I might be able to work out some kind of deal. Anyway, I'll have the G.I. Bill when I come out."

156   "*If* you come out." We stared at each other. "Sonny, please. Be reasonable. I know the setup is far from perfect. But we got to do the best we can."

157   "I ain't learning nothing in school," he said. "Even when I go." He turned away from me and opened the window and threw his cigarette out into the narrow alley. I watched his back. "At least, I ain't learning nothing you'd want me to learn." He slammed the window so hard I thought the glass would fly out, and turned back to me. "And I'm sick of the stink of these garbage cans!"

158   "Sonny," I said, "I know how you feel. But if you don't finish school now, you're going to be sorry later that you didn't." I grabbed him by the shoulders. "And you only got another year. It ain't so bad. And I'll come back and I swear I'll help you do *whatever* you want to do. Just try to put up with it till I come back. Will you please do that? For me?"

159   He didn't answer and he wouldn't look at me.

160   "Sonny. You hear me?"

161   He pulled away. "I hear you. But you never hear anything *I* say."

162   I didn't know what to say to that. He looked out of the window and then back at me. "OK," he said, and sighed. "I'll try."

163   Then I said, trying to cheer him up a little, "They got a piano at Isabel's. You can practice on it."

164   And as a matter of fact, it did cheer him up for a minute. "That's

right," he said to himself. "I forgot that." His face relaxed a little. But the worry, the thoughtfulness, played on it still, the way shadows play on a face which is staring into the fire.

165   But I thought I'd never hear the end of that piano. At first, Isabel would write me, saying how nice it was that Sonny was so serious about his music and how, as soon as he came in from school, or wherever he had been when he was supposed to be at school, he went straight to that piano and stayed there until suppertime. And, after supper, he went back to that piano and stayed there until everybody went to bed. He was at that piano all day Saturday and all day Sunday. Then he bought a record player and started playing records. He'd play one record over and over again, all day long sometimes, and he'd improvise along with it on the piano. Or he'd play one section of the record, one chord, one change, one progression, then he'd do it on the piano. Then back to the record. Then back to the piano.

166   Well, I really don't know how they stood it. Isabel finally confessed that it wasn't like living with a person at all, it was like living with sound. And the sound didn't make any sense to her, didn't make any sense to any of them—naturally. They began, in a way, to be afflicted by this presence that was living in their home. It was as though Sonny were some sort of god, or monster. He moved in an atmosphere which wasn't like theirs at all. They fed him and he ate, he washed himself, he walked in and out of their door; he certainly wasn't nasty or unpleasant or rude, Sonny isn't any of those things; but it was as though he were all wrapped up in some cloud, some fire, some vision all his own; and there wasn't any way to reach him.

167   At the same time, he wasn't really a man yet, he was still a child, and they had to watch out for him in all kinds of ways. They certainly couldn't throw him out. Neither did they dare to make a great scene about that piano because even they dimly sensed, as I sensed, from so many thousands of miles away, that Sonny was at that piano playing for his life.

168   But he hadn't been going to school. One day a letter came from the school board, and Isabel's mother got it—there had, apparently, been other letters but Sonny had torn them up. This day, when Sonny came in, Isabel's mother showed him the letter and asked where he'd been spending his time. And she finally got it out of him that he'd been down in Greenwich Village, with musicians and other characters, in a white girl's apartment. And this scared her and she started to scream at him, and what came up, once she began—though she denies it to this day—was what sacrifices they were making to give Sonny a decent home and how little he appreciated it.

169   Sonny didn't play the piano that day. By evening, Isabel's mother had calmed down but then there was the old man to deal with, and Isabel herself. Isabel says she did her best to be calm but she broke down and

started crying. She says she just watched Sonny's face. She could tell, by watching him, what was happening with him. And what was happening was that they penetrated his cloud, they had reached him. Even if their fingers had been a thousand times more gentle than human fingers ever are, he could hardly help feeling that they had stripped him naked and were spitting on that nakedness. For he also had to see that his presence, that music, which was life or death to him, had been torture for them and that they had endured it, not at all for his sake, but only for mine. And Sonny couldn't take that. He can take it a little better today than he could then but he's still not very good at it and, frankly, I don't know anybody who is.

170   The silence of the next few days must have been louder than the sound of all the music ever played since time began. One morning, before she went to work, Isabel was in his room for something and she suddenly realized that all of his records were gone. And she knew for certain that he was gone. And he was. He went as far as the navy would carry him. He finally sent me a postcard from someplace in Greece, and that was the first I knew that Sonny was still alive. I didn't see him any more until we were both back in New York and the war had long been over.

171   He was a man by then, of course, but I wasn't willing to see it. He came by the house from time to time, but we fought almost every time we met. I didn't like the way he carried himself, loose and dreamlike all the time, and I didn't like his friends, and his music seemed to be merely an excuse for the life he led. It sounded just that weird and disordered.

172   Then we had a fight, a pretty awful fight, and I didn't see him for months. By and by I looked him up, where he was living, in a furnished room in the Village, and I tried to make it up. But there were lots of other people in the room, and Sonny just lay on his bed, and he wouldn't come downstairs with me, and he treated these other people as though they were his family and I weren't. So I got mad and then he got mad, and then I told him that he might just as well be dead as live the way he was living. Then he stood up and he told me not to worry about him any more in life, that he *was* dead as far as I was concerned. Then he pushed me to the door, and the other people looked on as though nothing were happening, and he slammed the door behind me. I stood in the hallway, staring at the door. I heard somebody laugh in the room and then the tears came to my eyes. I started down the steps, whistling to keep from crying, I kept whistling to myself, *You going to need me, baby, one of these cold, rainy days.*

173   I read about Sonny's trouble in the spring. Little Grace died in the fall. She was a beautiful little girl. But she only lived a little over two years. She died of polio and she suffered. She had a slight fever for a couple of days, but it didn't seem like anything and we just kept her in bed. And we would certainly have called the doctor, but the fever

dropped, she seemed to be all right. So we thought it had just been a cold. Then, one day, she was up, playing, Isabel was in the kitchen fixing lunch for the two boys when they'd come in from school, and she heard Grace fall down in the living room. When you have a lot of children you don't always start running when one of them falls, unless they start screaming or something. And, this time, Grace was quiet. Yet, Isabel says that when she heard that *thump* and then that silence, something happened in her to make her afraid. And she ran to the living room and there was little Grace on the floor, all twisted up, and the reason she hadn't screamed was that she couldn't get her breath. And when she did scream, it was the worst sound, Isabel says, that she'd ever heard in all her life, and she still hears it sometimes in her dreams. Isabel will sometimes wake me up with a low, moaning, strangled sound, and I have to be quick to awaken her and hold her to me and where Isabel is weeping against me seems a mortal wound.

174   I think I may have written Sonny the very day that little Grace was buried. I was sitting in the living room in the dark, by myself, and I suddenly thought of Sonny. My trouble made his real.

175   One Saturday afternoon, when Sonny had been living with us, or, anyway, been in our house, for nearly two weeks, I found myself wandering aimlessly about the living room, drinking from a can of beer, and trying to work up the courage to search Sonny's room. He was out, he was usually out whenever I was home, and Isabel had taken the children to see their grandparents. Suddenly I was standing still in front of the living-room window, watching Seventh Avenue. The idea of searching Sonny's room made me still. I scarcely dared to admit to myself what I'd be searching for. I didn't know what I'd do if I found it. Or if I didn't.

176   On the sidewalk across from me, near the entrance to a barbecue joint, some people were holding an old-fashioned revival meeting. The barbecue cook, wearing a dirty white apron, his conked hair reddish and metallic in the pale sun, and a cigarette between his lips, stood in the doorway, watching them. Kids and older people paused in their errands and stood there, along with some older men and a couple of very tough-looking women who watched everything that happened on the avenue, as though they owned it, or were maybe owned by it. Well, they were watching this, too. The revival was being carried on by three sisters in black, and a brother. All they had were their voices and their Bibles and a tambourine. The brother was testifying and while he testified two of the sisters stood together, seeming to say, Amen, and the third sister walked around with the tambourine outstretched and a couple of people dropped coins into it. Then the brother's testimony ended, and the sister who had been taking up the collection dumped the coins into her palm and transferred them to the pocket of her long black robe. Then she raised both hands, striking the tambourine against the air, and then against one hand, and she started to sing. And the two other sisters and the brother joined in.

177   It was strange, suddenly, to watch, though I had been seeing these street meetings all my life. So, of course, had everybody else down there. Yet, they paused and watched and listened and I stood still at the window. "*'Tis the old ship of Zion*," they sang, and the sister with the tambourine kept a steady, jangling beat, "*it has rescued many a thousand!*" Not a soul under the sound of their voices was hearing this song for the first time, not one of them had been rescued. Nor had they seen much in the way of rescue work being done around them. Neither did they especially believe in the holiness of the three sisters and the brother, they knew too much about them, knew where they lived, and how. The woman with the tambourine, whose voice dominated the air, whose face was bright with joy, was divided by very little from the woman who stood watching her, a cigarette between her heavy, chapped lips, her hair a cuckoo's nest, her face scarred and swollen from many beatings, and her black eyes glittering like coal. Perhaps they both knew this, which was why, when, as rarely, they addressed each other, they addressed each other as Sister. As the singing filled the air, the watching, listening·faces underwent a change, the eyes focusing on something within; the music seemed to soothe a poison out of them; and time seemed, nearly, to fall away from the sullen, belligerent, battered faces, as though they were fleeing back to their first condition, while dreaming of their last. The barbecue cook half shook his head and smiled, and dropped his cigarette and disappeared into his joint. A man fumbled in his pockets for change and stood holding it in his hand impatiently, as though he had just remembered a pressing appointment further up the avenue. He looked furious. Then I saw Sonny, standing on the edge of the crowd. He was carrying a wide, flat notebook with a green cover, and it made him look, from where I was standing, almost like a schoolboy. The coppery sun brought out the copper in his skin, he was very faintly smiling, standing very still. Then the singing stopped, the tambourine turned into a collection plate again. The furious man dropped in his coins and vanished, so did a couple of the women, and Sonny dropped some change in the plate, looking directly at the woman with a little smile. He started across the avenue, toward the house. He has a slow, loping walk, something like the way Harlem hipsters walk, only he's imposed on this his own half-beat. I had never really noticed it before.

178   I stayed at the window, both relieved and apprehensive. As Sonny disappeared from my sight, they began singing again. And they were still singing when his key turned in the lock.

179   "Hey," he said.

180   "Hey, yourself. You want some beer?"

181   "No. Well, maybe." But he came up to the window and stood beside me, looking out. "What a warm voice," he said.

182   They were singing *If I could only hear my mother pray again!*

183   "Yes," I said, "and she can sure beat that tambourine."

184   "But what a terrible song," he said, and laughed. He dropped his notebook on the sofa and disappeared into the kitchen. "Where's Isabel and the kids?"

185   "I think they went to see their grandparents. You hungry?"

186   "No." He came back into the living room with his can of beer. "You want to come someplace with me tonight?"

187   I sensed, I don't know how, that I couldn't possibly say no. "Sure. Where?"

188   He sat down on the sofa and picked up his notebook and started leafing through it. "I'm going to sit in with some fellows in a joint in the Village."

189   "You mean, you're going to play, tonight?"

190   "That's right." He took a swallow of his beer and moved back to the window. He gave me a sidelong look. "If you can stand it."

191   "I'll try," I said.

192   He smiled to himself, and we both watched as the meeting across the way broke up. The three sisters and the brother, heads bowed, were singing *God be with you till we meet again.* The faces around them were very quiet. Then the song ended. The small crowd dispersed. We watched the three women and the lone man walk slowly up the avenue.

193   "When she was singing before," said Sonny, abruptly, "her voice reminded me for a minute of what heroin feels like sometimes—when it's in your veins. It makes you feel sort of warm and cool at the same time. And distant. And—and sure." He sipped his beer, very deliberately not looking at me. I watched his face. "It makes you feel—in control. Sometimes you've got to have that feeling."

194   "Do you?" I sat down slowly in the easy chair.

195   "Sometimes." He went to the sofa and picked up his notebook again. "Some people do."

196   "In order," I asked, "to play?" And my voice was very ugly, full of contempt and anger.

197   "Well"—he looked at me with great, troubled eyes, as though, in fact, he hoped his eyes would tell me things he could never otherwise say—"they *think* so. And *if* they think so—!"

198   "And what do *you* think?" I asked.

199   He sat on the sofa and put his can of beer on the floor. "I don't know," he said, and I couldn't be sure if he were answering my question or pursuing his thoughts. His face didn't tell me. "It's not so much to *play*. It's to *stand* it, to be able to make it at all. On any level." He frowned and smiled: "In order to keep from shaking to pieces."

200   "But these friends of yours," I said, "they seem to shake themselves to pieces pretty goddamn fast."

201   "Maybe." He played with the notebook. And something told me that I should curb my tongue, that Sonny was doing his best to talk, that I should listen. "But of course you only know the ones that've gone to

pieces. Some don't—or at least they haven't *yet* and that's just about all *any* of us can say." He paused. "And then there are some who just live, really, in hell, and they know it and they see what's happening and they go right on. I don't know." He sighed, dropped the notebook, folded his arms. "Some guys, you can tell from the way they play, they on something *all* the time. And you can see that, well, it makes something real for them. But of course," he picked up his beer from the floor and sipped it and put the can down again, "they *want* to, too, you've got to see that. Even some of them that say they don't—*some*, not all."

202   "And what about you?" I asked—I couldn't help it. "What about you? Do *you* want to?"

203   He stood up and walked to the window and remained silent for a long time. Then he sighed. "Me," he said. Then: "While I was downstairs before, on my way here, listening to that woman sing, it struck me all of a sudden how much suffering she must have had to go through—to sing like that. It's *repulsive* to think you have to suffer that much."

204   I said: "But there's no way not to suffer—is there, Sonny?"

205   "I believe not," he said, and smiled, "but that's never stopped anyone from trying. He looked at me. "Has it?" I realized, with this mocking look, that there stood between us, forever, beyond the power of time or forgiveness, the fact that I had held silence—so long!—when he had needed human speech to help him. He turned back to the window. "No, there's no way not to suffer. But you try all kinds of ways to keep from drowning in it, to keep on top of it, and to make it seem—well, like *you*. Like you did something, all right, and now you're suffering for it. You know?" I said nothing. "Well you know," he said, impatiently, "why *do* people suffer? Maybe it's better to do something to give it a reason, *any* reason."

206   "But we just agreed," I said, "that there's no way not to suffer. Isn't it better, then, just to—take it?"

207   "But nobody just takes it," Sonny cried, "that's what I'm telling you! *Everybody* tries not to. You're just hung up on the *way* some people try—it's not *your* way!"

208   The hair on my face began to itch, my face felt wet. "That's not true," I said, "that's not true. I don't give a damn what other people do, I don't even care how they suffer. I just care how *you* suffer." And he looked at me. "Please believe me," I said, "I don't want to see you—die—trying not to suffer."

209   "I won't," he said, flatly, "die trying not to suffer. At least, not any faster than anybody else."

210   "But there's no need," I said, trying to laugh, "is there, in killing yourself?"

211   I wanted to say more, but I couldn't. I wanted to talk about will power and how life could be—well, beautiful. I wanted to say that it was

all within; but was it? Or, rather, wasn't that exactly the trouble? And I wanted to promise that I would never fail him again. But it would all have sounded—empty words and lies.

212   So I made the promise to myself and prayed that I would keep it.

213   "It's terrible sometimes, inside," he said, "that's what's the trouble. You walk these streets, black and funky and cold, and there's not really a living ass to talk to, and there's nothing shaking, and there's no way of getting it out—that storm inside. You can't talk it and you can't make love with it, and when you finally try to get with it and play it, you realize *nobody's* listening. So *you've* got to listen. You got to find a way to listen."

214   And then he walked away from the window and sat on the sofa again, as though all the wind had suddenly been knocked out of him. "Sometimes you'll do *anything* to play, even cut your mother's throat." He laughed and looked at me. "Or your brother's." Then he sobered. "Or your own." Then: "Don't worry. I'm all right now and I think I'll *be* all right. But I can't forget—where I've been. I don't mean just the physical place I've been, I mean where I've *been*. And *what* I've been."

215   "What have you been, Sonny?" I asked.

216   He smiled—but sat sideways on the sofa, his elbow resting on the back, his fingers playing with his mouth and chin, not looking at me. "I've been something I didn't recognize, didn't know I could be. Didn't know anybody could be." He stopped, looking inward, looking helplessly young, looking old. "I'm not talking about it now because I feel *guilty* or anything like that—maybe it would be better if I did, I don't know. Anyway, I can't really talk about it. Not to you, not to anybody." And now he turned and faced me. "Sometimes, you know, and it was actually when I was most out of the world, I felt that I was in it, that I was *with* it, really, and I could play or I didn't really have to *play*, it just came out of me, it was there. And I don't know how I played, thinking about it now, but I know I did awful things, those times, sometimes, to people. Or it wasn't that I *did* anything to them—it was that they weren't real." He picked up the beer can; it was empty; he rolled it between his palms: "And other times—well, I needed a fix, I needed to find a place to lean, I needed to clear a space to *listen*—and I couldn't find it, and I—went crazy, I did terrible things to *me*, I was terrible *for* me." He began pressing the beer can between his hands, I watched the metal begin to give. It glittered, as he played with it, like a knife, and I was afraid he would cut himself, but I said nothing. "Oh well. I can never tell you. I was all by myself at the bottom of something, stinking and sweating and crying and shaking, and I smelled it, you know? *My* stink, and I thought I'd die if I couldn't get away from it and yet, all the same, I knew that everything I was doing was just locking me in with it. And I didn't know," he paused, still flattening the beer can, "I didn't know, I still *don't* know, something kept telling me that maybe it was good to smell your own stink, but I didn't think that *that* was what

I'd been trying to do—and—who can stand it?" And he abruptly dropped the ruined beer can, looking at me with a small, still smile, and then rose, walking to the window as though it were the lodestone rock. I watched his face, he watched the avenue. "I couldn't tell you when Mama died—but the reason I wanted to leave Harlem so bad was to get away from drugs. And then, when I ran away, that's what I was running from—really. When I came back, nothing had changed, I hadn't changed, I was just—older." And he stopped, drumming with his fingers on the windowpane. The sun had vanished, soon darkness would fall. I watched his face. "It can come again," he said, almost as though speaking to himself. Then he turned to me. "It can come again," he repeated. "I just want you to know that."

217   "All right," I said at last. "So it can come again. All right."

218   He smiled, but the smile was sorrowful. "I had to try to tell you," he said.

219   "Yes," I said. "I understand that."

220   "You're my brother," he said, looking straight at me, and not smiling at all.

221   "Yes," I repeated, "yes. I understand that."

222   He turned back to the window, looking out. "All that hatred down there," he said, "all that hatred and misery and love. It's a wonder it doesn't blow the avenue apart."

223   We went to the only night club on a short, dark street, downtown. We squeezed through the narrow, chattering, jam-packed bar to the entrance of the big room, where the bandstand was. And we stood there for a moment, for the lights were very dim in this room and we couldn't see. Then, "Hello, boy," said a voice, and an enormous black man, much older than Sonny or myself, erupted out of all that atmospheric lighting and put an arm around Sonny's shoulder. "I been sitting right here," he said, "waiting for you."

224   He had a big voice, too, and heads in the darkness turned toward us.

225   Sonny grinned and pulled a little away, and said, "Creole, this is my brother. I told you about him."

226   Creole shook my hand. "I'm glad to meet you, son," he said, and it was clear that he was glad to meet me *there*, for Sonny's sake. And he smiled. "You got a real musician in *your* family," and he took his arm from Sonny's shoulder and slapped him, lightly, affectionately, with the back of his hand.

227   "Well. Now I've heard it all," said a voice behind us. This was another musician, and a friend of Sonny's, a coal-black, cheerful-looking man, built close to the ground. He immediately began confiding to me, at the top of his lungs, the most terrible things about Sonny, his teeth gleaming like a lighthouse and his laugh coming up out of him like the beginning of an earthquake. And it turned out that everyone at the bar knew Sonny, or almost everyone; some were musicians, working there, or nearby, or not working, some were simply hangers-on, and some were

there to hear Sonny play. I was introduced to all of them and they were all very polite to me. Yet, it was clear that, for them, I was only Sonny's brother. Here, I was in Sonny's world. Or, rather: his kingdom. Here, it was not even a question that his veins bore royal blood.

228   They were going to play soon, and Creole installed me, by myself, at a table in a dark corner. Then I watched them, Creole, and the little black man, and Sonny, and the others, while they horsed around, standing just below the bandstand. The light from the bandstand spilled just a little short of them and, watching them laughing and gesturing and moving about, I had the feeling that they, nevertheless, were being most careful not to step into that circle of light too suddenly: that if they moved into the light too suddenly, without thinking, they would perish in flame. Then, while I watched, one of them, the small, black man, moved into the light and crossed the bandstand and started fooling around with his drums. Then—being funny and being, also, extremely ceremonious—Creole took Sonny by the arm and led him to the piano. A woman's voice called Sonny's name, and a few hands started clapping. And Sonny, also being funny and being ceremonious, and so touched, I think, that he could have cried, but neither hiding it nor showing it, riding it like a man, grinned, and put both hands to his heart and bowed from the waist.

229   Creole then went to the bass fiddle and a lean, very bright-skinned brown man jumped up on the bandstand and picked up his horn. So there they were, and the atmosphere on the bandstand and in the room began to change and tighten. Someone stepped up to the microphone and announced them. Then there were all kinds of murmurs. Some people at the bar shushed others. The waitress ran around, frantically getting in the last orders, guys and chicks got closer to each other, and the lights on the bandstand, on the quartet, turned to a kind of indigo. Then they all looked different there. Creole looked about him for the last time, as though he were making certain that all his chickens were in the coop, and then he—jumped and struck the fiddle. And there they were.

230   All I know about music is that not many people ever really hear it. And even then, on the rare occasions when something opens within, and the music enters, what we mainly hear, or hear corroborated, are personal, private, vanishing evocations. But the man who creates the music is hearing something else, is dealing with the roar rising from the void and imposing order on it as it hits the air. What is evoked in him, then, is of another order, more terrible because it has no words, and triumphant, too, for that same reason. And his triumph, when he triumphs, is ours. I just watched Sonny's face. His face was troubled, he was working hard, but he wasn't with it. And I had the feeling that, in a way, everyone on the bandstand was waiting for him, both waiting for him and pushing him along. But as I began to watch Creole, I realized that it was Creole who held them all back. He had them on a short rein. Up there, keeping the beat with his whole body, wailing on the fiddle, with his eyes half

closed, he was listening to everything, but he was listening to Sonny. He was having a dialogue with Sonny. He wanted Sonny to leave the shore line and strike out for the deep water. He was Sonny's witness that deep water and drowning were not the same thing—he had been there, and he knew. And he wanted Sonny to know. He was waiting for Sonny to do the things on the keys which would let Creole know that Sonny was in the water.

231   And, while Creole listened, Sonny moved, deep within, exactly like someone in torment. I had never before thought of how awful the relationship must be between the musician and his instrument. He has to fill it, this instrument, with the breath of life, his own. He has to make it do what he wants it to do. And a piano is just a piano. It's made out of so much wood and wires and little hammers and big ones, and ivory. While there's only so much you can do with it, the only way to find this out is to try and make it do everything.

232   And Sonny hadn't been near a piano for over a year. And he wasn't on much better terms with his life, not the life that stretched before him now. He and the piano stammered, started one way, got scared, stopped; started another way, panicked, marked time, started again; then seemed to have found a direction, panicked again, got stuck. And the face I saw on Sonny I'd never seen before. Everything had been burned out of it, and, at the same time, things usually hidden were being burned in, by the fire and fury of the battle which was occurring in him up there.

233   Yet, watching Creole's face as they neared the end of the first set, I had the feeling that something had happened, something I hadn't heard. Then they finished, there was scattered applause, and then, without an instant's warning, Creole started into something else, it was almost sardonic, it was *Am I Blue*. And, as though he commanded, Sonny began to play. Something began to happen. And Creole let out the reins. The dry, low, black man said something awful on the drums, Creole answered, and the drums talked back. Then the horn insisted, sweet and high, slightly detached perhaps, and Creole listened, commenting now and then, dry, and driving, beautiful and calm and old. Then they all came together again, and Sonny was part of the family again. I could tell this from his face. He seemed to have found, right there beneath his fingers, a damn brand-new piano. It seemed that he couldn't get over it. Then, for a while, just being happy with Sonny, they seemed to be agreeing with him that brand-new pianos certainly were a gas.

234   Then Creole stepped forward to remind them that what they were playing was the blues. He hit something in all of them, he hit something in me, myself, and the music tightened and deepened, apprehension began to beat the air. Creole began to tell us what the blues were all about. They were not about anything very new. He and his boys up there were keeping it new, at the risk of ruin, destruction, madness, and death, in order to find new ways to make us listen. For, while the tale of how we suffer, and how we are delighted, and how we may triumph is never

new, it always must be heard. There isn't any other tale to tell, it's the only light we've got in all this darkness.

235   And this tale, according to that face, that body, those strong hands on those strings, has another aspect in every country, and a new depth in every generation. Listen, Creole seemed to be saying, listen. Now these are Sonny's blues. He made the little black man on the drums know it, and the bright, brown man on the horn. Creole wasn't trying any longer to get Sonny in the water. He was wishing him Godspeed. Then he stepped back, very slowly, filling the air with the immense suggestion that Sonny speak for himself.

236   Then they all gathered around Sonny, and Sonny played. Every now and again one of them seemed to say, Amen. Sonny's fingers filled the air with life, his life. But that life contained so many others. And Sonny went all the way back, he really began with the spare, flat statement of the opening phrase of the song. Then he began to make it his. It was very beautiful because it wasn't hurried and it was no longer a lament. I seemed to hear with what burning he had made it his, with what burning we had yet to make it ours, how we could cease lamenting. Freedom lurked around us and I understood, at last, that he could help us to be free if we would listen, that he would never be free until we did. Yet, there was no battle in his face now. I heard what he had gone through, and would continue to go through until he came to rest in earth. He had made it his: that long line, of which we knew only Mama and Daddy. And he was giving it back, as everything must be given back, so that, passing through death, it can live forever. I saw my mother's face again, and felt, for the first time, how the stones of the road she had walked on must have bruised her feet. I saw the moonlit road where my father's brother died. And it brought something else back to me, and carried me past it. I saw my little girl again and felt Isabel's tears again, and I felt my own tears begin to rise. And I was yet aware that this was only a moment, that the world waited outside, as hungry as a tiger, and that trouble stretched above us, longer than the sky.

237   Then it was over. Creole and Sonny let out their breath, both soaking wet, and grinning. There was a lot of applause and some of it was real. In the dark, the girl came by and I asked her to take drinks to the bandstand. There was a long pause, while they talked up there in the indigo light and after a while I saw the girl put a Scotch and milk on top of the piano for Sonny. He didn't seem to notice it, but just before they started playing again, he sipped from it and looked toward me, and nodded. Then he put it back on top of the piano. For me, then, as they began to play again, it glowed and shook above my brother's head like the very cup of trembling.

Study Questions

1. Why is this story narrated from the older brother's point of view rather than from Sonny's? What is conveyed from this perspective that couldn't be conveyed from Sonny's?
2. How do the brothers' differing reactions to the Indian way to wisdom serve to characterize them? Are their attitudes and actions in the rest of the story consistent with these reactions?
3. The long paragraph (94) in which Mama describes the death of her brother-in-law may be thought of as a descriptive or narrative essay. Why does Baldwin use short sentences in this paragraph? What kind of imagery predominates?
4. What is accomplished by the parallelism and repetition in the first paragraph?
5. What does the water metaphor in paragraph 230 express? Is this metaphor connected in any way with the ice metaphor used at the beginning of the story to describe the older brother's reaction to Sonny's drug addiction?

Jazz and the White Critic

Imamu Amiri Baraka (LeRoi Jones)

1   Most jazz critics have been white Americans, but most important jazz musicians have not been. This might seem a simple enough reality to most people, or at least a reality which can be readily explained in terms of the social and cultural history of American society. And it is obvious why there are only two or three fingers' worth of Negro critics or writers on jazz, say, if one understands that until relatively recently those Negroes who *could* become critics, who would largely have to come from the black middle class, have simply not been interested in the music. Or at least jazz, for the black middle class, has only comparatively recently lost some of its stigma (though by no means is it yet as popular among them as any vapid musical product that comes sanctioned by the taste of the white majority). Jazz was collected among the numerous skeletons the middle-class black man kept locked in the closet of his psyche, along with watermelons and gin, and whose rattling caused him no end of misery and self-hatred. As one Howard University philosophy professor said to me when I was an undergraduate, "It's fantastic how

much bad taste the blues contain!" But it is just this "bad taste" that this Uncle spoke of that has been the one factor that has kept the best of Negro music from slipping sterilely into the echo chambers of middle-brow American culture. And to a great extent such "bad taste" was kept extant in the music, blues or jazz, because the Negroes who were responsible for the best of the music, were always aware of their identities as black Americans and really did not, themselves, desire to become vague, featureless Americans as is usually the case with the Negro middle class. (This is certainly not to say that there have not been very important Negro musicians from the middle class. Since the Henderson era, their number has increased enormously in jazz.)

2   Negroes played jazz as they had sung blues or, even earlier, as they had shouted and hollered in those anonymous fields, because it was one of the few areas of human expression available to them. Negroes who felt the blues, later jazz, impulse, as a specific means of expression, went naturally into the music itself. There were fewer social or extra-expressive considerations that could possibly disqualify any prospective Negro jazz musician than existed, say, for a Negro who thought he might like to become a writer (or even an elevator operator, for that matter). Any Negro who had some ambition towards literature, in the earlier part of this century, was likely to have developed so powerful an allegiance to the sacraments of middle-class American culture that he would be horrified by the very idea of writing about jazz.

3   There were few "jazz critics" in America at all until the 30's and then they were influenced to a large extent by what Richard Hadlock has called "the carefully documented gee-whiz attitude" of the first serious European jazz critics. They were also, as a matter of course, influenced more deeply by the social and cultural mores of their own society. And it is only natural that their criticism, whatever its intention, should be a product of that society, or should reflect at least some of the attitudes and thinking of that society, even if not directly related to the subject they were writing about, Negro music.

4   Jazz, as a Negro music, existed, up until the time of the big bands, on the same socio-cultural level as the sub-culture from which it was issued. The music and its sources were *secret* as far as the rest of America was concerned, in much the same sense that the actual life of the black man in America was secret to the white American. The first white critics were men who sought, whether consciously or not, to understand this secret, just as the first serious white jazz musicians (Original Dixieland Jazz Band, Bix, etc.) sought not only to understand the phenomenon of Negro music but to appropriate it as a means of expression which they themselves might utilize. The success of this "appropriation" signaled the existence of an American music, where before there was a Negro music. But the white jazz musician had an advantage the white critics seldom had. The white musician's commitment to jazz, the *ultimate concern,* proposed that the sub-cultural attitudes that produced the

music as a profound expression of human feelings, could be *learned* and need not be passed on as a secret blood rite. And Negro music is essentially the expression of an attitude, or a collection of attitudes, about the world, and only secondarily an attitude about the way music is made. The white jazz musician came to understand this attitude as a way of making music, and the intensity of his understanding produced the "great" white jazz musicians, and is producing them now.

5   Usually the critic's commitment was first to his *appreciation* of the music rather than to his understanding of the attitude which produced it. This difference meant that the potential critic of jazz had only to appreciate the music, or what he thought was the music, and that he did not need to understand or even be concerned with the attitudes that produced it, except perhaps as a purely sociological consideration. This last idea is certainly what produced the reverse patronization that is known as Crow Jim. The disparaging "all you folks got rhythm" is no less a stereotype, simply because it is proposed as a positive trait. But this Crow Jim attitude has not been as menacing or as evident a flaw in critical writing about jazz as has another manifestation of the white critic's failure to concentrate on the blues and jazz attitude rather than his conditioned appreciation of the music. The major flaw in this approach to Negro music is that it strips the music too ingenuously of its social and cultural intent. It seeks to define jazz as an art (or a folk art) that has come out of no intelligent body of socio-cultural philosophy.

6   We take for granted the social and cultural milieu and philosophy that produced Mozart. As western people, the socio-cultural thinking of eighteenth-century Europe comes to us as a history legacy that is a continuous and organic part of the twentieth-century West. The socio-cultural philosophy of the Negro in America (as a continuous historical phenomenon) is no less specific and no less important for any intelligent critical speculation about the music that came out of it. And again, this is not a plea for narrow sociological analysis of jazz, but rather that this music cannot be completely understood (in critical terms) without some attention to the attitudes which produced it. It is the philosophy of Negro music that is most important, and this philosophy is only partially the result of the sociological disposition of Negroes in America. There is, of course, much more to it than that.

7   Strict musicological analysis of jazz, which has come into favor recently, is also as limited as a means of jazz criticism as a strict sociological approach. The notator of any jazz solo, or blues, has no chance of capturing what in effect are the most important elements of the music. (Most transcriptions of blues lyrics are just as frustrating.) A printed musical example of an Armstrong solo, or of a Thelonius Monk solo, tells us almost nothing except the futility of formal musicology when dealing with jazz. Not only are the various jazz effects almost impossible to notate, but each note *means something* quite in adjunct to musical notation. The notes of a jazz solo exist in a notation strictly for musical

390 Man, Play, and Creativity

reasons. The notes of a jazz solo, as they are coming into existence, exist as they do for reasons that are only concomitantly musical. Coltrane's cries are not "musical," but they *are* music and quite moving music. Ornette Coleman's screams and rants are only musical once one understands the music his emotional attitude seeks to create. This attitude is real, and perhaps the most singularly important aspect of his music. Mississippi Joe Williams, Snooks Eaglin, Lightnin' Hopkins have different emotional attitudes than Ornette Coleman, but all of these attitudes are continuous parts of the historical and cultural biography of the Negro as it has existed and developed since there was a Negro in America, and a music that could be associated with him that did not exist anywhere else in the world. The note *means something;* and the something is, regardless of its stylistic considerations, part of the black psyche as it dictates the various forms of Negro culture.

8   Another hopeless flaw in a great deal of the writing about jazz that has been done over the years is that in most cases the writers, the jazz critics, have been anything but intellectuals (in the most complete sense of that word). Most jazz critics began as hobbyists or boyishly brash members of the American petit bourgeoisie, whose only claim to any understanding about the music was that they knew it was *different;* or else they had once been brave enough to make a trip into a Negro slum to hear their favorite instrumentalist defame Western musical tradition. Most jazz critics were (and are) not only white middle-class Americans, but middle-brows as well. The irony here is that because the majority of jazz critics are white middle-brows, most jazz criticism tends to enforce white middle-brow standards of excellence as criteria for performance of a music that in its most profound manifestations is completely antithetical to such standards; in fact, quite often is in direct reaction against them. (As an analogy, suppose the great majority of the critics of Western formal music were poor, "uneducated" Negroes?) A man can speak of the "heresy of bebop" for instance, only if he is completely unaware of the psychological catalysts that made that music the exact registration of the social and cultural thinking of a whole generation of black Americans. The blues and jazz aesthetic, to be fully understood, must be seen in as nearly its complete human context as possible. People made bebop. The question the critic must ask is: *why?* But it is just this *why* of Negro music that has been consistently ignored or misunderstood; and it is a question that cannot be adequately answered without first understanding the necessity of asking it. Contemporary jazz during the last few years has begun to take on again some of the anarchy and excitement of the bebop years. The cool and hard bop/funk movements since the 40's seem pitifully tame, even decadent, when compared to the music men like Ornette Coleman, Sonny Rollins, John Coltrane, Cecil Taylor and some others have been making recently. And of the bop pioneers, only Thelonius Monk has managed to maintain without question the vicious creativity with which he first entered the jazz scene back in the 40's. The music has changed again, for many of the same basic reasons it changed

twenty years ago. Bop was, at a certain level of consideration, a reaction by young musicians against the sterility and formality of Swing as it moved to become a formal part of the mainstream American culture. The New Thing, as recent jazz has been called, is, to a large degree, a reaction to the hard bop-funk-groove-soul camp, which itself seemed to come into being in protest against the squelching of most of the blues elements in cool and progressive jazz. Funk (groove, soul) has become as formal and clichéd as cool or swing, and opportunities for imaginative expression within that form have dwindled almost to nothing.

9   The attitudes and emotional philosophy contained in "the new music" must be isolated and understood by critics before any consideration of the *worth* of the music can be legitimately broached. Later on, of course, it becomes relatively easy to characterize the emotional penchants that informed earlier aesthetic statements. After the fact, is a much simpler way to work and think. For example, a writer who wrote liner notes for a John Coltrane record mentioned how difficult it had been for him to appreciate Coltrane earlier, just as it had been difficult for him to appreciate Charlie Parker when he first appeared. To quote: "I wish I were one of those sages who can say, 'Man, I dug Bird the first time I heard him.' I didn't. The first time I heard Charlie Parker, I thought he was ridiculous . . ." Well, that's a noble confession and all, but the responsibility is still the writer's and in no way involves Charlie Parker or what he was trying to do. When that writer first heard Parker he simply did not understand *why* Bird should play the way he did, nor could it have been very important to him. But now, of course, it becomes almost a form of reverse snobbery to say that one did not think Parker's music was worth much at first hearing, etc. etc. The point is, it seems to me, that if the music is worth something now, it must have been worth something then. Critics are supposed to be people in a position to tell what is of value and what is not, and, hopefully, at the time it first appears. If they are consistently mistaken, what is their value?

10   Jazz criticism, certainly as it has existed in the United States, has served in a great many instances merely to obfuscate what has actually been happening with the music itself—the pitiful harangues that raged during the 40's between two "schools" of critics as to which was the "real jazz," the new or the traditional, provide some very ugly examples. A critic who praises Bunk Johnson at Dizzy Gillespie's expense is no critic at all; but then neither is a man who turns it around and knocks Bunk to swell Dizzy. If such critics would (or could) reorganize their thinking so that they begin their concern for these musicians by trying to understand why each played the way he did, and in terms of the constantly evolving and redefined philosophy which has informed the most profound examples of Nego music throughout its history, then such thinking would be impossible.

11   It has never ceased to amaze and infuriate me that in the 40's a European critic could be arrogant and unthinking enough to inform serious young American musicians that what they were feeling (a con-

sideration that exists before, and without, the music) was false. What had happened was that even though the white middle-brow critic had known about Negro music for only about three decades, he was already trying to formalize and finally institutionalize it. It is a hideous idea. The music was already in danger of being forced into that junk pile of admirable objects and data the West knows as *culture.*

12   Recently, the same attitudes have become more apparent in the face of a fresh redefinition of the form and content of Negro music. Such phrases as "anti-jazz" have been used to describe musicians who are making the most exciting music produced in this country. But as critic A. B. Spellman asked, "What does anti-jazz mean and who are these ofays who've appointed themselves guardians of last year's blues?" It is that simple, really. What does anti-jazz mean? And who coined the phrase? What is the definition of jazz? And who was authorized to make one?

13   Reading a great deal of old jazz criticism is usually like boning up on the social and cultural malaise that characterizes and delineates the bourgeois philistine in America. Even rereading someone as intelligent as Roger Pryor Dodge in the old *Record Changer* ("Jazz: its rise and decline," 1955) usually makes me either very angry or very near hysterical. Here is a sample: ". . . let us say flatly that there is no future in preparation for jazz through Bop . . . ," or, "The Boppists, Cools, and Progressives are surely stimulating a dissolution within the vagaries of a non-jazz world. The Revivalists, on the other hand have made a start in the right direction." It sounds almost like political theory. Here is Don C. Haynes in the April 22, 1946 issue of *Down Beat,* reviewing Charlie Parker's *Billie's Bounce* and *Now's The Time:* "These two sides are bad taste and ill-advised fanaticism. . . ." and, "This is the sort of stuff that has thrown innumerable impressionable young musicians out of stride, that has harmed many of them irreparably. This can be as harmful to jazz as Sammy Kaye." It makes you blush.

14   Of course there have been a few very fine writers on jazz, even as there are today. Most of them have been historians. But the majority of popular jazz criticism has been on about the same level as the quoted examples. Nostalgia, lack of understanding or failure to see the validity of redefined emotional statements which reflect the changing psyche of the Negro in opposition to what the critic might think the Negro ought to feel; all these unfortunate failures have been built many times into a kind of critical stance or aesthetic. An aesthetic whose standards and measure are connected irrevocably to the continuous gloss most white Americans have always made over Negro life in America. Failure to understand, for instance, that Paul Desmond and John Coltrane represent not only two very divergent ways of thinking about music, but more importantly two very different ways of viewing the world, is at the seat of most of the established misconceptions that are daily palmed off as intelligent commentary on jazz or jazz criticism. The catalysts and neces-

sity of Coltrane's music must be understood as they exist even before they are expressed as music. The music is the result of the attitude, the stance. Just as Negroes made blues and other people did not because of the Negro's peculiar way of looking at the world. Once this attitude is delineated as a continuous though constantly evolving social philosophy directly attributable to the way the Negro responds to the psychological landscape that is his Western environment, criticism of Negro music will move closer to developing as consistent and valid an aesthetic as criticism in other fields of Western art.

15   There have been so far only two American playwrights, Eugene O'Neill and Tennessee Williams, who are as profound or as important to the history of ideas as Louis Armstrong, Bessie Smith, Duke Ellington, Charlie Parker or Ornette Coleman, yet there is a more valid and consistent body of dramatic criticism written in America than there is a body of criticism about Negro music. And this is simply because there is an intelligent tradition and body of dramatic criticism, though it has largely come from Europe, that any intelligent American drama critic can draw on. In jazz criticism, no reliance on European tradition or theory will help at all. Negro music, like the Negro himself, is strictly an American phenomenon, and we have got to set up standards of judgment and aesthetic excellence that depend on our native knowledge and understanding of the underlying philosophies and local cultural references that produced blues and jazz in order to produce valid critical writing or commentary about it. It might be that there is still time to start.

Study Questions

1. Explain the significance of the words *skeletons, watermelons, gin,* and *Uncle* in the first paragraph.
2. Identify the paradox in the first paragraph.
3. How does the two-part definition of Negro music in the fourth paragraph contribute to the argument as a whole?
4. According to Baraka, what are the function and value of critics?
5. Why does Baraka use italics where he does?

Piano and Drums

Gabriel Okara

When at break of day at a riverside
I hear jungle drums telegraphing
the mystic rhythm, urgent, raw
like bleeding flesh, speaking of
primal youth and the beginning,
I see the panther ready to pounce,
the leopard snarling about to leap
and the hunters crouch with spears poised;

And my blood ripples, turns torrent,
topples the years and at once I'm   10
in my mother's laps a suckling;
at once I'm walking simple
paths with no innovations,
rugged, fashioned with the naked
warmth of hurrying feet and groping hearts
in green leaves and wild flowers pulsing.

Then I hear a wailing piano
solo speaking of complex ways
in tear-furrowed concerto;
of far away lands   20
and new horizons with
coaxing diminuendo, counterpoint,
crescendo. But lost in the labyrinth
of its complexities, it ends in the middle
of a phrase at a daggerpoint.

And I lost in the morning mist
of an age at a riverside keep
wandering in the mystic rhythm
of jungle drums and the concerto.

Study Questions

1. What device divides this poem into two structural sections? What are the differences in language and perception in these two sections?
2. Explain the significance of the figurative "wailing piano" and the "tear-furrowed concerto."
3. Can you apply Imamu Amiri Baraka's definition of Negro music (". . . essentially the expression of an attitude, or a collection of attitudes, about the world . . .") to the attitude implicit in this poem?
4. What does Okara mean by "*groping* hearts" and "wild flowers *pulsing*"?

Ode on a Grecian Urn

John Keats

1

Thou still unravished bride of quietness,
   Thou foster-child of silence and slow time,
Sylvan historian, who canst thus express
   A flowery tale more sweetly than our rhyme:
What leaf-fringed legend haunts about thy shape
   Of deities or mortals, or of both,
     In Tempe or the dales of Arcady?
   What men or gods are these? What maidens loath?
What mad pursuit? What struggle to escape?
     What pipes and timbrels? What wild ecstasy?   10

2

Heard melodies are sweet, but those unheard
   Are sweeter; therefore, ye soft pipes, play on;
Not to the sensual ear, but, more endeared,
   Pipe to the spirit ditties of no tone:

Fair youth, beneath the trees, thou canst not leave
  Thy song, nor ever can those trees be bare;
    Bold Lover, never, never canst thou kiss,
Though winning near the goal—yet, do not grieve;
    She cannot fade, though thou hast not thy bliss,
  Forever wilt thou love, and she be fair!   20

3

Ah, happy, happy boughs! that cannot shed
  Your leaves, nor ever bid the Spring adieu;
And, happy melodist, unwearièd,
  Forever piping songs forever new;
More happy love! more happy, happy love!
  Forever warm and still to be enjoyed,
    Forever panting, and forever young;
All breathing human passion far above,
  That leaves a heart high-sorrowful and cloyed,
    A burning forehead, and a parching tongue.   30

4

Who are these coming to the sacrifice?
  To what green altar, O mysterious priest,
Lead'st thou that heifer lowing at the skies,
  And all her silken flanks with garlands dressed?
What little town by river or sea shore,
  Or mountain-built with peaceful citadel,
    Is emptied of this folk, this pious morn?
And, little town, thy streets for evermore
  Will silent be; and not a soul to tell
    Why thou art desolate, can e'er return.   40

5

O Attic shape! Fair attitude! with brede
  Of marble men and maidens overwrought,
With forest branches and the trodden weed;
  Thou, silent form, dost tease us out of thought
As doth eternity: Cold Pastoral!
  When old age shall this generation waste,
    Thou shalt remain, in midst of other woe

Than ours, a friend to man, to whom thou say'st,
"Beauty is truth, truth beauty,—that is all
     Ye know on earth, and all ye need to know."   50

Study Questions

1. What is the urn's relationship to time?
2. What is the subject of each of the five stanzas, and how does each relate to the conclusion in the last couplet?
3. What three metaphors refer to the urn in lines 1–3? What connotations do they contribute?
4. Account for the variations in the rhyme scheme from stanza to stanza.
5. How effective is Keats's use of apostrophe?

Anecdote of the Jar

Wallace Stevens

I placed a jar in Tennessee,
And round it was, upon a hill.
It made the slovenly wilderness
Surround that hill.

The wilderness rose up to it,
And sprawled around, no longer wild.
The jar was round upon the ground
And tall and of a port in air.

It took dominion everywhere.
The jar was gray and bare.   10
It did not give of bird or bush,
Like nothing else in Tennessee.

Study Questions

1. What is the relationship of the jar to the wilderness surrounding it?
2. Why does the poet use internal rhyme in "round upon the ground"? What variations on *round* does Stevens use, and what does he accomplish by so doing?
3. How is color used in the third stanza?
4. Does this poem state the same relationship between life and art that Keats's "Ode on a Grecian Urn" states? Explain.
5. How does Stevens use *round* in line 7, and *give* in line 11?

Musée des Beaux Arts

W. H. Auden

About suffering they were never wrong,
The Old Masters: how well they understood
Its human position; how it takes place
While someone else is eating or opening a window or just walking
       dully along;
How, when the aged are reverently, passionately waiting
For the miraculous birth, there always must be
Children who did not specially want it to happen, skating
On a pond at the edge of the wood:
They never forgot
That even the dreadful martyrdom must run its course   10
Anyhow in a corner, some untidy spot
Where the dogs go on with their doggy life and the torturer's horse
Scratches its innocent behind on a tree.

In Brueghel's *Icarus,* for instance: how everything turns away
Quite leisurely from the disaster; the ploughman may
Have heard the splash, the forsaken cry,
But for him it was not an important failure; the sun shone
As it had to on the white legs disappearing into the green

Water; and the expensive delicate ship that must have seen
Something amazing, a boy falling out of the sky,   20
Had somewhere to get to and sailed calmly on.

Study Questions

1. Like the poems by Keats and Stevens, this poem describes the human realities
   in art. For Keats and Stevens, the subjects are a Grecian urn and a gray jar; for
   Auden, the subject is Peter Brueghel the Elder's "Landscape with the Fall of
   Icarus." What is the "human position" of suffering depicted in this painting?
2. Upon what contrasts is the poem built? Consider, for instance, "the aged" and
   "children," "dreadful martyrdom" and "untidy spot/Where the dogs go on with
   their doggy life."
3. What is the grammatical parallelism of the sentences in the first stanza?
4. Why does Auden vary from standard English word order in his first sentence?
5. What is the effect of "sailed calmly on" in the last line?

How to Tell a Major Poet from a Minor Poet

E. B. White

1   Among the thousands of letters which I received two years ago from
people thanking me for my article "How to Drive the New Ford" were
several containing the request that I "tell them how to distinguish a
major poet from a minor poet." It is for these people that I have prepared
the following article, knowing that only through one's ability to distinguish a major poet from a minor poet may one hope to improve one's
appreciation of, or contempt for, poetry itself.

2   Take the first ten poets that come into your head—the list might run
something like this: Robert Frost, Arthur Guiterman, Edgar Lee Masters,

Dorothy Parker, Douglas Fairbanks, Jr., Stephen Vincent Benét, Edwin Arlington Robinson, Lorraine Fay, Berton Braley, Edna St. Vincent Millay. Can you tell, quickly and easily, which are major and which minor? Or suppose you were a hostess and a poet were to arrive unexpectedly at your party—could you introduce him properly: "This is Mr. Lutbeck, the major poet," or "This is Mr. Schenk, the minor poet"? More likely you would have to say merely: "This is Mr. Masefield, the poet"—an embarrassing situation for both poet and hostess alike.

3   All poetry falls into two classes: serious verse and light verse. Serious verse is verse written by a major poet; light verse is verse written by a minor poet. To distinguish the one from the other, one must have a sensitive ear and a lively imagination. Broadly speaking, a major poet may be told from a minor poet in two ways: (1) by the character of the verse, (2) by the character of the poet. (Note: it is not always advisable to go into the character of the poet.)

4   As to the verse itself, let me state a few elementary rules. Any poem starting with "And when" is a serious poem written by a major poet. To illustrate—here are the first two lines of a serious poem easily distinguished by the "And when":

> And when, in earth's forgotten moment, I
> Unbound the cord to which the soul was bound . . .

5   Any poem, on the other hand, ending with "And how" comes under the head of light verse, written by a minor poet. Following are the *last* two lines of a "light" poem, instantly identifiable by the terminal phrase:

> Placing his lips against her brow
> He kissed her eyelids shut. And how.

All poems of the latter type are what I call "light by degrees"—that is, they bear evidences of having once been serious, but the last line has been altered. The above couplet, for example, was unquestionably part of a serious poem which the poet wrote in 1916 while at Dartmouth, and originally ended:

> Placing his lips against her brow
> He kissed her eyelids shut enow.

It took fourteen years of knocking around the world before he saw how the last line could be revised to make the poem suitable for publication.

6   While the subject-matter of a poem does not always enable the reader to classify it, he can often pick up a strong clue. Suppose, for instance, you were to run across a poem beginning:

> When I went down to the corner grocer
> He asked would I like a bottle of Welch's grape juice
> And I said, "No, Sir."

You will know that it is a minor poem because it deals with a trademarked product. If the poem continues in this vein:

> "Then how would you like a package of Jello,
> A can of Del Monte peaches, some Grape Nuts,
> And a box of Rinso—
> Or don't you thin' so?"

you may be reasonably sure not only that the verse is "light" verse but that the poet has established some good contacts and is getting along nicely.

7   And now we come to the use of the word "rue" as a noun. All poems containing the word "rue" as a noun are serious. This word, rhyming as it does with "you," "true," "parvenu," "emu," "cock-a-doodle-doo," and thousands of other words, and occupying as it does a distinguished place among nouns whose meaning is just a shade unclear to most people— this word, I say, is the sort without which a major poet could not struggle along. It is the hallmark of serious verse. No minor poet dares use it, because his very minority carries with it the obligation to be a little more explicit. There are times when he would like to use "rue," as, for instance, when he is composing a poem in the A. E. Housman manner:

> When drums were heard in Pelham,
>   The soldier's eyes were blue,
> But I came back through Scarsdale,
>   And oh the . . .

8   Here the poet would like to get in the word "rue" because it has the right sound, but he doesn't dare.

9   So much for the character of the verse. Here are a few general rules about the poets themselves. All poets who, when reading from their own works, experience a choked feeling, are major. For that matter, all poets who read from their own works are major, whether they choke or not. All women poets, dead or alive, who smoke cigars are major. All poets who have sold a sonnet for one hundred and twenty-five dollars to a magazine with a paid circulation of four hundred thousand are major. A sonnet is composed of fourteen lines; thus the payment in this case is eight dollars and ninety-three cents a line, which constitutes a poet's majority. (It also indicates that the editor has probably been swept off his feet.)

10   All poets whose work appears in "The Conning Tower" of the *World* are minor, because the *World* is printed on uncoated stock— which is offensive to major poets. All poets named Edna St. Vincent Millay are major.

11   All poets who submit their manuscripts through an agent are major. These manuscripts are instantly recognized as serious verse. They come enclosed in a manila folder accompanied by a letter from the agent: "Dear Mr. ———: Here is a new group of Miss McGroin's poems, called 'Seven Poems.' We think they are the most important she has done yet,

and hope you will like them as much as we do." Such letters make it a comparatively simple matter for an editor to distinguish between serious and light verse, because of the word "important."

12   Incidentally, letters from poets who submit their work directly to a publication without the help of an agent are less indicative but are longer. Usually they are intimate, breezy affairs, that begin by referring to some previously rejected poem that the editor has forgotten about. They begin: "Dear Mr. ————: Thanks so much for your friendly note. I have read over 'Invulnerable' and I think I see your point, although in line 8 the word 'hernia' is, I insist, the only word to quite express the mood. At any rate, here are two new offerings, 'Thrush-Bound' and 'The Hill,' both of which are rather timely. I suppose you know that Vivien and I have rented the most amusing wee house near the outskirts of Sharon—it used to be a well-house and the well still takes up most of the living-room. We are as poor as church mice but Vivien says, etc., etc."

13   A poet who, in a roomful of people, is noticeably keeping at a little distance and "seeing into" things is a major poet. This poet commonly writes in unrhymed six-foot and seven-foot verse, beginning something like this:

> When, once, finding myself alone in a gathering of people,
> I stood, a little apart, and through the endless confusion of voices. . . .

This is a major poem and you needn't give it a second thought.

14   There are many more ways of telling a major poet from a minor poet, but I think I have covered the principal ones. The truth is, it is fairly easy to tell the two types apart; it is only when one sets about trying to decide whether what they write is any good or not that the thing really becomes complicated.

Study Questions

1. Some readers feel that White's introduction and conclusion are too pat, or not subtle enough. Comment.
2. What incongruity lends humor to the introductory paragraph?
3. Is distinguishing a major poet from a minor poet really the point of White's remarks? Consider the last line of the essay.
4. How has White used brand names, surnames, and social stereotypes to satirize the request stated in the first paragraph?

Kubla Khan

Samuel Taylor Coleridge

In Xanadu did Kubla Khan
A stately pleasure-dome decree:
Where Alph, the sacred river, ran
Through caverns measureless to man
   Down to a sunless sea.
So twice five miles of fertile ground
With walls and towers were girdled round:
And here were gardens bright with sinuous rills,
Where blossomed many an incense-bearing tree;
And here were forests ancient as the hills,   10
Enfolding sunny spots of greenery.

But oh! that deep romantic chasm which slanted
Down the green hill athwart a cedarn cover!
A savage place! as holy and enchanted
As e'er beneath a waning moon was haunted
By woman wailing for her demon-lover!
And from this chasm, with ceaseless turmoil seething,
As if this earth in fast thick pants were breathing,
A mighty fountain momently was forced:
Amid whose swift half-intermitted burst   20
Huge fragments vaulted like rebounding hail,
Or chaffy grain beneath the thresher's flail:
And 'mid these dancing rocks at once and ever
It flung up momently the sacred river.
Five miles meandering with a mazy motion
Through wood and dale the sacred river ran,
Then reached the caverns measureless to man,
And sank in tumult to a lifeless ocean:
And 'mid this tumult Kubla heard from far
Ancestral voices prophesying war!   30
   The shadow of the dome of pleasure
    Floated midway on the waves;
    Where was heard the mingled measure
    From the fountain and the caves.
It was a miracle of rare device,
A sunny pleasure-dome with caves of ice!

A damsel with a dulcimer
In a vision once I saw:
It was an Abyssinian maid,
And on her dulcimer she played,   40
Singing of Mount Abora.
Could I revive within me
Her symphony and song,
To such a deep delight 'twould win me.
That with music loud and long,
I would build that dome in air,
That sunny dome! those caves of ice!
And all who heard should see them there,
And all should cry, Beware! Beware!
His flashing eyes, his floating hair!   50
Weave a circle round him thrice,
And close your eyes with holy dread,
For he on honey-dew hath fed,
And drunk the milk of Paradise.

Study Questions

1. On a manuscript copy of this poem, Coleridge wrote: "This fragment, with a good deal more, not recoverable, composed, in a sort of Reverie brought on by two grains of Opium, taken a check a dysentery . . . in the fall of the year, 1797." What qualities or sounds might indicate that this poem is a dream vision?

2. In his preface to "Kubla Khan," Coleridge described himself as falling asleep just when he was reading the following in Samuel Purchas's *Purchase His Pilgrimage* (1613): "In Xamdu did Cublai Can build a stately Palace, encompassing sixteene miles of plaine ground with a wall, wherein are fertile meddowes, pleasant Springs, delightful Streames, and all sorts of beasts of chase and game, and in the midst thereof a sumptuous house of pleasure." How does the poem vary from this description? Upon what major object does it focus? Is the object real or figurative?

3. What does the simile "like rebounding hail" signify?

4. What is the effect of the alliteration in the line, "Five miles meandering with a mazy motion"?

5. What are the three structural divisions of the poem, and how are they related to each other?

6. If this poem can be read as a personal statement, what is Coleridge's attitude toward the poet?

For Black Poets Who Think of Suicide

Etheridge Knight

Black Poets should live—not leap
From steel bridges (like the white boys do).
Black Poets should live—not lay
Their necks on railroad tracks (like the white boys do).
Black Poets should seek—but not search too much
In sweet dark caves, nor hunt for snipes
Down psychic trails (like the white boys do).

For Black Poets belong to Black People. Are
The Flutes of Black Lovers. Are
The Organs of Black Sorrows. Are   10
The Trumpets of Black Warriors.
Let all Black Poets die as trumpets,
And be buried in the dust of marching feet.

Study Questions

1. What rhetorical and grammatical features mark the structural divisions of this poem?
2. What is *antithesis*? Explain the loose kind of antithesis used in the first stanza.
3. How do alliteration and the refrain bind the first stanza together?
4. By what means does the poet achieve assertiveness in the second stanza? How does the shift in mood contribute to this assertiveness?
5. How does the injunction in the last two lines relate to the imagery in the second stanza?

On First Looking into Chapman's Homer

John Keats

Much have I travelled in the realms of gold,
  And many goodly states and kingdoms seen;
  Round many western islands have I been
Which bards in fealty to Apollo hold.
Oft of one wide expanse had I been told
  That deep-browed Homer ruled as his demesne;
  Yet did I never breathe its pure serene
Till I heard Chapman speak out loud and bold:
Then felt I like some watcher of the skies
  When a new planet swims into his ken;   10
Or like stout Cortez when with eagle eyes
  He stared at the Pacific—and all his men
Looked at each other with a wild surmise—
  Silent, upon a peak in Darien.

Study Questions

1. What is the subject of the octet of this sonnet? Of the sestet? How are the two related?
2. In his sonnet Keats describes his artistic perception of George Chapman's translation of Homer's poetry. Try to describe Keats's feelings in a single declarative sentence.
3. Identify and comment upon the grammatical construction of "its pure serene."
4. Why does the poet allude to Apollo?
5. Knowing that Cortez did not discover the Pacific, what is your attitude toward Keats's error? Should it affect your appreciation of the poem?

The Lady of Shalott

Alfred, Lord Tennyson

Part I

On either side the river lie
Long fields of barley and of rye,
That clothe the wold and meet the sky;
And thro' the field the road runs by
   To many-tower'd Camelot;
And up and down the people go,
Gazing where the lilies blow
Round an island there below,
   The island of Shalott.

Willows whiten, aspens quiver,   10
Little breezes dusk and shiver
Thro' the wave that runs for ever
By the island in the river
   Flowing down to Camelot.
Four gray walls, and four gray towers,
Overlook a space of flowers,
And the silent isle imbowers
   The Lady of Shalott.

By the margin, willow-veil'd,
Slide the heavy barges trail'd   20
By slow horses; and unhail'd
The shallop flitteth silken-sail'd
   Skimming down to Camelot:
But who hath seen her wave her hand?
Or at the casement seen her stand?
Or is she known in all the land,
   The Lady of Shalott?

Only reapers, reaping early
In among the bearded barley,
Hear a song that echoes cheerly   30
From the river winding clearly,
   Down to tower'd Camelot;

And by the moon the reaper weary,
Piling sheaves in uplands airy,
Listening, whispers "'Tis the fairy
   Lady of Shalott."

Part II

There she weaves by night and day
A magic web with colors gay.
She has heard a whisper say,
A curse is on her if she stay
   To look down to Camelot.   40
She knows not what the curse may be,
And so she weaveth steadily,
And little other care hath she,
   The Lady of Shalott.

And moving thro' a mirror clear
That hangs before her all the year,
Shadows of the world appear.
There she sees the highway near
   Winding down to Camelot;   50
There the river eddy whirls,
And there the surly village-churls,
And the red cloaks of market girls,
   Pass onward from Shalott.

Sometimes a troop of damsels glad,
An abbot on an ambling pad,
Sometimes a curly shepherd-lad,
Or long-hair'd page in crimson clad,
   Goes by to tower'd Camelot;
And sometimes thro' the mirror blue   60
The knights come riding two and two:
She hath no loyal knight and true,
   The Lady of Shalott.

But in her web she still delights
To weave the mirror's magic sights,
For often thro' the silent nights
A funeral, with plumes and lights
   And music, went to Camelot;
Or when the moon was overhead,
Came two young lovers lately wed: 70
"I am half sick of shadows," said
   The Lady of Shalott.

Part III

A bow-shot from her bower-eaves,
He rode between the barley-sheaves,
The sun came dazzling thro' the leaves,
And flamed upon the brazen greaves
   Of bold Sir Lancelot.
A red-cross knight for ever kneel'd
To a lady in his shield,
That sparkled on the yellow field,   80
   Beside remote Shalott.

The gemmy bridle glitter'd free,
Like to some branch of stars we see
Hung in the golden Galaxy.
The bridle bells rang merrily
   As he rode down to Camelot;
And from his blazon'd baldric slung
A might silver bugle hung,
And as he rode his armor rung,
   Beside remote Shalott.   90

All in the blue unclouded weather
Thick-jewell'd shone the saddle-leather,
The helmet and the helmet-feather
Burn'd like one burning flame together,
   As he rode down to Camelot;
As often thro' the purple night,
Below the starry clusters bright,
Some bearded meteor, trailing light,
   Moves over still Shalott.

His broad clear brow in sunlight glow'd;   100
On burnished hooves his war-horse trode;
From underneath his helmet flow'd
His coal-black curls as on he rode,
   As he rode down to Camelot.
From the bank and from the river
He flash'd into the crystal mirror,
"Tirra lirra," by the river
   Sang Sir Lancelot.

She left the web, she left the loom,
She made three paces thro' the room,   110
She saw the water lily bloom,
She saw the helmet and the plume,

She look'd down to Camelot.
Out flew the web and floated wide;
The mirror crack'd from side to side;
"The curse is come upon me," cried
   The Lady of Shalott.

Part IV

In the stormy east-wind straining,
The pale yellow woods were waning,
The broad stream in his banks complaining,
Heavily the low sky raining   120
   Over tower'd Camelot;
Down she came and found a boat
Beneath a willow left afloat,
And round about the prow she wrote
   The Lady of Shalott.

And down the river's dim expanse
Like some bold seër in a trance,
Seeing all his own mischance—
With a glassy countenance   130
   Did she look to Camelot.
And at the closing of the day
She loosed the chain, and down she lay;
The broad stream bore her far away,
   The Lady of Shalott.

Lying, robed in snowy white
That loosely flew to left and right—
The leaves upon her falling light—
Thro' the noises of the night
   She floated down to Camelot;   140
And as the boat-head wound along
The willowy hills and fields among,
They heard her singing her last song,
   The Lady of Shalott.

Heard a carol, mournful, holy,
Chanted loudly, chanted lowly,
Till her blood was frozen slowly,
And her eyes were darken'd wholly,
   Turned to tower'd Camelot.

For ere she reach'd upon the tide   150
The first house by the water-side,
Singing in her song she died,
    The Lady of Shalott.

Under tower and balcony,
By garden-wall and gallery,
A gleaming shape she floated by,
Dead-pale between the houses high,
    Silent into Camelot.
Out upon the wharfs they came,
Knight and burgher, lord and dame,   160
And round the prow they read her name,
    The Lady of Shalott.

Who is this: and what is here?
And in the lighted palace near
Died the sound of royal cheer;
And they cross'd themselves for fear,
    All the knights of Camelot:
But Lancelot mused a little space;
He said, "She has a lovely face;
God in his mercy lend her grace,   170
    The Lady of Shalott."

Study Questions

1. Identify the rhyme scheme of the poem. Is it regular throughout? How do the rhyme scheme and meter of this poem lend it an incantatory aspect?
2. What is the curse in the poem?
3. What structural divisions constitute the poem? Describe the events in Part III.
4. Write a literal plot summary of the events of this poem. What is lost in such a translation?
5. Some critics see the Lady as a symbol of the poet or artist. Others view the poem as a comment on the position of women in society. Discuss both interpretations.

To Make a Prairie It Takes a Clover and One Bee

Emily Dickinson

To make a prairie it takes a clover and one bee,
One clover, and a bee,
And revery.
The revery alone will do,
If bees are few.

Study Questions

1. Why are the taciturn phrasing and the reductive description appropriate in this five-line poem?
2. How does rhyme echo sentence structure?
3. How does this poem narrow its focus to a simple statement about art and imagination?

Very Like a Whale

Ogden Nash

One thing that literature would be greatly the better for
Would be a more restricted employment by authors of simile and
    metaphor.
Authors of all races, be they Greeks, Romans, Teutons or Celts,

Can't seem just to say that anything is the thing it is but have to go
   out of their way to say that it is like something else.
What does it mean when we are told
That the Assyrian came down like a wolf on the fold?
In the first place, George Gordon Byron had had enough experi-
   ence
To know that it probably wasn't just one Assyrian, it was a lot of
   Assyrians.
However, as too many arguments are apt to induce apoplexy and
   thus hinder longevity,
We'll let it pass as one Assyrian for the sake of brevity.   10
Now then, this particular Assyrian, the one whose cohorts were
   gleaming in purple and gold,
Just what does the poet mean when he says he came down like a
   wolf on the fold?
In heaven and earth more than is dreamed of in our philosophy
   there are a great many things,
But I don't imagine that among them there is a wolf with purple and
   gold cohorts or purple and gold anythings.
No, no, Lord Byron, before I'll believe that this Assyrian was actually like a wolf I must have some kind of proof;
Did he run on all fours and did he have a hairy tail and a big red
   mouth and big white teeth and did he say Woof woof
   woof?
Frankly I think it very unlikely, and all you were entitled to say, at
   the very most,
Was that the Assyrian cohorts came down like a lot of Assyrian
   cohorts about to destroy the Hebrew host.
But that wasn't fancy enough for Lord Byron, oh dear me no, he had
   to invent a lot of figures of speech and then interpolate
   them,
With the result that whenever you mention Old Testament soldiers
   to people they say Oh yes, they're the ones that a lot of
   wolves dressed up in gold and purple ate them.   20
That's the kind of thing that's being done all the time by poets, from
   Homer to Tennyson;
They're always comparing ladies to lilies and veal to venison.
How about the man who wrote,
Her little feet stole in and out like mice beneath her petticoat?
Wouldn't anybody but a poet think twice
Before stating that his girl's feet were mice?
Then they always say things like that after a winter storm.
The snow is a white blanket. Oh it is, is it, all right then, you sleep
   under a six-inch blanket of snow and I'll sleep under a
   half-inch blanket of unpoetical blanket material and we'll
   see which one keeps warm,

And after that maybe you'll begin to comprehend dimly
What I mean by too much metaphor and simile.   30

Study Questions

1. In spite of the humor in the strained rhyme of the first two lines, do these lines contain a serious thesis?
2. With how many different metaphors and similes does Nash specifically quarrel?
3. From what source has Nash taken, "In heaven and earth more than is dreamed of in our philosophy there are a great many things"? Why has he butchered the quotation?
4. How is Nash satirizing the literal-minded reader of verse?

A Conversation with My Father

Grace Paley

1   My father is eighty-six years old and in bed. His heart, that bloody motor, is equally old and will not do certain jobs anymore. It still floods his head with brainy light. But it won't let his legs carry the weight of his body around the house. Despite my metaphors, this muscle failure is not due to his old heart, he says, but to a potassium shortage. Sitting on one pillow, leaning on three, he offers last-minute advice and makes a request.

2   "I would like you to write a simple story just once more," he says, "the kind de Maupassant wrote, or Chekhov, the kind you used to write. Just recognizable people and then write down what happened to them next."

3   I say, "Yes, why not? That's possible." I want to please him, though I don't remember writing that way. I *would* like to try to tell such a story, if he means the kind that begins: "There was a woman . . ." followed by plot, the absolute line between two points which I've always despised.

Not for literary reasons, but because it takes all hope away. Everyone, real or invented, deserves the open destiny of life.

4   Finally I thought of a story that had been happening for a couple of years right across the street. I wrote it down, then read it aloud. "Pa," I said, "how about this? Do you mean something like this?"

5   Once in my time there was a woman and she had a son. They lived nicely, in a small apartment in Manhattan. This boy at about fifteen became a junkie, which is not unusual in our neighborhood. In order to maintain her close friendship with him, she became a junkie too. She said it was part of the youth culture with which she felt very much at home. After a while, for a number of reasons, the boy gave it all up and left the city and his mother in disgust. Hopeless and alone, she grieved. We all visit her.

6   "O.K., Pa, that's it," I said, "an unadorned and miserable tale."

7   "But that's not what I mean," my father said. "You misunderstood me on purpose. You know there's a lot more to it. You know that. You left everything out. Turgenev wouldn't do that. Chekhov wouldn't do that. There are in fact Russian writers you never heard of, you don't have an inkling of, as good as anyone, who can write a plain ordinary story, who would not leave out what you have left out. I object not to facts, but to people sitting in trees talking senselessly, voices from who knows where . . ."

8   "Forget that one, Pa, what have I left out now? In this one?"

9   "Her looks, for instance."

10   "Oh. Quite handsome, I think. Yes."

11   "Her hair?"

12   "Dark, with heavy braids, as though she were a girl or a foreigner."

13   "What were her parents like, her stock? That she became such a person. It's interesting, you know."

14   "From out of town. Professional people. The first to be divorced in their county. How's that? Enough?" I asked.

15   "With you, it's all a joke," he said. "What about the boy's father? Why didn't you mention him? Who was he? Or was the boy born out of wedlock?"

16   "Yes," I said. "He was born out of wedlock."

17   "For Godsakes, doesn't anyone in your stories get married? Doesn't anyone have the time to run down to City Hall before they jump into bed?"

18   "No," I said. "In real life, yes. But in my stories, no."

19   "Why do you answer me like that?"

20   "Oh, Pa, this is a simple story about a smart woman who came to N.Y.C. full of interest love trust excitement very uptodate and about her son, what a hard time she had in this world. Married or not, it's of small consequence."

21   "It is of great consequence," he said.

22   "O.K.," I said.

23   "O.K. O.K. yourself," he said, "but listen. I believe you that she's good-looking but I don't think she was so smart."

24   "That's true," I said. "Actually that's the trouble with stories. People start out fantastic. You think they're extraordinary, but it turns out as the work goes along, they're just average with a good education, sometimes the other way around, the person's a kind of dumb innocent, but he outwits you and you can't even think of an ending good enough."

25   "What do you do then?" he asked. He had been a doctor for a couple of decades and then an artist for a couple of decades and he's still interested in details, craft, technique.

26   "Well, you just have to let the story lie around till some agreement can be reached between you and the stubborn hero."

27   "Aren't you talking silly, now?" he asked. "Start again," he said. "It so happens I'm not going out this evening. Tell the story again. See what you can do this time."

28   "O.K.," I said. "But it's not a five-minute job." Second attempt:

29   Once across the street from us, there was a fine handsome woman, our neighbor. She had a son whom she loved because she'd known him since birth (in helpless chubby infancy, and in the wrestling, hugging ages, seven to ten, as well as earlier and later). This boy when he fell into the fist of adolescence became a junkie. He was not a hopeless one. He was in fact hopeful, an ideologue, and successful converter. With his busy brilliance, he wrote persuasive articles for his high school newspaper. Seeking a wider audience, using important connections, he drummed into Lower Manhattan newsstand distribution a periodical called *Oh! Golden Horse!*

30   In order to keep him from feeling guilty (because guilt is the stony heart of nine-tenths of all clinically diagnosed cancers in America today, she said), and because she had always believed in giving bad habits room at home where one could keep an eye on them, she too became a junkie. Her kitchen was famous for a while—a center for intellectual addicts who knew what they were doing. A few felt artistic like Coleridge and others were scientific and revolutionary like Leary. Although she was often high herself, certain good mothering reflexes remained, and she saw to it that there was lots of orange juice around and honey and milk and vitamin pills. However she never cooked anything but chili, and that no more than once a week. She explained, when we talked to her, seriously, with neighborly concern, that it was her part in the youth culture and she would rather be with the young, it was an honor, than with her own generation.

31   One week, while nodding through an Antonioni film, this boy was severely jabbed by the elbow of a stern proselytizing girl, sitting beside him. She offered immediate apricots and nuts for his sugar level, spoke to him sharply, and took him home.

32   She had heard of him and his work and she herself published, edited, and wrote a competitive journal called *Man Does Live by Bread Alone*. In the organic heat of her continuous presence he could not help but become interested once more in his muscles, his arteries, and nerve connections. In

fact he began to love them, treasure them, praise them with funny little songs in *Man Does Live* . . .

> the fingers of my flesh transcend
> my transcendental soul
> the tightness in my shoulders end
> my teeth have made me whole

33   To the mouth of his head (that glory of will and determination) he brought hard apples, nuts, wheat germ, and soybean oil. He said to his old friends: From now on, I guess I'll keep my wits about me. I'm going on the natch. He said he was about to begin a spiritual deep-breathing journey. How about you too, Mom? he asked kindly.

34   His conversion was so radiant, splendid, that neighborhood kids his age began to say that he had never been a real addict at all, only a journalist along for the smell of the story. The mother tried several times to give up what had become without her son and his friends a lonely habit. This effort only brought it to supportable levels. The boy and his girl took their electronic mimeograph and moved to the bushy edge of another borough. They were very strict. They said they would not see her again until she had been off drugs for sixty days.

35   At home alone in the evening, weeping, the mother read and reread the seven issues of *Oh! Golden Horse!* They seemed to her as truthful as ever. We often crossed the street to visit and console. But if we mentioned any of our children who were at college or in the hospital or dropouts at home, she would cry out, My baby! My baby! and burst into terrible, face-scarring, time-consuming tears. The End.

36   First my father was silent, then he said, "Number One: You have a nice sense of humor. Number Two: I see you can't tell a plain story. So don't waste time." Then he said, sadly, "Number Three: I suppose that means she was alone, she was left like that, his mother. Alone. Probably sick?"

37   I said, "Yes."

38   "Poor woman. Poor girl, to be born in a time of fools, to live among fools. The end. The end. You were right to put that down. The end."

39   I didn't want to argue, but I had to say, "Well, it is not necessarily the end, Pa."

40   "Yes," he said, "what a tragedy. The end of a person."

41   "No, Pa," I begged him. "It doesn't have to be. She's only about forty. She could be a hundred different things in this world as time goes on. A teacher or a social worker. An ex-junkie! Sometimes it's better than having a Master's in education."

42   "Jokes," he said. "As a writer that's your main trouble. You don't want to recognize it. Tragedy! Plain tragedy! Historical tragedy! No hope.The end."

43   "Oh, Pa," I said. "She could change."

44   "In your own life, too, you have to look it in the face." He took a couple of nitroglycerin. "Turn to five," he said pointing to the dial on the

oxygen tank. He inserted the tubes into his nostrils and breathed deep. He closed his eyes and said, "No."

45   I had promised the family to always let him have the last word when arguing, but in this case I had a different responsibility. That woman lives across the street. She's my knowledge and my invention. I'm sorry for her. I'm not going to leave her there in that house crying. (Actually neither would Life, which unlike me has no pity.)

46   Therefore: She did change. Of course her son never came home again. But right now, she's the receptionist in a storefront community clinic in the East Village. Most of the customers are young people, some old friends. The head doctor has said to her—"if we only had three people in this clinic with your experiences . . ."

47   "The doctor said that?" my father took the oxygen tubes out of his nostrils and said. "Jokes. Jokes again."

48   "No, Pa, it could really happen that way, it's a funny world nowadays."

49   "No," he said. "Truth first, She will slide back. A person must have character. She does not."

50   "No, Pa," I said. "That's it. She's got a job. Forget it. She's in that storefront working."

51   "How long will it be?" he asked. "Tragedy! You too. When will you look it in the face?"

Study Questions

1. According to the narrator's father, what are the deficiencies of the two versions of her short story? Do you agree?
2. What does the father mean by "a plain ordinary story"? Are human concerns, fleshed out by realistic detail, his major requirements? Which writers does he admire? Why?
3. What is the dictionary definition of *tragedy*? The father's definition?
4. Who seems to have the most realistic attitude toward human character and fate—the father or the narrator?
5. Does the conversation seem real to you?
6. How appropriate are the metaphors and similes Paley uses?

Toys and the Imagination of Children

Rose K. Goldsen

1   The games children play and the toys they play with feed their imaginations in the same sense that the meals children eat feed their muscles. It's the community's business to make sure our suppliers keep the food supply wholesome, and we know that when we fail we're in trouble. What about the supply of toys and games that feed developing imaginations? Are we in trouble in that department, too?

2   I think we are. My students and I are systematically analyzing the offerings that go to make up the stockpile of toys and games available for children's imaginations to grow on, and what we see adds up to a dismal story. This article is an interim report.

3   By far the vast majority of toys and games entering the nation's homes are bought from a handful of companies that mass-produce these commodities for a national, even an international, market. (See "The Little Old Toymakers," p. 430.) Their catalogs list hundreds of items: but when you squeeze out all the water it shrinks to about a dozen categories. The same items are repeated over and over, with but minor variations. They all even feel the same and smell the same—which is scarcely odd since virtually all are poured from the same vat of polyvinyl chloride polymers, the plastic gunk from which they're made.

4   The companies producing toys and games for the mass market see essentially two separate "children's markets," which is the way they customarily describe the nation's children. There's an "over-six market" and a "preschool market," and each, in turn, is divided into the "boys market" and "girls market." Preschoolers get essentially riding toys, pull toys, baby dolls and fanciful animals. But what we're dealing with here are the toys and games targeted to the much larger "market" of children about five·or six and over.

5   The Mattel catalog is a good place to start, since Mattel is the biggest toy company in the world. Their 1976 catalog lists about 400 items this single company targets to children from five or six on. About 250 of the salable items listed are dolls, their gear and accessories, even total environments to put them in: houses, shopping centers, space stations, race tracks, fortresses and the like. *Playsets* is the term the business uses for these prepackaged environments. About a hundred

419

items in the Mattel catalog emulate gasoline burning vehicles. mainly automobiles, but also some aircraft. There are a few craft items and "activity toys." The rest are guns. All the Mattel toys are made of plastic, in some cases soft and pliable—baby dolls, for example. Others, like the guns and playsets, are rigid and inflexible. Whether soft or rigid, however, there is little difference in texture, and they all feel essentially the same to a child's sense of touch.

6   Missing from the Mattel catalog are board games (Milton Bradley Company specializes in these) and model kits (Aurora Products is one of the companies turning them out). Add a "miscellaneous" category for such items as magic kits, construction sets and train sets, and that's not a bad description of what goes into the nation's stockpile of toys these businesses press upon children over preschool age.

7   Mattel's best-known contribution to the stockpile is the doll they began to promote for girls about 18 years ago: Barbie. To Barbie the company owes its great leap forward to number-one position in the trade, a success story that has meant that by now a whole generation of little girls has been drilled in the special virtues of the Barbie line. *The World of Barbie,* Mattel calls it—140 salable items of *collectables and interchangeables.* That's another trade term that means that a single purchase generates successive buys—a marketing strategy all the toy companies try to emulate.

8   Once Barbie enters a family or a play group, whether by purchase or as a gift, Mattel counts on her to awaken a child's further hankerings—for boyfriend Ken, for P.J., Francie, Cara, Skipper, Ginger. They're Barbie's supporting cast—friends or perhaps her sisters. There's certainly a strong family resemblance among them all. Cara might be a special case, since she's a black—or at least chocolate brown. Still, she's a dead ringer for Barbie—identical features, identical build. Like twins, they could be cast from the same mold—as, indeed, they probably are.

9   Barbie is what the trade calls a fashion doll. Like all dolls, fashion dolls started out "for real," not as children's playthings. In a day before cheap printing and saturation advertising made mass-circulation magazines possible, a convenient way to show fashionable ladies the latest modes was to send them a doll clothed in exact scale models of the season's latest. After the lady of the family was through with her, it was not unusual for the doll to end up in the nursery for the little girls of the house to play with. A child could dress and undress her, converse with her and for her, poke her and examine her, name her and endow her with an imaginary personality, take her on imaginary visits, share imaginary adventures with her, love her and punish her—in short, weave all kinds of fantasies around her. That's how toys nourish imaginations; they act as props for dramas the children work out in fantasy and practice in play.

10   After the fashion doll's original clothes had worn out, the little girl was typically expected to make do with homemade doll clothes, even to make the clothes herself. That's another job toys take on: encouraging

not only dexterity, but also the sense of mastery a child feels as he or she embarks on a task and works it through to its conclusion.

11   The aim of the original fashion dolls was to persuade the ladies to buy the wardrobe for themselves, not for the dolls. That children played with them was just an unintended side effect. Doll companies noted, however, that the by-product could be promoted in its own right. Mattel caught on early to the further realization that saturation advertising, especially by coast-to-coast television, could develop a "child market" for such merchandise. The company began to produce and promote a few items in what is by now Barbie's seemingly endless wardrobe and accoutrements.

12   The modest start led to such spectacular success that at this point Mattel could give away the first Barbie and still not jeopardize its leading position in the industry. Their current catalog lists 34 changes for Barbie, 18 changes for Skipper and 10 for Ken. A "shoe set" alone includes a dozen pairs of boots and shoes. There are three special carrying cases for toting the stuff, as well as a set of special hangers for putting it all away. There are four hair-grooming sets, wigs and hairpieces ("Different lengths for different moods . . . and lots of makeup!"). In the single year 1976, the World of Barbie line offered, and the company promoted, two fully equipped houses—a town house and a country house—four "room sets" that the children are assured have been "decorator designed" and "Fashion Plaza," a complete shopping center.

13   Mattel's competitors got the message, and Tuesday Taylor, another fashion doll, appeared on the market, complete with consort Eric and their penthouse. "By Ideal," as the commercials say.

14   The Mego Corporation, then, not to be outdone, countered with a plastic replica of Cher, television star and show business "personality," accompanied by her consort. Mego had to face up to a knotty problem. Should the consort be Sonny Bono, Cher's current costar on "The Sonny and Cher Show," her former husband and father of her first child? Or should it be rock star Gregg Allman, Cher's current husband and father of her second child?

15   Since coast-to-coast television exposure guarantees that Sonny's "recognition factor" beats out Gregg's in the "child market," it was never even a horse race—which is how it came to pass that Sonny's plastic replica joined Cher's as Mego's tie-in sale. Oh yes, the playset Mego promotes with Sonny and Cher is "an exciting playset . . . styled just like the real thing in CBS Television City in Hollywood." Cher's wardrobe—24 changes in just her first year's edition—includes a sequined, bare-midriff, hotpants costume: feather boas; zippered jumpsuits; lounging pajamas. It's a wardrobe appropriate to the combination *Playboy/Playgirl*-show business lifestyle suggested by the scenarios that publicize these fashion doll pairs. Tuesday Taylor is said to be a model; so is T.J., in Barbie's retinue ("I'm so glad I'm a fashion model," says the tape tucked away in the insides of "Talking T.J.").

16   Mattel's 1976 Barbie scenario took the whole gang to Malibu Beach, and publicity for "Malibu Barbie" describes her as beautifully sun bronzed, with an especially flexible waist and especially bendable limbs. In the catalog, there she stands alongside "Malibu Ken" and the rest of the girls, who are equally bendable (the children are assured). Awaiting them on the next page is their Beach Bus Vehicle (here Ken is seen as a surfer), and on the page after that, their Pool Party Set. The play houses and room sets are loaded with ultramodern equipment and furnishings that could have been bought just yesterday; ordered, perhaps, by mail from *Playboy's* advertisers; paid for, perhaps, by Ken's credit card.

17   Since the wardrobe features a bridal costume for Barbie and a groom's formal wear for Ken—and the shopping plaza boasts a special bridal boutique—I'm assuming that sooner or later this pair plans to make it legal. I'm willing to guess, too, that Mattel's research teams are testing a "Maternity Barbie" in successive editions that will take her through to parturition. (Think of all those maternity clothes!) There's the further possibility, too, of new cast members such natural population increase can introduce.

18   Barbie is what the business calls a "full-figured doll," which means she has breasts. So does Tuesday, so does Cher, so do all these fashion dolls. Skipper is a special case. When a child first encounters Skipper, she's just a weeny bopper and quite flat-chested. Twist her arm, though, and she's a teeny bopper. She shoots up tall, her little girl's waist narrows, and—lo and behold!—a pair of tiny, pointed breasts thrusts forward. They make no pretense of being anatomically correct, of course: no nipples, no pigmentation, no network of veins. These breasts are strictly to drape clothes around, to suggest fantasies having to do with self-decoration. They have nothing to do with fantasies about providing milk for infants, nothing to do with succorance and nurturance of babies. The fashion-doll scenario the toy companies target to girls casts their vote for number-one female sex role, and it's not the role of wife and mother, not by a long shot. Sex object in charge of consumption is more to the point.

19   *Anatomically correct* is a term I picked up from the toy business' own trade journals where it's bandied about a lot these days, what with three big companies promoting baby dolls they describe as "anatomically correct." The term was cooked up by the Madison Avenue crowd handling the research that informs the industry whether a product idea is salable. It also provides the basis for the publicity that talks it up once the product is on the market. Ideal's baby doll is named Joey Stivic, after the infant son of Michael Stivic and Gloria Bunker Stivic. (I think of Joey as twice born, the country having had not just one but two opportunities to share in imagination his journey through the birth canal as Gloria delivered him originally on an episode of "All in the Family" shown in 1975, repeated in 1976. Total, about 80 million Americans on the same emotional jag.) Joey's rival baby dolls are Mattel's Baby Brother Tender-

love and Horseman Dolls' Li'l David and Li'l Ruthie. The three boys have plastic penises and scrotums, and Li'l Ruthie sports an unmistakable vagina.

20   Releases sent out by the advertising agencies retained by these companies and by their trade organizations mention the liberalism and liberation these dolls are said to herald. A new maturity; abandonment of the sexual hypocrisy we've lived with for so long in this country. Here's an opportunity, they say, to introduce a generation of children fairly and squarely to the realization that little boys *are* different from little girls and let's face up to it instead of playing silly charades. Frankness and realism and psychological health, they say, that's the name of the game.

21   Yet, even a cursory inspection of the dolls promoted as "anatomically correct" reveals that the term promises more than it delivers. The little boys have penis and scrotum, to be sure, but there's not a single navel among the lot, not an anus, nor are their nipples pigmented. These dolls have no tongue, no gums, not a tooth or suggestion of a tooth; their painted lips rim a gaping hole. Ears are molded in a piece with the head, eyebrows are painted on. Eyelids, eyelashes, they have none. No anatomically correct nostrils. Their arms and legs are not articulated. Fingers are not jointed nor are toes. Poor Li'l Ruthie's vagina lacks what might be called labial flexibility.

22   Dr. Brian Sutton-Smith, chairperson of the Psychology Department at Columbia University's Teachers College, acts as a consultant of the Toy Manufacturers Association, trade and lobbying organization of the toy business. He's consultant, as well, to their consultants, Harshe-Rotman and Druck, public relations specialists, who distribute Dr. Sutton-Smith's paper subtitled, "Questions and Answers About Toys and Play." The paper discusses the pros and cons of providing children with such so-called anatomically correct dolls in a tone that is circumspect and cautious. Dr. Sutton-Smith told me with enthusiasm, however, that he is "delighted" these dolls are finally available, and he believes that they "may well signal an important step in the direction of greater cultural sanity about sex."

23   I doubt that this is the principal signal these dolls are beaming to us about the direction our culture is moving in. It's one thing to craft a doll with such attention to detail that every organ is fashioned with care and artistry, in literal and lifelike miniature. A doll so carefully and lovingly worked would certainly possess literal sex organs along with literal everything else. But these poor deformed creatures have been stamped out by the tens of thousands. The molds that shape them simplify details for the sake of low-cost production. Of all apertures in the human body, only one is chosen for such literal representation—the boy's penis, the girl's vagina.

24   Such deliberate selectiveness is reminiscent of priapic dolls I've seen recovered from archaeological sites. The term refers to the exaggerated emphasis on primary sex organs that often goes with ritualistic cult

behavior. Of course, the plastic manikins I have just described are scarcely in that league, any more than *Playboy* and its many imitators are. But they're all off to a good start: the magazines using sexual titillation to glorify mass consumption; the toy industry doing its bit to ease the children into the cult with fashion dolls and "anatomically correct" infants. Even the odor of the plastic helps usher them into the cult of consumption; an odor so distinctive that it has been baptized with a name of its own, "the new car smell."

25   Dolls for boys, a post-World War II contribution, are heavily represented in the nation's stockpile of toys. Little boys have typically refused to play with dolls, parents having viewed them as sissy stuff. But not toy soldiers. Aha! Someone made a connection, and thus was GI Joe born. Transitional form between toy soldier and doll, Hasbro turns him out complete with canned scripts and an ever-expanding supporting cast. Other companies followed suit and imitations burgeoned.

26   Marketing strategists warned that these manikins must not be called *dolls;* so now we're blessed with a new term, *action figure*. Call a doll an "action figure," and it's easy to persuade little boys that it's not really a doll. Thus, in less than a generation, decisions taken in a few corporate boardrooms have legitimated dolls as playthings for boys. It's a cultural revolution; whether major or minor remains to be seen as history plays itself out.

27   GI Joe's supporting cast includes stock characters such as Atomic Man, the Defender, Bullet Man, Intruder Warrior. Canned scenarios are: "Dive to Danger," "Challenge of Savage River"—a whole shelf of stock plots patterned after stock formulas that stock comic books, stock pulps and stock television series drill all children in. Kenner produces a variety of "action figures," among them Maskatron. "Strike Maskatron in the right places, and *pow*—his arms, legs, even his head, fly off," says their publicity.

28   Mattel produces Torpedo Fist. In place of a right arm, he sports a deadly prosthesis; "Vroom! . . . It lashes out." Dr. Steel's right hand is another prosthesis; the plastic has been treated to look like steel. The Whip is a mustachioed, beared, macho figure carrying not only a *bola*— the gaucho's "lasso" that can bring down game on the hoof, even a man—but he also carries the prop that accounts for his name: a huge, thick, black, snaky bullwhip! They're all good guys, though, members of P.A.C.K. (Professional Agents/Crime Killers), whose emblem is a snarling wolf's head. Leader of P.A.C.K. is the hero of Mattel's script, Big Jim.

29   Toy companies vie among themselves, each trying to hit upon a gimmick to distinguish its own little robots for boys from the rest. Maskatron's head flies off; Torpedo Fist's prosthesis "strikes like lightning"; and Big Jim is activated by what Mattel calls its "double-trouble feature." The same mechanism that endows Growing-up Skipper with instant breasts now provides Big Jim with two different apparitions:

"Crank his arm, press his back. Instantly his face changes! One minute he's all tough P.A.C.K. commander. The next: fierce leader in action!" As tough P.A.C.K. commander, the doll's visage is lantern-jawed, complexion ruddy, brow serene. Then, presto, chango! Eyebrows draw together, lips part, teeth bare, face contorts, complexion changes—to bright green!

30   Mattel also features Zorak, the Enemy, who goes through a similar transformation. This doll's head and shoulders are shrouded in a deep black hood, something like those worn by interrogators in the Spanish Inquisition. The face that shows through the opening in repose is "the evil face of genius." The child has only to activate the "double-trouble mechanism," whereupon Zorak's lips, too, draw back; Zorak's teeth, too, are bared; Zorak's visage, too, contorts into a snarl; Zorak's complexion, too, turns bright green; and—*voila!*— "Mad Scientist." The purple cape draped around Zorak's bare torso is held in place by a heavy link chain.

31   Chains are big among these "action figures," as are bare torsos, tattoos and heavy boots. Cofeatured costumes and props are Sam Browne belts, uniforms and guns—both traditional and ray types, including ever-popular laser guns, even laser cannons. They are joined by craft kits and models claiming to be authentic reproductions of whole fleets of warships, warplanes, submarines and helicopters, plus materiel, from every known war. Certain recent enemies are featured here—Imperial Japan and Nazi Germany, for example; others are downplayed, such as Fascist Italy. In the same way, certain allies are featured—Soviet Russia and Great Britain—while others are downplayed or ignored such as Canada and Australia.

32   Into the nation's stockpile go these images and the scenarios they suggest. Into the nation's stockpile go the arsenals of war that, while never slighting the entertainment value of face-to-face violence, celebrate the joys of push-button destruction by remote control.

33   Action figures for boys follow the marketing principles laid down by the World of Barbie: star and supporting cast in multiple manifestation, costume changes and gear. GI Joe comes in a talking version; another endows him with movable eyes. He is equipped with combat jeep and trailer; pivoting, recoilless rifle; a ray gun turret; a cage to hold the Invader (whose special feature is "Crusher Arms"). Secret Mountain Outpost playset, jungle fighting equipment, mountain climbing equipment, paratrooper equipment and all appropriate costume changes are pressed upon the child. Big Jim joins this parade: as a karate fighter, on ski patrol, as a frogman. More equipment, more costumes, more arms, more scenarios—into the stockpile they go.

34   Cars, race sets, vehicles of all kinds are another principal contribution to the nation's stockpile of toys. They're fast-moving "collectables and interchangeables" and most of the big companies turn them out in complete fleets. Detroit is well represented here, many of the cars made to resemble familiar models and bearing their trademark symbols. Sports

cars, both foreign and domestic, are likewise well represented, not only the kinds of fast cars *Playboy* likes, but also real racers (Ferraris, Maseratis and so on) along with fanciful ones.

35   The "race sets" are recent additions. These are battery-run cars with special tracks and total environments to go with them. They enable the children to run the cars in real races, by way of the push-button, remote-control devices the toy producers like so well. (Batteries may or may not be included.) Production of race sets is catching up with production of model railroads in the toy industry, although the latter are still very much in evidence. (Lionel and Tyco are two of the major companies specializing in such rolling stock.)

36   Mattel puts out a "Hot Wheels" fleet of cars plus race sets. Aurora's race sets are XLerators, Screechers and AFX. Kenner makes motorcycle race sets as well as Lightnin' SSP (for Supersonic Speed) along with Smash-Up Derby ("Real demolition derby thrills in the spirit of '76 colors"). "Speed around corners on two wheels," is their advice to the children. It's a counsel that is pretty standard among most of the major toy companies. Indeed, the men and women their advertising agencies call "creative staff" are kept busy thinking up appealing ways to drill children in the same lessons: the joys of superspeed, of daredevil driving, risk and never-ending acquisition of nonbiodegradable consumer items bought on credit, plus promotional material suggesting appropriate scenarios.

37   The toy business is a growth industry, expanding since 1968 at the rate of about 10 percent per year, with just occasional blips in the curve but no change in direction. A good measure of this expansion can be laid at the doorstep of a marketing strategy that takes advantage of the "merchandising circle" based on franchises and called *character merchandising*.

38   Here's how it works. The television business introduces every family in America to characters engineered in New York or Hollywood, including sports figures. Since there are more television homes than bathtub homes in the United States, there is no way for a child to escape getting to know and recognize the cast, getting to learn their vices and their virtues. Their initial attention-getting potential has already been pretested; and they enjoy a total support system that provides something like what ecologists call "biological concentrators" or what economists call "multipliers."

39   Buying franchises allows the toy business to invest in known successes, thus limiting risk. The Joey Stivic doll is an example: Ideal pays the TAT Production Company's franchising division for the privilege of allowing their baby doll to bask in the aura lent by a character "All in the Family" has made known to everyone. Carroll O'Connor, the star who plays Archie Bunker in that series, even appears on the package Joey comes in, beckoning from it to both parents and children. The strategy works particularly well with kids, who are known to respond uncritically

to beckoning, without reflection or deliberation. The Cher doll is another example. Mego produces her as a fashion doll just like Barbie, but without the expense of the long advertising buildup Mattel had to undertake to make her familiar to most little girls.

40   "Six Million Dollar Man" and "Bionic Woman," two relatively new television series, introduce still further economy into the hand-in-glove arrangement between the toy business and the television business. Jaime Sommers, leading character of "Bionic Woman," turns up as a fashion doll; Steve Austin, leading character in "Six Million Dollar Man," is her consort. Steve, however, is an updated version of Superman, so he does double duty for the company that bought his franchise. As consort, he does for Kenner what Ken has done for Mattel; as superhero action figure, he does what GI Joe has done for Hasbro.

41   Both Steve and Jaime happen to be multiple amputees: the poor man has lost the use of both legs and his right arm and the sight of an eye; the poor woman has also lost both legs and an arm, and she is hard of hearing. They are joined by Ideal's Jay J. Armes™ "The world's most successful private eye despite the fact that he has no hands!" Advertising, television and the toy trade in tandem drill American children in the appropriate feelings: not compassion at the suffering such mutilation entails but admiration at the good luck it represents. It's the opposite of such classic children's stories as "The Little Lame Prince," for example, who deserves admiration because his human qualities—love, compassion, understanding—eclipse the tragedy of his physical impairment in a story that never forgets that even if his lameness can take a back seat, it still costs him pain to walk.

42   Scenarios for Steve, Jaime and Jay J., however, take quite a different slant. Their prostheses are promoted as replacement parts—more collectables and interchangeables. "Special snap-on right arms for the Six Million Dollar Man's™ critical assignments. 'Laser Arm' shoots safe red beam; 'Neutralizer Arm' delivers crushing karate chop. 'Sonic Stunner' disables enemies. . . . Roll back skin to reveal modules that can be removed for Bionic surgery." For Jay J. (Ideal claims he's scheduled to star in a CBS crime series), the spring-loaded hooks that serve as his everyday hands may be replaced by "a pair of suction cups for climbing walls, a magnet for hanging on to steel structures, a machete for cutting his way out of tough situations. . . . But the niftiest weapon of all is the hook that flips over to become a pistol!" Jaime just trails along with "Bionic™ modules in ears, right arm and both legs . . ." and "pinging noise when she uses her Bionic ears."

43   She still gives Barbie a run for the money, though, whether in her "official stylish jogging outfit and tennis shoes," her "gold evening gown with matching wrap and shoes," or her "silky white pantsuit" shown with scarf and platform sandals. Her address book includes telephone numbers of about a dozen men but only one woman. Her playset is the usual doll house where she can wear another "beautiful two-piece eve-

ning outfit" as she gets "ready for the party," or even for just "relaxing after a mission with Steve."

44   Another playset offers the children the usual beauty salon scenario (". . . arrange her beautiful hair . . . for an evening out with Steve . . ."). But there's a difference. Jaime's beauty salon is run by a computer that checks out her various protheses the way a service garage checks replacement parts for an automobile. I'm betting that just as GI Joe was the transitional form converting toy soldiers into robots for boys to weave their fantasies around, Jaime will turn out to be the transitional form converting toy women into mechanical warriors girls can identify with their own wishes, aspirations, dreams, self-images and body images.

45   Kenner purchases the franchise to keep effigies of Steve and Jaime in its own corporate fold; but franchisers for Universal Studios are kept busy elsewhere, too. All kinds of businesses seek the licenses to link whatever admiration Steve and Jaime may engender to their own merchandise, from T-shirts and underpants to board games for children. Parker Brothers promotes a Six Million Dollar Man Game in which the winner must prove his right to "handle assignments for NASA, Interpol and the CIA." In Bionic Crisis, Parker invites each player to assume the role of a doctor whose task is to complete a circuit on one part or another of Steve's poor mutilated body.

46   Similar franchises for dolls and games have been sold by the production companies handling "Kojak," "The Rookies," "Columbo," "Kung Fu," "McCloud," "Ironside," "Baretta," "Starsky and Hutch," "S.W.A.T." and other shows that, catering to the rough trade, have been banned from network television's so-called family hour.

47   Production companies turning out television's game shows are also big franchisers. "Concentration" (by Milton Bradley) is in its 18th edition as a board game for children and families; "Password" is in its 15th; "Jeopardy," in its 11th. "Beat the Clock," Musical Chairs, Twenty Questions, "Truth or Consequences"—all these games that spring from sources in the folk culture have been preempted, industrially produced, and are being sold back to the people, their original creators.

48   Television programs made to attract children to the set, including "Sesame Street," are a lucrative source of the character-merchandise franchises the toy business buys. There's an "Addams Family" game, "Fat Albert and the Cosby Kids," "The Flintstones," "The Oddball Couple," "Planet of the Apes"— dolls and games and merchandise in these images line up alongside their ancestors: Lone Ranger, Superman, Batman, Davy Crockett and, of course, Mickey and his entire entourage.

49   The franchising division handling Paramount's sale of licenses that allow "Star Trek" images to be attached to merchandise has negotiated dozens of different licenses and still keeps coming up with new ones even though the series has been off network television for years. (A full-length movie is planned for release in the near future.) It's a franchising success that vies with the success of Walt Disney Productions,

the company that first thrust the nation's children inside the merchandising circle.

50   As the television shows, their stars and their props move into the nation's playrooms, so do the businesses that use them as envelopes to tuck their commercials into. Grandstands, grease pits and lengths of track in race sets are adorned with billboards advertising Gulf, Exxon, Mobil, Coca-Cola, Pepsi—all among television's major advertisers. Even television's ex-advertisers appear: Chesterfield, Marlboro, L & M cigarette ads turn up on the toy grandstands and cars urged upon children.

51   McDonald's is well represented: winner of a McDonald's board game is the child who first serves up the items the McDonald Corporation features on its fast-food menus. Remco sells dolls in the image of Ronald McDonald, the clown who is the company's corporate symbol, as well as dolls patterned after the rest of the cast of puppets who act in McDonald television commercials. A complete plastic environment goes along with Ronald and gang: "Welcome to the fun and excitement of McDonaldland. Cross the Filet-O-Fish Lake via the Golden Arch Bridge. . . . Serve a tray of McDonald's hamburgers and shakes at the famous McDonald Family Restaurant."

52   Kentucky Fried Chicken has taken a leaf from the same book; so has Pizza Hut and Holiday Inn, among others. Le Sueur Industries moves its corporate symbol, the Jolly Green Giant, into the home and into children's play groups; Child Guidance provides the playset—an agribusiness complex.

53   Books on 18th-century toys describe little guillotines used by French children who played at beheading toy aristocrats. A "comic toy" of the same era was a hollowed-out figure into which a child could place a live bird. Its frantic struggles activated the toy so cleverly that "one would suppose it was run by a clockwork. . . ." As late as 1930, Montgomery Ward's catalog described "Number 48 E 3988, Mammy's Black-Faced Boy. See him wiggle his ears . . . he sure is a funny feller!"

54   I suppose the people who produced these monstrosities must have believed that their creations were all right for children to play with, and this was just another way to make a buck. There's no accounting for tastes, and not everyone is endowed with the same portion of wit, wisdom and sensibility. Since earlier toymakers did not enjoy the advantages modern merchandising knowhow bestows, subgroups that did not share their views could still shield themselves and their children from forced exposure to incessant drilling in their values by way of their playthings. Today, nobody can escape. Television shows from which toys are recruited receive blanket coverage. Promotional inserts for Kenner's 1976 line were stuffed "inside 13 million boxes of General Mills' top-selling kids' cereals . . . breakfast-table billboards amounting to 26 million free ads." Add their "comic ads hitting 120 million in over 240 newspapers" in a single day. Add their commercials spliced into "four great CBS network specials designed to hit over 150 million"—the same

commercials that are shown repeatedly through routine network and spot buys. In 1976, Milton Bradley planned a three-month campaign just for its race sets designed "to reach 90 percent of all six- to 11-year-olds an average of 24 times." Mattel is among the top hundred advertisers in the world.

55   In the face of onslaughts on this scale, what child can avoid admitting these scenarios, these images, to consciousness? Even the slowest learners pick them up and store them. Where? In the place where human beings store imagery and images: in imagination. There they settle, waiting, waiting, colonists in those young minds that are ever in the making.

The Little Old Toymakers

1   Aurora Products Corporation makes and markets dolls, cars, model kits and other toys and games for children. It is a subsidiary of the Nabisco Corporation, a food and agricultural conglomerate. Nabisco is 33rd on the list of U.S. companies ranked in order of their outlays for all advertising. In 1975, Aurora spent $2.6 million on network television promotion.

2   Child Guidance Toys is owned by Questor Company, a corporation that makes and markets instructional technology systems.

3   Creative Playthings is owned by the Columbia Broadcasting System, a media conglomerate with international reach. Creative Playthings makes and markets preschool toys. It owns five major retail toy stores.

4   Daisy Toy Division is owned by the Victor Comptometer Corporation.

5   Elmex Corporation distributes toys and hobby crafts to retailers for toy, game and doll manufacturers, including Kenner and Bradley. In addition, they operate Fun City toy retail stores. Elmex is owned by W. R. Grace and Co., which began as a steamship line and ended up as a multinational conglomerate owning subsidiaries from plantations to factories.

6   X-Acto, Inc., makes hobby and craft products. It is owned by the Columbia Broadcasting System.

7   Fisher-Price Toys is owned by Quaker Oats, the food and agricultural conglomerate with international reach and interests.

8   Hasbro Industries, Inc., began specializing in "Romper Room" toys for preschool children, then produced GI Joe. Hasbro's business burgeoned and so did its expenditures for advertising—$4 million for selected network commercials in 1975.

9   Hasbro owns International Telecable Productions, Inc.; two pen and pencil manufacturing subsidiaries; another that produces home products; and (until 1972) a subsidiary that operated a chain of private nursery schools, Romper Room Schools, Inc.

10   Ideal Toy Corporation was second to Mattel in terms of share of the market in 1974. In 1975, $10 million went just to network and spot television commercials. The 1976 figure: $12 million.

11   Kenner Products Co. makes and markets toys, games and dolls such as Dusty, the teenage fashion doll; Jaime, the Bionic Woman; and Six Million Dollar Man. It is owned by General Mills, the food and agricultural conglomerate.

12   Kohner Brothers, Inc., makes and markets infant and preschool toys, instructional games and board games. Until 1975, it was owned by General Foods, the food and agricultural conglomerate. It is now a division of Gabriel Industries, ranked as the 17th largest toy and sporting goods corporation.

13   Lionell Corporation, the company that is known for those toy trains, is a subsidiary of General Mills. The Lionel Corporation also owns Lionel Leisure, Inc. (retail toy stores). Other subsidiaries are engaged in the manufacture of primary industrial products such as power transmission systems, hydraulic aircraft systems and automatic car wash equipment.

14   Louis Marx and Company—the famous toy company—until this year, was owned by Quaker Oats, the food and agricultural conglomerate.

15   Mattel, Inc., is the biggest toy company in the world, 91st on a list of all companies ranked in order of the amount of money they spend on advertising. Mattel owns Barnum and Bailey Combined Shows; Metaframe Corp. (aquariums and related products); Monogram Models, Inc. (model kits). Subsidiary divisions are spotted throughout the world, turning out toys, games and dolls in about a dozen different countries. Mattel spent $22.3 million on advertising in 1975 alone—most of it on television commercials.

16   Milton Bradley Company, manufacturer of toys and games, was second after Mattel in terms of share of the market in 1975. Among its international subsidiaries is Arrow Games, Ltd. Ranking companies in terms of all advertising commissioned, bought and paid for on network radio throughout the country, Milton Bradley is 20th on the list.

17   Playskool makes and markets toys and games especially for preschool children. It is owned by the Milton Bradley Company.

18   Parker Brothers makes and markets games. Among their products is the decades-old game Monopoly, and games cashing in on the success of the "Six Million Dollar Man" television series: Six Million Dollar Man Game, Bionic Woman Game and Bionic Crisis game. General Mills owns the company.

19   Playtime Products, Inc.—the parent company of Playtime is Coleco, manufacturer of recreational products as well as games and toys. They specialize in sport action games, play popcorn poppers and cotton candy makers.

20   Tonka Corporation makes and markets children's toys, including Vogue Dolls, one of its subsidiaries. Tonka also owns Ceramichrome,

Inc. Tonka's international division produce their wares in a half-dozen foreign countries.

21   Tyco Industries produces toy trains. It is owned by Consolidated Foods Corporation, the food and agricultural conglomerate.

22   Wilson Sporting Goods is owned by Pepsico, the food and agricultural conglomerate.

Study Questions

1. Is the analogy opening the essay defensible?
2. What rhetorical form does this essay take? Is this form suitable to the subject?
3. What are the implications of the advertisers' use of *action figure* instead of *doll*?
4. How do the television networks figure in this analysis? Can it be said that they are the real topic of this essay? Why or why not?
5. What is the tone of the essay? How is it achieved?

The Toys of Peace

"Saki" (H. H. Munro)

1   "Harvey," said Eleanor Bope, handing her brother a cutting from a London morning paper[1] of the 19th of March, "just read this about children's toys, please; it exactly carries out some of our ideas about influence and upbringing."

2   "In the view of the National Peace Council," ran the extract, "there are grave objections to presenting our boys with regiments of fighting men, batteries of guns, and squadrons of 'Dreadnoughts.' Boys, the Council admits, naturally love fighting and all the panoply of war . . . but that is no reason for encouraging, and perhaps giving permanent form to, their primitive instincts. At the Children's Welfare Exhibition, which opens at Olympia in three weeks' time, the Peace Council will make an alternative suggestion to parents in the shape of an exhibition of 'peace

[1] An actual extract from a London paper of March 1914.

toys.' In front of a specially painted representation of the Peace Palace at The Hague will be grouped, not miniature soldiers but miniature civilians, not guns but ploughs and the tools of industry. . . . It is hoped that manufacturers may take a hint from the exhibit, which will bear fruit in the toy shops."

3   "The idea is certainly an interesting and very well-meaning one," said Harvey; "whether it would succeed well in practice—"

4   "We must try," interrupted his sister; "you are coming down to us at Easter, and you always bring the boys some toys, so that will be an excellent opportunity for you to inaugurate the new experiment. Go about in the shops and buy any little toys and models that have special bearing on civilian life in its more peaceful aspects. Of course you must explain the toys to the children and interest them in the new idea. I regret to say that the 'Siege of Adrianople' toy, that their Aunt Susan sent them, didn't need any explanation; they knew all the uniforms and flags, and even the names of the respective commanders, and when I heard them one day using what seemed to be the most objectionable language they said it was Bulgarian words of command; of course it *may* have been, but at any rate I took the toy away from them. Now I shall expect your Easter gifts to give quite a new impulse and direction to the children's minds; Eric is not eleven yet, and Bertie is only nine-and-a-half, so they are really at a most impressionable age."

5   "There is primitive instinct to be taken into consideration, you know," said Harvey doubtfully, "and hereditary tendencies as well. One of their great-uncles fought in the most intolerant fashion at Inkerman—he was specially mentioned in dispatches, I believe—and their great-grandfather smashed all his Whig neighbours' hothouses when the great Reform Bill was passed. Still, as you say, they are at an impressionable age. I will do my best."

6   On Easter Saturday Harvey Bope unpacked a large, promising-looking red cardboard box under the expectant eyes of his nephews. "Your uncle has brought you the newest thing in toys," Eleanor had said impressively, and youthful anticipation had been anxiously divided between Albanian soldiery and a Somali camel-corps. Eric was hotly in favour of the latter contingency. "There would be Arabs on horseback," he whispered; "the Albanians have got jolly uniforms, and they fight all day long, and all night too, when there's a moon, but the country's rocky, so they've got no cavalry."

7   A quantity of crinkly paper shavings was the first thing that met the view when the lid was removed; the most exciting toys always began like that. Harvey pushed back the top layer and drew forth a square, rather featureless building.

8   "It's a fort!" exclaimed Bertie.

9   "It isn't, it's the palace of the Mpret of Albania," said Eric, immensely proud of his knowledge of the exotic title; "it's got no windows, you see, so that passers-by can't fire in at the Royal Family."

10   "It's a municipal dust-bin," said Harvey hurriedly; "you see all the refuse and litter of a town is collected there, instead of lying about and injuring the health of the citizens."

11   In an awful silence he disinterred a little lead figure of a man in black clothes.

12   "That," he said, "is a distinguished civilian, John Stuart Mill. He was an authority on political economy."

13   "Why?" asked Bertie.

14   "Well, he wanted to be; he thought it was a useful thing to be."

15   Bertie gave an expressive grunt, which conveyed his opinion that there was no accounting for tastes.

16   Another square building came out, this time with windows and chimneys.

17   "A model of the Manchester branch of the Young Women's Christian Association," said Harvey.

18   "Are there any lions?" asked Eric hopefully. He had been reading Roman history and thought that where you found Christians you might reasonably expect to find a few lions.

19   "There are no lions," said Harvey. "Here is another civilian, Robert Raikes, the founder of Sunday schools, and here is a model of a municipal wash-house. These little round things are loaves baked in a sanitary bakehouse. That lead figure is a sanitary inspector, this one is a district councillor, and this one is an official of the Local Government Board."

20   "What does he do?" asked Eric wearily.

21   "He sees to things connected with his Department," said Harvey. "This box with a slit in it is a ballot-box. Votes are put into it at election times."

22   "What is put into it at other times?" asked Bertie.

23   "Nothing. And here are some tools of industry, a wheelbarrow and a hoe, and I think these are meant for hoppoles. This is a model beehive, and that is a ventilator, for ventilating sewers. This seems to be another municipal dustbin—no, it is a model of a school of art and a public library. This little lead figure is Mrs. Hemans, a poetess, and this is Rowland Hill, who introduced the system of penny postage. This is Sir John Herschel, the eminent astrologer."

24   "Are we to play with these civilian figures?" asked Eric.

25   "Of course," said Harvey, "these are toys; they are meant to be played with."

26   "But how?"

27   It was rather a poser. "You might make two of them contest a seat in Parliament," said Harvey, "and have an election—"

28   "With rotten eggs, and free fights, and ever so many broken heads!" exclaimed Eric.

29   "And noses all bleeding and everybody drunk as can be," echoed Bertie, who had carefully studied one of Hogarth's pictures.

30   "Nothing of the kind," said Harvey, "nothing in the least like that.

Votes will be put in the ballot-box, and the Mayor will count them—the district councillor will do for the Mayor—and he will say which has received the most votes, and then the two candidates will thank him for presiding, and each will say that the contest has been conducted throughout in the pleasantest and most straightforward fashion, and they part with expressions of mutual esteem. There's a jolly game for you boys to play. I never had such toys when I was young."

31   "I don't think we'll play with them just now," said Eric, with an entire absence of the enthusiasm that his uncle had shown; "I think perhaps we ought to do a little of our holiday task. It's history this time; we've got to learn up something about the Bourbon period in France."

32   "The Bourbon period," said Harvey, with some disapproval in his voice.

33   "We've got to know something about Louis the Fourteenth," continued Eric; "I've learnt the names of all the principal battles already."

34   This would never do. "There were, of course, some battles fought during his reign," said Harvey, "but I fancy the accounts of them were much exaggerated; news was very unreliable in those days, and there were practically no war correspondents, so generals and commanders could magnify every little skirmish they engaged in till they reached the proportions of decisive battles. Louis was really famous, now, as a landscape gardener; the way he laid out Versailles was so much admired that it was copied all over Europe."

35   "Do you know anything about Madame Du Barry?" asked Eric; "didn't she have her head chopped off?"

36   "She was another great lover of gardening," said Harvey evasively; "in fact, I believe the well-known rose Du Barry was named after her, and now I think you had better play for a little and leave your lessons till later."

37   Harvey retreated to the library and spent some thirty or forty minutes in wondering whether it would be possible to compile a history, for use in elementary schools, in which there should be no prominent mention of battles, massacres, murderous intrigues, and violent deaths. The York and Lancaster period and the Napoleonic era would, he admitted to himself, present considerable difficulties, and the Thirty Years' War would entail something of a gap if you left it out altogether. Still, it would be something gained if, at a highly impressionable age, children could be got to fix their attention on the invention of calico printing instead of the Spanish Armada or the Battle of Waterloo.

38   It was time, he thought, to go back to the boys' room, and see how they were getting on with their peace toys. As he stood outside the door he could hear Eric's voice raised in command; Bertie chimed in now and again with a helpful suggestion.

39   "That is Louis the Fourteenth," Eric was saying, "that one in knee-breeches, that Uncle said invented Sunday schools. It isn't a bit like him, but it'll have to do."

40   "We'll give him a purple coat from my paintbox by and by," said
Bertie.

41   "Yes, an' red heels. That is Madame de Maintenon, that one he
called Mrs. Hemans. She begs Louis not to go on this expedition, but he
turns a deaf ear. He takes Marshal Saxe with him, and we must pretend
that they have thousands of men with them. The watchword is *Qui vive?*
and the answer is *L'état c'est moi*—that was one of his favourite remarks,
you know. They land at Manchester in the dead of night, and a Jacobite
conspirator gives them the keys of the fortress."

42   Peeping in through the doorway Harvey observed that the municipal dust-bin had been pierced with holes to accommodate the muzzles of
imaginary cannon, and now represented the principal fortified position
in Manchester; John Stuart Mill had been dipped in red ink, and apparently stood for Marshal Saxe.

43   "Louis orders his troops to surround the Young Women's Christian
Association and seize the lot of them. 'Once back at the Louvre and the
girls are mine,' he exclaims. We must use Mrs. Hemans again for one of
the girls; she says 'Never,' and stabs Marshal Saxe to the heart."

44   "He bleeds dreadfully," exclaimed Bertie, splashing red ink liber-
ally over the facade of the Association building.

45   "The soldiers rush in and avenge his death with the utmost savage-
ry. A hundred girls are killed"—here Bertie emptied the remainder of
the red ink over the devoted building—"and the surviving five hundred
are dragged off to the French ships. 'I have lost a Marshal,' says Louis,
'but I do not go back empty-handed.'"

46   Harvey stole away from the room, and sought out his sister.

47   "Eleanor," he said, "the experiment—"

48   "Yes?"

49   "Has failed. We have begun too late."

Study Questions

1. Comment on the naiveté of the two adults in the story.
2. Are Eric and Bertie individuals? That is, do they have personal characteristics
    which distinguish them from one another?
3. Do the children seem like real children? Why or why not?
4. Is there internal evidence for concluding that this story was written by an
    Englishman?

Mousemeal

Howard Nemerov

My son invites me to witness with him
a children's program, a series of cartoons,
on television. Addressing myself to share
his harmless pleasures, I am horrified
by the unbridled violence and hostility
of the imagined world he takes in stride,
where human beings dressed in the skins of mice
are eaten by portcullises and cowcatchers,
digested through the winding corridors
or organs, overshoes, boa constrictors   10
and locomotive boilers, to be excreted
in waters where shark and squid and abalone
wait to employ their tentacles and jaws.
It seems there is no object in this world
unable to become a gullet with great lonely teeth;
sometimes a set of teeth all by itself
comes clacking over an endless plain
after the moving mouse; and though the mouse
wins in the end, the tail of one cartoon
is spliced into the mouth of the next, where his   20
rapid and trivial agony repeats itself
in another form. My son has seen these things
a number of times, and knows what to expect;
he does not seem disturbed or anything more
than mildly amused. Maybe these old cartoons
refer to my childhood and not to his
(The ogres in them wear Mussolini's face),
so that when mice are swallowed by skeletons
or empty suits of armor, when a tribe
of savage Negro mice is put through a wringer   30
and stacked flat in the cellar, he can take
the objective and critical view, while I
am shaken to see the giant picassoid
parents eating and voiding their little mice
time and again. And when the cheery announcer
cries, "Well, kids, that's the end," my son gets up
obediently and runs outside to play.

437

I hope he will ride over this world as well,
and that his crudest and most terrifying dreams
will not return with such wide publicity.   40

Study Questions

1. How do the imagery and metaphors of the second.sentence culminate in one generalized statement?
2. How is the father's perspective of the cartoons broader than his son's?
3. What is the irony in the child's "objective and critical view"? Does the father have this objectivity? Why not?
4. What verb tense does Nemerov use? What does he accomplish by this?
5. How do you know that "Mousemeal" is poetry?

Television: The Splitting Image

Marya Mannes

1   A bride who looks scarcely fourteen whispers, "Oh, Mom, I'm so *happy!*" while a doting family adjust her gown and veil and a male voice croons softly, "A woman is a harder thing to be than a man. She has more feelings to feel." The mitigation of these excesses, it appears, is a feminine deodorant called Secret, which allows our bride to approach the altar with security as well as emotion.

2   Eddie Albert, a successful actor turned pitchman, bestows his attention on a lady with two suitcases, which prompt him to ask her whether she has been on a journey. "No," she says, or words to that effect, as she opens the suitcases. "My two boys bring back their soiled clothes every weekend from college for me to wash." And she goes into the familiar litany of grease, chocolate, mud, coffee, and fruit-juice stains, which presumably record the life of the average American male from two to fifty. Mr. Albert compliments her on this happy device to

bring her boys home every week and hands her a box of Biz, because "Biz *is* better."

3   Two women with stony faces meet cart to cart in a supermarket as one takes a jar of peanut butter off a shelf. When the other asks her in a voice of nitric acid why she takes that brand, the first snaps, "Because I'm choosy for my family!" The two then break into delighted smiles as Number Two makes Number One taste Jiffy for "mothers who are choosy."

4   If you have not come across these dramatic interludes, it is because you are not home during the day and do not watch daytime television. It also means that your intestinal tract is spared from severe assaults, your credibility unstrained. Or, for that matter, you may look at commercials like these every day and manage either to ignore them or find nothing—given the fact of advertising—wrong with them. In that case, you are either so brainwashed or so innocent that you remain unaware of what this daily infusion may have done and is doing to an entire people as the long-accepted adjunct of free enterprise and support of "free" television.

5   "Given the fact" and "long-accepted" are the key words here. Only socialists, communists, idealists (or the BBC) fail to realize that a mass television system cannot exist without the support of sponsors, that the massive cost of maintaining it as a free service cannot be met without the massive income from selling products. You have only to read of the unending struggle to provide financial support for public, noncommercial television for further evidence.

6   Besides, aren't commercials in the public interest? Don't they help you choose what to buy? Don't they provide needed breaks from programing? Aren't many of them brilliantly done, and some of them funny? And now, with the new sexual freedom, all those gorgeous chicks with their shining hair and gleaming smiles? And if you didn't have commercials taking up a good part of each hour, how on earth would you find enough program material to fill the endless space/time void?

7   Tick off the yesses and what have you left? You have, I venture to submit, these intangible but possibly high costs: the diminution of human worth, the infusion and hardening of social attitudes no longer valid or desirable, pervasive discontent, and psychic fragmentation.

8   Should anyone wonder why deception is not an included detriment, I suggest that our public is so conditioned to promotion as a way of life, whether in art or politics or products, that elements of exaggeration or distortion are taken for granted. Nobody really believes that a certain shampoo will get a certain swain, or that an unclogged sinus can make a man a swinger. People are merely prepared to hope it will.

9   But the diminution of human worth is much more subtle and just as pervasive. In the guise of what they consider comedy, the producers of television commercials have created a loathsome gallery of men and women patterned, presumably, on Mr. and Mrs. America. Women liberationists have a major target in the commercial image of woman

flashed hourly and daily to the vast majority. There are, indeed, only four kinds of females in this relentless sales procession: the gorgeous teen-age swinger with bouncing locks; the young mother teaching her baby girl the right soap for skin care; the middle-aged housewife with a voice like a power saw; and the old lady with dentures and irregularity. All these women, to be sure, exist. But between the swinging sex object and the constipated granny there are millions of females never shown in commercials. These are—married or single—intelligent, sensitive women who bring charm to their homes, who work at jobs as well as lend grace to their marriage, who support themselves, who have talents or hobbies or commitments, or who are skilled at their professions.

10   To my knowledge, as a frequent if reluctant observer, I know of only one woman on a commercial who has a job; a comic plumber pushing Comet. Funny, heh? Think of a dame with a plunger.

11   With this one representative of our labor force, which is well over thirty million women, we are left with nothing but the full-time house-wife in all her whining glory: obsessed with whiter wash, moister cakes, shinier floor, cleaner children, softer diapers, and greaseless fried chicken. In the rare instances when these ladies are not in the kitchen, at the washing machine, or waiting on hubby, they are buying beauty shops (fantasy, see?) to take home so that their hair will have more body. Or out at the supermarket being choosy.

12   If they were attractive in their obsessions, they might be bearable. But they are not. They are pushy, loud-mouthed, stupid, and—of all things now—bereft of sexuality. Presumably, the argument in the tenets of advertising is that once a woman marries she changes overnight from plaything to floor-waxer.

13   To be fair, men make an equivalent transition in commercials. The swinging male with the mod hair and the beautiful chick turns inevitably into the paunchy slob who chokes on his wife's cake. You will notice, however, that the voice urging the viewer to buy the product is nearly always male: gentle, wise, helpful, seductive. And the visible presence telling the housewife how to get shinier floors and whiter wash and lovelier hair is almost invariably a man: the Svengali in modern dress, the Trilby (if only she were!), his willing object.

14   Woman, in short, is consumer first and human being fourth. A wife and mother who stays home all day buys a lot more than a woman who lives alone or who—married or single—has a job. The young girl hell-bent on marriage is the next most susceptible consumer. It is entirely understandable, then, that the potential buyers of detergents, foods, polishes, toothpastes, pills, and housewares are the housewives, and that the sex object spends most of *her* money on cosmetics, hair lotions, soaps, mouthwashes, and soft drinks.

15   Here we come, of course, to the youngest class of consumers, the swinging teen-agers so beloved by advertisers keen on telling them (and us) that they've "got a lot to live, and Pepsi's got a lot to give." This

affords a chance to show a squirming, leaping, jiggling group of beautiful kids having a very loud high on rock and—of all things—soda pop. One of commercial TV's most dubious achievements, in fact, is the reinforcement of the self-adulation characteristic of the young as a group.

16   As for the aging female citizen, the less shown on her the better. She is useful for ailments, but since she buys very little of anything, not having a husband or any children to feed or house to keep, nor—of course—sex appeal to burnish, society and commercials have little place for her. The same is true, to be sure, of older men, who are handy for Bosses with Bad Breath or Doctors with Remedies. Yet, on the whole, men hold up better than women at any age—in life or on television. Lines on their faces are marks of distinction, while on women they are signatures of decay.

17   There is no question, in any case, that television commercials (and many of the entertainment programs, notably the soap serials that are part of the selling package) reinforce, like an insistent drill, the assumption that a woman's only valid function is that of wife, mother, and servant of men: the inevitable sequel to her earlier function as sex object and swinger.

18   At a time when more and more women are at long last learning to reject these assumptions as archaic and demeaning, and to grow into individual human beings with a wide option of lives to live, the sellers of the nation are bent upon reinforcing the ancient pattern. They know only too well that by beaming their message to the Consumer Queen they can justify her existence as the housebound Mrs. America: dumber than dumb, whiter than white.

19   The conditioning starts very early: with the girl child who wants the skin Ivory soap has reputedly given her mother, with the nine-year-old who brings back a cake of Camay instead of the male deodorant her father wanted. (When she confesses that she bought it so she could be "feminine," her father hugs her, and, with the voice of a child-molester, whispers, "My little girl is growing up on me, huh.") And then, before long, comes the teen-aged bride who "has feelings to feel."

20   It is the little boys who dream of wings, in an airplane commercial; who grow up (with fewer cavities) into the doers. Their little sisters turn into *Cosmopolitan* girls, who in turn become housewives furious that their neighbors' wash is cleaner than theirs.

21   There is good reason to suspect that this manic obsession with cleanliness, fostered, quite naturally, by the giant soap and detergent interests, may bear some responsibility for the cultivated sloppiness of so many of the young in their clothing as well as in their chosen hideouts. The compulsive housewife who spends more time washing and vacuuming and polishing her possessions than communicating to, or stimulating her children creates a kind of sterility that the young would instinctively reject. The impeccably tidy home, the impeccably tidy lawn are—in a very real sense—unnatural and confining.

22   Yet the commercials confront us with broods of happy children, some of whom—believe it or not—notice the new fresh smell their clean, white sweatshirts exhale thanks to Mom's new "softener."

23   Some major advertisers, for that matter, can even cast a benign eye on the population explosion. In another Biz commercial, the genial Eddie Albert surveys with surprise a long row of dirty clothes heaped before him by a young matron. She answers his natural query by telling him gaily they are the products of her brood of eleven "with one more to come!" she adds as the twelfth turns up. "That's great!" says Mr. Albert, curdling the soul of Planned Parenthood and the future of this planet.

24   Who are, one cannot help but ask, the writers who manage to combine the sales of products with the selling-out of human dreams and dignity? Who people this cosmos of commercials with dolts and fools and shrews and narcissists? Who know so much about quirks and mannerisms and ailments and so little about life? So much about presumed wants and so little about crying needs?

25   Can women advertisers so demean their own sex? Or are there no women in positions of decision high enough to see that their real selves stand up?

26   Do they not know, these extremely clever creators of commercials, what they could do for their audience even while they exploit and entertain them? How they could raise the levels of manners and attitudes while they sell their wares? Or do they really share the worm's-eye view of mass communication that sees, and addresses, only the lowest common denominator?

27   It can be argued that commercials are taken too seriously, that their function is merely to amuse, engage, and sell, and that they do this brilliantly. If that were all to this wheedling of millions, well and good. But it is not. There are two more fallouts from this chronic sales explosion that cannot be measured but that at least can be expected. One has to do with the continual celebration of youth at the expense of maturity. In commercials only the young have access to beauty, sex, and joy in life. What do older women feel, day after day, when love is the exclusive possession of a teenage girl with a bobbing mantle of hair? What older man would not covet her in restless impotence?

28   The constant reminder of what is inaccessible must inevitably produce a subterranean but real discontent, just as the continual sight of things and places beyond reach has eaten deeply into the ghetto soul. If we are constantly presented with what we are not or cannot have, the dislocation deepens, contentment vanishes, and frustration reigns. Even for the substantially secure, there is always a better thing, a better way, to buy. That none of these things makes a better life may be consciously acknowledged, but still the desire lodges in the spirit, nagging and pulling.

29   This kind of fragmentation works in potent ways above and beyond the mere fact of program interruption, which is much of the time more of

a blessing than a curse, especially in those rare instances when the commercial is deft and funny: the soft and subtle sell. Its overall curse, due to the large number of commercials in each hour, is that it reduces the attention span of a people already so conditioned to constant change and distraction that they cannot tolerate continuity in print or on the air.

30   Specifically, commercial interruption is most damaging during that 10 percent of programing (a charitable estimate) most important to the mind and spirit of a people: news and public affairs, and drama.

31   To many (and among these are network news producers), commercials have no place or business during the vital process of informing the public. There is something obscene about a newscaster pausing to introduce a deodorant or shampoo commercial between an airplane crash and a body count. It is more than an interruption; it tends to reduce news to a form of running entertainment, to smudge the edges of reality by treating death or disaster or diplomacy on the same level as household appliances or a new gasoline.

32   The answer to this would presumably be to lump the commercials before and after the news or public affairs broadcasts—an answer unpalatable, needless to say, to the sponsors who support them.

33   The same is doubly true of that most unprofitable sector of television, the original play. Essential to any creative composition, whether drama, music, or dance, are mood and continuity, both inseparable from form and meaning. They are shattered by the periodic intrusion of commercials, which have become intolerable to the serious artists who have deserted commercial television in droves because the system allows them no real freedom of autonomy. The selling comes first, the creation must accommodate itself. It is the rare and admirable sponsor who restricts or fashions his commercials so as to provide a minimum of intrusion or damaging inappropriateness.

34   If all these assumptions and imponderables are true, as many suspect, what is the answer or alleviation?

35   One is in the course of difficult emergence: the establishment of a public television system sufficiently funded so that it can give a maximum number of people an alternate diet of pleasure, enlightenment, and stimulation free from commercial fragmentation. So far, for lack of funds to buy talent and equipment, this effort has been in terms of public attention a distinctly minor operation.

36   Even if public television should, hopefully, greatly increase its scope and impact, it cannot in the nature of things and through long public conditioning equal the impact and reach the size of audience now tuned to commercial television.

37   Enormous amounts of time, money, and talent go into commercials. Technically they are often brilliant and innovative, the product not only of the new skills and devices but of imaginative minds. A few of them are both funny and endearing. Who, for instance, will forget the miserable young man with the appalling cold, or the kids taught to use—as an

initiation into manhood—a fork instead of a spoon with a certain spaghetti? Among the enlightened sponsors, moreover, are some who manage to combine an image of their corporation and their products with accuracy and restraint.

38   What has to happen to mass medium advertisers as a whole, and especially on TV, is a totally new approach to their function not only as sellers but as social influencers. They have the same obligation as the broadcast medium itself: not only to entertain but to reflect, not only to reflect but to enlarge public consciousness and human stature.

39   This may be a tall order, but it is a vital one at a time when Americans have ceased to know who they are and where they are going, and when all the multiple forces acting upon them are daily diminishing their sense of their own value and purpose in life, when social upheaval and social fragmentation have destroyed old patterns, and when survival depends on new ones.

40   If we continue to see ourselves as the advertisers see us, we have no place to go. Nor, I might add, has commercial broadcasting itself.

Study Questions

1. What is the thesis statement of this essay? How many parts does it have?
2. What is the effect of the three paragraphs of rhetorical questions near the middle (paragraphs 24–26)? Do you feel that Mannes overuses questions as a device?
3. How effective is Mannes's use of detail? Are her examples real or fictitious? How can you tell?
4. What does the title of the essay mean?
5. Provide an outline for Mannes's essay. What does it tell you about how she constructed the piece?

A Newspaper Is a Collection of Half-Injustices

Stephen Crane

A newspaper is a collection of half-injustices
Which, bawled by boys from mile to mile,
Spreads it curious opinion
To a million merciful and sneering men,
While families cuddle the joys of the fireside
When spurred by tale of dire lone agony.
A newspaper is a court
Where everyone is kindly and unfairly tried
By a squalor of honest men.
A newspaper is a market   10
Where wisdom sells its freedom
And melons are crowned by the crowd.
A newspaper is a game
Where his error scores the player victory
While another's skill wins death.
A newspaper is a symbol;
It is feckless life's chronicle,
A collection of loud tales
Concentrating eternal stupidities,
That in remote ages lived unhaltered,   20
Roaming through a fenceless world.

Study Questions

1. What five words in this poem define a newspaper?
2. Is there any order or accumulation in the presentation of the definitions?
3. What irony do you find in each definition?
4. What is the effect of *feckless* in the concluding sentence?

Choosing a Dream

Choosing a Dream includes representative writings with wide universal appeal from a variety of cultures. The first subsection is about childhood and youth. Some authors, looking back on those periods of their lives, are able to recapture the essence of youthful experience—the sense of being unique and the reasons for feeling that uniqueness. At the same time, most of these reminiscences possess a great deal of universality; we can all say, at one place or another, "Oh, yes! That reminds me. . . ." Nikki Giovanni feels that her childhood experience is understandable only to blacks, while Piri Thomas's account of a boy's search for acceptance in a new environment will be familiar to many who changed neighborhoods as children. Most readers, however, will not have known the intensity of the situation as Thomas describes it. Mario Puzo and Jade Snow Wong present positive views of two different ethnic youth experiences; both are able to resolve the conflicts between cultures, while both seem aware of something lost as well as something gained. Gwendolyn Brooks sees youth as a time fraught with danger—"cool" may not be quite the answer to everything. Don L. Lee, on the other hand, speaks of ultimate "cool." But he also speaks a cautionary word: The "cool" black youth in America today may be "very-hot."

In the second subsection of *Choosing a Dream* two Native Americans, a Chinese-American, a nisei, and a black American speak of tradition. Each of these authors finds it possible to retain a strong sense of the past and to relate that past to the present environment. Kuangchi C. Chang, a refugee from the People's Republic of China, discovers that although he is removed by continents and light-years from his childhood garden, he will be able to recreate that garden in his new land. Bruce Ignacio wonders where the culture of his people has gone; Leslie Silko denies, in her story of the merging of the white man's and Native American's burial customs, that Native American culture is any less pertinent or powerful than it ever was. Kenneth Yasuda (Shosōn), an American-born descendant of Japanese forbears, offers six poems in the haiku style of his ancestors. Each, restricted in form and content, is as highly polished and as traditional as any written by a sixteenth-century emperor. And finally, Claude McKay, in a city that bears no resemblance to his beloved homeland, nevertheless finds similarities that keep alive his memories of Jamaica.

447

From tradition we turn to alienation, the expressions of writers who have been turned off, in one way or another, by their attempts to choose a dream. William Eastlake speaks for the Native American who sees a bitter contrast between man's reaching the moon and his people's futile striving for a better life on earth. José Angel Gutiérrez traces his growing awareness of his position as an alien in his own country through his reactions, at different ages, to the word "Mexican." Victor Hernández Cruz suggests that the Hispanic-American is out of place in any part of the American culture and can only cling to its edges. Richard Wright, in closing the section, offers a short story on a theme that, in the last analysis, transcends the mistreatment of one race by another and becomes a universal statement of man's inhumanity to man.

The visionaries are the last to speak in this section. They are led by Martin Luther King, Jr., who had a dream, and who lived to see it slowly coming true. He is followed by Peter La Farge, whose vision is of a future that cannot bear the slightest resemblance to the past, and by Chiang Yee, who has travelled a great distance since leaving China and who anticipates greater distances yet to travel. Enrique Hank Lopez then discusses his attempts to look back, and finds that he must look ahead instead. We chose the poem by Langston Hughes for its prophetic tone; Hughes saw the 1960s clearly some fifteen years before Watts became anything more than a name on a Los Angeles city map to many people.

All of these writers are moderns who represent ethnic groups within the melting pot of America today. Some of them choose assimilation, others opt for the retention of their own worlds and customs. But most of them speak with voices that transcend barriers of race and culture, and thus reach all who read their words.

Nikki-Rosa

Nikki Giovanni

childhood remembrances are always a drag
if you're Black
you always remember things like living in Woodlawn
with no inside toilet
and if you become famous or something
they never talk about how happy you were to have your mother
all to yourself and
how good the water felt when you got your bath from one of
those big tubs that folk in chicago barbecue in
and somehow when you talk about home   10
it never gets across how much you
understood their feelings
as the whole family attended meetings about Hollydale
and even though you remember
your biographers never understand
your father's pain as he sells his stock
and another dream goes
and though you're poor it isn't poverty that
concerns you
and though they fought a lot   20
it isn't your father's drinking that makes any difference
but only that everybody is together and you
and your sister have happy birthdays and very good christmasses
and I really hope no white person ever has cause to write
about me because they never understand Black love is Black
wealth and they'll probably talk about my hard childhood
and never understand that all the while I was quite happy

Study Questions

1. What is the thesis of this poem? Why does it logically appear at the end of the poem?
2. What are the sources of comfort and community for the child in this poem?

3. How many of Giovanni's memories are directly related to her black heritage? How many have universality?
4. Why does the poem seem to jump from one topic to the next? Why is there a lack of transition, with the exception of *and*?

If You Ain't Got Heart, You Ain't Got Nada

Piri Thomas

1   We were moving—our new pad was back in Spanish Harlem—to 104th Street between Lex and Park Avenue.

2   Moving into a new block is a big jump for a Harlem kid. You're torn up from your hard-won turf and brought into an "I don't know you" block where every kid is some kind of enemy. Even when the block belongs to your own people, you are still an outsider who has to prove himself a down stud with heart.

3   As the moving van rolled to a stop in front of our new building, number 109, we were all standing there, waiting for it—Momma, Poppa, Sis, Paulie, James, José, and myself. I made out like I didn't notice the cats looking us over, especially me—I was gang age. I read their faces and found no trust, plenty of suspicion, and a glint of rising hate. I said to myself, *These cats don't mean nothin'. They're just nosy.* But I remembered what had happened to me in my old block, and that it had ended with me in the hospital.

4   This was a tough-looking block. That was good, that was cool; but my old turf had been tough, too. *I'm tough enough.* A voice within said. *I hope I'm tough enough. I am tough enough. I've got* mucho corazón, *I'm king wherever I go. I'm a killer to my heart. I not only* can *live, I* will *live, no punk out, no die out, walk bad; be down, cool breeze, smooth.* My mind raced, and thoughts crashed against each other, trying to reassemble themselves into a pattern of rep. I turned slowly and with eyelids half-closed I looked at the rulers of this new world and with a cool shrug of my shoulders I followed the movers into the hallway of number 109 and dismissed the coming war from my mind.

5   The next morning I went to my new school, called Patrick Henry, and strange, mean eyes followed me.

6   "Say, pops," said a voice belonging to a guy I later came to know as Waneko, "where's your territory?"

7   In the same tone of voice Waneko had used, I answered, "I'm on it, dad, what's shaking?"

8   "Bad, huh?" He half-smiled.

9   "No, not all the way. Good when I'm cool breeze and bad when I'm down."

10   "What's your name, kid?"

11   "That depends. 'Piri' when I'm smooth and 'Johnny Gringo' when stomping time's around."

12   "What's your name now?" he pushed.

13   "You name me, man," I answered, playing my role like a champ.

14   He looked around, and with no kind of words, his boys cruised in. Guys I would come to know, to fight, to hate, to love, to take care of. Little Red, Waneko, Little Louie, Indio, Carlito, Alfredo, Crip, and plenty more. I stiffened and said to myself, *Stomping time, Piri boy, go with heart.*

15   I fingered the garbage-can handle in my pocket—my homemade brass knuckles. They were great for breaking down large odds into small, chopped-up ones.

16   Waneko, secure in his grandstand, said. "We'll name you later, *panin.*"

17   I didn't answer. Scared, yeah, but wooden-faced to the end, I thought, *Chévere, panin.*

18   It wasn't long in coming. Three days later, at about 6 p.m., Waneko and his boys were sitting around the stoop at number 115. I was cut off from my number 109. For an instant I thought, *Make a break for it down the basement steps and through the back yards—get away in one piece!* Then I thought, *Caramba! Live punk, dead hero. I'm no punk kid. I'm not copping any pleas.* I kept walking, hell's a-burning, hell's a-churning, rolling with cheer. *Walk on, baby man, roll on without fear. What's he going to call?*

19   "Whatta ya say, Mr. Johnny Gringo?" drawled Waneko.

20   *Think, man,* I told myself, *think your way out of a stomping. Make it good.* "I hear you 104th Street coolies are supposed to have heart," I said. "I don't know this for sure. You know there's a lot of streets where a whole 'click' is made out of punks who can't fight one guy unless they all jump him for the stomp." I hoped this would push Waneko into giving me a fair one. His expression didn't change.

21   "Maybe we don't look at it that way."

22   *Crazy, man. I cheer inwardly, the* cabrón *is falling into my setup. We'll see who gets messed up first, baby!* "I wasn't talking to you," I said. "Where I come from, the pres is president 'cause he got heart when it comes to dealing."

23   Waneko was starting to look uneasy. He had bit on my worm and felt like a sucker fish. His boys were now light on me. They were no longer so much interested in stomping me as in seeing the outcome between Waneko and me. "Yeah," was his reply.

24   I smiled at him. "You trying to dig where I'm at and now you got me interested in you. I'd like to see where you're at."

25   Waneko hesitated a tiny little second before replying, "Yeah."

26   I knew I'd won. Sure, I'd have to fight; but one guy, not ten or fifteen. If I lost I might still get stomped, and if I won I might get stomped. I took care of this with my next sentence. "I don't know you or your boys," I said, "but they look cool to me. They don't feature as punks."

27   I had left him out purposely when I said "they." Now his boys were in a separate class. I had cut him off. He would have to fight me on his own, to prove his heart to himself, to his boys, and most important, to his turf. He got away from the stoop and asked, "Fair one, Gringo?"

28   "Uh-uh," I said, "roll all the way—anthing goes." I thought, *I've got to beat him bad and yet not bad enough to take his prestige all away.* He had *corazón.* He came on me. *Let him draw first blood,* I thought, *it's his block.* Smish, my nose began to bleed. His boys cheered, his heart cheered, his turf cheered. "Waste this chump," somebody shouted.

29   *Okay, baby, now it's my turn.* He swung. I grabbed innocently, and my forehead smashed into his nose. His eyes crossed. His fingernails went for my eye and landed in my mouth—crunch, I bit hard. I punched him in the mouth as he pulled away from me, and he slammed his foot into my chest.

30   We broke, my nose running red, my chest throbbing, his finger— well, that was his worry. I tied up with body punching and slugging. We rolled onto the street. I wrestled for acceptance, he for rejection or, worse yet, acceptance on his terms. It was time to start peace talks. I smiled at him. "You got heart, baby," I said.

31   He answered with a punch to my head. I grunted and hit back, harder now. I had to back up my overtures of peace with strength. I hit him in the ribs, I rubbed my knuckles in his ear as we clinched. I tried again. "You deal good," I said.

32   "You too," he muttered, pressuring out. And just like that, the fight was over. No more words. We just separated, hands half up, half down. My heart pumped out, *You've established your rep. Move over, 104th Street. Lift your wings, I'm one of your baby chicks now.*

33   Five seconds later my spurs were given to me in the form of introductions to streetdom's elite. There were no looks of blankness now; I was accepted by heart.

34   "What's your other name, Johnny Gringo?"

35   "Piri."

36   "Okay, Pete, you wanna join my fellows?"

37   "Sure, why not?"

Study Questions

1. Thomas uses standard English, the street jargon of Harlem, and Spanish in this sketch. How do these different linguistic levels contribute to the theme?
2. Define *gang age* and *corazón*.
3. Does Thomas imply that "heart" is cross-cultural? Explain.

Choosing a Dream: Italians in Hell's Kitchen

Mario Puzo

1   As a child and in my adolescence, living in the heart of New York's Neapolitan ghetto, I never heard an Italian singing. None of the grown-ups I knew were charming or loving or understanding. Rather they seemed coarse, vulgar, and insulting. And so later in my life when I was exposed to all the clichés of lovable Italians, singing Italians, happy-go-lucky Italians, I wondered where the hell the movie-makers and story-writers got all their ideas from.

2   At a very early age I decided to escape these uncongenial folk by becoming an artist, a writer. It seemed then an impossible dream. My father and mother were illiterate, as were their parents before them. But practicing my art, I tried to view the adults with a more charitable eye and so came to the conclusion that their only fault lay in their being foreigners; I was an American. This didn't really help because I was only half right. I was the foreigner. They were already more "American" than I could ever become.

3   But it did seem then that the Italian immigrants, all the fathers and mothers that I knew, were a grim lot; always shouting, always angry, quicker to quarrel than embrace. I did not understand that their lives were a long labor to earn their daily bread and that physical fatigue does not sweeten human natures.

4   And so even as a very small child I dreaded growing up to be like the adults around me. I heard them saying too many cruel things about

their dearest friends, saw too many of their false embraces with those they had just maligned, observed with horror their paranoiac anger at some small slight or a fancied injury to their pride. They were, always, too unforgiving. In short, they did not have the careless magnanimity of children.

5   In my youth I was contemptuous of my elders, including a few under thirty. I thought my contempt special to their circumstances. Later when I wrote about these illiterate men and women, when I thought I understood them, I felt a condescending pity. After all, they had suffered, they had labored all the days of their lives. They had never tasted luxury, knew little more economic security than those ancient Roman slaves who might have been their ancestors. And alas, I thought, with newfound artistic insight, they were cut off from their children because of the strange American tongue, alien to them, native to their sons and daughters.

6   Already an artist but not yet a husband or father, I pondered omnisciently on their tragedy, again thinking it special circumstance rather than a constant in the human condition. I did not yet understand why these men and women were willing to settle for less than they deserved in life and think that "less" quite a bargain. I did not understand that they simply could not afford to dream; I myself had a hundred dreams from which to choose. For I was already sure that I would make my escape, that I was one of the chosen. I would be rich, famous, happy. I would master my destiny.

7   And so it was perhaps natural that as a child, with my father gone, my mother the family chief, I, like all the children in all the ghettos of America, became locked in a bitter struggle with the adults responsible for me. It was inevitable that my mother and I became enemies.

8   As a child I had the usual dreams. I wanted to be handsome, specifically as cowboy stars in movies were handsome. I wanted to be a killer hero in a worldwide war. Or if no wars came along (our teachers told us another was impossible), I wanted at the very least to be a footloose adventurer. Then I branched out and thought of being a great artist, and then, getting ever more sophisticated, a great criminal.

9   My mother, however, wanted me to be a railroad clerk. And that was her *highest* ambition; she would have settled for less. At the age of sixteen, when I let everybody know that I was going to be a great writer, my friends and family took the news quite calmly, my mother included. She did not become angry. She quite simply assumed that I had gone off my nut. She was illiterate, and her peasant life in Italy made her believe that only a son of the nobility could possibly be a writer. Artistic beauty after all could spring only from the seedbed of fine clothes, fine food, luxurious living. So then how was it possible for a son of hers to be an artist? She was not too convinced she was wrong even after my first two books were published many years later. It was only after the commercial success of my third novel that she gave me the title of poet.

10   My family and I grew up together on Tenth Avenue, between Thirtieth and Thirty-first streets, part of the area called Hell's Kitchen. This particular neighborhood could have been a movie set for one of the Dead End Kid flicks or for the social drama of the East Side in which John Garfield played the hero. Our tenements were the western wall of the city. Beneath our windows were the vast black iron gardens of the New York Central Railroad, absolutely blooming with stinking boxcars freshly unloaded of cattle and pigs for the city slaughterhouse. Steers sometimes escaped and loped through the heart of the neighborhood followed by astonished young boys who had never seen a live cow.

11   The railroad yards stretched down to the Hudson River, beyond whose garbagey waters rose the rocky Palisades of New Jersey. There were railroad tracks running downtown on Tenth Avenue itself to another freight station called St. Johns Park. Because of this, because these trains cut off one side of the street from the other, there was a wooden bridge over Tenth Avenue, a romantic-looking bridge despite the fact that no sparkling water, no silver flying fish darted beneath it; only heavy dray carts drawn by tired horses, some flat-boarded trucks, tin lizzie automobiles and, of course, long strings of freight cars drawn by black, ugly engines.

12   What was really great, truly magical, was sitting on the bridge, feet dangling down, and letting the engine under you blow up clouds of steam that made you disappear, then reappear all damp and smelling of fresh ironing. When I was seven years old, I fell in love for the first time with the tough little girl who held my hand and disappeared with me in that magical cloud of steam. This experience was probably more traumatic and damaging to my later relationships with women than one of those ugly childhood adventures Freudian novelists use to explain why their hero has gone bad.

13   My father supported his wife and seven children by working as a trackman laborer for the New York Central Railroad. My oldest brother worked for the railroad as a brakeman; another brother was a railroad shipping clerk in the freight office. Eventually I spent some of the worst months of my life as the railroad's worst messenger boy.

14   My oldest sister was just as unhappy as a dressmaker in the garment industry. She wanted to be a schoolteacher. At one time or another my other two brothers also worked for the railroad—it got all six males in the family. The two girls and my mother escaped, though my mother felt it her duty to send all our bosses a gallon of homemade wine on Christmas. But everybody hated their jobs except my oldest brother, who had a night shift and spent most of his working hours sleeping in freight cars. My father finally got fired because the foreman told him to get a bucket of water for the crew and not to take all day. My father took the bucket and disappeared forever.

15   Nearly all the Italian men living on Tenth Avenue supported their large families by working on the railroad. Their children also earned

pocket money by stealing ice from the refrigerator cars in summer and coal from the open stoking cars in the winter. Sometimes an older lad would break the seal of a freight car and take a look inside. But this usually brought down the "Bulls," the special railroad police. And usually the freight was "heavy" stuff, too much work to cart away and sell, something like fresh produce or boxes of cheap candy that nobody would buy.

16   The older boys, the ones just approaching voting age, made their easy money by hijacking silk trucks that loaded up at the garment factory on Thirty-first Street. They would then sell the expensive dresses door to door, at bargain prices no discount house could match. From this some graduated into organized crime, whose talent scouts alertly tapped young boys versed in strong arm. Yet despite all this, most of the kids grew up honest, content with fifty bucks a week as truck drivers, deliverymen, and white-collar clerks in the Civil Service.

17   I had every desire to go wrong but I never had a chance. The Italian family structure was too formidable.

18   I never came home to an empty house; there was always the smell of supper cooking. My mother was always there to greet me, sometimes with a policeman's club in her hand (nobody ever knew how she acquired it). But she was always there, or her authorized deputy, my older sister, who preferred throwing empty milk bottles at the heads of her little brothers when they got bad marks on their report cards. During the great Depression of the 1930's, though we were the poorest of the poor, I never remember not dining well. Many years later as a guest of a millionaire's club, I realized that our poor family on home relief ate better than some of the richest people in America.

19   My mother would never dream of using anything but the finest imported olive oil, the best Italian cheeses. My father had access to the fruits coming off ships, the produce from railroad cars, all before it went through the stale process of middlemen; and my mother, like most Italian women, was a fine cook in the peasant style.

20   My mother was as formidable a personage as she was a cook. She was not to be treated cavalierly. My oldest brother at age sixteen had his own tin lizzie Ford and used it to further his career as the Don Juan of Tenth Avenue. One day my mother asked him to drive her to the market on Ninth Avenue and Fortieth Street, no more than a five minute trip. My brother had other plans and claimed he was going to work on a new shift on the railroad. Work was an acceptable excuse even for funerals. But an hour later when my mother came out of the door of the tenement, she saw the tin lizzie loaded with three pretty neighborhood girls, my Don Juan brother about to drive them off. Unfortunately there was a cobblestone lying loose in the gutter. My mother dropped her black leather shopping bag and picked up the stone with both hands. As we all watched in horror, she brought the boulder down on the nearest fender of the tin lizzie, demolishing it. Then she picked up her bag and

marched off to Ninth Avenue to do her shopping. To this day, forty years later, my brother's voice still has a surprised horror and shock when he tells the story. He still doesn't understand how she could have done it.

21   My mother had her own legends and myths on how to amass a fortune. There was one of our uncles who worked as an assistant chef in a famous Italian-style restaurant. Every day, six days a week, this uncle brought home, under his shirt, six eggs, a stick of butter, and a small bag of flour. By doing this for thirty years he was able to save enough money to buy a fifteen-thousand-dollar house on Long Island and two smaller houses for his son and daughter. Another cousin, blessed with a college degree, worked as a chemist in a large manufacturing firm. By using the firm's raw materials and equipment he concocted a superior floor wax which he sold door to door in his spare time. It was a great floor wax, and with his low overhead, the price was right. My mother and her friends did not think this stealing. They thought of it as being thrifty.

22   The wax-selling cousin eventually destroyed his reputation for thrift by buying a sailboat; this was roughly equivalent to the son of a Boston Brahmin spending a hundred grand in a whorehouse.

23   As rich men escape their wives by going to their club, I finally escaped my mother by going to the Hudson Guild Settlement House. Most people do not know that a settlement house is really a club combined with social services. The Hudson Guild, a five-story field of joy for slum kids, had ping-pong rooms and billiard rooms, a shop in which to make lamps, a theater for putting on amateur plays, a gym to box and play basketball in. And then there were individual rooms, where your particular club could meet in privacy. The Hudson Guild even suspended your membership for improper behavior or failure to pay the tiny dues. It was a heady experience for a slum kid to see his name posted on the billboard to the effect that he was suspended by the Board of Governors.

24   There were young men who guided us as counselors whom I remember with fondness to this day. They were more like friends than adults assigned to watch over us. I still remember one helping us eat a box of stolen chocolates rather than reproaching us. Which was exactly the right thing for him to do; we trusted him after that. The Hudson Guild kept more kids out of jail than a thousand policemen. It still exists today, functioning for the new immigrants, the blacks, and the Puerto Ricans.

25   There was a night when the rich people of New York, including the Ethical Culture Society, attended a social function at the Hudson Guild in order to be conned into contributing huge sums of money for the settlement house program. I think it was a dinner and amateur theater presentation that was costing them a hundred bucks a head. Their chauffeurs parked the limousines all along the curbs of Twenty-seventh Street and Tenth Avenue. Us deprived kids, myself the leader, spent the night letting the air out of our benefactors' tires. *Noblesse oblige.*

26   But we weren't all bad. In our public schools one year an appeal

was made to every child to try to bring a can of food to fill Thanksgiving baskets for the poor. The teachers didn't seem to realize *we* were the poor. We didn't either. Every kid in that public school, out of the goodness of his heart, went out and stole a can of food from a local grocery store. Our school had the best contributor record of any school in the city.

27   Some of the most exciting days in my life were spent at the Hudson Guild. At the age of eleven I became captain of my club football team for seven years and president of the Star Club, an office I held for five. I enjoyed that success more than any other in my life. And learned a great deal from it. At the age of fifteen I was as thoroughly corrupted by power as any dictator until I was overthrown by a coalition of votes; my best friends joining my enemies to depose me. It was a rare lesson to learn at fifteen.

28   The Star Club was made up of boys my own age, a gang, really, which had been pacified by the Hudson Guild Settlement House. We had a football team, a baseball team, a basketball team. We had a yearbook. We had our own room, where we could meet, and a guidance counselor, usually a college boy. We had one named Ray Dooley whom I remember with affection to this day. He took us for outings in the country, to the Hudson Guild Farm in New Jersey for winter weekends, where we hitched our sleds to his car, towed at thirty miles an hour. We repaid him by throwing lye into his face and almost blinding him. We thought it was flour. He never reproached us and it wound up OK. We idolized him after that. I liked him because he never tried to usurp my power, not so that I could notice.

29   The Hudson Guild was also responsible for absolutely the happiest times of my childhood. When I was about nine or ten they sent me away as a Fresh Air Fund kid. This was a program where slum children were boarded on private families in places like New Hampshire for two weeks.

30   As a child I knew only the stone city. I had no conception of what the countryside could be. When I got to New Hampshire, when I smelled grass and flowers and trees, when I ran barefoot along the dirt country roads, when I drove the cows home from pasture, when I darted through fields of corn and waded through clear brooks, when I gathered warm brown-speckled eggs in the henhouse, when I drove a hay wagon drawn by two great horses—when I did all these things—I nearly went crazy with joy of it. It was quite simply a fairy tale come true.

31   The family that took me in, a middle-aged man and woman, childless, were Baptists and observed Sunday so religiously that even checker playing was not allowed on the Lord's day of rest. We went to church on Sunday for a good three hours, counting Bible class, then again at night. On Thursday evenings we went to prayer meetings. My guardians, out of religious scruple, had never seen a movie. They disapproved of dancing, they were no doubt political reactionaries; they were everything that I came later to fight against.

32   And yet they gave me those magical times children never forget. For two weeks every summer from the time I was nine to fifteen I was happier than I have ever been before or since. The man was good with tools and built me a little playground with swings, sliding boards, seesaws. The woman had a beautiful flower and vegetable garden and let me pick from it. A cucumber or strawberry in the earth was a miracle. And then when they saw how much I loved picnics, the sizzling frankfurters on a stick over the wood fire, the yellow roasted corn, they drove me out on Sunday afternoons to a lovely green grass mountainside. Only on Sundays it was never called a picnic; it was called "taking our lunch outside." I found it then—and now—a sweet hypocrisy.

33   The Baptist preacher lived in the house a hundred yards away, and sometimes he, too, took his lunch "out" with us on a Sunday afternoon, he and his wife and children. Outside of his church he was a jolly fat man, a repressed comedian. Also a fond father, he bought his children a great many toys. I borrowed those toys and on one late August day I sailed his son's huge motor launch down a quiet, winding brook, and when it nosed into a wet mossy bank, I buried the toy there to have the following year when I came back. But I never found it.

34   There came a time, I was fifteen, when I was told I was too old to be sent away to the country as a Fresh Air Fund kid. It was the first real warning that I must enter the adult world, ready or not. But I always remembered that man and woman with affection, perhaps more. They always bought me clothing during my visits, my very first pajamas. They sent me presents at Christmastime, and when I was about to go into the Army, I visited them as a young man of twenty-one. The young were excessively grateful then, so I did not smoke in their house nor did I follow up on a local maid who seemed promising.

35   I believed then, as a child, that the state of New Hampshire had some sort of gates at which all thieves and bad guys were screened out. I believed this, I think, because the house was left unlocked when we went to church on Sundays and Thursday nights. I believed it because I never heard anyone curse or quarrel with raised voices. I believed it because it was beautiful to believe.

36   When I returned home from these summer vacations I had a new trick. I said grace with bowed head before eating the familiar spaghetti and meat balls. My mother always tolerated this for the few days it lasted. After all, the two weeks' vacation from her most troublesome child was well worth a Baptist prayer.

37   From this Paradise I was flung into hell. That is, I had to help support my family by working on the railroad. After schools hours of course. This was the same railroad that had supplied free coal and free ice to the whole Tenth Avenue when I was young enough to steal with impunity. After school finished at 3 P.M. I went to work in the freight office as a messenger. I also worked Saturdays and Sundays when there was work available.

38   I hated it. One of my first short stories was about how I hated that job. But of course what I really hated was entering the adult world. To me the adult world was a dark enchantment, unnatural. As unnatural to the human dream as death. And as inevitable.

39   The young are impatient about change because they cannot grasp the power of time itself; not only as the enemy of flesh, the very germ of death, but as a benign cancer. As the young cannot grasp really that love must be a victim of time, so too they cannot grasp that injustices, the economic and family traps of living, can also fall victim to time.

40   And so I really thought that I would spend the rest of my life as a railroad clerk. That I would never be a writer. That I would be married and have children and go to christenings and funerals and visit my mother on a Sunday afternoon. That I would never own an automobile or a house. That I would never see Europe, the Paris and Rome and Greece I was reading about in books from the public library. That I was hopelessly trapped by my family, by society, by my lack of skills and education.

41   But I escaped again. At the age of eighteen I started dreaming about the happiness of my childhood. As later at the age of thirty I would dream about the joys of my lost adolescence, as at the age of thirty-five I was to dream about the wonderful time I had in the Army which I had hated being in. As at the age of forty-five I dreamed about the happy, struggling years of being a devoted husband and loving father. I had the most valuable of human gifts, that of retrospective falsification: remembering the good and not the bad.

42   I still dreamed of future glory. I still wrote short stories, one or two a year. I still *knew* I would be a great writer, but I was beginning to realize that accidents could happen and my second choice, that of being a great criminal, was coming up fast. But for the young everything goes so slowly, I could wait it out. The world would wait for me. I could still spin out my life with dreams.

43   In the summertime I was one of the great Tenth Avenue athletes, but in the wintertime I became a sissy. I read books. At a very early age I discovered libraries, the one in the Hudson Guild and the public ones. I loved reading in the Hudson Guild where the librarian became a friend. I loved Joseph Altsheler's (I don't even have to look up his name) tales about the wars of the New York State Indian tribes, the Senecas and the Iroquois. I discovered Doc Savage and the Shadow and then the great story-teller Sabatini. Part of my character to this day is Scaramouche, I like to think. And then maybe at the age of fourteen or fifteen or sixteen I discovered Dostoevski. I read books, all of them I could get. I wept for Prince Myshkin in *The Idiot,* I was as guilty as Raskolnikov. And when I finished *The Brothers Karamazov* I understood for the first time what was really happening to me and the people around me. I had always hated religion even as a child, but now I became a true believer. I believed in art. A belief that has helped me as well as any other.

44   My mother looked on all this reading with a fishy Latin eye. She saw no profit in it, but since all her children were great readers, she was a good enough general to know she could not fight so pervasive an insubordination. And there may have been some envy. If she had been able to, she would have been the greatest reader of us all.

45   My direct ancestors for a thousand years have most probably been illiterate. Italy, the golden land, so loving to vacationing Englishmen, so majestic in its language and cultural treasures (they call it, I think, the cradle of civilization), has never cared for its poor people. My father and mother were both illiterates. Both grew up on rocky, hilly farms in the countryside adjoining Naples. My mother remembers never being able to taste the ham from the pig they slaughtered every year. It brought too high a price in the marketplace and cash was needed. My mother was also told the family could not afford the traditional family gift of linens when she married, and it was this that decided her to emigrate to America to marry her first husband, a man she barely knew. When he died, in a tragic work accident on the docks, she married my father, who assumed responsibility for a widow and her four children perhaps out of ignorance, perhaps out of compassion, perhaps out of love. Nobody ever knew. He was a mystery, a Southern Italian with blue eyes, who departed from the family scene three children later when I was twelve. But he cursed Italy even more than my mother did. Then again, he wasn't too pleased with America either. My mother never heard of Michelangelo; the great deeds of the Caesars had not yet reached her ears. She never heard the great music of her native land. She could not sign her name.

46   And so it was hard for my mother to believe that her son could become an artist. After all, her one dream in coming to America had been to earn her daily bread, a wild dream in itself. And looking back she was dead right. Her son an artist? To this day she shakes her head. I shake mine with her.

47   America may be a Fascistic, warmongering, racially prejudiced country today. It may deserve the hatred of its revolutionary young. But what a miracle it once was! What has happened here has never happened in any other country in any other time. The poor, who had been poor for centuries—hell, since the beginning of Christ—whose children had inherited their poverty, their illiteracy, their hopelessness, achieved some economic dignity and freedom. You didn't get it for nothing, you had to pay a price in tears, in suffering, but why not? And some even became artists.

48   Not even my gift for retrospective falsification can make my eighteenth to twenty-first years seem like a happy time. I hated my life. I was being dragged into the trap I feared and had foreseen even as a child. It was all there, the steady job, the nice girl who would eventually get knocked up, and then the marriage and fighting over counting pennies to make ends meet. I noticed myself acting more unheroic all the time. I had to tell lies in pure self-defense, I did not forgive so easily.

49   But I was delivered. When World War II broke out, I was delighted. There is no other word, terrible as it may sound. My country called. I was delivered from my mother, my family, the girl I was loving passionately but did not love. And delivered WITHOUT GUILT. Heroically. My country called, ordered me to defend it. I must have been one of millions—sons, husbands, fathers, lovers—making their innocent getaway from baffled loved ones. And what an escape it was. The war made all my dreams come true. I drove a jeep, toured Europe, had love affairs, found a wife, and lived the material for my first novel. But of course it is perhaps for the best that the revolutionary young make their escape by attacking their own rulers.

50   Then why five years later did I walk back into the trap with a wife and child and a Civil Service job I was glad to get? After five years of the life I had dreamed about, plenty of women, plenty of booze, plenty of money, hardly any work, interesting companions, travel, etc., why did I walk back into that cage of family and duty and a steady job?

51   For the simple reason, of course, that I had never really escaped, not my mother, not my family, not the moral pressures of our society. Time again had done its work. I was back in my cage and I was, I think, happy. In the next twenty years I wrote three novels. Two of them were critical successes but I didn't make much money. The third novel, not as good as the others, made me rich. And free at last. Or so I thought.

52   Then why do I dream of those immigrant Italian peasants as having been happy? I remember how they spoke of their forebears, who spent all their lives farming the arid mountain slopes of Southern Italy. "He died in that house in which he was born," they say enviously. "He was never more than an hour from his village, not in all his life." They sigh. And what would they make of a phrase like "retrospective falsification"?

53   No, really, we are all happier now. It is a better life. And after all, as my mother always said, "Never mind about being happy. Be glad you're alive."

54   When I came to my "autobiographical novel," the one every writer does about himself, I planned to make myself the sensitive, misunderstood hero, much put upon by his mother and family. To my astonishment my mother took over the book and instead of my revenge I got another comeuppance. But it is, I think, my best book. And all those old-style grim conservative Italians whom I hated, then pitied so patronizingly, they also turned out to be heroes. Through no desire of mine, I was surprised. The thing that amazed me most was their courage. Where were their Congressional Medals of Honor? Their Distinguished Service Crosses? How did they ever have the balls to get married, have kids, go out to earn a living in a strange land, with no skills, not even knowing the language? They made it without tranquilizers, without sleeping pills, without psychiatrists, without even a dream. Heroes. Heroes all around me. I never saw them.

55   But how could I? They wore lumpy work clothes and handlebar

mustaches, they blew their noses on their fingers, and they were so short that their high school children towered over them. They spoke a laughable broken English and the furthest limit of their horizon was their daily bread. Brave men, brave women, they fought to live their lives without dreams. Bent on survival, they narrowed their minds to the thinnest line of existence.

56   It is no wonder that in my youth I found them contemptible. And yet they had left Italy and sailed the ocean to come to a new land and leave their sweated bones in America. Illiterate Colombos, they dared to seek the promised land. And so they, too, dreamed a dream.

57   Forty years ago, in 1930, when I was ten, I remember gas light, spooky, making the tenement halls and rooms alive with ghosts.

58   We had the best apartment on Tenth Avenue, a whole top floor of six rooms, with the hall as our storage cellar and the roof as our patio. Two views, one of the railroad yards backed by the Jersey shore, the other of a backyard teeming with tomcats everybody shot at with BB guns. In between these two rooms with a view were three bedrooms without windows—the classic railroad flat pattern. The kitchen had a fire escape that I used to sneak out at night. I liked that apartment, though it had no central heating, only a coal stove at one end and an oil stove at the other. I remember it as comfortable, slum or not.

59   My older brothers listened to a crystal radio on homemade headsets. I hitched a ride on the backs of horses and wagons; my elders daringly rode the trolley cars. Only forty years ago in calendar time, it is really a thousand years in terms of change in our physical world. There are the jets, TV, penicillin for syphilis, cobalt for cancer, equal sex for single girls; yet still always the contempt of the young for their elders.

60   But maybe the young are on the right track this time. Maybe they know that the dreams of our fathers were malignant. Perhaps it is true that the only real escape is in the blood magic of drugs. All the Italians I knew and grew up with have escaped, have made their success. We all are Americans now, we all are successes now. And yet the most successful Italian man I know admits that, though the one human act he never could understand was suicide, he understood it when he became a success. Not that he ever would do such a thing; no man with Italian blood ever commits suicide or becomes a homosexual in his belief. But suicide has crossed his mind. And so to what avail the finding of the dream? He went back to Italy and tried to live like a peasant again. But he can never again be unaware of more subtle traps than poverty and hunger.

61   There is a difference between having a good time in life and being happy. My mother's life was a terrible struggle and yet I think it was a happy life. One tentative proof is that at the age of eighty-two she is positively indignant at the thought that death dares approach her. But it's not for everybody that kind of life.

62   Thinking back, I wonder why I became a writer. Was it the poverty or the books I read? Who traumatized me, my mother or the Brothers Karamazov? Being Italian? Or the girl sitting with me on the bridge as the engine steam deliciously made us vanish? Did it make any difference that I grew up Italian rather than Irish or black?

63   No matter. The good times are beginning, I am another Italian success story. Not as great as DiMaggio or Sinatra but quite enough. It will serve. Yet I can escape again. I have my retrospective falsification (how I love that phrase). I can dream now about how happy I was in my childhood, in my tenement, playing in those dirty but magical streets— living in the poverty that made my mother weep. True, I was a deposed dictator at fifteen but they never hanged me. And now I remember all those impossible dreams strung out before me, waiting for me to choose, not knowing that the life I was living then, as a child, would become my final dream.

Study Questions

1. What is the thesis of Puzo's autobiographical essay? What details and ideas lead up to the thesis?
2. What, apart from the major events in Puzo's life, is the subject of the essay?
3. Explain the contrast between the popular conception of the warm, singing Italian and the child's firsthand perceptions of dour, coarse Italians.

A Measure of Freedom

Jade Snow Wong

1   Of her college courses, Latin was the easiest. This was a surprise, for everyone had told her of its horrors. It was much more logical than French, almost mathematical in its orderliness and precision, and actually a snap after nine years of Chinese.

2   Chemistry, true to the instructor's promise, was difficult, although

the classes were anything but dull. It turned out that he was a very nice person with a keen sense of humor and a gift for enlivening his lectures with stories of his own college days. There were only two girls in a class of more than fifty men—a tense blonde girl from Germany, who always ranked first; and Jade Snow, who usually took second place.

3   But if Latin was the easiest course and chemistry the most difficult, sociology was the most stimulating. Jade Snow had chosen it without thought, simply to meet a requirement; but that casual decision completely revolutionized her thinking, shattering her Wong-constructed conception of the order of things. This was the way it happened:

4   After several uneventful weeks during which the class explored the historical origins of the family and examined such terms as *norms, mores, folkways,* there came a day when the instructor stood before them to discuss the relationship of parents and children. It was a day like many others, with the students listening in varying attitudes of interest or indifference. The instructor was speaking casually of ideas to be accepted as standard. Then suddenly upon Jade Snow's astounded ears there fell this statement:

5   "There was a period in our American history when parents had children for economic reasons, to put them to work as soon as possible, especially to have them help on the farm. But now we no longer regard children in this way. Today we recognize that children are individuals, and that parents can no longer demand their unquestioning obedience. Parents should do their best to understand their children, because young people also have their rights."

6   The instructor went on talking, but Jade Snow heard no more, for her mind was echoing and re-echoing this startling thought. "Parents can no longer demand unquestioning obedience from their children. They should do their best to understand. Children also have their rights." For the rest of the day, while she was doing her chores at the Simpsons', while she was standing in the streetcar going home, she was busy translating the idea into terms of her own experience.

7   "My parents demand unquestioning obedience. Older Brother demands unquestioning obedience. By what right? I am an individual besides being a Chinese daughter. I have rights too."

8   Could it be that daddy and mama, although they were living in San Francisco in the year 1938, actually had not left the Chinese world of thirty years ago? Could it be that they were forgetting that Jade Snow would soon become a woman in a new America, not a woman in old China? In short, was it possible that daddy and mama could be wrong?

9   For days Jade Snow gave thought to little but her devastating discovery that her parents might be subject to error. As it was her habit always to act after reaching a conclusion, she wondered what to do about it. Should she tell daddy and mama that they needed to change their ways? One moment she thought she should; the next she thought not. At last she decided to overcome her fear in the interests of education and

better understanding. She would at least try to open their minds to modern truths. If she succeeded, good! If not, she was prepared to suffer the consequences.

10   In this spirit of patient martyrdom she waited for an opportunity to speak.

11   It came, surprisingly, one Saturday. Ordinarily that was a busy day at the Simpsons', a time for entertaining, so that Jade Snow was not free until too late to go anywhere, even had she had a place to go. But on this particular Saturday the Simpsons were away for the weekend, and by three in the afternoon Jade Snow was ready to leave the apartment with unplanned hours ahead of her. She didn't want to spend these rare hours of freedom in any usual way. And she didn't want to spend them alone.

12   "Shall I call Joe?" she wondered. She had never telephoned to a boy before, and she debated whether it would be too forward. But she felt too happy and carefree to worry much, and she was confident that Joe would not misunderstand.

13   Even before reporting to mama that she was home, she ran downstairs to the telephone booth and gave the operator Joe's number. His mother answered and then went to call him while Jade Snow waited in embarrassment.

14   "Joe." She was suddenly tongue-tied. "Joe, I'm already home."

15   That wasn't at all what she wanted to say. What did she want to say?

16   "Hello! Hello!" Joe boomed back. "What's the matter with you! Are you all right?"

17   "Oh, yes, I'm fine. Only, only . . . well, I'm through working for the day." That was really all she had to say, but now it sounded rather pointless.

18   "Isn't that wonderful? It must have been unexpected." That was what was nice and different about Joe. He always seemed to know without a lot of words. But because his teasing was never far behind his understanding, he added quickly, "I suppose you're going to study and go to bed early."

19   Jade Snow was still not used to teasing and didn't know how to take it. With an effort she swallowed her shyness and disappointment. "I thought we might go for a walk . . . that is, if you have nothing else to do . . . if you would care to . . . if. . . ."

20   Joe laughed. "I'll go you one better. Suppose I take you to a movie. I'll even get all dressed up for you, and you get dressed up too."

21   Jade Snow was delighted. Her first movie with Joe! What a wonderful day. In happy anticipation she put on her long silk stockings, lipstick, and the nearest thing to a suit she owned—a hand-me-down jacket and a brown skirt she had made herself. Then with a bright ribbon tying back her long back hair she was ready.

22   Daddy didn't miss a detail of the preparations as she dashed from room to room. He waited until she was finished before he demanded, "Jade Snow, where are you going?"

23   "I am going out into the street," she answered.

24   "Did you ask my permission to go out into the street?"

25   "No, daddy."

26   "Do you have your mother's permission to go out into the street?"

27   "No, daddy."

28   A sudden silence from the kitchen indicated that mama was listening.

29   Daddy went on: "Where and when did you learn to be so daring as to leave this house without permission of your parents? You did not learn it under my roof."

30   It was all very familiar. Jade Snow waited, knowing that daddy had not finished. In a moment he came to the point.

31   "And with whom are you going out into the street?"

32   It took all the courage Jade Snow could muster, remembering her new thinking, to say nothing. It was certain that if she told daddy that she was going out with a boy whom he did not know, without a chaperone, he would be convinced that she would lose her maidenly purity before the evening was over.

33   "Very well," daddy said sharply. "If you will not tell me, I forbid you to go! You are now too old to whip."

34   That was the moment.

35   Suppressing all anger, and in a manner that would have done credit to her sociology instructor addressing his freshman class, Jade Snow carefully turned on her mentally rehearsed speech.

36   "That is something you should think more about. Yes, I am too old to whip. I am too old to be treated as a child. I can now think for myself, and you and mama should not demand unquestioning obedience from me. You should understand me. There was a time in America when parents raised children to make them work, but now the foreigners regard them as individuals with rights of their own. I have worked too, but now I am an individual besides being your fifth daughter."

37   It was almost certain that daddy blinked, but after the briefest pause he gathered himself together.

38   "Where," he demanded, "did you learn such an unfilial theory?"

39   Mama had come quietly into the room and slipped into a chair to listen.

40   "From my teacher," Jade Snow answered triumphantly, "who you taught me is supreme after you, and whose judgment I am not to question."

41   Daddy was feeling pushed. Thoroughly aroused, he shouted: "A little learning has gone to your head! How can you permit a foreigner's theory to put aside the practical experience of the Chinese, who for thousands of years have preserved a most superior family pattern? Confucius had already presented an organized philosophy of manners and conduct when the foreigners were unappreciatively persecuting Christ. Who brought you up? Who clothed you, fed you, sheltered you, nursed

you? Do you think you were born aged sixteen? You owe honor to us before you satisfy your personal whims."

42   Daddy thundered on, while Jade Snow kept silent.

43   "What would happen to the order of this household if each of you four children started to behave like individuals? Would we have one peaceful moment if your personal desires came before your duty? How could we maintain our self-respect if we, your parents, did not know where you were at night and with whom you were keeping company?"

44   With difficulty Jade Snow kept herself from being swayed by fear and the old familiar arguments. "You can be bad in the daytime as well as at night," she said defensively. "What could happen after eleven that couldn't happen before?"

45   Daddy was growing excited. "Do I have to justify my judgment to you? I do not want a daughter of mine to be known as one who walks the streets at night. Have you no thought for our reputations if not for your own? If you start going out with boys, no good man will want to ask you to be his wife. You just do not know as well as we do what is good for you."

46   Mama fanned daddy's wrath. "Never having been a mother, you cannot know how much grief it is to bring up a daughter. Of course we will not permit you to run the risk of corrupting your purity before marriage."

47   "Oh, mama!" Jade Snow retorted. "This is America, not China. Don't you think I have any judgment? How can you think I would go out with just any man?"

48   "Men!" daddy roared. "You don't know a thing about them. I tell you, you can't trust any of them."

49   Now it was Jade Snow who felt pushed. She delivered the balance of her declaration of independence: "Both of you should understand that I am growing up to be a woman in a society greatly different from the one you knew in China. You expect me to work my way through college—which would not have been possible in China. You expect me to exercise judgment in choosing my employers and my jobs and in spending my own money in the American world. Then why can't I choose my friends? Of course independence is not safe. But safety isn't the only consideration. You must give me the freedom to find some answers for myself."

50   Mama found her tongue first. "You think you are too good for us because you have a little foreign book knowledge."

51   "You will learn the error of your ways after it is too late," daddy added darkly.

52   By this Jade Snow knew that her parents had conceded defeat. Hoping to soften the blow, she tried to explain: "If I am to earn my living, I must learn how to get along with many kinds of people, with foreigners as well as Chinese. I intend to start finding out about them now. You must have confidence that I shall remain true to the spirit of your teachings. I shall bring back to you the new knowledge of whatever I learn."

53   Daddy and mama did not accept this offer graciously. "It is as useless for you to tell me such ideas as 'The wind blows across a deaf ear.' You have lost your sense of balance," daddy told her bluntly. "You are shameless. Your skin is yellow. Your features are forever Chinese. We are content with our proven ways. Do not try to force foreign ideas into my home. Go. You will one day tell us sorrowfully that you have been mistaken."

Study Questions

1. How does American life represent chaos and meaninglessness to Jade Snow's father?
2. What events in this narrative contribute to the anxiety experienced by immigrant or first-generation children in America?
3. What academic discipline more than any other gives Jade Snow the objectivity to examine her own life?
4. Could you call this an argumentative narrative? Is the author successful in getting you to accept her argument? What audience is she addressing? In what ways does or doesn't her diction influence the reader? Does the argument seem dated?

We Real Cool

Gwendolyn Brooks

The Pool Players.
Seven at the Golden Shovel.

We real cool. We
Left school. We

Lurk late. We
Strike straight. We

Sing sin. We
Think gin. We

Jazz June. We
Die soon.   10

Study Questions

1. What is the significance of the pool hall's name?
2. Why are all the sentences in the poem simple declarative ones?
3. Why are stanzas concluded with "We" at each break?
4. Does Brooks adequately prepare you for the poem's conclusion?
5. This poem suggests that many dropouts from school or conventional society act as they do because of despair and helplessness, rather than because of hatred or proud defiance. Do you agree with this view?

But He Was Cool
or: He Even Stopped for Green Lights

Don L. Lee

super-cool
ultrablack
a tan/purple
had a beautiful shade.

he had a double-natural
that wd put the sisters to shame.
his dashikis were tailor made
& his beads were imported sea shells
    (from some blk/country i never heard of)
he was triple-hip.   10

his tikis were hand carved
out of ivory
& came express from the motherland.
he would greet u in swahili
& say good-by in yoruba.
wooooooooooooo-jim he bes so cool & ill tel li gent
        cool-cool is so cool he was un-cooled by other nig-
            gers' cool
        cool-cool ultracool was bop-cool/ice box cool so
            cool cold cool
        his wine didn't have to be cooled, him was air
            conditioned cool
        cool-cool/real cool made me cool—now ain't that
            cool   20
        cool-cool so cool him nick-named refrigerator.

cool-cool so cool
he didn't know,
after detroit, newark, chicago &c.,
we had to hip
        cool-cool/ super-cool/ real cool
   that
to be black
is
to be   30
very-hot.

Study Questions

1. This poem parodies the clichéd use of the word *cool*. Explain.
2. How does the author satirize the trappings of the cool street black?
3. How does the author use street language?
4. What is the effect of the abbreviations?

Garden of My Childhood

Kuangchi C. Chang

"Run, run, run,"
Whispered the vine,
"A horde is on the march no Great Wall can halt."
But in the garden of my childhood
The old maple was painting a sunset
And the crickets were singing a carol;
No, I had no wish to run.

"Run, run, run,"
Gasped the wind,
"The horde has entered the Wall."   10
Down the scorched plain rode the juggernaut
And crossed the Yangtse as if it were a ditch;
The proverbial rats had abandoned the ship
But I had no intention of abandoning
The garden of my childhood.

"Run, run, run,"
Roared the sea,
"Run before the bridge is drawn."
In the engulfed calm after the storm
The relentless tom-tom of the rice-sprout song   20
Finally ripped my armor,
And so I ran.

I ran past the old maple by the terraced hall
And the singing crickets under the latticed wall,
And I kept on running down the walk
Paved with pebbles of memory big and small
Without turning to look until I was out of the gate
Through which there be no return at all.

Now, eons later and worlds away,
The running is all done   30
For I am at my destination: Another garden,
Where the unpebbled walk awaits tomorrow's footprints,
Where my old maple will come with the sunset's glow
And my crickets will sing under the wakeful pillow.

Study Questions

1. Which lines in the first three stanzas exhort the speaker to move? What is the effect of beginning the first three stanzas with the same three words?
2. How do movement and time change in the last two stanzas?
3. What are the possible meanings of the central metaphor, the garden?
4. Discuss the relevance of the allusions to the world of nature in this poem.

Lost

Bruce Ignacio

I know not of my forefathers
nor of their beliefs
For I was brought up in the city.
Our home seemed smothered and surrounded
as were other homes on city sites.
When the rain came
I would slush my way to school
as though the street were a wading pool.
Those streets were always crowded.
I brushed by people with every step,   10
Covered my nose once in awhile,
Gasping against the smell of perspiration on humid days.
Lights flashed everywhere
until my head became a signal, flashing on and off.
Noise so unbearable
I wished the whole place would come to a standstill,
leaving only peace and quiet

And still, would I like this kind of life? . . .
The life of my forefathers
who wandered, not knowing where they were going,   20
but just moving, further and further
from where they had been,

To be in quiet,
to kind of be lost in their dreams and wishing,
as I have been to this day,
I awake.

Study Questions

1. The speaker seems to react to the pressures of the city to an unusual degree. Why might this be so?
2. Besides length, what contrasts can be seen between the two stanzas? Are they structurally different?
3. Why might a Native American reader be particularly sensitive to the images in the poem?
4. Is there an answer to the question posed by the poet?

Six Haiku

Kenneth Yasuda (Shosōn)

The Rainbow

From the clearing space
Arched with rainbow, falls the rain
On a lifted face.

The Poppy-Field

Circling again
Flies the hill-side poppy-field
Far, far from the train.

At Tacoma, Washington

Shadows from the hills
Lengthen half-across a field
Of gold daffodils.

The Lizard

A lizard swam over
The undulating waves
Of the fresh green clover.

The Mississippi River

Under the low grey
Winter skies water pushes
Water on its way.

Summer Shower

The green breeze passes,
Accompanied by summer shower
Across the grasses.

Study Questions

1. Haiku is a form of poetry created by the Japanese. Although these haiku were written by a moden, native-born Japanese-American poet, the form dates to antiquity. Why would haiku be considered a form pertinent to an anthology for writers?
2. Do these poems share any common structural devices besides the rhyme of the first and third lines?
3. In "The Rainbow," what metaphor serves to define the earth upon which the rain falls?
4. In "The Poppy-Field," from what visual vantage point does the field seem to "circle" and to "fly"?
5. In each haiku, what predominant element makes the reader see, even in such a short description, the picture the poet seeks to reveal?
6. What element in each haiku contributes to the senses of stillness, immobility, and calm?

The Man to Send Rain Clouds

Leslie Silko

One

1   They found him under a big cottonwood tree. His Levi jacket and pants were faded light-blue so that he had been easy to find. The big cottonwood tree stood apart from a small grove of winterbare cottonwoods which grew in the wide, sandy arroyo. He had been dead for a day or more, and the sheep had wandered and scattered up and down the arroyo. Leon and his brother-in-law, Ken, gathered the sheep and left them in the pen at the sheep camp before they returned to the cottonwood tree. Leon waited under the tree while Ken drove the truck through the deep sand to the edge of the arroyo. He squinted up at the sun and unzipped his jacket—it sure was hot for this time of year. But high and northwest the blue mountains were still deep in snow. Ken came sliding down the low, crumbling bank about fifty yards down, and he was bringing the red blanket.

2   Before they wrapped the old man, Leon took a piece of string out of his pocket and tied a small gray feather in the old man's long white hair. Ken gave him the paint. Across the brown wrinkled forehead he drew a streak of white and along the high cheekbones he drew a strip of blue paint. He paused and watched Ken throw pinches of corn meal and pollen into the wind that fluttered the small gray feather. Then Leon painted with yellow under the old man's broad nose, and finally, when he had painted green across the chin, he smiled.

3   "Send us rain clouds, Grandfather." They laid the bundle in the back of the pickup and covered it with a heavy tarp before they started back to the pueblo.

4   They turned off the highway onto the sandy pueblo road. Not long after they passed the store and post office they saw Father Paul's car coming toward them. When he recognized their faces he slowed his car and waved for them to stop. The young priest rolled down the car window.

5   "Did you find old Teofilo?" he asked loudly.

6   Leon stopped the truck. "Good morning, Father. We were just out to the sheep camp. Everything is O.K. now."

7   "Thank God for that. Teofilo is a very old man. You really shouldn't allow him to stay at the sheep camp alone."

8   "No, he won't do that any more now."

476

9   "Well, I'm glad you understand. I hope I'll be seeing you at Mass this week—we missed you last Sunday. See if you can get old Teofilo to come with you." The priest smiled and waved at them as they drove away.

Two

10   Louise and Teresa were waiting. The table was set for lunch, and the coffee was boiling on the black iron stove. Leon looked at Louise and then at Teresa.

11   "We found him under a cottonwood tree in the big arroyo near sheep camp. I guess he sat down to rest in the shade and never got up again." Leon walked toward the old man's bed. The red plaid shawl had been shaken and spread carefully over the bed, and a new brown flannel shirt and pair of stiff new Levis were arranged neatly beside the pillow. Louise held the screen door open while Leon and Ken carried in the red blanket. He looked small and shriveled, and after they dressed him in the new shirt and pants he seemed more shrunken.

12   It was noontime now because the church bells rang the Angelus. They ate the beans with hot bread, and nobody said anything until after Teresa poured the coffee.

13   Ken stood up and put on his jacket. "I'll see about the gravediggers. Only the top layer of soil is frozen. I think it can be ready before dark."

14   Leon nodded his head and finished his coffee. After Ken had been gone for a while, the neighbors and clanspeople came quietly to embrace Teofilo's family and to leave food on the table because the gravediggers would come to eat when they were finished.

Three

15   The sky in the west was full of pale-yellow light. Louise stood outside with her hands in the pockets of Leon's green army jacket that was too big for her. The funeral was over, and the old men had taken their candles and medicine bags and were gone. She waited until the body was laid into the pickup before she said anything to Leon. She touched his arm, and he noticed that her hands were still dusty from the corn meal that she had sprinkled around the old man. When she spoke, Leon could not hear her.

16   "What did you say? I didn't hear you."

17   "I said that I had been thinking about something."

18   "About what?"

19   "About the priest sprinkling holy water for Grandpa. So he won't be thirsty."

20   Leon stared at the new moccasins that Teofilo had made for the

ceremonial dances in the summer. They were nearly hidden by the red blanket. It was getting colder, and the wind pushed gray dust down the narrow pueblo road. The sun was approaching the long mesa where it disappeared during the winter. Louise stood there shivering and watching his face. Then he zipped up his jacket and opened the truck door. "I'll see if he's there."

Four

21   Ken stopped the pickup at the church, and Leon got out; and then Ken drove down the hill to the graveyard where people were waiting. Leon knocked at the old carved door with its symbols of the Lamb. While he waited he looked up at the twin bells from the king of Spain with the last sunlight pouring around them in their tower.

22   The priest opened the door and smiled when he saw who it was. "Come in! What brings you here this evening?"

23   The priest walked toward the kitchen, and Leon stood with his cap in his hand, playing with the earflaps and examining the living room—the brown sofa, the green armchair, and the brass lamp that hung down from the ceiling by links of chain. The priest dragged a chair out of the kitchen and offered it to Leon.

24   "No thank you, Father. I only came to ask you if you would bring your holy water to the graveyard."

25   The priest turned away from Leon and looked out the window at the patio full of shadows and the dining-room windows of the nuns' cloister across the patio. The curtains were heavy, and the light from within faintly penetrated; it was impossible to see the nuns inside eating supper. "Why didn't you tell me he was dead? I could have brought the Last Rites anyway."

26   Leon smiled. "It wasn't necessary, Father."

27   The priest stared down at his scuffed brown loafers and the worn hem of his cassock. "For a Christian burial it was necessary."

28   His voice was distant, and Leon thought that his blue eyes looked tired.

29   "It's O.K. Father, we just want him to have plenty of water."

30   The priest sank down into the green chair and picked up a glossy missionary magazine. He turned the colored pages full of lepers and pagans without looking at them.

31   "You know I can't do that, Leon. There should have been the Last Rites and a funeral Mass at the very least."

32   Leon put on his green cap and pulled the flaps down over his ears. "It's getting late, Father. I've got to go."

33   When Leon opened the door Father Paul stood up and said, "Wait." He left the room and came back wearing a long brown overcoat. He followed Leon out the door and across the dim churchyard to the adobe

steps in front of the church. They both stooped to fit through the low adobe entrance. And when they started down the hill to the graveyard only half of the sun was visible above the mesa.

34   The priest approached the grave slowly, wondering how they had managed to dig into the frozen ground; and then he remembered that this was New Mexico, and saw the pile of cold loose sand beside the hole. The people stood close to each other with little clouds of steam puffing from their faces. The priest looked at them and saw a pile of jackets, gloves, and scarves in the yellow, dry tumbleweeds that grew in the graveyard. He looked at the red blanket, not sure that Teofilo was so small, wondering if it wasn't some perverse Indian trick—something they did in March to ensure a good harvest—wondering if maybe old Teofilo was actually at sheep camp corraling the sheep for the night. But there he was, facing into a cold dry wind and squinting at the last sunlight, ready to bury a red wool blanket while the faces of his parishioners were in shadow with the last warmth of the sun on their backs.

35   His fingers were stiff, and it took him a long time to twist the lid off the holy water. Drops of water fell on the red blanket and soaked into dark icy spots. He sprinkled the grave and the water disappeared almost before it touched the dim, cold sand; it reminded him of something—he tried to remember what it was, because he thought if he could remember he might understand this. He sprinkled more water; he shook the container until it was empty, and the water fell through the light from sundown like August rain that fell while the sun was still shining, almost evaporating before it touched the wilted squash flowers.

36   The wind pulled at the priest's brown Franciscan robe and swirled away the corn meal and pollen that had been sprinkled on the blanket. They lowered the bundle into the ground, and they didn't bother to untie the stiff pieces of new rope that were tied around the ends of the blanket. The sun was gone, and over on the highway the eastbound lane was full of headlights. The priest walked away slowly. Leon watched him climb the hill, and when he had disappeared within the tall, thick walls, Leon turned to look up at the high blue mountains in the deep snow that reflected a faint red light from the west. He felt good because it was finished, and he was happy about the sprinkling of the holy water; now the old man could send them big thunderclouds for sure.

Study Questions

1. This story delineates the contrast between two civilizations. Its immediate subject is the death and burial of an old Native American man and the contrast

between the Native Americans' and the white people's burial practices. How
does Silko show the meeting of the two cultures?
2.   Why does Silko divide the story into four sections?
3.   Why does the point of view in the last section shift to the mind of the priest?
4.   What is the misunderstanding about the uses of holy water?

The Tropics in New York

Claude McKay

Bananas ripe and green, and ginger root,
    Cocoa in pods and alligator pears,
And tangerines and mangoes and grape fruit,
    Fit for the highest prize at parish fairs,

Set in the window, bringing memories
    Of fruit-trees laden by low-singing rills,
And dewy dawns, and mystical blue skies
    In benediction over nun-like hills.

My eyes grew dim, and I could no more gaze;
    A wave of longing through my body swept,
And, hungry for the old, familiar ways,   10
    I turned aside and bowed my head and wept.

Study Questions

1.   Stanzas 1 and 2 form one long noun phrase. Stanza 3 is the vision evoked by the
images of stanzas 1 and 2. Explain the relationships between the stanzas.
2.   Explain the simile "nun-like hills."
3.   What images describe "the tropics"?
4.   Explain the function of color, smell, and texture in the images of stanzas 1 and 2.

Whitey's on the Moon Now

William Eastlake

1   I had a Papago Indian intellectual friend over to watch the first man on the moon.

2   The Papago Indian intellectual brought over a Papago Indian cowboy to watch too.

3   "They are about to land," I said.

4   "You said something about beer."

5   "Wait."

6   "What for?"

7   "Till they get on the moon."

8   "Are they on the moon yet?"

9   "Yes."

10   "Can I have the beer?"

11   "The white man on the moon said one small step for a man and one giant step for mankind."

12   "That's nice," the Papago cowboy said. "Can I have the beer now?"

13   "What he means," my friend the Papago Indian intellectual said, "is that his people are starving. He's not interested in the white man on the moon."

14   I got the Papago cowboy the beer.

15   The Papago cowboy, now that he had the beer can, smiled and said, "How much did it cost to go to the moon?"

16   "Twenty billion."

17   The Papago cowboy smiled and shook his head at the white man on the moon.

18   "What he means," the Papago intellectual said, "is that he hopes they are happy on the moon."

19   "Who that?" the Indian cowboy said.

20   "President Nixon."

21   "Why?"

22   "He says it's the biggest thing since creation."

23   "Why?"

24   "What he means is he hopes President Nixon is very happy on the moon."

25   "Would you like all white people to go to the moon?"

26   "Yes."

27   "Never come back from the moon?"

28   "Yes."

29   "Would you like some more beer?"

30   "Yes."

31   When the Papago Indian cowboy got the beer he thought a while and then said, "No."

32   The intellectual Papago said, "He means why do you want to destroy another planet."

33   "Curiosity."

34   The cowboy Indian Papago thought about that and laughed.

35   "He laughs because the Papago are all cried out," his friend said.

36   "They will bring back moonstones," I said.

37   "Will they kill all the people there?" the Papago Indian cowboy said.

38   "No."

39   "Put them on reservations?"

40   "No. Because there are no people on the moon," I said.

41   "Will the white people come back?"

42   "Yes."

43   The Papago Indian cowboy got up.

44   "Where are you going?"

45   "To the moon."

46   "Of course you can't," the intellectual Papago said.

47   The Indian sat down.

48   "You see," the Papago intellectual said, "the Indian would very much like to get off this planet. If you will not get off his land."

49   "One small step for a man on earth . . . ?"

50   "And forget the moon."

51   "Yes."

52   "What he means," the intellectual Papago said, "is he would like another beer." That is why they call my Indian friend an intellectual Papago. All over Arizona they laugh at him because he does not want to settle for Overkill Rockets at Tucson or a dam on the Grand Canyon or the London Bridge over the Havasupai or for mankind to take their first giant step on the moon.

53   "Why can't they take it here?" he said.

54   "Would you like a beer?"

55   "Why can't we take it here?"

56   Like all Indians my intellectual Indian Papago friend and the Papago Indian cowboy are mad, not mad crazy, but just plain damn mad. Not moonstruck. Just two hungry, angry Indians watching Whitey on the moon.

Study Questions

1. What is the point of view of this piece? Does the speaker ever lapse from his objectivity?
2. Why is the Papago Indian cowboy so bored with the moon landing?
3. Why does the Papago Indian intellectual speak for the cowboy?
4. What tone does the title convey?

22 Miles . . .

José Angel Gutiérrez

From 22 I see my first 8 weren't.
   Around the 9th, I was called "meskin".
      By the 10th, I knew and believed I was.
         I found out what it meant to know, to believe. . .before my
         13th.

Through brown eyes, seeing only brown colors and feeling only
brown feelings. . .I saw. . .I felt. . .I hated. . .I cried. . .I
tried. . .I didn't understand during these 4.
      I rested by just giving up.

While, on the side. . .I realized I BELIEVED in
   white as pretty,
      my being governor,
         blond blue eyed baby Jesus,
            cokes and hamburgers,
               equality for all regardless of race, creed, or color,
                 Mr. Williams, our banker.
            I had to!
         That was all I had.
      Beans and Communism were bad.
         Past the weeds, atop the hill, I looked back.

10

Pretty people, combed and squeaky clean, on arrowlike roads.   20
Pregnant girls, ragged brats, swarthy machos, rosary beads,
and friends waddle clumsily over and across hills, each other,
mud, cold, and woods on caliche ruts.
At the 19th mile, I fought blindly at everything and anything.
   Not knowing, Not caring about WHY, WHEN, or FOR WHAT.
     I fought. And fought.
       By the 21st, I was tired and tried.

                But now. . . . .
I've been told that I am dangerous.
That is because I am good at not being a Mexican.   30
That is because I know now that I have been cheated.
That is because I hate circumstances and love choices.

     You know. . .chorizo tacos y tortillas ARE good, even at school.
   Speaking Spanish is a talent.
Being Mexican IS as good as Rainbo bread.
And without looking back, I know that there are still too many. . .
   brown babies,
      pregnant girls,
         old 25 year-old women,
            drunks,   40
               who should have lived but didn't,
                 on those caliche ruts.

         It is tragic that my problems during these past 21 miles
         were/are/might be. . .
            looking into blue eyes,
          wanting to touch a gringita,
        ashamed of being Mexican,
      believing I could not make it at college,
     pretending that I liked my side of town,
    remembering the Alamo,   50
  speaking Spanish in school bathrooms only,
and knowing that Mexico's prostitutes like Americans better.
At 22, my problems are still the same but now I know I am your
        problem.
That farm boys, Mexicans and Negro boys are in Vietnam is but one
        thing
I think about:

   Crystal City, Texas 78839
   The migrant worker;
   The good gringo:

Staying Mexican enough;   60
Helping;
Looking at the world from the back of a truck.

The stoop labor with high school rings on their fingers;
The Anglo cemetery,
Joe the different Mexican,
                    Damn.
                    Damn.
                    Damn.

Study Questions

1. The poet was twenty-two years old when he wrote this poem. How are the events
    of the poem ordered?
2. Does the poem have a thesis statement?
3. How are commercial images, political language, street slang, bigotry, and color
    used in this poem?
4. What prejudices has the speaker encountered that have limited his sense of
    self-worth?

The Cha Cha Cha at Salt Lake City Bus Terminal

Victor Hernández Cruz

flys ate the apple pie
as I waited for my two eggs
in this gorgeous spaceship waiting
room . . . which is open all night
long . . . the street outside was trampled

by pigeons . . . who seemed to be the only
ones doing the cha cha cha

the juke box was blue
and looked like a computer
sitting under a mid western   10
landscape painting . . .

I played the Supremes "Baby Love"
a couple of years off . . . but it was
there . . . the closest thing to cha cha
there was nothing more . . . one more
selection . . . the light was still on . . .

I took a chance with the *Salt Lake City
Country Boys* (number M-5) "The House
By The Hill, Is Our Dream House Baby"

Study Questions

1. What is the theme of this poem?
2. What concrete details contribute to the picture you have of this bus terminal?
3. What is the tone of the poem, and how is it established?
4. Why does Cruz use ellipses so heavily in the first three stanzas and not at all in the fourth?

Bright and Morning Star

Richard Wright

I

She stood with her black face some six inches from the moist windowpane and wondered when on earth would it ever stop raining. It might keep up like this all week, she thought. She heard rain droning upon the roof and high up in the wet sky her eyes followed the silent rush of a bright shaft of yellow that swung from the airplane beacon in far off Memphis. Momentarily she could see it cutting through the rainy dark; it would hover a second like a gleaming sword above her head, then vanish. She sighed, troubling, Johnny-Boys been trampin in this slop all day wid no decent shoes on his feet. . . . Through the window she could see the rich black earth sprawling outside in the night. There was more rain than the clay could soak up; pools stood everywhere. She yawned and mumbled: "Rains good n bad. It kin make seeds bus up thu the ground, er it kin bog things down lika watah-soaked coffin." Her hands were folded loosely over her stomach and the hot air of the kitchen traced a filmy vein of sweat on her forehead. From the cook stove came the soft singing of burning wood and now and then a throaty bubble rose from a pot of simmering greens.

"Shucks, Johnny-Boy coulda let somebody else do all tha runnin in the rain. Theres others bettah fixed fer it than he is. But, naw! Johnny-Boy ain the one t trust nobody t do nothin. Hes gotta do it *all* hissef. . . ."

She glanced at a pile of damp clothes in a zinc tub. Waal, Ah bettah git to work. She turned, lifted a smoothing iron with a thick pad of cloth, touched a spit-wet finger to it with a quick, jerking motion: *smiiitz!* Yeah; its hot! Stooping, she took a blue work-shirt from the tub and shook it out. With a deft twist of her shoulders she caught the iron in her right hand; the fingers of her left hand took a piece of wax from a tin box and a frying sizzle came as she smeared the bottom. She was thinking of nothing now; her hands followed a life-long ritual of toil. Spreading a sleeve, she ran the hot iron to and fro until the wet cloth became stiff. She was deep in the midst of her work when a song rose up out of the far off days of her childhood and broke through half-parted lips:

> *Hes the Lily of the Valley, the Bright n Mawnin Star*
> *Hes the Fairest of Ten Thousand t ma soul . . .*

4   A gust of wind dashed rain against the window. Johnny-Boy oughta c mon home n eat his suppah. Aw, Lawd! Itd be fine ef Sug could eat wid us tonight! Itd be like ol times! Mabbe aftah all it wont be long fo he comes back. Tha lettah Ah got from im last week said *Don give up hope.* . . . Yeah; we gotta live in hope. Then both of her sons, Sug and Johnny-Boy, would be back with her.

5   With an involuntary nervous gesture, she stopped and stood still, listening. But the only sound was the lulling fall of rain. Shucks, ain no usa me ackin this way, she thought. Ever time they gits ready to hol them meetings Ah gits jumpity. Ah been a lil scared ever since Sug went t jail. She heard the clock ticking and looked. Johnny-Boys a *hour* late! He sho must be havin a time doin all tha trampin, trampin thu the mud. . . . But her fear was a quiet one; it was more like an intense brooding than a fear; it was a sort of hugging of hated facts so closely that she could feel their grain, like letting cold water run over her hand from a faucet on a winter morning.

6   She ironed again, faster now, as if she felt the more she engaged her body in work the less she would think. But how could she forget Johnny-Boy out there on those wet fields rounding up white and black Communists for a meeting tomorrow? And that was just what Sug had been doing when the sheriff had caught him, beat him, and tried to make him tell who and where his comrades were. Po Sug! They sho musta beat the boy somethin awful! But, thank Gawd, he didnt talk! He ain no weaklin, Sug ain! Hes been lion-hearted all his life long.

7   That had happened a year ago. And now each time those meetings came around the old terror surged back. While shoving the iron a cluster of toiling days returned; days of washing and ironing to feed Johnny-Boy and Sug so they could do party work; days of carrying a hundred pounds of white folks' clothes upon her head across fields sometimes wet and sometimes dry. But in those days a hundred pounds was nothing to carry carefully balanced upon her head while stepping by instinct over the corn and cotton rows. The only time it had seemed heavy was when she had heard of Sug's arrest. She had been coming home one morning with a bundle upon her head, her hands swinging idly by her sides, walking slowly with her eyes in front of her, when Bob, Johnny-Boy's pal, had called from across the fields and had come and told her that the sheriff had got Sug. That morning the bundle had become heavier than she could ever remember.

8   And with each passing week now, though she spoke of it to no one, things were becoming heavier. The tubs of water and the smoothing iron and the bundles of clothes were becoming harder to lift, with her back aching so; and her work was taking longer, all because Sug was gone and she didn't know just when Johnny-Boy would be taken too. To ease the ache of anxiety that was swelling her heart, she hummed, then sang softly:

He walks wid me, He talks wid me
He tells me Ahm His own. . . .

9   Guiltily, she stopped and smiled. Looks like Ah just cant seem t fergit them ol songs, no mattah how hard Ah tries. . . . She had learned them when she was a little girl living and working on a farm. Every Monday morning from the corn and cotton fields the slow strains had floated from her mother's lips, lonely and haunting; and later, as the years had filled with gall, she had learned their deep meaning. Long hours of scrubbing floors for a few cents a day had taught her who Jesus was, what a great boon it was to cling to Him, to be like Him and suffer without a mumbling word. She had poured the yearning of her life into the songs, feeling buoyed with a faith beyond this world. The figure of the Man nailed in agony to the Cross, His burial in a cold grave, His transfigured Resurrection, His being breath and clay, God and Man—all had focused her feelings upon an imagery which had swept her life into a wondrous vision.

10   But as she had grown older, a cold white mountain, the white folks and their laws, had swum into her vision and shattered her songs and their spell of peace. To her that white mountain was temptation, something to lure her from her Lord, a part of the world God had made in order that she might endure it and come through all the stronger, just as Christ had risen with greater glory from the tomb. The days crowded with trouble had enhanced her faith and she had grown up to love hardship with a bitter pride; she had obeyed the laws of the white folks with a soft smile of secret knowing.

11   After her mother had been snatched up to heaven in a chariot of fire, the years had brought her a rough workingman and two black babies, Sug and Johnny-Boy, all three of whom she had wrapped in the charm and magic of her vision. Then she was tested by no less than God; her man died, a trial which she bore with the strength shed by the grace of her vision; finally even the memory of her man faded into the vision itself, leaving her with two black boys growing tall, slowly into manhood.

12   Then one day grief had come to her heart when Johnny-Boy and Sug had walked forth demanding their lives. She had sought to fill their eyes with her vision, but they would have none of it. And she had wept when they began to boast of the strength shed by a new and terrible vision.

13   But she had loved them, even as she loved them now; bleeding, her heart had followed them. She could have done no less, being an old woman in a strange world. And day by day her sons had ripped from her startled eyes her old vision, and image by image had given her a new one, different, but great and strong enough to fling her into the light of another grace. The wrongs and sufferings of black men had taken the

place of Him nailed to the Cross; the meager beginning of the party had become another Resurrection; and the hate of those who would destroy her new faith had quickened in her a hunger to feel how deeply her new strength went.

14   "Lawd, Johnny-Boy," she would sometimes say, "Ah jus wan them white folks t try t make me tell *who* is *in* the party n who *ain!* Ah jus wan em t try, Ahll show em somethin they never thought a black woman could have!"

15   But sometimes like tonight, while lost in the forgetfulness of work, the past and the present would become mixed in her; while toiling under a strange star for a new freedom the old songs would slip from her lips with their beguiling sweetness.

16   The iron was getting cold. She put more wood into the fire, stood again at the window and watched the yellow blade of light cut through the wet darkness. Johnny-Boy ain here yit. . . . Then, before she was aware of it, she was still, listening for sounds. Under the drone of rain she heard the slosh of feet in mud. Tha ain Johnny-Boy. She knew his long, heavy footsteps in a million. She heard feet come on the porch. Some woman. . . . She heard bare knuckles knock three times, then once. Thas some of them comrades! She unbarred the door, cracked it a few inches, and flinched from the cold rush of damp wind.

17   "Whos tha?"
18   "Its me!"
19   "Who?"
20   "Me, Reva!"
21   She flung the door open.
22   "Lawd, chile, c mon in!"
23   She stepped to one side and a thin, blond-haired white girl ran through the door; as she slid the bolt she heard the girl gasping and shaking her wet clothes. Somethings wrong! Reva wouldna walked a mil t mah house in all this slop fer nothin! That gals stuck onto Johnny-Boy. Ah wondah ef anythin happened t im?

24   "Git on inter the kitchen, Reva, where its warm."
25   "Lawd, Ah sho is wet!"
26   "How yuh reckon yuhd be, in all tha rain?"
27   "Johnny-Boy aint here *yit?*" asked Reva.
28   "Naw! N ain no usa yuh worryin bout im. Jus yuh git them shoes off! Yuh wanna ketch yo deatha col?" She stood looking absently. Yeah; its somethin about the party er Johnny-Boy thas gone wrong. Lawd, Ah wondah ef her pa knows how she feels bout Johnny-Boy? "Honey, yuh hadn't oughta come out in sloppy weather like this."

29   "Ah had t come, An Sue."
30   She led Reva to the kitchen.
31   "Git them shoes off n git close t the stove so yuhll git dry!"
32   "An Sue, Ah got somethin t tell yuh . . ."

33   The words made her hold her breath. Ah bet its somethin bout Johnny-Boy!

34   "Whut, honey?"

35   "The sheriff wuz by our house tonight. He come t see pa."

36   "Yeah?"

37   "He done got word from somewheres about tha meetin tomorrow."

38   "Is it Johnny-Boy, Reva?"

39   "Aw, naw, An Sue! Ah ain hearda word bout im. Ain yuh seen im tonight?"

40   "He ain come home t eat yit."

41   "Where kin he be?"

42   "Lawd knows, chile."

43   "Somebodys gotta tell them comrades that meetings off," said Reva. "The sheriffs got men watchin our house. Ah had t slip out t git here widout em followin me."

44   "Reva?"

45   "Hunh?"

46   "Ahma ol woman n Ah wans yuh t tell me the truth."

47   "Whut, An Sue?"

48   "Yuh ain tryin t fool me, is yuh?"

49   "*Fool* yuh?"

50   "Bout Johnny-Boy?"

51   "Lawd, naw, An Sue!"

52   "Ef theres anythin wrong jus tell me, chile. Ah kin stan it."

53   She stood by the ironing board, her hands as usual folded loosely over her stomach, watching Reva pull off her water-clogged shoes. She was feeling that Johnny-Boy was already lost to her; she was feeling the pain that would come when she knew it for certain; and she was feeling that she would have to be brave and bear it. She was like a person caught in a swift current of water and knew where the water was sweeping her and did not want to go on but had to go on to the end.

54   "It ain nothin bout Johnny-Boy, An Sue," said Reva. "But we gotta do somethin er we'll all git inter trouble."

55   "How the sheriff know about tha meetin?"

56   "Thas whut pa wants t know."

57   "Somebody done turned Judas."

58   "Sho looks like it."

59   "Ah bet it wuz some of them new ones," she said.

60   "Its hard t tell," said Reva.

61   "Lissen, Reva, yuh oughta stay here n git dry, but yuh bettah git back n tell yo pa Johnny-Boy ain here n Ah don know when hes gonna show up. *Some*bodys gotta tell them comrades t stay erway from yo pas house."

62   She stood with her back to the window, looking at Reva's wide, blue eyes. Po critter! Gotta go back thu all tha slop! Though she felt sorry

for Reva, not once did she think that it would not have to be done. Being a woman, Reva was not suspect; she would *have* to go. It was just as natural for Reva to go back through the cold rain as it was for her to iron night and day, or for Sug to be in jail. Right now, Johnny-Boy was out there on those dark fields trying to get home. Lawd, don let em git im tonight! In spite of herself her feelings became torn. She loved her son and, loving him, she loved what he was trying to do. Johnny-Boy was happiest when he was working for the party, and her love for him was for his happiness. She frowned, trying hard to fit something together in her feelings: for her to try to stop Johnny-Boy was to admit that all the toil of years meant nothing; and to let him go meant that sometime or other he would be caught, like Sug. In facing it this way she felt a little stunned, as though she had come suddenly upon a blank wall in the dark. But outside in the rain were people, white and black, whom she had known all her life. Those people depended upon Johnny-Boy, loved him and looked to him as a man and leader. Yeah; hes gotta keep on; he cant stop now. . . . She looked at Reva; she was crying and pulling her shoes back on with reluctant fingers.

63   "Whut yuh carryin on tha way fer, chile?"

64   "Yuh done los Sug, now yuh sending Johnny-Boy . . ."

65   "Ah got t, honey."

66   She was glad she could say that. Reva believed in black folks and not for anything in the world would she falter before her. In Reva's trust and acceptance of her she had found her first feelings of humanity; Reva's love was her refuge from shame and degradation. If in the early days of her life the white mountain had driven her back from the earth, then in her last days Reva's love was drawing her toward it, like the beacon that swung through the night outside. She heard Reva sobbing.

67   "Hush, honey!"

68   "Mah brothers in jail too! Ma cries ever day . . ."

69   "Ah know, honey."

70   She helped Reva with her coat; her fingers felt the scant flesh of the girl's shoulder. She don git ernuff t eat, she thought. She slipped her arms around Reva's waist and held her close for a moment.

71   "Now, yuh stop that cryin."

72   "A-a-ah c-c-cant hep it. . . ."

73   "Everythingll be awright; Johnny-Boyll be back."

74   "Yuh think so?"

75   "Sho, chile. Cos he will."

76   Neither of them spoke again until they stood in the doorway. Outside they could hear water washing through the ruts of the street.

77   "Be sho n send Johnny-Boy t tell the folks t stay erway from pas house," said Reva.

78   "Ahll tell im. Don yuh worry."

79   "Good-bye!"

80   "Good-bye!"

81   Leaning against the door jamb, she shook her head slowly and watched Reva vanish through the falling rain.

II

82   She was back at her board, ironing, when she heard feet sucking in the mud of the back yard; feet she knew from long years of listening were Johnny-Boy's. But tonight, with all the rain and fear, his coming was like a leaving, was almost more than she could bear. Tears welled to her eyes and she blinked them away. She felt that he was coming so that she could give him up; to see him now was to say good-bye. But it was a good-bye she knew she could never say; they were not that way toward each other. All day long they could sit in the same room and not speak; she was his mother and he was her son. Most of the time a nod or a grunt would carry all the meaning that she wanted to convey to him, or he to her. She did not even turn her head when she heard him come stomping into the kitchen. She heard him pull up a chair, sit, sigh, and draw off his muddy shoes; they fell to the floor with heavy thuds. Soon the kitchen was full of the scent of his drying socks and his burning pipe. Tha boys hongry! She paused and looked at him over her shoulder; he was puffing at his pipe with his head tilted back and his feet propped up on the edge of the stove; his eyelids drooped and his wet clothes steamed from the heat of the fire. Lawd, tha boy gits mo like his pa every day he lives, she mused, her lips breaking in a slow, faint smile. Hols tha pipe in his mouth just like his pa usta hol his. Wondah how they woulda got erlong ef his pa hada lived? They oughta liked each other, they so mucha like. She wished there could have been other children besides Sug, so Johnny-Boy would not have to be so much alone. A man needs a woman by his side. . . . She thought of Reva; she liked Reva; the brightest glow her heart had ever known was when she had learned that Reva loved Johnny-Boy. But beyond Reva were cold white faces. Ef theys caught it means *death*. . . . She jerked around when she heard Johnny-Boy's pipe clatter to the floor. She saw him pick it up, smile sheepishly at her, and wag his head.

83   "Gawd, Ahm sleepy," he mumbled.

84   She got a pillow from her room and gave it to him.

85   "Here," she said.

86   "Hunh," he said, putting the pillow between his head and the back of the chair.

87   They were silent again. Yes, she would have to tell him to go back out into the cold rain and slop; maybe to get caught; maybe for the last time; she didn't know. But she would let him eat and get dry before telling him that the sheriff knew of the meeting to be held at Lem's tomorrow. And she would make him take a big dose of soda before he went out; soda always helped to stave off a cold. She looked at the clock.

It was eleven. Theres time yit. Spreading a newspaper on the apron of the stove, she placed a heaping plate of greens upon it, a knife, a fork, a cup of coffee, a slab of cornbread, and a dish of peach cobbler.

88 "Yo suppahs ready," she said.

89 "Yeah," he said.

90 He did not move. She ironed again. Presently, she heard him eating. When she could no longer hear his knife tickling against the edge of the plate, she knew he was through. It was almost twelve now. She would let him rest a little while longer before she told him. Till one er'clock, mabbe. Hes so tired. . . . She finished her ironing, put away the board, and stacked the clothes in her dresser drawer. She poured herself a cup of black coffee, drew up a chair, sat down and drank.

91 "Yuh almos dry," she said, not looking around.

92 "Yeah," he said, turning sharply to her.

93 The tone of voice in which she had spoken had let him know that more was coming. She drained her cup and waited a moment longer.

94 "Reva wuz here."

95 "Yeah?"

96 "She lef bout a hour ergo."

97 "Whut she say?"

98 "She said old man Lem hada visit from the sheriff today."

99 "Bout the meetin?"

100 She saw him stare at the coals glowing red through the crevices of the stove and run his fingers nervously through his hair. She knew he was wondering how the sheriff had found out. In the silence he would ask a wordless question and in the silence she would answer wordlessly. Johnny-Boys too trustin, she thought. Hes trying to make the party big n hes takin in folks fastern he kin git t know em. You cant trust ever white man yuh meet. . . .

101 "Yuh know, Johnny-Boy, yuh been takin in a lotta them white folks lately . . ."

102 "Aw, ma!"

103 "But, Johnny-Boy . . ."

104 "Please, don't talk t me bout tha now, ma."

105 "Yuh ain t ol t lissen n learn, son," she said.

106 "Ah know whut yuh gonna say, ma. N yuh wrong. Yuh cant judge folks just by how yuh feel bout em n by how long yuh done knowed em. Ef we start that we wouldnt have *no*body in the party. When folks pledge they word t be with us, then we gotta take em in. Wes too weak to be choosy."

107 He rose abruptly, rammed his hands into his pockets, and stood facing the window; she looked at his back in a long silence. She knew his faith; it was deep. He had always said that black men could not fight the rich bosses alone; a man could not fight with every hand against him. But he believes so hard hes blind, she thought. At odd times they had had these arguments before; always she would be pitting her feelings against

the hard necessity of his thinking, and always she would lose. She shook her head. Po Johnny-Boy; he don know . . .

108   "But ain nona our folks tol, Johnny-Boy," she said.

109   "How yuh know?" he asked. His voice came low and with a tinge of anger. He still faced the window and now and then the yellow blade of light flicked across the sharp outline of his black face.

110   "Cause Ah know em," she said.

111   "*Any*body mighta tol," he said.

112   "It wuznt nona *our* folks," she said again.

113   She saw his hand sweep in a swift arc of disgust.

114   "*Our* folks! Ma, who in Gawds name is *our* folks?"

115   "The folks we wuz born n raised wid, son. The folks we *know!*"

116   "We cant make the party grow tha way, ma."

117   "It mighta been Booker," she said.

118   "Yuh don know."

119   ". . . er Blattberg . . ."

120   "Fer Chrissakes!"

121   " . . . er any of the fo-five others whut joined las week."

122   "Ma, yuh just don wan me t go out tonight," he said.

123   "Yo ol ma wans yuh t be careful, son."

124   "Ma, when yuh start doubtin folks in the party, then there ain no end."

125   "Son, Ah knows ever black man n woman in this parta the country," she said, standing too. "Ah watched em grow up; Ah even heped birth n nurse some of em; Ah knows em *all* from way back. There ain none of em that *coulda* tol! The folks Ah know jus don open they dos n ast death t walk in! Son, it wuz some of them *white* folks! Yuh just mark mah word n wait n see!"

126   "Why is it gotta be *white* folks?" he asked. "Ef they tol, then theys just Judases, thas all."

127   "Son, look at whuts befo yuh."

128   He shook his head and sighed.

129   "Ma, Ah done tol yuh a hundred times. Ah cant see white n Ah cant see black," he said. "Ah sees rich men n Ah sees po men."

130   She picked up his dirty dishes and piled them in a pan. Out of the corners of her eyes she saw him sit and pull on his wet shoes. Hes goin! When she put the last dish away he was standing fully dressed, warming his hands over the stove. Jus a few mo minutes now n hell be gone, like Sug, mabbe. Her throat tightened. This black mans fight takes *ever*thin! Looks like Gawd put us in this world jus t beat us down!

131   "Keep this, ma," he said.

132   She saw a crumpled wad of money in his outstretched fingers.

133   "Naw, yuh keep it. Yuh might need it."

134   "It ain mine, ma. It berlongs t the party."

135   "But, Johnny-Boy, yuh might hafta go erway!"

136   "Ah kin make out."

137 "Don fergit yosef too much, son."

138 "Ef Ah don come back theyll need it."

139 He was looking at her face and she was looking at the money.

140 "Yuh keep tha," she said slowly. "Ahll give em the money."

141 "From where?"

142 "Ah got some."

143 "Where yuh git it from?"

144 She sighed.

145 "Ah been savin a dollah a week for Sug ever since hes been in jail."

146 "Lawd, ma!"

147 She saw the look of puzzled love and wonder in his eyes. Clumsily, he put the money back into his pocket.

148 "Ahm gone," he said.

149 "Here; drink this glass of soda watah."

150 She watched him drink, then put the glass away.

151 "Waal," he said.

152 "Take the stuff outta yo pockets!"

153 She lifted the lid of the stove and he dumped all the papers from his pocket into the fire. She followed him to the door and made him turn round.

154 "Lawd, yuh tryin to maka revolution n yuh cant even keep yo coat buttoned." Her nimble fingers fastened his collar high around his throat. "There!"

155 He pulled the brim of his hat low over his eyes. She opened the door and with the suddenness of the cold gust of wind that struck her face, he was gone. She watched the black fields and the rain take him, her eyes burning. When the last faint footstep could no longer be heard, she closed the door, went to her bed, lay down, and pulled the cover over her while fully dressed. Her feelings coursed with the rhythm of the rain: Hes gone! Lawd, Ah *knows* hes gone! Her blood felt cold.

III

156 She was floating in a grey void somewhere between sleeping and dreaming and then suddenly she was wide awake, hearing and feeling in the same instant the thunder of the door crashing in and a cold wind filling the room. It was pitch black and she stared, resting on her elbows, her mouth open, not breathing, her ears full of the sound of tramping feet and booming voices. She knew at once: They lookin fer im! Then, filled with her will, she was on her feet, rigid, waiting, listening.

157 "The lamps burnin!"

158 "Yuh see her?"

159 "Naw!"

160 "Look in the kitchen!"

161 "Gee, this place smells like niggers!"

162   "Say, somebodys here er been here!"

163   "Yeah; theres fire in the stove!"

164   "Mabbe hes been here n gone?"

165   "Boy, look at these jars of jam!"

166   "Niggers make good jam!"

167   "Git some bread!"

168   "Heres some cornbread!"

169   "Say, lemme git some!"

170   "Take it easy! Theres plenty here!"

171   "Ahma take some of this stuff home!"

172   "Look, heres a pota greens!"

173   "N some hot cawffee!"

174   "Say, yuh guys! C mon! Cut it out! We didn't come here fer a feas!"

175   She walked slowly down the hall. They lookin fer im, but they ain got im yit! She stopped in the doorway, her gnarled, black hands as always folded over her stomach, but tight now, so tightly the veins bulged. The kitchen was crowded with men in glistening raincoats. Though the lamp burned, their flashlights still glowed in red fists. Across her floor she saw the muddy track of their boots.

176   "Yuh white folks git outta mah house!"

177   There was a quick silence; every face turned toward her. She saw a sudden movement, but did not know what it meant until something hot and wet slammed her squarely in the face. She gasped, but did not move. Calmly, she wiped the warm, greasy liquor of greens from her eyes with her left hand. One of the white men had thrown a handful of greens out of the pot at her.

178   "How they taste, ol bitch?"

179   "Ah ast yuh t git outta mah house!"

180   She saw the sheriff detach himself from the crowd and walk toward her.

181   "Now, Anty . . ."

182   "White man, don yuh *Anty* me!"

183   "Yuh ain got the right sperit!"

184   "Sperit hell! Yuh git these men outta mah house!"

185   "Yuh ack like yuh don like it!"

186   "Naw, Ah don like it, n yuh knows dam waal Ah don!"

187   "What yuh gonna do about it?"

188   "Ahm telling yuh t git outta mah house!"

189   "Gittin sassy?"

190   "Ef telling yuh t git outta mah house is sass, then Ahm sassy!"

191   Her words came in a tense whisper; but beyond, back of them, she was watching, thinking, judging the men.

192   "Listen, Anty," the sheriff's voice came soft and low. "Ahm here t hep yuh. How come yuh wanna ack this way?"

193   "Yuh ain never heped yo *own* sef since yuh been born," she flared. "How kin the likes of yuh hep me?"

194   One of the white men came forward and stood directly in front of her.

195   "Lissen, nigger woman, yuh talkin t *white* men!"

196   "Ah don care who Ahm talkin t!"

197   "Yuhll wish some day yuh did!"

198   "Not t the likes of yuh!"

199   "Yuh need somebody t teach yuh how t be a good nigger!"

200   "*Yuh* cant teach it t me!"

201   "Yuh gonna change yo tune."

202   "Not longs mah bloods warm!"

203   "Don git smart now!"

204   "Yuh git outta mah house!"

205   "Spose we don go?" the sheriff asked.

206   They were crowded around her. She had not moved since she had taken her place in the doorway. She was thinking only of Johnny-Boy as she stood there giving and taking words; and she knew that they, too, were thinking of Johnny-Boy. She knew they wanted him, and her heart was daring them to take him from her.

207   "Spose we don go?" the sheriff asked again.

208   "Twenty of yuh running over one ol woman! Now, ain yuh white men glad yuh so brave?"

209   The sheriff grabbed her arm.

210   "C mon, now! Yuh don did ernuff sass fer one night. Wheres tha nigger son of yos?"

211   "Don't yuh wished yuh knowed?"

212   "Yuh wanna git slapped?"

213   "Ah ain never seen one of yo kind that wuznt too low fer . . ."

214   The sheriff slapped her straight across her face with his open palm. She fell back against a wall and sank to her knees.

215   "Is tha whut white men do t nigger women?"

216   She rose slowly and stood again, not even touching the place that ached from his blow, her hands folded over her stomach.

217   "Ah ain never seen one of yo kind tha wuznt too low fer . . ."

218   He slapped her again; she reeled backward several feet and fell on her side.

219   "Is tha whut we too low to do?"

220   She stood before him again, dry-eyed, as though she had not been struck. Her lips were numb and her chin was wet with blood.

221   "Aw, let her go! Its the nigger we wan!" said one.

222   "Wheres that nigger son of yos?" the sheriff asked.

223   "Find im," she said.

224   "By Gawd, ef we hafta find im well kill im!"

225   "He wont be the only nigger yuh ever killed," she said.

226   She was consumed with a bitter pride. There was nothing on this earth, she felt then, that they could not do to her but that she could take. She stood on a narrow plot of ground from which she would die before

she was pushed. And then it was, while standing there feeling warm blood seeping down her throat, that she gave up Johnny-Boy, gave him up to the white folks. She gave him up because they had come tramping into her heart demanding him, thinking they could get him by beating her, thinking they could scare her into making her tell where he was. She gave him up because she wanted them to know that they could not get what they wanted by bluffing and killing.

227   "Wheres this meetin gonna be?" the sheriff asked.

228   "Don yuh wish yuh knowed?"

229   "Ain there gonna be a meetin?"

230   "How come yuh astin me?"

231   "There *is* gonna be a meetin," said the sheriff.

232   "Is it?"

233   "Ah gotta great mind t choke it outta yuh!"

234   "Yuh so smart," she said.

235   "We ain playing wid yuh!"

236   "Did Ah say yuh wuz?"

237   "Tha nigger son of yos is erroun here somewheres n Ah aim to find im," said the sheriff. "Ef yuh tell us where he is n ef he talks, mabbe hell git off easy. But ef we hafta find im, well kill im! Ef we hafta find im, then yuh git a sheet t put over im in the mawnin, see? Git yuh a sheet, cause hes gonna be dead!"

238   "He wont be the only nigger yuh ever killed," she said again.

239   The sheriff walked past her. The others followed. Yuh didnt git whut yuh wanted! she thought exultingly. N yuh ain gonna *never* git it! Hotly, something arched in her to make them feel the intensity of her pride and freedom; her heart groped to turn the bitter hours of her life into words of a kind that would make them feel that she had taken all they had done to her in stride and could still take more. Her faith surged so strongly in her she was all but blinded. She walked behind them to the door, knotting and twisting her fingers. She saw them step to the muddy ground. Each whirl of the yellow beacon revealed glimpses of slanting rain. Her lips moved, then she shouted:

240   "Yuh didnt git whut yuh wanted! N yuh ain gonna nevah git it!"

241   The sheriff stopped and turned; his voice came low and hard.

242   "Now, by Gawd, thas ernuff outta yuh!"

243   "Ah know when Ah done said ernuff!"

244   "Aw, naw, yuh don!" he said. "Yuh don know when yuh done said ernuff, but Ahma teach yuh ternight!"

245   He was up the steps and across the porch with one bound. She backed into the hall, her eyes full on his face.

246   "Tell me when yuh gonna stop talkin!" he said, swinging his fist.

247   The blow caught her high on the cheek; her eyes went blank; she fell flat on her face. She felt the hard heel of his wet shoes coming into her temple and stomach.

248   "Lemme hear yuh talk some mo!"

249   She wanted to, but could not; pain numbed and choked her. She lay still and somewhere out of the grey void of unconsciousness she heard someone say: *Aw fer chrissakes leave her erlone, its the nigger we wan. . . .*

IV

250   She never knew how long she had lain huddled in the dark hallway. Her first returning feeling was of a nameless fear crowding the inside of her, then a deep pain spreading from her temple downward over her body. Her ears were filled with the drone of rain and she shuddered from the cold wind blowing through the door. She opened her eyes and at first saw nothing. As if she were imagining it, she knew she was half lying and half sitting in a corner against a wall. With difficulty she twisted her neck and what she saw made her hold her breath—a vast white blur was suspended directly above her. For a moment she could not tell if her fear was from the blur or if the blur was from her fear. Gradually the blur resolved itself into a huge white face that slowly filled her vision. She was stone still, conscious really of the effort to breathe, feeling somehow that she existed only by the mercy of that white face. She had seen it before; its fear had gripped her many times; it had for her the fear of all the white faces she had ever seen in her life. *Sue . . .* As from a great distance, she heard her name being called. She was regaining consciousness now, but the fear was coming with her. She looked into the face of a white man, wanting to scream out for him to go; yet accepting his presence because she felt she had to. Though some remote part of her mind was active, her limbs were powerless. It was as if an invisible knife had split her in two, leaving one half of her lying there helpless, while the other half shrank in dread from a forgotten but familiar enemy. *Sue its me Sue its me . . .* Then all at once the voice came clearly.

251   "Sue, its me! Its Booker!"

252   And she heard an answering voice speaking inside of her. Yeah, its Booker . . . The one whut just joined . . . She roused herself, struggling for full consciousness; and as she did so she transferred to the person of Booker the nameless fear she felt. It seemed that Booker towered above her as a challenge to her right to exist upon the earth.

253   "Yuh awright?"

254   She did not answer; she started violently to her feet and fell.

255   "Sue, yuh hurt!"

256   "Yeah," she breathed.

257   "Where they hit yuh?"

258   "Its mah head," she whispered.

259   She was speaking even though she did not want to; the fear that had hold of her compelled her.

260   "They beat yuh?"

261   "Yeah."

262   "Them bastards! Them Gawddam bastards!"

263   She heard him saying it over and over; then she felt herself being lifted.

264   "Naw!" she gasped.

265   "Ahma take yuh t the kitchen!"

266   "Put me down!"

267   "But yuh cant stay here like this!"

268   She shrank in his arms and pushed her hands against his body; when she was in the kitchen she freed herself, sank into a chair, and held tightly to its back. She looked wonderingly at Booker. There was nothing about him that should frighten her so, but even that did not ease her tension. She saw him go to the water bucket, wet his handkerchief, wring it, and offer it to her. Distrustfully, she stared at the damp cloth.

269   "Here; put this on yo fohead . . ."

270   "Naw!"

271   "C mon; itll make yuh feel bettah!"

272   She hesitated in confusion. What right had she to be afraid when someone was acting as kindly as this toward her? Reluctantly, she leaned forward and pressed the damp cloth to her head. It helped. With each passing minute she was catching hold of herself, yet wondering why she felt as she did.

273   "Whut happened?"

274   "Ah don know."

275   "Yuh feel bettah?"

276   "Yeah."

277   "Who all wuz here?"

278   "Ah don know," she said again.

279   "Yo head still hurt?"

280   "Yeah."

281   "Gee, Ahm sorry."

282   "Ahm awright," she sighed and buried her face in her hands.

283   She felt him touch her shoulder.

284   "Sue, Ah got some bad news fer yuh . . ."

285   She knew; she stiffened and grew cold. It had happened; she stared dry-eyed, with compressed lips.

286   "Its mah Johnny-Boy," she said.

287   "Yeah; Ahm awful sorry t hafta tell yuh this way. But Ah thought yuh oughta know . . ."

288   Her tension eased and a vacant place opened up inside of her. A voice whispered, Jesus, hep me!

289   "W-w-where is he?"

290   "They got im out t Foleys Woods trying t make him tell who the others is."

291   "He ain gonna tell," she said. "They jus as waal kill im, cause he ain gonna nevah tell."

292   "Ah hope he don," said Booker. "But he didnt have a chance t tell the others. They grabbed im just as he got t the woods."

293   Then all the horror of it flashed upon her; she saw flung out over the rainy countryside an array of shacks where white and black comrades were sleeping; in the morning they would be rising and going to Lem's; then they would be caught. And that meant terror, prison, and death. The comrades would have to be told; she would have to tell them; she could not entrust Johnny-Boy's work to another, and especially not to Booker as long as she felt toward him as she did. Gripping the bottom of the chair with both hands, she tried to rise; the room blurred and she swayed. She found herself resting in Booker's arms.

294   "Lemma go!"

295   "Sue, yuh too weak t walk!"

296   "Ah gotta tell em!" she said.

297   "Set down, Sue! Yuh hurt! Yuh sick!"

298   When seated, she looked at him helplessly.

299   "Sue, lissen! Johnny-Boys caught. Ahm here. Yuh tell me who they is n Ahll tell em."

300   She stared at the floor and did not answer. Yes; she was too weak to go. There was no way for her to tramp all those miles through the rain tonight. But should she tell Booker? If only she had somebody like Reva to talk to! She did not want to decide alone; she must make no mistake about this. She felt Booker's fingers pressing on her arm and it was as though the white mountain was pushing her to the edge of a sheer height; she again exclaimed inwardly, Jesus, hep me! Booker's white face was at her side, waiting. Would she be doing right to tell him? Suppose she did not tell and then the comrades were caught? She could not ever forgive herself for doing a thing like that. But maybe she was wrong; maybe her fear was what Johnny-Boy had always called "jus foolishness." She remembered his saying, Ma, we cant make the party grow ef we start doubtin everbody. . . .

301   "Tell me who they is, Sue, n Ahll tell em. Ah just joined n Ah don know who they is."

302   "Ah don know who they is," she said.

303   "Yuh *gotta* tell me who they is, Sue!"

304   "Ah tol yuh Ah don know!"

305   "Yuh *do* know! C mon! Set up n talk!"

306   "Naw!"

307   "Yuh wan em all t git *killed?*"

308   She shook her head and swallowed. Lawd, Ah don believe in this man!

309   "Lissen, Ahll call the names n yuh tell me which ones is in the party n which ones ain, see?"

310   "Naw!"

311   "Please, Sue!"

312   "Ah don know," she said.

313   "Sue, yuh ain doin right by em. Johnny-Boy wouldnt wan yuh t be this way. Hes out there holdin up his end. Les hol up ours . . ."

314   "Lawd, Ah don know . . ."

315   "Is yuh scared a me cause Ahm *white?* Johnny-Boy ain like tha. Don let all the work we don go fer nothin."

316   She gave up and bowed her head in her hands.

317   "Is it Johnson? Tell me, Sue?"

318   "Yeah," she whispered in horror, a mounting horror of feeling herself being undone.

319   "Is it Green?"

320   "Yeah."

321   "Murphy?"

322   "Lawd, Ah don know!"

323   "Yuh gotta tell me, Sue!"

324   "Mistah Booker, please leave me erlone . . ."

325   "Is it Murphy?"

326   She answered yes to the names of Johnny-Boy's comrades; she answered until he asked her no more. Then she thought, How he know the sheriffs men is watching Lems house? She stood up and held onto her chair, feeling something sure and firm within her.

327   "How yuh know about Lem?"

328   "Why . . . How Ah know?"

329   "What yuh doin here this tima night? How yuh know the sheriff got Johnny-Boy?"

330   "Sue, don yuh believe in me?"

331   She did not, but she could not answer. She stared at him until her lips hung open; she was searching deep within herself for certainty.

332   "You meet Reva?" she asked.

333   "Reva?"

334   "Yeah; Lems gal?"

335   "Oh, yeah. Sho, Ah met Reva."

336   "She tell yuh?"

337   She asked the question more of herself than of him; she longed to believe.

338   "Yeah," he said softly. "Ah reckon Ah oughta be goin t tell em now."

339   "Who?" she asked. "Tell *who?*"

340   The muscles of her body were stiff as she waited for his answer; she felt as though life depended upon it.

341   "The comrades," he said.

342   "Yeah," she sighed.

343   She did not know when he left; she was not looking or listening. She just suddenly saw the room empty and from her the thing that had made her fearful was gone.

V

344   For a space of time that seemed to her as long as she had been upon the earth, she sat huddled over the cold stove. One minute she would say to herself, They both gone now; Johnny-Boy n Sug . . . Mabbe Ahll never see em ergin. Then a surge of guilt would blot out her longing. "Lawd, Ah shouldna tol!" she mumbled. "But no man kin be so low-down as to do a thing like that . . ." Several times she had an impulse to try to tell the comrades herself; she was feeling a little better now. But what good would that do? She had told Booker the names. He jus couldnt be a Judas to po folks like us . . . He *couldn't!*

345   "An Sue!"

346   Thas Reva! Her heart leaped with an anxious gladness. She rose without answering and limped down the dark hallway. Through the open door, against the background of rain, she saw Reva's face lit now and then to whiteness by the whirling beams of the beacon. She was about to call, but a thought checked her, Jesus, hep me! Ah gotta tell her bout Johnny-Boy . . . Lawd, Ah cant!

347   "An Sue, yuh there?"

348   "C mon in, chile!"

349   She caught Reva and held her close for a moment without speaking.

350   "Lawd, Ahm sho glad yuh here," she said at last.

351   "Ah thought somethin had happened t yuh," said Reva, pulling away. "Ah saw the do open . . . Pa told me to come back n stay wid yuh tonight . . ." Reva paused and started, "W-w-whuts the mattah?"

352   She was so full of having Reva with her that she did not understand what the question meant.

353   "Hunh?"

354   "Yo neck . . ."

355   "Aw, it ain nothin, chile. C mon in the kitchen."

356   "But theres blood on yo neck!"

357   "The sheriff wuz here . . ."

358   "Them fools! Whut they wanna bother yuh fer? Ah could kill em! So hep me Gawd, Ah could!"

359   "It ain nothing," she said.

360   She was wondering how to tell Reva about Johnny-Boy and Booker. Ahll wait a lil while longer, she thought. Now that Reva was here, her fear did not seem as awful as before.

361   "C mon, lemma fix you head, An Sue. Yuh hurt."

362   They went to the kitchen. She sat silent while Reva dressed her scalp. She was feeling better now; in just a little while she would tell Reva. She felt the girl's fingers pressing gently upon her head.

363   "That hurt?"

364   "A lil, chile."

365   "Yuh po thing."

366   "It ain nothin."

367   "Did Johnny-Boy come?"

368   She hesitated.

369   "Yeah."

370   "He done gone t tell the others?"

371   Reva's voice sounded so clear and confident that it mocked her. Lawd, Ah cant tell this chile . . .

372   "Yuh tol im, didnt yuh, An Sue?"

373   "Y-y-yeah . . ."

374   "Gee! Thas good! Ah tol pa he didnt hafta worry ef Johnny-Boy got the news. Mabbe thingsll come out awright."

375   "Ah hope . . ."

376   She could not go on; she had gone as far as she could. For the first time that night she began to cry.

377   "Hush, An Sue! Yuh awways been brave. Itll be awright!"

378   "Ain nothing awright, chile. The worls jus too much fer us, Ah reckon."

379   "Ef yuh cry that way itll make me cry."

380   She forced herself to stop. Naw; Ah cant carry on this way in fronta Reva . . . Right now she had a deep need for Reva to believe in her. She watched the girl get pine-knots from behind the stove, rekindle the fire, and put on the coffee pot.

381   "Yuh wan some cawffee?" Reva asked.

382   "Naw, honey."

383   "Aw, c mon, An Sue."

384   "Jusa lil, honey."

385   "Thas the way to be. Oh, say, Ah fergot," said Reva, measuring out spoonsful of coffee. "Pa tol me t tell yuh t watch out fer tha Booker man. Hes a stool."

386   She showed not one sign of outward movement or expression, but as the words fell from Reva's lips she went limp inside.

387   "Pa tol me soon as Ah got back home. He got word from town . . ."

388   She stopped listening. She felt as though she had been slapped to the extreme outer edge of life, into a cold darkness. She knew now what she had felt when she had looked up out of her fog of pain and had seen Booker. It was the image of all the white folks, and the fear that went with them, that she had seen and felt during her lifetime. And again, for the second time that night, something she had felt had come true. All she could say to herself was, Ah didnt like im! Gawd knows, Ah didnt! Ah tol Johnny-Boy it wuz some of them white folks . . .

389   "Here; drink yo cawffee . . ."

390   She took the cup; her fingers trembled, and the steaming liquid spilt onto her dress and leg.

391   "Ahm sorry, An Sue!"

392   Her leg was scalded, but the pain did not bother her.

393   "Its awright," she said.

394   "Wait; lemma put some lard on tha burn!"

395   "It don hurt."

396   "Yuh worried bout somethin."

397   "Naw, honey."

398   "Lemma fix yuh so mo cawffee."

399   "Ah don wan nothin now, Reva."

400   "Waal, buck up. Don be tha way . . ."

401   They were silent. She heard Reva drinking. No; she would not tell Reva; Reva was all she had left. But she had to do something, some way, somehow. She was undone too much as it was; and to tell Reva about Booker or Johnny-Boy was more than she was equal to; it would be too coldly shameful. She wanted to be alone and fight this thing out with herself.

402   "Go t bed, honey. Yuh tired."

403   "Nah; Ahm awright, An Sue."

404   She heard the bottom of Reva's empty cup clank against the top of the stove. Ah *got* t make her go t bed! Yes; Booker would tell the names of the comrades to the sheriff. If she could only stop him some way! That was the answer, the point, the star that grew bright in the morning of new hope. Soon, maybe half an hour from now, Booker would reach Foleys Woods. Hes boun t go the long way, cause he don know no short cut, she thought. Ah could wade the creek n beat im there. . . . But what would she do after that?

405   "Reva, honey, go t bed. Ahm awright. Yuh need res."

406   "Ah ain sleepy, An Sue."

407   "Ah knows whuts bes fer yuh, chile. Yuh tired n wet."

408   "Ah wanna stay up wid yuh."

409   She forced a smile and said:

410   "Ah don think they gonna hurt Johnny-Boy . . ."

411   "Fer *real*, An Sue?"

412   "Sho, honey."

413   "But Ah wanna wait up wid yuh."

414   "Thas mah job, honey. Thas what a mas fer, t wait up fer her chillun."

415   "Good night, An Sue."

416   "Good night, honey."

417   She watched Reva pull up and leave the kitchen; presently she heard the shucks in the mattress whispering, and she knew that Reva had gone to bed. She was alone. Through the cracks of the stove she saw the fire dying to grey ashes; the room was growing cold again. The yellow beacon continued to flit past the window and the rain still drummed. Yes; she was alone; she had done this awful thing alone; she must find some way out, alone. Like touching a festering sore, she put her finger upon that moment when she had shouted her defiance to the sheriff, when she had shouted to feel her strength. She had lost Sug to save others; she had let Johnny-Boy go to save others; and then in a moment of weakness that came from too much strength she had lost all. If she had

not shouted to the sheriff, she would have been strong enough to have resisted Booker; she would have been able to tell the comrades herself. Something tightened in her as she remembered and understood the fit of fear she had felt on coming to herself in the dark hallway. A part of her life she thought she had done away with forever had had hold of her then. She had thought the soft, warm past was over; she had thought that it did not mean much when now she sang: *"Hes the Lily of the Valley, the Bright n Mawnin Star"* . . . The days when she had sung that song were the days when she had not hoped for anything on this earth, the days when the cold mountain had driven her into the arms of Jesus. She had thought that Sug and Johnny-Boy had taught her to forget Him, to fix her hope upon the fight of black men for freedom. Through the gradual years she had believed and worked with them, had felt strength shed from the grace of their terrible vision. That grace had been upon her when she had let the sheriff slap her down; it had been upon her when she had risen time and again from the floor and faced him. But she had trapped herself with her own hunger; to water the long, dry thirst of her faith; her pride had made a bargain which her flesh could not keep. Her having told the names of Johnny-Boy's comrades was but an incident in a deeper horror. She stood up and looked at the floor while call and counter-call, loyalty and counter-loyalty struggled in her sould. Mired she was between two abandoned worlds, living, but dying without the strength of the grace that either gave. The clearer she felt it the fuller did something well up from the depths of her for release; the more urgent did she feel the need to fling into her black sky another star, another hope, one more terrible vision to give her the strength to live and act. Softly and restlessly she walked about the kitchen, feeling herself naked against the night, the rain, the world; and shamed whenever the thought of Reva's love crossed her mind. She lifted her empty hands and looked at her writhing fingers. Lawd, whut kin Ah do now? She could still wade the creek and get to Foleys Woods before Booker. And then what? How could she manage to see Johnny-Boy or Booker? Again she heard the sheriff's threatening voice: Git yuh a sheet, cause hes gonna be dead! The sheet! Thas it, the *sheet!* Her whole being leaped with will; the long years of her life bent toward a moment of focus, a point. Ah kin go wid mah sheet! Ahll be doin whut he said! Lawd Gawd in Heaven, Ahma go lika nigger woman wid mah windin sheet t git mah dead son! But then what? She stood straight and smiled grimly; she had in her heart the whole meaning of her life; her entire personality was poised on the brink of a total act. Ah know! Ah *know!* She thought of Johnny-Boy's gun in the dresser drawer. Ahll hide the gun in the sheet n go aftah Johnny-Boy's body. . . . She tiptoed to her room, eased out the dresser drawer, and got a sheet. Reva was sleeping; the darkness was filled with her quiet breathing. She groped in the drawer and found the gun. She wound the gun in the sheet and held them both under her apron. Then she stole to the bedside and watched Reva. Lawd, hep her! But mabbe shes bettah off. This had t happen sometime . . . She n Johnny-Boy couldna been together in this here South . . . N Ah couldnt tell her about Booker. Itll come out awright n she wont nevah know. Reva's trust would never be shaken. She caught her breath as the shucks in the mattress rustled dryly; then all was quiet and she breathed easily again. She tiptoed to the door, down the hall, and stood on the porch. Above her the yellow beacon whirled through the rain. She went over muddy ground, mounted a slope, stopped and looked back at her house. The lamp glowed in her window, and the yellow beacon that swung every few seconds seemed to feed it with light. She turned and started across the fields, holding the gun and sheet tightly, thinking, Po Reva . . . Po critter . . . Shes fas ersleep . . .

VI

418   For the most part she walked with her eyes half shut, her lips tightly compressed, leaning her body against the wind and the driving rain, feeling the pistol in the sheet sagging cold and heavy in her fingers. Already she was getting wet; it seemed that her feet found every puddle of water that stood between the corn rows.

419   She came to the edge of the creek and paused wondering at what point was it low. Taking the sheet from under her apron, she wrapped the gun in it so that her finger could be upon the trigger. Ahll cross here, she thought. At first she did not feel the water; her feet were already wet. But the water grew cold as it came up to her knees; she gasped when it reached her waist. Lawd, this creeks high! When she had passed the middle, she knew that she was out of danger. She came out of the water, climbed a grassy hill, walked on, turned a bend and saw the lights of autos gleaming ahead. Yeah; theys still there! She hurried with her head down. Wondah did Ah beat im here? Lawd, Ah *hope* so! A vivid image of Booker's white face hovered a moment before her eyes and a surging will rose up in her so hard and strong that it vanished. She was among the autos now. From nearby came the hoarse voices of the men.

420   "Hey, yuh!"

421   She stopped, nervously clutching the sheet. Two white men with shotguns came toward her.

422   "Whut in hell yuh doin out here?"

423   She did not answer.

424   "Didnt yuh hear somebody speak t yuh?"

425   "Ahm comin aftah mah son," she said humbly.

426   "Yo *son?*"

427   "Yessuh."

428   "What yo son doin out here?"

429   "The sheriffs got im."

430   "Holy Scott! Jim, its the niggers ma!"

431 "What yuh got there?" asked one.

432 "A sheet."

433 "A *sheet?*"

434 "Yessuh."

435 "Fer whut?"

436 "The sheriff tol me to bring a sheet t git his body."

437 "Waal, waal . . ."

438 "Now, ain tha somethin?"

439 The white men looked at each other.

440 "These niggers sho love one ernother," said one.

441 "N tha ain no lie," said the other.

442 "Take me t the sheriff" she begged.

443 "Yuh ain givin us *orders*, is yuh?"

444 "Nawsuh."

445 "Well take yuh when wes good n ready."

446 "Yessuh."

447 "So yuh wan his body?"

448 "Yessuh."

449 "Waal, he ain dead yit."

450 "They gonna kill im," she said.

451 "Ef he talks they wont."

452 "He ain gonna talk," she said.

453 "How yuh know?"

454 "Cause he ain."

455 "We got ways of makin niggers talk."

456 "Yuh ain got no way fer im."

457 "Yuh thinka lot of that black Red, don yuh?"

458 "Hes mah son."

459 "Why don yuh teach im some sense?"

460 "Hes mah son," she said again.

461 "Lissen, ol nigger woman, yuh stand there wid yo hair white. Yuh got bettah sense than t believe tha niggers kin make a revolution . . ."

462 "A black republic," said the other one, laughing.

463 "Take me t the sheriff," she begged.

464 "Yuh his ma," said one. "Yuh kin make im talk n tell whose in this thing wid im."

465 "He ain gonna talk," she said.

466 "Don yuh wan im t live?"

467 She did not answer.

468 "C mon, les take her t Bradley."

469 They grabbed her arms and she clutched hard at the sheet and gun; they led her toward the crowd in the woods. Her feelings were simple; Booker would not tell; she was there with the gun to see to that. The louder became the voices of the men the deeper became her feeling of wanting to right the mistake she had made; of wanting to fight her way back to solid ground. She would stall for time until Booker showed up.

Oh, ef theyll only lemma git close t Johnny-Boy! As they led her near the crowd she saw white faces turning and looking at her and heard a rising clamor of voices.

470   "Whose tha?"

471   "A nigger woman!"

472   "Whut she doin out here?"

473   "This is his ma!" called one of the men.

474   "Whut she wan?"

475   "She brought a sheet t cover his body!"

476   "He ain dead yit!"

477   "They tryin to make im talk!"

478   "But he will be dead soon ef he don open up!"

479   "Say, look! The niggers ma brought a sheet t cover up his body!"

480   "Now, ain that sweet?"

481   "Mabbe she wans t hol a prayer meetin!"

482   "Did she git a preacher?"

483   "Say, go git Bradley!"

484   "O.K.!"

485   The crowd grew quiet. They looked at her curiously; she felt their cold eyes trying to detect some weakness in her. Humbly, she stood with the sheet covering the gun. She had already accepted all that they could do to her.

486   The sheriff came.

487   "So yuh brought yuh sheet, hunh?"

488   "Yessuh," she whispered.

489   "Looks like them slaps we gave yuh learned yuh some sense, didnt they?"

490   She did not answer.

491   "Yuh don need tha sheet. Yo son ain dead yit," he said, reaching toward her.

492   She backed away, her eyes wide.

493   "Naw!"

494   "Now, lissen, Anty!" he said. "There ain no use in yuh ackin a fool! Go in there n tell tha nigger son of yos t tell us whos in this wid im, see? Ah promise we wont kill im ef he talks. We'll let im git outta town."

495   "There ain nothing Ah kin tell im," she said.

496   "Yuh wan us to kill im?"

497   She did not answer. She saw someone lean toward the sheriff and whisper.

498   "Bring her erlong," the sheriff said.

499   They led her to a muddy clearing. The rain streamed down through the ghostly glare of the flashlights. As the men formed a semi-circle she saw Johnny-Boy lying in a trough of mud. He was tied with rope; he lay hunched and one side of his face rested in a pool of black water. His eyes were staring questioningly at her.

500   "Speak t im," said the sheriff.

501   If she could only tell him why she was here! But that was impossible; she was close to what she wanted and she stared straight before her with compressed lips.

502   "Say, nigger!" called the sheriff, kicking Johnny-Boy. "Heres yo ma!"

503   Johnny-Boy did not move or speak. The sheriff faced her again.

504   "Lissen, Anty," he said. "Yuh got mo say wid im than anybody. Tell im t talk n hava chance. Whut he wanna pertect the other niggers n white folks fer?"

505   She slid her finger about the trigger of the gun and looked stonily at the mud.

506   "Go t him," said the sheriff.

507   She did not move. Her heart was crying out to answer the amazed question in Johnny-Boy's eyes. But there was no way now.

508   "Waal, yuhre astin fer it. By Gawd, we gotta way to *make* yuh talk t im," he said, turning away. "Sam, Tim, git one of them logs n turn that nigger upside-down n put his legs on it!"

509   A murmur of assent ran through the crowd. She bit her lips; she knew what that meant.

510   "Yuh wan yo nigger son crippled?" she heard the sheriff ask.

511   She did not answer. She saw them roll the log up; they lifted Johnny-Boy and laid him on his face and stomach, then they pulled his legs over the log. His kneecaps rested on the sheer top of the log's back and the toes of his shoes pointed groundward. So absorbed was she in watching that she felt that it was she who was being lifted and made ready for torture.

512   "Git a crowbar!" said the sheriff.

513   A tall, lank man got a crowbar from a nearby auto and stood over the log. His jaws worked slowly on a wad of tobacco.

514   "Now, its up t yuh, Anty," the sheriff said. "Tell the man whut to do!"

515   She looked into the rain. The sheriff turned.

516   "Mebba she think wes playin. Ef she don say nothin, then break em at the kneecaps!"

517   "O.K., Sheriff!"

518   She stood waiting for Booker. Her legs felt weak; she wondered if she would be able to wait much longer. Over and over she said to herself, Ef he came now Ahd kill em both!

519   "She ain sayin nothin, Sheriff!"

520   "Waal, Gawddammit, let im have it!"

521   The crowbar came down and Johnny-Boy's body lunged in the mud and water. There was a scream. She swayed, holding tight to the gun and sheet.

522   "Hol im! Git the other leg!"

523   The crowbar fell again. There was another scream.

524   "Yuh break em?" asked the sheriff.

525   The tall man lifted Johnny-Boy's legs and let them drop limply again, dropping rearward from the kneecaps. Johnny-Boy's body lay still. His head had rolled to one side and she could not see his face.

526   "Jus lika broke sparrow wing," said the man, laughing softly.

527   Then Johnny-Boy's face turned to her; he screamed.

528   "Go way, ma! Go way!"

529   It was the first time she had heard his voice since she had come out to the woods; she all but lost control of herself. She started violently forward, but the sheriff's arm checked her.

530   "Aw, naw! Yuh had yo chance!" He turned to Johnny-Boy. "She kin go ef yuh talk."

531   "Mistah, he ain gonna talk," she said.

532   "Go way, ma!" said Johnny-Boy.

533   "Shoot im! Don make im suffah so," she begged.

534   "He'll either talk or he'll never hear yuh ergin," the sheriff said. "Theres other things we kin do t im."

535   She said nothing.

536   "Whut yuh come here fer, ma?" Johnny-Boy sobbed.

537   "Ahm gonna split his eardrums," the sheriff said. "Ef yuh got anythin to say t im yuh bettah say it *now!*"

538   She closed her eyes. She heard the sheriffs feet sucking in mud. Ah could save im! She opened her eyes; there were shouts of eagerness from the crowd as it pushed in closer.

539   "Bus em, Sheriff!"

540   "Fix im so he cant hear!"

541   "He knows how t do it, too!"

542   "He busted a Jew boy tha way once!"

543   She saw the sheriff stoop over Johnny-Boy, place his flat palm over one ear and strike his fist against it with all his might. He placed his palm over the other ear and struck again. Johnny-Boy moaned, his head rolling from side to side, his eyes showing white amazement in a world without sound.

544   "Yuh wouldnt talk t im when yuh had the chance," said the sheriff. "Try n talk now."

545   She felt warm tears on her cheeks. She longed to shoot Johnny-Boy and let him go. But if she did that they would take the gun from her, and Booker would tell who the others were. Lawd, hep me! The men were talking loudly now, as though the main business was over. It seemed ages that she stood there watching Johnny-Boy roll and whimper in his world of silence.

546   "Say, Sheriff, heres somebody lookin fer yuh!"

547   "Who is it?"

548   "Ah don know!"

549   "Bring em in!"

550   She stiffened and looked around wildly, holding the gun tight. Is tha Booker? Then she held still, feeling that her excitement might betray

her. Mabbe Ah kin shoot em both! Mabbe Ah kin shoot *twice!* The sheriff stood in front of her, waiting. The crowd parted and she saw Booker hurrying forward.

551 "Ah know em all, Sheriff!" he called.

552 He came full into the muddy clearing where Johnny-Boy lay.

553 "Yuh mean yuh got the names?"

554 "Sho! The ol nigger . . ."

555 She saw his lips hang open and silent when he saw her. She stepped forward and raised the sheet.

556 "Whut . . ."

557 She fired, once; then, without pausing, she turned, hearing them yell. She aimed at Johnny-Boy, but they had their arms around her, bearing her to the ground, clawing at the sheet in her hand. She glimpsed Booker lying sprawled in the mud, on his face, his hands stretched out before him; then a cluster of yelling men blotted him out. She lay without struggling, looking upward through the rain at the white faces above her. And she was suddenly at peace; they were not a white mountain now; they were not pushing her any longer to the edge of life. Its awright . . .

558 "She shot Booker!"

559 "She hada gun in the sheet!"

560 "She shot im right thu the head!"

561 "Whut she shoot im fer?"

562 "Kill the bitch!"

563 "Ah *thought* somethin wuz wrong bout her!"

564 "Ah wuz fer givin it t her from the firs!"

565 "Thas whut yuh git fer treatin a nigger nice!"

566 "Say, Bookers dead!"

567 She stopped looking into the white faces, stopped listening. She waited, giving up her life before they took it from her; she had done what she wanted. Ef only Johnny-Boy . . . She looked at him; he lay looking at her with tired eyes. Ef she could only tell im! But he lay already buried in a grave of silence.

568 "Whut yuh kill im fer, hunh?"

569 It was the sheriff's voice; she did not answer.

570 "Mabbe she wuz shootin at yuh, Sheriff!"

571 "Whut yuh kill im fer!"

572 She felt the sheriff's foot come into her side; she closed her eyes.

573 "Yuh black bitch!"

574 "Let her have it!"

575 "Yuh reckon she foun out bout Booker?"

576 "She mighta."

577 "Jesus Chris, whut yuh dummies *waitin* on!"

578 "Yeah; kill her!"

579 "Kill em *both!*"

580 "Let her know her nigger sons dead firs!"

581   She turned her head toward Johnny-Boy; he lay looking puzzled in a world beyond the reach of voices. At leas he cant hear, she thought.

582   "C mon, let im have it."

583   She listened to hear what Johnny-Boy could not. They came, two of them, one right behind the other: so close together that they sounded like one shot. She did not look at Johnny-Boy now; she looked at the white faces of the men, hard and wet in the glare of the flashlights.

584   "Yuh hear tha, nigger woman?"

585   "Did tha surprise im? Hes in hell now wonderin whut hit im!"

586   "C mon! Give it t her, Sheriff!"

587   "Lemma shoot her, Sheriff! It wuz mah pal she shot!"

588   "Awright, Pete! Thas fair ernuff!"

589   She gave up as much of her life as she could before they took it from her. But the sound of the shot and the streak of fire that tore its way through her chest forced her to live again, intensely. She had not moved, save for the slight jarring impact of the bullet. She felt the heat of her own blood warming her cold, wet back. She yearned suddenly to talk. "Yuh didnt git whut yuh wanted! N yuh ain gonna nevah git it! Yuh didnt kill me; Ah come here by mahsef . . ." She felt rain falling into her wide-open, dimming eyes and heard faint voices. Her lips moved soundlessly. *Yuh didnt git yuh didnt yuh didnt . . .* Focused and pointed she was, buried in the depths of her star, swallowed in its peace and strength; and not feeling her flesh growing cold, cold as the rain that fell from the invisible sky upon the doomed living and the dead that never dies.

Study Questions

1. What is the basic similarity between Sue's two faiths? The basic difference between them?
2. Is she able to reconcile the two faiths? How do you know?
3. Why does Wright present the dialogue in dialect?
4. What Christian event is metaphorically treated in this story?

I Have a Dream

Martin Luther King, Jr.

1   Five score years ago, a great American, in whose symbolic shadow we stand, signed the Emancipation Proclamation. This momentous decree came as a great beacon light of hope to millions of Negro slaves who had been seared in the flames of withering injustice. It came as a joyous daybreak to end the long night of captivity.

2   But one hundred years later, we must face the tragic fact that the Negro is still not free. One hundred years later, the life of the Negro is still sadly crippled by the manacles of segregation and the chains of discrimination. One hundred years later, the Negro lives on a lonely island of poverty in the midst of a vast ocean of material prosperity. One hundred years later, the Negro is still languished in the corners of American society and finds himself an exile in his own land. So we have come here today to dramatize an appalling condition.

3   In a sense we have come to our nation's Capital to cash a check. When the architects of our republic wrote the magnificent words of the Constitution and the Declaration of Independence, they were signing a promissory note to which every American was to fall heir. This note was a promise that all men would be guaranteed the unalienable rights of life, liberty, and the pursuit of happiness.

4   It is obvious today that America has defaulted on this promissory note insofar as her citizens of color are concerned. Instead of honoring this sacred obligation, America has given the Negro people a bad check; a check which has come back marked "insufficient funds." But we refuse to believe that the bank of justice is bankrupt. We refuse to believe that there are insufficient funds in the great vaults of opportunity of this nation. So we have come to cash this check—a check that will give us upon demand the riches of freedom and the security of justice. We have also come to this hallowed spot to remind America of the fierce urgency of *now*. This is no time to engage in the luxury of cooling off or to take the tranquilizing of gradualism. *Now* is the time to make real the promises of Democracy. *Now* is the time to rise from the dark and desolate valley of segregation to the sunlit path of racial justice. *Now* is the time to open the doors of opportunity to all of God's children. *Now* is the time to lift our nation from the quicksands of racial injustice to the solid rock of brotherhood.

5   It would be fatal for the nation to overlook the urgency of the moment and to underestimate the determination of the Negro. This

sweltering summer of the Negro's legitimate discontent will not pass until there is an invigorating autumn of freedom and equality. 1963 is not an end, but a beginning. Those who hope that the Negro needed to blow off steam and will now be content will have a rude awakening if the nation returns to business as usual. There will be neither rest nor tranquility in America until the Negro is granted his citizenship rights. The whirlwinds of revolt will continue to shake the foundation of our nation until the bright day of justice emerges.

6   But there is something that I must say to my people who stand on the warm threshold which leads into the palace of justice. In the process of gaining our rightful place we must not be guilty of wrongful deeds. Let us not seek to satisfy our thirst for freedom by drinking from the cup of bitterness and hatred. We must forever conduct our struggle on the high plane of dignity and discipline. We must not allow our creative protest to degenerate into physical violence. Again and again we must rise to the majestic heights of meeting physical force with soul force. The marvelous new militancy which has engulfed the Negro community must not lead us to a distrust of all white people, for many of our white brothers, as evidenced by their presence here today, have come to realize that their destiny is tied up with our destiny and their freedom is inextricably bound to our freedom. We cannot walk alone.

7   And as we walk, we must make the pledge that we shall march ahead. We cannot turn back. There are those who are asking the devotees of civil rights, "When will you be satisfied?" We can never be satisfied as long as the Negro is the victim of the unspeakable horrors of police brutality. We can never be satisfied as long as our bodies, heavy with the fatigue of travel, cannot gain lodging in the motels of the highways and the hotels of the cities. We cannot be satisfied as long as the Negro's basic mobility is from a smaller ghetto to a larger one. We can never be satisfied as long as a Negro in Mississippi cannot vote and a Negro in New York believes he has nothing for which to vote. No, no, we are not satisfied, and we will not be satisfied until justice rolls down like waters and righteousness like a mighty stream.

8   I am not unmindful that some of you have come here out of great trials and tribulations. Some of you have come fresh from narrow jail cells. Some of you have come from areas where your quest for freedom left you battered by the storms of persecution and staggered by the winds of police brutality. You have been the veterans of creative suffering. Continue to work with the faith that unearned suffering is redemptive.

9   Go back to Mississippi, go back to Alabama, go back to South Carolina, go back to Georgia, go back to Louisiana, go back to the slums and ghettos of our northern cities, knowing that somehow this situation can and will be changed. Let us not wallow in the valley of despair.

10   I say to you today, my friends, that in spite of the difficulties and frustrations of the moment I still have a dream. It is a dream deeply rooted in the American dream.

11   I have a dream that one day this nation will rise up and live out the true meaning of its creed: "We hold these truths to be self-evident; that all men are created equal."

12   I have a dream that one day on the red hills of Georgia the sons of former slaves and the sons of former slaveowners will be able to sit down together at the table of brotherhood.

13   I have a dream that one day even the state of Mississippi, a desert state sweltering with the heat of injustice and oppression, will be transformed into an oasis of freedom and justice.

14   I have a dream that my four little children will one day live in a nation where they will not be judged by the color of their skin but by the content of their character.

15   I have a dream today.

16   I have a dream that one day the state of Alabama, whose governor's lips are presently dripping with the words of interposition and nullification, will be transformed into a situation where little black boys and black girls will be able to join hands with little white boys and white girls and walk together as sisters and brothers.

17   I have a dream today.

18   I have a dream that one day every valley shall be exalted, every hill and mountain shall be made low, the rough places will be made plain, and the crooked places will be made straight, and the glory of the Lord shall be revealed, and all flesh shall see it together.

19   This is our hope. This is the faith with which I return to the South. With this faith we will be able to hew out of the mountain of despair a stone of hope. With this faith we will be able to transform the jangling discords of our nation into a beautiful symphony of brotherhood. With this faith we will be able to work together, to pray together, to struggle together, to go to jail together, to stand up for freedom together, knowing that we will be free one day.

20   This will be the day when all of God's children will be able to sing with new meaning

> My country, 'tis of thee,
> Sweet land of liberty,
>   Of thee I sing:
> Land where my fathers died,
> Land of the pilgrims' pride,
> From every mountain-side
>   Let freedom ring.

21   And if America is to be a great nation this must become true. So let freedom ring from the prodigious hilltops of New Hampshire. Let freedom ring from the mighty mountains of New York. Let freedom ring from the heightening Alleghenies of Pennsylvania!

Let freedom ring from the snowcapped Rockies of Colorado!

Let freedom ring from the curvacious peaks of California!

But not only that; let freedom ring from Stone Mountain of Georgia!
Let freedom ring from Lookout Mountain of Tennessee!

Let freedom ring from every hill and molehill of Mississippi. From every mountainside, let freedom ring.

22   When we let freedom ring, when we let it ring from every village and every hamlet, from every state and every city, we will be able to speed up that day when all of God's children, black men and white men, Jews and Gentiles, Protestants and Catholics, will be able to join hands and sing in the words of the old Negro spiritual, "Free at last! free at last! thank God almighty, we are free at last!"

Study Questions

1. This essay was originally a speech delivered in 1963. How much of King's dream has come true? How much of it seems impossibly idealistic today?
2. What word would King probably substitute for the word *Negro* today?
3. Parallelism is used very effectively in this selection. Cite examples. Can parallelism perhaps be used to greater effect in oral than in written presentations? Explain.
4. How effective is the use of a closing quotation? Is this generally good practice in the writing of freshman themes?

Vision of a Past Warrior

Peter La Farge

I have within me such a dream of pain
That all my silver horseman hopes rust still—
Beyond quick silver mountains, on the plain,
The buffalo are gone, none left to kill.

I see the plains grow blackened with that dawn,
No robes for winter warmth, no meat to eat—
The ghost white buffalos' medicine gone,
No hope for Indians then; I see defeat.

Then there will be changes to another way,
We will fight battles that are legends long.   10
But of all our glory none will stay—
Who will remember that I sang this song?

Study Questions

1. These lyrics reflect a concern for the Native American's heritage. Can this poem in any way be called "positive"?
2. What are "silver horseman hopes"? Why do they "rust"? Is there a pun in the phrase "quick silver mountains"?
3. How is color used in the song? In "the plains grow blackened with that dawn," why is the natural course of events reversed?
4. How do the ideas in the song lead up to the bitterness of the last line?

Arrival at Boston

Chiang Yee

Originally I lived in Mount Lu,
A dumbman well-acquainted with travels.
Riding the storm and braving the waves
    I reached the Western land,
Having seen all the winds and rains of the human world.

After twenty years stay in Oxford, England,
I now drifted towards the Star-flag.
With no definite purpose
I stop at Boston temporarily,
Tracing at leisure the origin of the Yankees.   10

Study Questions

1. What does Yee mean by *dumbman*?
2. What does "twenty years stay in Oxford, England" suggest?
3. Why does Yee suddenly switch to present verb tense in line 9?
4. What words specifically suggest that Yee is in no hurry to end his journies?

Back to Bachimba

Enrique Hank Lopez

1   I am a *pocho* from Bachimba, a rather small Mexican village in the
state of Chihuahua, where my father fought with the army of Pancho
Villa. He was, in fact, the only private in Villa's army.

2   *Pocho* is ordinarily a derogatory term in Mexico (to define it succinctly, a *pocho* is a Mexican slob who has pretensions of being a gringo
sonofabitch), but I use it in a very special sense. To me that word has
come to mean "uprooted Mexican," and that's what I have been all my
life. Though my entire upbringing and education took place in the
United States, I have never felt completely American; and when I am in
Mexico, I sometimes feel like a displaced gringo with a curiously Mexican name—Enrique Preciliano Lopez y Martinez de Sepulveda de Sa-
pien (—de Quien-sabe-quien). One might conclude that I'm either a
schizo-cultural Mexican or a cultured schizoid American.

3   In any event, the schizo-ing began a long time ago, when my father
and many of Pancho Villa's troops fled across the border to escape the
oncoming *federales* who eventually defeated Villa. My mother and I,

traveling across the hot desert plains in a buckboard wagon, joined my father in El Paso, Texas, a few days after his hurried departure. With more and more Villistas swarming into El Paso every day, it was quickly apparent that jobs would be exceedingly scarce and insecure; so my parents packed our few belongings and we took the first available bus to Denver. My father had hoped to move to Chicago because the name sounded so Mexican, but my mother's meager savings were hardly enough to buy tickets for Colorado.

4   There we moved into a ghetto of Spanish-speaking residents who chose to call themselves Spanish-Americans and resented the sudden migration of their brethren from Mexico, whom they sneeringly called *surumatos* (slang for "southerners"). These so-called Spanish-Americans claimed direct descent from the original conquistadores of Spain. They also insisted that they had *never* been Mexicans, since their region of New Spain (later annexed to the United States) was never a part of Mexico. But what they claimed most vociferously—and erroneously— was an absence of Indian ancestry. It made no difference that any objective observer could see by merely looking at them the results of considerable fraternization between the conquering Spaniards and the Comanche and Navaho women who crossed their paths. Still, these *manitos,* as they were snidely labeled by the *surumatos,* stubbornly refused to be identified with Mexico, and would actually fight anyone who called them Mexican. So intense was this intergroup rivalry that the bitterest "race riots" I have ever witnessed—and engaged in—were between the look-alike, talk-alike *surumatos* and *manitos* who lived near Denver's Curtis Park. In retrospect the harsh conflicts between us were all the more silly and self-defeating when one recalls that we were all lumped together as "spiks" and "greasers" by the Anglo-Saxon community.

5   Predictably enough, we *surumatos* began huddling together in a sub-neighborhood within the larger ghetto, and it was there that I became painfully aware that my father had been the only private in Pancho Villa's army. Most of my friends were the sons of captains, colonels, majors, and even generals, though a few fathers were admittedly mere sergeants and corporals. My father alone had been a lowly private in that famous Division del Norte. Naturally I developed a most painful complex, which led me to all sorts of compensatory fibs. During one brief spell I fancied my father as a member of the dreaded *los dorados,* the "golden ones," who were Villa's favorite henchmen. (Later I was to learn that my father's cousin, Martin Lopez, was a genuine and quite notorious *dorado.*) But all my inventions were quickly uninvented by my very own father, who seemed to take a perverse delight in being Pancho's only private.

6   No doubt my chagrin was accentuated by the fact that Pancho Villa's exploits were a constant topic of conversation in our household. My entire childhood seems to be shadowed by his presence. At our

dinner table, almost every night, we would listen to endlessly repeated accounts of this battle, that stratagem, or some great act of Robin Hood kindness by *el centauro del norte.* I remember how angry my parents were when they saw Wallace Beery in *Viva Villa!* "Garbage by stupid gringos" they called it. They were particularly offended by the sweaty, unshaven sloppiness of Beery's portrayal. "Pancho Villa was clean and orderly, no matter how much he chased after women. This man's a dirty swine."

7   As if to deepen our sense of *Villismo,* my parents also taught us "Adelita" and "*Se llevaron el cañon para Bachimba*" ("They took the cannons to Bachimba"), the two most famous songs of the Mexican revolution. Some twenty years later (during my stint at Harvard Law School), while strolling along the Charles River, I would find myself softly singing "*Se llevaron el cañon para Bachimba, para Bachimba, para Bachimba*" over and over again. That's all I could remember of that poignant rebel song. Though I had been born there, I had always regarded "Bachimba" as a fictitious, made-up, Lewis Carroll kind of word. So that eight years ago, when I first returned to Mexico, I was literally stunned when I came to a crossroad south of Chihuahua and saw an old road marker: "Bachimba 18 km." Then it really exists—I shouted inwardly—Bachimba is a real town! Swinging onto the narrow, poorly paved road, I gunned the motor and sped toward the town I'd been singing about since infancy. It turned out to be a quiet, dusty village with a bleak worn-down plaza that was surrounded by nondescript buildings of uncertain vintage.

8   Aside from the songs about Bachimba and Adelita and all the folk tales about Villa's guerrilla fighters, my early years were strongly influenced by our neighborhood celebrations of Mexico's two most important patriotic events: Mexican Independence Day on September 16, and the anniversay of the battle of Puebla on May 5. On those two dates Mexicans all over the world are likely to become extremely chauvinistic. In Denver we would stage annual parades that included three or four floats skimpily decorated with crepe-paper streamers, a small band, several adults in thread-bare battle dress, and hundreds of kids marching in wild disorder. It was during one of these parades—I was ten years old then—that I was seized with acute appendicitis and had to be rushed to a hospital. The doctor subsequently told my mother that I had made a long, impassioned speech about the early revolutionist Miguel Hidalgo while the anesthetic was taking hold, and she explained with pardonable pride that it was the speech I was to make at Turner Hall that evening. Mine was one of the twenty-three *discursos* scheduled on the postparade program, a copy of which my mother still retains. My only regret was missing the annual *discurso* of Don Miguel Gomez, my godfather, a deep-throated orator who would always climax his speech by falling to his knees and dramatically kissing the floor, almost weeping as he loudly proclaimed: "*Ay, Mexico! Beso tu tierra, tu mero corazón*" ("Ah,

Mexico! I kiss your sacred soil, the very heart of you"). He gave the same oration for seventeen years, word for word and gesture for gesture, and it never failed to bring tears to his eyes. But not once did he return to Chihuahua, even for a brief visit.

9   My personal Mexican-ness eventually produced serious problems for me. Upon entering grade school I learned English rapidly and rather well, always ranking either first or second in my class; yet the hard core of me remained stubbornly Mexican. This chauvinism may have been a reaction to the constant racial prejudice we encountered on all sides. The neighborhood cops were always running us off the streets and calling us "dirty greasers," and most of our teachers frankly regarded us as totally inferior. I still remember the galling disdain of my sixth-grade teacher, whose constant mimicking of our heavily accented speech drove me to desperate study of *Webster's Dictionary* in the hope of acquiring a vocabulary larger than hers. Sadly enough, I succeeded only too well, and for the next few years I spoke the most ridiculous high-flown rhetoric in the Denver public schools. One of my favorite words was "indubitably," and it must have driven everyone mad. I finally got rid of my accent by constantly reciting "Peter Piper picked a peck of pickled peppers" with little round pebbles in my mouth. Somewhere I had read about Demosthenes.

10   During this phase of my childhood the cultural tug of war known as "Americanization" almost pulled me apart. There were moments when I would identify completely with the gringo world (what could have been more American than my earnest high-voiced portrayal of George Washington, however ridiculous the cotton wig my mother had fashioned for me?); then quite suddenly I would feel so acutely Mexican that I would stammer over the simplest English phrase. I was so ready to take offense at the slightest slur against Mexicans that I would imagine prejudice where none existed. But on other occasions, in full confidence of my belonging, I would venture forth into social areas that I should have realized were clearly forbidden to little *chicanos* from Curtis Park. The inevitable rebuffs would leave me floundering in self-pity; it was small comfort to know that other minority groups suffered even worse rebuffs than we did.

11   The only non-Mexican boy on our street was a Negro named Leroy Logan, who was probably my closest childhood friend. Leroy was the best athlete, the best whistler, the best liar, the best horseshoe player, the best marble shooter, the best mumblety-pegger, and the best shoplifter in our neighborhood. He was also my "partner," and I thus entitled myself to a fifty-fifty share of all his large triumphs and petty thefts. Because he considered "Mexican" a derogatory word bordering on obscenity, Leroy would pronounce it "Mesican" so as to soften its harshness. But once in a while, when he'd get angry with me, he would call me a "lousy Mesican greasy spik" with the most extraordinarily effective hissing one can imagine. And I'm embarrassed to admit that I would

retaliate by calling him "alligator bait." As a matter of fact, just after I had returned from the hospital, he came to visit me, and I thoughtlessly greeted him with a flippant "Hi, alligator ba—" I never finished the phrase because Leroy whacked me on the stomach with a Ping-pong paddle and rushed out of my house with great, sobbing anger.

12   Weeks later, when we had re-established a rather cool rapport, I tried to make up for my stupid insult by helping him steal cabbages from the vegetable trucks that rumbled through our neighborhood on their way to the produce markets. They would come down Larimer Street in the early dawn, and Leroy and I would sneak up behind them at the 27th Street stop sign, where they were forced to pause for cross traffic. I would be waiting below to catch them with an open gunny sack. Our system was fabulously successful for a while, and we found a ready market for the stolen goods; but one morning, as I started to unfurl my sack, a fairly large cabbage conked me on the head. Screaming with pain, I lunged at Leroy and tried to bite him. He, laughing all the while—it was obviously a funny scene—glided out of my reach, and finally ran into a nearby alley. We never engaged in commercial affairs thereafter.

13   Still and all, I remember him with great affection and a touch of sadness. I say sadness because eventually Leroy was to suffer the misery of being an outsider in an already outside ghetto. As he grew older, it was apparent that he longed to be a Mexican, that he felt terribly dark and alone. "Sometimes," he would tell me, "I feel like my damn skin's too tight, like I'm gonna bust out of it." One cold February night I found him in the coal shed behind Pacheco's store, desperately scraping his forearm with sandpaper, the hurt tears streaming down his face. "I got to get this off, man. I can't stand all this blackness." We stood there quietly staring at the floor for a long, anguished moment, both of us miserable beyond word or gesture. Finally he drew a deep breath, blew his nose loudly, and mumbled half audibly, "Man, you sure lucky to be a Mesi-can."

14   Not long after this incident Leroy moved out of Denver to live with relatives in Georgia. When I saw him off at the bus station, he grabbed my shoulder and whispered huskily, "You gonna miss me, man. You watch what I tellya." "Indubitably," I said. "Aw, man, cut that stuff. You the most fancy-pants Mesican I know." Those were his last words to me, and they caused a considerable dent in my ego. Not enough, however, to diminish my penchant for fancy language. The dictionary continued to be my comic book well into high school.

15   Speaking of language, I am reminded of a most peculiar circumstance: almost every Mexican-American lawyer that I've ever met speaks English with a noticeable Spanish accent, this despite the fact that they have all been born, reared, and educated exclusively in America. Of the forty-eight lawyers I have in mind, only three of us are free of any accent. Needless to say our "cultural drag" has been weighty and persistent.

And one must presume that our ethnic hyphens shall be with us for many years to come.

16   My own Mexican-ness, after years of decline at Harvard University, suddenly burst forth again when I returned to Chihuahua and stumbled on the town of Bachimba. I had long conversations with an uncle I'd never met before, my father's younger brother, Ramon. It was Tio Ramon who chilled my spine with eyewitness stories about Pancho Villa's legendary *dorados*, one of whom was Martin Lopez. "He was your second cousin. The bravest young buck in Villa's army. And he became a *dorado* when he was scarcely seventeen years old because he dared to defy Pancho Villa himself. As your papa may have told you, Villa had a bad habit of burying treasure up in the mountans and also burying the man he took with him to dig the hole for it. Well, one day he chose Martin Lopez to go with him. Deep in the mountains they went, near Parral. And when they got to a suitably lonely place, Pancho Villa told him to dig a hole with pick and shovel. Then, when Martin had dug down to his waist, Villa leveled a gun at the boy. "Say your prayers, *muchacho*. You shall stay here with the gold—forever." But Martin had come prepared. In his large right boot he had a gun, and when he rose from his bent position, he was pointing that gun at Villa. They stood there, both ready to fire, for several seconds, and finally Don Pancho started to laugh in that wonderful way of his. *"Bravo, bravo, muchacho!* You've got more guts than a man. Get out of that hole, boy. I need you for my *dorados*."

17   Tio Ramon's eyes were wet with pride. "But what is more important, he died with great valor. Two years later, after he had terrorized the *federales* and Pershing's gringo soldiers, he was finally wounded and captured here in Bachimba. It was a bad wound in his leg, finally turning to gangrene. Then one Sunday morning they hauled Martin Lopez and three other prisoners to the plaza. One by one they executed the three lesser prisoners against that wall. I was up on the church tower watching it all. Finally it was your uncle's turn. They dragged him off the buckboard wagon and handed him his crutches. Slowly, painfully, he hobbled to the wall and stood there. Very straight he stood. 'Do you have any last words?' said the captain of the firing squad. With great pride Martin tossed his crutches aside and stood very tall on his one good leg. "Give me, you yellow bastards, give me a gun—and I'll show you who is the man among . . .' Eight bullets crashed into his chest and face, and I never heard that final word. That was your second cousin. You would have been proud to know him."

18   As I listened to Tio Ramon's soft nostalgic voice that evening, there in the sputtering light of the kerosene lamp on his back patio, I felt as intensely Mexican as I shall ever feel.

19   But not for long. Within six weeks I was destined to feel *less* Mexican than I had ever felt. The scene of my trauma was the Centro

Mexicano de Escritores, where the finest young writers of Mexico met regularly to discuss works in progress and to engage in erudite literary and philosophical discussions. Week after week I sat among them, dumb struck by my inadequacy in Spanish and my total ignorance of their whole frame of reference. How could I have possibly imagined that I was Mexican? Those conversations were a dense tangle of local and private allusions, and the few threads I could grasp only magnified my ignorance. The novelist Juan Rulfo was then reading the initial drafts of his *Pedro Páramo*, later to be acclaimed the best avant-garde fiction in Mexican literature. Now that I have soaked myself in the *ambiance* of Mexico, Rulfo's novel intrigues me beyond measure; but when he first read it at the Centro, he might just as well have been reading "Jabber-wocky" in Swahili for all I understood of it. And because all of the other Mexican writers knew and greatly appreciated *Páramo*, I could only assume that I was really "too gringo" to comprehend it. For this reason, I, a person with no great talent for reticence, never opened my mouth at the Centro. In fact, I was so shell-shocked by those sessions that I even found it difficult to converse with my housekeeper about such simple matters as dirty laundry or the loose doorknob in the bathroom.

20   Can any of us really go home again? I, for one, am convinced that I have no true home, that I must reconcile myself to a schizo-cultural limbo, with a mere hyphen to provide some slight cohesion between my split selves. This inevitable splitting is a plague and a pleasure. Some mornings as I glide down the Paseo de la Reforma, perhaps the most beautiful boulevard in the world, I am suddenly angered by the *machismo*, or aggressive maleness, of Mexican drivers who crowd and bully their screeching machines through dense traffic. What terrible insecurity, what awful dread of emasculation, produces such assertive bully-boy conduct behind a steering wheel? Whatever the reasons, there is a part of me that can never accept this much-celebrated *machismo*. Nor can I accept the exaggerated nationalism one so frequently encounters in the press, on movie screens, over the radio, in daily conversations—that shrill barrage of slogans proclaiming that "there is only one Mexico."

21   Recently, when I expressed these views to an old friend, he smiled knowingly: "Let's face it, Hank, you're not really a Mexican—despite that long, comical name of yours. You're an American through and through." But that, of course, is a minority view and almost totally devoid of realism. One could just as well say that Martin Luther King is not a Negro, that he's merely an American. But the plain truth is that neither I nor Martin Luther King can escape the fact that we are a Mexican and a Negro whose roots are so deeply planted in the United States that we have grown those strong little hyphens that make us Mexican-American and Negro-American. This assertion may not please some idealists who would prefer to blind themselves to our obvious ethnic and racial differ-ences, who are unwittingly patronizing when they insist that we are all alike and indistinguishable. But the politicians, undoubtedly the most

pragmatic creatures in America, are completely aware that ethnic groups *do* exist and that they seem to huddle together, and sometimes vote together.

22   When all is said and done, we hyphenated Americans are here to stay, bubbling happily or unhappily in the great nonmelting pot. Much has been gained and will be gained from the multiethnic aspects of the United States, and there is no useful purpose in attempting to wish it away or to homogenize it out of existence. In spite of the race riots in Watts and ethnic unrest elsewhere, there would appear to be a kind of modus vivendi developing on almost every level of American life.

23   And if there are those of us who may never feel completely at home, we can always make that brief visit to Bachimba.

Study Questions

1. This essay uses alternating paragraphs of description and analysis, and the development leads to the thesis paragraph, paragraph 22. Explain the progression of ideas to this point.
2. Why does Lopez allude twice to Lewis Carroll to describe his experiences with language?
3. What elements in this essay contribute to an understanding of the writer's emotions?
4. How do the events in paragraph 13 contribute to the writer's understanding of racial prejudice?

Dream Boogie

Langston Hughes

Good morning, daddy!
Ain't you heard
The boogie-woogie rumble
Of a dream deferred?

Listen closely:
You'll hear their feet
Beating out and beating out a—

    You think
    It's a happy beat?

Listen to it closely: 10
Ain't you heard
something underneath
like a—

    What did I say?

Sure,
I'm happy!
Take it way!

    Hey, pop!
    Re-bop!
    Mop!   20

    Y-e-a-h!

Study Questions

1. What is *boogie-woogie*? How does the title relate to it?
2. What type of rhythm is Hughes approximating in "Dream Boogie?"
3. Why does Hughes italicize the words he does?
4. What incongruity of black life does Hughes project here? Do you find this incongruity in other works in this section?
5. Have you found music to be a way of soothing or covering up some discontent or frustration you have had?

Biographies

Conrad Aiken

Conrad Aiken (1889–1973) was born in Savannah, Georgia. He received his B.A. from Harvard, graduating in the class that included T.S. Eliot, Heywood Broun, Robert Benchley, and Walter Lippmann. A prolific writer, he published dozens of volumes, including poetry: *Priapus and the Pool* (1922), *Preludes for Memnon* (1931), *Brownstone Eclogues* (1942), *The Morning Song of Lord Zero* (1963), and *Cats and Bats and Things with Wings* (1965); novels: *Blue Voyage* (1927), *A Heart for the Gods of Mexico* (1939); a play: *Mr. Arcularis;* short stories; and his autobiography: *Ushant: An Essay.* His collected poems were published in 1953, his collected short stories in 1960, and his collected novels in 1964. Among the many honors awarded him have been the Pulitzer Prize, the National Book Award, the Bollingen Prize, and the Brandeis Medal.

Woody Allen

Woody Allen, or Allen Stewart Konigsberg, was born in Brooklyn in 1935. Although he has described himself as a student at both the Neighborhood School for Bit Players and The House of Vocal Cords, Allen actually attended New York University and City College of New York. Best known as the writer and star of such films as *Play It Again, Sam* (1972), *Everything You Always Wanted to Know About Sex But Were Afraid to Ask* (1972), *Sleeper* (1973), *Love and Death* (1975), and *Annie Hall* (1977), Allen also writes for television and stage. He is in addition a contributor to several magazines, notably the *New Yorker* and *Playboy.* Two collections of his magazine pieces have been published: *Getting Even* (1971) and *Without Feathers* (1975). In the program for the stage production of *Play It Again, Sam,* Allen claims to have played the title role in *Lady Windemere's Fan,* Porgy in *Porgy and Bess,* and Willy Loman in *Mr. Roberts.*

Matthew Arnold

Matthew Arnold (1822–1888) was born in Laleham, the son of Thomas Arnold, who later became headmaster of Rugby School. He attended Balliol College, Oxford, where he won the Newdigate Prize for Poetry in 1843 and from which he graduated in 1844. He was elected a fellow of Oriel College, Oxford, before taking a position as private secretary to Lord Lansdowne. Arnold was subsequently appointed an inspector of schools, a position he held while also serving as Professor of Poetry at Oxford. Among his works are *The Strayed Reveller and Other Poems* (1849), *Empedocles on Etna* (1852), *Poems* (1853), *On Translating Homer* (1861), *Essays in Criticism* (1865), *Culture and Anarchy* (1869), and *Literature and Dogma* (1873). Today Arnold is considered more important as a critic than as a poet, but his small output of poems has nonetheless won him a secure niche in English literature.

W. H. Auden

Editor, lyricist, dramatist, and poet, Wystan Hugh Auden (1907–1973) was born in Rok, England. He came to the United States in 1939 and was naturalized in 1946. Prior to his entry into the United States, Auden attended Oxford (1925–1928), was a schoolmaster in Britain (early 1930s), served as a stretcher bearer for the Loyalists in the Spanish civil war (1937), and made trips to Iceland (1936) and China (1938). Auden was a professor of English at many American schools, and served as editor of the Yale Series of Younger Poets from 1947 until his death in 1973. He received the Pulitzer Prize for poetry in 1948 for *The Age of Anxiety,* the Bollingen Prize for poetry in 1954, and the National Book Award in 1955 for *The Shield of Achilles.*

Francis Bacon

Francis Bacon (1561–1626), English statesman, scholar, and writer, is best known today for his pithy essays that are models of conciseness and symmetry. Bacon served in Parliament, rising to the position of Lord High Chancellor of England under James I. He was accused, tried, and found guilty of bribery but spent only two days in prison; although he was pardoned in 1621, he finished his life more or less in disgrace. Bacon is generally included in histories of science as the father of the scientific method. He died of bronchitis, the result of an experiment with the preservative qualities of snow. Among his many works are *Essays or Counsels, Civil and Moral* (1597), *The Advancement of Learning* (1605), the *Novum Organum* (1620), and *The New Atlantis* (1627).

James Baldwin

James Baldwin (b. 1924) has established a reputation as one of America's outstanding contemporary writers. Born and raised in Harlem, Baldwin received a Eugene F. Saxton Fellowship in 1945 that enabled him to devote his time to writing. Active in civil rights activities, he has lectured in numerous colleges and universities. He is a member of the national advisory board of the Congress of Racial Equality. He has won Rosenthal, Guggenheim, and National Institute of Arts and Letters awards. Baldwin has authored the novels *Go Tell It on the Mountain* (1953), *Giovanni's Room* (1958), and *Another Country* (1962), and the essay collections *Notes of a Native Son* (1955), *Nobody Knows My Name* (1960), *The Fire Next Time* (1963), *The Devil Finds Work* (1976), and *Little Man, Little Man* (1976).

Imamu Amiri Baraka (LeRoi Jones)

LeRoi Jones, a leading spokesperson for black nationalism, was born in Newark, New Jersey in 1934. A convert to the Islamic faith, he changed his name to Imamu Amiri Baraka, the name under which he is often anthologized. His writings include plays, poetry, short stories, and essays, and he has recorded his work for the Library of Congress. Among his plays are *The Dutchman* and *The Slave,* produced off-Broadway in 1964 and in London in 1967; *Four Black Revolutionary Plays: All Praises to the Black Man* (1969); and two anthologized plays: *The Death of Malcolm X* (1969) and *BA-KA-RA* (1972). Also published have been such poetry collections as *Black Art* (1966), *Spirit Reach* (1972), and *Afrikan Revolution: A Poem* (1973). Baraka received the John Whitney Foundation Fellowship in 1962, the Obie Award for *Dutchman* in 1964, and a Guggenheim Fellowship in 1965–1966.

Donald Barthelme

Born in 1931 in Philadelphia, Donald Barthelme is considered by critics to be one of America's most gifted writers. He has had a varied career—working as a newspaper writer, a museum director, and as editor of *Location,* a literary magazine. In 1974–1975 he was Distinguished Visiting Professor of English at City College of the City University of New York. His awards include the Guggenheim Fellowship (1966), the National Book Award for children's literature (1972), and the Morton Dauwen Zabel Award from the National Institute of Arts and Letters (1972). In addition to writing short stories, novels, and children's books, Barthelme contributes regularly to the *New Yorker.* Among his works are *Come Back, Dr. Caligari* (1964), *City Life* (1970), *Sadness* (1972), and *The Dead Father* (1975).

Ray Bradbury

One of the country's foremost science fiction writers, Ray Bradbury was born in Waukegan, Illinois in 1920. He graduated from high school in California, and shortly thereafter founded *Futuria Fantasia,* a mimeographed science fiction quarterly. Bradbury estimates that he has written over a thousand short stories. His work has been published in a dozen languages. He received the Benjamin Franklin Short Story Award in 1953, the Commonwealth Club of California's Gold Medal for his antiutopian novel, *Fahrenheit 451,* in 1954, and an Academy Award for his short film "Icarus Montgolfier Wright" in 1963. Bradbury publishes in many popular, as well as science fiction, magazines. His latest publication is *When Elephants Last in Dooryard Bloomed* (1973), and in progress is *The Best of Bradbury.*

Richard Brautigan

Richard Brautigan, born in 1935, declines generally to discuss himself or his life for biographers. About his own work he does say that he doesn't like to be considered a humorist, although he may be one of the best social commentators writing in the United States today. His novels include *A Confederate General from Big Sur* (1965), *The Abortion: An Historical Romance* (1971), and *Trout Fishing in America* (1967). He has also published two collections of poetry: *The Return of the Rivers* (1957) and *Rommel Drives on Deep into Egypt* (1970).

Robert Bridges

Born in Walmer, England, Robert Bridges (1844–1930) attended Eton and Christ College, Oxford. He graduated from Oxford with a degree in medicine, a profession which he practiced for a time. An essayist and poet, Bridges in his later years was associated with the Oxford University Press in an advisory capacity, overseeing matters of taste and accuracy as well as the more prosaic questions of form and mechanics. He is best remembered for his series of *Shorter Poems,* published in the 1870s and 1880s. His longer works include *Prometheus, the Firegiver* (1884), *Eros and Psyche* (1894), and *Demeter* (1905). An oratorio, *Eden,* appeared in 1891, and a collection of *Chants for the Psalter* in 1899. Although Bridges is considered a difficult poet to read, his work has always found an audience; one of his last poems, *The Testament of Beauty* (1929), was reprinted fourteen times in the year of its issue.

Gwendolyn Brooks

Born in Topeka, Kansas in 1917, Gwendolyn Brooks has made a career of writing and lecturing at colleges and universities. She received Guggenheim Fellowships in 1946 and 1947, and the Pulitzer Prize for poetry in 1950 for the collection *Annie Allen* (1949). Her other books of poetry include *A Street in Bronzeville* (1945), *Bronzeville Boys and Girls* (1956), *The Bean Eaters* (1960), and *The Tiger Who Wore White Gloves* (1974). She contributed to *A Capsule Course in Black Poetry Writing* (1975).

Robert Browning

Robert Browning (1812–1889) was born in Camberwell, a suburb of London. Although he attended private schools as a child and later entered the University of London, most of Browning's education came from his father's library of six thousand volumes. The critical reception accorded Browning's first two publications—*Pauline* (1833) and *Paracelsus* (1835)—temporarily diverted the poet's energies into the composition of dramas, which were as unsuccessful as his early poems. All of Browning's major works came after his famous courtship and elopement with Elizabeth Barrett. These major works include *Men and Women* (1855), *Dramatis Personæ* (1864), and *The Ring and the Book* (1868), in all of which Browning demonstrated his mastery of the dramatic monologue. Elizabeth Barrett Browning is buried in Florence, where the famous couple lived after their marriage; Browning died in Venice but is buried in Westminster Abbey.

Anthony Burgess

Anthony Burgess was born in 1917 in Manchester, England. He received a B.A. from Manchester University. He has taught school, served as an officer in Malaya and Borneo, produced plays, and been a jazz pianist. His critical works include *English Literature: A Survey for Students* (1958), *The Novel Today* (1963), *Language Made Plain* (1964), *Re Joyce* (1965), and *Shakespeare* (1970). His more important novels are *Time for a Tiger* (1956), *The Doctor Is Sick* (1960), *A Clockwork Orange* (1962), *The Wanting Seed* (1962), *Honey for the Bears* (1963), *Inside Mr. Enderby* (1963), *Nothing Like the Sun* (1964), *The Long Day Wanes* (1965), *A Vision of Battlements* (1966), *The Clockwork Testament, or Enderby's End* (1976), and *A Long Trip to Tea Time* (1976).

Kuangchi C. Chang

Born in Shanghai, China, Kuangchi C. Chang was educated there before coming to the United States to attend Columbia University. After receiving a degree in architecture he returned to China. In 1949 he became a refugee from the People's Republic of China, and has remained in the United States since that time. He has worked as an architect in New York and has been a professor of Oriental art at the University of Oklahoma. His poems have appeared in various American journals.

Walter Van Tilburg Clark

Walter Van Tilburg Clark (1901–1971) was born in East Orland, Maine. He was highly regarded both as a writer and as a teacher of creative writing. His stories and novels about the West helped rescue Western fiction from the popularizers of the Western "myth." He was writer-in-residence at the University of Nevada, and visiting lecturer at Reed College, Stanford University, and the Universities of Iowa, Utah, Wyoming, California, Washington, and Oregon. In 1945 he won the O. Henry Memorial Award for "The Wind and the Snow of Winter." His *Ox-Bow Incident* (1940) is considered a classic Western novel. Among his other well-known works are *The City of Trembling Leaves* (1945), *The Track of the Cat* (1949), and *The Watchful God, and Other Stories* (1950).

Arthur C. Clarke

Arthur C. Clarke (b. 1917) is a native of Somersetshire, England. He was educated at Kings College, University of London, and served in the British Civil Service and the Royal Air Force. At home in both space and undersea explorations, Clarke's writings encompass both areas; he suggested the use of space satellites for communications as early as 1945. His nonfiction works include *The Challenge of the Spaceship* (1959), *The Challenge of the Sea* (1960), *Man and Space* (1964), *Earthlight* (1972), and *Rendezvous with Rama* (1973). He is perhaps best known to the public for his screenplay *2001: A Space Odyssey*, written with Stanley Kubrick. Clarke's honors include the International Fantasy Award (1952), the Kalinga Prize (1961), and the Franklin Institute Ballentine Medal (1963).

Samuel Taylor Coleridge

Samuel Taylor Coleridge (1772–1834) was born in Ottery St. Mary, England, and educated at Christ's Hospital and Jesus College, Cambridge. One of the great English Romantic poets, he first published in the *Morning Chronicle* in 1793. He met and formed a lifelong friendship with William Wordsworth in 1795. Their joint *Lyrical Ballads* (1798) includes Coleridge's most famous poems, among them "The Rime of the Ancient Mariner." Coleridge's poetry remains popular. His disillusionment with revolutionary movements is reflected in "France, An Ode" and "Dejection," but his best-known poems are probably those which deal with the supernatural, poems (in addition to "Ancient Mariner") such as "Christabel" and "Kubla Khan." Coleridge was founder of two short-lived newspapers, wrote literary criticism that is still considered important, and was a playwright.

Judy Collins

Judy Collins was born in Seattle, Washington in 1939 and raised in Boulder and Denver, Colorado. She was hailed while still in grade school as a prodigy, and was being groomed for a career as a concert pianist when she discovered the guitar. She started entertaining at nineteen, staying close to home until the early 1960s, when she sought greener fields in New York. Collins's first hit record was *The Judy Collins Concert* (1964). Not a devoted political activist, Collins nevertheless was one of the spokespeople, through her songs, of the revolutionary movements of the late 1960s. She is today one of America's leading folk singers, commanding huge audiences wherever she appears. Her latest albums include *Colors of the Day: The Best of Judy Collins* (1972), *Judith* (1975), and *Bread and Roses* (1976).

Stephen Crane

Few writers attain the distinction of being revolutionaries in the prose or verse of their literatures; Stephen Crane (1871–1900) was a radical as a writer of both fiction and poetry. Born in Newark, New Jersey, Crane spent two years in college; he quit in 1891 to go to New York City as a freelance writer. Unable to hold a steady job as a journalist because of his unconventional, impressionistic style of reporting, Crane published *Maggie: a Girl of the Streets* in 1893 without notice, even though the book was the first pure example of American naturalism. *The Red Badge of Courage* brought him instant fame in 1895 and allowed him to live the hectic life of an international correspondent that hastened his early death from tuberculosis. His poetry, collected in 1899 in the volume *War Is Kind,* was even more revolutionary than his prose. Its imagistic technique and violent despair anticipated the avant-garde poetry of the twenties and was entirely without precedent in American verse.

Victor Hernández Cruz

One of the rising young Puerto Rican poets in the United States today, Victor Hernández Cruz was born in Aguas Buenas, Puerto Rico in 1949. His poetry was first published when he was in high school; his first accepted poem was "Papo Got His Gun," printed in *Evergreen Review* in 1967. He has published two collections of poetry: *Snaps* (1969) and *Mainland* (1973).

Emily Dickinson

Emily Dickinson (1830–1886) was born in Amherst, Massachusetts, and spent most of her life there. She attended the Mt. Holyoke Female Academy in 1847, and made brief visits to Washington, Philadelphia, and Boston. She may have had two unhappy love affairs—with Ben Newton and the Reverend Charles Wadsworth. Family tradition supported the legend that Miss Dickinson spent eight years as a recluse, dressing only in white. She was encouraged in her writing by Helen Hunt Jackson and Thomas Wentworth Higginson. Only seven of her poems were published in her lifetime. Her *Poems* (1890) included 114 of her brilliantly brief lyrics. A second series of poems was published in 1891, and her letters in 1894. The standard edition is *The Poems of Emily Dickinson,* edited by Thomas H. Johnson.

John Donne

Born in London, John Donne (1571?–1631) matriculated at Oxford and Cambridge, but received no degree because his religion (Roman Catholic) prevented him from taking the required oaths. Subsequently, he read for the law at Lincoln's Inn, and added to his already flourishing reputation as a dandy, wit, and poet. Participation in Essex's first strike expedition against the Spanish fleet at Cadiz led eventually to Donne's appointment as secretary to the Lord Chancellor in 1597. He was dismissed from this post, however, when he married the young niece of his employer's wife in 1601. For a number of years, Donne made his way as a resident intellectual at the court of James I. He had rejected the teachings of the Church of Rome, and when the secular preferment he desired never came, Donne finally yielded to the King's urging and entered the priesthood of the Church of England in 1615. In 1621 he became the Dean of St. Paul's Cathedral. Donne never published his poetry—it circulated in manuscript among the intelligentsia during his life, and was printed for the first time in a collected edition shortly after his death. His fame rests primarily on such short poems as "A Valediction: Forbidding Mourning" and "Batter My Heart, Three-Person'd God." Donne's early love poetry and late religious verse both embody the abstract sensuousness that perpetuated his name.

William Eastlake

William Eastlake was born in New York City in 1917, and was educated at the Alliance Française in Paris. He served four years in the U.S. Army infantry and has lectured at the Universities of Eastern New Mexico and Arizona. His work, chiefly on the Native American, is noted for its compassionate approach to Native American problems. He writes with a great deal of humor, albeit humor tinged with irony, and sometimes with sarcasm. His writings include *The Bronc People* (1958), *Castle Keep* (1965), *Dancers in the Scalp House* (1975), and *The Long Naked Descent into Boston* (1977). In addition to these novels, Eastlake's short stories and articles have been published in various magazines and anthologized widely. His *Castle Keep,* a novel about World War II, was made into a film for which Eastlake wrote the script. His awards include a Ford Foundation grant in 1963–1964 and a Rockefeller Foundation grant in 1966–1967.

Loren Eiseley

Loren Eiseley (1907–1977) was born in Lincoln, Nebraska. He received his B.A. from the University of Nebraska, and his M.A. and Ph.D. from the University of Pennsylvania. He taught at the University of Kansas and Oberlin College before returning, in 1947, to the University of Pennsylvania where he was, for the remainder of his life, University Professor in anthropology and history of science and head of the Department of the History and Philosophy of Science. A Guggenheim Fellow, he was published widely in popular periodicals and learned journals. *Darwin's Century* received the Phi Beta Kappa science award in 1959, and *The Firmament of Time* (1960) received the John Burroughs medal and the Lecomte de Nouy award. His other books include *The Immense Journey* (1951), *Francis Bacon and the Modern Temper* (1952), *Galapagos: The Flow of Wilderness* (1968), *Invisible Pyramid* (1972), and *All the Strange Hours* (1975).

T. S. Eliot

Born in St. Louis, Missouri, the son of an industrial executive, Thomas Stearns Eliot (1888–1965) migrated East: first to Harvard, where, in attendance intermittently from 1906 to 1914, he took the B.A., M.A., and completed the requirements for the Ph.D., though he never applied for the degree; then to Europe where, after a short stay in France, he settled permanently in Britain. Eliot revolutionized Anglo-American poetry with the publication of the poem *The Waste Land* in 1922. A long life of scant but exquisite literary production resulted in his acceptance of the 1948 Nobel Prize for literature. Following a distinguished career as an editor and publisher, Eliot died with his place in literary history secure. His major works, besides *The Waste Land* (1922), include "The Love Song of J. Alfred Prufrock," *Four Quartets* (1944), *Ash Wednesday* (1930), and the verse dramas *Murder in the Cathedral* and *The Cocktail Party.*

Eugene Field

Eugene Field (1850–1895) was born in St. Louis, Missouri. In 1868 he attended Knox College and later the University of Missouri without receiving a degree. From 1875 to 1895 he held editorial positions on various midwestern newspapers, ending his career with the Chicago *Morning News,* for which he was a columnist. Field was a prolific writer, producing dialect sketches, fables, and fairy tales in prose, and jingles, translations, and sentimental poems for and about children in verse. His "children" poems retain for him a small place in the history of American letters as a pure example of the sentimental poet.

Robert Frost

Robert Frost (1874–1963) was born in San Francisco, California. He attended Dartmouth College for one term, and Harvard University for two years. During his lifetime Frost was awarded nearly fifty honorary degrees by American universities, and in 1957 he received honorary degrees from Oxford, Cambridge, and the National University of Ireland. He taught or lectured at Amherst College, the University of Michigan, Wesleyan, Darmouth, Yale, and Harvard. In 1954 he served as an American good-will ambassador to South America, and in 1961 to Greece. Frost read his "The Gift Outright" and represented the arts at the inauguration of John F. Kennedy in 1961. His poetry earned four Pulitzer Prizes. Frost's books include *A Boy's Will* (1913), *North of Boston* (1914), *West-Running Brook* (1928), *A Further Range* (1936), *A Witness Tree* (1942), and *A Masque of Mercy* (1947).

Nikki Giovanni

Nikki Giovanni was born in 1943 in Knoxville, Tennessee, received her B.A. from Fisk University, and has done graduate work at the University of Pennsylvania and at the Columbia University School of the Arts. She has taught English at Rutgers and Livingston College, and has lectured widely. Her awards include grants from the Harlem Cultural Council, the Ford Foundation, and the National Council of the Arts. A political writer, Giovanni's poetry is for the most part concerned with black revolutionary themes, and she has emerged as one of the chief spokespeople for the black movement of the late 1960s and the 1970s. In addition to children's poetry, she has written *Black Feeling, Black Talk* (1968), *Black Judgment* (1968), *Re: Creation* (1970), *Extended Autobiographical Statement on My Twenty-Seven Years of Being a Black Poet* (1971), *My House* (1972), and *The Women and the Men* (1975).

Rose K. Goldsen

A native of Newark, New Jersey, where she was born in 1918, Rose Goldsen received her bachelor's degree from New York University and her master's and doctorate from Yale. Chiefly involved with writing for professional journals, her works include *Puerto Rican Journey* (1950) and *What College Students Think* (1960). In addition to teaching at Columbia, Yale, and Cornell, Goldsen served as Fulbright lecturer in France in 1957–1958.

José Angel Gutiérrez

One of the foremost Chicano spokespeople today, José Angel Gutiérrez was born in Crystal City, Texas in 1945. His education includes degrees from Texas College of Arts and Industry of the University of Houston and St. Mary's University. He is working toward a doctorate in political science at the University of Texas at Austin, and is county judge for the county of Savala, Texas. Gutiérrez was one of the founders of the Mexican American Youth Organization (MAYO) and of La Raza Unida. He has served with the Texas Migrant Council, United Migrants for Opportunity, and other Chicano-oriented organizations, and as president of the Crystal City School Board. His poetry has been published in various Chicano and professional journals and anthologies.

Nathaniel Hawthorne

Nathaniel Hawthorne (1804–1864) was born in Salem, Massachusetts. He was a descendent of Judge Hawthorne, who presided over the Salem witch trials. Among his classmates at Bowdoin College were Henry Wadsworth Longfellow and Franklin Pierce. After graduation he served as surveyor at the Boston Custom House. He was named consul to Liverpool in 1852. Hawthorne's first novel, *Fanshawe*, was published in 1828. Among his better-known works are *The Scarlet Letter* (1850), *The House of Seven Gables* (1851), and *The Blithedale Romance* (1852).

Adrian Henri

Adrian Henri was born in 1932 at Birkenhead, Cheshire, England, and educated in North Wales. He was awarded a B.A. in Fine Arts by King's College, Newcastle, Durham University, in 1955. His major works include *Tonight at Noon* (1968), *City* (1969), and *Autobiography* (1971), but his poems have also appeared in *Penguin Modern Poets, No. 10* (1967), *The Liverpool Scene* (1967), *Love, Love, Love* (1968), and *Total Art: Environment, Happenings, and Performance,* (1974).

Eric Hoffer

A philosophical writer who has had a lifelong passion for books, Eric Hoffer has been compared to such diverse personalities as Machiavelli and the duc de La Rochefoucauld. Born in New York City in 1902, Hoffer early felt the stifling complexities of the big city, and moved to California at the first opportunity. There he worked in a box factory, in the fields, in the gold mines, and in construction, finally coming to rest in San Francisco, where he was a longshoreman for some twenty years. At present he holds weekly seminars at the University of California at Berkeley, where he has refused a full-time professorship. A logical, somewhat cold, and pessimistic writer, Hoffer nonetheless sees great potential for growth in man. His first book, *The True Believer* (1951), won for him the Commonwealth Club of California's Gold Medal in 1952. Other publications include *The Passionate State of Mind* (1955), *First Things, Last Things* (1971), *Reflections on the Human Condition* (1973), and a journal of his waterfront days published in 1969.

Robert Hogan

Born in Oakland, California in 1927, Robert Hogan received degrees from the University of California at Santa Barbara and Berkeley, and a doctorate from the University of Illinois. He has taught English at the high school and college levels, and has been Executive Secretary for the National Council of Teachers of English since 1968. He contributes widely to professional journals and other publications, and was coeditor in 1963 of Arthur Koestler's *Darkness at Noon*.

Gerard Manley Hopkins

Born at Stratford, Essex, England into a British family of gifted amateurs of the arts who were moderate Anglicans, Gerard Manley Hopkins (1844–1889) both perfected and severed his paternal inheritance by becoming a major British poet and a Jesuit priest. Hopkins entered Oxford in 1863, where he came under the influence of Cardinal Newman, and he was converted to Roman Catholicism in 1866. After his graduation with honors in 1867 from Oxford, Hopkins entered the Jesuit novitiate, and was ordained a priest in the Society of Jesus in 1877. After serving in various capacities for the Order about England, Hopkins became, in 1884, Professor of Classics at University College, Dublin, where he remained until his death from malaria in 1889. Hopkins left a small body of manuscript poetry that was published in a selected edition by his friend and fellow poet Robert Bridges in 1918. Though estimates of his excellence as a poet and his psychological integrity as a person have varied, Hopkins is now generally recognized as the first British poet to break with the stultifying tradition of the Romantic genteel embodied by Tennyson, and he is acknowledged as a germinating influence on British and American poetry in the 1920s.

Arthur Hoppe

A native of Honolulu, Arthur Hoppe graduated cum laude from Harvard. He served in the U.S. Navy in World War II, and has built a career as a reporter and columnist since that time. He is syndicated today in some seventy newspapers. Although best known for his acerbic comments on the political scene, Hoppe discusses many aspects of life and people in his columns. He is witty, satiric, and quite often irreverent. His writings include *The Love Everybody Crusade* (1963), a novel, *Dreamboat* (1964), and *The Perfect Solution to Absolutely Everything* (1968).

Langston Hughes

Author, playwright, song lyricist, and lecturer, James Langston Hughes (1902–1967) was born in Joplin, Missouri. A student at Columbia University in 1921 and 1922, Hughes took a B.A. at Lincoln University in 1929. He received a Guggenheim Fellowship for creative work, the Amisfield-Wolfe Award, and a Spingarn Medal. His collections of poetry included *The Weary Blues* (1926), *The Dream Keeper* (1932), *Jim Crow's Last Stand* (1943), *Montage of a Dream Deferred* (1957), and *Ask Your Mama* (1961).

Ted Hughes

Ted Hughes was born in 1930 in Mytholmroyd, a small town in West Yorkshire, near Haworth (where the Brontes lived). He won an Open Exhibition to Cambridge University in 1948, but served two years in the RAF before actually attending. He was a rose gardener, a nightwatchman, and reader for the Rank Corporation before becoming a teacher. He has a son and daughter by the late Sylvia Plath, noted American poet. Among the awards he has received are the First Publication Award of the New York Poetry Centre (1957), and the International Poetry Prize of the City of Florence (1969). Hughes' books include *The Hawk in the Rain* (1957), *Lupercal* (1960), *The Earth Owl and Other Moon People* (1963), *Wodwo* (1967); *Crow* (1971), *Season's Songs* (1975), and *Moon Whales and Other Poems* (1976). He has also written a number of children's books.

Bruce Ignacio

Bruce Ignacio, a full-blooded Ute Indian, was born on the Utah and Duray Reservation in Fort Duchene, Utah, where he presently resides. Ignacio attended the Institute of American Indian Arts, majoring in both creative writing and jewelry. He has been successful in both fields; his poetry is widely anthologized, and his first exhibited jewelry at Scottsdale, Arizona in 1971 won the top prize.

Shirley Jackson

Shirley Jackson (1919–1965) was born in California. She received her education at Syracuse University and lived for most of her adult life in Vermont. Her writings are concerned with disturbed, sometimes psychopathic, people and weird events, generally presented in understated, realistic settings. Among her novels are *The Road Through the Wall* (1948), *Hangsman* (1951), *The Bird's Nest* (1954), *The Sundial* (1958), and *The Haunting of Hill House* (1959). A short story collection, *The Lottery* (1949), contains the story of the same title, probably her most famous work.

Randall Jarrell

Randall Jarrell (1914–1965) was another of the Southern formalist poets who constituted a major force in modern American poetry. Born in Nashville, Tennessee, Jarrell took his B.A. and his M.A. from Vanderbilt University. Except for a military hiatus—service in the U.S. Army Air Force during World War II—Jarrell was a professional academic. He taught at Kenyon College, the University of Texas, Sarah Lawrence, and the University of North Carolina, among others. Jarrell received the National Book Award in 1961 for his volume of poetry *The Woman at the Washington Zoo* (1960). He was editor of many anthologies and was poetry critic for the *Partisan Review* from 1949 to 1951. Jarrell's other major collections of verse include *Blood for a Stranger* (1942) and *Losses* (1948).

Robinson Jeffers

Robinson Jeffers (1887–1962) was born in Pittsburgh, Pennsylvania. After traveling widely on the Continent with his academic family, Jeffers took a B.A. from Occidental College and an M.A. from the University of Southern California. An inheritance assured him of financial independence in 1912, and with his new bride he settled on the Monterey peninsula in California in 1913, where he lived for the rest of his life. Jeffers combined an intuitive feeling for Greek tragedy, primitive culture, and the natural world into a harsh philosophy embodied in a poetic style at once spare and fiercely exuberant. His tragic narratives, such as "Roan Stallion" and "The Tower Beyond Tragedy," illustrate this power most clearly. His principal volumes of verse include *Tamar and Other Poems* (1924), *Give Your Heart to the Hawks and Other Poems* (1933), *The Double Ax* (1948), and *The Beginning and the End and Other Poems* (1963).

Erica Jong

Erica Jong is a feminist who sees in poetry the power to free both women and men from long held self-destructive beliefs and patterns. Born in New York City in 1942, Jong was educated at Barnard and Columbia. She enjoys reading her poetry aloud, and has done so at schools, a women's prison, and in parks and city squares. She received a grant from the New York State Council on the Arts in 1971, and that same year won *Poetry* magazine's Bess Hokins Prize for her first book of poems, *Fruits and Vegetables*. Jong's other publications include *Half-Lives* (1973), her best-selling novel *Fear of Flying* (1974), and her latest novel, *How to Save Your Own Life* (1977).

James Joyce

James Joyce (1882–1941) was born in Dublin. He received a B.A. from University College, Dublin. Although he had been working on other projects, *Chamber Music* (1907), a book of poems, was the first of his major works to see print. *Dubliners* was published in 1914, the same year that saw serial publication of *A Portrait of the Artist as a Young Man* begin. *Portrait* was published in book form in 1916. This was followed by a play, *Exiles* (1918), and by *Ulysses* (1922), and *Finnegan's Wake* (1939). Nearly all of Joyce's works were controversial; the Irish found *Dubliners* obscene and degrading, and *Ulysses* had to await the decision of a court in 1933 before an American edition could be authorized. However, Joyce's influence on contemporary literature was immediate; indeed, many critics consider him the most important of contemporary literary figures.

Barbara Katz

Barbara Katz, staff writer for the *National Observer,* was born in 1942 in Cleveland, Ohio. Her academic degrees include a B.A. from Brown University and M.A.s from the University of Chicago and Columbia University Graduate School of Journalism. Katz has worked as a reporter for United Press International and the *Los Angeles Times,* as speechwriter and assistant press secretary for Indiana Senator Birch Bayh, and as writer-reporter for CBS radio. She has won awards from the National Association of Science Writers, the American Psychological Foundation, and the National Press Club.

John Keats

John Keats (1795–1821) was born in London. He spent a short time in a small country school but was soon apprenticed to a surgeon. After four years as an apprentice, he entered Guy's Hospital as a medical student, but he was more interested in becoming a poet. His major works were *Poems* (1817), *Endymion* (1818), and *Lamia, Isabella, The Eve of St. Agnes, and Other Poems* (1820). Shelley helped create the legend, in *Adonais,* that Keats was killed by unsympathetic reviewers, but Keats actually died of tuberculosis, which he probably had contracted while nursing his brother Tom. He died in Rome, having watched most of his family die and having experienced an unhappy love affair with a girl named Fanny Brawne. He asked that his grave bear no name but only the words, "Here lies one whose name was writ in water."

Daniel Keyes

Daniel Keyes was born in 1927 in Brooklyn. He attended Brooklyn College where he received a B.A. and an M.A. He has taught both high school and college, and is now on the faculty of Ohio State University. "Flowers for Algernon" was expanded into a novel in 1966, and it appeared as a movie ("Charly") in 1968. Keyes published a second novel, *Touch,* in 1966.

Martin Luther King, Jr.

Born in Atlanta, Georgia, the son of a Baptist minister, Martin Luther King (1929–1968) received his B.A. from Morehouse College, his B.D. from Crozier Theological Seminary, and his Ph.D. in systematic theology from Boston University. President of the Southern Christian Leadership Conference from its formation in 1957, Dr. King received the Nobel Peace Prize in 1964. The quest for justice and equality for his people that began with the Montgomery bus boycott in 1955 ended for Martin Luther King, Jr. when he was killed in a political assassination in Nashville, Tennessee thirteen years later. He reached his summit as a charismatic figure in 1963, when he delivered his address—"I have a Dream"—to 250,000 persons assembled at the Lincoln Memorial during the mammoth March on Washington. His writings include *Stride Toward Freedom* (1958) and *Why We Can't Wait* (1964), accounts of the civil rights movement, and *Strength to Love* (1963), a collection of sermons.

Etheridge Knight

At times writer- and poet-in-residence for the Universities of Pittsburgh, Hartford, and Lincoln, Etheridge Knight has also served an eight-year sentence at Indiana State Prison. Knight was born in 1931 in Corinth, Mississippi, and is self-educated. His awards include a National Endowment for the Arts grant (1972), National Book Award and Pulitzer Prize nominations (1973), and a Guggenheim Fellowship (1974). Knight strongly believes that whites and blacks must write widely diverging poetry because of the divergence in their racial experiences. Whites, he suggests, write of beauty; blacks cannot. Knight's poetry has appeared in *Black Digest, Essence, Motive, American Report, American Poetry,* and other journals, and he has been poetry editor of *Motive* and contributing editor of *New Letters.* Collections of his work include *Poetry from Prison* (1968) and *Belly Song and Other Poems* (1973); his work is also widely anthologized.

Maxine Kumin

Born in Philadelphia in 1925, Maxine Kumin received both an A.B. and an A.M. from Radcliffe College. She has taught at Tufts University and is at present teaching a seminar in creative writing at Sacred Heart. Among her awards are the Lowell Mason Palmer Award and a grant from the National Council on the Arts and the Humanities. Kumin writes both poetry and novels as well as books for children; most critics agree, however, that poetry is her real forte. Among her many poetry collections are *Halfway* (1961), *The Privilege* (1965), *Up Country: Poems of New England* (1973), and *House, Bridge, Fountain, Gate* (1975).

Peter La Farge

Peter La Farge (1931–1965) was born in Colorado. Of part Native American ancestry, he became known throughout the United States as a folk singer and composer. He was considered one of the major spokespeople for the Native American because of his concern with Native American heritage. Nearly all of his work, including "Vision of a Past Warrior," was written to be sung; however, it loses little, if anything, when presented as poetry. His albums included *As Long as the Grass Shall Grow, Peter La Farge Sings of the Cowboys, On the Warpath,* and *Poems and Ballads.*

D. H. Lawrence

One of Great Britain's important twentieth-century writers, David Herbert Lawrence (1885–1930) was born in the heart of the coal-mining midlands of England. His birthplace, Nottingham, and his mining background were to figure strongly in Lawrence's writing. Very much concerned with the dreary life, deprivations, and exploitation of the miner, he treated these themes repeatedly in his books. Lawrence was a prolific writer of short stories and poetry; however, he is best known today for his novels. Among his best works are *The White Peacock* (1911), *Sons and Lovers* (1913), *Women in Love* (1920), *Aaron's Rod* (1922), *The Plumed Serpent* (1926), and the 1928 novel, banned in England and the United States until 1960, *Lady Chatterley's Lover.* Lawrence's short stories are widely anthologized; his *Collected Poems* appeared in 1928.

Don L. Lee

Don L. Lee was born in Little Rock, Arkansas in 1942, received an A.A. degree from Chicago City College, and attended Roosevelt University. He has worked as a museum curator, stock clerk, and junior executive, and has served four years in the U.S. Army. Presently writer-in-residence at Howard University, he has served in the same capacity at Cornell, Northeastern

Illinois State College, and Morgan State College. Lee's honors include a National Endowment for the Arts grant in 1969 and the Kuumba Workshop Black Liberation Award in 1973. Lee has published numerous poetry collections and has made one recording, *Rappin' and Readin'* (1971). His recent poetry publications include *We Walk the Way of the New World* (1970), *Directionscore: Selected and New Poems* (1971), and *Book of Life* (1973).

Denise Levertov

Denise Levertov was born in 1923 in Ilford, Essex, England. She was privately educated, and during the war she worked as a civilian nurse, experiencing nearly all of the air raids in London. She and her husband settled in New York in 1948, and in 1955 she became an American citizen. She was an associate scholar at the Radcliffe Institute for Independent Study in 1964, and was visiting lecturer at Drew University (1965), City College of New York (1965), and Vassar College (1966). In 1965 she initiated the "Writers' and Artists' Protest Against the War in Vietman." Levertov received the Bess Hokins Prize in 1959, the Longview Award in 1960, the Inez Boulton Prize in 1964, and a National Institute of Arts and Letters grant in 1965. She was poetry editor of *Nation* in 1961 and from 1963 to 1965. Her collections of verse include *The Double Image* (1946), *Here and Now* (1957), *The Jacob's Ladder* (1962), *O Taste and See* (1964), *The Sorrow Dance* (1967), *Footprints* (1972), *The Poet in the World* (1973), and *The Freeing of the Dust* (1975).

Enrique Hank Lopez

Enrique Hank Lopez, a naturalized U.S. citizen who travelled to the United States from Mexico chiefly by wagon, graduated from Harvard Law School, and has subsequently studied at Harvard's Graduate School of Economics and at the Universidad Nacional de Mexico. He has been active in both United States and international law, and has worked as an interviewer, actor, and field representative for the Migratory Labor Office of the Coordinator for Inter-American Affairs. Lopez's articles and essays have appeared in many international journals, and in such American magazines as the *Atlantic, Harper's, Horizon, Nation, Look,* and *American Heritage.*

John McCrae

Born in Guelph, Ontario, Canada, John McCrae (1872–1918) studied medicine at the University of Toronto and served in the South African War from 1899 to 1900. On returning home, he became a pathologist at McGill University. He died in 1918 while serving as a medical officer in World War I. His one enduring poem, "In Flanders' Fields," originally appeared in *Punch* in 1915, and posthumously in the collection *In Flanders' Fields and Other Poems* (1919).

Claude McKay

A leading poet of the "Harlem Renaissance," Claude McKay (1891–1948) was born in Jamaica. He attended Tuskegee Institute and Kansas State University from 1912 to 1914, and then went to New York City, where he became active as a writer and editor. An expatriate in Europe from 1922 to 1932, his volumes of poetry include *Spring in New Hampshire* (1920), *Harlem Shadows* (1922), and *Selected Poems of Claude McKay* (1953), issued posthumously.

Bernard Malamud

Born in 1914 in Brooklyn, Bernard Malamud has used his intimate knowledge of the Jewish experience to create fiction that has universal appeal. Malamud received his B.A. from City College of New York, and his M.A. from Columbia University. After some years as a high school teacher, Malamud became a college instructor and has been a professor of English at Bennington College since 1961. A member of the National Institute of Arts and Letters, Malamud has been a Ford Fellow in the Humanities and Arts and was a recipient of the National Book Award in fiction in 1959 for his collection of short stories, *The Magic Barrel* (1958). He received both the National Book Award and the Pulitzer Prize in 1967 for his novel *The Fixer* (1967). His other major novels include *The Natural* (1952), *The Assistant* (1957), and *Rembrandt's Hat* (1973).

Marya Mannes

Marya Mannes—magazine writer, editor, television personality, and lecturer—was born in New York City in 1904. She has received awards from, among others, the Federation of Jewish Women's Organizations and Theta Sigma Phi. Mannes had her own television program, "I Speak For Myself," in New York in the late 1950s, and since that time has been a frequent guest on other television programs. She has been feature editor of *Vogue* and *Glamour,* and writes for such magazines as *Esquire, Harper's,* and *New York Herald Tribune Book Week.* Her published works include a novel, *Message from a Stranger* (1948); a book of verse, *Subverse;* and several collections of essays, the latest of which is *Last Rights* (1974).

Margaret Mead

Margaret Mead (b. 1901) became a public figure because of her testimony before the United States Senate on various social issues. This public notice had been preceded by a professional prominence as an anthropologist that was world-wide. Born in Philadelphia, she received a B.A. from Barnard College, an M.A. and a Ph.D. from Columbia University. She has been associated with the American Museum of Natural History as a curator of ethnology since 1942, and with Columbia University since 1954 as adjunct professor of anthropology. Mead is past president of the American Anthropological Association, the Society for Applied Anthropology, and the World Federation of Mental Health. She is past vice-president of the American Council of Learned Societies, and a board member of the American Association for the Advancement of Science. She holds numerous honorary degrees. Among her most important books are *Coming of Age in Samoa* (1928), *The Changing Culture of an Indian Tribe* (1932), *Male and Female* (1949), *Continuities in Cultural Evolution* (1964), *Culture and Commitment* (1970), *An Anthropologist at Work* (1973), and *Blackberry Winter* (1973).

George Meredith

George Meredith (1828–1909) was born in Portsmouth, England. He attended schools in Portsmouth and Southsea, and in Neuwied on the Rhine. After being articled to a lawyer, he married the daughter of novelist Thomas Love Peacock. This marriage ended in 1858 and is reflected in the poems that make up *Modern Love.* He is as famous for his novels as his poems. The most famous of the novels are *The Ordeal of Richard Feverel* (1859), *Evan Harrington* (1861), *Beauchamp's Career* (1875), *The Egoist* (1879), and *Diana of the Crossways* (1885). His essay "On the Idea of Comedy and the Uses of the Comic Spirit" (1877) greatly influenced modern literary theory.

Edna St. Vincent Millay

Born in Maine, Edna St. Vincent Millay (1892–1950) had already published her first poem, "Renascence," when she graduated from Vassar. Known for her use of Elizabethan forms and for her technical control, particularly with the sonnet and the lyric, Millay was soon recognized as one of the leading American poets of the early twentieth century. Her publications include *Renascence and Other Poems* (1912); *A Few Figs from Thistles* (1920); the Pulitzer Prize–winning *The Harp-Weaver and Other Poems* (1923); *The Buck in the Snow* (1928); the Elizabethan sonnet sequence, *Fatal Interview* (1931); *Make Bright the Arrows* (1940); a ballad written for radio, *Murder of Lidice* (1942); and collected editions of her sonnets in 1941, lyrics in 1943, and poems in 1956. In addition to her poetry, Millay wrote several plays, none of which achieved fame; the libretto of an opera; and, under the pseudonym Nancy Boyd, a volume of prose sketches, *Distressing Dialogues* (1942).

John Milton

John Milton (1608–1674), England's greatest poet after Shakespeare, was born in London, where he later achieved fame both as a poet and rhetorical disputant for Cromwell's government. After taking his M.A. at Cambridge in 1632, Milton retired to his father's estate at Horton to self-consciously prepare himself for a career as a poet. In the ten-year period between his degree and the outbreak of the Civil War, Milton produced "L'Allegro," "Il Penseroso," "Comus," and "Lycidas," giving promise of his later sublimity. From 1642 to the Restoration in

1660, Milton wrote prose, at first concerning himself independently with the issues of God, divorce, and freedom of the press, and later—as Cromwell's Latin Secretary—with the various foes of the theocratic state. Only after blindness and penury had overtaken him did Milton create his greatest works: *Paradise Lost*—the last viable European epic—during the period from 1658 to 1663, and *Paradise Regained* and *Samson Agonistes,* both published in 1671.

Joni Mitchell

Joni Mitchell was born in 1943 in McLeod, Alberta, a small Canadian town, and was reared in Saskatoon, Saskatchewan. Her chosen career was that of a commercial artist, but she discovered early that her talents lay in a different field. While still at the Alberta College of Art she began playing and singing in coffeehouses to augment her college funds, and shortly abandoned art for music. Although she commands large audiences whenever she appears in concert, Mitchell prefers to compose and record her songs, reaching her listeners through her records rather than in person. Her latest recordings include *Miles of Aisles, Court and Spark, The Hissing of Summer Lawns,* and *Hejira.*

Jessica Mitford

Jessica Mitford was born in 1917 in Batsford, Gloucestershire, England, and was educated at home. After coming to the United States in 1939, she worked variously as a sales clerk, bartender, investigator for the wartime Office of Price Administration, and executive secretary for the Civil Rights Congress. Beginning a new career in writing at the age of 38, Mitford was following in the footsteps of her sister Nancy. In addition to articles in *Life, Esquire, The Nation,* and other magazines and periodicals, her published work includes *Lifeitselfmanship* (1956), *Daughters and Rebels* (1960), the widely anthologized *The American Way of Death* (1963), and *Kind and Usual Punishment: The Prison Business* (1973).

Marianne Moore

Once considered the grande dame of American poetry, Marianne Moore (1887–1972) was born in St. Louis and graduated from Bryn Mawr. Her collected poetry includes *Poems* (1921), *Observations* (1924), *The Pangolin, and Other Verse* (1936), *What Are Years?* (1941), *Nevertheless* (1944), *Like a Bulwark* (1956), and *O To Be a Dragon* (1959). Her *Collected Poems* (1951) won for her the Pulitzer Prize. Moore edited *The Dial* for several years in the 1920s, translated *The Fables of La Fontaine* (1954), and published *Predilections* (1955), a group of essays about her favorite writers.

Jim Morrison

Jim Morrison's death at the age of twenty-seven in July, 1971 in Paris, following those of Jimi Hendrix and Janis Joplin, seemed to many to confirm what has become a truism of the hard-rock scene: that success not only metaphorically kills the music, but literally kills the man. In four years Morrison, as lead singer and songwriter for the Los Angeles group The Doors, went from oblivion to underground fame to commercial success to death in France of what police described as a heart attack. An album, *The Doors,* and an on-stage act that seemed to be a cross between a black mass and a drug freak-out made The Doors famous among connoisseurs as inventors, along with the Jefferson Airplane, of a new, more sophisticated rock. After a single—"Light My Fire"—that became a national hit, the publicity circus diluted the quality of The Doors' music and drove Morrison to desperate vulgarity on the stage. But as a writer ("Twentieth Century Fox," "Light My Fire," "The End," "Crystal Ship," "Horse Latitudes,") and, in the early days, as one of the leading lights in rock-theatre (*cf.* his enactment, complete with shrieks, of the parricide episode in "The End") Morrison was a real talent.

Ogden Nash

Ogden Nash (1902–1971) was born in New York City. Except for one essay into the theater in collaboration with Kurt Weill and S. J. Perelman on the muscial comedy *One Touch of Venus* (1943), Nash spent his working years producing outrageously punning, slightly mad, invariably good-humored light verse. He ignored the conventions of poetry, or followed them only when he chose; as a result of his idiosyncratic versifying, his poetry is immediately recognizable, usually delightfully so. Among his collections are *Free Wheeling* (1931), *Hard Lines* (1931), *Happy Days* (1933), *I'm a Stranger Here Myself* (1938), *Family Reunion* (1950), *You Can't Get There from Here* (1957), and *Everyone but Thee and Me* (1962).

Howard Nemerov

A writer of novels, short stories, and criticism, Howard Nemerov has earned his place in American letters chiefly through his poetry. Nemerov was born in New York City in 1920, and received his A.B. from Harvard. He has taught or served as poet-in-residence at Bennington College, Brandeis University, the University of Minnesota, and Hollins College, and was Consultant in Poetry to the Library of Congress. His only excursions outside the field of letters were World War II tours of duty with the Royal Canadian Air Force and the U.S. Army Air Force. Nemerov's poems are generally long, developed dialogues, in which he uses puns, fantasy, and rhythm to develop his probing, metaphysical themes. His first poetry collection was *The Image and the Law* (1948), and his most recent works have been the collection of essays, *Reflections on Poetry and Poetics* (1972), *Gnomes and Occasions* (1973), and *The Western Approaches* (1975).

Frank O'Connor

Frank O'Connor (1903–1966), whose real name was Michael O'Donovan, was born in Cork, Ireland, into a family too poor to provide him with a formal education. As a young man he worked as a librarian. His genius as a short story writer was first recognized by George Russell, already established as a leader in Irish literary movements. Among O'Connor's many books are *Guest of a Nation* (1931), *Bones of Contention* (1936), *Towards an Appreciation of Literature* (1945), *Selected Stories* (1946), *The Art of the Theatre* (1947), *Domestic Relations* (1957), *The Lonely Voice* (1963), and *The Backward Look* (1967). He has also published several books of verse, and critical studies of Turgenev and Michael Collins and the Irish Revolution. O'Connor has said: "Story telling is the nearest thing one can get to the quality of a pure lyric poem. It doesn't deal with problems; it doesn't have any solutions to offer; it just states the human condition."

Gabriel Okara

Gabriel Imomotime Gbaingbaing Okara was born in Nigeria in 1921. He received his education at Government College in Umuahia, where he was trained as a bookbinder. After working at his trade for a period of time, he became a civil servant, working at Enugu in Nigeria. Okara is a regular contributor to *Black Orpheus;* his contribution to the first issue of that publication was the winner of the Nigerian Festival of the Arts main prize in 1953. He has published one novel, *The Voice* (1964), and has translated several works from his native Ijaw into English.

Grace Paley

Grace Paley (b. 1922) was born in New York City. She attended Hunter College and has taught at Columbia University, Syracuse University, and Sarah Lawrence College. Her short stories have appeared in the *Atlantic, Esquire, Ikon, Genesis West,* and *Accent,* among other periodicals. Her books include *The Little Disturbances of Man* (1959) and *Enormous Changes at the Last Minute* (1975). In 1970 the National Institute of Arts and Letters named her a recipient of one of its literary awards.

Sylvia Plath

Sylvia Plath (1932–1963) was educated at Smith College and studied at Cambridge University in England before returning to Smith to teach. She was married to poet Ted Hughes. A tortured woman, pursued by private devils, Plath wrote one novel and much intense, personal poetry before taking her own life in London. Her highly autobiographical novel, *The Bell Jar,* was published under the name Victoria Lucas in 1963. Her poetry was collected in *The Colossus* (1962) and, posthumously, in *Ariel* (1966).

Edgar Allan Poe

Edgar Allan Poe (1809–1849) was born in Boston, but lived in England and Scotland from 1815 to 1820. He attended school at Stoke Newington and later, after his return to the States, in Richmond, Virginia. His guardian removed him from the University of Virginia because of the gambling debts the boy had accrued. Poe ran away to Boston where he published *Tamerlane and Other Poems* in 1827. Most of his famous short stories were originally published in newspapers and periodicals, but he collected them into *Tales of the Grotesque and Arabesque* in 1840. His place in American letters is secure, not only because of his poems ("The Raven," "The Bells," and "Annabel Lee") and short stories ("The Fall of the House of Usher," "The Gold Bug," "The Murders in the Rue Morgue," and "The Pit and the Pendulum") but also because of his literary criticism, particularly the views on the short story, which he expounded in his examination of Nathaniel Hawthorne's *Twice-Told Tales*.

Katherine Anne Porter

Katherine Anne Porter was born in Texas in 1890. Educated in private schools, she travelled widely in Mexico and Europe as a young woman; the settings for many of her stories are taken from places she visited then. Her first book of short stories, *Flowering Judas* (1930), brought her instant critical recognition; the title story from that collection is still widely anthologized. Other volumes include *Hacienda* (1934), *Noon Wine* (1937), *Pale Horse, Pale Rider* (1939), *The Leaning Tower* (1944), and *Collected Stories* (1965). In addition to short stories, Porter has published her essays, articles, and book reviews in two volumes: *The Days Before* (1952) and *Collected Essays and Occasional Writings* (1970). Porter's best-known work is her 1962 novel, *Ship of Fools,* an allegory on the voyage of life in which she writes about a group of people, mostly German nationals, travelling from Mexico to Germany in 1931.

Mario Puzo

Mario Puzo was born in 1920 in New York City and received his formal education at the New School for Social Research. His most notable work to date has been *The Godfather,* the story of the Mafia that was made into an award-winning film. Besides *The Godfather* (1969), Puzo has published *The Dark Arena* (1955), *The Fortunate Pilgrim* (1964), and *The Godfather Papers and Other Confessions* (1972).

John Crowe Ransom

John Crowe Ransom (1888–1973) was one of a group of Southern writers whose creative writing and criticism dominated American letters in the 1930s and 1940s. Born in Pulaski, Tennessee, he took his B.A. at Vanderbilt University; as a Rhodes scholar, he also earned a B.A. at Oxford. Ransom served on the Vanderbilt University faculty from 1914 to 1937; in 1938 he moved to Kenyon College, where he was professor of poetry and editor of the *Kenyon Review* until 1959. Ransom received the Bollingen Prize for poetry in 1951, and the National Book Award for *Selected Poems* in 1964. Ransom's book on philosophical literary criticism, *The New Criticism,* provided the primary theoretical justification for the classicism that ruled American poetry and its interpretation for some twenty years.

Richard Rhodes

Richard Rhodes was born in Kansas City in 1937. He holds a B.A. cum laude from Yale University. Rhodes served in the U.S. Air Force Reserve as a surgical technician, has taught college English, writes films for television, and contributes widely to magazines. He won the *Playboy* Editorial Award in 1972, and his most recent publication is *The Ungodly: A Novel of the Donner Party* (1973).

Edwin Arlington Robinson

Edwin Arlington Robinson (1869–1935) was born in Head Tide, Maine. He studied at Harvard University for two years, but the death of his father necessitated his withdrawal. This inaugurated a period of severe mental depression, which was intensified by a chronically painful abscessed ear, financial problems, the death of both his brothers and his mother, and the end of a serious love affair. *The Torrent and the Night Before* was printed at his own expense in 1896, as was *The Children of the Night* in 1897. Through the intercession of a friend, President Roosevelt appointed him to a clerkship in the New York Custom House and urged Scribner's to publish Robinson's *The Town Down the River* (1910). Thereafter Robinson led a comfortable if not luxurious existence. Robinson was awarded three Pulitzer Prizes—for his *Collected Poems* (1921), *The Man Who Died Twice* (1924), and *Tristram* (1927).

Theodore Roethke

Theodore Roethke (1908–1963) was born in Michigan and graduated from Michigan State University. A teacher of English at the university level, Roethke published his first book of poetry, *Open House,* in 1941. His most important works are *The Waking,* for which he received the Pulitzer Price in 1953, and *Words for the Wind,* for which he won the Bollingen Prize in 1958. Other works include *Praise to the End* (1951), *I Am! Says the Lamb* (1961), and, posthumously, *The Far Field* (1964) and *On the Poet and His Craft* (1965), a compilation of essays and lectures.

"Saki" (H. H. Munro)

Hector Hugh Munro (1870–1916) published his first collection of short stories, *Reginald,* in 1904 under the pseudonym "Saki." Earlier he had worked as a political satirist for the *Westminster Gazette;* later he served as correspondent in Russia and France for the *Morning Post.* Although "Saki" is best remembered for his short stories, he published one novel, *The Unbearable Bassington* (1912). His short story collections include *Reginald in Russia* (1910), *The Chronicles of Clovis* (1911), and *Beasts and Superbeasts* (1914).

Carl Sandburg

Carl Sandburg (1878–1967) has been perhaps the writer most successful at reconciling the leveling demands of a mass democratic audience and those of art. Born in Galesburg, Illinois, he attended Lombard College in his home town, leaving to fight in the Spanish-American War. Upon returning he held a variety of journalistic and political positions before becoming a professional poet, historian, novelist, and folklorist. Sandburg's memory will live longest because of his multi-volumed biography of Abraham Lincoln. The four volumes entitled *The War Years* won the Pulitzer Prize for history in 1940. His *Complete Poems* won the Pulitzer Prize for poetry in 1951.

Anne Sexton

Anne Sexton (1928–1974) was a modern poet who, in her outspoken frankness, was compared to Robert Lowell and W. D. Snodgrass. She never hesitated to acknowledge that both poets influenced her, and felt complimented by the comparisons. Sexton was born in Newton, Massachusetts, and was educated at Rogers Hall, Garland Junior College, and the Radcliffe Institute for Independent Study. She received the Robert Frost Fellowship in 1959, the *Audience* Poetry Prize in 1959, the Levinson Prize in 1962, an American Academy of Arts and Letters travelling fellowship in 1963–1964, and a Ford Foundation grant in 1964–1965. Her collections include *To Bedlam and Part Way Back* (1960), *All My Pretty Ones* (1962), *Live or Die* (1966), *The Death of Notebooks* (1974), and, edited posthumously by her daugher Linda, *Forty-Five Mercy Street* (1975). She committed suicide in 1974.

William Shakespeare

William Shakespeare (1564–1616) was born in Stratford-on-Avon. Nearly all of what we think we know about his early years is conjecture. We do know that he was married and the father of three children before he left for London and a career in the theater. He may have started as a horseboy. But before too long he was actor, playwright, and part-owner of a theater. He retired to a wealthy, middle-class existence in a comfortable home in Stratford. Critics have tried to find Shakespeare-the-man in his works, but Shakespeare remains an enigma—the greatest writer the English-speaking world has ever known, and the most mysterious. Although we cannot be sure exactly when the plays were written, most of the major tragedies, including *Hamlet,* probably date from 1602 to 1608.

Gail Sheehy

Born in 1937 in New York City, Gail Sheehy graduated from the University of Vermont and has done graduate work at Columbia University. She has worked as a newspaper fashion editor and feature writer, and as a contributing editor to *New York* magazine. Her many awards include the Front Page Award of the Newswomen's Club of New York (1964); the National Magazine Award (1972); and the Alicia Patterson Foundation Fellowship Award (1974). Sheehy publishes in numerous popular magazines both in the United States and in Britain, and is anthologized in many collections. Her first book, *Lovesounds,* was published in 1970, and was followed by *Hustling: Prostitution in our Wide Open Society* (1973) and the best-selling *Passages* (1976).

Percy Bysshe Shelley

Percy Bysshe Shelley (1792–1822), one of the great English Romantic poets, was born in Sussex, and educated at Eton and University College, Oxford. Married to sixteen-year-old Harriet Westbrook in 1811, Shelley immediately began a lifelong wandering existence, accompanied usually by Mary Godwin (whom he married after Harriet drowned herself in despair) and Mary's sister, Claire Clairmont. Shelley was deeply concerned with revolutionary movements of the period; he went to Greece to share in the struggles of the Greek people in 1821. The next year he drowned while sailing. Shelley's first work, *Queen Mab,* appeared in 1821. He is best remembered today for his magnificent lyrical odes, chief among them "Ode to the West Wind," "To A Skylark," "Ode to Naples," and "Ode to Liberty." Other important works include a tragedy, *The Cenci;* the lyrical dramas *Prometheus Unbound* and *Hellas;* his elegy on the death of John Keats, *Adonais;* and *Epipsychidion,* a defense of free love addressed by Shelley to a lady of his acquaintance.

Jon Silkin

Jon Silkin was born in London in 1930. He was educated at the University of Leeds, where he graduated with first class honors. After service in the British National Service, Education Corps, he worked for several years as a manual laborer in London and then became a teacher of English as a second language. He was Leeds University's Gregg Fellow in Poetry, 1958–1960. Silkin is considered a far cry from an establishment poet. His poetry is not easy to read; it is extremely intense and full of self-examination. He contributes to such periodicals as *Botteghe Oscure, Poetry, Encounter, New Statesman, London* magazine, and *Jewish Quarterly,* among others. His publications include *The Peaceable Kingdom* (1954), *The Two Freedoms* (1958), *The Re-ordering of the Stones* (1961), *Nature With Man* (1965), *Amana Grass* (1971), *Out of the Battle: The Poetry of the Great War* (1972), *Poetry of the Committed Individual* (1973), and *The Principle of Water* (1974).

Leslie Silko

Leslie Silko was born in New Mexico in 1948, and now lives in Alaska. Silko received her B.A. from the University of New Mexico at Albuquerque, and was elected to Phi Beta Kappa. A Native American story teller and poet, Silko captures the conflicts and confusions of the Native American living in an alien culture—the white culture—with compassion and warmth. She contributes to the *Chicago Review,* the *Southern Review,* the *Northwest Review,* and *Quetzal.* Her published works also include the stories in *Stories of the Southwest* (1973) and *The Man to Send Rain Clouds* (1974); and *Laguna Woman* (1974) and *Ceremony* (1977).

Alan Sillitoe

Alan Sillitoe was born in 1928 in Nottingham, England and educated in Nottingham schools. He was a factory worker for four years, and served as a radio operator in the RAF. Sillitoe has published short stories—*The Loneliness of the Long Distance Runner* (1959), poems—*The Rats* (1960), and a travel book—*Road to Volgograd* (1964). However, he is most famous for his novels, among which are *Saturday Night and Sunday Morning* (1958), *The Ragman's Daughter* (1963), *A Falling Out of Love* (1964), and *A Start in Life* (1970).

Paul Simon

Born in Queens, New York in 1941, composer-singer Paul Simon began his performing career singing with his sixth grade classmate Art Garfunkel. The partnership formed then was not interrupted until the young men parted to attend different colleges, and was resumed following their college years. "The Sound of Silence," a cut from their first album, *Wednesday Morning, 3 A.M.* brought Simon and Garfunkel to the front of the blossoming folk-rock movement in the mid-sixties, where they remained until the dissolution of their partnership in 1971. Simon has continued to produce successful music; his recent albums include *There Goes Rhymin' Simon, Still Crazy After All These Years,* and *Paul Simon in Concert: Live Rhymin'.*

John Steinbeck

John Steinbeck (1902–1969) was born in Salinas, California. He attended Salinas High School and was a student at Stanford University. His devastating picture of the Joads in *The Grapes of Wrath* (1939) brought him literary immortality. Among his other books are *Cup of Gold* (1929), *Tortilla Flat* (1935), *Of Mice and Men* (1937), *The Red Pony* (1937), *The Moon is Down* (1942), *Cannery Row* (1945), *East of Eden* (1952), and *The Winter of Our Discontent* (1961). He was the recipient of a Pulitzer Prize, the Nobel Prize, and the Presidential Medal of Freedom. "The Snake" is only one of many short stories and novels set in the Salinas Valley.

Gloria Steinem

Gloria Steinem was born in Ohio in 1936. After graduating from Smith College magna cum laude, she became a Chester Bowles Asian Fellow at the Universities of Delhi and Calcutta. A freelance writer and a contributing editor of *New York* magazine for several years, Steinem founded *Ms.* magazine in 1972. One of the foremost proponents of the women's movement, she was a founding member of the National Women's Political Caucus and has been chairperson and member of the board of the Women's Action Alliance. Her awards include the Penney-Missouri journalism award for 1970 and an honorary doctorate in human justice from Simmons College in 1973. A contributor to many magazines, including *Esquire, Ms., Harper's, Vogue,* and *Time,* Steinem's writings include *The Thousand Indias* (1957) and *The Beach Book* (1963). She also has written for television, including the series popular in the early 1960s, "That Was the Week That Was."

Cat Stevens

Cat Stevens, né Steven Georgiou, was born in London in 1948. Although brought up hearing the native Greek music from his parent's homeland, by his high school years he had turned to the music of his own generation, rock and roll. He started singing in public while still in school, and quickly reached the top of British popularity lists. After a prolonged illness in the late 1960s, he returned to the music scene with a style that was unique. Since then, he has become a favorite in the United States as well as in Europe. One of Stevens's most popular records was the 1971 *Tea for the Tillerman;* it remains one of his best-selling records today. Other recent albums include *Buddha and the Chocolate Box, Catch Bull at Four,* and *Teaser and the Firecat.*

Wallace Stevens

Wallace Stevens (1879–1955) was an executive in an insurance firm by vocation and a poet by avocation. Born in Pennsylvania and educated at Harvard and New York University Law School, Stevens published his first poetry at forty-three; most of his poems were written after he passed fifty. His work has wit, imagination, and passion, and shows great insight into life. His first collection, *Harmonium* (1923), was followed by *Ideas of Order* (1935), *Owl's Clover* (1936), *The Man with the Blue Guitar* (1937), *Parts of a World* (1942), *Transport to Summer* (1947), *The Auroras of Autumn* (1950), and *Collected Poems* (1954).

Dabney Stuart

A teacher and writer, Dabney Stuart was born in 1937 in Richmond, Virginia and has spent most of his life in the South. A modern poet, Stuart comments succinctly on many aspects of American life and society. He has published several books of poetry, among them *The Diving Bell* (1966), *A Particular Place* (1969), *The Other Hand* (1975), and *Round and Round* (1977); now in progress is *Nabokov: The Dimensions of Parody*.

Jonathan Swift

Born in Dublin after his father's death, Jonathan Swift (1667–1745) was destined to spend his life in clashes with what would be termed today the "establishment." He was almost expelled from Trinity College, Dublin, for rebelling against discipline, and after a short attempt at being a secretary in England, was ordained and received a small living in Ireland. He eventually became dean of St. Patrick's in Dublin after some stormy years divided between Ireland and England. Swift's first important work, like most of his publications, was a satire, *A Tale of a Tub,* (1704). Swift wrote many political pamphlets, usually for the purpose of pointing out to the Whigs their unfair policies in regard to Ireland. His masterpiece, *Gulliver's Travels,* was published in 1726; among his other important works are *Journal to Stella* (1766–68), *A Complete Collection of Polite and Ingenious Conversation* (1738), and *Directions to Servants* (1745). Although Swift wrote some poetry, it was never as well received as his satirical prose. Most of Swift's work was published after his death; the only work he was ever paid for was *Gulliver's Travels,* and for that he received £200.

Sara Teasdale

Sara Teasdale (1884–1933) was born in Missouri but lived most of her life in New York City. Her poetry is straightforward and lyrical, and for the most part seeks to express a mood rather than to pursue universal questions. Her poetry was collected in *Sonnets to Duse and Other Poems* (1907), *Helen of Troy* (1911), *Rivers to the Sea* (1915), *Love Songs* (1917), *Flame and Shadow* (1920), *Dark of the Moon* (1926), and *Strange Victory* (1933). The posthumous *Collected Poems* was issued in 1937. Teasdale's *Love Songs* was awarded a special Pulitzer Prize in 1917.

Alfred, Lord Tennyson

Alfred, Lord Tennyson (1809–1892) was born at Somersby in Lincolnshire. His father was a rector, who educated his son at home and later at private schools and the Louth Grammar School. Tennyson's earliest books included *Poems by Two Brothers* (1827), *Poems Chiefly Lyrical* (1830), and *Poems* (1842). Probably the most important events in Tennyson's life stem from his friendship with Arthur Henry Hallam, whom he met at Trinity College, Cambridge. Hallam's death sent Tennyson into a long period of intense depression, which he described in *In Memoriam A.H.H.* (1850). With the publication of *In Memoriam,* Tennyson was named Poet Laureate and was able to marry Emily Sellwood, after an engagement of almost twenty years. Tennyson's Arthurian epic, *The Idylls of the King,* was published in sections between 1859 and 1885. Other important volumes were *Maud* (1855), *Enoch Arden* (1864), and *Locksley Hall Sixty Years After* (1886).

Dylan Thomas

Dylan Thomas was born in Swansea, Wales in 1914, and died in the United States in 1953. An important poet of the first half of the twentieth century, Thomas has had a great deal of influence on later poets. A rebel against establishment views, Thomas is remembered as an outspoken bohemian. His volumes include *Twenty-five Poems* (1936), *The Map of Love* (1939), *Death and Entrances* (1946), and *Collected Poems* (1952). His play for voices, *Under Milkwood* (1954), was first performed in public by Thomas himself. Lesser-known prose works include the semiautobiographical *Portrait of the Artist as a Young Dog* (1940) and *Adventures in the Skin Trade* (1955).

Piri Thomas

Born in 1928 in New York City, Piri Thomas received most of his education in the streets of Spanish Harlem. After serving a prison term, Thomas became interested in drug rehabilitation, and founded several drug rehabilitation centers in New York City and in Puerto Rico, where he also attended the University of Puerto Rico. Thomas's writings include his autobiographical novel *Down These Mean Streets* (1967), *Savior, Savior, Hold My Hand* (1973), *Seven Long Times* (1974), and the narration for the 1964 prize-winning film *Petey and Johnny,* a documentary of life in Spanish Harlem.

Henry David Thoreau

American writer, mystic, transcendentalist, and naturalist, Henry David Thoreau (1817–1862) was born in Concord, Massachusetts. After graduation from Harvard he returned to Concord, where he and his brother ran a school for a brief period of time. He later lived for a while with Emerson, at which time his interest in transcendentalism developed and matured. Thoreau's definitive work, *Walden,* was written during an 1845–1847 sojourn at Walden Pond in Concord, where he built himself a hut and lived a simple life, close to nature. A strong believer in passive resistance, Thoreau wrote his essay on "Civil Disobedience" in 1849 to explain his belief. Another important essay, espousing his faith in the individual, "Life Without Principle," appeared in 1863. Thoreau's works, all published posthumously, include his complete *Journal* (1906), *Consciousness in Concord* (1958), *The Collected Poems* (1948) and *Correspondence* (1958).

James Thurber

James Thurber (1894–1961) was born in Columbus, Ohio. He graduated from Ohio State University, worked as a code clerk in the Department of State, and then as a newspaper reporter. He joined the staff of the *New Yorker* in 1926. In 1929, with E. B. White, he co-authored *Is Sex Necessary?* Among his many stories, fables, and essays are *The Owl in the Attic* (1931), *The Seal in the Bedroom* (1932), *My Life and Hard Times* (1933), *Fables for Our Time* (1940), *The Thurber Carnival* (1945), *The Thirteen Clocks* (1950), and *Thurber Country* (1953).

Jean Toomer

Jean Toomer (1894–1977) was born in Washington, D.C. He graduated from New York University. His writing career started soon thereafter with the publication of *Cane* (1923); this collection included short stories, verse, and a play about the emotional problems of blacks. *Essentials* was published in 1913, *Portage Potential* in 1932, and a new edition of *Cane* in 1975.

Lionel Trilling

Though his short stories have been recognized as works of genuine artistic merit, Lionel Trilling (1905–1975) is known primarily as a scholar and critic. Born in New York City, he received a B.A., M.A., and Ph.D. from Columbia University and taught there from 1931 until his death. Author of the best critical biography of Matthew Arnold, *Matthew Arnold* (1939), he also wrote *The Liberal Imagination* (1950), *Freud and the Crisis of Our Culture* (1955), and *Literary Criticism: An Introductory Reader* (1970). His novel, *The Middle of the Night,* earned wide acclaim.

Judith Viorst

Born in the mid-1930s in Newark, New Jersey, Judith Viorst graduated with honors from Rutgers University. Her awards include, in addition to membership in Phi Beta Kappa, an Emmy Award received in 1970 for poetic monologues written for the CBS special program, "Annie: the Women in the Life of a Man." Best known for her poetry, Viorst also writes children's books, and since 1972 has written a regular column for *Redbook* magazine. She also contributes to various periodicals and magazines, including *New York,* the *New York Times, Holiday,* and

Venture. Her poetry collections include *The Village Square* (1965), *People and Other Aggravations* (1971), and *How Did I Get to Be Forty . . . and Other Atrocities* (1976). Viorst has also published several prose collections, and collaborated with her husband on *It's Hard to Be Hip Over Thirty, and Other Tragedies of Married Life,* a collection of poetry published in 1968.

E. B. White

Elwyn Brooks White was born in 1899 in Mount Vernon, New York, and has spent most of his life in the northeastern United States. He was educated at Cornell University. His essays have long been familiar to readers of the *New Yorker* and other periodicals; White writes with great warmth about his life, his family, and his country. His awards would encompass a page of their own; chief among them are honorary degrees from Dartmouth, Yale, the University of Maine, Bowdoin College, Hamilton College, Harvard, and Colby College. He has also received awards from the Limited Editions Club, the National Association of Independent Schools, the Institute of Arts and Letters, the American Library Association, and the National Book Committee. He received the Presidential Medal of Freedom in 1963. White's first publication was a book of poetry, *The Lady is Cold* (1929). This was followed by *One Man's Meat* (1942), *Here is New York* (1949), *The Second Tree From the Corner* (1954), and *The Points of My Compass* (1962), among others. White will probably be best remembered, however, for the two children's books that have become classics in his time: *Charlotte's Web* (1952) and *Stuart Little* (1945).

Walt Whitman

Walt Whitman (1819–1892) was born on Long Island and educated in Brooklyn. He worked as a printer's devil, compositor, and schoolteacher, and as editor of the *Long Islander,* the *Brooklyn Eagle,* and other newspapers including the *Brooklyn Times.* His first collected poetry was published as *Leaves of Grass* in 1855. His celebration of nature and man's place in nature as a free spirit, and his use of free verse to expound his message were some fifty years ahead of their time; *Leaves of Grass,* printed privately, was poorly received in the United States. Among Whitman's peers, Ralph Waldo Emerson recognized the volume's worth. A second edition was published in 1856, but it was not until 1860 that a commercial publisher was found who would handle the work. Whitman's other poetry has been collected in many modern volumes; among those published during his lifetime were *Memoranda During the War* (1875), and his two other important collections of Civil War poetry: *Drum-Taps* (1865) and *Sequel to Drum-Taps* (1866). Other publications spanned his life; his final collection was *Good-bye My Fancy* (1891).

Nancy Willard

Nancy Willard (b. 1936) lives in Poughkeepsie, New York, and teaches English at Vassar College. She writes books for children and has also published a book of essays—*Testimony of the Invisible Man*—on, among others, Rilke and Neruda. Her poetry collections include *Skin of Grace* (1967), *Nineteen Masks for a Naked Poet* (1971), and *Carpenter of the Sun* (1974).

William Carlos Williams

William Carlos Williams (1883–1963) was born in Rutherford, New Jersey. A graduate of the University of Pennsylvania Medical School, Williams became a pediatrician in his home town, where he remained throughout his life. Williams published his first collection, *Poems,* in 1909. Other volumes include *The Tempers* (1913), *Sour Grapes* (1921), *Collected Poems* (1934), *Complete Collected Poems* (1938), *The Broken Span* (1941), *Journey to Love* (1955), and the 1964 Pulitzer Prize–winning *Pictures from Brueghel.* Williams also wrote essays, published in several volumes including *Selected Essays* (1954), and plays collected in, among others, *Many Loves* (1961), *Make Light of It* (1950), and *The Farmers' Daughters* (1961). His novels include *A Voyage to Pagany* (1928), *White Mule* (1937), and *The Build Up* (1952). Williams's autobiography was published in 1951.

Samuel T. Williamson

Reporter, biographer, book reviewer, and freelance writer, Samuel T. Williamson (1891–1962) was born in Augusta, Maine. After graduating from Harvard in 1916, Williamson entered the U.S. Army as a lieutenant and served in France in several World War I campaigns. Most of his writing career was spent with the *New York Times*, where he was chiefly a book reviewer. He left the *Times* to become the first editor of *Newsweek*, returning to the newspaper with contributions to the *New York Times Magazine*. Many of his short stories written for that publication were about the imaginary town of "Salt Harbor," and included discussions on such subjects as the proper method of making clam chowder and the habits of sand fleas. Williamson's work has never been collected for publication in book form, but many of his essays and stories are anthologized.

Terrance Withers

Terrance Withers was born in 1948 in Warren, Ohio, and "pushed westward" to Arizona in 1953. He received a B.A. from Arizona State University. Presently he works as a fabric librarian with an interior decorating firm in San Francisco. His poems have been published in *Inscape* and *Catalyst*.

Jade Snow Wong

Jade Snow Wong, born in 1922 in San Francisco, was the daughter of first-generation Chinese-Americans who were still steeped in the traditions of their parents' home. Wong's perceptive autobiographical novel, *Fifth Chinese Daughter* (1945), depicts the conflict between cultures and generations. Wong herself became wholly Americanized while still recognizing her parents' ties to China. After graduating from Mills College in 1942 she worked for the Navy throughout World War II, then began writing and working in ceramics.

William Wordsworth

William Wordsworth (1770–1850) was born in Cockermouth, Cumberland, England. Raised in the Lake District, he developed an affinity for nature that later gave his poetry its distinctive tinge. Wordsworth took his degree from Cambridge in 1791, and immediately thereafter embarked for France, where he supported the Revolution. In 1795 he set up house in rural environs with his sister Dorothy and began the association with Coleridge that resulted in the publication in 1798 of *Lyrical Ballads*, the collection of poetry and critical commentary that Wordsworth wrote along with Coleridge, and that announced a new age for British poetry. Wordsworth's period of highest creativity lasted through 1805. Thereafter he lived in mediocrity as a poet and tranquility as a person.

Richard Wright

Born in Natchez, Mississippi and self-educated, Richard Wright (1908–1960) was a very important twentieth-century American author. Wright was at various times a manual laborer, a writer for the Federal Writers' Project, and, for a brief period of time, a member of the Communist party. This last experience he recorded in *The God That Failed* (1950). Among his most important books was *Uncle Tom's Children* (1938), which won the *Story* prize in that year. Wright's best-selling autobiography, *Black Boy*, appeared in 1945. In the same year Wright became an expatriate, living in Paris. While in France he wrote *The Outsider* (1953) and *The Long Dream* (1958). Among his other publications are two issued posthumously: *Eight Men* (1963) and *Lawd Today* (1963).

Kenneth Yasuda (Shosōn)

Kenneth Yasuda, an American of Japanese descent, was born in Auburn, California in 1914. He graduated from the University of Washington and did graduate work in Japan and at Columbia University. After World War II, part of which he spent in relocation centers, he worked in various capacities for the U.S. government in Japan. In 1956 Yasuda received a doctorate in Literature in Japanese at Tokyo University. He was the first American to receive this degree. Yasuda has taught at the University of Hawaii and Indiana University. One of the first poets to write haiku in English, he also translates this poetry from the Japanese. Awards received by Yasuda include the Imperial Decoration of the Sacred Treasure of the Third Order of Japan. His first publication was *A Pepper Pod* (1947). It was follwed by *The Japanese Haiku* (1957), *Land of the Reed Plains: Ancient Japanese Lyrics from the Manyoshu* (1961), and *Six Noh Plays* (1967–1968).

William Butler Yeats

Like Gerard Manley Hopkins, W. B. Yeats (1865–1939) is one of a small group of poets whose work constructed a bridge for Anglo-American letters from a nineteenth-century traditionalism to the new idiom of the twentieth century. Born in Sandymount, a suburb of Dublin, Yeats came early to London with his father, a minor painter active in Pre-Raphaelite circles. From the beginning Yeats wished to be and was a professional writer. As an adult he returned to Ireland where, with the patronage of Lady Isabella Augusta Gregory, he helped to create and sustain the Irish Renaissance, literary and political. His poetic style transforms from a languid, imitative amalgam of Keats, the early Tennyson, Pre-Raphaelitism, and Irish myth into the taut philosophical meditation, the heady cultivation of ambiguity embodied in such poems as "The Second Coming" and "Among School Children."

Chiang Yee

A native of Kiukiang, China, Chiang Yee was born in 1903, the son of an important Chinese painter. Yee received his B.S. from the National South-Eastern University of Nanking, taught for a short period of time, and then served as governor and director of four districts. He has lived in the west since 1935, going first to London as a lecturer at London University, and then to the United States. He has written a number of *Silent Traveller* volumes; the first, *Silent Traveller in Lakeland* (1937), was followed by *The Silent Traveller in New York* (1950), *The Silent Traveller in Boston* (1959), and *The Silent Traveller in San Francisco* (1964).

Zitkala-Ša (Gertrude Bonnin)

Zitkala-Ša (1876–1938) was an early spokesperson not only for Native Americans but also for women. She was a full-blooded Dakota Sioux and the granddaughter of Sitting Bull. After attending Earlham College in Indiana, she taught for a short period at the Carlisle Indian School. Then she worked for the Bureau of Indian Affairs under the U.S. Department of the Interior before marrying Captain Raymond T. Bonnin. In 1918 she was the chief speaker at the first women's open discussion ever held at the National Arts Club in Washington, a notable achievement for that time. The founder of the American Indians Council, she was an indefatigable champion of Indian causes throughout her life. In addition to numerous contributions to periodicals, she published two books: *Old Indian Legends* and *Indian Stories*.

Index

A

B

C

D

E

F